SECRETS

OF

HEAVEN

SECRETS

OF

HEAVEN

The Portable New Century Edition

EMANUEL SWEDENBORG

Volume 3

Translated from the Latin by Lisa Hyatt Cooper

SWEDENBORG FOUNDATION

West Chester, Pennsylvania

Originally published in Latin as *Arcana Coelestia,* London, 1749–1756. The volume contents of this and the original Latin edition, along with ISBNs of the annotated version, are as follows:

Volume number in this edition	Text treated	Volume number in the Latin first edition	Section numbers	ISBN (of hardcover except where noted)
1	Genesis 1–8	1	§§1–946	978-0-87785-486-9 978-0-87785-504-0 (pb)
2	Genesis 9–15	1	§§947–1885	978-0-87785-487-6
3	Genesis 16–21	2 (in 6 fascicles)	§§1886–2759	978-0-87785-488-3
4	Genesis 22–26	3	§§2760–3485	978-0-87785-489-0
5	Genesis 27–30	3	§§3486–4055	978-0-87785-490-6
6	Genesis 31–35	4	§§4056–4634	978-0-87785-491-3
7	Genesis 36–40	4	§§4635–5190	978-0-87785-492-0
8	Genesis 41–44	5	§§5191–5866	978-0-87785-493-7
9	Genesis 45–50	5	§§5867–6626	978-0-87785-494-4
10	Exodus 1–8	6	§§6627–7487	978-0-87785-495-1
11	Exodus 9–15	6	§§7488–8386	978-0-87785-496-8
12	Exodus 16–21	7	§§8387–9111	978-0-87785-497-5
13	Exodus 22–24	7	§§9112–9442	978-0-87785-498-2
14	Exodus 25–29	8	§§9443–10166	978-0-87785-499-9
15	Exodus 30–40	8	§§10167–10837	978-0-87785-500-2

ISBN (Portable)   **Volume 3: 978-0-87785-418-0**
ISBN (e-book of Portable Edition)   Volume 3: 978-0-87785-689-4

(The ISBN in the Library of Congress data shown below is that of volume 1.)

Library of Congress Cataloging-in-Publication Data

Swedenborg, Emanuel, 1688–1772.
    [Arcana coelestia. English]
    Secrets of heaven / Emanuel Swedenborg ; translated from the Latin by
Lisa Hyatt Cooper. — Portable New Century ed.
      p. cm.
    Includes bibliographical references and indexes.
    ISBN 978-0-87785-408-1 (alk. paper)
    1. New Jerusalem Church—Doctrines. 2. Bible. O.T. Genesis—Commentaries—Early works to 1800. 3. Bible. O.T. Exodus—Commentaries—Early works to 1800. I. Title.
    BX8712.A8 2010
    230'.94—dc22

        2009054171

Senior copy editor, Alicia L. Dole
Text designed by Joanna V. Hill
Typesetting by Alicia L. Dole and Sarah Dole
Ornaments from the first Latin edition, 1750
Cover design by Karen Connor

For information about the New Century Edition of the Works of Emanuel Swedenborg, contact the Swedenborg Foundation, 320 North Church Street, West Chester, PA 19380 U.S.A.
Telephone: (610) 430-3222 • Web: www.swedenborg.com • E-mail: info@swedenborg.com

Contents

Volume 3

Genesis Chapter 19

Genesis Chapter 20

Genesis Chapter 21

Conventions Used in This Work

MOST of the following conventions apply generally to the translations in the New Century Edition Portable series. For introductory material on the content and history of *Secrets of Heaven,* and for annotations on the subject matter, including obscure or problematic content, and extensive indexes, the reader is referred to the Deluxe New Century Edition volumes.

Volume designation *Secrets of Heaven* was originally published in eight volumes; in this edition all but this, the second original volume, have been divided into two. Thus Swedenborg's eight volumes now fill fifteen volumes. The second volume is a special case. The first volume had not sold well, and Swedenborg was apparently eager to try new formats to spark interest among readers. He commissioned an English translation of volume 2 that was published in the same year as the original Latin volume, and he arranged to have the six chapters of the Latin version printed and sold separately. The present edition represents the separate printings by giving an individual part title page for each chapter.

Section numbers Following a practice common in his time, Swedenborg divided his published theological works into sections numbered in sequence from beginning to end. His original section numbers have been preserved in this edition; they appear in boxes in the outside margins. Traditionally, these sections have been referred to as "numbers" and designated by the abbreviation "n." In this edition, however, the more common section symbol (§) is used to designate the section numbers, and the sections are referred to as such.

Subsection numbers Because many sections throughout Swedenborg's works are too long for precise cross-referencing, Swedenborgian scholar John Faulkner Potts (1838–1923) further divided them into subsections; these have since become standard, though minor variations occur from one edition to another. These subsections are indicated by bracketed numbers that appear in the text itself: [2], [3], and so on. Because the beginning of the first *subsection* always coincides with the beginning of the section proper, it is not labeled in the text.

Citations of Swedenborg's text As is common in Swedenborgian studies, text citations of Swedenborg's works refer not to page numbers but to section numbers, which unlike page numbers are uniform in most editions. In citations the section symbol (§) is generally omitted after the title of a work by Swedenborg. Thus "*Secrets of Heaven* 29" refers to section 29 (§29) of Swedenborg's *Secrets of Heaven,* not to page 29 of any edition. Subsection numbers are given after a colon; a reference such as "29:2" indicates subsection 2 of section 29. The reference "29:1" would indicate the first subsection of section 29, though that subsection is not in fact labeled in the text. Where section numbers stand alone without titles, their function is indicated by the prefixed section symbol; for example, "§29:2".

Citations of the Bible Biblical citations in this edition follow the accepted standard: a semicolon is used between book references and between chapter references, and a comma between verse references. Therefore "Matthew 5:11, 12; 6:1; 10:41, 42; Luke 6:23, 35" would refer to Matthew chapter 5, verses 11 and 12; Matthew chapter 6, verse 1; Matthew chapter 10, verses 41 and 42; and Luke chapter 6, verses 23 and 35. Swedenborg often incorporated the numbers of verses not actually represented in his text when listing verse numbers for a passage he quoted; these apparently constitute a kind of "see also" reference to other material he felt was relevant. This edition includes these extra verses and also follows Swedenborg where he cites contiguous verses individually (for example, John 14:8, 9, 10, 11), rather than as a range (John 14:8–11). Occasionally this edition supplies a full, conventional Bible reference where Swedenborg omits one after a quotation.

Quotations in Swedenborg's works Some features of the original Latin text of *Secrets of Heaven* have been modernized in this edition. For example, Swedenborg's first edition generally relies on context or italics rather than on quotation marks to indicate passages taken from the Bible or from other works. The manner in which these conventions are used in the original suggests that Swedenborg did not feel it necessary to belabor the distinction between direct quotation and paraphrase; neither did he mark his omissions from or changes to material he quoted, a practice in which this edition generally follows him. One exception consists of those instances in which Swedenborg did not include a complete sentence at the beginning or end of a Bible quotation. The omission in such cases has been marked in this edition with added points of ellipsis.

Italicized terms Any words in indented scriptural extracts that are here set in italics reflect a similar emphasis in the first edition.

Special use of vertical rule The opening passages of the chapters treating Genesis 1–15, as well as the ends of all chapters, contain material that derives in some way from Swedenborg's experiences in the spiritual world. Swedenborg specified that the text of these passages be set in continuous italics to distinguish it from exegetical and other material. For this edition, the heavy use of italic text was felt to be antithetical to modern tastes, as well as difficult to read, and so such passages are instead marked by a vertical rule in the inside margin.

Changes to and insertions in the text This translation is based on the first Latin edition, published by Swedenborg himself (1749–1756); it also reflects emendations in the third Latin edition, edited by P. H. Johnson, John E. Elliott, and others, and published by the Swedenborg Society (1949–1973). It incorporates the silent correction of minor errors, not only in the text proper but in Bible verse references. The text has also been changed without notice where the verse numbering of the Latin Bible cited by Swedenborg differs from that of modern English Bibles. Throughout the translation, references or cross-references that were implied but not stated have been inserted in brackets; for example, [John 3:27]. In many cases, it is very difficult to determine what Swedenborg had in mind when he referred to other passages giving evidence for a statement or providing further discussion on a topic. Because of this difficulty, the missing references that are occasionally supplied in this edition should not be considered definitive or exhaustive. In contrast to such references in square brackets, references that occur in parentheses are those that appear in the first edition; for example, (1 Samuel 30:16), (see §42 above). Occasionally square brackets signal an insertion of other material that was not present in the first edition. These insertions fall into two classes: words likely to have been deleted through a copying or typesetting error, and words supplied by the translator as necessary for the understanding of the English text, though they have no direct parallel in the Latin. The latter device has been used sparingly, however, even at the risk of some inconsistency in its application. Unfortunately, no annotations concerning these insertions can be supplied in this Portable edition.

Biblical titles Swedenborg refers to the Hebrew Scriptures as the Old Testament and to the Greek Scriptures as the New Testament; his terminology has been adopted in this edition. As was the custom in his day, he refers to the Pentateuch (Genesis, Exodus, Leviticus, Numbers, and Deuteronomy) as the books of Moses, or simply as "Moses"; for example, in

§1947 he writes "as described in Moses," and then quotes a passage from Exodus. Similarly, in sentences or phrases introducing quotations he sometimes refers to the Psalms as "David," to Lamentations as "Jeremiah," and to the Gospel of John, the Epistles of John, and the Book of Revelation as simply "John." Conventional references supplied in parentheses after such quotations specify their sources more precisely.

Problematic content Occasionally Swedenborg makes statements that, although mild by the standards of eighteenth-century theological discourse, now read as harsh, dismissive, or insensitive. The most problematic are assertions about or criticisms of various religious traditions and their adherents—including Judaism, ancient or contemporary; Roman Catholicism; Islam; and the Protestantism in which Swedenborg himself grew up. These statements are far outweighed in size and importance by other passages in Swedenborg's works earnestly maintaining the value of every individual and of all religions. This wider context is discussed in the introductions and annotations of the Deluxe edition mentioned above. In the present format, however, problematic statements must be retained without comment. The other option—to omit them—would obscure some aspects of Swedenborg's presentation and in any case compromise its historicity.

SECRETS
OF
HEAVEN

A Disclosure of

SECRETS OF HEAVEN

Contained in

SACRED SCRIPTURE

or

THE WORD OF THE LORD

Continuing with Those in

Genesis
Chapter 16

Together with Amazing Things Seen
in the World of Spirits & in the Heaven of Angels

First seek God's kingdom and its justice
and you will gain all.

—Matthew 6:33

Preface

THE first two volumes explain [the first] fifteen chapters of Genesis and say what is contained in their inner meaning. Attached to each chapter [in those volumes] is a record of what the Lord in his divine mercy has given me the opportunity to see and hear in the world of spirits and the heaven of angels. Now comes the third volume, which includes similar reports likewise attached to each chapter. The article appended to the current chapter, Genesis 16 [§§1966–1983], concerns visions and dreams (including prophetic dreams) in the Word.

I know few will believe that anyone can see into the other world or report from there on the state of souls after death, because few believe in the resurrection, and this is the case with even fewer of the well-educated than of the uneducated. It is true that they say with their lips that they will rise again, because this accords with church doctrine, but they deny it at heart.

[2] Some even confess openly that they would believe it if someone were to rise from the dead and they were to see, hear, and touch the person. If this happened, though, it would be an isolated experience and would fail to convince those who at heart deny the resurrection. A thousand objections would occur to them and harden them in their negative frame of mind.

Others do claim to believe they will rise again, but only on the day of the Last Judgment. The picture they have formed of this is that everything in the visible world will cease to exist on that day; and since they have been awaiting it in vain for so many centuries, they too are dubious. What is meant by the Last Judgment mentioned in the Word, however, will be summarized at the end of the next chapter, Genesis 17 [§§2117–2133], the Lord in his divine mercy willing.

[3] These attitudes indicate what kind of people make up the Christian world today. The Sadducees told of in Matthew 22:23 and the verses

that follow openly denied the resurrection; but that was better than people today who claim they believe it (since it is church doctrine, as noted) but actually deny it at heart. Such people's words contradict their beliefs, and their beliefs contradict their words.

To prevent them from growing even more firmly entrenched in this misguided opinion, the Lord in his divine mercy has given me the privilege of experiencing the next world in spirit while bodily present in this world (since a human being is a spirit clothed with a body). There I have spoken with souls recently revived after death, and in fact with almost everyone I knew during physical life who had since died. Every day now for several years I have also talked with spirits and angels and seen astounding sights that it has never occurred to anyone even to imagine. No illusion of any kind was involved.

[4] Many people say that if someone comes to them from the other life, they will believe, so we shall see now whether they can be persuaded despite their hard hearts.

I can attest that people who come into the next life from the Christian world are the worst of all. They hate their neighbor, they hate the religion, they deny the Lord (since it is the heart rather than the mouth that does the talking in the other world), not to mention the fact that they are more adulterous than anyone else. Because heaven is starting to move away from people in the Christian church as a result, clearly the last days are at hand, as I have learned for certain.

To learn the identity and nature of the Word's inner meaning, see the statements and illustrations in the first two volumes, §§1–5, 64, 65, 66, 167, 605, 920, 937, 1143, 1224, 1404, 1405, 1408, 1409, 1502 at the end, 1540, 1659, 1756, 1767–1777 and 1869–1879 (particularly), 1783, 1807; and in the current volume, §§1886–1889.

Genesis 16

1886

T HIS chapter has to do with Hagar and Ishmael, but until now no one has recognized what they represent and symbolize on an inner level. No one *could* have recognized it, because so far the world (even the scholarly world) has supposed that the stories of the Word are mere narratives, with no deeper implications. They have said that every jot is divinely inspired, but they do not mean much by it. All they mean is that the contents have been revealed [by God] and that some amount of doctrine relevant to their theology can be drawn from it and used by teachers and students. Because the stories have been divinely inspired (the world reasons), they have divine force in people's minds and do them more good than any other history.

Taken at face value, however, the narratives do little to improve us. They have no effect at all on our eternal life, because in the other world historical detail is obliterated from memory. What good would it do us there to know about Hagar the slave, about the fact that Sarai gave her to Abram, about Ishmael, or even about Abram? In order to go to heaven and partake of its joy (that is, of eternal life), our souls need only what belongs to and comes from the Lord. This is what his Word is for, and this is what it contains in its depths.

1887

To call the Word inspired is to say that everything in it, both the narratives and the other parts, contains heavenly qualities (which relate to love and goodness) and spiritual qualities (which relate to faith and truth). In other words, the contents are divine.

What the Lord inspires comes down from him through the heaven of angels and so through the world of spirits all the way to humankind. Among human beings it presents itself in its literal form, but in its first origins it is radically different. In heaven there is no such thing as a plain, ordinary narrative; instead, everything there represents something divine, and no one there perceives it any other way. This can be recognized from the fact that what it holds is inexpressible [2 Corinthians 12:4]. Consequently, unless the narratives represent divine matters and are therefore heavenly, they cannot possibly be divinely inspired.

Only the inner meaning reveals what the Word is like in the heavens, because *that is what the Lord's Word in the heavens is.*

1888   Let the following two examples demonstrate how the Word's literal meaning represents divine secrets and forms a repository and hiding place for the heavenly and spiritual dimensions of the Lord. The first example will be that "David" means not David but the Lord. The second will be that names have no meaning other than a symbolic one (implying that nothing else has any other meaning either).

This is what Ezekiel says about David:

> My servant David will be king over them, and there will be a single shepherd for them all. They will live on that land—they and their children and their children's children—forever. And David my servant will be chief over them forever. (Ezekiel 37:24, 25)

And in Hosea:

> The children of Israel will return and seek Jehovah their God and David their king. (Hosea 3:5)

Those prophets wrote these words after David's time, and yet they say explicitly that he will be their king and chief, from which anyone can see that in an inner sense David means the Lord. This is true in all other passages that mention David, even the narrative ones.

[2] It is clear to see in the Prophets that the names of kingdoms, regions, cities, and men have a symbolic meaning. Take for example just this one selection in Isaiah:

> This is what the Lord Jehovih Sabaoth has said: "You are not to be afraid of Assyria, my people, who reside in Zion. With a rod he will strike you; and a staff he will lift over you on the way to Egypt." Jehovah Sabaoth will stir up a whip upon him (as in the blow dealt to Midian at the rock

of Oreb) and [lift] his staff over the sea, and he will lift it on the way to Egypt. He will come against Aiath. He will cross into Migron. At Michmash he will command his weapons. They will cross Mabara. Gibeah will be a way station for us. Hormah will tremble. Gibeah of Saul will flee. Bellow with your voice, daughter of Gallim! Listen carefully, Laishah! Anathoth will be wretched. Madmenah will wander. The residents of Gebim will huddle together. It is still the day to stand firm in Nob. The mountain of the daughter of Zion will wave its hand, the hill of Jerusalem. [The Lord] will chop down the thickets of the forest with iron; and Lebanon will be felled by the Majestic One. (Isaiah 10:24, 26–34)

[3] This passage consists almost exclusively of names, which would have no meaning unless each one of them symbolized some deeper reality. If your mind were to become stuck on those names, you would never acknowledge that this was the Lord's Word.

Yet who would believe that they all contain secrets of heaven in their inner meaning? Who would believe that they depict the state of people attempting to pry into the mysteries of faith by sophistic arguments based on secular knowledge? That each name portrays some particular facet of that state? Or that heavenly attributes of love and spiritual elements of faith received from the Lord do away with such arguments?

Explanations concerning Assyria in §§119, 1186 make it quite clear that Assyria symbolizes the sophistry being treated of here. Explanations at §§1164, 1165, 1462 make it clear that Egypt symbolizes secular knowledge. Read and examine the discussions there to see whether this is not so. The same is true with all other names and with every single word [in Scripture].

The same is true in the current chapter with the names of Abram, Sarai, Hagar, and Ishmael. What they mean can be seen from the summary below and then from the verse-by-verse explanation that follows. By its very nature, though, the meaning will be difficult to explain intelligibly, because the theme discussed under the guise of these figures is the Lord's rational mind—how it was conceived and born, and what it was like before it became one with his inner self, which was Jehovah.

The reason the subject is not easy to explain intelligibly is that people today have not heard of the inner self, intermediate self, and outer self. The term *rational mind,* or *rational self,* does have some meaning; but if you say that the rational mind is midway between the inner and outer self, few if any understand.

1889

Still, the inner meaning here speaks of the Lord's rational self, and how it was conceived and born as the result of an inflow from his inner self into his outer self, and this is what the story of Abram, Hagar, and Ishmael involves. So to prevent the explanation that follows from seeming completely alien, it needs to be pointed out that everyone has an inner self, an outer self, and a rational self in between, each of which is perfectly distinct from the next. For more on this subject, see the earlier discussion in §978.

Genesis 16

1. And Sarai, wife of Abram, had not borne [a child] for him. And she had an Egyptian slave, and her name was Hagar.

2. And Sarai said to Abram, "Consider, please: Jehovah has closed me off from giving birth. Go in, please, to my slave; maybe I will be built up from her." And Abram listened to the voice of Sarai.

3. And Sarai, wife of Abram, took Hagar, her Egyptian slave, at the end of ten years of Abram's residing in the land of Canaan, and gave her to Abram, her husband, to be his woman.

4. And he went in to Hagar, and she conceived, and she saw that she had conceived, and the woman who owned her was contemptible in her eyes.

5. And Sarai said to Abram, "My wrong be on you: I gave my slave into your embrace, and she saw that she had conceived, and I am contemptible in her eyes. Jehovah judge between me and you!"

6. And Abram said to Sarai, "Here, now, your slave is in your hand; do to her what is good in your eyes." And Sarai humbled her, and she fled from Sarai's face.

7. And the angel of Jehovah found her at a spring of water in the wilderness, at the spring on the way to Shur.

8. And he said, "Hagar, Sarai's slave, where are you coming from and where are you going?" And she said, "From the face of Sarai, my owner, I am fleeing."

9. And the angel of Jehovah said to her, "Go back to your owner and humble yourself under her hands."

10. And the angel of Jehovah said to her, "I will greatly multiply your seed, and they will be too abundant to count."

11. And the angel of Jehovah said to her, "Here, you are pregnant, and you will bear a son, and you shall call his name Ishmael, because Jehovah has listened to your affliction.

12. And he will be a wild donkey of a person, his hand against everyone, and everyone's hand against him, and he will dwell defiantly in the face of all his brothers."

13. And she called the name of Jehovah, the one speaking to her, "You are a God who sees me"; because she said, "Even in this place, did I see behind the one seeing me?"

14. Therefore they called the spring "the spring of the living one who sees me"; here, it is between Kadesh and Bered.

15. And Hagar bore Abram a son, and Abram called the name of his son, whom Hagar bore, Ishmael.

16. And Abram was a son of eighty-six years when Hagar bore Ishmael to Abram.

Summary

THIS chapter deals with the Lord's first rational capacity, which was **1890** conceived by an inflow of his inner self into the desire his outer self had for knowledge. His inner self is Abram. The desire his outer self had for knowledge is the Egyptian slave Hagar. The rational capacity developing out of it is Ishmael. The nature of this capacity is described, and chapter 21 then depicts its banishment from home after the Lord's divine rationality, represented by Isaac, was born.

The Lord's first rational abilities were conceived in an orderly way, **1891** when his inner self flowed into or joined forces with the vital energy of his outer self in its desire for knowledge (verses 1, 2, 3). Since this rationality developed from his outer self, however, by nature it despised intuitive truth (verse 4). As a result the Lord had thoughts about the subduing of it (verses 5, 6, 7, 8, 9), and about the fact that it would become spiritual and heavenly when subdued (verses 10, 11). A portrayal of its nature if not subdued is provided (verse 12). The Lord looked at the reason for this from the viewpoint of his intermediate self (verses 13, 14). The character of his rational mind is therefore depicted, as is the stage he had reached when his rational mind emerged (verses 15, 16).

Inner Meaning

1892 GENESIS 16:1. *And Sarai, wife of Abram, had not borne [a child] for him. And she had an Egyptian slave, and her name was Hagar.*

Sarai, wife of Abram, had not borne [a child] for him means that a rational self did not yet exist [in the Lord]. *Sarai* is truth that is attached to goodness; *Abram* is the Lord's inner self, which was Jehovah. *And she had an Egyptian slave* symbolizes a desire for knowledge. *And her name was Hagar* symbolizes vital energy in the outer (earthly) self.

1893 The fact that *Sarai, wife of Abram, had not borne [a child] for him* means that a rational self did not yet exist [in the Lord] will become clear later, where Isaac is discussed.

As mentioned before [§1889], each of us has an inner self, an outer self (more properly referred to as an earthly self), and a rational self in between. In the Lord's case these were represented by Abraham, Isaac, and Jacob—his inner self, by Abraham; his rational self, by Isaac; and his earthly self, by Jacob.

The Lord's inner self was Jehovah himself, because he was conceived of Jehovah. That is why he called Jehovah his Father so many times, and that is why the Word calls him the Only-Born of God, and God's only Son [John 1:14, 18; 3:16, 18].

We are not born rational but only with the ability to become rational, as anyone can see by considering that newborn babies are not equipped with reason. They become rational over time, with the help of their outer and inner senses, as they absorb secular and religious knowledge.

Adolescents do seem to possess rationality, but it is not actual rationality; it is merely a kind of starting point. This can be recognized from the consideration that it is adults, young and old, who are rational.

[2] The subject of the current chapter is the Lord's rational self. Divine rationality in its genuine form is represented by Isaac; but in its early form, before it became divine, that rationality is represented by Ishmael. The statement here, then, that Sarai, wife of Abram, had not borne [a child] for him, means that there was no divine rationality yet.

As noted earlier [§§1414, 1444, 1573], the Lord was born like any other person and resembled any other person in what he inherited from his mother, Mary. The rational mind is shaped by secular and religious knowledge, which enter through the outer senses, the senses that belong to the outer self, so early rationality was born in the Lord the same way it is in any other person. But since he made every human quality in himself divine, by his own power, he made his rationality divine as well.

The current chapter paints a picture of the Lord's early rationality, as does Genesis 21:4–21, which also treats of Hagar and Ishmael, and the latter's banishment when Isaac, representing divine rationality, started to grow up.

It has already been stated and shown that *Sarai* means truth attached to goodness (§1468 and elsewhere), and that *Abram* means the Lord's inner self, [or inner human,] which was Jehovah.

1894

The reason the Lord's inner self is referred to as human, although it was Jehovah, is that no one but Jehovah is human. "Human being" in its true sense means the core reality from which humanness comes. That core reality from which humanness comes is divine, and consequently it is heavenly and spiritual. If we lack what is divinely heavenlike and spiritual, nothing in us is human; all we have is something analogous to the soul animals have.

It is from the core essence of Jehovah, or the Lord, that every human is human and can be called human. The heavenly trait that makes us human is loving the Lord and loving our neighbor. To love others is to be human, because for one thing, to love them is to be an image of the Lord, and for another, that love is something we receive from the Lord. Without it, we are wild beasts.

[2] The fact that Jehovah, or the Lord, is the only human, that our being referred to as human is something we acquire from him, and that one person can be more human than another may be seen in §§49, 288, 477, 565. It may also be seen from the fact that Jehovah, or the Lord, appeared as a human to our ancestors in the very earliest church and afterward to Abraham and the prophets as well. So when there was no longer any human on the earth—no longer anything heavenly or spiritual in people—the Lord saw fit to take on a human nature by being born like any other person and to render this humanity divine, making it the only true human.

In the Lord's eyes the whole of heaven reflects the image of a human being, because it reflects him. Heaven is called the universal human, primarily because the Lord is the all-in-all there.

And she had an Egyptian slave symbolizes a desire for knowledge, as can be seen from the symbolism of a female *slave* and of *Egypt.*

1895

Sarai, the slave's owner, or mistress, represents and symbolizes truth attached to goodness, as noted above [§1892]. Truth attached to goodness is [intuitive truth, or] truth that is genuinely understood. Truth seen by a process of reasoning, on the other hand, is on a lower level and so is lesser. It is born of secular learning and religious knowledge that has been brought to life by an emotional response to the knowledge. Because this emotion belongs to our outer self, it ought to serve the intuitive truth in our inmost depths, as a slave serves her owner or a servant serves her mistress. That emotion, then, is what the *slave* Hagar represents and symbolizes.

[2] It is not very easy to explain how these things work in a way that can be grasped. First you need to know what truth that is genuinely understood is. Then you need to know how rationality is born from the inner self as its father and the outer or earthly self as its mother, since unless these two selves unite, no rational capacity can possibly emerge.

Rationality is born not of secular learning and religious knowledge, as people think it is, but of an emotion: the *desire* for learning and knowledge. This can be seen simply from the fact that no one can possibly become rational without feeling some kind of pleasure in learning and knowledge, or some desire for it. This desire is the actual living force that plays the role of the mother, while heavenliness and spirituality itself, within this desire, is the living force that plays the role of the father. The stronger the desire, then, the more rational the person becomes; and the nobler the desire, the better the rationality. Facts and knowledge in themselves are simply dead things, or instrumental causes; it is the vital energy of desire that brings them to life. This is how everyone's rational self is conceived.

The reason the slave was Egyptian and the reason it is mentioned in the text is that *Egypt* symbolizes secular learning, as shown earlier, in §§1164, 1165, 1186, 1462.

1896   *Her name was Hagar* symbolizes vital energy in the outer (earthly) self, as can be seen from the discussion just above. It can also be seen from the meaning of "Hagar" as an immigrant or foreigner. Immigrants represented people who were being taught. Living somewhere as an immigrant represented instruction and the customs of a person's life, as shown before, in §1463.

When the Word says, "so-and-so's name is" (as in "*her name was Hagar*"), it means that the name involves something worth noting. To call someone by name is to recognize what the person is like, as shown before, in §§144, 145, 340. Not a single syllable appears in the Word without a reason or without symbolizing some inner phenomenon.

Genesis 16:2. And Sarai said to Abram, "Consider, please: Jehovah has closed me off from giving birth. Go in, please, to my slave; maybe I will be built up from her." And Abram listened to the voice of Sarai. **1897**

Sarai said to Abram means that this situation was perceived. *Consider, please: Jehovah has closed me off from giving birth* symbolizes conditions as they were before the intermediate self (the divinely rational self) had been born. *Go in, please, to my slave* symbolizes union with the outer self. *Maybe I will be built up from her* means that then rationality could be born. *And Abram listened to the voice of Sarai* means it could not have happened any other way.

Sarai said to Abram means that this situation was perceived. This can **1898** be seen from the symbolism of *Sarai* and *Abram: Sarai* symbolizes truth attached to goodness, and *Abram* symbolizes the inner self. In an inner sense, then, what Sarai said to Abram must mean a perception rather than any spoken words.

When the Lord perceived things at this stage, he was listening to truth connected with goodness, which told him how matters stood.

Heavenly people with the gift of perception experience something similar: there is a kind of truth connected with goodness that dictates to them. Later it is from goodness itself (or by means of goodness itself) that they perceive truth.

For the fact that on an inner level *saying* symbolizes perceiving, see §§1791, 1815, 1819, 1822.

Consider, please: Jehovah has closed me off from giving birth symbolizes **1899** conditions as they were before the intermediate self (the divinely rational self) had been born. This is established by statements above regarding the conception and birth of the rational self [§1893]. Specifically, Isaac represents the Lord's divinely rational self, but Ishmael represents his first rational self, which was to become divine. As a representation of this circumstance, Sarai remained infertile until Ishmael became a young man, as recounted in Genesis 21. That is why it says here that *Jehovah closed her off from giving birth.*

Go in, please, to my slave symbolizes union with the outer self. This **1900** too can be seen from remarks above, to the effect that a person's rationality is conceived and born from the inner self as father and the outer self as mother [§1895]. Our actual life comes from our inner self, which cannot communicate with our outer self in more than the vaguest fashion until vessels for receiving it are formed in the memory. They are formed by means of religious knowledge and secular learning. [2] The inner self influences the knowledge and learning of the outer self by means of emotion. In the interval before we acquire knowledge and learning, the inner self does communicate with the outer, but only by means of emotions, through which it governs the outer self. This produces only the most general impulses and certain appetites and blind instincts, like those seen in small children.

This life gradually becomes more distinct, though, as vessels are formed in the [outer] memory by means of knowledge, and in the inner memory by means of rational thinking. As these vessels are being formed and organized in series (in such a fashion that they interrelate the way close and distant relatives do, or the way communities and clans do), the outer self comes into fuller and fuller correspondence with the inner self. Rational thinking, which is a bridge between the inner and outer selves, is even better at bringing them into correspondence. Still, the two do not come into agreement with each other unless the religious knowledge that forms the vessels is accurate. [3] The heavenly and spiritual facets of the inner self find counterparts to themselves only among true ideas. True ideas impressed on the organic forms of both kinds of memory are real vessels, into which the heavenly qualities of love and the spiritual qualities of faith can pour themselves.

At that point, you see, the Lord arranges them to match a vision and image of the communities in heaven (his kingdom). As a result, the person becomes a miniature heaven, a miniature kingdom of the Lord. The minds of people devoted to the heavenliness of love and the spirituality of faith are in fact referred to as heaven (the Lord's kingdom) in the Word.

But these things are said for those who love to think deeply.

1901   *And maybe I will be built up from her* means that then rationality could be born. This can be seen from the meaning of *being built up* when it has to do with birth, so there is no need for explanation. Sarai, as noted, symbolizes intuitive truth, which is attached to goodness as its spouse [§§1402, 1468–1469, 1475, 1495, 1895].

Before there is any rationality for it to flow into or flow through, intuitive truth, which exists at the inmost depths, is totally bereft of offspring, like a mother without children. Without rationality as a means, it cannot bring any truth to the outer self. Take little children, for example. They cannot see any truth at all until they have absorbed religious knowledge. The better and fuller the knowledge they gain, as just said, the better and fuller the communication of intuitive truth, which lives in their inmost depths, or in goodness.

[2] This intuitive truth represented by Sarai is spirituality itself, which comes to us through heaven and so by an inner path. It comes to every one of us, and is constantly seeking out the knowledge we have gained through our senses and planted in our memory. We are unaware of this kind of truth, because it is too pure for our indistinct manner of thinking to perceive. It is like a light that shines in the mind and gives us the ability to learn, think, and understand.

Rationality, on the other hand, cannot emerge unless the intuitive truth that Sarai represents reaches us. As a consequence, it functions in every way as her child, as long as it is formed of true ideas that are connected with various kinds of good, and even more so when it is formed of goodness that gives rise to true ideas. Under those circumstances, it is her own child. Up till then it is *acknowledged* as her child, but is in fact not her own; it is merely a child acquired from her slave. Nonetheless she adopts it, which is why it says here that she would be built up from her slave.

And Abram listened to the voice of Sarai means it could not have happened any other way. This can be seen from the train of thought in the inner meaning and from the unavoidable fact that rationality cannot be born in us in any other way.

1902

If we were not steeped in inherited evil, our rationality would be born directly from a marriage between the heavenly and the spiritual qualities of our inner self, and knowledge would be born through our rationality. We would come into the world already equipped with a full supply of rationality and knowledge. That is how we were originally designed. The evidence for this is the fact that all animals of every stripe are born into all the knowledge they need or can use—what to eat, how to stay safe, where to live, how to reproduce. Their nature harmonizes with their destiny. What would we be capable of, then, if our destiny were not destroyed in us? We are the only beings born without knowledge.

[2] What causes us to be born in this condition is the evil we inherit from our father and mother. Because of inherited evil, all our capacities are turned backward, away from truth and goodness. A direct stream of heavenly and spiritual influences from the Lord cannot reshape them to conform. This is the reason our rational mind needs to be created in an entirely different way, by entirely different means. It must be formed through secular facts and religious knowledge that are absorbed through the senses and therefore enter by an external route. So the proper order is reversed, and it is only through a miracle that the Lord makes us rational. That is what is meant by going in to Sarai's slave, which symbolizes the

joining of the inner with the outer self. It is also meant by *Abram listened to the voice of Sarai,* which symbolizes the fact that it could not have happened any other way.

[3] Because the Lord was born like any other person and had a heredity from his mother, he resembled other people in this way. The purpose was for him to reduce everything to order by fighting and winning his inward battles. His rational mind was consequently conceived and born as it is in other people, but with a difference: his divine nature, or Jehovah, was at the core of absolutely everything in him. So at his core lay the vital energy of love for the entire human race, and he fought for the human race and its salvation in all his trials.

1903   Genesis 16:3. *And Sarai, wife of Abram, took Hagar, her Egyptian slave, at the end of ten years of Abram's residing in the land of Canaan, and gave her to Abram, her husband, to be his woman.*

Sarai, wife of Abram, symbolizes a desire for truth, which is Sarai as wife in a positive sense. *Took Hagar, her Egyptian slave,* symbolizes the vital energy of the outer self and a desire for knowledge. *At the end of ten years of Abram's residing in the land of Canaan* symbolizes remaining traces of goodness and of truth that rises out of goodness, which the Lord acquired for himself and through which this kind of rationality was conceived. *And gave her to Abram, her husband, to be his woman* symbolizes a union urged by the desire for truth.

1904   *Sarai, wife of Abram,* symbolizes a desire for truth, which is Sarai as wife in a positive sense. This can be seen from the symbolism of *Sarai* as truth attached to goodness and from the symbolism of a *wife* as an emotion, as discussed earlier, in §§915, 1468.

The desire for what is good and the desire for what is true are two distinctly different emotions. When we are regenerating, the desire for truth takes precedence, because we desire truth for the sake of what is good. When we have been reborn, though, the desire for goodness takes precedence, and goodness gives us a desire for truth. A desire for goodness belongs to our will, a desire for truth to our intellect.

The earliest people established [a custom of referring to] these two emotions as partners in a kind of marriage, calling goodness or the love of goodness a husband, and truth or the love of truth a wife, as if they were people. The practice of comparing goodness and truth to marriage traces its origin to the heavenly marriage.

[2] Goodness and truth viewed in themselves have no life. It is from love or desire that they draw life. They are simply instruments used by

life. As a result, the quality of the love in us that desires goodness and truth is what determines the quality of our life, since all life is a matter of love or desire. That is why Sarai as wife in a positive sense symbolizes a desire for truth. Here, because intuition longed to have rationality as its offspring, and it speaks with longing or desire, the current verse explicitly says, "Sarai, *wife of Abram,* gave *Abram, her husband.*" There would have been no need to repeat the idea—since in themselves the latter words are superfluous—had such meanings not been involved on an inner level.

[3] Intuitive truth is distinguished from rational truth, and rational truth from factual truth, in the same way that the inner, intermediate, and outer planes are. Intuitive truth is on the inner plane, rational truth is intermediate, and factual truth is on the outer plane. These are distinctly different from each other, because each lies within the next. The intuitive truth that is inside, at our core, is never ours but the Lord's in us. So the Lord flows into our rational mind (where truth first seems to be ours) and through our rational mind into our store of facts. It follows from this that when we think on our own (as we seem to do), we cannot possibly think on the basis of intuitive truth but only on the basis of rational and factual truth, because these appear to be ours. [4] Only the Lord when he lived in the world based his thinking on intuitive truth, because that truth was his divine truth joined to goodness, or his divine spirituality joined to his divine heavenliness. In this the Lord was different from any other person. To think in divine terms, seemingly on one's own, is not something a human ever does or is ever capable of doing. Only the One who was conceived by Jehovah is capable of this. Because his thoughts grew out of intuitive truth, or rather out of a love or desire for intuitive truth, his longing for rationality did too. That is why it says here that Sarai, wife of Abram (meaning the desire for intuitive truth), took Hagar the Egyptian and gave her to Abram, her husband, to be his woman.

[5] The rest of the secrets hidden here cannot be unfolded and explained intelligibly, because people are in deep darkness about their inner reaches and do not have even the least idea of them. They mistake factual information for rationality and for higher intuition, failing to recognize that these are different things. In fact, the three are so distinct from each other that intuition can exist without rationality, and rationality based on intuition can exist without a supply of facts. This will inevitably bewilder people who dote on facts, but it is still the truth. On the other hand, it is not possible for a person to have reliable facts—specifically, a desire for reliable facts and a trust in them—without also having true rationality, so that the

Lord can flow into it (and through it) from the intuitive part of the mind. These secrets are not evident to people until they reach the other world.

1905   *Took Hagar, her Egyptian slave* symbolizes the vital energy of the outer self and a desire for knowledge. This is established by the symbolism of *Hagar* (discussed above in §§1895, 1896) and by the symbolism of an *Egyptian* and a *slave* (also discussed there).

1906   *At the end of ten years of Abram's residing in the land of Canaan* symbolizes remaining traces of goodness and of truth that rises out of goodness, which the Lord acquired for himself and through which this kind of rationality was conceived. This can be seen from the symbolism of *ten* as remaining traces (dealt with earlier, in §576). Remaining traces have been defined and illustrated in §§468, 530, 560, 561, 660, 661, 798, 1050. They are all the states in which goodness and truth affect us, states that the Lord gives us as a gift, starting in infancy and continuing to the end of life. These states he stores up in us for use in our life after death. All the states of our life return one after another in the next world, where they are modified by states of goodness and truth that the Lord has given us. The more of these traces we receive during bodily life, then, or in other words, the more goodness and truth we receive, the more pleasant and beautiful the rest of our states appear when they return.

Anyone who gives it some thought can see that this is so. When we are born, we have no goodness on our own. From head to toe we are polluted with inherited evil. Everything good about us—our love for our parents, caregivers, and peers, and the innocence of this love—comes from outside us. These are the things that flow from the Lord through the heaven of innocence and peace, which is the inmost heaven. That is how we come to be imbued with them while still very small.

[2] Later, as we grow up, this childish goodness, innocence, and gentleness dwindle bit by bit. The more we assimilate into society, the more we participate in its sensual pleasures, in greed, and therefore in evil. To the same extent, the good, heavenly tendencies of childhood start to fade, yet they stay with us, and these states modify the ones we later adopt as our own. Without them, we could not be the least bit human. If our states of appetite, or of evil, were not tempered by states of a desire for something good, they would be more monstrous than those of any animal. These good states are what are called remaining traces. The Lord gives them to us as a gift and plants them in our psyche without our awareness.

[3] At the next stage of life, we still receive new gifts, but they are states that have more to do with truth than with goodness. As we mature,

we absorb truth, which in a similar way is stored up in our intermediate self. This remnant of truth, which is born from a spiritual influence the Lord exerts on us, enables us to think and also to understand what is good and true in public and private life. In addition it enables us to accept spiritual truth, or religious truth, although for this we also need the remnant of goodness we received in childhood.

We have no idea that there is such a thing as a remnant or that we have one hidden away in our intermediate, rational mind, because we do not think that anything comes in from outside us. We imagine that it all comes naturally, that we are born with it, and therefore that it all exists inside us as children, when the truth of the matter is quite the opposite.

The Word speaks of a remnant in many places, and it symbolizes the states through which we become human, the Lord alone doing the work.

[4] The Lord's remnant, though, consisted of all the divine states he acquired for himself, which he used in making his human nature one with his divine nature. Our own remnant cannot compare with his, because ours is not divine but human.

That remnant is what the ten years of Abram's residence in the land of Canaan symbolize.

When angels hear Scripture, they do not know what "ten" means. No, as soon as a person on earth voices that word, the idea of a remnant immediately springs to the angels' minds instead, because "ten" and "tenths" in Scripture symbolize remaining traces. This is established by the remarks and illustrations in §§576, 1738. When angels perceive that a thing happened at the end of ten years of Abram's residing in the land of Canaan, they picture the Lord and at the same time the countless qualities meant by the remnant the Lord had when he was in the world.

And gave her to Abram, her husband, to be his woman symbolizes a union urged by the desire for truth. This can be seen from the description above of Sarai, wife of Abram, in a positive sense, as the desire for truth. It can also be seen from the discussion of the union between the inner self on one hand and vital energy and desire in the outer self on the other, which results in rationality.

Hagar was given to Abram not as a wife but as a woman, because the divine plan requires that marriage be restricted to one husband and one wife. The love in a marriage cannot possibly be divided. When it is divided among many, it is not married love but rather a collection of lusts. This will be discussed below, by the Lord's divine mercy [§2740].

1907

1908   Genesis 16:4. *And he went in to Hagar, and she conceived; and she saw that she had conceived, and the woman who owned her was contemptible in her eyes.*

He went in to Hagar symbolizes union of the inner self with the vital energy that a desire for knowledge entails. *And she conceived* symbolizes the first stirrings of the rational mind. *And she saw that she had conceived, and the woman who owned her was contemptible in her eyes* means that at its conception this rationality despised genuine truth attached to goodness.

1909   *He went in to Hagar* symbolizes union of the inner self with the vital energy that a desire for knowledge entails. This can be seen from the symbolism of *Hagar* as the vital energy of the outer or earthly self, discussed above at verse 1 [§1896]. This energy is the energy connected with a desire for knowledge, as can be seen from the symbolism of an Egyptian slave, also discussed above [§1895].

The outer self has many emotions, each devoted to its own purpose, but the best emotion it has is the desire for religious knowledge and secular learning, as long as one's aim is to become truly rational, since goodness and truth are then the end in view.

The actual life force of the inner self flows into all the emotions of the earthly self, but its nature changes there, depending on the earthly self's ends. When it flows into desires that look to the material world as their goal, it energizes this goal with its vital force and turns into a worldly type of energy. When it flows into desires that look to oneself as their goal, it energizes this goal with its vital force and turns into a bodily type of energy. And so on. That is why cravings and delusions do indeed have life, but the life they have opposes a desire for goodness and truth.

[2] The only object in us on which the inflowing life force acts is the end we have in view, because whatever we love is our individual goal, and love is the only thing that has life. Any other possible objects merely branch off from that goal and draw their life from it.

We can each see what kind of life we have in us simply by examining what kind of end we have in view—though not what ends we have, since they are as numerous as our intentions, and almost as numerous as the judgments and decisions forming our thoughts. These are intermediate goals, however, and they branch off from our main goal in different ways, or lead back to it. Instead, we need to examine the aim that we cherish above all others, the aim beside which all others seem unimportant.

If you aim at personal power or worldly advantages, be aware that your life is hellish. If in contrast you aim to benefit your neighbor, the larger community, the Lord's kingdom, and especially the Lord himself, know that your life is heavenly.

The symbolism of *and she conceived* as the first stirrings of the rational mind can be seen from the symbolism of *conception* as the beginning of life.

1910

The rational mind, as noted [§1895], receives life when the vital energy of the inner self acts on the vital energy of the outer self's desire for religious knowledge and secular learning. The latter kind of energy acts in effect as a body for the rational mind; it clothes the life force of the inner self as a body clothes a soul. This is precisely the function of knowledge and learning.

Something that appears like a soul and a body exists in every facet of our being—in every facet of our feelings and in every facet of our thinking. Nothing exists in us, no matter how simple it seems, that does not consist of many parts and does not emerge from something prior to itself.

And she saw that she had conceived, and the woman who owned her was contemptible in her eyes means that at its conception this rationality despised genuine truth attached to goodness. This can be seen from the symbolism of *the woman who owned her,* Sarai, as truth attached to goodness.

1911

At its conception, the rational mind cannot acknowledge intuitive truth (or spiritual truth) as true, because many misconceptions cling to the rational mind. These include illusions rising out of information gleaned from the world and from nature; they also include appearances rising out of knowledge acquired from the literal meaning of the Word; and none of them are accurate.

[2] For example, it is an intuitive truth that the Lord is the source of all life. At its conception, the rational mind does not grasp this. It thinks that if it did not have independent life, it would have no life at all. In fact, it becomes outraged if anyone says otherwise, as I have noticed many times in spirits who cling to the lies their senses tell them.

[3] It is an intuitive truth that the Lord is the source of everything good and true. At its conception, the rational mind does not grasp this either, because it perceives goodness and truth as originating in itself. The way the rational mind looks at it, if goodness and truth were not inherent in us, we would not be able to think anything good or true, let alone act on it. If they do come from somewhere else, it supposes, we should give up our own efforts and just wait perpetually for inspiration.

[4] It is an intuitive truth that what comes from the Lord is always good, never evil. At its conception, the rational mind rejects this idea too. It supposes that because the Lord is in absolute control, even evil

comes from him. Since he is omnipotent, is present everywhere, is goodness itself, and allows punishment to proceed for the evil in hell, the rational mind thinks that he wills the evil effects of punishment. The truth is, though, that the Lord never does evil to anyone and does not like to see anyone punished.

[5] It is an intuitive truth that the Lord gives heavenly people a perception of goodness and truth. The primitive rational mind either completely denies the existence of perception or argues that if perception came from outside us, not from ourselves, we would be lifeless automatons.

In fact, the more the rational mind bases its thinking on facts gleaned from sensory data and on philosophical reasoning, the more difficulty it has understanding these or any other intuitive truths. After all, the more the rational mind thinks this way, the more deeply the shadows thicken around the mistaken thinking that results. This is why the well-educated have less faith than others.

[6] Since the rational mind is like this at its conception, it plainly holds its owner in contempt, or in other words, despises intuitive truth.

Intuitive truth does not reveal itself—that is, we do not recognize it—until illusions and appearances dissolve, and they do not even begin to dissolve as long as we are wrangling over genuine truth on the basis of empirical evidence and facts. Intuitive truth first reveals itself when we believe in all simplicity of heart that something is true because the Lord has said so. Then the dark shadows of error scatter and there is nothing left in us to cause misunderstanding.

[7] The Lord, however, had no outright misconceptions. When his rationality was first conceived, what he fell prey to were notions that seemed to be true—"truth" that was not true in and of itself—as is evident from the remarks at §1661. So at its conception, even *his* rational mind despised intuitive truth; but as it gradually became divine, the cloud of appearances evaporated and intuitive truths revealed themselves to him in all their glory. This shift was represented and symbolized by Ishmael's being banished from home when Isaac started to grow up.

The Lord himself did not despise intuitive truth. Rather, he perceived and saw that his newly formed rationality despised it, as will become plain from what follows in §1914.

1912   Genesis 16:5. *And Sarai said to Abram, "My wrong be on you: I gave my slave into your embrace, and she saw that she had conceived, and I am contemptible in her eyes. Jehovah judge between me and you!"*

Sarai said to Abram means that the desire for truth perceived this. *My wrong be on you: I gave my slave into your embrace* means that the desire for truth was not willing to take the blame. *And she saw that she had conceived* symbolizes the first stirrings of rationality. *And I am contemptible in her eyes* here as above means that at its conception this rationality despised genuine truth attached to goodness. *Jehovah judge between me and you* symbolizes the Lord's indignation.

The fact that *Sarai said to Abram* means that the desire for truth perceived this, is established by the symbolism of *Sarai* as the desire for truth (§1904) and of *saying* on an inner level as perceiving (as noted above at §1898, where the same words occur).

1913

My wrong be on you: I gave my slave into your embrace means that the desire for truth was not willing to take the blame, as can be seen without explanation.

1914

In an inner sense these words involve the idea that the Lord perceived this primitive rationality to be such that it despised intuitive truth, so he denounced it. Intuitive truth was what he based his thinking on, as noted above at §1904, and since intuitive truth lies above the rational mind, he could perceive and see that the rational mind by its very nature held that truth in contempt.

[2] It was of course from within that the Lord was able to perceive and see what this budding rationality in him was like, since deeper levels can perceive what is happening on more superficial levels. To put it another way, higher levels are able to see what is happening on lower levels. (The reverse, however, is not true.) People with a conscience can and do experience this kind of insight from above, because when anything contrary to their principles springs to mind or urges itself on their will, they not only perceive it but also judge it to be wrong. In fact, it grieves them to know they are capable of such a thing. This is even more true of people with perception, because perception lies even deeper in the rational mind. What then of the Lord! Consider that the kind of perception he had was divinely heavenlike, and that his thinking was inspired by the desire for intuitive truth, which lies above the rational mind. He could not help feeling indignant, then, knowing that not a whisper of evil or falsity came from him and that because he loved truth he felt the gravest possible concern that the rational mind be pure.

This shows that the Lord himself did not despise intuitive truth but perceived that the primitive rationality within him did.

[3] Explaining intelligibly what it is to base one's thinking on intuitive truth is impossible, particularly because no one's thoughts have come from that love and that truth except the Lord's. One whose thoughts come from there is above the angelic heaven. The angels of the third heaven base their thinking not on intuitive truth but on a kind of rationality that is relatively deep. In the case of the Lord, though, the more fully he united his human nature with his divine nature, the more his thoughts were born of divine goodness itself, that is, of Jehovah.

[4] Our ancestors in the earliest church had perception and based their thinking on a relatively deep rationality. Our ancestors in the ancient church, who had conscience instead of perception, based their thinking on a more superficial or earthly rationality. But among those who lack conscience, none ever think at all rationally, because they have no rationality. Although they appear to be rational, they base their thinking on an earthly point of view tied to the senses and the body. The reason people devoid of conscience cannot think rationally is that they lack a rational mind, as just noted. Rational people are those who think what is good and true, never those who oppose goodness and truth. People who think what is evil and false think crazy thoughts, so they cannot be said to have any rationality at all.

1915   The symbolism of *and she saw that she had conceived* as the first stirrings of rationality can be seen from the symbolism of *conception* as the beginning of life, the same here as above at §1910.

1916   *I am contemptible in her eyes* means that at its conception this rationality despised genuine truth attached to goodness, as established by the remarks just above at §§1911, 1914.

1917   *Jehovah judge between me and you* symbolizes the Lord's indignation. This can be seen from the remarks just made and therefore needs no explanation.

The further ramifications of all this cannot be clearly grasped except by those who have been through the struggles involved in a spiritual crisis. When we are being tested, we experience times of devastation and desolation, times of despair, and consequently times of grief and anger, not to mention other deeply painful emotions. These come to us in different ways and at different times, depending on the states of evil and falsity that the evil demons and spirits arouse in us and that we fight. Devilish spirits love nothing more than to find some false idea within us. In fact, it is very common for them to plant their own false beliefs in us, then turn around and blame us for them. That is why the Lord responded to this with great indignation. In his case, his early rationality was incapable of containing any falsity, but it nevertheless contained some seeming truth that was not actually true in and of itself, as described previously at §§1661, 1911 (at the end).

Genesis 16:6. *And Abram said to Sarai, "Here, now, your slave is in your hand; do to her what is good in your eyes." And Sarai humbled her, and she fled from Sarai's face.*

1918

Abram said to Sarai symbolizes a perception. *Here, now, your slave is in your hand* means that this rationality was conceived under the authority of a desire for truth attached to goodness. *Do to her what is good in your eyes* symbolizes complete control over it. *And Sarai humbled her* symbolizes the conquest of it. *And she fled from Sarai's face* symbolizes the indignation felt by this newly conceived rationality.

The symbolism of *Abram said to Sarai* as a perception is established by statements above at §1898.

1919

The Lord's perceptions were represented by the words *Abram said to Sarai* and are symbolized by them. The thoughts inspired by these perceptions, however, were represented by the words *Sarai said to Abram*. Perception was what inspired the Lord's thoughts. When people have perception, that is the sole source of their thinking. Still, perception is not the same thing as thought.

To see that they are different, let conscience serve as an illustration. [2] Conscience is a general and therefore vague kind of inner dictate consisting of messages that stream in from the Lord by way of the heavens. These incoming messages present themselves to our intermediate, rational self, where they are more or less enveloped in a haze of appearances and fallacies concerning religious truth and goodness. Thought is different from conscience, but it nevertheless flows from conscience, because those who have conscience think and speak in accord with it. To think is nearly the same as to explain what our conscience is telling us—to split the message of conscience up into thoughts and then into words. As a result, people who have conscience are enabled by the Lord to think good thoughts about their neighbors consistently and are held back from thinking evil thoughts about them. Accordingly, conscience cannot possibly exist except in those who love their neighbor as themselves and think affirmatively about religious truth.

This example illustrates the difference between conscience and thought, and by extension, the difference between perception and thought.

[3] The Lord's perceptive abilities came directly from Jehovah and so from divine goodness. His thinking, however, was inspired by intuitive truth and a desire for this truth, as noted above in §§1904, 1914.

The Lord's divine perceptions cannot be captured in any thought, not even an angelic one, so they also cannot be described. The perceptive abilities of angels (described in §§1384 and following sections, 1394, 1395) are almost nothing compared to those the Lord had. Because the Lord's perceptions were divine, he was able to perceive everything in the heavens; and because he was able to perceive everything in the heavens, he was able to perceive everything on earth. The pattern in which the things of heaven and earth connect and interrelate ensures that anyone who perceives the former also perceives the latter.

[4] Ever since the Lord's human side united as one with his divine side and became Jehovah, though, the Lord has transcended what we call perception, because he is above the pattern in which the heavens and therefore the earth are arranged. He is Jehovah, the creator of the pattern, so it can be said that Jehovah is the pattern itself. He alone governs the pattern, not only in general, as people assume, but even in the smallest details. The smallest details, after all, are what make up the general whole. To speak of a general whole and remove the particulars from it would be exactly the same as speaking of a sum without parts. It would be speaking of a something that contains nothing. As a result, it is absolutely wrong and a mere figment of the imagination (as they say) to suggest that the Lord's providence is universal and not specific in the most minute way. To provide and govern in general and not in the smallest particulars is to provide for and govern exactly nothing.

This is a philosophical truth, but amazing to say, philosophers themselves—even the loftier ones—do not think or conceive of providence this way.

1920 *Here, now, your slave is in your hand* means that this rationality was conceived under the authority of a desire for truth attached to goodness. This can be seen from the symbolism of a *hand* as authoritative power (discussed before, at §878) and from that of Hagar the Egyptian as a desire for knowledge (also discussed before [§1895]).

Once the rational mind has been conceived as the result of an inflow from the inner self into the vital energy of the outer self and its desire for knowledge, the meaning of the slave includes the tender rationality that was still in her womb. Once it has been born and has matured, though, it is represented by Ishmael, as will be discussed later.

The Lord had power over the rationality in himself, and by his own power he subdued it, as will become clear from the discussion that now follows.

Do to her what is good in your eyes symbolizes complete control over it, **1921** as can be seen without explanation.

In an inner sense these words represent and symbolize the idea that the Lord used his own power to overcome, subdue, and banish the hereditary evil that had crept into this primitive rationality. As I said [§§1893, 1895], his rational mind was conceived from his inner self (which was Jehovah and served as its father) and born to his outer self (which served as its mother). Whatever came from his outer self brought this heredity with it, so it also brought evil. What came from his outer self is what the Lord overcame, subdued, and banished by his own power and ultimately made divine.

Each and every word in this verse establishes the fact that the Lord did these things by his own power. "Your slave is in your hand," for instance, means that this rationality was under his power. The current clause—"Do to her what is good in your eyes"—symbolizes his complete control over it. "Sarai humiliated her" just below symbolizes the conquest of it.

[2] These words were spoken to Sarai, who represents the intuitive truth which the Lord himself possessed and on which he based his thinking (as noted above in §§1904, 1914). This truth gave him complete control over his rational mind, and over his earthly mind, too, which was part of his outer self.

One whose thoughts originate in intuitive truth and whose perceptions originate in divine goodness necessarily acts under his own power. (Divine goodness was his too, since it was his Father's and he had no other soul than the Father.) Because it was by his own power that he mastered his hereditary evil and rid himself of it, then, it was also by his own power that he united his human nature with his divine nature. The one is a consequence of the other.

[3] The inner core, or in other words, the soul of one conceived of Jehovah, is nothing but Jehovah, so the Lord's very life was Jehovah himself. Jehovah—the divine nature, that is—cannot branch off the way the soul of a human father does in order for offspring to be conceived. The more human offspring depart from a resemblance to their father, the more they depart from their father himself, increasingly so as they mature. That is why fathers love their children less and less the older they grow. It was different with the Lord; as his human side grew up, he did not withdraw from his Father but continually drew closer, until they achieved perfect oneness. Clearly, then, he is identical with Jehovah the Father, as he himself also teaches plainly in John 14:6, 8, 9, 10, 11.

1922   The symbolism of *and she humbled her* as the conquest of that rationality follows from the discussion above.

1923   *And she fled from Sarai's face* symbolizes the indignation felt by this newly conceived rationality, as can be seen without explanation. *Fleeing from another's face* is the same as being unable to bear that person's presence, which is a consequence of indignation.

These words describe the anger this rationality felt against intuitive truth on account of the wish held by intuitive truth (the Lord, in other words) to humble or subdue it.

When the rational level of the mind rises up against the intuitional level, an internal battle ensues, followed by outrage on the part of the losing side. This happens during spiritual struggles, which amount to civil wars, consisting of quarrels and strife over power and control—evil power and control on one side and good power and control on the other.

1924   Genesis 16:7. *And the angel of Jehovah found her at a spring of water in the wilderness, at the spring on the way to Shur.*

The angel of Jehovah found her symbolizes the thinking of the intermediate self; the *angel of Jehovah* here is the intermediate-level thoughts that came from the Lord's inner self. *At a spring of water in the wilderness* means earthly truth that has not yet come alive. *At the spring on the way to Shur* means that this kind of truth developed out of the truth that results from a knowledge of facts.

1925   *The angel of Jehovah found her* symbolizes the thinking of the intermediate self—the Lord's intermediate self, specifically—as can be seen from the representation and symbolism of the *angel of Jehovah.*

The Word mentions the angel of Jehovah a number of times. Whenever the term is used in a positive sense, it represents and symbolizes something essential in the Lord or from the Lord. Context provides the key to that representation and symbolism.

There were angels who were sent to people and angels who spoke through the prophets, but the messages came *through* the angels rather than from them. In the state they were then in, they were wholly convinced that they were Jehovah (the Lord), but the moment they stopped speaking, they returned to their original state and spoke as if on their own.

[2] This is how it was with the angels who delivered the Word of the Lord, as I was allowed to learn from many similar experiences in the other world in my own times. (The experiences will be described later, with the Lord's divine mercy.) That is why angels were sometimes called Jehovah. One clear example is the angel who appeared to Moses in the bramble, as described in these words:

The *angel of Jehovah* appeared to Moses in a fiery flame from the middle of the bramble. *Jehovah* saw that he turned aside to see, and *God* cried out to him from the middle of the bramble. *God* said to Moses, "*I Am Who I Am.*" And *God* said further to Moses, "This is what you shall say to the children of Israel: '*Jehovah, God* of your ancestors, has sent me to you.'" (Exodus 3:2, 4, 14, 15)

These words clearly indicate that it was an angel who appeared to Moses as a flame in the bramble and that the angel spoke as Jehovah because the Lord (or Jehovah) was speaking through the angel.

[3] In order to speak to us in audible, articulated sounds on the lowest plane of creation, the Lord uses the help of angels. He fills them with his divinity and puts their own personalities to sleep, so that at the time they have no idea they are not Jehovah themselves. In this way Jehovah's divinity, which is on the highest of heights, filters down to the bottommost level of creation, where we see with our eyes and hear with our ears.

It was similar with the angel who talked to Gideon, as recounted this way in Judges:

The *angel of Jehovah* appeared to Gideon and said to him, "Jehovah be with you, a man mighty in strength!" And Gideon said to him, "Upon my life, my Lord! [Then] why has all this [trouble] found us?" And *Jehovah* faced him and said, "Go in your strength." Then *Jehovah* said to him, "Yet I will be with you." (Judges 6:12, 13, 14, 16)

And later:

Gideon saw that it was the *angel of Jehovah,* and Gideon said, "Oh no, Lord Jehovih! For I have seen the *angel of Jehovah* face to face!" And *Jehovah* said to him, "Peace to you. Do not be afraid." (Judges 6:22, 23)

Again it was an angel, but the angel was then in a state that prevented him from realizing he was not Jehovah, or the Lord. [4] Elsewhere in Judges:

The *angel of Jehovah* went up from Gilgal to Bochim and said, "I have caused you to come up out of Egypt and have brought you into the land that I swore [to give] to your ancestors, and I said, 'I will never, ever render my pact with you void.'" (Judges 2:1)

Here too an angel speaks in Jehovah's name, saying that he had led them out of the land of Egypt, when it was not an angel but Jehovah who led them out, as noted over and over in other places.

From this we can see how angels spoke through the prophets: it was the Lord himself speaking, although he spoke through angels. The angels did not say a thing on their own. Many passages prove that the Word is from the Lord, including this one from Matthew:

> . . . to fulfill what was *said by the Lord through the prophet,* who said, "Here, now, the virgin will become pregnant and deliver a child." (Matthew 1:22, 23)

Not to mention other places.

Since the Lord speaks through angels when he is talking to us, this explains why he himself is called an angel throughout the Word. In those cases, the angel symbolizes something essential in or from the Lord, as noted. Here, for instance, the angel symbolizes the Lord's intermediate-level thinking, so here too the angel is also called Jehovah and God. Verse 13 of the current chapter, for instance, says, "And Hagar called the name of *Jehovah,* the one speaking to her, 'You are a *God* who sees me.'"

[5] In other places, angels likewise symbolize something particular about the Lord, as in John:

> The seven stars are *angels* of the seven churches. (Revelation 1:20)

There is no such thing as "angels of the churches." The angels symbolize something about the church and therefore something about the Lord in relation to the churches. In the same author:

> I saw the wall of Jerusalem the Holy, big and high, having twelve gates and on the gates twelve *angels* and names written, which are those of the twelve tribes of the children of Israel. (Revelation 21:12)

The twelve angels have the same symbolism as the twelve tribes. They symbolize every aspect of faith, and so they symbolize the Lord, the source of faith and everything having to do with faith. In the same author:

> I saw an *angel* flying in midair, having the eternal gospel. (Revelation 14:6)

The angel symbolizes the Gospel, which is the Lord's alone. [6] In Isaiah:

> The *angel of his presence* saved us. On account of his love and on account of his compassion, he redeemed them and bore them and carried them all the days of eternity. (Isaiah 63:9)

The angel of his presence means the Lord's mercy toward the entire human race, in that he redeemed them. Similar words came from Jacob when he blessed Joseph's sons:

> May the *angel* who redeemed me from every evil bless the boys. (Genesis 48:16)

In this verse, redemption (which is the Lord's work) is symbolized by the angel. In Malachi:

> Suddenly to his Temple will come the Lord, whom you are seeking, and the *Angel of the Covenant,* whom you desire. (Malachi 3:1)

The symbolism of the angel as the Lord is obvious in this verse, where the term "angel of the covenant" is used on account of the Lord's Coming. It is still more obvious in Exodus that an angel symbolizes the Lord:

> Watch! I am sending an *angel* before you to guard you on the way and to lead you to the place that I have prepared. He will not tolerate your transgressing, because *my name is within him.* (Exodus 23:20, 21)

This now clarifies that in the Word an angel means the Lord but that the context of the inner meaning makes it clear what aspect of the Lord is meant.

The *angel of Jehovah* here is the intermediate-level thoughts that came from the Lord's inner self, which is clear from context, as noted. **1926**

The intermediate level here means the part of the Lord that became one with Jehovah (the Lord's inner self).

Oneness was not achieved instantly, at a single stroke, but gradually, from the Lord's early youth up till the last moment of his life in the world, and it was achieved mainly through repeated trials and victories. Every trial and every victory brought closer union. The more the Lord united himself to his inner self, or Jehovah, the deeper his thinking went and the more complete the oneness of intuitive truth and divine goodness within him.

This kind of thinking is what is meant by the Lord's intermediate-level thoughts, coming from his inner reaches; it is what the angel of Jehovah properly represents and symbolizes here.

At a spring of water in the wilderness symbolizes earthly truth that has not yet come alive, as can be seen from the following. A *spring of water* symbolizes truth. The *wilderness* symbolizes that which as yet has little life, as it also does in the inner meaning in Luke, which speaks of the Lord: **1927**

> The child grew and became strong in spirit, yet he was in the *wilderness* up to the days of his presentation to Israel. (Luke 1:80)

Many, many passages in the Word can be used to confirm that this is what a spring of water and a wilderness symbolize. Since both come up quite frequently later on, though, and with the same meaning, proof will be offered there, with the Lord's divine mercy.

What it means to say that truth has not yet come alive will become clear from the discussion just below.

1928   *At the spring on the way to Shur* means that this kind of truth developed out of the truth that results from a knowledge of facts, as can be seen from the symbolism of a *spring,* a *way,* and *Shur.* A *spring,* again, symbolizes truth. A *way* symbolizes a path that leads toward truth and also a path that starts at truth, as shown earlier, in §627. *Shur,* though, symbolizes the kind of factual information that is still "in the wilderness," or in other words, that has not yet come alive.

Truth that results from a knowledge of facts is said to come alive when it attaches or links itself to truth that heavenly love flows into. That is where the actual living force of truth comes from.

Real things—truths—interconnect the same way communities in heaven do, and they correspond to the communities of heaven as well. So far as our inner dimensions are concerned, each of us is a miniature heaven. Realities (or truths) that have not formed connections modeling the interconnection of heaven's communities have not yet come alive. Until they form those connections, heavenly love from the Lord has no suitable means of influencing them. They first receive life when the two models match—when the image of our miniature heaven corresponds to the image of the whole. Before reaching that stage, no one can be called a heavenly person.

[2] When the Lord (who was governing all of heaven by his own power) was in the world, he reorganized the true ideas and good impulses of his outer self (his human nature) into this pattern. But because he could tell that his rational mind did not fit the pattern at conception, as noted above at verses 4 and 5 [§§1911, 1914, 1916], he thought about the reason for it and perceived that the earthly truth he had gleaned from facts had not yet come alive. In other words, it had not yet been reorganized into the heavenly pattern.

What is more, religious truth has no life whatever if we are not living lives of love for our neighbor. All religious truth flows from our love for others and dwells in our love for others. When it dwells in that love and flows from that love, it has life. In love for our fellow humans there is life, but never in truth without that love.

[3] The symbolism of *Shur* shows it means facts that have not yet come alive. Shur was a wilderness not far from the Suph Sea and therefore lay in the direction of Egypt, as indicated in Moses:

> Moses caused Israel to set out from the Suph Sea, and they went away to the *wilderness of Shur*. From there they went three days in the *wilderness* and did not find water. (Exodus 15:22)

The fact that it lay in the direction of Egypt is also indicated in Moses, where he speaks of Ishmael's descendants:

> They lived from Havilah all the way to *Shur,* which is in *front of Egypt*. (Genesis 25:18)

And in Samuel:

> Saul struck Amalek starting in Havilah, where you come to *Shur,* which is in *front of Egypt*. (1 Samuel 15:7)

And in another place:

> David spread out [his forces] toward the Geshurite and Girzite and Amalekite who were living in the age-old land where you come into *Shur* and all the way to the *land of Egypt*. (1 Samuel 27:8)

These things show that Shur symbolizes first facts—facts of a type that is still in the wilderness, or not yet connected to the rest as heavenly communities are. After all, Egypt in all its senses symbolizes knowledge, as shown previously, in §§1164, 1165, 1186, 1462, and Shur was "in front of it."

This symbolism of "The angel of Jehovah found Hagar at a spring of water in the wilderness, at the spring on the way to Shur" cannot possibly be seen from the literal meaning, especially because it is a history. The narrative meaning seems very remote from this symbolism, yet the symbolic sense is the one that comes into an angel's mind when a person is reading the words. Angels never picture Hagar, a spring of water, a wilderness, a path, or Shur. None of these things penetrate to them but rather die away on the very threshold. What Hagar, the spring, the wilderness, the path, and Shur symbolize, however, is something angels understand, and from it they form heavenly ideas in their minds. That is how they perceive the Lord's Word, because the inner meaning *is* the Word to them. **1929**

Genesis 16:8. *And he said, "Hagar, Sarai's slave, where are you coming from and where are you going?" And she said, "From the face of Sarai, my owner, I am fleeing."* **1930**

He said, "Hagar, Sarai's slave," means learning something. *"Where are you coming from and where are you going?"* means about this state. *And she said, "From the face of Sarai, my owner, I am fleeing,"* symbolizes the answer, and indignation.

1931   *He said, "Hagar, Sarai's slave,"* means learning something, as the context shows, because the angel calls to Hagar as if he wanted to learn something.

In the Word, it is common for Jehovah to ask people questions and for them to respond, even though he already knows the answer. He knows not only what has happened but also the reasons and the purposes—in other words, all the deepest, most minute particulars involved. But we human beings are unaware of this and believe that no one can have any idea of the things we do in secret, unseen, still less what we are thinking. So the asking of these questions is adapted to our preconceptions.

Still, the truth of the matter is that ordinary spirits have a better idea of what we are thinking than we do ourselves. Angelic spirits pick up on deeper aspects of our thoughts, and angels pick up still deeper aspects—our reasons and purposes, which we know little of. This fact I have learned from a great deal of experience occurring constantly over many years. If spirits and angels perceive all this, what about the Lord, or Jehovah, who is infinite and gives all of us our ability to perceive?

1932   *Where are you coming from and where are you going?* means learning about this state, as the above indicates.

1933   *And she said, "From the face of Sarai, my owner, I am fleeing,"* means the answer, and indignation, as established by the remarks above. For an explanation of the indignation, see above at verse 6, where the same words occur [§1923].

Since a *face* symbolizes what lies inside, as shown before, in §358, it means indignation and more.

1934   Genesis 16:9. *And the angel of Jehovah said to her, "Go back to your owner and humble yourself under her hands."*

The angel of Jehovah said symbolizes the response on the part of the Lord's intermediate self. *Go back to your owner* means that it realized it should trust not in itself but in a deeper level of truth and in a desire for that truth. *And humble yourself under her hands* means that it should force itself to submit to the authority of that deeper truth.

1935   *The angel of Jehovah said* symbolizes a response on the part of the Lord's intermediate self. This is established by the symbolism of the *angel of Jehovah* as the Lord's intermediate-level thinking, as discussed above in §1925. Because it symbolizes his thinking, it also symbolizes his response.

The Lord's intermediate-level thoughts grew out of a desire for intuitive truth, and this desire grew out of divine goodness itself. Such thoughts, as noted earlier [§§1904, 1914, 1919], never do and never can occur in any human being.

Humans too have an intermediate level of thinking. It flows from the Lord by way of our inward self into our rational or intermediate self, provided we have a conscience. This can be seen from our ability to notice the evil and falsity in our outer selves that do battle with the goodness and truth in our intermediate selves. This kind of thinking occurs on a level so far below the Lord's, though, that it cannot be compared to it at all. The Lord's thinking sprang from a desire for intuitive truth and was his very own.

Those who have no conscience are incapable of intermediate-level thinking, so they are also free of all conflict, because their rational mind is on the very same level as their bodily senses. Although they too have goodness and truth constantly streaming into them from the Lord, they are never aware of it, because they immediately snuff it out and smother it. That is why they also fail to accept any religious truth.

Go back to your owner means that it realized it should trust not in itself but in a deeper level of truth and in a desire for that truth. This can be seen from the symbolism of a woman who is the *owner* of a slave as a desire for deep truth.

1936

The precise symbolism of Sarai as herself, as a wife, and as the owner of a slave cannot be explained, because it can by no means be grasped. As already noted [§§1914, 1919], these meanings lie beyond even an angel's comprehension. The current verse only hints at the Lord's thoughts about the appearances that held the attention of his dawning rationality. Those thoughts were that he should not trust in appearances but in divine truth itself, no matter how incredible it might seem to that early rationality.

This is the case with all divine truth. If you consult your rational mind about it, you will never accept divine truth, because it lies completely beyond the rational mind's grasp. Take, for example, the truth that humans, spirits, and angels have no life at all in themselves—only the Lord does; and the life they do have merely seems to be theirs. The rational mind fights this idea, judging as it does on the basis of illusions. Still, it ought to be believed, because it is true.

[2] It is a divine truth that every word of Scripture holds within it an unlimited number of ideas, even though the Word appears to us to be so uncomplicated and unpolished. In fact, every word embraces the whole of heaven and more. The mysteries hidden in it can be presented to the

view of angels by the Lord with unending variety forever. This is so unbelievable to the rational mind that it is totally unwilling to give credence to it; and yet it is true.

[3] It is a divine truth that none of us receives any reward whatever in the other life for the things we have done well, if we have claimed credit for them or if we have done them for the sake of wealth, position, or reputation. And none of us receives any punishment whatever for the things we have done badly, if we have done them for a genuinely good motive. It is our purposes that receive attention, and our deeds are viewed in light of them. The rational mind is unable to believe any of this either. Since it is true, however, we ought not to trust our rationality, which arrives at its conclusions on the basis of outward appearances rather than inward realities.

[4] It is a divine truth that whoever strives for the least joy in the next life receives the most from the Lord, and whoever strives for the most has the least. Heavenly joy, moreover, contains no trace of superiority over another person. The more superiority is present, the more hell is present. And heavenly glory contains not even the slightest hint of worldly glory. All of this again offends the rational mind but ought to be believed because it is true.

[5] It is also a divine truth that the more firmly we believe no wisdom at all originates in us, the wiser we are; and the more firmly we believe it does originate in us and so credit our own selves with prudence, the more insane we are. The rational mind denies this as well, imagining that anything that does not originate in us is nothing.

Countless other examples are possible. These few, offered by way of illustration, show that the rational mind deserves no trust. Our rational mind latches on to illusions and appearances and therefore rejects truth that has been stripped of illusions and appearances. The more wrapped up we become in self-love and selfish urges, in rationalizations, and in misguided assumptions regarding religion, the more we reject such truth.

See also the information offered above in §1911.

1937   *Humble yourself under her hands* means that it should force itself to submit to the authority of that deeper truth, as can be seen without explanation.

The idea of *humbling oneself* is expressed in the original language by a word that denotes *affliction*. Numerous passages in the Word illustrate that in an inner sense, afflicting oneself is compelling oneself, and this meaning of the phrase will be demonstrated below [§1947].

We ought to compel ourselves to do good, obey what the Lord has commanded, and speak truly. In so doing we are humbling ourselves under the Lord's hands, or in other words, submitting to the authority of divine goodness and truth. This fact embraces more hidden information than can possibly be explained in a few words.

[2] There are certain spirits who, while they lived in the world, refused on principle to compel themselves in any way. They adopted this principle because they had heard that everything good comes from the Lord and that we are incapable of doing any good on our own. Imagining that if this was the case all effort would be useless, they relaxed and waited for inspiration to spark an effort of the will directly. They did not make themselves do anything good. So radical were they in holding to this principle that when any evil crept in, sensing no inner resistance to it they abandoned themselves to it on the supposition that it was therefore acceptable. Their character, though, is such that they are almost devoid of selfhood, utterly lacking in self-determination, which makes them some of the more useless spirits. They are just as open to being led by the evil as by the good and suffer much at the hands of the evil.

[3] Others, however, have forced themselves to oppose evil and falsity. Although at first they thought they were doing so on their own or under their own power, they later gained sufficient light to see that their effort came from the Lord—even the slightest of all their exertions. In the next life they do not take direction from evil spirits but are among the blessed instead.

Obviously, then, we ought to force ourselves to do good and speak truth.

The secret here is that when we do, the Lord grants us a sense of autonomy that is heavenly in nature. A heavenly autonomy forms in us when we contemplate making an effort, and if we do not obtain the object of that effort through (apparent) self-compulsion, we certainly never do so through *lack* of self-compulsion.

[4] To explain the situation more clearly, whenever we feel compelled to do right, we enjoy a certain freedom. We are not aware of it while we are under the compulsion, but it is still present. The case is like that of a person who is ready to risk death for the sake of a particular goal, or like that of a person who is willing to suffer physical pain in order to get well. In those situations there is a willingness and so a certain freedom that causes us to act, even though the danger and the pain remove any sense of willingness or freedom at the time.

That is how it is when we compel ourselves to do right. Deep down, there is a willingness and so a freedom that form the basis and the reason for our self-compulsion. In other words, we aim to obey what the Lord has commanded and to gain the salvation of our soul after death. More deeply yet, unknown to us, we are acting for the sake of the Lord's kingdom and in fact for the sake of the Lord himself.

[5] This is especially true in times of spiritual crisis. If at those times we compel ourselves to resist the flood of evil and falsity that evil spirits unleash, we have more freedom than we ever do in any crisis-free state, although we are unable to grasp the fact at the time. The freedom lies deep inside. It gives us the will to subdue evil—a will strong enough to match the power and might of the evil attacking us. Otherwise we would never put up a fight.

This freedom comes from the Lord, who instills it in our conscience, where he uses it to give us victory over evil, a victory that we seem to have won on our own. The freedom allows us to adopt a sense of self on which the Lord can act to produce something good. Without a sense of self acquired—or rather, granted as a gift—through freedom, not one of us could ever reform, because not one of us could ever develop a new will, which is conscience. This gift of liberty is the actual receiving ground for goodness and truth flowing in from the Lord. That is why those of us who do not use our free will to fight back when we are being tested succumb.

[6] All of our freedom has our life at its center, because it has our love at its center. Whatever we do out of love seems free to us. Heavenly love is present within that freedom when we force ourselves to resist evil and falsity and to do good. At such a time, heavenly love is what the Lord introduces into us and uses to create a sense of autonomy in us. As a result, the Lord wants it to appear to us as if we have true self-determination, even though we do not. In the other world, the Lord takes this autonomy that we have acquired through apparent self-compulsion during the life of the body and fills it full of pleasure and happiness without limit. We also receive greater and greater enlightenment. In fact, we come to believe firmly in the truth of the idea that we have not really compelled ourselves at all, but that even the very smallest efforts of our will came from the Lord. It becomes clear to us that the purpose of our apparent independence was to enable us to receive a new will from the Lord as our own and in this way adopt a life of heavenly love. The Lord wants to share what is his—and therefore what is heavenly—with every single person. He wants it to feel as if it belongs to us and resides in us, even though it

does not. Angels have this sense of ownership. The more sure they are of the truth that everything good and true comes from the Lord, the more pleasure and happiness they gain from this sense of ownership.

[7] On the other hand, some people despise and reject everything good and true and refuse to believe anything that conflicts with their impulses and rationalizations. These people cannot compel themselves and so are unable to receive this personal sense of conscience, this new willpower.

The discussion above also makes it clear that compelling ourselves is not the same as being compelled. No good ever comes of being compelled, as for instance when one person forces another to do good. What is being referred to here as self-compulsion grows out of a freedom invisible to the person, because the Lord never forces anything on anyone. This is the source of the universal law that all seeds of goodness and truth are planted in freedom. Otherwise the soil would never come to receive or nurture goodness. There would not even be any soil in which the seed could grow.

Genesis 16:10. *And the angel of Jehovah said to her, "I will greatly multiply your seed, and they will be too abundant to count."*   **1938**

The angel of Jehovah said symbolizes the thinking of the intermediate self. *I will greatly multiply your seed* symbolizes the fruitfulness of the rational self when it places itself under the authority of intuitive truth that is attached to goodness. *And they will be too abundant to count* means increase beyond measure.

The symbolism of *the angel of Jehovah said* as the thinking of the intermediate self can be seen from the previous verse, where the same words occur.   **1939**

I will greatly multiply your seed symbolizes the fruitfulness of the rational self when it places itself under the authority of intuitive truth that is attached to goodness. This is established by the symbolism of seed as love and faith, a symbolism dealt with before, in §§1025, 1447, 1610. Here, though, the *multiplying of seed* symbolizes a fruitful increase in the heavenly qualities of love within the rational mind when it surrenders to a deeper kind of truth, namely, divine truth.   **1940**

Truth is usually said to *multiply,* while good qualities are said to be fruitful, as earlier statements and supporting quotations show; see §§43, 55, 913, 983. In this case, however, since the focus is on the Lord, multiplying means being fruitful. This is because every true idea in the Lord's rational mind turned into a good quality and so into something divine (and the words above are portraying it as divine).

The situation is different with humans: our rationality is formed by the Lord out of truth or a desire for truth. That desire is the good in us that moves us to act.

[2] To see how the contents of a person's rational mind multiply and become fruitful, you must first understand how spiritual inflow works. Here is a broad outline.

Each of us has an inner self, an outer self, and a rational self in between, as noted before [§978]. The inner self is at our core and is the source of our humanity. It distinguishes us from brute animals, which have no such core. Our inner self is also a gate or entryway into us for the Lord, or in other words, for the Lord's heavenly and spiritual qualities. What goes on at that level is something we are unable to grasp, because it lies completely above the rational level on which we do our thinking. Our rational mind, which seems to be ours, is in actuality subordinate to this core, this inner self. The heavenly aspects of love and faith that we receive from the Lord flow by way of the inner self into our rational mind and continue by way of it into the store of facts in our outer self. But how we receive these influences depends on our individual state.

[3] If our rational mind does not surrender to the Lord's goodness and truth, it smothers these influences or rejects them or corrupts them— especially when they reach the sense impressions stored as facts in our memory. That is the meaning of the seed that fell either on the path or on the stony ground or among the thorns, as the Lord teaches in Matthew 13:3–7; Mark 4:3–7; Luke 8:5–7. But when the rational mind does surrender and believes in the Lord—that is, in his Word—then it is like the good ground, the good earth, where the seed falls and bears much fruit.

1941   *And they will be too abundant to count* means increase beyond measure, as can be seen without explanation. These words refer to truth, which will grow in this kind of abundance under the influence of good.

Since everything in the Lord—the subject of the inner sense here—is divine and infinite, it cannot be described in words. So if the reader is to gain any idea of the way goodness causes truth to multiply, I will have to speak in terms of mere human beings.

If we are motivated by good, that is, by love and charity, the seed that the Lord plants bears fruit and multiplies so rapidly that it becomes too abundant to count. While we are living in the body this does not apply, but in the next life it is true to an unbelievable degree. [2] As long as we are still living in our bodies, the seed rests in bodily ground, where it lies among tangled thickets of facts and pleasures, cares and worries. These fall away, however, when we cross into the other world, and the seed is freed from them. It then grows the way the seed of a tree does, sprouting from the earth, developing into a sapling, then into a large tree, and finally multiplying into a whole grove of trees. All knowledge, understanding, and wisdom, along with the joy and happiness that accompany them, bear fruit and multiply this way and so keep growing to eternity. They begin with the smallest seed, like the mustard seed that the Lord teaches about in Matthew 13:31. After all, the knowledge, understanding, and wisdom that angels have were incomprehensible to them when they were on earth.

Genesis 16:11. *And the angel of Jehovah said to her, "Here, you are pregnant, and you will bear a son, and you shall call his name Ishmael, because Jehovah has listened to your affliction."*   **1942**

The angel of Jehovah said to her symbolizes the thoughts of the intermediate self. *Here, you are pregnant* symbolizes the vital energy of the rational self. *You will bear a son* symbolizes the truth known to that self. *And you shall call his name Ishmael* symbolizes the state of its vital energy. *Because Jehovah has listened to your affliction* means when it was becoming submissive.

The angel of Jehovah said symbolizes the thoughts of the intermediate self. This can be seen from remarks above at verses 7, 9, 10 [§§1925, 1926, 1935, 1939].   **1943**

Here, you are pregnant symbolizes the vital energy of the rational self. This can be seen from the discussion above about the conception of rationality [§1910] and also from what follows concerning Ishmael as the Lord's first rationality [§1964].   **1944**

Here are some general facts about the rational self that need to be known: The point at which our rationality is said to take life, grow in the womb, and be born is when we start to realize that we harbor evil and falsity, which contradict and resist what is true and good. Our rationality comes even more fully to life when we try to displace evil and falsity and subdue it. If we cannot see the evil and falsity or sense its presence in us, we have no rationality at all, no matter how rational we consider ourselves. The rational mind is the bridge linking the inner self to the outer, so with the Lord's aid it sees what is going on in our outer self and reduces it to obedience. In fact, it raises the outer self up out of the bodily and earthly concerns in which it wallows. Our rationality makes us human, enabling us to look toward heaven (our home), not just toward the earth (where we are merely visitors) as brute animals do—let alone toward hell. These, then, are the duties of the rational mind. Unless we are the kind of people who can think in the way described above, we cannot be said to have rationality. By determining whether that function or activity has any vitality in us, we can tell whether rationality exists in us or not.

[2] When we know what is good and true through hearing about it but deny it at heart, we can argue against it, but this is not the same as having rationality. Lots of people who plunge into all manner of unspeakable crime without restraint are capable of doing the same. The only difference is that those who consider themselves rational but are not, speak with a certain decorum and pretend to act with integrity. What forces them into this is external shackles—fear of the law and of losing wealth, rank, reputation, and life. If these restraints, which are superficial, were taken away, some of them would go even more insane than those others. Consequently no one can be described as possessing rationality merely on the basis of being able to make a strong argument. In fact, people who have no rational ability usually talk much more skillfully on the basis of empirical evidence and factual knowledge than people who are truly rational do.

[3] This is abundantly clear from certain evil spirits in the other life who were considered more rational than others when they lived in the body. External checks led them to speak appropriately and pretend to live honorably, but when these restraints are taken away—as is customary for everyone in the other life—then despite their former reputation they are more insane than those in the world who are obviously insane. They hurl themselves into every kind of wickedness without shame, fear, or horror. Those who were truly rational when they lived in the world, however, do not act this way. When external bonds are removed from them, they grow still more sane, because they have had internal bonds: the bonds of conscience. By these bonds the Lord anchored their thinking to the laws of truth and goodness, which were their rational principles.

1945 *You will bear a son* symbolizes the truth known to the rational mind that Ishmael symbolizes. This is established by the meaning of a *son* as truth, dealt with earlier, at §§264, 489, 491, 533, 1147. The following verse describes this truth [§§1949–1951].

1946 *And you shall call his name Ishmael* symbolizes the state of its vital energy.

In times long past, people gave their children names that indicated what conditions were like for the parents (especially for the mother in conceiving or in carrying the child or in giving birth) or for the baby (once born). So names were meaningful.

The current verse explains where Ishmael's name came from: "because Jehovah has listened to your affliction"—the state of his mother. The next verse explains what Ishmael represents.

Because Jehovah has listened to your affliction means when it was becoming submissive. This can be seen from remarks above in §1937 to the effect that humbling and afflicting oneself means submitting to the authority of the inner self. This surrender was discussed there. I showed that it means compelling oneself, and that *self-compulsion* contains the element of freedom, of a voluntary quality or willingness that distinguishes *self*-compulsion from *being* compelled. It was also shown that without this freedom—this voluntary choice or willingness—we cannot possibly be reformed or receive any heavenly autonomy. Furthermore it was demonstrated that in times of trial we have more freedom than we do outside of those times, although the opposite seems true. Our freedom then gains strength in proportion to the attacks of evil and falsity and is reinforced by the Lord so that we can be given the gift of a heavenly selfhood. As a result the Lord is also more intimately present in our struggles. All this was laid out, and also the fact that the Lord never compels anyone in any way. When we are forced to think what is true and do what is good, we do not reform. Rather, we then think what is false and wish what is evil more than ever. This is the inevitable consequence of all compulsion, as life experience can testify. Such experience reveals two constants: conscience refuses to be compelled, and we strive after the forbidden. What is more, we always long to move from nonliberty to liberty, because this is central to our life. [2] Obviously, then, what does not come of freedom, of voluntary choice or willingness, is in no way pleasing to the Lord. When we worship the Lord in nonfreedom, we worship him with nothing of our own. It is our outer shell that acts, or rather is forced to act. The inner core either is passive or else rebels and in fact cries out against it.

When we are regenerating, we take the Lord's gift of liberty and use it to compel ourselves. We humble and even afflict our rational mind so that it will submit. This gives us a heavenly sense of independence, and the Lord then gradually makes that sensation more and more complete. It grows freer and freer until it turns into a love for what is good and for

1947

the truth that comes of goodness. Pleasure is ours, and in the love and pleasure we find a happiness like that of the angels. This is the freedom the Lord himself spoke of in John when he said:

> The truth makes you *free*. If the Son makes you *free,* you are truly *free.* (John 8:32, 36)

[3] The nature of this freedom is wholly beyond the knowledge of people who lack conscience. They identify liberty with the unchecked license to think and speak what is false and to will and do what is evil, not to force or humble themselves in these matters, let alone afflict themselves. The reality, though, is just the opposite, as the Lord also teaches in John:

> Everyone doing sin is a *slave* of sin. (John 8:34)

Those of us devoid of conscience receive this "enslaved liberty" from the hellish spirits with us, who flood us with it. When we take on their life as our own, we take on their desires and cravings too, exhilarated as we are by the unclean, fecal pleasure of them. When we find ourselves carried away by the rushing torrent of these urges, we consider ourselves free, but it is a hellish freedom. The difference between this hellish freedom and heavenly freedom is that the former is deadly and drags us down to hell, while the latter (heavenly freedom) is revitalizing and lifts us up to heaven.

[4] All true, inner worship is offered in freedom, not under compulsion. If it is not offered in freedom, it is not inner worship. This is clear from the Word. It is clear from the various kinds of *sacrifice*—freewill offerings; offerings made in fulfillment of a vow; and peace offerings, or offerings of thanks. These sacrifices were called offerings and oblations and are described in Numbers 15:3 and the following verses; Deuteronomy 12:6; 16:10, 11; 23:23; and elsewhere. In David:

> With a *voluntary [sacrifice] I will sacrifice* to you; I will acclaim your name, Jehovah, because it is good. (Psalms 54:6)

The same thing is clear from the terumah, or contribution, they were to make for the tabernacle and for the holy garments, as described in Moses:

> Speak to the children of Israel and have them receive a contribution for me; from every man *whose heart has compelled him of its own accord* you shall take a contribution for me. (Exodus 25:2)

And in another place:

Everyone *willing at heart* shall bring it, a contribution for Jehovah. (Exodus 35:5)

[5] The humbling or afflicting of the rational self in freedom (just described) was represented by the afflicting of one's soul on holy days, as commanded in Moses:

It will serve you as an eternal statute: in the seventh month, on the tenth of the month, *you shall afflict your souls.* (Leviticus 16:29)

And in another place:

On the tenth of the seventh month, this is a day of atonement; a holy convocation it shall be for you, and you shall *afflict your souls.* All souls who have not *afflicted* themselves on that very day shall be cut off from their peoples. (Leviticus 23:27, 29)

This is why the unleavened bread, containing no yeast, is called *the bread of affliction* in Deuteronomy 16:2, 3. Affliction is spoken of this way in David:

Jehovah, who will abide in your tent? Who will live on your holy mountain? Those walking unblemished and doing justice, who swear *to afflict themselves* |and| do not change [their minds]. (Psalms 15:1, 2, 4)

[6] What has been said so far shows that afflicting ourselves means taming and subduing the evil and falsity that surge from our outer self into our rational self. It does not mean dragging ourselves down into poverty and misery or renouncing bodily pleasures. Self-denial does not tame or subdue our evils. Sometimes it even awakens another kind of evil: a sense of merit for making sacrifices. Besides, it is an assault on our freedom, and freedom is the only ground in which the seeds of religious goodness and truth can be sown.

For a discussion of the idea that affliction is also a time of trial, see §1846 above.

Genesis 16:12. *"And he will be a wild donkey of a person, his hand against everyone, and everyone's hand against him, and he will dwell defiantly in the face of all his brothers."*

He will be a wild donkey of a person symbolizes rational truth, which is what is being depicted. *His hand against everyone* means that it will fight anything that is not true. *And everyone's hand against him* means that falsity will fight back. *And he will dwell defiantly in the face of all his brothers*

1948

means that there will be constant strife over religious tenets but rational truth will win anyway.

1949   *He will be a wild donkey of a person* symbolizes rational truth, which is what is being depicted. This can be seen from the symbolism of a *wild donkey* as rational truth.

The Word very often mentions horses, riders, mules, and donkeys, and so far no one has recognized that they symbolize matters of intellect, reason, and fact. (By the Lord's divine mercy, this symbolism of them will be illustrated fully where each of them occurs.) A wild donkey belongs to the same category, because it is a mule that lives in the wilderness, a long-ear that lives in the forest, and it symbolizes human rationality. It does not symbolize the entire range of rational attributes, just rational truth.

Rationality consists of goodness and truth, that is, of qualities involving love for our neighbor and qualities involving faith. Rational truth is what a wild donkey symbolizes. That is what Ishmael represents here, and it is what the current verse describes.

[2] No one is likely to believe that rational truth separated from rational goodness is like this, and I myself would not have known if I had not learned by my own observation. Whether you speak of rational truth or of people with this kind of rationality, it amounts to the same thing.

People whose rational minds are such that they devote themselves exclusively to truth—even religious truth—and not at the same time to neighborly kindness are exactly like this. Such a person is a peevish, intolerant, universally belligerent man. He sees all others as wrongheaded, leaps to blame and criticize and punish them, lacks pity, and refuses to bother learning how to turn their minds gently in a better direction. This is because he views everything in terms of truth and never in terms of goodness. In short, such people are harsh.

The only thing that can soften their hardness is a goodness born of neighborly love. The soul of truth is goodness, and when goodness draws close to truth and works its way in, truth changes so radically that it can hardly be recognized.

Isaac represents the Lord's rational self, which developed out of goodness, not out of truth separated from goodness. That is why Ishmael was driven away to live in the wilderness and why his mother took him a wife from the land of Egypt (Genesis 21:9–21). All these details represent a person equipped with this kind of rationality.

[3] The prophetic books of the Word mention wild donkeys. In Isaiah, for instance:

The palace will be deserted; the throng of the city, abandoned. Mound and watchtower will be in place of caves. To eternity it will be the *joy of wild donkeys,* a pasture for flocks. (Isaiah 32:14)

This is about the devastation of our intellect to the point where we essentially lack a rational mind. When our intellect is stripped of true ideas, it is called the joy of wild donkeys, and when it is stripped of good impulses, it is called a pasture for flocks. In Jeremiah:

Wild donkeys stood on the hills; they gulped the wind like great sea creatures. Their eyes were spent, because there was no grass. (Jeremiah 14:6)

This is about a drought, or a lack of goodness and truth. The wild donkeys are said to gulp the wind when people grasp at hollow shams instead of ideas with real substance, or in other words, true ideas. The failing of their eyes stands for the fact that they do not understand what is true. [4] In Hosea:

For they have gone up to Assyria—a *lone wild donkey.* Ephraim has sought lovers for a harlot's wages. (Hosea 8:9)

This is about Israel, or the spiritual church. Ephraim stands for its intellect. Going up to Assyria stands for debating whether truth is true. The lone wild donkey stands for a rational mind that has accordingly been stripped of truth. In the same author:

Because he will be *like a wild donkey among his brothers,* Jehovah's east wind will come rising from the desert, and his fount will dry up, and his spring will evaporate. He will plunder the treasury of all its desirable vessels. (Hosea 13:15)

This is about Ephraim, who symbolizes the intellect of the spiritual church. Its rational capacity will be like the wild donkey whose ruin is discussed here. In David:

Jehovah God will send his springs out into rivers; among the mountains they will go. They supply drink to every wild animal of the fields; *wild donkeys* break their thirst. (Psalms 104:10, 11)

The springs stand for knowledge; wild animals of the fields, for good qualities; wild donkeys, for rational truth.

His hand against everyone means that it will fight anything that is not true; *and everyone's hand against him* means that falsity will fight back. This **1950** can be seen from the fact that Ishmael symbolizes rational truth separated from goodness, as noted. When such truth is described as having *his hand against everyone and everyone's hand against him,* clearly the meaning is the one mentioned.

It was pointed out earlier [§1893] that Abram represents the Lord's inner self or, to describe it another way, that which was divinely heaven-like and divinely spiritual in him. Isaac represents the Lord's intermediate self, or his divine rationality. Jacob represents the Lord's outer self, or his divine earthliness. The subject here is his rational mind and what it would be like if it did not unite as one with his inner self, or his divine heavenliness and spirituality. His rational mind drew its nature from the vital energy of his desire for knowledge, or in other words, from Hagar, Sarai's Egyptian slave. This energy was part of the Lord's outer self, and it contained a hereditary burden from his mother that he had to fight against and banish. As a consequence, this verse describes his rational mind as it would be if it had no rational-level goodness. Through the struggles and victories of his inner trials, though, the Lord humbled this heredity, or afflicted and subdued it, and he brought the true rationality in him to life with divine goodness. Then his rational mind becomes Isaac—or comes to be represented by Isaac—once Ishmael has been driven from the house, along with his mother Hagar.

[2] All genuine rationality consists of goodness and truth, that is, of what is heavenly and spiritual. Goodness, or heavenliness, is its actual soul or life. Truth, or spirituality, derives its life from that goodness. Rationality without the life imparted by heavenly goodness shows all the signs described in the current verse: it battles with everyone and everyone battles with it.

Rational-level goodness never fights, no matter how ferociously it is attacked. It is gentle and compassionate, tolerant and yielding, since it comes of love and mercy. Even though it does not fight, it conquers all. It never plans to fight and does not boast of its victory. This is because it is divine and inherently secure; nothing bad can assail goodness. Evil cannot even survive in the same environment with goodness. If goodness simply moves in its direction, evil spontaneously withdraws and sinks back down, because evil comes from hell, goodness from heaven.

The case is nearly the same with that which is heavenly-spiritual, or in other words, truth from a heavenly origin, or truth that grows out of goodness. This truth is truth formed from good, so it can be called a form of good. [3] But truth separated from good (represented here by Ishmael and depicted in this verse) is completely different; it resembles a wild donkey. It fights everyone and everyone fights it. In fact, it hardly ever thinks or dreams of anything but fighting. Its overarching pleasure or supreme desire is to win and, once it has won, to celebrate its victory. That is why it is portrayed as a wild donkey—a mule in the wilderness, a long-ear in the forest—which cannot coexist with others. This kind of life is the life of truth without goodness and in fact the life of faith without love for others. When we are being reborn, then, religious truth does play a role, but so does a life of love for our neighbor, which the Lord gradually infuses into us as we learn more and more religious truth.

He will dwell defiantly in the face of all his brothers means that there will be constant strife over religious tenets but rational truth will win anyway, as the discussion just above shows. Ishmael's future home is described even more fully in these words, which tell of his descendants: **1951**

> They lived from *Havilah* all the way to *Shur,* which is in front of *Egypt* as you come into *Assyria;* [the lot] fell [to him] in the face of all his brothers. (Genesis 25:18)

The inner meaning of these words is evident from the symbolism of Havilah, Shur, Egypt, and Assyria. Havilah symbolizes anything that is a matter of intelligence, as is clear from what was shown at §115. Shur symbolizes truth that develops out of facts, as mentioned above in §1928. Egypt symbolizes every aspect of scholarly learning (1164, 1165, 1186, 1462). And Assyria symbolizes anything that is a matter of reason (119, 1186). Reduce the symbolism of these into a single meaning and you will find that Ishmael represents the kind of rationality described.

This type of truth is portrayed by various kinds of representations in the other world. It is always presented as so strong, powerful, and hard that it cannot be resisted in the least. When spirits merely think about such truth, a certain terror rises in them, because its very nature prevents it from yielding or retreating. These considerations also reveal what *dwelling defiantly in the face of all his brothers* symbolizes.

Anyone can see that this description conceals a secret of some kind, but what that secret is has remained unknown until now.

Genesis 16:13, 14. *And she called the name of Jehovah, the one speaking to her, "You are a God who sees me"; because she said, "Even in this place, did I see behind the one seeing me?" Therefore they called the spring "the spring of the living one who sees me"; here, it is between Kadesh and Bered.* **1952**

And she called the name of Jehovah, the one speaking to her, means the state of the Lord's intermediate self when he had these thoughts. *"You are a God who sees me"* symbolizes an inflow. *Because she said, "Even in this place, did I see behind the one seeing me?"* symbolizes an inflow into the life of the outer self, but not through the rational mind. *Therefore they called the spring* symbolizes the state of truth that resulted. *"The spring of the living one who sees me"* symbolizes truth that was therefore quite clear to see. *Here, it is between Kadesh and Bered* symbolizes its quality.

1953   *And she called the name of Jehovah, the one speaking to her,* means the state of the Lord's intermediate self when he had these thoughts. This can be seen from remarks above [§§1889, 1925–1926, 1935] and below [§§1955, 1958] and from the symbolism of someone's *name* as a recognition of that person's nature (discussed previously, in §§144, 145, 1754).

These verses tell what the Lord's state was like, or what state he was in, when he thought this way about his rational mind. His rational mind could not think these thoughts, but a deeper or higher level of his being could, as mentioned above in §1926. The rational mind can never analyze its own nature, because it cannot look at itself. There has to be something deeper or higher to analyze it, since only this can really see it. The ear, for example, does not recognize let alone understand the speech it transmits; only the internal power of hearing does. The ear merely distinguishes the articulated sounds, or the words. It is the internal power of hearing that grasps what is said, and subsequently the internal power of sight, or "insight," that understands it. So it is through inner hearing that we discern the meaning of the words.

The case is similar with visual experiences. The first ideas to be drawn from the objects of sight are matter-based, which is why they are called material ideas. It is a deeper level of vision that really sees them and therefore thinks about them. It is the same with our rationality. The rational mind can never truly see itself, let alone examine its own nature. There has to be something deeper that does this. So whenever we find that we *can* do it—can sense a distortion in our rational mind or a truth that shines there, and especially something that fights and wins—we can assume that it is the Lord acting on us by way of our inner self. The Lord's intermediate self (described earlier, in §1926, and meant by the words above) was the part of him that was united to his inner self, or Jehovah. So it was on a far, far higher level than this rationality. It was from his inner self that he saw and perceived in heaven's light (so to speak) what his rational mind would be like if it devoted itself to truth alone and not to goodness.

You are a God who sees me symbolizes an inflow, as can be deduced 〔**1954**〕 from the remarks just above.

Insight from our higher self into our lower or, to say the same thing another way, from our deeper self into our shallower, is called an inflow, because that is how it operates. Take a person's deeper power of sight, for example. If our deeper power of sight did not constantly act on our outward eyesight, our eyes would never be able to seize on any object and make it out. It is our more inward power of sight that uses the eye to take in what the eye sees. It is never our eyes that do this, although they seem to.

This also shows how much our senses deceive those of us who believe that our eyes see. In reality, it is the vision of our spirit—our deeper vision— that sees things through our eyes.

[2] The spirits I have with me have seen the sights of the world through my eyes as clearly as I have, which is mentioned in §1880. Some of them, who still believed whatever their senses told them, thought they had seen those sights through their own eyes. I showed them otherwise, since when my eyes were closed they could see nothing in this world with its physical atmosphere. The same is true for us. It is our spirit that sees things, not our eyes, although it sees them *through* our eyes. Dreams illustrate the same point, since in them we sometimes see as clear as day. Even so, this deeper sight of our spirit functions in the same way. Our more inward eye does not see anything on its own but only from the still deeper sight of our rational mind. In fact, neither does this power see anything on its own; there has to be an even deeper power, which is that of our inner self (as discussed in §1940). Even then, it is not the inner self that sees but the Lord working through our inner self. He alone sees, because he alone lives and gives us the power to see—and to feel as though we see things on our own.

This is how matters stand with spiritual inflow.

Because she said, "Even in this place, did I see behind the one seeing me?" 〔**1955**〕 symbolizes an inflow into the life of the outer self, but not through the rational mind. This is established by the symbolism of *seeing behind the one seeing*. Seeing behind the one seeing is seeing from a deeper or higher level. (Whatever is *within* or *above* in an inner sense is expressed as *behind* in the literal sense, whenever that deeper or higher element appears in something outside or below it.) Hagar, the speaker, symbolizes the vital energy inherent in the knowledge the outer self possesses, as already shown [§§1895–1896]. The Lord's primitive rationality rose out of that energy, so when he looked at the reason for this [§1928], his outer self saw the answer from a deeper level of his being, without relying on rational analysis.

These words contain hidden dimensions, as anyone can see simply from the fact that no one could possibly know what *seeing behind the one seeing me* means except from its inner meaning. Even the inner meaning contains elements that cannot be explained intelligibly without the use of ideas like those that angels have. Angels' ideas do not fall into words, only into the meanings of words, divorced from the matter-based thinking from which an idea of the words' meaning comes. These things seem terribly obscure to us, but the picture angels have of them is so clear and distinct and so rich in representative meaning that it would take a whole book just to outline a small part of it.

1956 *Therefore they called the spring* symbolizes the state of truth that resulted. This can be seen from the current discussion and from the symbolism of a *spring* as truth (mentioned above in §1927).

The Lord saw this truth not in his rational mind but below it, so the word for *spring* in the original language here differs from the one used above [in verse 7], which is the usual word for it.

1957 *The spring of the living one who sees me* symbolizes truth that was therefore very clear to see. This too can be seen from the current discussion, specifically from the way the Lord saw very clearly that the truth adopted by this primitive rationality was not good.

The Lord's intermediate self, from which he saw this, is what is being called "the living one who sees." This intermediate self was united with his inner self, or Jehovah, who alone lives and who alone sees, as shown above in §1954.

1958 *Here, it is between Kadesh and Bered* symbolizes its quality. In other words, he saw what this truth was like and so what this rationality was like. This can be seen from the symbolism of *Kadesh* and *Bered. Kadesh* symbolizes truth and disputes about truth, as shown earlier, in §1678. *Bered,* though, symbolizes truth on a lower level, so it symbolizes truth in the form of facts, which is what the rational mind develops out of.

To see that names in the Word have symbolic meaning, see §§1876, 1888, 1889; and §§1224, 1264.

1959 Genesis 16:15. *And Hagar bore Abram a son, and Abram called the name of his son, whom Hagar bore, Ishmael.*

Hagar bore Abram a son means that the Lord's rational self was born of that joining together and conception. *And Abram called the name of his son, whom Hagar bore, Ishmael* symbolizes its character.

1960 *Hagar bore Abram a son* means that the Lord's rational self was born of that conception and joining together, as can be seen from the representation and symbolism of *Hagar, Abram,* and a *son. Hagar* symbolizes the vital energy of the outer self in its desire for knowledge, as noted above in §§1895, 1896. *Abram* symbolizes the Lord's inner self (§§1893, 1950). And a *son* symbolizes truth, and therefore the truth that belongs to this kind of rationality (§§264, 489, 491, 533, 1147). So "Hagar bore to Abram" means that his rational self was born of that conception and joining together.

The literal meaning changes into this meaning among the angels, when it reaches them.

And Abram called the name of his son, whom Hagar bore, Ishmael sym- **1961** bolizes its character. This can be seen from the symbolism of a *name* as a recognition of the character (dealt with in §§144, 145, 1754). It can also be seen from the representation and symbolism of *Ishmael* as rational truth, which is described in verses 11 and 12 in these words: "You shall call his name Ishmael, because Jehovah has heard your affliction. And he will be a wild donkey of a person, his hand against everyone, and everyone's hand against him; and he will dwell defiantly in the face of all his brothers." The meaning is discussed where these verses are explained [§§1946–1951]. The character of rational truth is what they portray.

Genesis 16:16. *And Abram was a son of eighty-six years when Hagar bore* **1962** *Ishmael.*

Abram was a son of eighty-six years symbolizes the state of the heavenly goodness the Lord had acquired through the battles he fought in times of trial. *When Hagar bore Ishmael* means once the vital energy of a desire for knowledge had given birth to rationality.

Abram was a son of eighty-six years symbolizes the state of the heavenly **1963** goodness the Lord had acquired through the battles he fought in times of trial, as can be seen from the following symbolism. *Eighty* involves the same thing as forty, which symbolizes times of trial, as shown earlier, in §§730, 862; and *six* symbolizes battle, also addressed previously, in §§720, 737, 900. Further, *ten* symbolizes a remnant, as discussed in §576. In the Lord, this remnant consisted of the heavenly goodness he had acquired, which enabled him to unite his human nature into one with his divine nature (§1906 at the end). These three numbers are part of the number eighty-six, which embraces their meanings and accordingly symbolizes the state of the heavenly goodness the Lord had acquired through his spiritual struggles.

All numbers in the Word have symbolic meaning, as shown before, in §§482, 487, 575, 647, 648, 755, 813.

It does not seem here as though the numbers could have this kind of significance, since what they are counting are years, and those years are assigned historically to Abram's life. Nothing is written in the Word, however, that does not pass into a spiritual, heavenly meaning as it crosses over to the angels. Angels think only spiritual, heavenly thoughts. When we on earth read the Word, angels do not know or perceive how many eighty-six is, and do not care how old Abram was when Hagar bore Ishmael to him. Instead, when we read a number like this, everything the number enfolds within it springs instantly to their minds. The same holds true for all the other particulars as explained in their inner sense.

1964   *When Hagar bore Ishmael to Abram* means once the vital energy of a desire for knowledge had given birth to rationality. This can be seen from the symbolism of *Hagar* as the vital energy of a desire for knowledge, and from the symbolism of *Ishmael* as the rational mind at its conception, both discussed above.

This chapter has focused on our rational mind, telling what it is like when it consists of truth alone and what it is like when it consists of goodness and the truth that comes of goodness. It needs to be known, then, that the rational mind can never be conceived or born (that is, it cannot form) without both secular and religious knowledge. The knowledge, however, must have usefulness as its goal. When it has usefulness as its goal, it has life as its goal, since life has everything to do with being useful, because it has everything to do with purpose. If we do not acquire knowledge for the sake of a useful life, the knowledge lacks any importance, because it lacks usefulness. [2] Secular and religious knowledge by itself, without a life of service, creates the kind of rationality depicted: wild-donkey-like, quick to criticize, and belligerent. What life it possesses is the parched and arid life imparted by a dubious pleasure in truth tainted with conceit. When knowledge seeks to be useful, on the other hand, it receives life from the services it performs; the more useful the service, the more life the knowledge has.

In its truest, most genuine form, faith is love for the Lord and for our neighbor, so when we acquire religious knowledge in order to perfect a loving faith, we are fulfilling the very purpose of all useful activity. Under those circumstances, we receive spiritual, heavenly life from the Lord, and when we come into this kind of life, we come into the ability to perceive everything of the Lord's kingdom. All angels have this kind of life, and because they do, they have true understanding and wisdom.

1965   This now is the inner meaning of all that the current chapter says about Abram, Hagar, and Ishmael. How rich that meaning is, though, or in other words, how limitless its contents are, can be seen from a single fact: Absolutely everything in the Word's inner sense looks to the Lord and speaks of the Lord. That is where the living quality of the Word comes from, because that is where the Word itself comes from. The inner meaning also tells about the Lord's kingdom in the heavens and about his kingdom on earth (the church). It treats of every individual who has the Lord's kingdom inside, too, and in addition it treats generally of anything that is heavenly or spiritual. All these layers of meaning come from the Lord.

That is why Abram also represents a heavenly church, a heavenly individual, heavenliness itself, and so on. Stretching the explanation out to cover these subjects as well, however, would make the work far too long.

Visions and Dreams in the Word, Including Those of the Prophets

FEW people today know how visions occur or which visions are genuine. Almost continually, though, for several years now, I have been present with those who are in the other world (as the first two volumes reveal clearly enough) and have seen the astounding sights there. Consequently I have learned about visions and dreams by personal experience. Let me relate the following things about them.   **1966**

Much attention is given to the visions of people who claim they have had many. They actually have seen things, but they were hallucinating. I have been taught about such visions and also shown how they occur. There are spirits who bring up imaginary images of seemingly real objects, like those seen in shadow, or by moonlight, or even by daylight out of the corner of one's eye. Then the spirits focus the person's mind without pause or letup on the thought of some object, whether it is an animal, a freak of nature, a forest, or something else. As long as the person's mind is fixed on this thought, the hallucination grows and develops until she or he finally becomes convinced: the person sees the object as absolutely real, when in fact it is nothing but an illusion.   **1967**

These visions afflict people who overindulge in fantasy to the point of mental illness and as a result are easily duped. They are fantasizers.

Fanatical spirits are similar, but their visions center on religious belief. They themselves are so firmly convinced of their beliefs (and work so   **1968** hard to persuade others) that they are capable of swearing to the truth of a falsehood or the validity of a delusion. I could say much about the nature of these spirits from experience but will deal with them in detail [elsewhere], the Lord in his divine mercy willing.

They have contracted this condition as a result of self-deceptions and false assumptions they entertained while alive in this world.

1969   In the other life, evil spirits consist almost entirely of cravings and delusions. They have acquired no other life for themselves. Their delusions are so strong that they have absolutely no idea things are not the way they perceive them.

The figments of our imagination cannot be compared to theirs; they are in a state that transcends ours, even in this regard.

Such fantasies occur constantly among spirits in hell, who use them to torture one another in dreadful ways.

1970   By genuine visions I mean the vision or sight of things that really do exist in the other life. They truly are objects that can be seen with the eyes of the spirit, not the eyes of the body. People on earth see them when the Lord activates their inner sight, that is, the sight of their spirit, the same sight they come into when they are released from their body and cross into the other world. After all, people are spirits clothed in bodies. These are the kinds of visions the prophets had.

When the eyes of our spirit open, then in daylight brighter than that of the noonday sun on earth we see what actually exists among spirits. We see not only representations but also the spirits themselves, and we perceive who they are, what they are like, where they are, where they come from, where they are going, how they feel, what they think, and even what they believe (§§1388, 1394). All these impressions are confirmed, without error, by audible speech that precisely resembles human speech.

1971   The visions that appear before good spirits serve to represent what exists in heaven. Anything that exists in the presence of angels in heaven turns into representations when it comes down into the world of spirits. The meaning of the representations is clear to see from and in the representations themselves.

This kind of experience occurs constantly among good spirits, with a beauty and sweetness that can hardly be expressed.

1972   In regard to the visions or rather sights that appear before the eyes of the spirit and not of the body, they exist at progressively deeper levels. When I saw things in the world of spirits, I saw them in clear light. What I saw in the heaven of angelic spirits was less clear, and still less clear in the heaven of angels. Rarely were the eyes of my spirit opened that far. Still, by means of a certain perception whose nature I cannot describe, I was able to tell what they were saying, often through intermediate spirits. Sometimes the objects there appeared in the shade cast by heaven's light. This shade is not like the shade cast by earthly light, because it is a thinning and weakening of the light that makes it as hard for the intellect as for the eye to grasp what it sees.

It would take too long to list all the different kinds of visions, as there are quite a few. Let me simply report on two visions by way of illustration. **1973** These two will show what visions are like and how spirits are affected by what they see. They will also show how evil spirits are tormented when they are prevented from seeing what others see and hear, because they cannot stand to miss out on anything of this kind at all. Instead of having a sense of taste, spirits have a craving to learn and know that resembles an appetite for food. For them, knowledge is like food, and it nourishes them (§1480). How the removal of this food distresses them can be seen from the following example.

Once, as I was first waking up after a poor night of sleep, the most charming sight presented itself. Garlands of greenery resembling laurel **1974** wreaths formed an exquisitely beautiful pattern, moving as if alive. Their shape and elegance were so beautiful and harmonious and radiated such a feeling of bliss that it cannot be described. The garlands were in two rows slightly separated, linked, and stretching out quite a distance, as the particular type of beauty kept changing and changing. The spirits—even the evil ones—had no trouble seeing this.

Another sight still more beautiful then took its place. This new scene contained heavenly gladness but was only dimly visible. It involved children playing heavenly games whose effect on my mind was indescribable.

[2] Afterward I talked about these sights with the spirits, who said they could see the first scene as clearly as I could but not the second, except in such a vague way that they could not tell what it was. This aroused their resentment. Later they began to feel more and more jealous, because they had been told that angels and little children *could* see it. I was given the opportunity to sense their envy palpably, so that I would have a full opportunity to learn from it. Their envy was so strong that it caused them not only intense annoyance but also distress and deep-seated pain—simply because they had not been able to see the second scene too. As a consequence they were led through all the varieties of jealousy until at last their insides ached. [3] While they were in this state,

I talked to them about jealousy. I maintained that they could have been content with seeing the first scene, and that they could also have seen the second if they had been worthy. At these words, outrage sharpened their envy, aggravating it to the point where they could no longer bear even the slightest reminder of it without being convulsed with anguish. The stages and progression of their envy was beyond description, with all its steps, increases, and variations, mingled with sickness of heart and soul.

This demonstrated how much torture simple envy puts the godless through when they see the blessings of good people from a distance and in fact when they merely think about such blessings.

1975   To turn now to dreams: People recognize that the Lord revealed secrets of heaven to the prophets not only through visions but also through dreams. The dreams were just as full of representation and symbolism as the visions and were almost the same type of thing. Dreams also disclosed the future to others besides the prophets; examples are the dreams that Joseph, Joseph's fellow inmates, Pharaoh, Nebuchadnezzar, and others had. All this people know, and from it they can see that dreams of this type flow from heaven just as much as visions do. The difference is that dreams occur when the body is asleep but visions occur when it is not.

I had a vivid demonstration of the way the prophetic dreams and other similar signs mentioned in the Word flow in and in fact come down from heaven. On this subject let me recount the following lessons from my experience.

1976   There are three kinds of dreams. The first kind comes indirectly from the Lord through heaven. The prophetic dreams mentioned in the Word were of this type.

The second comes through angelic spirits, especially those above, in front, and to the right, where the gardens of paradise are. This is where the people of the earliest church received their dreams from, and their dreams were instructive (§1122).

The third kind comes through the spirits nearby us when we sleep, and these dreams too are symbolic.

Incoherent dreams come from somewhere else.

1977   To learn for certain how dreams flowed in, I was put to sleep and dreamed that a ship laden with all kinds of delicious and savory things to eat had arrived. The cargo was not in sight but rather was hidden. On the deck stood two armed guards, and a third man besides, who was captain of the vessel. The ship was pulling into a kind of covered dock. At this point I woke up and thought about the dream. Then I was addressed by angelic spirits above me, in front, and to the right, who said that they had introduced the dream.

To see for certain that it had come from them, I was put into a state of simultaneous sleep and wakefulness, and they again introduced various charming and delightful sights. One was a tiny animal unknown to me that disappeared in a burst of light rays pulsing darker and lighter as they flew into my left eye with amazing speed. They also presented images of people and of children in various kinds of finery, and other scenes as well possessing a sweetness that defies words. These too I discussed with them. This happened not once but several times, and every time, they taught me about it using the spoken word.

[2] It is angelic spirits standing at the threshold of paradise who introduce these dreams. They are also charged with the duty of watching over certain people while they sleep, to prevent evil spirits from molesting them. This duty they perform with supreme pleasure, so much so that they compete for the privilege. They love to stir up in us the pleasures and delights they see in our desires and talents. Because they were people who in their physical lives had loved and enjoyed using every means and making every effort to render the lives of others happy, they eventually became angelic spirits. When one's [inner] ear is open to it, one can hear from there a seemingly distant sound, sweet and tuneful like a song. They said they did not know where these [skills] came from nor how such lovely, delightful representations arose in an instant, but they were told that heaven was the source.

These angelic spirits belong to the region of the cerebellum, because the cerebellum, as I have been taught, stays awake during times of sleep, while the cerebrum does not.

This is where the people of the earliest church received their dreams from, along with a perception of the meaning. From these dreams the ancients took most of the representational and symbolic forms they used to bring deeply hidden concepts to view.

In addition there are spirits who belong to the area of the left side of the chest and frequently try to interfere [with the dreams], as other spirits also do; but [the angelic spirits] do not worry about them. **1978**

Very often after these dreams I was allowed to talk with the spirits and angels who had sent them. They would describe what they had introduced, and I would describe what I had seen; but to cite all my experiences with them would take too long. **1979**

1980   Here is another thing worth mentioning: When I would wake up and report on what I had seen in my dreams—long stories, they were—a different group of angelic spirits than those described above would say that these agreed and coincided exactly with the subjects they had been discussing among themselves. There was absolutely no discrepancy. Yet it was not the themes themselves of their discussion that appeared in my dreams. Rather it was objects representing those themes—objects that their thoughts would be changed and transformed into, on reaching the world of spirits. (Angels' thoughts turn into representative images in the world of spirits.) As a result, each and every thing they discussed among themselves was represented this way in my dream.

Moreover they told me that the same conversation could have been represented in other ways as well, more like my dream or less like it, with unending variety. It was the state of the spirits around me and therefore the state I was then in that caused it to be represented the way it was, they said.

In short, many different dreams can develop out of the same conversation and so out of a single source. The reason, again, is that the things we remember and the things we love are vessels [§1977]. The thoughts contained in those vessels are received as various representations, according to differences in their form and changes in their state.

1981   Let me recount yet another experience of the same kind. I had a dream, but a common type of dream. When I woke up, I told some angels all about it from start to finish. They said my story perfectly matched a conversation they had been having. It was not the things they were discussing that showed up in my dream, but something completely different, which the thoughts they were discussing turned into. Yet the elements of my dream still represented and corresponded to their ideas, even down to the smallest details, so that nothing was missing.

I also talked with them about spiritual inflow—how these ideas flow into us and take on different forms.

There was a man who had struck me as being completely absorbed with earthly truth—an opinion I had formed from the way he lived his life. The angels were talking about earthly truth, so the image that came to me was of him. The things he said to me in the dream, and the actions he took, followed along in order with the conversation they were having among themselves, representing and corresponding to that conversation. Still, there was nothing exactly the same [in my dream as in their conversation].

1982   Some souls recently arrived from the world are eager to see the Lord's glory but are not yet ready to be let in [to heaven]. Their outer senses and lower faculties are lulled into a sweet type of sleep while their inner senses and faculties are roused to heightened wakefulness. In this state they are welcomed into heaven's glory. However, once their outer senses and faculties are restored to consciousness, they go back to their former state.

What evil spirits want more than anything else, what they burn to do, **1983** is to attack and harass us as we sleep; but that is a time when the Lord guards us with special care. Love does not sleep.

The spirits who harass us undergo terrible punishments. More times than I can tell I have heard their punishments, which consist of mutilation, as reported in §§829, 957, 959. This takes place under the heel of the left foot and sometimes lasts for hours at a time.

Sirens, who are inwardly devoted to sorcery, are the main ones to attack us by stealth during the night. They try to inject themselves into our deeper thoughts and feelings, but angels from the Lord always stop them, and eventually they are frightened off by severe punishments.

Sirens have also talked to various people by night exactly as though it was I who was speaking. Imitating my speech so perfectly that it could not be distinguished from mine, they have made foul suggestions and foisted falsehoods on their victims.

[2] One time I had the pleasantest possible night of sleep, filled entirely with sweet peace. When I woke up, though, certain good spirits started to chastise me for molesting them. They accused me of treating them so horribly that, in their words, they thought they were in hell. "I know nothing at all about it," I answered. "I was sleeping very peacefully, so I could not have bothered you in any way." Dumbfounded at this, they finally perceived that the sirens had used their sorceries to do it. The same demonstration was repeated later to teach me what that mob of sirens was like.

[3] For the most part sirens are women. During bodily life they poured all their energies into attracting friends by subtle wiles, using outward appearances to worm their way in and employing every available method to ensnare others' minds. They enter into everyone's desires and pleasures, but with ulterior motives, particularly that of gaining control. The result in the next life is that by their very nature they seem inherently capable of anything, imbibing and inventing various deceitful skills, which they seize on so readily. Just as sponges absorb water whether polluted or pure, they absorb both profane and sacred means and put them to work for the purpose (again) of gaining control.

I was allowed to sense how foul their deeper dimensions are, how defiled with adultery and hatred. I was also allowed to sense how powerful their aura is. They prepare themselves internally to sway others' minds, in an effort to coordinate their own inward and outward powers in pursuit of their aims. Then they forcefully compel spirits to think exactly the way they themselves do. [4] They do not appear to use reasoned argumentation; but there is still a certain accumulated force of argument, infused with negative emotion, that fills the same function. They also accommodate to others' personalities, gain access to their lower minds (which they take on as their own), and either entice or overpower them by the use of persuasion.

There is nothing they work harder at than destroying our conscience, and once it is destroyed, they take possession—total possession, in fact—of our inner depths, although we remain unaware of it. Outward possession no longer exists, as it once did, but inward possession by these spirits does. People on earth who are devoid of conscience are possessed in this way; deep down, their thinking is nearly as crazy, but they veil and conceal it with a superficial decency and false integrity for the sake of their status, prosperity, and reputation. Such people can recognize this tendency in themselves if they will only pay attention to the nature of their thoughts.

A Disclosure of

SECRETS OF HEAVEN

Contained in

SACRED SCRIPTURE

or

THE WORD OF THE LORD

Those in

Genesis
Chapter 17

*Together with Amazing Things Seen and Heard
in the World of Spirits & in the Heaven of Angels*

At the End of the Current Chapter, Those Having to Do with

The Last Judgment

First seek God's kingdom and its justice
and you will gain all.
—Matthew 6:33

Genesis 17

1984

THE Word has an inner meaning that does not reveal itself in the literal meaning at all because the inner meaning lies as far beyond the literal meaning as heaven lies beyond earth; but few will believe this. The literal meaning does contain an inner sense, however, and also represents and symbolizes hidden elements that no one sees but the Lord and angels, who have the Lord's help. This has been established by discussions throughout the first two volumes. The literal meaning relates to the inner meaning just as our body relates to our soul. As long as we inhabit our bodies and think in bodily terms, we know almost nothing of our soul. The functions of the body are different from those of the soul—so different that if we could detect the soul's functioning we would not recognize it as such. It is the same with the inner dimensions of the Word. The Word's inner levels are its soul, its life. These inner levels have to do exclusively with the Lord, his kingdom, the church, and the qualities in us that exemplify his kingdom and the church. When these ideas are uppermost in our thoughts, the Word is the Lord's, because life itself is then present in the inner levels. Much evidence for this appeared in the first two volumes; it is something I know for certain. Thoughts about bodily and worldly concerns can never reach the angels. Instead such thoughts are stripped away and completely removed as soon as they cross the threshold on their way out of our minds, as can be seen from actual experience in volume 2, §§1769–1772 inclusive. The way the thoughts change can be seen in §§1872–1876.

[2] This is sufficiently clear from many statements in the Word that are completely unintelligible in a literal sense. If there were no such soul

or life within them, they would not be acknowledged as the Lord's Word. They would not appear divine to anyone who had not been imbued from childhood with the belief that the Word was inspired and therefore holy.

Who would see in the literal text the meaning of the words in Genesis 49 that Jacob spoke to his sons before his death? "Dan will be a snake on the path, an asp on the track, biting the horse's heels, and its rider will fall off behind" (verse 17). "A troop will prey on Gad, and he will prey on their heel" (verse 19). "Naphtali is a doe let loose, delivering elegant words" (verse 21). "Judah will tie his young donkey to the grapevine, and his jenny's foal to a choice vine. He will wash his clothing in wine and his garment in the blood of grapes. He will have eyes redder than wine and teeth whiter than milk" (verses 11, 12).

The same is true of very many places in the Prophets. The meaning of these passages cannot be seen at all except in the inner sense, in which each and every detail hangs together in the most beautiful pattern.

[3] The same is true of the Lord's words in Matthew concerning the final days:

> At the close of the age the sun will go dark, and the moon will not shed its light; and the stars will fall down from the sky, and the powers of the heavens will be shaken. And then the sign of the Son of Humankind will appear; and then all the tribes of the earth will mourn. (Matthew 24:3, 29, 30)

Not for one moment is this talking about the darkening of sun and moon or the plummeting of stars from the sky or the mourning of the tribes. It is talking about love for our neighbor, and faith, which in an inner sense are the sun and moon that will go dark. It is talking about knowledge of what is good and true, which is the stars, here called "the powers of the heavens," which will therefore fall and vanish. And it is talking about faith, in all its manifestations, which are the tribes of the earth. This was demonstrated in volumes 1 and 2, §§31, 32, 1053, 1529, 1530, 1531, 1808.

These few examples now indicate what the Word's inner meaning is. They also show that it is distant from the literal meaning, and in some passages very distant indeed.

Still, the literal meaning does present the truth in visual form, and it also presents ideas that appear to be true, which we can rely on when we lack true light.

✿✿✿✿✿✿✿✿✿✿✿✿✿✿✿✿✿✿✿✿✿✿✿✿✿✿✿✿✿

Genesis 17

1. And Abram was a son of ninety-nine years, and Jehovah appeared to Abram and said to him, "I am God Shaddai. Walk before me and be upright.

2. And I will establish my pact between me and you, and I will multiply you very greatly."

3. And Abram dropped face down on the ground, and God spoke with him, saying,

4. "As for me, here now, my pact is with you, and you will become the father of an abundance of nations.

5. And no longer will they call you by your name 'Abram,' but your name will be 'Abraham,' because I have made you father of an abundance of nations.

6. And I will make you extremely fruitful and will turn you into nations, and monarchs will come from you.

7. And I will set up my pact between me and you and your seed after you, throughout their generations, as an eternal pact, to be God to you and to your seed after you.

8. And I will give you and your seed after you the land of your immigrant journeys—all the land of Canaan—as an eternal possession; and I will become their God."

9. And God said to Abraham, "And you shall keep my pact, you and your seed after you, throughout their generations.

10. This is my pact that you shall keep, between me and you and your seed after you: that every male among you be circumcised.

11. And you shall circumcise the flesh of your foreskin, and it will serve as a sign of the pact between me and you.

12. And a son of eight days among you shall be circumcised, every male, throughout your generations: [the slave] born in the house, and anyone purchased with silver, from every foreign son who is not of your seed.

13. Circumcision is absolutely required for [the slave] born in your house and anyone purchased with your silver; and my pact will be in your flesh as an eternal pact.

14. And the foreskinned male who is not circumcised of the flesh of his foreskin—that soul shall be cut off from his peoples; my pact he has rendered void."

15. And God said to Abraham, "You shall not call Sarai your wife by her name 'Sarai,' because 'Sarah' is her name.

16. And I will bless her and also give you a son from her; and I will bless him, and he will become nations; monarchs over the peoples will come from her."

17. And Abraham dropped face down on the ground and laughed and said in his heart, "Will a child be born to a son of a hundred years? And will Sarah, a daughter of ninety years, give birth?"

18. And Abraham said to God, "If only Ishmael could live in your sight!"

19. And God said, "Truly, Sarah your wife is bearing you a son, and you shall call his name Isaac; and I will set up my pact with him as an eternal pact, for his seed after him.

20. And as for Ishmael, I have heard you. Here now, I will bless him and make him fruitful and make him multiply very greatly; twelve chieftains he will father, and I will turn him into a great nation.

21. And my pact I will set up with Isaac, whom Sarah will bear to you at this set time in the following year."

22. And he finished talking with him, and God rose up from being with Abraham.

23. And Abraham took Ishmael his son, and all [the slaves] born in his house, and everyone purchased with his silver, every male among the men of Abraham's household, and circumcised the flesh of their foreskin, on this same day, as God had spoken with him.

24. And Abraham was a son of ninety-nine years when he circumcised the flesh of his foreskin.

25. And Ishmael his son was a son of thirteen years when the flesh of his foreskin was circumcised.

26. On this same day, Abraham was circumcised and Ishmael his son.

27. And all the men of his household—[the slave] born in the house, and anyone purchased with silver, from a foreign son—were circumcised with him.

Summary

1985 THIS has to do with the uniting of the Lord's divine nature with his human nature, and of his human nature with his divine. It also treats of the Lord's bond with the human race through his human side.

1986 Jehovah was revealed to the Lord in the Lord's human consciousness (verse 1). He was predicting their union (verses 2, 3)—the uniting of his divinity with his humanity and of his humanity with his divinity (verses 4, 5). Everything good and true would come from him (verse 6). Through him divinity would form a close connection with the human race (verse 7). He would have a heavenly kingdom, which he would give to those who believed in him (verses 8, 9). First, though, people have to be purified by ridding themselves of their [unclean] passions and of the foul cravings that go with those passions; this is what circumcision represented then and symbolizes now (verses 10, 11). This would lead to a bond both with people in the church and with people outside the church (verse 12). [2] Purification absolutely must come first—otherwise there would be no bond [with the Lord] but rather damnation—and yet such a bond cannot be formed except in the context of our impurity (verses 13, 14). The union of the Lord's human nature with his divine nature, or of truth with goodness, is predicted (verses 15, 16, 17). So is the creation of a bond between him and people devoted to the true ideas of the faith; he would form a bond with people in the spiritual church just as he would with those in the heavenly church (verses 18, 19). The former would also be imbued with various kinds of religious goodness (verse 20). To sum up, this would result from the union of the human and divine natures in the Lord (verse 21). The end of the prediction (verse 22). This is how it would happen, and this is how it did happen (verses 23, 24, 25, 26, 27).

Inner Meaning

GENESIS 17:1. *And Abram was a son of ninety-nine years, and Jehovah appeared to Abram and said to him, "I am God Shaddai. Walk before me and be upright."*

1987

Abram was a son of ninety-nine years symbolizes the time before the Lord had fully united his inner self with his rational self; *Abram* symbolizes the Lord in that phase and at that stage of his life. *And Jehovah appeared to Abram* symbolizes a manifestation to him. *And said to him* symbolizes a perception. *I am God Shaddai* in a literal sense means the name of Abram's God, by which the Lord was first represented to [Abram and his family]. *Walk before me* symbolizes religious truth. *And be upright* symbolizes goodness.

1988   *Abram was a son of ninety-nine years* symbolizes the time before the
Lord had fully united his inner self with his rational self. This can be seen
from the symbolism of *nine,* coming as it does before ten. Similarly, it
can be seen from the symbolism of *ninety-nine,* coming as it does before
a hundred. Abram was a hundred years old when Isaac was born to him.

Numbers (like names) reveal with special clarity the nature of the Word's
inner meaning. All the numbers in the Word have symbolic meaning, just
as the names do. There is nothing whatever in the Word that does not have
divinity within it, or in other words, that does not have an inner meaning.
Numbers show particularly well how far removed that inner meaning is
from the literal, because in heaven the inhabitants do not pay any attention
to names and numbers in the Word but only to what the names and numbers symbolize. For example, wherever the number seven comes up, the
concept of holiness immediately replaces that number in angels' minds.
Seven symbolizes holiness because a heavenly type of person is the seventh
day, or the Sabbath, the day the Lord rested (§§84–87, 395, 433, 716, 881).

It is the same with the other numbers; for example, twelve. Every time
twelve comes up, the thought of everything having to do with faith springs
to angels' minds, because that is what the twelve tribes of Israel symbolized
(§577). For a demonstration of the idea that numbers in the Word have
symbolic meaning, see §§482, 487, 488, 493, 575, 647, 648, 755, 813, 893 in
the first volume.

[2] It is the same with ninety-nine, which symbolizes the time before
the Lord had fully united his inner self with his rational self. This can
be seen from the symbolism of a hundred years, which was Abram's age
when Isaac was born to him, which in turn represents and symbolizes the
Lord's rational self as united to his inner or divine self. In the Word, one
hundred symbolizes the same thing as ten, because it is made up of ten
times ten, and ten symbolizes a remnant [of goodness and truth]. The
symbolism of ten was illustrated in volume 1 at §576. For a definition of
the remnant in a person, see §§468, 530, 561, 660, 1050. For a description
of the remnant in the Lord, see §1906.

These mysteries cannot be explained any further, but people everywhere can come to their own conclusions about them after finding out
what a remnant is, since that is currently unknown.

The key fact is this: the remnant in the Lord symbolizes the divine
goodness that he acquired for himself by his own power, through which
he made his human nature one with his divine.

[3] This discussion indicates what ninety-nine symbolizes. Because it comes before a hundred, it symbolizes a time before the Lord had fully united his inner self with his rational self. Ishmael represented the Lord's early rationality, whose nature was demonstrated more than amply in the previous chapter, Genesis 16 [§§1911, 1936, 1948–1951, 1964]. But Isaac represents the Lord's divine rationality, as later sections will establish [§§2632, 2658].

Abram has stayed in the land of Canaan for quite a while—twenty-four years now (ten before the year Ishmael was born and then thirteen after)—and still had not had a child by his wife Sarai. Only now, when he was ninety-nine, did he receive the promise of a son. Anyone can see that this has a secret meaning. The secret is that through these particulars he would represent the union of the Lord's divine nature with his human nature, and indeed that of the Lord's inner self—Jehovah—with his rational self.

The symbolism of *Abram* as the Lord in that phase and at that stage of his life can be seen from what has already been said about Abram.

1989

In an inner sense, Abram represents the Lord, because no other "Abram" is understood in heaven when that name is mentioned in the Word.

Admittedly, people coming into the other world do know who Abram was, if they have been born in the church and heard about him from the Word; but since he is like any other person and cannot help them one bit, he soon ceases to be their concern. They also learn that "Abram" in the Word means no one but the Lord. On the other hand, angels think heavenly thoughts, which they do not fix on any human being, so they know nothing of Abram. When we are reading the Word, then, and Abram is mentioned, they picture no one but the Lord. When the current phrase comes up, they picture the Lord in that phase and at that stage of his life, because here Jehovah talks to Abram, that is, to the Lord.

Jehovah appeared to Abram symbolizes a manifestation to him, as is clear without explanation, since *Abram* represents the Lord, as noted.

1990

Not one person in the entire world except the Lord has seen Jehovah, the Lord's Father, as he himself said in John:

> God has never been seen by anyone; the only-born Son, who is in the Father's embrace, is the one who has revealed him. (John 1:18)

In the same author:

> You have never heard his voice or seen his form. (John 5:37)

And again in the same author:

> No one has seen the Father, except the one who is with the Father; this
> one has seen the Father. (John 6:46)

[2] The Infinite itself, which is high above all the heavens and high
above our inmost reaches, cannot be revealed except through divine humanity, which exists only in the Lord. This is the only possible source of contact between the Infinite Being and finite beings. That is why Jehovah
revealed himself as a person to the people of the earliest church and later
to those of the ancient church that followed the Flood and finally to
Abraham and the prophets, when he appeared to them. This person was
the Lord, as he explicitly teaches in John:

> Abraham your father rejoiced to see my day; and he saw it and was glad.
> Truly, truly, I say to you: before Abraham was, I Am. (John 8:56, 58)

This can also be seen in the Prophets, for example, Daniel, to whom he
appeared as a "Son of Humankind" (Daniel 7:13). [3] This shows that
the Infinite Reality, which is Jehovah, never could have been revealed to
humankind except through a human nature—that is, except through the
Lord. As a result it never *was* revealed to anyone but the Lord alone. The
Divine sought a way to be present with humankind, and to connect with
us, even though we had completely alienated ourselves from it, as we sur-
rendered to our vile cravings and so to concerns centered purely on the
body and the world. For this purpose, then, it put on human nature itself
in a tangible way by being born, so that the Infinite Divine would be
able to form a connection with humankind despite our distance from it.
Otherwise humankind would have died the death of the damned forever.

There are other secrets about the way Jehovah manifested himself to
the Lord's human consciousness when the Lord was in a humbled state,
before he had made his human nature completely one with his divine and
glorified it. By the Lord's divine mercy, these will be explained (so far as
they can be understood) below [§§1999, 2147–2153, 2159, 2218, 2265].

1991   *He said to him* symbolizes a perception. This can be seen from the fact
that the Lord's perceptions came from Jehovah (as mentioned before in
§1919). It can also be seen from the fact that in an inner sense Jehovah's
saying (or God's *saying*) means perceiving (§§1602, 1791, 1815, 1819, 1822).

1992   *I am God Shaddai* in a literal sense means the name of Abram's God,
by which the Lord was first represented to them. This can be seen from

statements in the Word about Abram and his father's household to the effect that they worshiped other gods.

In Syria, where Abram came from, there were still survivors from the ancient church, and many clans there still retained their form of worship. This is evident from Eber, who came from there and who gave rise to the Hebrew nation, which likewise kept the use of the name Jehovah (as shown by the evidence offered in volume 2, §1343). It is also evident from Balaam, another native of Syria, who offered sacrifices and called his god Jehovah. (Numbers 23:7 shows that he was from Syria. Numbers 22:39, 40; 23:1, 2, 3, 14, 29 show that he offered sacrifices. Numbers 22:8, 13, 18, 31; 23:8, 12, 16 show that he called his god Jehovah.)

[2] The same was not true for the house of Terah, father of Abram and Nahor, however. Terah's house was among the clans of the nations there that not only forgot the name Jehovah but even served other gods. Instead of Jehovah they worshiped Shaddai, whom they called their god. The verses quoted in volume 2, §1343, show that they had forgotten Jehovah's name. The fact that they served other gods is stated explicitly in Joshua:

> Joshua said to all the people, "This is what Jehovah, God of Israel, has said: '*Your ancestors lived across the river* ages ago—*Terah, father of Abraham* and *father of Nahor*—and *served other gods.*' Now fear Jehovah and serve him in integrity and truth; and take away the *gods that your ancestors served across the river* and in Egypt and serve Jehovah. And if it is bad in your eyes to serve Jehovah, choose for yourselves today whom you would serve, whether it is the *gods that your ancestors who were across the river served* or the gods of the Amorites." (Joshua 24:2, 14, 15)

Nahor (Abram's brother) and the nation that sprang from him also served other gods, as can be seen from Laban the Syrian, who lived in Nahor's city and worshiped the images or teraphim that Rachel stole (Genesis 24:10; 31:19, 30, 32, 34; see the remarks on this in volume 2, §1356). In Moses it is said explicitly that in place of Jehovah the people worshiped Shaddai, whom they called their god:

> I, Jehovah, appeared to Abraham, Isaac, and Jacob as God Shaddai, and by my name "Jehovah" I was not known to them. (Exodus 6:[2,] 3)

[3] These considerations lead to several others. They show what Abram was like as a young man, namely, an idolater like others outside the church. They show that when he was living in the land of Canaan he had still not

removed God Shaddai from his heart and mind, "Shaddai" being the name of Abram's god in a literal sense. Finally they show that the Lord was first represented to them—to Abraham, Isaac, and Jacob—under the name of Shaddai, as is clear from the passage cited (Exodus 6:3).

[4] The reason the Lord chose to be represented to them at first under the name of Shaddai is that he wishes not to hastily disrupt, let alone instantly annihilate, the religion we were brought up on. To do so would be to tear it out by the roots and so destroy the reverent devotion and worship sown deeply in us. This reverence the Lord never breaks but bends. The reverent devotion rooted in us from our childhood is by nature unable to survive violence, only gentle, merciful bending. The same thing happens with non-Christians who worshiped idols during bodily life but lived lives of love for one another. In the other life their holy worship, rooted in them from their childhood, is not taken from them instantly but gradually. In those who have lived lives of love for one another, the seeds of the faith's good values and true ideas can easily be planted, and later on they receive these seeds with joy, because love for others is the soil that they grow in.

This is what happened with Abraham, Isaac, and Jacob; the Lord allowed them to keep the name God Shaddai. In fact, he even referred to himself as God Shaddai, because of the meaning of the name.

[5] Some translators render Shaddai as "Almighty"; others, as "the Thunderer." Strictly speaking, though, it means the one who tests us and who does good to us after we have been tested. This can be seen in Job, who mentions Shaddai as often as he does because of the trials he was undergoing, as the following passages there illustrate:

> Look, now, you who are fortunate: the person whom God chastises. And *you shall not reject correction by Shaddai.* (Job 5:17)

> The *arrows of Shaddai* are with me; the *terrors of God* draw up their ranks against me. (Job 6:4)

> They will abandon *fear of Shaddai.* (Job 6:14)

> I would speak to *Shaddai,* and with *God* I wish to argue. (Job 13:3)

> They stretch out their hand against *God,* and against *Shaddai* they strengthen themselves. (Job 15:25)

> Their eyes will see their ruin, and of the *fury of Shaddai they will drink.* (Job 21:20)

You will not find *Shaddai*. He is great in might and judgment and breadth of justice; *he will not afflict*. (Job 37:23)

And in Joel:

Oh no, the day! For the day of Jehovah is near, and it will come as *devastation from Shaddai*. (Joel 1:15)

The same meaning can also be seen from the word Shaddai itself, which means devastation and therefore times of trial, since trials are a form of devastation. Because the name had its origin among the nations of Syria, however, "God Shaddai" is expressed not as *Elohim Shaddai* but as *El Shaddai*. In Job he is called simply *Shaddai,* and *El* (God) is mentioned separately.

[6] Because it means comfort after our struggles as well, the same people also attributed to Shaddai the good that comes out of those struggles (as in Job 22:17, 23, 25, 26) and our understanding of truth (Job 32:8; 33:4), which also grows out of them. So he was considered a god of truth, since it is never goodness but truth that devastates, tests, punishes, and chastises people. For this reason, and because he represented the Lord to Abraham, Isaac, and Jacob, the name was kept, even in the Prophets. There, however, Shaddai means truth. In Ezekiel, for instance:

I heard the sound of the wings of the guardian beings, like the sound of many waters, like the *sound of Shaddai;* as they went [I heard] the sound of commotion, like the sound of a camp. (Ezekiel 1:24)

In the same author:

The courtyard was filled with the radiance of Jehovah's glory, and the sound of the wings of the guardian beings was heard all the way to the outer court, like the *voice of God Shaddai when he speaks.* (Ezekiel 10:4, 5)

Jehovah stands here for what is good; Shaddai, for what is true. On an inner level of the Word, wings likewise symbolize anything that has to do with truth.

[7] Isaac and Jacob likewise mention God Shaddai in a similar sense— as one who tries us, delivers us from our trials, and then does good to us. When Isaac's son Jacob fled from Esau, Isaac said to him:

God Shaddai bless you and make you fruitful and multiply you. (Genesis 28:3)

When Jacob's sons set out for Egypt to buy grain, despite their great fear of Joseph, Jacob said to them:

> *God Shaddai* give you mercy before the man and release to you your other brother and Benjamin. (Genesis 43:14)

In blessing Joseph, who had suffered more challenging evils than any of his brothers—and been delivered from them—Jacob (now Israel [Genesis 32:28]) said:

> . . . by the God of your father, who will help you, and with *Shaddai,* who will bless you. (Genesis 49:25)

This, then, is why the Lord chose to be represented at first as God Shaddai, the god Abram worshiped, when he said, "I am *God Shaddai.*" He said the same thing to Jacob later on:

> I am *God Shaddai;* be fruitful and multiply! (Genesis 35:11)

A further reason is that the story up to this point has dealt in an inner sense with times of trial.

[8] The worship of Shaddai among [Terah's family] traces its origin to this: Like a nation that will be discussed later (the Lord in his divine mercy willing), the people of the ancient church would often hear spirits upbraiding them and then spirits comforting them. The spirits who criticized them were perceived at their left side below their arm. At the same time angels were present by their head, controlling the spirits and tempering their accusations. Since the spirits said nothing to them that they did not take as a message from God, they named the accusatory spirit Shaddai. Because they also received consolation afterward, that too they named God Shaddai.

At that time, because they did not understand the Word's inner meaning, their religion (like that of the Jews) was that everything bad and therefore all trials came from God, just as everything good and therefore all comfort did. But that is not how it works; see §§245, 592, 696, 1093, 1874, 1875 in the first two volumes.

1993   *Walk before me* symbolizes religious truth. This is established by the symbolism of *walking* as living a life of obedience to religious truth (as discussed in §519), and by that of a path as truth (as discussed in §627; walking presupposes a path).

1994   *And be upright* symbolizes good that is done out of charity. This can be seen from the symbolism of being *upright* as being inspired by *truth* to do good, which is the same as being inspired by a true conscience to do it.

So it is doing good out of charity, since this forms a person's conscience. For this symbolism of uprightness, see §612. Since the subject on an inner level here is the Lord, though, uprightness in this case symbolizes *good* that is done out of charity, because charity produces good actions. In fact, even the truth it produces is a form of goodness.

Genesis 17:2. *"And I will establish my pact between me and you, and I will multiply you very greatly."* **1995**

I will establish my pact between me and you symbolizes the uniting of the Lord's inner self, which was Jehovah, with his intermediate self. *And I will multiply you very greatly* symbolizes the way a desire for truth bears infinite fruit.

I will establish my pact between me and you symbolizes the uniting of the Lord's inner self, which was Jehovah, with his intermediate self, as can be seen from the symbolism of a *pact* as union. Whenever the Word mentions a compact between Jehovah and humankind, it symbolizes no other pact on an inner level than the Lord's close connection with us. This is exactly what the pacts struck so often between Jehovah and Jacob's descendants represented. It would be redundant to prove so here, since it was already proved in volumes 1 and 2, §§665, 666, 1023, 1038, 1864. **1996**

The Lord's inner self was Jehovah, because he was conceived by Jehovah. His intermediate self, however, is represented here by Abram, so the *pact between me and you* symbolizes the uniting of the Lord's inner self, or Jehovah, with his intermediate self, and so with his human nature.

I will multiply you very greatly symbolizes the way a desire for truth bears infinite fruit. This can be seen from the significance of *multiplying* as a word that applies to truth, as explained in §§43, 55, 913, 983. Because it has to do with the Lord, here, it symbolizes the way truth that grows out of goodness bears infinite fruit, as explained above in §1940. **1997**

There are two basic categories of desire: the desire for what is good and the desire for what is true. To desire good is to do good because you love good. To desire truth is to do good because you love truth. At first glance, these two kinds of desire look as though they were the same, but they are inherently different, both in essence and in origin. The desire for good (doing good because you love good) is really a matter of the will. The desire for truth, though, (doing good because you love truth) is really a matter of the intellect. These two desires, then, differ from one another the same way the will and the intellect do.

A desire for what is good comes from heavenly love, but a desire for what is true comes from spiritual love. [2] Only those who are heavenly have a desire for what is good; those who are spiritual have a desire for truth instead. (The first two volumes showed at some length what a heavenly quality and a heavenly person are like, and what a spiritual quality or a spiritual person is like.)

The earliest church, before the Flood, was devoted to goodness, but the ancient church, after the Flood, was devoted to truth. The former, after all, was a heavenly church, while the latter was a spiritual one. All the angels in the heavens are divided into heavenly ones and spiritual ones. The heavenly ones are the ones devoted to goodness; the spiritual ones, to truth. The former see the Lord as the sun; the latter, as the moon (§§1529, 1530, 1531, 1838).

When the Lord united his human nature with his divine, he united this desire—the desire for truth—with a desire for goodness (that is, with the doing of good out of a love of goodness). As a result, *multiplying very greatly* symbolizes the way truth that grows out of goodness bears infinite fruit.

1998   Genesis 17:3. *And Abram dropped face down on the ground, and God spoke with him, saying, . . .*

Abram dropped face down on the ground symbolizes reverence. *And God spoke with him, saying,* symbolizes the level of perception. It says *God* because God Shaddai, whom Abram worshiped, represents the Lord, and because the subject here is truth that needed to be united to goodness.

1999   *Abram dropped face down on the ground* symbolizes reverence, as can be seen without explanation.

Dropping face down on the ground was a ritual way of expressing reverence in the earliest church and therefore among the ancient people. The *face* symbolized a person's inner depths, so dropping face down on the ground represented an inwardly humble attitude. That is why the representative Jewish religion had the same tradition. True reverence, or a humble heart, naturally and inherently causes us to prostrate ourselves before the Lord, face to the ground. A humble heart holds in itself an acknowledgment of our own nature, which is nothing but filth, and also an acknowledgment of the Lord's infinite mercy toward such a piece of filth. When these two acknowledgments occupy our thoughts, our mind sinks down toward hell of its own volition and prostrates our body. It does not lift itself up until the Lord lifts it. This happens in any true state of humility and brings with it a sense that the Lord in his mercy is raising us up. That is what humility was like for the people of the earliest church. The case is different, though, with devotion that does not arise out of a humble heart; see §1153.

[2] From the Word as written in the Gospels, people know that the Lord worshiped and prayed to Jehovah his Father [Matthew 11:25; Mark 14:36; Luke 23:34; John 11:41]. In doing so he addressed the Father as someone other than himself, even though Jehovah was actually within him. The state the Lord was then in, however, was his state of being humbled. The second volume described these low times as times when the frail humanity he inherited from his mother came to the fore [§§1414, 1444, 1573]. The more he divested himself of this humanity and put on divinity, though, the more he entered into another state, called his state of glorification. In the first stage he worshiped Jehovah as separate from himself, even though Jehovah was within him. (As mentioned before, his inner depths were Jehovah.) In the second stage, on the other hand—the state of his glorification—he talked to Jehovah as himself, because he *was* Jehovah.

[3] None of this can be understood, however, without the knowledge of several things: what the inner core is; how the inner core acts on the outer shell; and how the inner core and outer shell differ from one another and yet are joined. Nevertheless it can be illustrated by comparison, specifically comparison with our own inner core and the way it flows into and acts on our outer shell. (On the point that we have an inner level, an intermediate or rational level, and an outer level, see §§1889, 1940.) Our inner core is what makes us human and distinguishes us from animals. It is on account of this inner core that we live on after death forever and that the Lord can lift us up among the angels. It is the original [human] form itself from which we are and become human. Through this inner core the Lord unites with us. The heaven closest to the Lord is made up of these human interiors, but it exists above the inmost angelic heaven, so the interiors belong to the Lord himself. That is how the Lord keeps the human race directly under his gaze. (We are conscious of distance in this terrestrial world of ours, but no distance of that kind exists in heaven, let alone above heaven. See what I learned from experience in §§1275, 1277.)

[4] These inner dimensions of ours have no life of their own. They are merely forms that receive the Lord's life. The more awash in evil we are, then, whether it is evil we have done or only inherited, the greater the distance that seems to separate us from this inner core. And since our inner core is the Lord's and exists with him, the presence of evil in us also seems to separate us from the Lord. Although this core is fixed into us and is inseparable from us, we still seem to distance ourselves from it to the extent that we withdraw from the Lord (see §1594). Distance is

not the same as a complete rift, however. If we were cut off from it, we would not be able to survive death. Rather, our lower faculties—those of our rational self and outer self—come to clash and conflict with it. The more they clash and conflict, the more distant they grow. The less they clash and conflict, though, the more closely our inner core unites us with the Lord. This unity depends on the amount of love and charity we have, because love and charity unify. That is how the case stands with people's inner core.

[5] The Lord's inner core, on the other hand, was Jehovah himself, because he was conceived by Jehovah, who cannot branch off or be differentiated into a second person, as happens with a child conceived by a human father. Divinity is not divisible, as humanity is, but is and remains a single, uniform entity. This inner core is what the Lord made his human nature one with. Because the Lord's inner core was Jehovah, it was not a form for receiving life, as it is in us; it was life itself. Even the Lord's human nature became life itself through union with divinity, which is why the Lord said so many times that he is life. In John, for instance:

> Just as the Father has life in himself, so he has granted the Son to have life in himself. (John 5:26)

Other such passages in John are 1:4; 5:21; 6:33, 35, 48; 11:25.

The more conscious the Lord was of the humanity he inherited from his mother, then, the more he appeared to be separate from Jehovah and worshiped Jehovah as someone other than himself. The more he shed this humanity, though, the more he became not different from Jehovah but identical with him. The former state, again, was a humbled one for the Lord, but the latter was one of his glorification.

2000 *And God spoke with him* symbolizes the level of perception, which is established by the symbolism of Jehovah's *saying* as perceiving (§1898). Here it symbolizes the Lord's level of perception, because he was in a state of humility, or reverence. The further into this state he entered, the closer his connection and union with Jehovah became, because these are a natural result of humility. (To learn about the constant deepening of perception, see §1616.)

2001 The word *God* is used because God Shaddai, whom Abram worshiped, represents the Lord, and because the subject here is truth that needed to be united to goodness. This can be seen from previous remarks.

The Word refers to the Lord sometimes as Jehovah, sometimes as Jehovah God or the Lord Jehovah, and sometimes as God. In every case the inner meaning provides a hidden reason for the use of the particular name. Where the message has to do with love or goodness and with a heavenly religion, the Lord is called Jehovah; but where the message has to do with faith or truth and with a spiritual religion, he is called God (§§709, 732). This happens consistently. The reason for the distinction is that the central reality of the Lord is the reality of love, while the reality that emerges from it is that of faith. Here, then, he is called God because the topic is truth that needs to be united to goodness.

A second reason is the fact that the Lord chose to be represented as God Shaddai, whom Abram worshiped, so the name "God" is kept in subsequent verses. Notice that the chapter uses "Jehovah" only once but "God" a number of times, as in verses 7, 8, 15, 18, 19, 22, 23.

Genesis 17:4. *"As for me, here now, my pact is with you, and you will* **2002** *become the father of an abundance of nations."*

As for me, here now, my pact is with you symbolizes the uniting of his divine nature with his human nature. *And you will become the father of an abundance of nations* symbolizes the uniting of his human nature with his divine. A *father* symbolizes what comes from him; an *abundance* symbolizes truth; and *of nations* symbolizes the good that would result.

As for me, here now, my pact is with you symbolizes the uniting of his **2003** divine nature with his human nature, as is established by the symbolism of a *pact*, which means union (discussed in §§665, 666, 1023, 1038). In the current context, then, it symbolizes the uniting of the Lord's divine nature with his human, which also becomes clear from the inner meaning of the last few verses, and therefore from the words themselves: "My pact is with you."

And you will become the father of an abundance of nations symbolizes **2004** the uniting of his human nature with his divine. This cannot be seen very clearly from an explanation of the inner meaning of the individual words; one needs to look at them from a broad point of view to see this meaning. That is sometimes how it is with the inner meaning.

When the inner meaning requires a broad viewpoint, it can be described as more universal, because it is further from the surface. The most immediate meaning to spring from an explanation of the individual words is that the Lord would become the source of everything true and everything good. As will be explained below, a *father* symbolizes what comes from him (the Lord), an *abundance* symbolizes truth, and *of nations* symbolizes the good that would result. However, since these two—truth and goodness— are the means by which the Lord united his human nature to his divine, this union emerges as the more universal, less direct or immediate meaning. That is how angels understand the words, which they take to mean a reciprocal union—that of the Lord's divine nature with his human and of his human nature with his divine. *As for me, my pact is with you* symbolizes the uniting of his divine nature with his human, as noted, so the current words symbolize that of his human nature with his divine.

[2] The fact that each nature became united with the other is a secret never before disclosed, and one that can hardly be explained in an intelligible way, because no one knows yet how spiritual inflow works. Without that knowledge, the reciprocal uniting of the two can never be grasped in the least. To some extent, though, it can be illustrated by the spiritual inflow that affects us, since we too experience a reciprocal bond.

Life constantly flows in from the Lord through our inner core (discussed just above in §1999) into our rational mind and through this into our outer self—specifically, into the facts and religious knowledge we have learned. This inflow not only prepares our facts and knowledge to come alive but also organizes them, enabling us to think and eventually become rational. This is the way the Lord forms a bond with us, and without that bond, we could not think at all, much less rationally. Anyone can see the truth of this claim. Consider the fact that within our thoughts lie countless secret skills belonging to the science and art of analytic thinking—so many of them that eternity would not be enough time to get to the bottom of them. Never do they reach us through the physical senses of our outer self but through our inner depths. For our part, though, we meet this stream of life from the Lord halfway by acquiring facts and religious knowledge, and this is how we in turn form a bond with him.

[3] The uniting of the Lord's divine nature with his human and of his human with his divine, however, infinitely transcends our bond with him. The Lord's inner core was Jehovah himself and therefore life itself, but our inner core is not the Lord and so is not life but something that receives life. Between the Lord and Jehovah there was oneness, but between us and the Lord there is connection rather than oneness. The Lord made himself one with Jehovah by his own power, so he also became righteousness. We never unite with the Lord through our own power but through his; in other words, he binds us to himself.

This mutual union is what the Lord means where he attributes what is his to the Father and what is the Father's to himself, as in John:

> Jesus said, "*Whoever believes in me believes not in me but in him who sent me;* whoever sees me sees him who sent me. I have come into the world as the light, so that no one *who believes in me* should stay in the dark." (John 12:44, 45, 46)

These words conceal the deepest secrets, which have to do with the uniting of goodness with truth and of truth with goodness. To say the same thing another way, they have to do with the uniting of the divine nature with the human and of the human with the divine. That is why he says, "Whoever believes in me does not believe in me but in him who sent me," and then immediately refers to one "who believes in me." In between, he speaks of their oneness in these words: "Whoever sees me sees him who sent me." [4] In the same author:

> The words *that I speak to you I do not speak from myself;* the *Father* who dwells in me, *he does the works.* Believe me, that I am in the Father and the Father is in me. Truly, I say to you: those who *believe in me, the works that I do* . . . (John 14:10, 11, 12)

These words contain the same secrets concerning the uniting of goodness with truth and of truth with goodness, or to put it another way, the uniting of the Lord's divine nature with his human and of his human with his divine. That is why he says, "The words that I speak to you I do not speak from myself; the Father who is in me does the works," and directly afterward mentions "the works that I do." In between, he speaks here again of their union in these words: "I am in the Father and the Father is in me." This is the mystical union that many people speak of.

[5] The above evidence shows that the Lord was not a separate person from the Father even though he spoke of the Father as a separate person (which he did because of the reciprocal union that was to take place and actually did). After all, he explicitly says many times that he is one with the Father, as for instance in the passages just quoted:

> *Whoever sees me sees him who sent me.* (John 12:45)

And:

> *The Father who dwells in me, . . . Believe me, that I am in the Father and the Father is in me.* (John 14:10, 11)

Further in the same author:

> *If you knew me, you would also know my Father.* (John 8:19)

In the same author:

> "*If you know me, you also know my Father; and from now on you know him and have seen him.*" Philip says to him, "Show us the Father." Jesus says to him, "So much time I've spent with you, and you do not know

me, Philip? *Whoever has seen me has seen the Father.* How then can you say, 'Show us the Father'? Don't you believe *that I am in the Father and the Father is in me?"* (John 14:7, 8, 9, 10)

And in the same author:

> *I and the Father are one.* (John 10:30)

This is why in heaven they know no other Father than the Lord. As he said, the Father is in him, and he is one with the Father, and when they see him they see the Father. (See §15.)

2005   The symbolism of a *father* as what comes from the Lord can be seen from the meaning of *the Father* as discussed just above. To be specific, whatever came from the Father came from the Lord, because they were one.

In every individual, the inner core comes from the father and the outer shell from the mother. To put the same thing another way, the soul itself is from the father; the body that clothes it is from the mother. Soul and body nevertheless make a single unit together, because the soul belongs to the body and the body to the soul, so that they are inseparable.

The Lord's inner core was from the Father and therefore was the Father himself. That is why the Lord says, "The Father is in me," "I am in the Father and the Father is in me," "Whoever sees me sees the Father," and "I and the Father are one," as the passages quoted above show.

He is also called the Father in the Old Testament Word, as in Isaiah:

> A child has been born for us, a son has been given to us, and sovereignty will be on his shoulder, and his name will be called Miraculous, Counselor, God, Hero, *Eternal Father,* Prince of Peace. (Isaiah 9:6)

Anyone can see that the child born for us and the son given to us is the Lord, and he is being called the Eternal Father. In the same author:

> *You are our Father,* because Abraham does not know us and Israel does not acknowledge us. *You are Jehovah our Father, our Redeemer;* your name is from eternity. (Isaiah 63:16)

This too is speaking of the Lord, who is being called Jehovah our Father, because there is no other Redeemer. In Malachi:

> Do we not all have *one father?* Did not *one God create us?* (Malachi 2:10)

Creating stands for regenerating, as shown in the first volume, §§16, 88, 472.

Besides, everywhere in the Old Testament Word *Jehovah* means the Lord, because all religious rites represented him, and everything in the inner meaning of the Word has to do with him.

The symbolism of an *abundance* as truth can be seen from the previous discussion in §1941, which showed that an *abundance* or *multitude* symbolizes truth. It can also be seen from the significance of *multiplying* as a word used to describe truth, a subject discussed in §§43, 55, 913, 983.   **2006**

Of nations symbolizes the good that would result, which is established by the symbolism of *nations* as goodness, as discussed in the second volume, §§1159, 1258, 1259, 1260, 1416, 1849.   **2007**

Genesis 17:5. *"And no longer will they call you by your name 'Abram,' but your name will be 'Abraham,' because I have made you father of an abundance of nations."*   **2008**

No longer will they call you by your name "Abram" means that he would shed his human nature. *But your name will be "Abraham"* means that he would put on a divine nature. *Because I have made you father of an abundance of nations* here as before means that everything true and therefore good would come from him.

No longer will they call you by your name "Abram" means that he would shed his human nature. *But your name will be "Abraham"* means that he would put on a divine nature. This can be seen from the symbolism of a *name* and the symbolism of *Abram* and then *Abraham*.   **2009**

When the Word says, "Your name will be," it means a quality, or "This is what you will be like." Quotations in §§144, 145, 1754 of the first two volumes make this clear.

Because a name symbolizes a quality, it embraces everything in the person at once. Heaven pays no attention to a person's name. Instead, when anyone is named or a name is mentioned, an idea of the person's character springs to mind—a picture of everything that belongs to, exists with, or resides in the person. As a result, a name in the Word symbolizes a quality or character. To make this intelligible, let me bring forward yet another set of scriptural passages by way of proof.

In Moses' blessing, for example:

Jehovah bless you and guard you; Jehovah make his face shine on you and have mercy on you. Jehovah lift his face toward you and give you peace. So will they *put my name on the children of Israel.* (Numbers 6:24, 25, 26, 27)

This passage reveals what a name is and what putting Jehovah's name on the children of Israel means—namely, that Jehovah blesses, guards, enlightens, has mercy, and gives peace. So it means that Jehovah (the Lord) has these characteristics. [2] In the Ten Commandments:

> You shall not *utter the name of Jehovah your God for an evil purpose,* because Jehovah will not hold guiltless the person who *has uttered his name for an evil purpose.* (Exodus 20:7; Deuteronomy 5:11)

Uttering God's name *for an evil purpose* does not mean treating his name this way but treating absolutely everything that comes from him this way. The passage is talking about divine worship in each and every one of its facets, which we are not to scorn, much less blaspheme or pollute with filth. In the Lord's Prayer:

> *May your name be held sacred.* May your kingdom come. May your will be done—as in heaven, so on earth. (Luke 11:2)

Here too his name does not mean his name but every aspect of love and faith, because these are God's, or the Lord's, and have their origin in him. These are the things that are sacred, so when we hold them sacred, the Lord's kingdom comes and his will is done on earth as in the heavens.

[3] Every passage in the Word (Old Testament and New) that mentions his name reveals this symbolism. In Isaiah, for example:

> You will say on that day, "Acclaim Jehovah; *call on his name;* make his deeds known among the peoples. Make mention that *his name is exalted.*" (Isaiah 12:4)

Calling on Jehovah's name and making mention that it is exalted never means equating worship with the use of his name, or believing that we call on Jehovah by saying his name. No, we call on Jehovah by knowing what he is like and therefore by calling on each and every thing we receive from him. In the same author:

> Therefore honor Jehovah in the Urim; the *name of Jehovah, God of Israel,* in the islands of the sea. (Isaiah 24:15)

Honoring Jehovah in the Urim is honoring him with holy love. Honoring the name of Jehovah, God of Israel, in the islands of the sea is honoring him with holy faith. In the same author:

> Jehovah our God, [relying] only on you we will *mention your name.* (Isaiah 26:13)

[4] And in the same author:

> I will rouse one from the north who will come; from the rising of the
> sun, that one will *call on my name.* (Isaiah 41:25)

Mentioning and calling on Jehovah's name is worshiping him with the
good deeds of love and the true ideas of faith. The people from the north
are those who are outside the church and do not know Jehovah's name.
Yet they call on his name when they live lives of love for each other and
revere the spirit that created the universe. Calling on Jehovah consists not
in the use of a name but in worship and the quality of the worship. (For
the point that the Lord is also present with people outside the church, see
§§932, 1032, 1059.) [5] In the same author:

> The nations have seen your justice and all monarchs your glory. And
> *a new name will be given to you,* which the mouth of Jehovah will pro-
> nounce. (Isaiah 62:2)

"A new name will be given to you" stands for being changed, specifically
for being created anew, or reborn, and so for being this kind of person.
In Micah:

> All peoples will walk each *in the name of its god,* and we will walk *in the
> name of Jehovah our God* forever and ever. (Micah 4:5)

Walking in the name of one's own god obviously stands for profane worship, while walking in Jehovah's name stands for true worship. In Malachi:

> From the sun's rising to its setting, *my name is great among the nations;*
> and in every place, incense has been *offered to my name,* and a clean
> minha, because *my name is great among the nations.* (Malachi 1:11)

His name here does not mean a name but worship, or the quality for
which Jehovah (the Lord) wants us to revere him. [6] In Moses:

> The place that Jehovah your God chooses out of all the tribes, to *put
> his name* there and to *make his name dwell* there—to that place you will
> bring everything that I am commanding you. (Deuteronomy 12:5, 11,
> 14; 16:2, 6, 11)

Once again, putting his name there and making it dwell there is not about
his name but about worship and so about the quality for which we are to
worship Jehovah (the Lord). The Lord's nature comprises the good that
love inspires and the truth that faith teaches. People who share these qualities have Jehovah's name dwelling in them. In Jeremiah:

> Go to my place that is in Shiloh, where *I made my name dwell* at first. (Jeremiah 7:12)

Here too his name stands for worship and so for the teachings of true faith. Anyone can see that Jehovah does not dwell with people who simply know and use his name. His name alone, without any mental image of his nature, any knowledge of it, or any belief in it, is just a word. Clearly, then, his name means his nature and a recognition of his nature as well. [7] In Moses:

> At that time Jehovah set apart the tribe of Levi to minister to him and to *bless people in his name.* (Deuteronomy 10:8)

Blessing people in Jehovah's name is blessing them not through his name but through the qualities that belong to Jehovah's name, as described above. In Jeremiah:

> *This is his name* that they will call him: *Jehovah our Righteousness.* (Jeremiah 23:6)

The name stands for righteousness, and this quality belongs to the Lord, who is the subject here. In Isaiah:

> Jehovah called me from the womb, from my mother's belly, and *mentioned my name.* (Isaiah 49:1)

This too is about the Lord. Mentioning his name means teaching people what he is like.

[8] The symbolism of a name as a quality is even clearer to see in the Revelation of John:

> You have a *few names in Sardis* who have not defiled their clothes and will walk with me in white because they are worthy. Those who conquer will be dressed in white clothes, and *I will not delete their name from the book of life;* and *I will proclaim their name* before my Father and before the angels. Those who conquer, *I will write on them the name of God,* and the *name of the city of my God*—New Jerusalem, which is coming down out of heaven from my God—and *my new name.* (Revelation 3:4, 5, 12)

In this passage, a name obviously is not a name but an individual's character. A name in the book of life is nothing else. The same holds true for a person's name proclaimed before the Father; for the name of God, the name of the city, and the new name written on a person; and elsewhere for the names to be written in the book of life and in heaven (Revelation 13:8; 17:8; Luke 10:20). [9] In heaven people never recognize each other except by character, which the literal meaning of the Word expresses as a name. Anyone can see the truth of this by considering that whenever we refer to a person by name on earth, our listener forms an idea of that person's character—the quality by which the person is recognized and distinguished from others. In the next life (especially among angels) the name disappears; only the idea remains. That is why a name is a quality or the recognition of a person's nature in an inner sense. In the same author:

> On the head of the one who sat on a white horse were many crowns. *Having a name written* that no one knows but he, he was dressed in a garment dyed with blood, and *his name is called God's Word.* (Revelation 19:12, 13)

The words here explicitly say that his name is God's Word, so the name is the nature of the person who sat on the white horse.

[10] The following words of the Lord's make it clear that Jehovah's name means knowing what he is like, or knowing that he is all the good that love inspires and all the truth that faith teaches:

> Righteous Father, I know you, and these also have recognized that you sent me, because *I made your name known to them,* and I will make it known, so that the love with which you loved me can exist in them, and I in them. (John 17:25, 26)

[11] And the following words in the same Gospel make it clear that God's name (or the Lord's) is everything faith teaches about love and charity—a theology symbolized by "believing in his name":

> As many as did accept him, to them he gave the power to be God's children, *to those believing in his name.* (John 1:12)

> If you *ask* anything *in my name,* I will do it; *if you love me,* keep my commandments. (John 14:13, 14, 15)

> Whatever you *ask the Father in my name,* he gives it to you. These things I am *commanding you, to love one another.* (John 15:16, 17)

In Matthew:

> Where two or three are *gathered in my name,* there I am in their midst. (Matthew 18:20)

People gathered in the Lord's name mean those who live by faith's teachings on love and charity and therefore have love and charity themselves. In the same author:

> You will be hated by all the nations *because of my name*. (Matthew 10:22; 24:9, 10; Mark 13:13)

"Because of my name" obviously means "because of my teachings."

[12] The name itself is completely unimportant. All that matters is what the name implies—in other words, every expression of charity and faith. This is clear from the following words in Matthew:

> "Haven't we prophesied *in your name* and cast out demons *in your name* and exercised many powers *in your name?*" But then I'll proclaim to them, "I do not know you. Leave me, you evildoers!" (Matthew 7:22, 23)

This shows that people who equate worship with the use of a name (as Jews do with Jehovah's name and Christians do with the Lord's) are not any more worthy for having done so, because a name is unimportant. What matters is being the kind of people the Lord commanded us to be; to do this is to believe in his name. To say that salvation is to be found in no name but the Lord's is to say it is found in no other theology—none other than that of mutual love, which is the true theology. It is found in no one but the Lord, because he alone is the source of all love and of the faith that rises out of love.

2010   A name, then, symbolizes a quality, and recognition of a person's character. So when this verse says, *No longer will they call you by your name "Abram," but your name will be "Abraham,"* it must mean that he would now be not as he had been but as he would be in the future.

Abram served other gods and worshiped God Shaddai, as shown above (§1992). He was about to represent the Lord, though—not simply the Lord but the Lord's inner self, and therefore his heavenly love. So his former quality had to be done away with first; that is, the name "Abram" had to take on a new character capable of representing the Lord. As a result the letter *h* was taken from Jehovah's name and inserted, and he was called Abraham. (The letter *h* is the only letter in Jehovah's name that involves divinity, and it means the I Am, or Being.) Likewise for Sarai in a later verse [Genesis 17:15]; the same letter was added to her name, and she was called Sarah.

This demonstrates that in the Word's inner meaning Abraham represents Jehovah, or the Lord.

[2] It should be noted, however, that when people represent inner things, it does not matter what kind of people they are. Representation implies nothing about the person, only about the phenomenon represented, as stated and shown before (§§665, 1097 at the end, 1361). In an inner sense, then, these words mean that the Lord was shedding his humanity and putting on divinity. This continues seamlessly from what precedes, and it also continues on into what follows, since a promise is now made concerning Isaac, Abraham's son, who would represent the Lord's divine rationality.

Because I have made you father of an abundance of nations here as before   **2011** means that everything true and therefore good would come from him, as can be seen from the following symbolism: A *father* symbolizes what comes from the Lord; an *abundance* symbolizes truth; and *of nations* symbolizes the good that would result. These are discussed above at §§2005, 2006, 2007. In a more universal sense, farther from the surface, the same words symbolize the union of the Lord's human nature with his divine nature; see above at §2004.

The uniting of the Lord's human nature with his divine resembles that of truth with goodness, and the uniting of his divine nature with his human resembles that of goodness with truth. The union is reciprocal. The Lord harbored within him truth itself, which united with goodness, and goodness that united with truth. Infinite divinity cannot be described as anything but goodness and truth itself. So the human mind makes no mistake when it thinks of the Lord as goodness itself and truth itself.

Genesis 17:6. *"And I will make you extremely fruitful and will turn you*   **2012** *into nations, and monarchs will come from you."*

I will make you extremely fruitful symbolizes the way goodness bears infinite fruit. *And will turn you into nations* means that everything good would come from the Lord. *And monarchs will come from you* means that everything true would come from him.

I will make you extremely fruitful symbolizes the way goodness bears   **2013** infinite fruit. This is established by the significance of *being fruitful* as a word used to describe what is good, a subject discussed earlier, in §§43, 55, 913, 983. And because in talking about the Lord it says *extremely,* it means bearing infinite fruit.

I will turn you into nations means that everything good would come   **2014** from the Lord. This is established by the symbolism of *nations* in its genuine, original sense as goodness, as discussed in the second volume, §§1259, 1260, 1416, 1849.

2015   *Monarchs will come from you* means that everything true would come
from him. This can be seen from the symbolism of a *monarch,* which in
both the narrative and the prophetic parts of the Word means truth. Such
a symbolism was mentioned in §1672 but has not been demonstrated
very fully yet. The symbolism of nations as what is good and that of monarchs as what is true illuminates the nature of the Word's inner meaning
and the distance that separates that meaning from the literal meaning.

One who reads the Word, especially the narrative part, inevitably
believes that "nations" there are nations, that "monarchs" are monarchs,
and consequently that the Lord's own Word is talking about the nations
named there and their rulers. When angels take in that person's reading,
though, the idea of nations and rulers dies away completely and the concepts of goodness and truth take their place. This cannot help sounding
strange or even impossible, but it is still true. Anyone can see the truth of
it from this: If the nations in the Word meant nations and the rulers
meant rulers, the Lord's Word would contain hardly anything more than
any other history or document. It would be worldly. In reality, however,
the Word contains nothing that is not divine and therefore heavenly and
spiritual. [2] Take just the current verse, which says that Abraham would
be made fruitful, he would turn into nations, and monarchs would come
from him. Do you find anything here but what is purely secular and not
in the least transcendent? These predictions concern nothing more than
worldly glory, which is utterly worthless in heaven. If it is the Lord's Word,
though, the glory must be that of heaven, not of the world. That is why
the literal meaning is completely obliterated and vanishes when it crosses
into heaven. It is purified to the point where nothing of the world remains
to taint it. "Abraham" does not mean Abraham but the Lord. Being made
fruitful does not mean generations of descendants that would increase to
an extreme degree but goodness in the Lord's human nature, which would
grow to infinity. Nations do not mean nations but good qualities. And
monarchs do not mean monarchs but true concepts. At the same time,
the history of the literal meaning remains true; it was true that these
words were said to Abraham, that he did become fruitful in this way, and
that nations and monarchs did come from him.

[3] The following passages show that monarchs symbolize truth. In
Isaiah:

> The children of a foreigner will rebuild your walls, and *their monarchs*
> will tend to you. *You will suck the milk of the nations,* and *you will suck
> the nipple of monarchs.* (Isaiah 60:10, 16)

The literal meaning would never reveal what sucking the milk of the nations and the nipple of monarchs is; only the inner meaning would. In an inner sense, sucking the milk of the nations and the nipple of monarchs means being gifted with what is good and being taught what is true. In Jeremiah:

> Through the gates of this city will enter *monarchs* and chieftains, sitting on David's throne, riding a chariot and horses. (Jeremiah 17:25; 22:4)

"Riding a chariot and horses" is an oracular phrase that symbolizes a wealth of intellectual abilities, as many passages in the Prophets show. In an inner sense, then, "through the gates of the city will enter monarchs" means that people will learn religious truth. This is the heavenly meaning of the Word, into which the worldly, literal meaning passes. [4] In the same author:

> Jehovah in the outrage of his anger has spurned *monarch* and priest. The gates of Zion have sunk into the earth. He has destroyed and broken the *bars* on them. Its *monarch* and *chieftains* live among the nations; there is no law. (Lamentations 2:6, 9)

The monarch stands for religious truth; the priest, for neighborly kindness. Zion stands for religion, which is being destroyed and the bars of whose gates are being broken. The monarch and chieftains (truth and everything related to it) will go into exile among the nations, so much so that there will be no law (no body of religious teachings). In Isaiah:

> Before the child knows to spurn evil and choose good, the ground that you despise in the presence of *its two monarchs* will be abandoned. (Isaiah 7:16)

This is about the Lord's Coming. The ground that will be abandoned stands for a faith that would then disappear. The monarchs mean religious truths, which would be despised. [5] In the same author:

> I will lift my hand to the *nations,* and for the peoples I will raise my signal. And they will bring your sons in their embrace, and your daughters will be carried here on their shoulder. *Kings* will be your *nourishers,* and their ladies, your wet nurses. (Isaiah 49:22, 23)

Nations and daughters stand for goodness, while peoples and sons stand for truth, as shown in the first two volumes. Nations stand for goodness: §§1259, 1260, 1416, 1849. Daughters too: 489, 490, 491. Peoples stand for truth: 1259, 1260. Sons too: 489, 491, 533, 1147. Kings, then, stand for truth in general, which nourishes us. Their ladies stand for the goodness that nurses us. Whether you say goodness and truth or people who have goodness and truth, it is all the same. [6] In the same author:

> He will sprinkle many *nations; monarchs* will shut their mouth on account of him, because what was not told them, they have seen, and what they did not hear, they have understood. (Isaiah 52:15)

This is about the Lord's Coming. Nations stand for people who respond to what is good; monarchs, for people who respond to what is true. In David:

> Now, *monarchs,* be *intelligent;* be trained, you judges of the earth. Serve Jehovah with fear, and rejoice with trembling; kiss the Son, or he might grow angry and you might be destroyed along the way. (Psalms 2:10, 11, 12)

The monarchs stand for people who have true ideas, because of which they are also referred to as *royal offspring* in many passages. The Son stands for the Lord, who is being called a son because he is truth itself and the source of all truth. [7] In John:

> They will sing a new song: "You are worthy to take the book and open its seals. You have made us *monarchs* and priests to our God so that we may *rule* over the earth." (Revelation 5:9, 10)

People who have true ideas are called monarchs here. In Matthew the Lord also calls them children of the kingdom:

> The one who sows good seed is the Son of Humankind; the field is the world; the seeds are the *children of the kingdom;* and the tares are the children of the evil one. (Matthew 13:37, 38)

In John:

> The sixth angel poured out his bowl over the great river Euphrates, whose water was drained to prepare a *path for monarchs* who came from the rising of the sun. (Revelation 16:12)

You can see from this that the Euphrates does not mean the Euphrates and that the monarchs from the rising of the sun do not mean monarchs. See §§120, 1585, 1866 for the symbolism of the Euphrates. It is evident, then, that a path for monarchs who come from the rising of the sun is religious truth that comes from a loving goodness. [8] In the same author:

> The *nations* that are being saved will walk in its light, and the *monarchs of the earth* will bring their glory and honor into it. (Revelation 21:24)

The nations stand for people committed to goodness; the monarchs of the earth, for people committed to truth. Another clear indicator of this is the fact that the Book of Revelation contains prophecy, not history. In the same author:

> The *monarchs of the earth* have committed whoredom with the great whore who is sitting on many waters, and have become drunk on the wine of her whoredom. (Revelation 17:[1,] 2)

And in another place:

> Babylon has given all the nations something to drink from the wine of her whoredom, and the *monarchs of the earth* have committed whoredom with her. (Revelation 18:3, 9)

Here again the monarchs of the earth plainly do not mean monarchs, since the text is speaking of the way people falsify and adulterate religious teachings, or in other words, truth. This is the whoredom. These monarchs of the earth stand for truth falsified and adulterated. [9] In the same author:

> The ten horns that you saw are *ten monarchs* who have not yet received a *kingdom*. They receive authority as if for one hour alongside the beast. They will have a single mind and will hand their power and authority over to the beast. (Revelation 17:12, 13)

Here too anyone can easily see that the monarchs do not mean monarchs. Otherwise the statement that ten monarchs would receive authority as if for one hour would be completely incomprehensible. Something similar is true of these words in the same author:

> I saw the beast and the *monarchs of the earth* and their armies gathered to make war with the one sitting on the horse and with his army. (Revelation 19:19)

Verse 13 of that same chapter says explicitly that the one sitting on the horse is God's Word, which is what the monarchs of the earth are described as gathering against. The beast stands for the good deeds of love, profaned. The monarchs stand for the true ideas of faith, adulterated. They are called the monarchs of the earth because they are ideas in the church, and the earth is the church (§§662, 1066, 1068, 1262). A white horse stands for comprehension of truth. The one sitting on the horse stands for the Word.

The same thing is even clearer in Daniel 11, which deals with a war between a *monarch of the south* and a *monarch of the north,* symbolizing truth and falsity, which fought one another. There too the battles are depicted as an account of a war.

[10] The fact that a monarch symbolizes truth indicates what it means in an inner sense to say that the Lord is a king and also a priest. It also shows what it is in the Lord that monarchs represented and what priests represented. Monarchs represented his divine truth, and priests, his divine goodness. Every law of the plan by which the Lord as king governs the universe is an expression of truth. Every law by which he governs the universe as priest (and even governs truth itself) is an expression of goodness. Government by truth alone would damn everyone to hell, but government by goodness lifts us from hell and raises us to heaven (see §1728).

These two kinds of governance are united in the Lord, so in ancient times they were represented by a consolidation of monarchy and priesthood. Genesis 14:18 offers the example of Melchizedek, king of Salem and at the same time priest to God the Highest. Later examples among the Jewish people—who developed the outward form of a representative religion—were the judges and priests and eventually the kings. [11] The kings to come, however, would represent truth, and it was wrong for truth to take control, since it condemns people (as stated). As a result, the institution of the monarchy was so objectionable that kings were denounced in 1 Samuel 8:11–18; that passage uses the behavior of the king to portray the nature of truth when it is on its own. And earlier, in Deuteronomy 17:14–18, Moses had commanded the people to choose genuine truth (which comes of goodness) rather than counterfeit truth, and not to befoul it with rationalizations based on secular knowledge. That is what is involved in his instructions concerning a king in the passage cited. No one could possibly see this in the literal meaning, but it shines out from every detail of the inner meaning, as does the conclusion that monarchs and monarchy actually represented and symbolized truth.

2016   To return to the main point, it is an invariable truth that everything good and therefore everything true comes from the Lord. Angels are aware of this truth and even perceive that so far as a thing is from the Lord it is good and true, and so far as it is from themselves it is evil and false. They confess as much to newly arrived souls and doubtful spirits. What is more, they admit that it is the Lord who withholds them from the evil and falsity they themselves supply and maintains them in goodness and truth. His actual withholding of them and his actual inflow into them are perceptible to them. (See §1614.)

The reason we imagine we do good deeds on our own and think true thoughts on our own is appearances. We lack any perception, or any clarity about inflow, so we base our conclusions on appearances and even on illusions, from which we refuse to be delivered as long as we believe in our senses alone and use their evidence to figure out whether we have autonomy.

Yet even though this is so, we still ought to do good and think truth as if we were doing it on our own. There is no other way to reform or regenerate. The reason may be seen in §§1937, 1947.

[2] The current verse addresses the need for the Lord's human nature to become one with his divine nature. The only route by which we receive goodness and truth, then, is from his divine nature through his human nature, but this is a divine secret, which few people believe, because they do not understand it. They suppose that divine goodness can reach us even without any union between the Lord's humanity and divinity, but this is impossible, as briefly shown above (§§1676, 1990). To be specific, humankind alienated itself from the Supreme Divine by immersing itself in corrupt desires and blinding itself with false ideas. We removed ourselves to such a distance that no inflow from the Divine could ever have reached the rational level of our minds except through the humanity that the Lord made one with the divinity in himself. The Lord's humanity provided a point of contact. Through it, the Supreme Divine could come to us, as the Lord explicitly says in many places—that he is the way and that there is no access to the Father except through him. This, then, is what the current verse is saying: that everything good and everything true would come from him, that is, from his humanity united with his divinity.

Genesis 17:7. *"And I will set up my pact between me and you and your seed after you, throughout their generations, as an eternal pact, to be God to you and to your seed after you."*

I will set up my pact between me and you symbolizes oneness. *And your seed after you* symbolizes a close connection with people who believe in him. *Throughout their generations* symbolizes aspects of faith. *As an eternal pact* symbolizes a close connection with these. *To be God to you* symbolizes the divinity the Lord had within him. *And to your seed after*

2017

you symbolizes the resulting divine presence among people who believe in him.

2018   *I will set up my pact between me and you* symbolizes oneness. This is established by the symbolism of a *pact* as oneness, dealt with previously in §§665, 666, 1023, 1038. This oneness has been discussed in the current chapter and in many other places earlier, where it was shown that Jehovah, who is the speaker here, was within the Lord. He was one with the Lord from the time the Lord was first conceived and born, because the Lord was conceived by Jehovah, and as a result his inner depths *were* Jehovah, as I have illustrated by comparison with human beings (§1999). Our soul is one with our body; our inner core is one with our outer shell, even though they are distinct from one another. Sometimes the difference between them is so great that one fights the other, as commonly happens in times of trial. At those times, our inner core upbraids our outer shell and tries to get rid of the evil in our outer shell, and yet they are closely connected or form a single whole, because both soul and body belong to the same person.

Take, for instance, the times when we are thinking something else than what our face shows, our mouth says, and our body does. Under those circumstances, our inward parts disagree with our outward parts, but they still form a single whole, because our thoughts are just as much ours as the face, mouth, and deeds on the surface. Union, though, occurs when the latter—face, speech, and accomplishments—conform with what we really think. This is by way of illustration.

2019   *And your seed after you* symbolizes a close connection with people who believe in him, as can be seen from the following. A *seed* symbolizes faith (as discussed in §§1025, 1447, 1610). *After you* means the act of following someone. A familiar phrase in the Word is *following after someone,* as in Jeremiah 7:6; 8:2; Ezekiel 20:16; and Mark 8:34; Luke 9:23; 14:27. So *your seed after you* symbolizes people who believe in and follow the Lord. In an inner sense, it means people who are born from him.

2020   *Throughout their generations* symbolizes aspects of faith. This can be seen from the symbolism of *generations* as that which is generated and born from our love for others. In other words, it symbolizes every aspect of our faith. To put the same thing another way, it symbolizes everyone regenerated by the Lord and therefore everyone who has the faith that comes of love for others, which will be described later, the Lord in his divine mercy willing. This inner meaning of generations and also of births was demonstrated in the first two volumes, §§613, 1041, 1145, 1330.

As an eternal pact symbolizes a close connection with these. This can **2021**
be seen from the symbolism of a *pact* as a close connection (dealt with
previously in §§665, 666, 1023, 1038). The fact that this close connection is with the people called "seed" can be seen from the way it follows
directly after the mention of seed, and also from the repetition of *pact* in
the current verse. The first time, it refers to the oneness between Jehovah
and the Lord's human nature. The second time, it refers to his close connection with the people who are his "seed."

To give a clearer picture of the way the Lord's divine nature became
one with his human nature and of the way the Lord forms a close connection with the human race through the faith that comes of love for others, let me call the former a *oneness* and the latter a *connection* here and in
what follows. The Lord's divine nature did become one with his human
nature, and the Lord does connect with the human race by means of the
faith that comes of neighborly love. [2] This can be seen from the fact that
Jehovah (or the Lord) is life itself, and that his human nature became life
itself, as shown above [§2004]. Life unites with life. We human beings, on
the other hand, are not life but receive life, as also shown above [§§1999,
2004]. When life itself flows into a recipient of life, there is a connection,
because the former adapts to the latter, as an active force adapts to a passive one, or as something alive in itself adapts to something dead in itself,
which then comes alive. The principal cause does seem to come together
with the instrumental cause (as they are termed) as if they formed a single
whole, but despite the appearance, they are not a single whole. The principal cause is an entity to itself and the instrumental cause is too. We do
not live on our own, but the Lord in his mercy attaches us to himself and
in this way causes us to live forever. Because the Lord and a human being
are so different, their relationship is instead called connection.

To be God to you symbolizes the divinity the Lord had within him, as **2022**
can be seen from remarks above concerning the Lord's divine nature and
its presence within him.

And to your seed after you symbolizes the resulting divine presence **2023**
among people who believe in him, as can be seen from the following. A
seed symbolizes the faith that comes of charity (as discussed in §§1025,
1447, 1610). *After you* means following the Lord (as discussed just above in
§2019).

The divine presence among people who believe in the Lord is love
and charity. *Love* means love for the Lord. *Charity* means love for our
neighbor. Love for the Lord cannot possibly be separated from love for

our neighbor, because the Lord's own love goes out to the entire human race. He wants to save all of us forever and to attach us tightly to himself so that not one of us will perish. So anyone who loves the Lord has the Lord's own love and consequently cannot help loving others.

[2] People who love their neighbor do not necessarily love the Lord, however. Non-Christians who are upright may not know about the Lord, for instance, but the Lord is still present with them in the love they have for others, as shown in the second volume (§§1032, 1059). Even some within the church are in a similar situation.

Love for the Lord is a step higher. Those who love the Lord are people of heavenly character, but those who love their neighbor, or have charity, are spiritual. The earliest church, which predated the Flood and was heavenly, possessed love for the Lord. The ancient church, though, which followed the Flood and was spiritual, possessed neighborly love, or charity.

This distinction between love and charity will be observed where they are mentioned below.

2024   Genesis 17:8. *"And I will give you and your seed after you the land of your immigrant journeys—all the land of Canaan—as an eternal possession; and I will become their God."*

I will give you and your seed after you the land of your immigrant journeys means that the Lord gained everything for himself by the use of his own powers, the *land of your immigrant journeys* being everything he gained. *I will give you* is the fact that everything in the heavens and on earth is his; *and your seed after you* means that he would give it to people who believed in him. *All the land of Canaan* symbolizes the heavenly kingdom. *As an eternal possession* means forever. *And I will become their God* means that there is one God.

2025   *I will give you and your seed after you the land of your immigrant journeys* means that the Lord gained everything for himself by the use of his own powers, the *land of your immigrant journeys* being everything he gained. This can be seen from the symbolism of *being an immigrant* as being taught (discussed in §1463). We acquire a life for ourselves mostly by learning facts, doctrinal concepts, and religious knowledge, so being an immigrant symbolizes the life we acquire in this way.

As applied to the Lord, being an immigrant symbolizes the life that he acquired for himself through knowledge, inward battles, and victory in those battles. Because he acquired it by his own powers, this is symbolized by "the land of your immigrant journeys."

[2] The prophets make the following quite plain: the Lord used his own powers in gaining everything; he used his own powers to unite his human nature with his divine and his divine nature with his human; and in the process he alone became righteousness. In Isaiah, for instance:

> Who is this coming from Edom, marching in the *abundance of his strength?* The winepress I have trodden, *I alone,* and from among the peoples there was *not anyone with me.* I looked around, and *no one was helping;* and I was astounded that *no one was supporting me.* Therefore *my arm achieved salvation for me.* (Isaiah 63:1, 3, 5)

Edom stands for the Lord's human side. Strength and an arm stand for power. The passage says clearly that the power he used was his own, since no one was helping, no one was supporting him, and his arm achieved salvation for him. [3] In the same author:

> He saw *that there was not anyone* and was astounded that *no one was interceding;* and *his arm achieved salvation for him,* and his righteousness sustained him. And he *put on righteousness* like a coat of armor, and a helmet of salvation on his head. (Isaiah 59:16, 17)

This too says that the power was his own, and that in the process he became righteousness. Daniel says that the Lord became righteousness:

> Seventy weeks have been decreed, to atone for wickedness, and to *introduce everlasting righteousness,* and to seal up vision and prophet, and to anoint the Holiest Place. (Daniel 9:24)

And in Jeremiah:

> I will raise up for David a righteous offshoot, and he will reign as monarch, and he will act with understanding and exercise judgment and justice in the land. In his days Judah will be saved and Israel will live confidently. And this is his name that they will call him: *Jehovah our Righteousness.* (Jeremiah 23:5, 6; 33:15, 16)

For that reason he is also called the *dwelling place of righteousness* (Jeremiah 31:23; 50:7), and in Isaiah, *Miraculous* and *Hero* (Isaiah 9:6). [4] The reason the Lord so often attributes what is his to the Father is explained above (§§1999, 2004). Jehovah was within him, after all, and therefore within everything that was his. This can be illustrated by something similar (but not equal) in us. Our soul is within us, and since it is within us, it is within absolutely everything that is ours—in every single facet of our thoughts and deeds. Anything that does not have our soul within it is not ours. The Lord's soul was life itself, or reality itself, which is Jehovah, because he was conceived by Jehovah; so Jehovah was in absolutely everything of his. Since life itself or reality itself—which is Jehovah— was his, as our soul is ours, anything that was Jehovah's was his. That is what the Lord says: that he is in the Father's embrace (John 1:18), and that everything that the Father has is his (John 16:15; 17:10, 11). [5] Drawing on the strength of goodness, which is Jehovah's, he united his divine side with his human, and drawing on the strength of truth he united his human side with his divine. Accordingly, he accomplished the whole process entirely on his own. In fact, his human side was left to its own devices, to fight and conquer all the hells on its own. And since he had life in himself, as noted, and since it was his, it was by his own strength and power that he overcame them. The prophets clearly say as much in the passages quoted above.

The Lord, then, gained everything for himself by the use of his own powers; became righteousness; rescued the world of spirits from hellish demons and spirits; by this means delivered the human race from destruction (since the human race is governed through spirits); and so redeemed it. That is why the Old Testament Word so often calls him Deliverer and Redeemer, and also Savior, which is his name—Jesus.

2026   *I will give you* is the fact that everything in the heavens and on earth is his, as follows from the remarks just above. The literal meaning of "giving you" something would suggest that God, or Jehovah, would give it to the Lord. This is also what the Word according to the Gospels says—that his Father had given him everything in heaven and on earth. The inner meaning, though, which presents truth itself in its purity, is that the Lord acquired it for himself, because Jehovah was within him and within everything that was his, as noted. Again this can be illustrated by comparison. Our intermediate, rational self or our thoughts might say, for example, that our bodily dimension would have peace and quiet if it stopped doing this or that. Under those circumstances, the part that speaks is the same as the part spoken to, because both the rational side and the bodily side are ours. So when we say *it* would have peace, we mean *we* would.

[2] Moreover, many passages from the Word show that everything in the heavens and on earth is the Lord's. In addition to those in the Old Testament, there are these in the Gospels: Matthew 11:27; 28:18; Luke 10:22; John 3:34, 35; 17:2. Further support may be found in evidence

provided in the first two volumes, §§458, 551, 552, 1607; and since the Lord rules the whole of heaven, he also rules everything on earth. They are so tightly interconnected that whoever rules one part rules everything. On the heaven of angels depends the heaven of angelic spirits, on which depends the world of spirits, on which in turn depends the human race. Everything in the material world likewise depends on the heavens, because without inflow from the Lord, coming by way of the heavens, nothing in nature or its three kingdoms could ever emerge or survive. (See §1632.)

To your seed after you means that he would give it to people who believed in him. This can be seen from the symbolism of *seed* as faith (discussed in §§1025, 1447, 1610), specifically the faith that comes of charity (discussed in §§379, 389, 654, 724, 809, 916, 1017, 1162, 1176, 1258). People who take credit for their good deeds do not have the faith that comes of charity, so they are not the kind of seed meant here. They want to be saved by their own righteousness, not the Lord's. Their lack of charitable faith—that is, charity—can be seen from the fact that they put themselves ahead of others and therefore focus on themselves rather than others, unless those others are serving them. Any others who refuse to do so incur either their contempt or their hatred. So self-love cuts such people off from others rather than bringing them together, and destroys what is heavenly, or in other words, mutual love, which is the foundation of heaven. Heaven itself abides and consists in mutual love, as does all its good fellowship and like-mindedness. Anything in the other world that destroys unity violates the pattern of heaven itself and consequently aims at the destruction of the whole. That is what people are like when they take credit for the deeds of their life and claim righteousness as their own.

[2] The other world contains many people of this type. Sometimes their faces shine like little torches (although the light is swamp light produced by their self-justifications), but they are cold. Sometimes they are seen running around trying to prove their righteousness using literal statements from the Word, all the while nursing hatred for the truth that makes up its inner meaning (§1877). Their aura is one of self-absorption and so is destructive of any thinking that does not focus on them as something like minor deities. When a large number of them gather in one place, the atmosphere is so divisive that it consists of pure enmity and hostility. When we all have the same wish—to be served by others—we kill each other in our hearts.

[3] Some of these people are among those who claim to have labored in the Lord's vineyard. The fact of the matter is that in doing so they had

2027

always been dwelling on their own prominence, glory, high position, and even material gain, to the point of wanting to become greatest in heaven and in fact to be served by the angels. In their hearts they despise other people by comparison with themselves. As a result they are imbued not with the mutual love in which heaven consists but with self-love. This they equate with heaven because they do not realize what heaven is. For more on people like this, see §§450, 451, 452, 1594, 1679.

These people are among those who want to be first but end up last (Matthew 19:30; 20:16; Mark 10:31). They are also among those who say they had prophesied and performed many miracles in the Lord's name but are told [by the Lord], "I do not know you" (Matthew 7:22, 23).

[4] It is different with those who believed, in all simplicity of heart, that they were earning heaven, and lived lives of love for their neighbor. They regarded the earning of heaven as a promise and have no difficulty acknowledging it to be a result of the Lord's mercy. This is the natural consequence of a charitable life. Real charity loves everything that is true.

2028   *All the land of Canaan* symbolizes the heavenly kingdom. This is established by the symbolism, as discussed before in §§1413, 1437, 1607, of the *land of Canaan* as the heavenly kingdom.

2029   *As an eternal possession* means forever, as is self-evident.

The recipients are referred to as owners and heirs not on their own merits but out of mercy.

2030   *I will become their God* means that there is one God. This can be seen from the consideration that the text here is dealing with the Lord's human nature, which was to become one with his divine nature. In this way his human nature itself would also become God, so *I will become their God* on an inner level symbolizes one God.

2031   Genesis 17:9. *And God said to Abraham, "And you shall keep my pact, you and your seed after you, throughout their generations."*

God said to Abraham symbolizes a perception. *And you shall keep my pact* symbolizes even closer union. *You and your seed after you* means that he would form a bond with everyone who believes in him. *Throughout their generations* symbolizes aspects of faith.

2032   *God said to Abraham* symbolizes a perception. This is established by the symbolism of *God's saying,* when mentioned in the scriptural narrative, as perceiving (discussed before at §§1602, 1791, 1815, 1819, 1822).

2033   *You shall keep my pact* symbolizes even closer union. This is established by the symbolism of a *pact* as oneness and connection (discussed before at verses 2, 4, 7, and in §§665, 666, 1023, 1038 of volumes 1 and 2). The repetition here of the word *pact,* used so many times already, indicates an even closer union.

On the narrative level, which has to do with Abraham, there is no significance beyond the command for him to keep the pact. In the inner meaning, however, which tells about the Lord, the narrative disappears and the significance takes over, which is that of being united more closely.

The Lord's human nature did not become one with his divine nature all at once but throughout the course of his life from childhood to his last moment in the world. So he ceaselessly climbed toward glorification— that is, toward oneness—which is what he says in John:

> Jesus said, "Father, *glorify* your name." A voice went out from heaven: "I both *have glorified it* and *will glorify it* again." (John 12:28)

See the previous remarks at §§1690, 1864.

You and your seed after you means that he would form a bond with everyone who believes in him, as can be seen from the following: A *seed* symbolizes faith, as discussed several times above. *After you* means following the Lord, as discussed above in §2019.

Before this, the subject has been the uniting of the divine nature with the human and of the human with the divine. Now it becomes the Lord's connection with those who believe in him. For this reason, *you* is said twice: "*You* shall keep my pact, *you* and your seed." The repetition and the link with *seed* show that a connection—the connection with people who are "the seed"—is symbolized on an inner level. Seed symbolizes the faith that comes of charity (as demonstrated in §§1025, 1447, 1610), and this faith actually is charity (as demonstrated in §§30–38, 379, 389, 654, 724, 809, 916, 1017, 1076, 1077, 1162, 1176, 1258, 1798, 1799, 1834, 1844 of volumes 1 and 2).

[2] When the Lord talks about his uniting with the Father, he always turns next to his bond with the human race, because this was the reason for their union. An example appears in John:

> . . . that they may all be one; as you, Father, are in me, and I in you, that they too may be one in us. I have given them the glory that you have given me, so that they can be one as we are one—I in them and you in me. For I made your name known to them, and I will make it known, so that the love with which you loved me can exist in them. (John 17:21, 22, [23,] 26)

2034

This passage makes it clear that in becoming one with his Father the Lord was looking to his connection with the human race. It also shows that this connection was precious to him because it was what he loved. All bonds are formed through love, after all. Love is the essential bond. [3] Elsewhere in the same author:

> Because I live, you will also live. On that day you will know that I am in the Father and you are in me and I am in you. Whoever has my commandments and does them, that person loves me. (John 14:19, 20, 21)

This passage likewise makes it clear that in making his human nature one with his divine the Lord was looking to his connection with the human race, this connection being his goal, since it was the object of his love. He loved us so much that his inmost joy was to save the human race, which is what he sought in becoming one with his Father. The same passage also explains what unites us to him: having his commandments, doing them, and in this way loving him. [4] In the same author:

> "Father, glorify your name." So a voice went out from heaven: "I both have glorified it and will glorify it again." Jesus said, "This voice occurred not for my sake but for your sake. But I, when I have been raised up from the earth, will draw everyone toward me." (John 12:28, 30, 32)

Glorifying his name means achieving oneness, as noted above [§2033]. This passage says explicitly that in uniting with his Father he sought a close connection with the human race: "When I have been raised up, I will draw everyone toward me."

[5] The infinite divine being—the Supreme Divine—became joined to the human race by means of the Lord's humanity, once it had been made divine, and this bond was the reason the Lord came into the world; but the fact is a secret. Many people ask themselves about it inwardly, and because they do not understand it, they do not believe. Since failure to understand keeps them from believing it, the idea becomes a stumbling block for them. Much experience with people coming into the next life has taught me that this is so. There are very many of them, including most, perhaps, of those considered the world's cleverest people. When they simply think about the fact that the Lord became a human being and resembled other people in outward form, that he suffered and yet controls the universe, they immediately fill the air with objections. The reason for their negative reaction is that this idea was an impediment to them during bodily life, even though at the time they revealed nothing of their doubt and worshiped the Lord with outward piety. In the other

life, one's inner depths lie open and make themselves visible by the aura they give off, as described in the second volume, §§1048, 1053, 1316, 1504. From this aura, others can plainly tell what kind of faith these people had possessed and what they had thought about the Lord.

[6] Since this is the situation, let me explain briefly how it stands. After humankind had lost everything heavenly—that is, all love for God— so that it no longer had any will to do good, the human race was separated from the Divine. Nothing but love brings people together, and when love dies, a rift occurs; when a rift occurs, death and annihilation follow. So at that point a promise was made that the Lord would come into the world to unite his humanity with his divinity and by this means bind the human race together in himself through the faith that comes of love and charity. [7] Beginning with the first promise, recorded in Genesis 3:15, what created the bond was a faith rising out of love for the Lord who was to come. When no trace of a loving faith remained anywhere in the world, then the Lord came and united his human nature to his divine nature, so that they became completely one, as he himself clearly says. At the same time he taught the path of truth: all who believed in him would form a connection with him and be saved. That is, all who loved him and everything he stands for, who shared his love for the entire human race and so for the individual neighbor, would be saved.

[8] When humanity became divine and divinity became human in the Lord, the infinite divine being—the Supreme Divine—established an inflow into us. That inflow could never have come into existence in any other way. The same inflow drove away the dreadfully persuasive lies and equally dreadful cravings for evil that filled the world of spirits and continued to fill it as a result of new souls arriving from the world. The spirits who had devoted their lives to those lies and cravings were thrown into hell and in the process separated from the others. Had this not been done, the human race would have died out, because the Lord governs us through spirits. What is more, the lies and cravings could not have been driven off by any other means. Divinity was unable to act through our rational thoughts on our inner sense impressions, because until the Supreme Divine became one with humanity, these things lay far, far below it.

I pass by other secrets still deeper that cannot possibly be expressed in a manner intelligible to any human being. For other passages [concerning such secrets], see §§1676, 1990, 2016. The Lord appears as the sun in the heaven of heavenly angels and as the moon in the heaven of spiritual angels; the sun is the heavenly side of his love and the moon is the spiritual side (§§1053, 1521, 1529, 1530, 1531). Absolutely everything is under his gaze (§§1274 at the end, 1277 at the end).

2035   *Throughout their generations* symbolizes aspects of faith. This can be seen from the symbolism of *generations* and births as different aspects of faith (dealt with in §§613, 1145, 1255, 1330). It can also be seen from the fact that different forms of love and faith interrelate the way blood relatives and kin of different generations do (§§685, 917).

2036   Genesis 17:10. *"This is my pact that you shall keep, between me and you and your seed after you: that every male among you be circumcised."*

This is my pact that you shall keep, between me and you means a mark of the bond everyone can have with the Lord. *And your seed after you* symbolizes people who believe in him. *That every male among you be circumcised* symbolizes purity.

2037   *This is my pact that you shall keep, between me and you* means a mark of the bond everyone can have with the Lord. This is established by the symbolism of a *pact* as union, which has already been treated of [§2033]. Here it is a mark of the bond, as can be seen in the next verse, where it is called a sign of the pact, in these words: "You shall circumcise the flesh of your foreskin, and it will serve as a *sign of the pact* between me and you."

All the outward rituals of religion were signs of the compact and were to be held in reverence because they symbolized something deeper. Circumcision too—the sign referred to here—was actually a ritual with representative and symbolic meaning, as discussed below [§2039]. [2] Still, the Word is always referring to such rituals themselves as the pact, because the outward actions represented and therefore symbolized inward realities. What is inside us is part of the pact, because it unites us to the Lord, but what is on the surface does not, except through what is inside. Outward acts were merely signs of the pact, or marks of unity, which reminded people of something deeper and so united them with the Lord through those deeper values. (For more on signs of the pact, see §1038.) All the inner values of the pact (all inner values that create a bond) have to do with love and charity. They also arise out of love and charity, because on these two (loving the Lord more than ourselves and our neighbor as ourselves) depend all the Law and all the Prophets (meaning the whole of theology; Matthew 22:35–40; Mark 12:28–34).

2038   The symbolism of *and your seed after you* as people who believe in him is established by the symbolism of *seed* as the faith that comes of charity, which has already been discussed.

2039   *That every male be circumcised* symbolizes purity. This can be seen from the representation and so the symbolism of *circumcision* on an inner level. Circumcision, or cutting off the foreskin, symbolized nothing else than removing and banishing the things that block and defile heavenly love. These impediments and pollutants are the evils we crave (especially those that our love for ourselves craves) and the distortions they give rise to. The reason for this symbolism is that the genitals of both sexes represent heavenly love.

There are three categories of love that make up the heavenly aspects of the Lord's kingdom: marriage love, love for children, and fellowship (mutual love). Marriage love is the highest love of all, because it includes the most useful possible goal: propagation of the human race and so of the Lord's kingdom, for which it provides the breeding ground. Love for children is next, because it develops out of marriage love. Then comes fellowship, or mutual love. Anything that cloaks, hampers, or contaminates these three types of love is symbolized by the foreskin, and that is why its removal, or circumcision, came to have a representative meaning. The more the evils we crave are removed, along with the distortions they lead to, the more pure we grow and the more manifest heavenly love becomes in us.

Sections 760, 1307, 1308, 1321, 1594, 2045, 2057 describe and illustrate how utterly opposed to heavenly love and how unclean self-love is.

These considerations make it quite clear that circumcision on an inner level symbolizes purity.

[2] The status of circumcision as a mere sign of the pact (or of union) is clear from the fact that circumcision of the foreskin is completely worthless without circumcision of the heart. Circumcision of the heart—purification from those unclean passions—is what it symbolizes. The following passages in the Word make this very clear. In Moses:

> Jehovah God will circumcise your heart and the heart of your seed, [to cause you] to love Jehovah your God with all your heart and with all your soul, so that you will live. (Deuteronomy 30:6)

These words prove that circumcising the heart means being purified of vile passions so that we can love Jehovah God, or the Lord, with all our heart and with all our soul. [3] In Jeremiah:

> Till untilled ground for yourselves, and do not sow among thorns. *Circumcise yourselves to Jehovah* and *remove the foreskin of your heart,* man of Judah and inhabitants of Jerusalem! (Jeremiah 4:3, 4)

Again, circumcising themselves to Jehovah and removing the foreskins of their heart actually means removing the kinds of things that block heavenly love. This passage too proves that circumcising the heart is what circumcising the foreskin means inwardly. In Moses:

> You shall *circumcise the foreskin of your heart,* and your neck you shall no longer harden. [Jehovah] is passing judgment in favor of the orphan and widow and loves the immigrant, to give the immigrant bread and clothing. (Deuteronomy 10:16, 18)

Here too it is quite plain that circumcising the foreskin of the heart is being purified from the evil of unclean passions and from the false thinking they lead to. Heavenly deeds of love are depicted as acts of charity—passing judgment in favor of the orphan and widow, and loving immigrants, to give them bread and clothing. [4] In Jeremiah:

> Watch! The days are coming when I will inflict punishment on everyone *circumcised in the foreskin*—on Egypt and on Judah and on Edom and on the children of Ammon and on Moab and on all who have trimmed the corners [of their hair and beard] and live in the wilderness, because *all the nations are foreskinned,* and the whole house of Israel is *foreskinned at heart.* (Jeremiah 9:25, 26)

This passage as well makes it plain that circumcision is a symbol of purification. The people are said to have their foreskins circumcised but are still called "foreskinned nations," Judah among them, and Israel is described as being foreskinned at heart. In Moses:

> . . . or then *their foreskinned heart* will be brought low. (Leviticus 26:41)

This is similar.

[5] A foreskin and being foreskinned symbolizes something unclean, as can be seen in Isaiah:

> Wake up! Wake up! Put on your strength, Zion! Put on *your finest clothes,* Jerusalem, you holy city, because the *foreskinned* and *unclean* will not come into you any longer. (Isaiah 52:1)

Zion means a heavenly religion, and Jerusalem, a spiritual one, which the foreskinned—that is, anything unclean—will not enter.

[6] A very clear indication that circumcision is simply a *sign of the pact,* or a mark of union, is the fact that trees also had to be "circumcised" of their fruit, which had a similar representation. This is what Moses says about it:

> When you come into the land and plant any food tree, you shall *foreskin its foreskin, its fruit.* For three years it shall be *foreskinned* to you—it

shall not be eaten—and in the fourth year all its *fruit* shall be consecrated to the praises of Jehovah. (Leviticus 19:23, 24)

Fruit likewise represents and symbolizes charity, as many passages in the
Word can confirm, so its foreskin symbolizes uncleanness that hinders
and contaminates charity.

[7] Amazing to say, when angels in heaven think about purification
from earthly uncleanness, then almost immediately something like circumcision is represented in the world of spirits. Angelic thoughts, you
see, turn into representations in the world of spirits.

Some of the representative practices in the Jewish religion originated
in the world of spirits, but others did not.

There were some in the world of spirits who saw this instant representation of circumcision; they had been trying to gain admittance to heaven.
This representation occurred and then they were let in. This explains why
Joshua was commanded to circumcise the people as they were about to cross
the Jordan and enter the land of Canaan. Their entry into that land represented exactly that—the admittance of the faithful into heaven, [8] which
is why a second circumcision was commanded, as recorded in Joshua:

> Jehovah said to Joshua, "Make yourself *swords of flint; circumcise the chil-
> dren of Israel a second time.*" And Joshua made himself *swords of flint* and
> *circumcised the children of Israel at the Hill of Foreskins.* And Jehovah said
> to Joshua, "Today I have rolled the taunt of Egypt away from you." And
> he called the name of the place Gilgal [a rolling]. (Joshua 5:2, 3, 9)

Swords of flint symbolize the truth they needed to absorb in order to dis-
cipline and drive away foul passions. Without a knowledge of truth, there
can never be any purification. Stone, or flint, symbolizes truth, as shown
before (§§643, 1298). A sword relates to true ideas that punish evil, as the
Word reveals.

Genesis 17:11. *"And you shall circumcise the flesh of your foreskin, and it*   **2040**
will serve as a sign of the pact between me and you."

You shall circumcise the flesh of your foreskin symbolizes the removal of
self-love and materialism. *And it will serve as a sign of the pact between me
and you* means an act representing and symbolizing purity.

You shall circumcise the flesh of your foreskin symbolizes the removal of   **2041**
self-love and materialism, as can be seen from the following: *Circumcision*
represents and symbolizes purification from vile passions, as explained
just above in §2039. *Flesh* symbolizes human selfhood, as explained above
in §999. Human selfhood is nothing but self-love and love of the material

world, so it is every kind of greed that results from those two passions. The first two volumes showed how sordid it is, in §§141, 150, 154, 210, 215, 694, 731, 874, 875, 876, 987, 1047. Because this selfhood is what flesh symbolizes, and because it needs to be removed, the current verse refers to it as the *flesh of the foreskin.*

[2] It is these two kinds of so-called love, along with their cravings, that block the inflow of the Lord's heavenly love. When they take control of our intermediate and outer selves and overrun us, they either reject or smother the inflow of heavenly love. They also corrupt and pollute it, because they are absolutely opposed to heavenly love. (With the Lord's divine mercy, I will demonstrate the complete opposition of these two below [§2045].) The more they are set aside, on the other hand, the more the heavenly love that is flowing in from the Lord starts to grow visible and even to gleam in our intermediate self. To the same extent, we start to see that we are beset with evil and falsity, in fact that we harbor what is unclean and filthy, and finally that this is what our selfhood has been. People who are being reborn are the ones from whom these things are removed.

[3] Even the unregenerate can see this. Sometimes the urgings of these two passions quiet down in them (as can happen during religious meditation) or go to sleep (as happens during times of misfortune, illness, and disease, and especially at the point of death). In those moments, because their bodily and worldly concerns are asleep and seemingly dead, they sense something of a heavenly glow, which comforts them. With these people, however, selfish cravings have not been removed but only put to sleep. The instant such people return to their original condition, they fall back into their old compulsions.

[4] The bodily and worldly preoccupations of evil people can also be put to sleep, and then such people can be raised into a place that resembles heaven. This sometimes happens with souls in the other world, particularly those who have recently arrived. They want very badly to see the Lord's glory because they had heard so much about heaven when they were alive in the world. Their shallow concerns are put to sleep, and in this condition they are lifted up into the first heaven, where they fulfill their desire. They cannot stay long, though, because bodily and worldly preoccupations have only subsided in them, not disappeared as they have in angels. For more about these souls, see §§541, 542.

It needs to be known that heavenly love constantly flows into us from the Lord and that nothing hinders it, blocks it, or keeps it from being accepted but the obsessions of those two loves and the distortions that come from them.

And it will serve as a sign of the pact between me and you means an act representing and symbolizing purity. This is established by the remarks just above in §2039 showing that circumcision did nothing more than represent purification from unclean passions. As it was merely an outward ritual representing and symbolizing something deeper, it was not a pact but a *sign of the pact.*

2042

Genesis 17:12. *"And a son of eight days among you shall be circumcised, every male, throughout your generations: [the slave] born in the house, and anyone purchased with silver, from every foreign son who is not of your seed."*

2043

A son of eight days symbolizes the start of purification, each time it occurs. *Among you shall be circumcised* symbolizes purification. *Every male* symbolizes people who know religious truth. *Throughout your generations* symbolizes aspects of faith. *[The slave] born in the house* symbolizes heavenly people; *anyone purchased with silver* symbolizes spiritual people, who are within the church. *From every foreign son who is not of your seed* symbolizes those who are outside the church.

And a son of eight days symbolizes the start of purification, each time it occurs, as can be seen from the symbolism of *eight days.* A week, or seven days, symbolizes the entire span of any state or period, such as those of reformation, rebirth, or spiritual challenge, whether for a single individual or a whole religious movement. So any span of time is called a week, no matter whether it is a thousand, a hundred, or ten years, days, hours, or minutes, and so on, as the passages quoted in §728 of the first volume indicate. The eighth day is the first day of the next week, so in the current verse it symbolizes every new beginning.

2044

A further conclusion from this is that the timing on the eighth day represented purification, just as circumcision itself did. It was not that the circumcised would then enter a purer state, or that circumcision would purify them. Rather, since the eighth day symbolized purification just as circumcision did, it meant that they had an obligation to become purer all the time, as if they were constantly starting afresh.

Among you shall be circumcised symbolizes purification. This is established by the representation and symbolism of *circumcision* as purification from foul passions, as discussed above at §2039.

2045

People who love themselves and worldly advantages can never believe that the activities they are involved in are as foul and unclean as they really are. These things have a certain pleasure and delight that strokes, coddles, and flatters them. It makes them love this kind of life and prefer it to every other kind of life, so they imagine that there is nothing wrong with it. Whatever caters to the things we love and therefore to the way we live we believe to be good. As a result our rational mind also goes along and offers falsities to support our stance, blinding us so completely that we cannot see what heavenly love is at all. If we could see it, we would say in our hearts that it was something wretched, or a worthless trifle, or a delusion like the ones that seize our minds when we are sick.

[2] In reality a life of self-love and materialism is impure and unclean, for all its pleasures and satisfactions. Anyone can see the truth of this; you only need to be willing to use the rational ability you were born with and think about it. Self-love is the source of all the evils that destroy society. From it as from a polluted well rise all hatred, all vengefulness, all cruelty, and even all adultery. If we love ourselves, we either despise, condemn, or hate anyone who does not serve us or pay us respect or cater to us. When we hate others, all we can do is plot revenge and cruelty, and the more we love ourselves, the more we scheme. Self-love, then, is destructive of human society and humankind. To recognize the truth of this, see comments on the same subject in the first two volumes, §§693, 694, 760, 1307, 1308, 1321, 1506, 1594, 1691, 1862.

The fact that self-love is extremely disgusting in the other life, and diametrically opposed to mutual love, which makes up heaven, will come up again below, by the Lord's divine mercy [§2057]. [3] Because it breeds hatred, vengefulness, cruelty, and adultery, it breeds everything we call sin, crime, abomination, and profanation. When self-love is present in our rational mind, then, and in the compulsions and delusions of our outer self, the inflow of the Lord's heavenly love is constantly being choked off, twisted, and defiled. It is like a stinking heap of dung that dispels and even befouls any sweet fragrance. It is also like a physical object that takes the rays of light steadily streaming into it and turns them into horrible, dark colors. Again, it is like a tiger or snake that rebuffs the kindly words of its feeders and kills them by tooth or fang. Or it is like a misanthrope who takes even the best intentions of other people and their very deeds of kindness and interprets them as insults and wickedness.

This shows that the passions of self-love and materialism are what foreskins represent and symbolize and that they need to be cut away.

2046   *Every male* symbolizes people who know religious truth. This can be seen from the symbolism of a *male* as truth (discussed in §§672, 749).

The reason it says a male, meaning religious truth, is that the only people who can be purified of those filthy passions are people who know truth. Truth enables them to recognize what is pure and what is impure, what is sacred and what is profane. Until they know this, the heavenly love that is continually flowing in from the Lord has no means that it can operate into or through. Nothing but truth is capable of receiving that love. As a consequence, it is a knowledge of truth that allows us to reform and regenerate, which we do not do until we have become steeped in that knowledge. Conscience itself is formed by religious truth, because conscience is a consciousness of what is true and right that we receive as a gift when we have been reborn. For more on this, see §§977, 986 at the end, 1033, 1076, 1077. This is also the reason stone knives (or "swords of flint"), symbolizing truth, were used for circumcision. See above at the end of §2039.

Throughout your generations symbolizes aspects of faith. This is established by the symbolism of *generations* and births, both of which have to do with faith (dealt with in §§613, 1145, 1255, 2020, 2035).

2047

[The slave] born in the house symbolizes heavenly people; *anyone purchased with silver* symbolizes spiritual people; so they both symbolize people within the church. This can be seen from the meaning of *[the slave] born in the house* as those who are within the household. A *house* in the Word symbolizes heavenliness, because the heavenly level is the inmost level. As a result, the house of God in the broadest sense symbolizes the Lord's kingdom. In a less broad sense it symbolizes the church, and in a narrow sense it symbolizes an individual who has the Lord's kingdom or the Lord's church inside. When individuals are called a house, it symbolizes a heavenly kind of faith in them. When they are called a temple, it symbolizes religious truth in them. So [the slave] born in the house here symbolizes heavenly people.

2048

On the other hand, someone *purchased with silver* symbolizes spiritual people, which can be seen from the symbolism of *silver* as truth and so as a spiritual kind of faith. This is treated of in §1551 of the second volume.

[2] People who love the Lord are referred to as heavenly; and because the earliest church (the church predating the Flood) had that love, it was a heavenly church. People who love their neighbor and gain religious truth from that love are described as spiritual; this is what the ancient church (the church following the Flood) was like. The first two volumes discussed the difference between heavenly and spiritual people many times.

Anyone can see that secrets of heaven are contained in all this—in the requirement of circumcision for those born in the house, for those purchased with silver, and also for the foreign son; and in the listing of these categories, which are repeated several times, as below in verses 13,

23, 27. The secrets hidden in such details cannot be seen except from the inner meaning—from the symbolism of those born in the house and of those purchased with silver as heavenly and spiritual people, and so as people within the church; and from that of a foreign son who was not of Abraham's seed as people outside the church.

2049   *From every foreign son who is not of your seed* symbolizes those who are outside the church. This can be seen from the symbolism of a *foreign son* as people who were not born within the church and who consequently do not have the good values and true ideas taught by the faith because they do not know about them.

Foreign sons can also symbolize people whose worship is superficial, as described in §1097, but that is when the text is talking about people inside the church. Here it is talking about the Lord's church in the broadest sense, so the foreign sons are people born outside the church, that is, non-Christians.

Non-Christians, who are outside the church, can have truth, but not the truth taught by the faith. The true ideas they do have are the Ten Commandments: the need to honor one's parents; to refrain from murder, theft, adultery, and envy of other people's possessions; and to worship a divine being. The truth of the faith includes everything doctrine teaches about eternal life, the Lord's kingdom, and the Lord. Non-Christians cannot know these teachings, because they do not have the Word. [2] These are the people symbolized by the *foreign sons not of Abraham's seed* who were to be circumcised, or in other words, purified. Clearly, then, they too can be purified, just like people within the church, and this fact was represented by their circumcision. They become pure when they rid themselves of unclean passions and live together in charity. When they do, they live by true principles, since all truth has to do with charity. The principles they live by, though, are the kind just mentioned. When they live by these principles, it is easy for them to absorb the faith's truth—at least in the next life, if not during bodily life—because the faith's truth is the deep truth of charity. In the other life, non-Christians love nothing more than being introduced to the inner truth of charity. The deeper elements of charity are what compose the Lord's kingdom. For more on non-Christians, see §§932, 1032, 1059, 1327, 1328, 1366.

[3] Knowing religious concepts counts for nothing in the other world. Very evil and even hellish people can learn them, sometimes better than others. It is living by what you know that counts for something, since life is the point of all such knowledge. If we did not learn it in order to

put it into practice, it would have no use beyond that of allowing us to talk about it and in this way come across to the world as well educated, rise to high rank, earn a good reputation, and amass wealth. These considerations show that a life of religious knowledge is nothing other than a life of charity. The Law and the Prophets—the whole of theology, with everything there is to know about it—consists in love for the Lord and for our neighbor, as anyone can clearly see from the Lord's words in Matthew 22:35–40 and Mark 12:28–34.

[4] However, doctrinal concepts (or religious knowledge) are still indispensable in forming a charitable life; it cannot be formed without them. This life is what saves us after death. A life of supposed faith without charity is definitely not what saves us, because without charity there is no such thing as a life of faith. People who live a life of love and charity live the Lord's life. No one can be united to him by any other kind of life.

From this you can also see that unless religious truth is implanted in charity we cannot possibly acknowledge it as true—we cannot make the acknowledgment people talk so much about—except with our lips, for outward show. Inwardly, at heart, we deny the truth. As mentioned above, all truth has charity as its goal, and if charity is not present in us, deep down we reject the truth. When our outer shell is taken away, as it is in the other life, our inner dimensions reveal themselves in their true character, in this case as utterly opposing all religious truth.

In no way is it possible for us to accept a life of charity or to welcome mutual love in the next world if we lacked it completely during physical life. The life we led in the world awaits us after death. People devoid of charity loathe and despise mutual love. Let them merely approach a community whose members live in mutual love and they quake and shudder and feel tortured.

[5] People like this, even if they were born into the church, are called foreign sons, foreskinned at heart and foreskinned in the flesh, who are not to be admitted to the sanctuary (the Lord's kingdom). They are meant in Ezekiel:

> No foreign son, foreskinned at heart and foreskinned in the flesh, shall enter the sanctuary. (Ezekiel 44:7, 9)

And in the same author:

> Whom have you been made to resemble this way, in glory and in greatness, among the *trees of Eden?* And you were made to go down with the

trees of Eden into the underground realm. In the *midst of the foreskinned,* you will lie down with those stabbed by the sword. (Ezekiel 31:18)

This is about Pharaoh, who symbolizes knowledge in general (§§1164, 1165, 1186, 1462). The trees of Eden that they would go down with into the underground realm also symbolize knowledge, but knowledge of religious concepts.

This now clarifies what a foreskinned person is in an inner sense: someone who revels in unclean passions and in the life that goes with them.

2050   Genesis 17:13. *"Circumcision is absolutely required for [the slave] born in your house and anyone purchased with your silver; and my pact will be in your flesh as an eternal pact."*

Circumcision is absolutely required means that they positively must remove self-love and materialism from themselves. *For [the slave] born in your house and anyone purchased with your silver* symbolizes both kinds of people in the church. *And my pact will be in your flesh* symbolizes the Lord's bond with us in our impurity; it is also a symbolic act. *As an eternal pact* symbolizes that bond.

2051   *Circumcision is absolutely required* means that they positively must remove self-love and materialism from themselves. ("They" means the people in the church symbolized by one who is born in the house and one who is purchased with silver.) This can be seen from the representation of *circumcision* as purification from self-love and materialism, as discussed above at §2039. The current verse repeats that they were to be circumcised, with the words *Circumcision is absolutely required,* which express necessity. In other words, they positively had to be purified of those passions. Because it is talking about people in the church, foreign sons are not mentioned this time. Foreign sons symbolize people outside the church, as shown above in §2049.

[2] This verse repeats what the last says about those born in the house and those purchased with silver, which shows that it contains some divine secret not apparent in the literal meaning, as anyone can see. The secret is that purification from those unclean passions is utterly necessary within the church. People in the church are capable of defiling what is genuinely holy; people outside it (non-Christians) are not, so the danger that the former will damn themselves is greater. What is more, people inside the church have the opportunity to formulate and adopt false premises that directly contradict the truth of the faith. People outside the church do not, because they are ignorant of that truth. So the former are capable of

profaning sacred truth, but the latter are not. For more on this subject, see §§1059, 1327, 1328 in the second volume.

For [the slave] born in your house and anyone purchased with your sil-   **2052**
ver symbolizes both kinds of people in the church—the heavenly *([the slave] born in the house)* and the spiritual *(anyone purchased with silver)*, as shown above in §2048.

My pact will be in your flesh symbolizes the Lord's bond with us in   **2053**
our impurity, as established by the following: A *pact* symbolizes a bond, as discussed already [§2033]. *Flesh* symbolizes human selfhood, as also discussed above (§2041). The same section describes how impure our selfhood is, and the first two volumes demonstrate the same thing in §§141, 150, 154, 210, 215, 694, 731, 874, 875, 876, 987, 1047.

This is how it comes about that "my pact in your flesh" means the Lord's bond with us in our impurity: In human beings, there is no pure form of intuitive truth, or in other words, divine truth. The religious truth we have is only apparent truth. Illusions of the senses attach themselves to it, and distortions urged by our selfish and materialistic cravings attach themselves to the illusions. That is what the truth we have is like. The fact that illusions and distortions attach themselves to it shows how impure it is. [2] The Lord still binds himself to us in those impurities, however, animating and enlivening them with innocence and charity to form a conscience in us.

The truth that forms our conscience varies from person to person, depending on our religious beliefs. Because we have been steeped in that truth and have considered it holy, the Lord does not want to hurt it, as long as it does not violate the good actions taught by faith. He does not break anyone but instead bends us, as can be seen from the consideration that the gift of conscience can be found among adherents of every theological viewpoint in the church. Still, the closer we come to possessing genuine religious truth, the better our conscience is. Since religious truth of whatever type is what forms our conscience, clearly it is in our intellectual side that our conscience forms. The intellectual side is what takes in religious truth, which is why the Lord performed the miracle of separating it from our volitional side. This is a secret that has not been known till now. For more on it, see §§863, 875, 895, 927, 1023 in the first two volumes.

A *pact in your flesh* is also a symbolic act, specifically an act symbolic of purification, as can be seen from the points made in §2039 concerning circumcision.

2054   *As an eternal pact* symbolizes that bond. This can be seen from the symbolism of a *pact* as a bond, which has been discussed before [§2033].

The word *pact* is repeated here, and it is now described as an *eternal* one, because the current verse is talking about people inside the church. There are two reasons for this. One is that it is of the utmost necessity for people inside the church to be "circumcised" or purified of self-love and materialism, as shown above in §2051. The other is that the closest bond the Lord and his heaven have with people is with those who are in the church, because the good values and true ideas of the faith are what bind them. It is true that a bond also exists with people outside the church, but it is a looser one, because they do not have the good values and true ideas taught by the faith, as noted above in §2049.

The church is to the Lord's kingdom as the heart and lungs are to us. Our heart and lungs connect our insides to our outsides, keeping all the organs around them alive. It is the same with the human race; the connection of the Lord and his heaven with humankind is closest with the church. The connection is looser with people outside the church, who play the part of organs dependent on the heart and lungs for life.

Heavenly individuals resemble the heart, while spiritual ones resemble the lungs.

The need both groups have [for purification] is the reason this verse discusses people inside the church specifically and uses the word *pact* twice.

2055   Genesis 17:14. *"And the foreskinned male, who is not circumcised of the flesh of his foreskin—that soul shall be cut off from his peoples; my pact he has rendered void."*

The foreskinned male symbolizes people who lack religious truth. *Who is not circumcised of the flesh of his foreskin* symbolizes people who love themselves and worldly advantages. *That soul shall be cut off from his peoples* symbolizes eternal death. *My pact he has rendered void* means that they cannot be united.

2056   *And the foreskinned male* symbolizes people who lack religious truth. This can be seen from the symbolism of a *male* as religious truth (discussed above at §2046). A *foreskinned male* here, then, symbolizes people who lack religious truth and as a result accept falsity. Anything that blocks or pollutes is described as *foreskinned* or uncircumcised, as noted before [§2039]. When it is applied to the word *male*, it is anything that blocks or pollutes truth. When applied to something else, it likewise symbolizes the beclouding and tainting of that thing. Take the "foreskinned ear" in Jeremiah, for example:

> To whom shall I speak and testify and they will listen? Look, now, *their ear is foreskinned* and they cannot hear. Look, now, Jehovah's word has become a reproach; they do not want it. (Jeremiah 6:10)

A foreskinned ear stands for no ability to hear and for the reproach that the Word had become to them.

[2] Once again here in verse 14, the topic is people inside the church, occurring as it does after the previous verse. It is talking about those immersed not only in falsity but also in the impurity of self-love and materialism, which is why it speaks of a foreskinned male, who is not circumcised of the flesh of his foreskin. The theme, then, is falsity wedded to an impure life. The remarks of §2051 above show how great a risk of eternal damnation is incurred by people like this.

The current verse refers especially to those in the church who profane what the faith espouses as true and good, saying of them, "that soul shall be cut off from his peoples." People in the church are capable of committing profanation, but those outside it are not, as §§593, 1008, 1010, 1059 of the first two volumes show.

Who is not circumcised of the flesh of his foreskin symbolizes people who love themselves. This can be seen from discussions above about the symbolism of *circumcision* and the *foreskin* (§§2039, 2049 at the end) and that of *flesh* (§2041). The *flesh of the foreskin* here symbolizes self-love. People in the church who are immersed in falsity and at the same time in self-love profane what is holy to the greatest extent. Those with other passions of whatever kind do less to profane it. Love for ourselves is the vilest passion of all, because it destroys society and therefore the human race, as shown above in §2045. It is also diametrically opposed to mutual love, the sum and substance of heaven, so it destroys the heavenly pattern itself. This can be seen from evil spirits and demons in the other life and from the hells, where self-love is the all-in-all and reigns supreme. Since self-love reigns supreme there, all kinds of hatred, vengefulness, and cruelty do too, because these are bred by self-love.

[2] The mutual love of heaven consists in loving one's neighbor more than oneself. The whole of heaven presents the image of a single human being, since mutual love received from the Lord brings all the inhabitants together. The result is that the happiness of everyone in general

2057

is communicated to each individual in particular; and the happiness of each individual is communicated to everyone. The basic form of heaven, then, is such that everyone there is a kind of center point. Everyone is a kind of center to which all the happiness of everyone else is communicated, in accord with all the variations of that love, which are countless. People who reciprocate the love of others find their supreme happiness in the opportunity to share with others what they themselves receive, and to do so from the heart. As a consequence, the sharing goes on perpetually and eternally, so that the larger the Lord's kingdom grows, the more the happiness of the individual members grows. Because the angels are divided up into various communities and neighborhoods, they do not consciously think about the larger context, but the Lord arranges the whole and all the parts to create such a pattern. That is what the Lord's kingdom in the heavens is like.

[3] Self-love is the only force that actively tries to destroy this form and pattern. Without exception, people in the other life who love themselves are more profoundly hellish than others. Self-love shares nothing with others but snuffs out and smothers their pleasure and happiness. Whenever selfish people receive any kind of pleasure from others, they grab it, focus it on themselves, besmirch it with self-centeredness, and make sure it does not spread any further. In this way they destroy all unity and fellowship, creating division and consequently destruction. Because they each want others to serve them, worship them, and revere them, and they love none but themselves, they alienate everyone. This isolation manifests and expresses itself as horrible states of mind in which nothing gives them greater pleasure than torturing others in dreadful ways, by causing appalling hallucinations, out of sheer hatred, vengefulness, and cruelty. Any pleasure that flows into self-absorbed people comes to a halt in them, so if they come into a community of mutual love, they spontaneously plummet like foul, dead weight falling through pure, living air. Since they exude sordid thoughts of their own importance, as they fall their feeling of pleasure turns into a corpselike stench, and from it they sense the hell of self. In addition, they suffer excruciating pain.

[4] All of this shows what self-love is like. Not only does it work to destroy the human race, as shown above (§2045), it also works to destroy heaven's fundamental structure. So it contains nothing that is not impure, filthy, and profane, nothing that is not hell itself, despite the fact that self-love looks quite different to anyone afflicted with it.

Self-loving people are those who despise others by comparison with themselves and hate anyone who does not support them, serve them, and offer them some kind of worship. They take savage pleasure in revenge and in depriving others of position, reputation, wealth, and life. People under the sway of self-love are like this; and people who are like this need to realize that they are under the sway of self-love.

That soul shall be cut off from his peoples symbolizes eternal death, as can be seen from the following: A *soul* symbolizes life, as treated of in §§1000, 1040, 1742. *Peoples* symbolize truth, as treated of in §§1259, 1260; therefore they also symbolize those who live in truth—angels, in other words. To be a soul cut off from them is to be damned, that is, to die an eternal death.   **2058**

My pact he has rendered void means that they cannot be united. This can be seen from the symbolism of a *pact* as union, which has been dealt with before [§2033]. So rendering a pact void is making such a complete break that union is no longer possible.   **2059**

Genesis 17:15. *And God said to Abraham, "You shall not call Sarai your wife by her name 'Sarai,' because 'Sarah' is her name."*   **2060**

God said to Abraham symbolizes a perception. *Sarai your wife* here as before symbolizes truth united with goodness. *You shall not call her by her name "Sarai"* means that the Lord would shed his human nature. *Because "Sarah" is her name* means that he would put on a divine nature.

God said to Abraham symbolizes a perception. This is established by the symbolism of *God's saying* (on the level of the narrative) as perception (in the inner meaning), which has been discussed before, in §§1791, 1815, 1819, 1822, 1898, 1919.   **2061**

The focus now changes to the subject matter symbolized by Sarai and Sarah, by the promise of a son born of Sarah, and by Ishmael, who was to become a great nation. The text accordingly starts with a new perception by the Lord, expressed here (as in many other places) in the phrase *God said to Abraham.*

Sarai your wife symbolizes truth united with goodness. This can be seen from the symbolism of *Sarai* as intuitive truth. Since *wife* is added here, she symbolizes intuitive truth united with goodness. The fact that Sarai and Sarai as wife symbolize truth united with goodness was shown earlier, in §§1468, 1901, and many other places.   **2062**

You shall not call her by her name "Sarai," because "Sarah" is her name means that the Lord would shed his human nature and put on a divine   **2063** nature. This can be seen from remarks about Abraham above at verse 5, where these words occur: *No longer will they call you by your name "Abram," but your name will be "Abraham."* These words likewise mean that he would shed his human nature and put on a divine one, as §2009 says. The letter *h* that was added to Sarah's name was taken from Jehovah's in order for Sarah, like Abraham, to represent a divine quality of the Lord. What was represented was a divine marriage of goodness and truth in the Lord— Abraham representing divine goodness, and Sarah, divine truth—which would give birth to divine rationality, or Isaac.

[2] Divine goodness is love, and in regard to the entire human race it is mercy. This was the Lord's inner core, or in other words, Jehovah, who is goodness itself. That is what Abraham represents. The truth that was to unite with divine goodness was represented by *Sarai,* and once it has actually become divine, it is represented by *Sarah.* The Lord advanced in stages to oneness with Jehovah, as I have said in various places above. Before truth had become so completely one with goodness as to have its origin in goodness, it was not yet divine and was represented by Sarai. When it had become so completely one with goodness as to be a product of goodness, it was divine. After that, the truth actually *was* goodness, because it became an integral part of it. Truth that leads toward goodness because it seeks to unite with it is one thing; truth that has united with goodness so completely that it originates entirely in goodness is another. Truth that leads toward goodness retains a human quality, but truth that has become absolutely one with goodness has shed everything human and put on divinity.

[3] Once again, this can be illustrated by a similar process in human beings. When we are being reborn—that is, when we have yet to form a bond with the Lord—we move toward that bond by means of truth, or religious concepts that are true. No one can be reborn without learning what religion teaches, and this religious knowledge is the truth that enables us to move toward union. The Lord meets such truth along the way with goodness, that is, with neighborly love, which he inserts into our religious knowledge, or in other words, into the truth we know. All truths are vessels designed to receive what is good. The more genuine our truths are, and the more plentiful they are, the greater the capacity goodness has for taking them as vessels, organizing them, and eventually revealing itself [through them]. Ultimately, truth disappears, except as the medium that transmits the light of goodness. In this way, truth becomes both heavenly and spiritual. Only in goodness, which is strictly a matter of neighborly love, is the Lord present, so the same process unites us with the Lord, and through

goodness, or neighborly love, we receive the gift of conscience. Conscience then leads us to think truly and act rightly, though only by standards of truth and rightness that have been infused with the goodness that is charity.

Genesis 17:16. *"And I will bless her and also give you a son from her; and I will bless him, and he will become nations; monarchs over the peoples will come from her."*   **2064**

I will bless her symbolizes the multiplication of truth. *And also give you a son from her* symbolizes rationality. *And I will bless him* symbolizes the multiplication of it. *And he will become nations* means the good things that would result. *Monarchs over the peoples will come from her* symbolizes the truth produced by a uniting of true ideas and good impulses; such truths are the *monarchs over the peoples.*

I will bless her symbolizes the multiplication of truth. This can be seen from the symbolism of being *blessed* as being enriched with every kind of goodness and truth (discussed in §§981, 1096, 1420, 1422 of volume 2). Here it is Sarah who is being told that God would bless her, so the symbolism is the enrichment or multiplication of truth. Sarah, after all, represents and symbolizes the truth that comes of goodness, as shown already. The truth that comes of goodness is intuitive truth, and this truth and the multiplication of it is the subject of the current verse. For a definition of intuitive truth, see above at §1904.   **2065**

And I will also give you a son from her symbolizes rationality. This can be seen from the symbolism of a *son* as truth, which has been discussed in §§489, 491, 533, 1147. Since all rationality starts with truth, a son here symbolizes rationality.   **2066**

The Lord's earliest rational ability was represented and symbolized by Ishmael, born to Hagar the slave, as mentioned in the previous chapter, Genesis 16 [§1893]. His subsequent rational ability, which is the subject here, is represented and symbolized by Isaac, who would be born of Sarah. The former ability—the one represented by Ishmael—was one that was later driven from home. The latter ability, however, represented by Isaac, is one that remained at home, because it was divine.

By the Lord's divine mercy, however, more will be said about this rationality in the next chapter, which deals with Isaac [§§2189, 2194–2196, 2198–2200, 2203–2204, 2216].

And I will bless him symbolizes the multiplication of it—of the rationality meant by the son. This is established by the symbolism of being *blessed* as being enriched with every kind of goodness and truth, as noted just above.   **2067**

2068   *And he will become nations* means the good things that would result. This is established by the symbolism of *nations* as good qualities, which was discussed in volume 2, §§1259, 1260, 1416, 1849.

2069   *Monarchs over the peoples will come from her* symbolizes the truth produced by a uniting of true ideas and good impulses; such truths are the *monarchs over the peoples.* This can be seen from the symbolism of *monarchs* as all truth in general (discussed above in §2015) and from that of *peoples* too as truth, and as anything spiritual in general. Monarchs are described [in the Word] as ruling over peoples and not for the most part as ruling over nations, except when nations symbolize evil; this is discussed in §§1259, 1260.

The prophetic part of the Word very frequently mentions monarchs and peoples, but the meaning is never about them. God's own Word itself (which is to say, its inner meaning) contains nothing about monarchs and peoples but only about the heavenly and spiritual concerns of his kingdom. In other words, it speaks about goodness and truth. The literal meaning provides objects, in the form of words of human language, merely as an aid to understanding the meaning that emerges from them.

[2] When the current verse says that from her would come monarchs over the peoples, it is referring to Sarah, who symbolizes divine truth possessed by the Lord. This indicates that monarchs over the peoples symbolize the truths produced by a uniting of truth and goodness. All the truth known to the inner church—all deep religious truth—is this kind of truth. Because such truth comes from the Lord, the Word often refers to it as a monarch or as royal offspring, as shown above in §2015.

[3] Anyone can see that something deep and divine lies hidden in these words predicting that monarchs over the peoples would come from Sarah. After all, the verse speaks of Isaac, saying, "I will bless him, and he will become nations," but of Sarah it says, "Monarchs over the peoples will come from her." What is more, verse 6 above says almost the same thing about Abraham—that monarchs would come from him, but not, as with Sarah, that monarchs over the peoples would. The secret in this lies too deeply hidden to explain and illustrate in a few words. Abraham's representation and symbolism as divine goodness, and Sarah's representation and symbolism as divine truth, reveal a little. They show that all heavenly truth will come from the Lord's divine goodness (meant by Abraham) and that all spiritual truth will come from the Lord's divine truth (meant by Sarah). Heavenly truth is the truth that heavenly angels

have, and spiritual truth is the truth that spiritual angels have. To say the same thing another way, heavenly truth was the truth known to the people of the earliest church (the church predating the Flood), which was a heavenly church. Spiritual truth was the truth known to the people of the ancient church, which came after the Flood and was a spiritual church. Angels, like religious people in this world, are divided into heavenly ones and spiritual ones. Heavenly ones are distinguished from spiritual ones by love for the Lord; spiritual ones are distinguished from heavenly ones by love for their neighbor.

[4] Nothing more can be said about heavenly truth or spiritual truth until the reader knows what the difference is between heavenliness and spirituality, or in other words, between a heavenly religion and a spiritual one. For more on this, see the discussion in the first two volumes, §§202, 337, 1577. To learn what the earliest and ancient churches were like, see §§597, 607, 640, 765, 1114–1125, and many other places. On the fact that loving the Lord is heavenly, while loving one's neighbor is spiritual, see §2023.

[5] Now the secret becomes clear: The monarchs that would come from Abraham, mentioned in verse 6, symbolize heavenly truths that flow into us from the Lord's divine goodness. The monarchs over the peoples that would come from Sarah, mentioned in this verse, symbolize spiritual truths that flow into us from the Lord's divine truth. The Lord's divine goodness can flow only into heavenly people, because it acts on their volitional side, as it did in the earliest church. The Lord's divine truth, however, flows into spiritual people because it acts only on their intellectual side, which has been detached from their volitional side (§2053 at the end). In other words, heavenly goodness affects heavenly people; spiritual goodness affects spiritual people. This is why the Lord appears to heavenly angels as a sun, but to spiritual angels as a moon (§§1529, 1530).

Genesis 17:17. *And Abraham dropped face down on the ground and* **2070** *laughed and said in his heart, "Will a child be born to a son of a hundred years? And will Sarah, a daughter of ninety years, give birth?"*

Abraham dropped face down on the ground symbolizes reverence. *And laughed* symbolizes an emotional response to truth. *And said in his heart* means that this is what he thought. *Will a child be born to a son of a hundred years?* means that the rational capacity of the Lord's human side would now become one with his divine side. *And will Sarah, a daughter of ninety years, give birth?* means that truth united with goodness would accomplish it.

2071   *Abraham dropped face down on the ground* symbolizes reverence. This is established by the symbolism of *dropping face down on the ground* as revering, as mentioned above in §1999.

2072   *And laughed* symbolizes an emotional response to truth, as can be seen from the origin and essence of *laughter.* Laughter actually starts as either a response to truth or a response to falsity. This develops into gladness and good cheer, which reveals itself in the face as laughter. The essence of laughter, then, is obviously the same as its origin. Admittedly, laughter is something external, a reaction of the body and the face. But in the Word, external things express and symbolize inward attributes. All the deeper movements of heart and mind, for instance, are symbolized by the face; inward hearing and obedience, by the ear; inner sight, or comprehension, by the eye; power and strength, by the hand and arm; and so on. Likewise, a response to truth is symbolized by laughter.

[2] Our rational mind contains truth as its main component. It does also contain a desire for goodness, but this lies within the desire for truth, serving as its soul. The desire for goodness that we have in our rational mind does not express itself in laughter but in a kind of joy, and so in a delight and pleasure that do not laugh. (Laughter commonly contains an element that is not very good.)

The reason truth is the main ingredient of our rational mind is that rationality forms itself out of ideas whose truth we recognize. Unless a knowledge of truth forms our rationality, we cannot possibly become rational. (Anything we know about goodness is just as much a truth as knowledge of truth is.)

[3] The symbolism of laughter as an emotional response to truth can be seen here from the statement that Abraham laughed, which Sarah too is said to have done, both before and after Isaac was born. It can also be seen from the fact that Isaac was named for laughter, since that is what the name means. The current verse reveals that Abraham *laughed* when he heard about Isaac, because it says that when he heard he would have a son from Sarah he *laughed.* Sarah did the same before Isaac was born, when she heard from Jehovah that she would deliver a child. This is what is said of her:

> When she listened at the doorway of the tent, *Sarah laughed within herself,* saying, "After I have aged, will there be pleasure for me? And

my lord is old." And Jehovah said to Abraham, "Why did *Sarah laugh* at this, saying, 'Will I really, truly give birth, when I have aged?'" Sarah denied it, saying, "*I did not laugh,*" because she was afraid. And he said, "No, *but you did laugh.*" (Genesis 18:[10,] 12, 13, 15)

Then again when Isaac had been born:

Abraham called the name of his son *Isaac [laughter].* Sarah said, "*God has made laughter for me;* everyone who hears will *laugh for me.*" (Genesis 21:3, 6)

Had laughter not involved these elements—as Isaac's name also did, since it means laughter—it never would have been mentioned.

He said in his heart means that this is what he thought, as is clear without explanation. **2073**

Will a child be born to a son of a hundred years? means that the rational capacity of the Lord's human side would now become one with his divine side. This can be seen from the symbolism of a *hundred* as discussed above at §1988. **2074**

Will Sarah, a daughter of ninety years, give birth? means that truth united with goodness would accomplish it. This can be seen from the representation and symbolism of *Sarah* as truth united with goodness, or divine truth, and from the symbolism of *ninety* or, similarly, of nine. No one can help being amazed to hear that Abraham's hundred years mean that the rational powers of the Lord's human side would become one with his divine side, or that Sarah's ninety years mean that truth united with goodness would accomplish it. Since the Lord's Word contains only what is heavenly and divine, though, even the numbers there hold something heavenly and divine. The first two volumes demonstrated that every number in the Word has symbolic meaning, just as each of the names does (§§482, 487, 488, 493, 575, 647, 648, 755, 813, 893, 1988). **2075**

[2] Nine, then, symbolizes union. *Ninety,* the product of nine times ten, is an even stronger symbol of union, because ten symbolizes a remnant [of goodness and truth], and a remnant is the means to union, as is evident from earlier remarks at the end of §1988. This symbolism of ninety can also be seen from the representative and symbolic numbers in the following examples.

It was commanded that on the *tenth day of the seventh month* there was to be a day of atonement, and that this was to be an absolute Sabbath; and on the *ninth of the seventh month* in the evening, from evening to evening, they were to celebrate the Sabbath (Leviticus 23:27, 32). [3] On an inner level these things symbolize union through a remnant, *nine* symbolizing union, and *ten,* a remnant. If you look at the months and days of the year that were to be considered holy, you see plainly that a divine secret lies hidden in such numbers. Every seventh day, for instance, was to be a Sabbath; the seventh month (as mentioned here) was to contain an absolute Sabbath, as was the seventh year; and seven times seven years was when the jubilee was to start [Leviticus 23:3, 27–32; 25:4, 8–9]. It is similar with all the other numbers in the Word: three, which has almost the same symbolism as seven; twelve, which symbolizes all aspects of faith; ten, which (like tenths) symbolizes a remnant (§576); and so on. So in this passage in Leviticus if the numbers ten and nine had not held secrets inside them, the people would hardly have been ordered to hold this absolute Sabbath on the tenth of the seventh month or to celebrate it on the ninth of the month. That is what the Word of the Lord is like in its inner sense, even though nothing of the kind is apparent in the literal narrative.

[4] Something similar is meant by the tale told of the siege of Jerusalem by Nebuchadnezzar in the ninth year of Zedekiah, and of the city's breach in the eleventh year on the ninth day of the month. This is how it is told in the second book of Kings:

> It happened in the *ninth year* of Zedekiah's reign, in the *tenth month,* on the *tenth of the month,* that Nebuchadnezzar king of Babylon came against Jerusalem, and the city came into a siege lasting till the *eleventh year* of King Zedekiah. On the *ninth of the month* the famine grew strong in the city and there was no bread for the people of the land, and the city was breached. (2 Kings 25:1, [2,] 3, 4)

The ninth year in the tenth month, and the eleventh year on the ninth of the month, when there was famine in the city and no bread for the people of the land—in an inner sense these mean that no attributes of faith or charity created a bond anymore. Famine in the city and a lack of bread for the people of the land means that no faith or charity was left. Such is the inner meaning of these words, which does not show at all in the letter. Symbolism of this type is even harder to see in the narrative parts of the Word than in the prophetic parts, because the story captures the attention so completely that the reader can hardly believe any deeper import lies hidden there. The fact of the matter, though, is that everything in

Scripture is representative, and the words themselves are invariably symbolic. This is incredible but true. See §§1769–1772.

Genesis 17:18. *And Abraham said to God, "If only Ishmael could live in your sight!"* | 2076

Abraham said to God symbolizes what the Lord perceived from love. *If only Ishmael could live in your sight!* symbolizes a wish that others, whose rationality is based on truth, may not be destroyed.

Abraham said to God symbolizes what the Lord perceived from love. | 2077
This can be seen from the symbolism of *saying to God* as perceiving, which has been discussed many times before. At §1989 above, it was said that *Abraham* here symbolizes the Lord in that phase and at that stage of his life.

It is easy to see that the Lord said this with love. A sense of love radiates from the very words, when the text says, "*If only* Ishmael could live in your sight!"

The Lord's yearning or love was divine, which is to say that it extended to the entire human race. By uniting his human and divine natures, he sought to attach all of humankind wholeheartedly to himself and save us forever. (For more about this love, see §1735 in volume 2. Moved by this love, he fought the hells unceasingly: §§1690, 1789, 1812. In uniting his humanity with his divinity, his only goal was to create a bond between the Divine and the human race: §2034 above.)

[2] Love like the Lord's surpasses all human understanding. The people who find it hardest to believe in that love are those who do not know what the heavenly love of the angels is like. Heavenly angels would think nothing of dying in order to save a soul from hell. In fact, if they could, they would undergo hell themselves for that soul. As a consequence, their deepest joy is to bring anyone who is rising from the dead into heaven. They confess, however, that this love is not theirs at all, that every single bit of it comes from the Lord alone. In fact, they become angry if anyone suggests otherwise.

If only Ishmael could live in your sight! symbolizes a wish that others, | 2078
whose rationality is based on truth, may not be destroyed. This can be seen from the representation and so the symbolism of *Ishmael* as rationality, a subject discussed in the previous chapter, which dealt with Ishmael [§§1893, 1949–1951].

There are two kinds of people in the church: spiritual and heavenly. Spiritual people gain rationality from truth; heavenly people, on the other hand, gain it from goodness. For the difference between spiritual and heavenly individuals, see above at §2069 and in many places in the first two volumes.

Ishmael here means the former—spiritual people, who become rational through truth. Ishmael in a positive sense, after all, is rational truth, as shown before, in §§1893, 1949, 1950, 1951. When goodness desires and chooses rational truth, as the Lord (meant by Abraham) does here, Ishmael symbolizes spirituality and therefore a spiritual person. In other words, he symbolizes a spiritual religion. It is the salvation of spiritual people that the Lord in his divine love sought, as noted directly above in §2077 and as expressed in the words *If only Ishmael could live in your sight!*

2079   Genesis 17:19. *And God said, "Truly, Sarah your wife is bearing you a son, and you shall call his name Isaac; and I will set up my pact with him as an eternal pact, for his seed after him."*

God said symbolizes the answer that he perceived. *Truly Sarah your wife* symbolizes divine truth united to goodness. *Is bearing you a son* means that it would produce rationality. *And you shall call his name Isaac* symbolizes divine rationality. *And I will set up my pact with him* symbolizes oneness. *As an eternal pact* symbolizes eternal oneness. *For his seed after him* symbolizes those who would believe in the Lord.

2080   *God said* symbolizes the answer that he perceived. This can be seen from the symbolism of *saying* as perceiving, which was discussed just above in §2077. In the previous verse, Abraham said something, which symbolized a perception. Here, God said something, or answered, so it follows that this symbolizes a perceived response, or the answer to his perception. In all perception there is both a proposing of something and a response. The perception of both is expressed in the story here by what Abraham said to God and what God said.

For *God's saying* as perceiving, see §§1791, 1815, 1819, 1822, 1898, 1919, and several places earlier in the current chapter [§§1991, 2000, 2032, 2061].

2081   *Truly Sarah your wife* symbolizes divine truth united to goodness. This is established by the representation and so the symbolism of *Sarah* as divine truth united to goodness, as dealt with above in §2063.

2082   *Is bearing you a son* means that it would produce rationality, which can be seen from the symbolism of a *son* as truth—here, rational truth. This too was discussed above, in §2066.

2083   *And you shall call his name Isaac* symbolizes divine rationality. This can be seen from the representation of *Isaac* and from the symbolism of his name on an inner level.

As for the representation of Isaac: Abraham represents the Lord's inner self, as noted many times before. Isaac, however, represents his rational self, and Jacob, his earthly self. The Lord's inner self was Jehovah himself. His rational self was conceived as the result of an inflow from his inner self into his outer self and its desire for knowledge (§§[1895,] 1896, 1902, 1910), so it was a product of this union between his divinity and his humanity. The first rationality produced—which Ishmael represented—was human, but the Lord made it divine, and in this form it is represented by Isaac.

As for the symbolism of his name: Isaac was named for laughter, and on an inner level, laughter symbolizes an emotional response to truth. It is the rational mind that responds to truth, as shown before in §2072, so here the name Isaac symbolizes divine rationality.

[2] By his own power, the Lord made everything that was human in himself divine. So he transformed not only his rationality but also his inner and outer senses and accordingly his very body. In this way he made his humanity one with his divinity.

It has already been shown that the Lord's sensory capacity and so his whole body as well as his rationality was made divine and became Jehovah [§§1414, 1428]. Anyone can see so from the fact that he alone rose from the dead with his body and sits on the right hand of God's power with all his divinity and all his humanity. (To sit at the right hand of God's power means to have all authority in the heavens and on earth.)

And I will set up my pact with him as an eternal pact symbolizes oneness and in fact eternal oneness. This is established by the symbolism of a *pact* as a close bond and, in relation to the Lord, as the union of his divine nature with his human and of his human nature with his divine. This symbolism of a pact has been demonstrated before, in §§665, 666, 1023, 1038, 1864, and many times in the current chapter [§§1996, 2003, 2018, 2021, 2033, 2037, 2053, 2054].

2084

For his seed after him symbolizes those who would believe in the Lord. This can be seen from the symbolism of *seed* as faith, which has been dealt with before, in §§1025, 1447, 1610, 2034.

2085

Seed here symbolizes people whose faith in the Lord is born of love, or in other words, people who love the Lord. So it symbolizes heavenly people, or people in a heavenly church. The reason is that the seed is Isaac's. There are others, however, whose faith is born of charity, that is, who love their neighbor and so are spiritual, or are in a spiritual church. They are symbolized by Ishmael, whom the very next verse speaks of.

For the difference between the heavenly and the spiritual, see above at §§2069, 2078. For the difference between loving the Lord and feeling charity for one's neighbor, see §2023.

2086   Genesis 17:20. *"And as for Ishmael, I have heard you. Here now, I will bless him and make him fruitful and make him multiply [very greatly]; twelve chieftains he will father, and I will turn him into a great nation."*

As for Ishmael, I have heard you means that people whose rationality develops out of truth are to be saved. *Here now, I will bless him* means that they will be imbued and gifted. *I will make him fruitful* means with various kinds of religious goodness. *And make him multiply* means with the religious truth that comes from that goodness. *Very greatly* means beyond measure. *Twelve chieftains he will father* symbolizes the main precepts of a faith born of charity. *And I will turn him into a great nation* symbolizes the enjoyment, and increase, of what is good.

2087   *As for Ishmael, I have heard you* means that people whose rationality develops out of truth are to be saved. This can be seen from the representation of *Ishmael* here as people whose rationality develops out of truth, or spiritual people, given above at §2078. The fact that they are to be saved can be seen from the symbolism of *hearing you,* which is clear without explanation.

2088   *Here now, I will bless him, make him fruitful, and make him multiply, very greatly* means that they will be imbued and gifted with various kinds of religious goodness and the religious truth that comes from it, beyond measure. This can be seen from the symbolism of *being blessed, being fruitful,* and *multiplying. Being blessed* means receiving goodness of all kinds as a gift, as shown in the second volume, §§981, 1096, 1420, 1422. *Being fruitful* symbolizes the kinds of goodness they would receive from their faith, and *multiplying* symbolizes the truth that would come from it, as also shown in the first two volumes, §§43, 55, 913, 983.

[2] It would take too long to identify and describe heavenly people and spiritual ones here. The task has already been done, as may be seen in such places as §§81, 597, 607, 765, 2069, 2078, and many others. To speak generally, the heavenly are those who love the Lord, while the spiritual are those who feel charity for their neighbor. (For the difference between loving the Lord and having charity for your neighbor, see above at §2023.) Heavenly people are those who love goodness for its own sake, but spiritual people are those who love goodness for the sake of truth.

In the beginning, everyone had a heavenly character, because everyone loved the Lord. As a result, all of them received the power of perception, which enabled them to perceive goodness not from the standpoint of truth but from that of a desire for goodness.

[3] Later on, though, when love for the Lord ceased to be universal, spiritual people took over. They were called spiritual when they loved their neighbor, or in other words, felt charity. Love for their neighbor, or charity, however, was implanted by means of truth. Through it they received the power of conscience, which led them to act not from a desire for goodness but from a desire for truth. Charity in this kind of person looks like a desire for goodness, but it is a desire for truth. Because of the appearance, their charity is still called a form of goodness as well, but the goodness is that of their faith. These are the people the Lord meant in John:

> I am the doorway; if any come in through me, they will be saved, and go in and out, and find pasture. I am the good shepherd, and I recognize my own and am recognized by my own. *And other sheep I have that are not from this fold; those too I must bring,* and they will hear my voice, and there will come to be one flock and one shepherd. (John 10:9, 14, 16)

Twelve chieftains he will father symbolizes the main precepts of [a faith born of] charity. This can be seen from the symbolism of *twelve* as all aspects of faith, and from that of *chieftains* as main principles. **2089**

The Word refers to monarchs and *chieftains* throughout, yet in the inner sense they never mean monarchs or chieftains but whatever is the main feature of the subject they are connected with. Monarchs symbolize all truth collectively, as shown above in §2015. Chieftains symbolize main truths, which are precepts, §1482. That is why angels—even spiritual ones—are called principalities, because they possess truth. It is truth having to do with charity that is referred to as a chieftain, since, as noted above at §2088, it is through truth, or at least what seems to be true to them, that spiritual people receive their feelings of charity from the Lord; and through charity, a conscience.

[2] The symbolism of *twelve* as all aspects of faith has so far been unknown to the world, and yet every time it comes up in either the narrative or the prophetic parts of the Word, that is exactly what it symbolizes. The twelve sons of Jacob and therefore the twelve tribes named for them symbolize nothing else. Likewise the Lord's twelve disciples. Each of the former and the latter represented one of faith's main essentials. The representation of each son of Jacob and so of each tribe of Israel will be

given later, where the story of Jacob's sons in Genesis 29 and 30 comes up for discussion, the Lord in his divine mercy willing.

2090   *And I will turn him into a great nation* symbolizes the enjoyment, and increase, of what is good. This is established by the symbolism of nations as what is good (discussed in §§1159, 1258, 1259, 1260, 1416, 1849 of volume 2). So *turning someone into a great nation* means both the enjoyment of what is good and increases in goodness.

2091   Genesis 17:21. *"And my pact I will set up with Isaac, whom Sarah will bear to you at this set time in the following year."*

My pact I will set up with Isaac symbolizes oneness with divine rationality. *Whom Sarah will bear to you* symbolizes divine truth united to goodness, from which that rationality will emerge. *At this set time in the following year* means the state of oneness that will then occur.

2092   *My pact I will set up with Isaac* symbolizes oneness with divine rationality. This is established by the symbolism of a *pact* as oneness, as discussed before, and from the representation of Isaac as divine rationality, as discussed above at §2083.

2093   *Whom Sarah will bear to you* symbolizes divine truth united to divine goodness, from which that rationality will emerge. This can be seen from the representation of *Sarah* as divine truth (discussed above at §§2063, 2081) and that of Abraham as divine goodness (discussed in §2063 and many other places).

[2] The previous chapter told how the Lord's earliest rationality was conceived and born, where it spoke of Ishmael, who represented that rational ability. The current chapter and the next now tell how the Lord made that capacity divine by means of a bond resembling marriage between divine goodness and divine truth. A person's earliest rational ability can be conceived only through an inflow from the inner self into the outer self and its desire for knowledge, a desire that Sarai's slave Hagar represented, as shown in the previous chapter (§§[1895,] 1896, 1902, 1910, and other sections there). [3] The second stage of rationality, or divine rationality, however, is not conceived and born by these means but through the union of the inner self's truth with the inner self's goodness and an inflow from them both. In the Lord's case, this union was achieved by his own power, which came from divinity itself, that is, from Jehovah. As noted many times before, the Lord's inner self was Jehovah. Goodness itself, represented by Abraham, belonged to his inner self, and truth itself, represented by Sarah, also belonged to his inner self, so both were divine. From them the Lord's divine rationality was now conceived and born—specifically as the result of an inflow of goodness into truth, and

so through truth. Truth is the main component of rationality, as noted above at §2072. That is why it says here "whom Sarah will bear to you," symbolizing the divine truth united to goodness from which rationality will emerge. And above at verse 17 [§2075], it is said that "Sarah, a daughter of ninety years," means that truth united to goodness will accomplish it.

[4] Because we were all created in the likeness and image of God, something analogous (though not equal) happens in each of us. Our earliest rationality too is conceived and born as the result of an inflow from our inner self into the vital energy of our outer self and its desire for knowledge. The second stage of our rationality, on the other hand, is conceived and born as the result of an inflow of goodness and truth from the Lord through our inner self. This second rationality is something we receive from the Lord when we are being reborn, because our rational mind then senses what religious goodness and truth are.

The inner self in us lies above our rational mind and is the Lord's, as noted in §§1889, 1940.

The previous chapter, and the current one up to this point, have spoken of the conception and birth of rationality in the Lord; the way it was made divine is dealt with further below [§§2188–2196, 2551, 2557, 2625, 2636]. Some might be thinking that knowing these things does not much help us believe, as long as we know that the Lord's human nature became divine and that the Lord is God in both his humanity and his divinity. The fact of the matter is this: People who believe these things in all simplicity do indeed have no need to know how it was done, because the only reason for knowing *how* it happened is to learn to believe *that* it did.

[2] Today, though, many people believe nothing unless they can see rationally that it is so. This is obvious from the fact that few believe in the Lord, even though they pay lip service to belief in him because their theology requires them to do so. Still, they say to themselves and each other that if they could see the possibility of truth in it, they would believe. The reason they disbelieve and talk this way is that the Lord was born like other people and resembled others in outward appearance. Such people will never believe unless they first grasp in some measure how it could be so. It is for them that this explanation is provided.

People who believe the Word in simplicity have no need to know any of this, because they have already arrived at the goal that the others I mentioned can reach only through such knowledge.

[3] Besides, these are the contents of the inner meaning, and the inner meaning is the Lord's Word in the heavens; the inhabitants of the heavens perceive the Word this way. When we have access to truth, that is,

2094

to the inner meaning, we can think in unison with heaven's inhabitants, even though our thoughts are extremely vague and obscure by comparison. Heavenly angels, who have genuine faith, look at the inner content from the standpoint of goodness and think, "Yes." Spiritual angels, on the other hand, look at it from the standpoint of truth. The kinds of details contained in the inner meaning also confirm their thoughts and so perfect them, but the process requires thousands of deeply reasoned ideas that cannot enter into human thinking in any discernible way.

2095   *At this set time in the following year* means the state of oneness that will then occur. This can be seen from the remarks about Abraham's age (that he was a son of a hundred years) and Sarah's (that she was a daughter of ninety years) when Isaac was born. This symbolized the fact that the rational mind of the Lord's human side would then unite with his divine side, and that truth combined with goodness would accomplish it. These things are discussed above at §§1988, 2074, 2075. The *following year,* then, is a state of oneness.

2096   Genesis 17:22. *And he finished talking with him, and God rose up from being with Abraham.*

He finished talking with him symbolizes the end of this perception. *And God rose up from being with Abraham* symbolizes the Lord's return to his former state.

2097   *He finished talking with him* symbolizes the end of this perception. This can be seen from the symbolism of *talking* and saying on an inner level as perceiving, as mentioned several times before. So *to finish talking* is not to be in the same state of perception any longer.

2098   *And God rose up from being with Abraham* symbolizes the Lord's return to his former state. This follows from the above and so can be seen without explanation.

While the Lord was alive in the world, he experienced two states, one of being humbled and another of being glorified, as shown before in §§1603, [1999,] 2033. As there were two states, it stands to reason that he also experienced two states of perception. He was in a state of glorification—a state in which his humanity became one with his divinity—when he perceived everything contained in the inner meaning of the current chapter so far. "He finished talking with him, and God rose up from being with Abraham" expresses the idea that he was not in the same state of perception any longer.

2099   Genesis 17:23. *And Abraham took Ishmael his son, and all [the slaves] born in his house, and everyone purchased with his silver, every male among*

the men of Abraham's household, and circumcised the flesh of their foreskin, on this same day, as God had spoken with him.
    Abraham took Ishmael his son symbolizes people who are truly rational. *And all [the slaves] born in his house, and everyone purchased with his silver, and every male among the men of Abraham's household,* here as before symbolizes people in the church whose religious truth is united with goodness. *And circumcised all the flesh of their foreskin* means that the Lord purifies them and makes them righteous. *On this same day* symbolizes the very state being discussed. *As God had spoken with him* means in accord with his perception.

Abraham took Ishmael his son symbolizes people who are truly rational. This can be seen from the symbolism of *Ishmael* as people whose rationality is based on truth, or in other words, spiritual people, a symbolism discussed above at §§2078, 2087, 2088.

2100

All [the slaves] born in his house, and everyone purchased with his silver, every male among the men of Abraham's household symbolizes people in the church whose religious truth has been united with goodness, as can be seen from the following: *Those born in the house* symbolize heavenly people, *those purchased with silver* symbolize spiritual people, and both symbolize people in the church, as discussed earlier, in §§2048, 2051, 2052. A *male* symbolizes people who know religious truth, as also discussed earlier, in §2046. These remarks show that the people meant are those in the church in whom religious truth has been united with goodness.

2101

And circumcised the flesh of their foreskin means that the Lord purifies them and makes them righteous, as can be seen from the following: Being *circumcised* means being purified of self-love and materialism, as mentioned above in §2039. [Circumcision of] the *flesh of the foreskin* symbolizes the removal of those [unclean] passions, as also mentioned above at §§2041, 2053, 2057. Those passions are the only things that prevent the Lord's goodness and truth from entering us and doing their work, as the same sections also show. So they are the only things that prevent the Lord's righteousness from being bestowed on us.

2102

[2] The whole seventeenth chapter talks about the union of the Lord's divine nature with his human nature and about the Lord's bond with us through his human nature once it had become divine. It also talks about circumcision, or in other words, purification from what is unclean in us. These three form a series, and one follows from the other. The purpose in the union of the divine nature with the human nature in the Lord was to make it possible for his divinity to form a bond with humankind.

The bond cannot be formed, however, unless we are purified of those [unclean] passions. As soon as we are purified of them, the Lord's divine humanity acts on us and in this way binds us to him. This fact clearly indicates the nature of the Word: when its inner-level meaning is understood, it connects in a beautiful, elegant series.

2103   *On this same day* symbolizes the very state being discussed. This can be seen from the inner-level symbolism of a *day* as a state, which is dealt with in §§23, 487, 488, 493, 893.

2104   *As God had spoken with him* means in accord with his perception. This can be seen from the symbolism of *God's* saying and *speaking* as perceiving, a symbolism dealt with in §§1791, 1815, 1819, 1822, 1898, 1919, 2097.

2105   Genesis 17:24, 25, 26. *And Abraham was a son of ninety-nine years when he circumcised the flesh of his foreskin. And Ishmael his son was a son of thirteen years when the flesh of his foreskin was circumcised. On this same day, Abraham was circumcised and Ishmael his son.*

Abraham was a son of ninety-nine years symbolizes the state and period before the Lord's divine nature had become one with his human nature. *When he circumcised the flesh of his foreskin* means when he had completely driven away the evil in his outer self. *And Ishmael his son* symbolizes people who gain rationality as a result of religious truth from the Lord. *Was a son of thirteen years* symbolizes a holy remnant. *When the flesh of his foreskin was circumcised* again symbolizes purification. *On this same day* means then. *Abraham was circumcised and Ishmael his son* means that when the Lord had united his human nature to his divine, he also united to himself the rest of those who gain rationality from truth, and saved them.

2106   *Abraham was a son of ninety-nine years* symbolizes the state and period before the Lord's divine nature had become one with his human nature. This can be seen from the symbolism of *ninety-nine years* as the period before the Lord had fully united his inner self with his rational self (dealt with above at §1988).

As I have said several times before, the Lord's inner self was Jehovah himself, that is, divinity itself. When divinity becomes one with humanity, it becomes one with the rational mind, because humanity begins in the deepest reaches of the rational faculty and extends from there to the person's outer nature.

2107   *When he circumcised the flesh of his foreskin* means when he had completely driven away the evil in his outer self. This is established by the symbolism of being *circumcised* as being purified of self-love and materialism, or of evil, which is the same thing, since these are the source of all evil. (This symbolism was discussed above at §§2039, 2041, 2053, 2057.) The Lord drove evil out by his own might and in the process made his human nature divine, as the second volume demonstrated many times [§§1444, 1573, 1607, 1616, 1661, 1692, 1707–1708, 1737, 1752, 1787, 1793, 1813, 1820]. The same thing was shown above at §2025.

Ishmael his son symbolizes people who gain rationality from religious truth. This can be seen from the representation of *Ishmael* here as people who become rational, or in other words, spiritual, by means of truth. This too was discussed above, at §§2078, 2087, 2088.   **2108**

Was a son of thirteen years symbolizes a holy remnant. This can be seen from the symbolism of ten as a remnant (dealt with previously, at §§576, 1988) and that of three as holiness (dealt with at §§720, 901). *Thirteen*, then, symbolizes a holy remnant, since it is the sum of ten and three. (In the Word, numbers have symbolic meanings; see §§482, 487, 488, 493, 575, 647, 648, 755, 813, 893. Sections 468, 530, 561, 660, 1050, 1906 say what the remnant in a person is.)   **2109**

When the flesh of his foreskin was circumcised symbolizes purification, as established by the following: Being *circumcised* symbolizes being purified of self-love and materialism, as discussed in §2039. [Circumcision of] the *flesh of the foreskin* symbolizes the removal of those passions, as mentioned at §§2041, 2053, 2057.   **2110**

On this same day means then, which can be seen from the symbolism of a *day* as a period and state. This too has been discussed already, in §§23, 487, 488, 493, 893.   **2111**

Abraham was circumcised and Ishmael his son means that when the Lord had united his human nature to his divine, he also united to himself the rest of those who gain rationality from truth, and saved them, as can be seen from the following: In the current chapter, *Abraham* represents the Lord in that state and at that stage of his life, as noted above at §1989. *Ishmael* here represents people who gain rationality from truth, as discussed above, at §§2078, 2087, 2088. And being *circumcised* symbolizes being purified, as discussed above at §2039. In regard to the Lord, it symbolizes being glorified, or in other words, shedding his humanity and putting on divinity. (For the fact that being glorified is putting on divinity, see above at §2033.) After that the Lord also united to himself those who become rational, or in other words, spiritual, by means of truth; see above at §§2034, 2078, 2088.   **2112**

Genesis 17:27. *And all the men of his household—[the slave] born in the house, and anyone purchased with silver, from a foreign son—were circumcised with him.*   **2113**

All the men of his household—[the slave] born in the house, and anyone purchased with silver means everyone in the church. *From a foreign son* means everyone outside the church who is rational. *Were circumcised by him* means that the Lord makes them righteous.

2114   *All the men of his household—[the slave] born in the house, and anyone purchased with silver* means everyone in the church. This can be seen from the symbolism of *those born in the house* as heavenly people and that of *those purchased with silver* as spiritual people, as discussed above at §§2048, 2051, 2052. The same sections also state that these are people in the church. Everyone in the church—everyone who goes to make up the church, in other words—is either heavenly or spiritual. What the heavenly are like and what the spiritual are like may be seen above at §2088.

This final verse of the chapter summarizes everything said above, which is that when people either within or outside the church are purified of self-love and materialism, the Lord makes them righteous.

Both kinds are being called *men of the household,* because on an inner level a *household* symbolizes the Lord's kingdom (§2048).

2115   *From a foreign son* means everyone outside the church who is rational. This can be seen from the symbolism of a *foreign son* as people outside the church (discussed above in §2049) and so as non-Christians, who do not have the Word and therefore know nothing about the Lord. When they are rational—that is, when they live together in charity, or in mutual love, and have received a measure of conscience in line with their religion—they too are saved. (This was shown in §§593, 932, 1032, 1059, 1327, 1328 of the first two volumes.)

2116   *Were circumcised by him* means that the Lord makes them righteous. This can be seen from the representation and so the symbolism of *circumcision* as purification, which was dealt with above at §2039. The fact that they were circumcised *by him* (Abraham) represented something too: the fact that it was the Lord who purified them and in this way made them righteous.

As far as making people righteous is concerned, the process does not work the way popular opinion says it does. Most people think that all their evil and sin is wiped away and completely erased when they "believe," even if belief should come in the last hour before death, and even if they devoted the entire course of their life to wickedness and crime. I have been thoroughly taught that not even the slightest evil thing we have contemplated or actually committed in bodily life is wiped away or completely obliterated. Everything remains, down to its very smallest part.

[2] The truth is that people who have plotted and carried out acts of hatred, revenge, cruelty, and adultery have accordingly lived a life devoid of love for others, and the life that awaits them after death is the one they developed along the way. Every single detail of that life remains and returns to them, one after another. Such is the source of their torment in hell.

People who have lived lives of love for the Lord and charity for their neighbor also retain everything evil they have done in their lives, but it is mitigated by the good qualities they received from the Lord through living a life of charity when they were in the world. As a result, they are lifted into heaven and are withheld from the evil they have in them, so that it does not show. If any in the other world come to doubt that they still have evil in them, because it does not show, they are forced to return into it until they see that it is so. Then they are lifted back up into heaven. This, then, is to be made righteous, since under these circumstances we acknowledge not our own righteousness but the Lord's.

[3] Some say that people who have faith are saved, and this is true, but when the Word speaks of faith it actually means love for the Lord and charity for our neighbor. So it means a life based on love and charity. The doctrines and dogmas of faith are not faith itself but a part of faith. The point of each and every one of the doctrines is for us to become the kind of people they teach us to be. This is quite plain from the Lord's words that all the Law and the Prophets (the whole of theology) consists in loving God and our neighbor (Matthew 22:35–40; Mark 12:28–34).

The first two volumes show that there is no other kind of faith that is really faith, in §§30–38, 379, 389, 724, 809, 896, 904, 916, 989, 1017, 1076, 1077, 1121, 1158, 1162, 1176, 1258, 1285, 1316, 1608, 1798, 1799, 1834, 1843, 1844. They also show that heaven itself consists in love for the Lord and mutual love, in §§537, 547, 553, 1112, 2057.

The Last Judgment

FEW today know what the Last Judgment is. Most think it will come with the end of the world. As a result, they speculate that the whole wide world, along with everything visible in it, will be destroyed by fire. **2117**

The dead will then rise for the first time and be presented for judgment, they believe, and evil people will be thrown into hell, while good people will go up into heaven.

These theories come from scriptural prophecies that mention a new heaven and earth and a new Jerusalem as well. The theorizers do not realize that the meaning of scriptural prophecies in an inner sense differs radically from their evident meaning in the literal sense. They fail to see that heaven does not mean the sky, or the earth, the earth, but the Lord's church as a whole and as it exists with every individual in particular.

2118   The last judgment means the last days of the church and also the end of each individual's life.

The last days of the church. The earliest church, which predated the Flood, had its last judgment when its descendants were destroyed; their end is portrayed as a flood. The ancient church, which came after the Flood, had its last judgment when almost all in that church became idolaters and were dispersed. The representative church, which took the place of the ancient church among Jacob's descendants, had its last judgment when ten of the tribes were taken into captivity and scattered among the surrounding nations, and again after the Lord's Coming when the Jews were exiled from the land of Canaan and dispersed throughout the world. The last judgment of the current church, which is called Christian, is what the new heaven and the new earth in John's Revelation mean.

2119   *The end of each individual's life.* It does not escape some people that the end of life for each individual that dies is that person's last judgment. Still, few actually believe it. Nonetheless it is unalterably true that after death every person rises into the other life and is presented for judgment.

This is how individual judgment works: As soon as our body elements grow cold (which happens after several days), the Lord revives us by means of heavenly angels, who are the first to join us. If our nature is such that we cannot coexist with them, however, we are received by spiritual angels and then in turn by good spirits. Everyone who enters the other world, without exception, is a wanted, welcomed newcomer. Our desires come with us, though, so if we have led an evil life, we cannot stay long with angels or good spirits but gradually move away from them. The process continues until we reach spirits whose lives resemble and harmonize with the life we ourselves led in the world. Then we feel as though we are back in bodily life, and in fact [our new life] is actually an extension of our previous one. With this life, our judgment begins. If we have lived an evil life, we move down into hell over a period of time. If we have led a good life, the Lord lifts us step by step into heaven.

This is what every individual's last judgment is like, and the first two volumes offer lessons on it from my experience [§§900, 931, 1850].

In speaking of the last days, the Lord said sea and surf would then **2120** make noise, the sun would go dark, the moon would not shed its light, the stars would fall down from the sky, nation would be roused against nation, and kingdom against kingdom, and so on (Matthew 24:7, 29; Luke 21:25). Together and individually, these images symbolize what the condition of the church would be at its last judgment. What is meant by the noise of sea and surf is a comparable din of heresies and strife, in the church in general and in each individual in particular. What is meant by the sun is love for the Lord and charity for one's neighbor; by the moon, faith; and by the stars, religious knowledge. In the final days, then, these will go dark, fail to shed their light, and fall down from the sky, which is to say that they will vanish. (The Lord says something similar in Isaiah 13:10.) The one thing meant by the rousing of nation against nation and kingdom against kingdom is the rousing of evil against evil and falsity against falsity. The same with the other images.

The Lord spoke this way for many hidden reasons.

The fact that seas, sun, moon, stars, nations, and kingdoms symbolize these things is something I know for certain. What they symbolize has been demonstrated in the first two volumes.

The Last Judgment is at hand, but the fact is not as apparent on the **2121** earth and in the church as it is in the other life, where all souls arrive and converge. Today the world of spirits is full of evil demons and evil spirits, by and large from the Christian world. Unmitigated hatred, revenge, cruelty, lewdness, and treacherous plots run rampant among them.

The area in the world of spirits where souls who have just come from the world first arrive is not the only place full of these demons and spirits. So is the inner realm of that world, where spirits whose intents and purposes have been more deeply evil are found. This area too is now packed full, so full that I have wondered how such large numbers of them could possibly exist.

No one is thrown into the hells immediately. The laws of order require that all such spirits return to the life they lived in their body and be let down from there into hell step by step. [2] The Lord sends no one to hell; everyone sends himself or herself there. Both realms of the world of spirits are therefore extremely crowded, because a great many evil people are arriving and staying there for the time being. Souls coming from the world are viciously harassed by them, as are the spirits who keep people on earth company. (The Lord governs each of us by means of spirits and angels.) More than ever those demons and spirits are driven to hurt us. In fact, the angels present with us can hardly fend them off and so are forced to exert a less direct influence on us.

As a result, it is obvious in the other world that the final days are at hand.

2122   To say more about souls newly come from the world: Those that arrive from the Christian world think about hardly anything else and work at hardly anything else than rising to the top and amassing all the possessions they can. In other words, they have all been ensnared by self-love and materialism, which are totally opposed to the pattern of heaven (§2057). Furthermore, the thoughts of very many of them are monopolized by things that are filthy, obscene, and profane, which is all they talk to each other about, too. They completely discount anything that has to do with charity or faith and feel utter contempt for it. The Lord himself they fail to acknowledge. In fact, they hate anyone who claims to believe in him, since in the other life minds and hearts speak. In addition, the wicked lives of parents are lending greater and greater malevolence to the evil the next generation inherits. Like a fire hidden deep within and constantly stoked, it urges humankind to worse and worse blasphemies than ever against all that is upright and godly. At the present day, such people are arriving in droves in the other world and filling up both the outer and the inner realms of the world of spirits, as noted.

When evil starts to dominate in this way and the balance starts to tilt in its direction, anyone can plainly tell that the last days are close at hand and that balance can be restored only by casting out Christians and replacing them with non-Christians.

2123   There is another sign in the next world that the last days are imminent. Everything good that is coming into the world of spirits from the Lord by way of heaven is instantly being turned into something evil, obscene, and profane there. Everything true is instantly being turned into something false. So mutual love is converted to hatred, honesty to deceit, and so on, with the result that the spirits there are no longer capable of perceiving anything good or true.

Similar effects result for people on earth, who are governed by spirits in contact with those who are there [in the inner realm].

This phenomenon has become well known to me through abundant experience, which would fill many pages if I were to report on all of it. Very frequent opportunities were given to me to perceive and hear how the goodness and truth coming from heaven were turned into evil and falsity, and to sense the amount and type of evil and falsity as well.

I have been told that the people of the earliest church had a spontaneous kind of goodness that died out among those who lived just before the Flood. A more intellectual kind of goodness among people in the Christian church today is starting to disappear, I have also learned, to the point where little of it is left. It is disappearing because people believe nothing they cannot grasp with their senses. Moreover they currently reason about divine secrets not only on the basis of sensory evidence but also in terms of a philosophy unknown to the ancients. These things form a cloud that blots out all light in the intellect, the cloud by its very nature being almost impossible to disperse.

2124

The character of people in the Christian church today was displayed for me to see by means of representations.

2125

I saw spirits so dark they scared me, surrounded by a black cloud. Afterward I saw others less horrifying. To me this meant that I was about to have a vision.

The first thing I saw then was some adolescents whose hair was being combed by their mothers so viciously that blood flowed, which represented the way children are raised these days.

Next I saw a tree that seemed to me to be the tree of knowledge. Crawling up into it was a large viper so ghastly that it terrified me. It appeared to lie lengthwise along the trunk.

Tree and viper vanished, and a dog appeared. Then a door opened into a room lit with the yellowish glimmer of a coal fire, where there were two women. I could tell it was a kitchen but am not allowed to mention what I saw there.

I was told that the tree the viper climbed into represented the condition of people in the church and their character nowadays. In place of love and charity they harbor a murderous hatred, although it is completely cloaked behind honorable appearances and other forms of deceit. They also entertain unspeakable thoughts about religious matters. What I saw in the kitchen represented further characteristics of that hatred and those thoughts.

A further representation showed how people in the church today oppose innocence itself.

2126

A beautiful, innocent baby appeared, and when it did, the outward restraints keeping evil demons and spirits from committing their crimes were relaxed slightly. Then they started to abuse the child horribly, stomping on it and trying to kill it, one by this method and another by that. (In the other life, babies represent innocence.)

I said that this is not the kind of behavior people like them display during their bodily life, but was told that this *is* what they are like inside. If they were not prevented by law and by other superficial restraints as well (fear of losing wealth, status, and reputation, and fear for their life), they would attack any innocent being with the same kind of frenzy.

When the culprits themselves heard this response, they ridiculed it.

This account, then, reveals the nature of people today and also the fact that the final days are at hand.

2127   In the other life, it sometimes seems as though a kind of Last Judgment is taking place. For the evil it seems that way when groups of them are breaking up; for the good, when they are being let into heaven. Let me report on my experience of both.

2128   The picture of the Last Judgment presented to the evil, which I have seen two or three times, was as follows:

Some spirits around me banded together in fiendish groups in order to make themselves invincible. They refused to be controlled by the preordained law of balance, but arrogantly harassed other communities instead and used their power advantage to begin damaging them. Then a fairly large troop of spirits appeared out in front, above, and slightly off to the right. As it approached, it created an uproar, loud and pulsating, and when the spirits heard it, dismay and terror arose among them, producing mass confusion. Those who had banded together now scattered, one this way and one that, running from each other, and companions lost track of each other. While it lasted, it looked to the spirits exactly like the Last Judgment with its universal destruction. Some wept; some in their fright lost heart. In short, fear of some final peril gripped the minds of all. [2] The noise of the advancing company struck different listeners' ears differently. Some heard it as armed cavalry, others heard it another way, depending on their fears and imaginings. To me it sounded like a constant whispering carried on by many voices simultaneously, with a throb that came and went.

I learned from the spirits near me that troops like this one come from the same quarter whenever spirits gang up for evil as described. These troops know how to break up such gangs, sever the individuals from one another, and strike such terror into them that the only thing they can think of is running away. Through this fragmentation and dispersion the

Lord eventually reduces them all to order. That is what the east wind symbolizes in the Word.

There are other kinds of commotion or rather of conflict that also present an image of the Last Judgment. These too dissolve the evil bonds that inwardly hold such gangs together. Let me say the following things about them:

2129

Such spirits find themselves forced into a state of mind that prevents them from thinking as a group, as part of the whole, the way they usually do. Instead they each have to think for themselves. The resulting variance in their thoughts and discrepancy in their mumblings produces a kind of roar, like that of water in great quantities crashing onto itself. The conflict cannot be described, but it rises out of a confusion of opinions concerning certain axioms that are topics of current thought and conversation. The confusion is such that it can be called spiritual chaos.

[2] The sound made by their confused and clashing mutterings was threefold. One strain swirled around my head, and I was told that this was the sound of their thoughts. A second streamed toward my left temple, and I was told that this was the clash of their rationalizations concerning certain axioms that they did not want to believe in. The third flowed down from above toward the right. It was grating but less confused. The grating sound turned back and forth, and I was told that this was because they were resisting those axioms, turning them back and forth as they debated them.

Despite these conflicts, and for as long as they lasted, I had spirits talking to me, explaining what the different aspects symbolized. Their words cut through the noise quite easily.

[3] These were the main subjects they were arguing over: Should we take literally the statement that the twelve apostles will sit on twelve thrones and judge the twelve tribes of Israel? And will any others be allowed into heaven than those who have suffered persecution and misery?

The participants each argued according to the misconceptions they had acquired during bodily life. Some of them, however, were later taught that the statement regarding the apostles should be taken in a completely different way. These were the ones who had been restored to their group and brought back into order, and this is what they were taught: The apostles do not mean apostles, the thrones do not mean thrones, and the tribes do not mean tribes; not even twelve means itself. Instead, all of these—the apostles, thrones, tribes, and even the number twelve—symbolize the main precepts of faith (§2089). The judgment is carried out on everyone on the basis of those precepts and in accord with them. Moreover, as they were shown, the apostles cannot judge a single, solitary person; all judgment is the Lord's alone.

[4] As for the second biblical statement, neither should it be taken to mean that only those who have suffered persecution and misery will enter heaven. The rich are welcomed there just as much as the poor, the high-ranking just as much as the lowly. The Lord shows mercy to everyone, especially those who have been through spiritual miseries and trials, which is what persecution by evil people means. So he takes special pity on those who acknowledge that left to themselves they are wretched and who attribute their salvation to his mercy alone.

2130   To turn to an explanation of the other picture of the Last Judgment, the one good spirits face when they are being let into heaven, let me report the following:

The Word says that a door was closed so that people could not be let in any longer [Matthew 25:1–13]. It says that their oil ran out, that they came too late, and that for this reason they would not be admitted. These images too symbolize conditions at the Last Judgment. The implications and the way to understand it all were shown to me.

[2] I heard whole societies of spirits, one after another, saying in a clear voice that the wolf had wanted to carry them off but the Lord had rescued them, so that they were restored to him, for which they rejoiced from the bottom of their hearts. They had been in despair and consequently in fear, thinking that the door would shut, that they had come too late to be allowed in. Spirits referred to as wolves had instilled this thought into them, but it evaporated when they did get in, or in other words, when they were accepted by angelic communities. That is all that entry into heaven is.

I seemed to see societies being let in, one after another, until there were twelve. The twelfth had a harder time getting in, or being accepted, than the first eleven. Afterward, what appeared to be eight more societies were also admitted, and I was informed that they were made up of women.

After watching, I was told that this is what the process of entry (acceptance into heavenly communities) looks like. I learned that it goes on constantly, as newcomers go in order from one location to the next. Heaven will never, ever fill up completely, nor will the door be closed. The more numerous the arrivals, the more of a blessing and a joy it is to the inhabitants of heaven, since it strengthens their unity.

[3] After these spirits had entered, it did seem as though heaven closed, because there were others who then wanted to be allowed in too, or accepted, but were told they could not enter now. That is what is symbolized by their late arrival, the shutting of the door, their knocking on it, and the lack of oil in their lamps. The reason they were not let in was that they were not yet ready to participate in angelic communities, where love is shared with all. As noted above at the end of §2119, the Lord *gradually* raises people into heaven if their life in the world was one of charity for their neighbor.

[4] There was yet another group of spirits, who had no idea what heaven was or that it consisted in shared love and who also wanted to be let into heaven immediately. Their thought was that it is just a matter of getting in. The answer they received, however, was that it was not the right time for them yet, that they would be allowed in another time, when they were ready.

The reason I saw twelve societies was that twelve symbolizes all aspects of faith, as noted above near the end of §2129.

People who enter heaven are accepted by angelic communities with the deepest affection and an accompanying joy. Unstinting love and friendship is shown to them. If they do not freely choose to remain in the communities they first visit, they are welcomed by others, one after another, until they finally reach the community they harmonize with best. The way they have shared love with others in their lives is what determines how well they harmonize with the community. There they stay until they reach an even higher level of development, at which point they are lifted and raised to greater happiness. It is the Lord's mercy that raises them, and it is the love and charity they incorporated into their life in the world that determines how high they go. **2131**

When spirits leave one community for another, it is never because the community they are staying with rejects them. Rather it is due to a voluntary impulse instilled in them by the Lord that matches their own desires, and since it matches their desires, they feel a freedom throughout the entire process.

The Word says that there was also one who came in not wearing wedding clothes and was thrown out (Matthew 22:11, 12, 13). I was shown what the case is with this too. **2132**

There are people who adopted the trick during their bodily life of imitating angels of light. When they enter the same hypocritical frame of mind in the other life, they are able to steal their way into the communities that are nearest heaven. They do not stay there long, though, because as soon as they sense the atmosphere of mutual love there, fear and horror take hold of them and they race away. In the world of spirits it looks as if they have been *thrown* out—some toward a pool, some toward Gehenna, some into some other hell.

2133 Two or three times, by the Lord's divine mercy, heaven has opened so wide to me that I have heard the whole of it praising the Lord's glory. The process involves many communities praising him all together, with one heart, while at the same time each individual community participates by itself, with its own distinctive feelings and so its own thoughts. A heavenly sound could be heard far and wide, a sound so vast that my ears failed to reach its outer bounds, as the eye does when it observes the universe. The experience brought the deepest possible joy and happiness.

At times I also perceived heaven's praise of the Lord's glory as resembling a ray of light streaming down and touching the inner reaches of the mind.

Angels praise the Lord this way when they feel calm and peaceful, because then their praise flows from their very deepest joys and true happiness.

2134 The state of children in the other world will be the subject at the end of the next chapter, the Lord in his divine mercy willing [§§2289–2309].

A Disclosure of

SECRETS OF HEAVEN

Contained in

SACRED SCRIPTURE

or

THE WORD OF THE LORD

Those in

Genesis

Chapter 18

Together with Amazing Things Seen and Heard
in the World of Spirits & in the Heaven of Angels

At the End of the Current Chapter, Those Having to Do with
The State of Children in the Other World

First seek God's kingdom and its justice
and you will gain all.
—Matthew 6:33

Preface

THE end of the previous chapter discussed the Last Judgment and showed what it means: not the end of the world but the final days of the church. The Lord says that when this time is imminent he will "come in the clouds of the heavens with strength and glory" (Matthew 24:30; Mark 13:26; Luke 21:27). No one so far has realized what the clouds of the heavens mean, but it has been made clear to me that they actually mean the literal sense of the Word. I have also been shown that the strength and glory mean the Word's inner sense. The Word's inner meaning is where its glory lies, because everything in it speaks of the Lord and his kingdom. (See §§1769–1772 in the second volume.)

[2] The cloud that surrounded Peter, James, and John when the Lord appeared to them in his glory means the same thing. Luke says this of it:

> A voice came from the cloud saying, "This is my beloved Son; listen to him!" But when the voice had finished, Jesus was found alone. (Luke 9:35, 36)

In that scene, Moses and Elijah, who were talking with the Lord, represented the Old Testament Word, which is even *called* "Moses and the Prophets." Moses represented the books of Moses and the narrative books in general; the prophet Elijah represented all the books of the prophets. Peter, James, and John represented faith, charity, and the good actions that charity inspires, as they do everywhere else they are mentioned in the Gospels. The fact that they were the only witnesses meant that people who are devoted to faith, the charity that comes of faith, and the good actions that come from charity are the only ones who can see the glory of the Lord in his Word. It is true that others could see it, but in fact they do not see it, because they do not believe. This is the inner meaning in regard to [the clouds and glory]. Throughout the Prophets as well, a cloud symbolizes the Word in its letter, while glory symbolizes the Word as a living thing.

I have defined and described the Word's inner meaning in many places and illustrated it in the explanations of the individual words.

The people of the Lord's day least likely to believe that anything written in the Word had to do with him were the experts in [divine] law. Their counterparts today do know that the Word speaks of him, but they will perhaps be the last to believe that it contains any other glory than the kind that appears in the letter. Yet the letter is merely the cloud in which the glory lies.

Genesis 18

THE current chapter makes it especially clear what the Word's inner meaning is like and what angels perceive in it when people on earth read it.

This is all that can be gleaned from the literal meaning of the narrative: Jehovah appeared to Abraham in the form of three men, and Sarah, Abraham, and his houseboy prepared food for them—cakes of flour-meal, the young of an ox, and butter and milk.

Although such details are historically true—this really did happen—that is not what angels perceive in it. They see what the details represent and symbolize (as outlined in the summary below) in complete isolation from the literal meaning. The images presented as part of the story there are replaced by the state of perception the Lord's human side had achieved and the way it communicated with his divine side at that time. (This was before his divine nature had become completely one with his human nature, or his human nature with his divine.) That is the same state the Lord refers to in these words:

> God has never been seen by anyone; his only Son, who is in the Father's embrace, is the one who has revealed him. (John 1:18)

[2] What the foods mentioned in the current chapter mean to the angels are heavenly and spiritual kinds of goodness, as discussed in the explanation [§§2177, 2180, 2184].

To go further, they take what is said about the child Sarah would bear at the set time the next year to be purely and simply about the fact that the Lord's human rationality would become divine.

Finally, Abraham's conversation with Jehovah about the overthrow of Sodom and Gomorrah suggests nothing to them but the Lord's intervention on behalf of the human race. The numbers fifty, forty-five, forty, thirty, twenty, and ten there suggest his intervention on behalf of people in whom truth was attached to goodness and who acquired goodness as a result of trials and struggles or other conditions.

It is the same with all other images in the Word. This can be seen more clearly from the explanations of individual words, in which those words are shown to involve similar meanings in both the narrative and the prophetic parts of the Word.

[3] The inner meaning speaks exclusively of the Lord, of his kingdom in the heavens, of his church on earth and in each individual person there, and so of the good that love inspires and the truth that leads to faith. By looking at the Gospels' quotations from the Old Testament, anyone can see that this kind of meaning exists throughout the Word. In Matthew, for instance:

> The Lord said to my Lord, "Sit on my right till I make your enemies your footstool." (Matthew 22:44; Psalms 110:1)

The literal meaning of the cited verse from Psalms likewise does not make it at all clear that the subject is the Lord, but the verse does refer to him and him alone, as he himself teaches here in Matthew. [4] In the same author:

> You, Bethlehem, land of Judah, are by no means the least among the rulers of Judah, since from you will emerge a ruler who will shepherd my people Israel. (Matthew 2:6; Micah 5:2)

Even people who stick to the literal meaning, such as Jews, see from this that the Lord was to be born in that place. However, they are waiting for a ruler and monarch who will take them back to the land of Canaan, so they interpret the words according to their literal meaning. They equate the land of Judah with the land of Canaan, and Israel with Israel, even though they do not know where the Israelites are; and they still assume the ruler will be their Messiah. Nonetheless Judah and Israel mean something else; specifically, Judah means heavenly people and Israel means spiritual ones, in heaven and on earth. The ruler means the Lord. [5] In the same author:

A voice was heard in Ramah—mourning, crying, and much wailing, Rachel weeping for her children; and she refused to be comforted, because they are no more. (Matthew 2:18; Jeremiah 31:15)

People who stay in the literal meaning never grasp the meaning that lies within those words, but it is there, as the Gospel makes clear. In the same author:

Out of Egypt I called my child. (Matthew 2:15; Hosea 11:1)

The original statement in Hosea reads as follows:

When Israel was a boy, I loved him, and out of Egypt I called my child. They called them, so they went from their presence. And I made Ephraim go. (Hosea 11:1, [2, 3])

People who do not realize there is an inner meaning cannot see that this passage is not talking about Jacob's move to Egypt or his descendants' departure or that Ephraim does not mean the tribe of Ephraim. They assume the subjects are the same as in the Word's narrative books, and yet the Gospel scripture above makes it clear that such things symbolize the Lord. No one would be able to see what each of them symbolizes, though, unless it were revealed through the inner meaning.

Genesis 18

1. And Jehovah appeared to [Abraham] in the oak groves of Mamre, and he was sitting at the door of the tent as the day grew hot.

2. And he raised his eyes and looked, and here, now, three men standing near him; and he saw and ran from the door of the tent to meet them and bowed down toward the earth.

3. And he said, "My lord, please, if I have found favor in your eyes, please do not pass by your servant.

4. Please let a little water be taken, and wash your feet, and recline under the tree.

5. And let me take a morsel of bread, and you, sustain your heart. Afterward you may pass on, since this is the reason you have passed over to your servant." And they said, "You should do as you have spoken."

6. And Abraham hurried toward the tent, to Sarah, and said, "Bring three pecks of flour-meal in a hurry, knead it, and make cakes."

7. And Abraham ran to the herd and took the young of an ox, tender and good, and gave it to the houseboy, and he hurried to prepare the animal.

8. And [Abraham] took butter and milk and the young of an ox that he had prepared and placed it before them (and he was standing before them under the tree), and they ate.

9. And they said to him, "Where is Sarah, your wife?" and he said, "Look—she is in the tent."

10. And [the man] said, "I will definitely return to you about this time of life, and look: a son for Sarah your wife!" And Sarah was listening at the door of the tent, and it was behind him.

11. And Abraham and Sarah were old, advancing in days; the way it is with women had ceased to be with Sarah.

12. And Sarah laughed within herself, saying, "After I have aged, will there be pleasure for me? And my lord is old."

13. And Jehovah said to Abraham, "Why did Sarah laugh at this, saying, 'Will I really, truly give birth, when I have aged?'

14. Will anything be [too] amazing for Jehovah? At the set time I will come back to you, about this time of life; and to Sarah, a son."

15. And Sarah denied it, saying, "I did not laugh," because she was afraid. And he said, "No, because you did laugh."

16. And the men rose up from there and looked out toward the face of Sodom. And Abraham was going with them, to send them off.

17. And Jehovah said, "Shall I be hiding from Abraham what I am doing?

18. And Abraham will unquestionably become a large and numerous nation, and all the nations of the earth will be blessed in him.

19. For I know him, because he will command his sons and his household after him, and they will keep the way of Jehovah, to perform justice and judgment, in order for Jehovah to bring on Abraham that which he spoke concerning him."

20. And Jehovah said that the outcry of Sodom and Gomorrah had become great and that their sin had become very heavy.

21. "Let me go down, please, and I will see whether they have made an end of it according to its outcry, which has come to me. And if not, I will know it."

22. And the men looked out from there and went toward Sodom. And Abraham was still standing before Jehovah.

23. And Abraham came near and said, "Will you also destroy the just with the ungodly?

24. Perhaps there are fifty just people in the middle of the city. Will you still destroy it and not spare the place for the sake of the fifty just people who are in the middle of it?

25. Far be it from you to do according to this thing—to put the just to death with the ungodly and that it should be the same for the just as for the ungodly. Far be it from you; won't the judge of the whole earth perform judgment?"

26. And Jehovah said, "If I find in Sodom fifty just people in the middle of the city, I will spare the whole place for their sake."

27. And Abraham answered and said, "Here, I beg you, I have undertaken to speak to my lord, and I am dust and ash.

28. Maybe the fifty just people will lack five; will you ruin the whole city over five?" And he said, "I will not ruin it if I find forty-five there."

29. And [Abraham] went on to speak to him further and said, "Maybe forty will be found there." And he said, "For the sake of forty, I will not do it."

30. And he said, "Please let anger not blaze in my lord and let me speak; maybe thirty will be found there." And he said, "I will not do it if I find thirty there."

31. And he said, "Here, I beg you, I have undertaken to speak to my lord; perhaps twenty will be found there." And he said, "For the sake of twenty, I will not ruin it."

32. And he said, "Please let anger not blaze in my lord and let me speak just this once; maybe ten will be found there." And he said, "For the sake of ten, I will not ruin it."

33. And Jehovah went, when he had finished speaking to Abraham. And Abraham returned to his place.

Summary

THE first topic here is the state of perception the Lord's human side **2136** had achieved and the way it communicated with his divine side at that time, before his human nature had become completely one with his divine nature. That is the same state the Lord refers to in these words:

> God has never been seen by anyone; the only-born Son, who is in the Father's embrace, is the one who has revealed him. (John 1:18)

2137   The oak groves of Mamre symbolize the state of perception the Lord's human side would achieve at that time (verse 1). In that state the Lord would sense his divinity, which would reveal itself to his human side (verse 2). This would bring him joy (verse 3), and he would ask his divine side to come closer to his human side and take on a physical dimension (verse 4). He would also want his human side to move closer to his divine side and take on a heavenly dimension (verse 5). The three pecks of flour-meal made into cakes symbolize the heavenly quality he took on and the spiritual quality that rose out of it (verse 6). The young of an ox symbolizes the earthly aspect he would take on to match it (verse 7). As a result, his divinity would achieve harmony and communication with his humanity, and his humanity with his divinity (verse 8).

2138   The second topic is the perception the Lord had during that state that his rational mind would shed its human quality and become divine.

2139   The child that Sarah was to bear symbolizes the divine transformation of his rationality (verse 10). Sarah's laughter at the door of the tent, which was behind the man, means that the rational truth (of a human kind) in him would not perceive this and so would not believe it (verses 10, 11, 12, 13, 15). He had confirmation that he would also lay aside this human truth and put divine truth on in its place (verse 14).

2140   The third topic is the Lord's grief and distress over the human race because it would be so deeply immersed in self-love and consequently in an appetite for dominating other people, at the urging of evil and falsity. In that state he intervened on behalf of humankind and obtained a promise that people possessing goodness and truth would be saved. The identities of these people are listed in order.

2141   The Lord perceived that the human race had fallen prey to evil and falsity; Sodom is self-love and a resulting desire for control, inspired by evil, while Gomorrah is the same inspired by falsity (verses 16, 20). The perception could not be hidden from the Lord in that phase, because all salvation comes through him and from him (verses 17, 18, 19). What could not be hidden was the fact that punishment would be inflicted when human wickedness had reached its zenith (verses 20, 21). While the awareness of this was upon him (verse 22), he intervened on behalf of humankind. First he intervened for people who knew truth and whose truth was full of goodness, symbolized by the number fifty (verses 23, 24, 25, 26). Next he intervened for people who had less goodness, although the goodness was still united with truth, symbolized by the number forty-five (verses 27, 28). Then he did so for people who were suffering times of trial, symbolized by forty (verse 29), and for those who struggled against evil to some extent, symbolized by thirty (verse 30). Then for those who responded to goodness for some other reason, symbolized by twenty (verse 31), and finally for those who could respond to truth, symbolized by ten (verse 32). In all cases he was told that they would be saved (verses 26, 28, 29, 30, 31, 32). These negotiations complete, the Lord went back to his original state of perception (verse 33). These secrets reside in the inner meaning of the chapter without being visible in the letter.

Inner Meaning

G ENESIS 18:1. *And Jehovah appeared to [Abraham] in the oak groves of Mamre, and he was sitting at the door of the tent as the day grew hot.* **2142**

Jehovah appeared to him symbolizes the Lord's perception. *In the oak groves of Mamre* symbolizes the nature of the perception. *He was sitting at the door of the tent* symbolizes the type of holiness he had then. *As the day grew hot* means that love imparted it.

Jehovah appeared to him symbolizes the Lord's perception, as can be **2143** seen from the fact that scriptural narratives are entirely representative, and the words of which they are composed symbolize the subject matter of the inner meaning. The inner meaning here has to do with the Lord and his perception, represented by Jehovah's appearing to Abraham. Any time someone appears or speaks or acts in scriptural stories, it represents something, but just what it represents is not obvious. The only way to see the representation is to regard the historical details precisely like visual objects that provide us the opportunity or ability to think about higher things. When we look at a garden, for example, we can think about fruit and the purposes it serves, or about the pleasure it gives us in our lives, or—still more sublimely—about the happiness of paradise (heaven). When we concentrate on these subjects, we do still see the individual objects in the garden but in such a passing way that we hardly notice them.

It is the same with scriptural narratives: When we think about the heavenly and spiritual matters contained in their inner meaning, this is exactly how we look on the historical details and the words themselves.

2144   *In the oak groves of Mamre* symbolizes the nature of the perception, as can be seen from the representation and symbolism of *oak groves* and from that of *Mamre*. Sections 1442, 1443 in the second volume showed what *oak groves* represented and symbolized in general, and §1616 showed what the *oak groves of Mamre* meant in particular. They represented and symbolized perceptions, but human ones based on secular facts and on rational ideas growing directly out of them.

[2] No one today has any idea what perception is, because no one today perceives things the way the ancient and more particularly the very earliest people did. Perception told the earliest people whether a thing was good and therefore whether it was true. The Lord flowed into their rational mind by way of heaven, and as a result, when they considered any holy thought, they could tell instantly whether it was true or not.

Later on, when people no longer had heavenly thoughts but only worldly and body-centered ones, this kind of perception died out in humankind, to be replaced by conscience. Conscience too is a kind of perception, because acting in opposition to it or in accord with it is a matter of sensing from it whether a thing is true or not and whether it ought to be done. [3] Still, the perception of conscience comes not from the influence of goodness but from that of truth. The truth espoused by our religious culture is planted in our rational mind from our earliest years on and later reinforced. At that point it becomes the only thing we can see as good.

As a result, conscience is a type of perception, but a type that is based on this kind of truth. When the Lord injects charity and innocence into it, goodness springs into being in that conscience. These brief remarks indicate what perception is. Even so, there is a big difference between perception and conscience. See the discussion of perception in the first two volumes, §§104, 125, 371, 483, 495, 503, 521, 536, 597, 607, 784, 865, 895, 1121, 1616. The perceptive ability of spirits and angels is discussed in §§202, 203, 1008, 1383, 1384, 1390, 1391, 1392, 1394, 1397, 1504. The well-educated do not know what perception is, §1387.

[4] In respect to the Lord when he lived in the world, all his thinking was based on divine perception. He alone was a divine, heavenly person, because he alone had Jehovah himself within him giving him the ability to perceive. This was discussed in the second volume, §§1616, 1791.

His perceptions gradually deepened as he drew nearer and nearer to oneness with Jehovah. What his perception was like at this point can be seen from remarks concerning the oak groves of Mamre in §1616 of the second volume. How it changed when he perceived the things contained in the current chapter will be described just below [§§2191–2213].

Sitting at the door of the tent symbolizes the type of holiness he had then—holiness imparted by the love that the growing heat of the day symbolizes, as dealt with below. This can be seen from the symbolism of a *tent* as holiness (discussed in §§414, 1102, 1566). The reason tents symbolized what was holy may be seen in the same passages.

2145

The Lord then had the kind of perception symbolized by the oak groves of Mamre, which is perception on a relatively low rational plane but still a deeper plane than that symbolized by the oak grove of Moreh (discussed in §§1442, 1443). So this is represented and accordingly symbolized here by the fact that he *sat at the door of the tent,* or in other words, at the entry to holiness.

The fact that different types of perception exist on deeper and shallower levels can be illustrated by the types the earliest people experienced. I have heard from them that the more they focused on secular facts derived from what they heard and saw, the less exalted their perceptions were. The more their minds rose out of secular facts into the heavenly concerns of charity and love, however, the deeper their perceptions were, because the closer they then were to the Lord.

As the day grew hot means that love imparted it, which can be seen from the inner-level symbolism of *heat* as love. Since heat comes with either the time of day or the time of year, either the heat of the day or the heat of the year can represent love, depending on the terms in which the story is couched.

2146

The symbolism of heat as love can be seen from the fact that love is called spiritual warmth, and heat means any kind of emotional response, even in everyday language. What is more, at our deeper and shallower levels, and even on the level of our body, love and the emotions that compose it manifest themselves as a kind of heat. In fact, when we feel heat that comes from inside us, love is its only source.

The type of heat depends on the type of love. Heavenly love and spiritual love are what give off real warmth. Any other kind, whether it results from self-love or worldly love or some other foul love, is unclean and decays into excrement in the other life. See §1773.

In addition, it needs to be realized that the only properties that make a thing holy are love and charity. Faith does not do this, except to the extent that its truth contains either love or charity. Religious truth is not sacred otherwise. See the remarks above at §2049.

2147   Genesis 18:2. *And he raised his eyes and looked, and here, now, three men standing near him; and he saw and ran from the door of the tent to meet them and bowed down toward the earth.*

He raised his eyes means that he saw within himself. *And here, now, three men standing near him* symbolizes divinity itself, divine humanity, and their holy influence. *And he saw* means when he sensed this. *And ran to meet them* means that in thought he moved closer to the things he was perceiving. *From the door of the tent* means from the type of holiness he had then. *And bowed down toward the earth* means an outward effect of humility, inspired by joy over this.

2148   *He raised his eyes* means that he saw within himself, as established by the symbolism of *raising one's eyes*. In the Word, eyes symbolize inner sight, or comprehension, as the passages quoted in §212 show. So raising one's eyes is seeing and perceiving what is above. In the Word, deeper dimensions are expressed in terms of height, in such phrases as looking up, lifting one's eyes to heaven, or thinking lofty thoughts. The reason for this imagery is that people suppose heaven to be somewhere high up above them, although it is not high up but deep inside. When loving, heavenly influences hold sway over us, for instance, our heaven is inside us; see §450. From this it is clear that raising one's eyes means seeing within oneself.

2149   *Here, now, three men standing near him* symbolizes divinity itself, divine humanity, and their holy influence. This can be seen without explanation, because everyone knows that this is the Trinity and that the three are one. The current chapter makes it unmistakably plain that they are one. Verse 3 just below does so, where it says [in the singular]:

He said, "*My lord,* please, if I have found favor in *your* eyes, please do not *pass* by."

—this being addressed to the three men. In addition:

And *he said,* "*I will* definitely *return* to you." (verse 10)

And *Jehovah said* to Abraham, . . . (verse 13)

He said, "No, because you did laugh." (verse 15)

And *Jehovah said,* "*Shall I be hiding* from Abraham what *I am doing?*" (verse 17)

". . . for *I know* him . . ." (verse 19)

And *Jehovah said* . . . (verse 20)

"*Let me go down,* and *I will see* whether they have made an end of it according to its outcry, which has come to *me,* and if not, *I will know* it." (verse 21)

Abraham said, "Will *you* also *destroy* the just with the ungodly?" (verse 23)

"Far be it from *you* to do according to this thing; far be it from *you.*" (verse 25)

And *Jehovah said,* "If *I find* fifty just people, *I will spare* the whole place for their sake." (verse 26)

"I have undertaken to speak to *my lord.*" (verse 27)

"*Will you ruin* the whole city over five?" And *he said, "I will not ruin* it if *I find* forty-five there." (verse 28)

[Abraham] went on to speak to *him* further. *He said,* "For the sake of forty, *I will not do* it." (verse 29)

"Let anger not blaze in *my lord.*" *He said, "I will not do* it if *I find* thirty there." (verse 30)

"I have undertaken to speak to *my lord.*" *He said,* "For the sake of twenty, *I will not ruin* it." (verse 31)

"Please let anger not blaze in *my lord.*" And *he said,* "For the sake of ten, *I will not ruin* it." (verse 32)

And *Jehovah went,* when *he had finished* speaking to Abraham. (verse 33)

This shows that the three men who appeared to Abraham symbolized divinity itself, divine humanity, and their holy influence, and that in themselves the three are one.

The inner meaning here has to do with Jehovah. It says that he appeared to the Lord and that the Lord perceived it, but not visually, as Abraham did. It is historically true that Abraham saw three men, but this represents a divine perception (a perception from his divinity) that the Lord had when conscious as a human. This perception will be described below [§2171].

And he saw means when he sensed this. This can be seen from the inner-level symbolism of *seeing* as understanding and perceiving and also as being enlightened (treated of in §1584). Nothing is more common in

2150

the Word than this symbolism of seeing. Here it symbolizes his awareness that perception would come from his divinity, as just noted.

2151   *Abraham ran to meet them* means that he moved closer to the things he was perceiving, as can be seen from the train of thought in the inner sense. The previous verse described the kind of perception the Lord was experiencing. This verse says that he noticed a perception coming from his divine side. Now in the phrase before us his running to meet the men represents and therefore symbolizes his moving closer to it.

2152   *From the door of the tent* means from the type of holiness he had then. This is established by the symbolism of a *tent* as holiness and by the symbolism of a *door* as entry to holiness. These are discussed above at §2145.

2153   *And bowed down toward the earth* means an outward effect of humility, inspired by joy over this, which can be seen from the symbolism of *bowing down* as being humble.

All the feelings inside us have outward, physical gestures that correspond to them. These gestures are the effects of those feelings, which function as efficient causes of the gestures. So a feeling of humility has as its gesture the act of bowing and even full prostration. Clearly the gesture here was inspired by joy, since the Lord sensed that his perception came from his divine side, as noted.

The humility the Lord felt when conscious only of his human nature has already been discussed in many places and will be discussed again later in this chapter, with the Lord's divine mercy [§§1785, 1990, 1999–2000, 2098, 2159, 2250, 2265, 2288].

2154   Genesis 18:3. *And he said, "My lord, please, if I have found favor in your eyes, please do not pass by your servant."*

And he said means that this is what he thought. *My lord* means three in one. *Please, if I have found favor in your eyes* symbolizes the Lord's deferential attitude when he became aware of that perception. *Please do not pass by your servant* symbolizes his intense desire that what he was starting to perceive not pass him by; the *servant* is the Lord's humanity before it became divine.

2155   *He said* means that this is what he thought, which can be seen from the meaning of *saying* on the narrative level as perceiving. This has been discussed earlier, at §§1898, 1919, 2080.

2156   *My lord* means three in one—divinity itself, divine humanity, and their holy influence, which are three in one. As a consequence, Abraham here says "lord" in the singular, as he does again further on: "Here, I beg you, I have undertaken to speak with *my lord*" (verses 27, 31). "Please let anger not blaze in *my lord*" (verses 30, 32). The three men are also called Jehovah: "*Jehovah* said to Abraham" (verse 13). "Will anything be [too] amazing for *Jehovah?*" (verse 14). "Abraham was still standing before *Jehovah*" (verse 22). "And *Jehovah* went, when he had finished speaking to Abraham" (verse 33). This shows that the three men—in other words, divinity itself, divine humanity, and their holy influence—are the same as the Lord, and that the Lord is the same as Jehovah.

The statement of Christian faith that is called the [Athanasian] Creed acknowledges the same thing where it explicitly says, "There are not three uncreated beings, not three infinite beings, not three eternal beings, not three omnipotent beings, not three Lords, but one." The only people who divide up this three-in-one are those who claim to acknowledge a single Supreme Being, the creator of the universe. People outside the church can be excused for talking this way, but people inside the church who do so do not acknowledge *any* god, let alone the Lord, even though they claim to and sometimes even think they do.

Please, if I have found favor in your eyes symbolizes the Lord's deferential attitude when he became aware of that perception. This can be seen from the feeling of humility present in the very words themselves and also in the next clause: "Please do not pass by your servant." These words also display humility.

The individual words of Scripture contain both feelings and subject matter. Heavenly angels perceive the Word according to the emotion of its inner meaning. Spiritual angels perceive it according to the subject matter of its inner meaning. Those who perceive the emotion of Scripture's inner meaning pay no attention to the words, which express subject matter. Instead they shape their ideas from the feelings there and from the order in which the feelings arise, with unlimited variety. When they reach these words here, for instance—"Please, if I have found favor in your eyes, please do not pass by your servant"—they perceive the humility of the Lord's attitude as a human, but only the *feeling* of humility. From this, in an indescribable way and with indescribable variety and abundance, they form heavenly ideas for themselves that can hardly even be called ideas. Rather they are simply so many lamps shining on their feelings and perceptions, which follow one another in an unending series that matches the series of feelings expressed by the subject matter in the part of the Word being read. [2] You can see, then, that the perception, thought, and speech of heavenly angels is harder to describe and much richer than the perception, thought, and speech of spiritual angels. Spiritual angels are limited to the thought expressed by the series of phrases. For the speech of heavenly angels being like this, see §1647 in the second volume. That is

2157

why these words, "Please, if I have found favor in your eyes," in a heavenly sense symbolize the Lord's deferential attitude when he became aware of that [divine] perception.

Furthermore, to "find favor in your eyes" was a common expression to use whenever people were showing respect. This can be seen from Laban's deference toward Jacob: "Laban said to him, *'Please, if I have found favor in your eyes'*" (Genesis 30:27). [It can also be seen from] Jacob's deference toward Esau: "Jacob said, 'Please, no; *please, if I have found favor in your eyes'*" (Genesis 33:10). Similar phrases appear elsewhere in the Word.

2158   *Please do not pass by your servant* symbolizes his intense desire. The remarks just above fit the case here too. Deference is again being expressed, along with a feeling of desire that what he was starting to perceive not pass him by.

2159   The *servant* is the Lord's humanity before it became divine, as can be seen from many passages in the Prophets. The reason, as discussed several times before [§§2154, 2157], is that the Lord's humanity was nothing more than a servant until he rid himself of it and made it divine.

The humanity in him came from his mother, so it was weak, containing her heredity as it did. Through his spiritual struggles he overcame this heredity and eliminated it completely—so completely that he kept no trace of the weaknesses he had inherited from her. In fact, ultimately he kept nothing at all of his mother's. So he rid himself entirely of anything from her and was no longer her son, as he himself also says in Mark:

> They said to Jesus, "Look—your mother and your siblings! They are looking for you outside." And he answered them, saying, "Who is my mother or my siblings?" And looking all around [at those] who were sitting about him he said, "Look: my mother and my siblings. For whoever does the will of God is my brother and my sister and my mother." (Mark 3:32, 33, 34, 35; Matthew 12:46, 47, 48, 49, 50; Luke 8:20, 21)

[2] When he had shed this humanity he put on a divine humanity, for which reason he called himself the *Son of Humankind* (many times in the New Testament Word) and also the *Son of God*. By Son of Humankind he meant truth itself, and by Son of God, goodness itself, which was a trait of his human nature once it had become divine. The earlier state was one of humility for the Lord, but this was one of his glorification, as discussed above at §1999.

[3] In the earlier state—the state of humility, when he still had human weaknesses in him—he revered Jehovah as someone other than himself. He even regarded himself as a servant to Jehovah, because that is exactly

what his human side is by comparison. So the Word also refers to this human side of his as a servant. In Isaiah, for instance:

> I will provide protection over this city to preserve it, for my own sake and the sake of *David my servant.* (Isaiah 37:35)

This has to do with the Assyrians in whose camp an angel struck one hundred eighty-five thousand soldiers. David stands for the Lord, and because the Lord had yet to come, his human part is called a servant. To see that David stands for the Lord in the Word, see §1888. [4] In the same prophet:

> Look: *my servant,* on whom I lean; the one I have chosen, [in whom] my soul takes pleasure. I have set my spirit on him. He will bring judgment to the nations. (Isaiah 42:1)

This is obviously about the Lord, who is described as a chosen servant in the times when his human nature was uppermost. In the same author:

> Who is blind except *my servant,* and as deaf as the angel I will send? Who is as blind as the perfect one or as blind as *Jehovah's servant?* (Isaiah 42:19)

This too is about the Lord, and again he is referred to as a servant and angel at the times when he was functioning only as a human. [5] In the same author:

> "You are my witnesses," says Jehovah, "and *my servant,* whom I have chosen, in order that you may all know and believe me and understand that I am he." (Isaiah 43:10)

In the same author:

> Jehovah has said—who formed me from the *womb into a servant to him,* to bring Jacob back to him, and for Israel to be gathered to him— he has said, "It is too trifling that *you should be a servant to me,* to raise up the tribes of Jacob; I have made you a light for the nations, to be my salvation all the way to the end of the earth." (Isaiah 49:5, 6)

This too is plainly about the Lord and his human side before he had become the light of the nations and salvation to the end of the earth. In the same author:

> Who among you is fearing Jehovah, is hearing the voice of *his servant?* Let those who walk in darkness and have no light trust in Jehovah's name and lean on their God. (Isaiah 50:10)

Here again the servant stands for the human side of the Lord. The voice of Jehovah's servant means times when he taught the path of truth while his human side was predominant. [6] In the same author:

> Jehovah is going before you, and the God of Israel is gathering you in. Watch: *my servant* will act prudently. He will be lifted and raised and elevated greatly. (Isaiah 52:12, 13)

Clearly the servant refers to the Lord when his human side was predominant, since it says that he will be lifted, raised, and elevated. In the same author:

> He had no form and received no honor. We saw him, but he had no looks. He was despised, *a man in pain, knowing sickness.* Jehovah wished to crush him; he *weakened* him. If he makes his soul a guilt [offering], he will see his seed, he will lengthen his days, and the will of Jehovah will prosper through his hand. *Out of the toil of his soul* he will see; he will receive his fill. By his knowledge *my* righteous *servant* will make many others righteous, and their wickedness he has carried. (Isaiah 53:2, 3, 10, 11)

This passage openly describes the Lord's humbled state, as that whole chapter does. It says outright that his human weaknesses were dominant by depicting him as a man of pain, knowing sickness, weak, and toiling in his soul, not to mention other attributes typical of a state that can be described as servitude.

2160   Genesis 18:4. *"Please let a little water be taken, and wash your feet, and recline under the tree."*

Please let a little water be taken means that they would move nearer, lowering themselves from divine heights down closer to his intellectual abilities. *And wash your feet* means that they would take on something earthly, so that he could perceive them better in the state he was then in. *And recline under the tree* means down to where he could perceive them in the state he was then in; a *tree* is perception.

2161   *Please let a little water be taken* means that they would move nearer, lowering themselves from divine heights down closer to his intellectual abilities. This can be seen not so much from the words *let a little water be taken* alone as from the series of ideas in the current verse and its connection with the verses above and below. The words of the verse themselves could never reveal to anyone that "Please let a little water be taken, and wash your feet, and recline under the tree" meant that the Lord's divine side would lower itself down closer to the state of perception he was then in and adopt a kind of physical plane so that he could perceive it better. Not a trace of this secret is visible in the words, if they are taken at face value, but I know for certain that this is what they mean in an inner sense and that this is the way the angels perceive them. [2] These considerations indicate how awesome the secrets in the Word are and how deeply they lie hidden.

The meaning can also be seen from the symbolism of the words on an inner level. *Water* symbolizes matters of intellect, *feet* symbolize physical elements, and a *tree* symbolizes perception. Once you understand these, the series of ideas and its connection with the verses above and below can show you what they symbolize on an inner level. It shows that they have the meaning given.

Sections 28, 680 in the first volume showed the symbolism of *water* as facts and as rational ideas and so as matters of intellect. Many other passages in the Word can show the same thing, but quoting them would take too long.

Wash your feet means that [his divine nature] would take on something earthly, so that he could perceive it better in the state he was then in. This can be seen from the symbolism of *feet* as physical elements and again from the series of ideas. To some extent, Abraham's behavior indicates that secrets lie hidden in this material, since he begged the three men to take a little water and wash their feet and recline under the tree, even though he realized it was the Lord, or Jehovah. Another indication is the fact that otherwise these particulars would not have been mentioned.

[2] The symbolism of *feet* as physical elements can be seen from representational scenes in the other world, consequently from the way the earliest people used representation, and therefore from the way the Word uses it. The head and everything in the head represents what is heavenly and spiritual. The chest and everything in the chest represents rational ideas and everything connected with them. The feet and the parts adjoining them represent physical elements and everything connected with them. The foot itself and the heel, then, symbolize the very lowest physical elements; see the discussion in §259. A shoe symbolizes the very lowest attributes of all, which are unclean, as discussed in §1748.

[3] Images presented in the dreams and visions of the prophetic books have much the same symbolism. The statue that Nebuchadnezzar saw is an example, with its head of fine gold, chest and arms of silver, belly and thighs of bronze, legs of iron, and *feet partly of iron and partly of clay*

2162

(Daniel 2:32, 33). Its head symbolizes heavenly qualities, which are the deepest ones and are gold, as shown in §§113, 1551, 1552. Its chest and arms symbolize spiritual traits, or rational ideas, which are silver, as shown in §1551. Its feet, though, symbolize lower elements, which are earthly ones. Iron symbolizes earthly truth, and clay, earthly goodness. (For the symbolism of iron as truth, see §§425, 426, and for that of clay as goodness, §1300. Both are on the earthly or physical plane here.) The same hierarchy exists in the Lord's kingdom in the heavens, and in the church, which is the Lord's kingdom on earth, and also in each individual who is a kingdom of the Lord.

[4] The case is the same with the vision of Daniel's reported in these words:

> I raised my eyes and looked. Here, now, a lone man clothed in linen, and his hips were circled with the gold of Uphaz, and his body was like tarshish, and his face, like the appearance of lightning, and his eyes, like lamps of fire, and his arms and *feet, like the radiance of burnished bronze.* (Daniel 10:5, 6)

The particular symbolism of this vision is the inner dimensions of the Word as they relate to goodness and truth. The arms and feet are its outward aspects, or aspects of the literal meaning, because the literal meaning contains earthly features, referring as it does to earthly objects. Beyond this, the symbolism of the individual parts (the hips, body, face, eyes, and other parts of the human anatomy) can be seen from representations in the other life. The symbolism, by the Lord's divine mercy, will be laid out in the description of the universal human (which is the Lord's heaven) and of representations based on it in the world of spirits.

[5] Of Moses, Aaron, Nadab, Abihu, and the seventy elders we read:

> They saw the God of Israel, *under whose feet was something like a work of sapphire stone,* and it looked like the substance of the sky for purity. (Exodus 24:9, 10)

The symbolism here is that they saw only the superficial aspects of the church, represented by physical objects. They also saw the literal meaning of the Word, whose surface features are likewise represented by physical objects, as noted, which are the feet, under which there was a seeming work of sapphire stone and something like the substance of the sky. Clearly it was the Lord who appeared to them (though only in those lower, earthly aspects). After all, he is here called the God of Israel, whom everything in the church represented and everything in the Word symbolized on an inner level. The way the Lord is presented in a vision depends on the symbolism involved. An example may be seen in John, where the Lord is revealed as a man on a white horse and it says in plain language that this meant the Word (Revelation 19:11, 13).

[6] The living creatures or guardian beings that Ezekiel saw are portrayed in their heavenly and spiritual aspects by their faces and wings and other details. They are portrayed in their physical attributes, on the other hand, by these words:

> *Their feet, the right foot,* and the *sole* of their *feet* were like the *sole of a calf's foot,* and they were gleaming like the radiance of burnished bronze. (Ezekiel 1:7)

The reason their feet—their earthly aspects—are said to have gleamed like burnished bronze is that bronze symbolizes earthly goodness, as mentioned in §§425, 1551.

It means something similar that the Lord appeared to John as the Son of Humankind, "whose eyes were like a fiery flame and whose *feet resembled fine brass*" (Revelation 1:14, 15; 2:18).

[7] More evidence for the symbolism of feet as physical or earthly things can be seen in the following words from John, who saw:

> . . . a strong angel coming down from heaven wrapped in a cloud—and a rainbow was around his head, and his face was like the sun, and *his feet were like pillars of fire*—having in his hand a little book open, and putting *his right foot on the sea, his left,* on *the land.* (Revelation 10:1, 2)

This angel likewise symbolizes the Word. The rainbow around his head and the resemblance of his face to the sun symbolize the nature of the Word in its inner meaning, but his feet symbolize the outward or literal meaning. The sea is earthly truth; the land, earthly goodness; which suggests what it means that he put his right foot on the sea and his left on the land.

[8] The Word often mentions a *footstool*, as in Isaiah, but people do not know what it symbolizes on an inner level:

> Jehovah has said, "The heavens are my throne; and the *earth, my footstool.* Where is this house you will build me, and where is this place of my repose?" (Isaiah 66:1)

The heavens are heavenly and spiritual dimensions and therefore the deepest dimensions of both the Lord's kingdom in the heavens and his kingdom on earth, or in the church. They are also the same dimensions of his kingdom as it exists in each individual who is a kingdom of the Lord, or a church. By the same token, they are heavenly and spiritual dimensions regarded in themselves, which are facets of love and charity and resulting faith. So they are all possible facets of inward worship, and again all possible facets of the Word's inner meaning. All these are the heavens and are called the Lord's throne.

The earth, however, is all the lower planes corresponding to them. For instance, it is rational ideas on a lower level, and earthly endeavors. These too can be described as heavenly or spiritual by correspondence. They are heavenly or spiritual the way things in the lower heavens, in the church, in outward worship, or in the Word's literal meaning are. In short, they are everything that emerges on the surface as a result of inner forces. Because they are physical, they are called the earth and the Lord's footstool. For the inner meaning of heaven and earth, see also §§82, 1733. For that of the new heaven and the new earth, §§2117, 2118 at the end. To see that a person is a miniature heaven, §§911, 978, 1900.

[9] Again in Jeremiah:

> In his anger the Lord overclouds the daughter of Zion; he has thrown the beauty of Israel down from the heavens to the earth and has not remembered *his footstool on the day of his anger.* (Lamentations 2:1)

And again in David:

> Exalt Jehovah our God and bow down at *his footstool;* he is holy. (Psalms 99:5)

Elsewhere in the same author:

> We will enter his dwelling places; we will bow down at *his footstool.* (Psalms 132:7)

People in the representative church (Jews, that is) thought the House of God or the Temple was his footstool, not realizing that the House of God or Temple symbolized outward, representative worship. They had no idea at all what the deeper religious concerns symbolized by heaven (God's throne) were. [10] In the same author:

> Jehovah said to my Lord, "Sit at my right till I have made your enemies *your footstool.*" (Psalms 110:1; Matthew 22:44; Mark 12:36; Luke 20:42, 43)

Here too the footstool symbolizes what we get from the physical world—both sense impressions and facts—and the rational ideas that we build on it. These things are called enemies when they corrupt our worship (using the letter of the Word to do it), so that our worship is purely superficial, having no central core or only a foul one. This kind of worship is treated of in §§1094, 1175, 1182. When earthly things have been corrupted and polluted in this way, they are called enemies. Viewed in themselves, however, they relate to inward worship, so when real inward worship is restored, they become the Lord's footstool, as already noted. That includes earthly things both in outward worship and in the literal meaning of the Word.

[11] In Isaiah:

> The glory of Lebanon will come to you; fir, pine, boxwood together [will come] to beautify the place where my sanctuary is, and *I will make the place where my feet are honorable.* (Isaiah 60:13)

This has to do with the Lord's kingdom and the church. The heavenly qualities it possesses that are spiritual are "the glory of Lebanon" or in other words, cedars. Those oriented toward the earthly world, though, are the fir, pine, and boxwood, as elsewhere in the Word. These three are the outward signs of worship, too, then, of which it says, "I will make the place where my feet are honorable." Fir, pine, and boxwood cannot make it honorable; only the things they symbolize can.

[12] Certain representative acts and objects of the Jewish religion also illustrate this symbolism of feet. One example is the fact that Aaron and his sons were to *wash* their *hands* and *feet* before they entered the tabernacle (Exodus 30:19, 20; 40:31, 32). It is impossible not to see that this had some hidden representation, because what is hand- and foot-washing but a superficial trifle? It does no good if a person's inner depths are not already clean and pure, and a person's inner depths cannot be cleaned or purified by this kind of washing. All the rituals of that religion symbolized inner values, however, and inner values are heavenly and spiritual ones. So the same is true here. The washing was a symbol for making outward worship clean, and worship is clean when the outward display of it has an inner core. That is why their lavers were made of bronze, including the large one called the bronze sea, along with ten smaller washbowls of bronze set around Solomon's temple (1 Kings 7:23, 38). Bronze represented what is good in outward worship, which is the same as earthly goodness. For more on this symbolism of bronze, see §§425, 1551.

[13] A representative rule of the same kind was the one that prevented a man who had a *broken foot* or broken hand, of Aaron's lineage, from approaching to offer fire offerings to Jehovah (Leviticus 21:19, 21). Broken feet and hands represented people whose outward worship is corrupt.

[14] The symbolism of feet as earthly or physical aspects is evident in many other places in the Prophets as well, as in these enigmatic words in Moses:

A blessing on Asher because of his sons! Let him be accepted by his brothers and dip *his foot* into oil; iron and bronze are *your shoes*. (Deuteronomy 33:24, 25)

These words must be completely incomprehensible except to someone who knows what a foot, oil, iron, bronze, and a shoe symbolize on an inner level. A foot is something earthly or physical. A shoe is something earthly or physical but on a still lower plane (see §1748), like the physical senses. Oil is the quality of heaven (886); iron is earthly truth (425, 426); and bronze is earthly goodness (425, 1551). This list shows what the passage involves.

[15] In Nahum:

For Jehovah in windstorm and tempest there is a path, and *cloud is the dust of his feet*. (Nahum 1:3)

The dust of his feet symbolizes what is earthly and bodily in us, which generates clouds. These words in David symbolize the same thing:

Jehovah bent the heavens and came down, and *darkness was under his feet*. (Psalms 18:9)

[16] When worldly light, as people call it, perverts religious goodness and truth, the Word depicts it in terms of feet and animal hooves that churn water and trample food, as in Ezekiel:

You have emerged into the rivers and *churned the waters with your feet* and trampled their rivers. I will obliterate every animal of the place from beside many waters, and the *foot of a human* will not *churn [the waters] any longer*, nor will the *hoof of an animal*. (Ezekiel 32:2, 13)

This passage has to do with Egypt, which symbolized secular knowledge, as shown in §§1164, 1165, 1462. The feet and hooves that churn the rivers and waters, then, symbolize facts drawn from sense impressions and other earthly sources, on which people base their reasoning concerning religious mysteries. They also refuse to believe anything until they grasp it in those terms. This is the same as never believing it, because the more such people reason, the less they believe. See what is said in §§128, 129, 130, 215, 232, 233, 1072, 1385.

All this evidence now shows that feet in the Word symbolize earthly phenomena. What more they symbolize is evident from the series of ideas.

Recline under the tree means down to where he could perceive it in the state he was then in. This can be seen from the symbolism of a *tree* as perception (mentioned in §103). The meaning itself, then, can be seen from the series of ideas as being just this. 〔2163〕

The reason *trees* symbolized perceptions was that paradise, or the Garden of Eden, was a metaphor and simile for heavenly people, so the trees in the garden were a metaphor and simile for their perception of heavenly influences.

Genesis 18:5. *"And let me take a morsel of bread, and you, sustain your heart. Afterward you may pass on, since this is the reason you have passed over to your servant." And they said, "You should do as you have spoken."* 〔2164〕

Let me take a morsel of bread means something of heaven attached to it. *Sustain your heart* means a suitable amount. *Afterward you may pass on* means that when he stopped perceiving, he would be content. *Since this is the reason you have passed over to your servant* means that was why they had come. *And they said, "You should do as you have spoken,"* means so it would be.

Let me take a morsel of bread means something of heaven attached to it. This can be seen from the symbolism of *bread* as something heavenly, which has been discussed before, in §§276, 680, 681, 1798. The reason bread symbolizes something heavenly is that it means all food in general. So in an inner sense it means all heavenly food. Sections 56, 57, 58, 680, 681, 1480, 1695 in the first two volumes told what heavenly food is. 〔2165〕

The following passages in the Word show that bread means all food in general. Of Joseph we read, "He told the one who was over his household to bring the men [his brothers] to the house, and to slaughter abundantly and prepare [the meat]." Later, when everything was ready and they were to eat, he said, *"Set the bread"* (Genesis 43:16, 31). By this he meant "Put the meal on," so bread stands for all kinds of food. Of Jethro we read:

> Aaron and all the elders of Israel came to *eat bread* with Moses' father-in-law before God. (Exodus 18:12)

Here too bread stands for all kinds of food. Of Manoah we read in Judges:

> Manoah said to the angel of Jehovah, "Please let us detain you and prepare a goats' kid before you." And the angel of Jehovah said to Manoah, "If you detain me, I will not *eat your bread.*" (Judges 13:15, 16)

The bread here stands for the goats' kid. When Jonathan ate some honeycomb, they told him that Saul had put the people under an oath, saying, "Cursed is the man who *eats bread* today" (1 Samuel 14:27, 28). Bread here stands for any kind of food. In another passage concerning Saul:

> When Saul sat to *eat bread,* he said to Jonathan, "Why hasn't the son of Jesse come *to the bread* either yesterday or today?" (1 Samuel 20:24, 27)

Coming to the bread stands for coming to the table, which holds all kinds of food. Of David we read that he said to Mephibosheth, son of Jonathan, "You will always *eat bread at my table*" (2 Samuel 9:7, 10). We read something similar of Evil-merodach, who said that Jehoiachin, king of Judah, *would always eat bread before him,* all the days of his life (2 Kings 25:29). Of Solomon we read this:

> *The bread of Solomon* for each day was thirty kors of flour and sixty kors of meal, ten heads of fattened cattle and twenty heads of ranging cattle and a hundred of the smaller livestock, besides deer and roe deer and fallow deer and fattened poultry. (1 Kings 4:22, 23)

Obviously bread here stands for everything listed. [2] Now, since bread means all kinds of food in general, in an inner sense it means everything that is called heavenly food. This is even clearer to see from the lambs, sheep, she-goats, kids, he-goats, young cattle, and adult cattle offered as burnt offerings and sacrifices. These animals were called by the single name "bread of the fire offering to Jehovah," as is plain to see from the following passages in Moses that deal with the various sacrifices. Of those animals he says:

> The priest shall burn them on the altar, the *bread of the fire offering to Jehovah,* as a restful smell. (Leviticus 3:11, 16)

All of those sacrifices and burnt offerings were referred to this way. In the same author:

> The sons of Aaron shall be holy to their God and not profane the name of their God, because they are offering *fire offerings to Jehovah, the bread of their God.* You shall consecrate him, because he is offering the *bread of your God.* The man of Aaron's seed in whom there is a blemish shall not approach to offer the *bread of his God.* (Leviticus 21:6, 8, 17, 21)

Here too the sacrifices and burnt offerings are "bread," as they also are in Leviticus 22:25. In another place:

Command the children of Israel, and you are to say to them, "My obla-
tion, *my bread,* you shall be careful to offer me at its set time, as fire
offerings for a restful smell." (Numbers 28:2)

Here again bread stands for all the sacrifices listed in the chapter. In
Malachi:

You are offering defiled *bread* on my altar. (Malachi 1:7)

This refers to the sacrifices as well. The food consecrated by sacrifice that
they ate was also called bread, as these words in Moses show:

No one who touches anything unclean shall eat any of the consecrated
items but in fact shall wash his flesh in water, and when the sun sets he
shall be clean, and afterward he shall eat some of the consecrated items,
because it is his bread. (Leviticus 22:6, 7)

[3] Burnt offerings and sacrifices in the Jewish religion had no other
meaning than the heavenly side of the Lord's kingdom in the heavens and
of his kingdom on earth or in the church, and also the heavenly side of his
kingdom or church in each individual. In general they represented everything having to do with love and charity, because these are what is heavenly, and each type of sacrifice represented a particular aspect of them.
Taken together they were called *bread* at that time. So when sacrifices
were done away with, to be replaced by other outward acts of worship,
the use of bread and wine was commanded. [4] As a result, the symbolism of bread is clear: bread symbolizes everything that the sacrifices represented. So on an inner level it symbolizes the Lord himself, and since it
symbolizes the Lord himself, it symbolizes love itself for the entire human
race, along with all that love implies. It also symbolizes the love we reflect
back to the Lord and to our neighbor. So it symbolizes everything that
is heavenly, and therefore wine symbolizes everything spiritual. This fact
the Lord teaches openly in John:

They said, "Our ancestors ate manna in the wilderness. As it is written,
'*Bread from heaven* he gave them to eat.'" Jesus said to them, "Truly
truly, I say to you: Moses did not give you *bread from heaven,* but my
Father *gives you* true *bread from heaven. For the bread of God is* the one
who comes down from heaven and gives life to the world." They said
to him, "Lord, always give us this *bread.*" Jesus said to them, "*I am the
bread of life;* no one who comes to me will hunger and no one who
believes in me will ever thirst." (John 6:31–35)

And in the same author:

> Truly, I say to you: anyone who believes in me has eternal life. *I am the bread of life.* Your ancestors ate manna in the wilderness and died. *This is the bread* that comes down from heaven, so that if anyone eats of it, that person will not die. *I am the living bread* who came down from heaven; if anyone *eats of this bread,* that person will live forever. (John 6:47–51)

[5] Now, since bread is the Lord, it has to do with the heavenly qualities that belong to love and to the Lord. The Lord, after all, is heavenliness itself, because he is love itself, or in other words, mercy itself. Since this is so, bread is also everything heavenly. In other words, it is all the love and charity we have in us, since these come from the Lord. People who do not possess love or charity, then, do not have the Lord in them, so they do not receive the good and blessed gifts symbolized by bread on an inner level.

This outward symbol was commanded because for most of the human race worship is an outward act. If these people did not have something outwardly holy, they would have almost nothing holy at all. When they live lives of love for the Lord and of charity for their neighbor, then, they do have depth, even though they do not know that this is the most central core of worship. So their outward worship strengthens them in the kinds of good symbolized by bread.

[6] In the Prophets as well, bread symbolizes heavenly qualities of love, as in Isaiah 3:1, 7; 30:23; 33:15, 16; 55:2; 58:7, 8; Lamentations 5:9; Ezekiel 4:16, 17; 5:16; 14:13; Amos 4:6; 8:11; Psalms 105:16. The same is true of the loaves of the bread of presence on the table, mentioned in Leviticus 24:5–9; Exodus 25:30; 40:23; Numbers 4:7; 1 Kings 7:48.

2166   *Sustain your heart* means a suitable amount. This is not very easy to see from the symbolism of these words on the next deeper level of meaning, but it *can* be seen from the series of ideas. What is being expressed here is a desire that divine perception come closer to the perception the Lord then experienced in his human side and lower itself down closer to his intellectual abilities. It would do this by taking on something physical and also something heavenly attached to it, in a suitable amount, which is what *sustaining one's heart* is. In the most direct sense, sustaining one's heart with bread means being refreshed and therefore enjoying just enough of heaven to be suitable.

2167   *Afterward you may pass on* means that when he stopped perceiving, he would be content. Again, this can be seen from the series.

Since this is the reason you have passed over to your servant means that was why they had come. This too can be seen without explanation.   **2168**

They said, "You should do as you have spoken," means so it would be. Likewise, this has no need to be explained.   **2169**

Genesis 18:6. *And Abraham hurried toward the tent, to Sarah, and said, "Bring three pecks of flour-meal in a hurry, knead it, and make cakes."*   **2170**

Abraham hurried toward the tent, to Sarah symbolizes the Lord's rational-level goodness united with his truth. *Abraham* here is the goodness the Lord had at that stage; *Sarah* is truth in him then; a *tent* is holy love in him then. *And said* symbolizes the relative state of perception in him then. *Bring three pecks of flour-meal in a hurry, knead it, and make cakes* symbolizes his heavenly love in that state. *Three* is holiness; *flour-meal* is the heavenly and spiritual sides of the rationality the Lord then had; *cakes* are these heavenly and spiritual sides when they are joined together.

Abraham hurried toward the tent, to Sarah symbolizes the Lord's rational-level goodness united with his truth, as can be seen from the representation of *Abraham* and *Sarah* and from the symbolism of a *tent*, which are about to be discussed.   **2171**

The meaning of these words depends on the subject at hand in the inner sense, as it always does. Here it relates to the divine perception the Lord came into when his human side was perceiving things. People who do not know what perception is also cannot see how it works. Still less can they see that there are deeper and deeper levels of it. There is earthly perception, rational perception, and finally inner perception, which is divine. Only the Lord had this last kind. People with perception—angels, for example—know with perfect accuracy what kind they have, whether it is earthly, rational, or still deeper. (For them, this deeper perception is essentially divine.) Imagine, then, what it was like for the Lord! His perception came from divinity itself at its highest level—the infinite divine being (as discussed at the end of §1616 and in §1791). No angels ever experience this kind of perception, because the perception they receive from the Lord's supreme, infinite divinity comes through his human nature.

The reason the Lord's perception is being depicted is this: When his human side was predominant, it was through perception that he learned how divinity itself, divine humanity, and their holy influence would become one in him. It was through perception that he learned how his rational mind would become divine. And finally it was through perception that he learned what the human race is like and how it would be saved by him that it would be saved through the uniting of the human nature with the divine nature in him. These are the themes of the current chapter. It is for the sake of these goals that the Lord's perception is depicted here at the beginning, and also for the sake of the union itself that was to take place.

2172   The fact that *Abraham* here is the goodness the Lord had at that stage can be seen from the representation of Abraham. When he converses with Jehovah, Abraham represents the Lord's human side. He does so here as he did earlier at §1989, where he represented the Lord in that phase and at that stage of his life, because then too he was talking with Jehovah. At other times Abraham represents the Lord's divine goodness (while Sarah represents his divine truth), so at this point he represents rational-level goodness.

2173   The fact that *Sarah* is truth in the Lord can be seen from her representation as intuitive truth that is attached to goodness. Here she represents rational truth, for the same reason just given for Abraham. For Sarah's representation as truth, see earlier at §§1468, 1901, 2063, 2065.

In the narrative portions of the Word, goodness and truth can be represented only by a marriage. This is the relation goodness and truth bear to one another, because there is a divine marriage between heavenly forces and spiritual ones or, what is the same, between the forces of love and those of faith or, what is again the same, between the forces of the will and those of the intellect. The former of each pair relates to goodness; the latter, to truth.

The same kind of marriage exists in the Lord's kingdom in the heavens. It also exists in the Lord's kingdom on earth, or in the church. It exists in each of us, in everything about us, and in fact in all our very smallest particulars. Anything that does not participate in such a marriage is not alive. For that reason, the same marriage (although different in form and kind) even exists throughout the physical world, with all its parts. Otherwise nothing in it would ever survive.

Since this kind of marriage exists everywhere, every subject that comes up in the Prophets (especially Isaiah) is expressed in twinned terms. One term relates to what is heavenly, or good; the other relates to what is spiritual, or true. (There is more on this in §§683, 793, 801. To see that something analogous to marriage is present everywhere, see §§718, 747, 917, 1432.) That is why Abraham represents the Lord's goodness, and Sarah, his truth.

2174   The fact that a *tent* is holy love in him can be seen from the symbolism of a tent as holiness. This has been discussed before, in §§414, 1102, 1566, 2145.

And said symbolizes the relative state of perception in him then. This can be seen from the symbolism of *saying* in the narrative sense as perceiving, as discussed before in §§1898, 1919, 2080. **2175**

Bring three pecks of flour-meal in a hurry, knead it, and make cakes symbolizes his heavenly love in that state, as can be seen from the symbolism of *meal, flour,* and a *cake,* to be dealt with just below. No one who concentrates on the literal meaning, the meaning of the words themselves, can possibly believe that these ideas are involved. Still less can anyone who focuses on the story the words tell, because such people are thinking not only about the preparations described but also about the men who came to Abraham. What they are not thinking about is the presence of a more hidden meaning. That is why they are less able to believe that secrets lie hidden in the individual words of Scripture, as much in the narrative books as in the prophetic. Stories have a powerful hold on the mind, and they throw a veil over any deeper content. The following consideration alone, though, shows that even the stories have secrets hidden deep inside them: the Word is the Lord's and was written not only for people on earth but also for heaven. In fact, it was written in such a way that when we read it here, angels glean heavenly images from it. In this way, the Word unites heaven with the human race. **2176**

The inner meaning of meal, flour, and cakes now follows.

Flour-meal is the heavenly and spiritual qualities the Lord then had, and *cakes* are both of these when they are joined together. This is obvious from the sacrifices of the representative church and from the minha used in them, which consisted of flour mixed with oil and made into cakes. **2177**

The main activity of representative worship was burnt offerings and sacrifices. The discussion of bread above at §2165 explains what these represented. They represented what is heavenly in the Lord's kingdom in the heavens, in his kingdom on earth (the church), and in his kingdom (or church) in each individual. In general, they represented every facet of love and charity, because these are heavenly, and at that time they were all called "bread." To these sacrifices were also added the minha (made of flour mixed with oil, as I said, with the addition of frankincense) and libations of wine as well. [2] It is also possible to see the representation of the last two; they represented approximately the same thing as the [animal] sacrifices, though at a lower level. So they represented qualities of the spiritual church and also of outward religion. Anyone can see that such rituals would never have been commanded had they not represented something divine, and that each of them represents something particular. If they had not represented something divine, they would not have differed from similar activities among non-Jewish nations, which also had their sacrifices, minhas, libations, offerings of frankincense, eternal flames, and so on. These they inherited from the ancient church, and especially from the Hebrew church. Because the inner, divine dimensions represented in them were stripped from the rituals, however, they were simply idolatrous. Such rituals also became so among the Jews, which is why the Jews fell into all kinds of idolatry.

From this anyone can clearly see that heavenly secrets lay behind every ritual, especially the sacrifices, and behind every element of every ritual.

[3] As for the minha, one whole chapter in Moses describes it and explains how it was made into cakes (Leviticus 2, as well as Numbers 15 and other places). The law of the minha is described in these words in Leviticus:

> Fire shall always be kindled on the altar; it shall not be put out. And this is the *law of the minha:* that the sons of Aaron bring it before Jehovah at the face of the altar, and [one of them] shall take up from it by his fistful *some of the flour of the minha*, and some of its oil, and all the frankincense that is on the *minha*, and he shall burn it on the altar. It is a restful smell, as a memorial to Jehovah. And the remainder of it Aaron and his sons shall eat; unleavened loaves shall be eaten in a holy place; in the courtyard of the meeting tent they shall eat [the minha]. It shall not be cooked with yeast. I have given it as their portion out of my fire offerings. It is most holy. (Leviticus 6:13, 14, 15, 16, 17)

[4] The fire that "shall always be kindled on the altar" represented love, or in other words, the Lord's mercy, perpetual and eternal. In the Word, fire symbolizes love (see §934), so fire offerings for a restful smell symbolize the pleasure the Lord takes in anything involving love or charity. (For the symbolism of a smell as good pleasure, or something pleasing, see §§925, 1519.) The requirement that they take the minha by the fistful represented the fact that they should love [the Lord] with all their might, that is, with all their soul. The hand, or its palm, symbolizes power, as shown in §878, so a fistful does too. Flour with oil and frankincense represented every aspect of charity; flour was its spiritual side, but oil was its heavenly side, and frankincense, the fact that it was therefore pleasing. (These remarks and others to follow show that flour represented something spiritual. For the representation of oil as something heavenly, or the good that charity inspires, see §886. For that of frankincense, with its good fragrance, as something pleasing and welcome, see §925.) [5] The

unleavened nature of the minha, or its lack of yeast, means that it should be sincere; it should be offered from a sincere heart, without impurities. The fact that Aaron and his sons ate the remainder represented what we give back, and what we make our own, so it represented being bound together by love and charity. That is the reason for the command that they eat it in a holy place, which is why it is called most holy. This is what the minha represented, and this is how the representative items themselves were perceived in heaven. When people in the church understood them this way, their thoughts mirrored the angels' perceptions; although still on the earth, the people were actually in the Lord's kingdom in the heavens.

[6] Further instructions concerning the minha tell how it had to be used in each type of sacrifice, how it was to be cooked into cakes, and how it was to be offered by people who were being purified, as well as on other occasions. Listing and explaining them all would take too long. See the treatment of these subjects at Exodus 29:39, 40, 41; Leviticus 5:11, 12, 13; 6:16, 17, 19, 20, 21; 10:12, 13; 23:10, 11, 12, 13, 16, 17; Numbers 5:15 and following verses; 6:15, 16, 17, 19, 20; throughout chapter 7; 28:5, 8, 9, 12, 13, 20, 21, 28, 29; 29:3, 4, 9, 10, 14, 15, 18, 21, 24, 27, 30, 33, 37.

[7] Flour made into cakes generally represented the same thing as bread, or in other words, the heavenly aspect of love, while meal represented its spiritual aspect, as can be seen in the passages referred to above.

The loaves called the bread of presence, or showbread, were made of flour, which was prepared as cakes that were then placed on the table. They served as a constant representation of the Lord's love or mercy toward the whole human race, and of the love we return. Moses says this of them:

> You shall take *flour* and *cook it* into twelve *cakes. One cake* shall be of two tenths [of an ephah]. And you shall put them in two rows, six in each row, on the clean table, before Jehovah. And you shall put pure frankincense on the row. And it shall serve as *loaves* for a memorial, a fire offering to Jehovah. On each Sabbath day [Aaron] shall arrange it before Jehovah continually, [an offering] from the children of Israel, by an eternal pact, and it shall be for Aaron and his sons, and they shall eat it in a holy place, because it is most holy to him from the fire offerings to Jehovah by an eternal statute. (Leviticus 24:5, 6, 7, 8, 9)

The individual elements of these preparations, down to the most minute facets, represented the holy quality of love and charity. The flour represented the same thing as flour-meal—heavenliness and the spirituality that goes with it—and a cake represented both of these united.

[8] This shows what kind of holiness the Word holds for people who think heavenly thoughts; in fact it shows what kind of holiness lay at the heart of this representative ritual itself. That is why the ritual is called most holy. By the same token, it shows what kind of holiness is lacking for people who imagine there is nothing heavenly in the passage and who remain strictly on the surface; for example, those who take the meal mentioned in the current verse simply as meal, the flour as flour, and the cake as a cake, and suppose that these things would have been mentioned without each of them involving something divine. They make the same mistake as those who think of the Holy Supper with its bread and wine as nothing more than a kind of ritual, with no sacred content. In reality its holiness is such that it unites human minds to heavenly minds, as long as they think with deep affection about the bread and wine as symbols of the Lord's love and of the love we give back to him. When human minds do this, they have a holiness from within.

[9] When the children of Israel came into the land, they were to give a *cake* from the first fruits of their dough as a raised offering to Jehovah (Numbers 15:20), which involved a similar meaning. The same symbolism can also be seen in the Prophets, though for the time being let me quote just one passage in Ezekiel:

> You were adorned in gold and silver, and your clothing was fine linen and silk and embroidery. *Flour,* honey, and oil you ate, and you became very, very beautiful and succeeded to royalty. (Ezekiel 16:13)

This is about Jerusalem, which symbolizes the church. This is the kind of finery it had in its first era, which was that of the ancient church and which is portrayed by the clothes and other forms of elegance. The flour, honey, and oil portray its desire for truth and goodness. Anyone can see that all these details mean something completely different in an inner sense than they do in the literal sense. So too, then, for the current words, which Abraham said to Sarah: "Bring three pecks of flour-meal in a hurry, knead it, and make cakes." The symbolism of *three* as what is holy was shown above in §§720, 901.

2178 Genesis 18:7. *And Abraham ran to the herd and took the young of an ox, tender and good, and gave it to the houseboy, and he hurried to prepare the animal.*

Abraham ran to the herd symbolizes earthly goodness. *And took the young of an ox, tender and good* symbolizes something heavenly on the earthly plane that would match, which his rationality procured for itself so that it would be able to unite with the perception received from his divine side. *And gave it to the houseboy, and he hurried to prepare the animal* symbolizes the union of goodness on the earthly plane with goodness on the rational plane; the *houseboy* is the earthly self.

Abraham ran to the herd symbolizes earthly goodness. This can be **2179** seen from the symbolism of the cattle both adult and young that form a herd, as will be discussed just below.

The animals that formed *herds* and the ones that formed flocks symbolize human attributes, as can be seen from explanations in §§45, 46, 142, 143, 246, 714, 715, 719, 776 of the first volume. See also the discussion of the animals used in sacrifices [in volume 2], §1823.

You may be surprised to hear that the animals named in the Word and those offered in sacrifice symbolized goodness and truth or, to say the same thing another way, heavenly and spiritual values. Let me say briefly why this is so.

[2] Various representative scenes appear in the world of spirits, and animals are often presented to the sight of the spirits there too. They include horses wearing different types of ornamental trappings, cattle, sheep, lambs, and other species—sometimes kinds never seen on earth—but they are simply representations. The prophets also saw animals like these (as mentioned in the Word), and they arose in the same way. The creatures that appear in the world of spirits represent different kinds of desire for goodness and truth and also for evil and falsity. Good spirits know exactly what they symbolize, and they also gather from them what the angels are discussing with each other. When angels' conversation floats down into the world of spirits, you see, it frequently manifests itself in this way. When horses appear, for instance, good spirits know that angels are talking about matters of intellect. When adult cattle and young cattle appear, they are talking about earthly kinds of goodness. When sheep do, they are talking about rational kinds of goodness and about integrity. When lambs do, they are talking about still deeper types of goodness and about innocence; and so on.

[3] The people of the earliest church communicated with spirits and angels and were constantly having visions and dreams like those of the prophets. For this reason, as soon as they saw an animal, an awareness of its symbolism immediately leapt to mind. This was the original source for their use of representation and symbolism, which survived a long while after their era ended. Eventually symbolism became revered so highly for its antiquity that authors wrote in a purely representative mode.

Books not written in this mode were dismissed as lacking worth, and even holiness (if they had been written in the church). Consequently—and as a result of other, secret causes that will be spoken of elsewhere [§§2558, 6516, 9407], with the Lord's divine mercy—the books of the Word were written in the same mode.

2180   *And took the young of an ox, tender and good* symbolizes something heavenly on the earthly plane, which his rationality procured for itself so that he would be able to unite with the perception received from his divine side. This can be seen from the scriptural symbolism of a young ox, or the *young of an ox,* as earthly goodness. Because this has to do with the Lord's rational mind, the ox is called *tender* (for its heavenly spirituality, or the truth that grows out of goodness) and *good* (for heavenliness itself, or goodness itself). Genuine rationality contains a desire for truth and a desire for goodness, but its primary ingredient is desire for truth, as shown before, in §2072. That is why "tender" comes first. As it usually does, though, the Word still mentions both, for the sake of the marriage between truth and goodness, which is discussed above in §2173.

[2] The symbolism of a *young ox* as something heavenly on the earthly plane—earthly goodness, in other words—stands out with special clarity from the sacrifices, which were the main representative acts of worship in the Hebrew church, and later in the Jewish. What were sacrificed were members either of the herd or of the flock, and so various kinds of clean animals: adult cattle, young cattle, he-goats, sheep, rams, she-goats, kids, and lambs, and in addition turtledoves and pigeon chicks.

All the sacrifices symbolized deeper dimensions of worship—that is, heavenly and spiritual dimensions (§§2165, 2177). Specifically, those involving herd animals symbolized heavenly qualities on the earthly plane, while those involving flock animals symbolized heavenly qualities on the rational plane. Both kinds—the earthly ones and the rational ones— occur at deeper and deeper levels and in various forms, which is why so many different genera and species of those animals were used in sacrifices. The same thing can also be seen from the rules laying out just what animals were to be offered in burnt offerings and in sacrifices of various kinds: daily, Sabbath, and feast day; freewill offerings, thanksgiving, and vows; atonement for guilt and sin; purification and cleansing; and ordination. The animals are explicitly named, as is the number of them to be used in each type of sacrifice, which would never have happened if each had not had its own symbolism. This is obvious to see in passages that discuss the sacrifices, such as Exodus 29; Leviticus 1, 3, 4, 9, 16, 23; Numbers 7, 8, 15, 29. This is not the place to explain the symbolism of each, however. The case is similar where the animals are mentioned in the Prophets. This evidence shows that young cattle symbolized heavenly qualities on the earthly plane.

[3] The fact that only heavenly things are symbolized can also be seen from the guardian beings seen by Ezekiel and from the living creatures that John saw before the throne. The prophet says this about the guardian beings:

> The likeness of their faces: the face of a human, and the face of a lion on the right for the four of them, and the *face of an ox* on the left for the four of them, and the face of an eagle for the four of them. (Ezekiel 1:10)

This is what John says about the four living creatures before the throne:

> Around the throne were four *living creatures;* the first *living creature* like a lion, the second *living creature like a young ox,* the third *living creature* having a face like a human, the fourth *living creature* like a flying eagle. They were saying, "Holy, holy, holy Lord God Almighty, who was and who is and who is to come." (Revelation 4:[6,] 7, 8)

Anyone can see that the guardian beings and these living creatures—including the ox and the young ox mentioned—represented something sacred. It is similar with the ones in Moses' prophecy concerning Joseph, of whom he says:

> Let [a blessing] come on the head of Joseph and on the crown of the head of the Nazirite among his brothers. The *firstborn* of his *ox* has honor, and the horns of the unicorn are his horn. With them he will strike all the peoples at once, to the ends of the earth. (Deuteronomy 33:16, 17)

No one could possibly understand these words without knowing what an ox, a unicorn, horns, and so on symbolize on an inner level.

[4] To take up sacrifices in general: It is true that they were demanded of the Israelite people by Moses, but the earliest church, which preceded the Flood, never knew anything about them. It never entered their minds to worship the Lord by slaughtering animals. The ancient church, which followed the Flood, was also ignorant of sacrifices. It did subscribe to

representative practices, but not to sacrifices. The first church to establish sacrifices was the next one, called the Hebrew church. From there the custom spread to the surrounding nations, from there again to Abraham, Isaac, and Jacob, and so to their descendants. Section 1343 showed that non-Jewish nations had sacrificial worship. So did Jacob's descendants before they left Egypt and therefore before Moses commanded sacrifices on Mount Sinai. This can be seen from Exodus 5:3; 10:25, 26; 18:12; 24:4, 5. [5] It is especially clear to see in their idolatry before the golden calf, which Moses reports on as follows:

> Aaron built an altar before the calf, and Aaron proclaimed and said, "A feast to Jehovah tomorrow!" And they got up the next morning and *offered burnt offerings* and *brought peace offerings.* And the people sat to eat and drink and got up to play. (Exodus 32:5, 6)

This happened while Moses was on Mount Sinai and so before any commandment concerning the altar and the sacrifices had reached them. The reason it came to be commanded was that their sacrificial worship had turned idolatrous, as it had among non-Jews. They could not be detached from this worship because they assigned supreme holiness to it. Once a thing has been implanted in us as holy during our childhood (especially if our forebears have implanted it) and so has taken root, the Lord refuses to break it but rather bends it, unless it violates the divine plan itself. This was the reason they were ordered to establish the sacrifices mentioned in the books of Moses. [6] Sacrifice was never welcome to Jehovah; he merely tolerated and put up with it for the reason given, as is plain to see in the Prophets. This is what Jeremiah says about the subject:

> Jehovah Sabaoth, the God of Israel, has said, "Add your burnt offerings to your sacrifices and eat the meat. *I did not speak to your ancestors or command them (on the day when I brought them out of the land of Egypt) concerning the matters of burnt offering and sacrifice,* but this word I commanded them, saying 'Obey my voice and I will become your God.'" (Jeremiah 7:21, 22, 23)

In David:

> Jehovah, *sacrifice and gift you have not wished for, burnt offering and sin sacrifices you have not sought.* I have desired to do your will, my God. (Psalms 40:6, 8)

In the same author:

> *You do not take pleasure in sacrifice, that I should give it; burnt offering*
> *you do not welcome.* The sacrifices of God are a chastened spirit. (Psalms
> 51:16, 17)

In the same author:

> *I will not accept a young ox from your house, he-goats from your folds.* Sac-
> rifice praise to God! (Psalms 50:9, 14; 107:21, 22; 116:17; Deuteronomy
> 33:19)

In Hosea:

> Mercy I wish for and *not sacrifice,* and the knowledge of God *rather*
> *than burnt offerings.* (Hosea 6:6)

Samuel said to Saul:

> *Does Jehovah take satisfaction in burnt offerings and sacrifices?* Look: sub-
> mission [is better] *than the sacrifice of oxen,* obedience *than the fat of*
> *rams.* (1 Samuel 15:22)

In Micah:

> With what am I to meet Jehovah [or] bow down to God on high? *Am*
> *I to meet him with burnt offerings, with calves that are offspring of a year?*
> Will Jehovah take satisfaction *in thousands of rams,* in myriads of tor-
> rents of oil? He has pointed out to you, friend, what is good and what
> Jehovah is requiring of you: merely to carry out judgment and love
> mercy and be humble walking with your God. (Micah 6:6, 7, 8)

[7] These passages now make it clear that sacrifices were not commanded
but tolerated. The only thing in the sacrifices that God paid attention
to was their inward intent; it was the inner content that was pleasing,
not what was happening on the outside. That is why the Lord abolished
them, as Daniel predicted in these words:

> In the middle of the week he will *put an end to sacrifice and oblation.*
> (Daniel 9:27)

This is about the Lord's Coming. See what was said about sacrifices in the
first two volumes, at §§922, 923, 1128, 1823.

As for the young of an ox that Abraham prepared for the three men,
its meaning was similar to that of the one used in sacrifices. The similarity

of its symbolism can be seen from Abraham's request to Sarah to take *three pecks* of flour. This is what Moses says about the proportion of flour to one young ox:

> When you come into the land: *When you prepare* the young of an ox as a burnt offering or sacrifice, calling it a vow or a peace offering to Jehovah, you shall offer on the *young of the ox* a minha of *flour—three tenths* [of an ephah] mixed with oil. (Numbers 15:[2,] 8, 9)

This passage likewise speaks of three: here, three tenths; there, three pecks. A ram, on the other hand, required only two tenths, and a lamb, one (Numbers 15:4, 5, 6).

2181   *And gave it to the houseboy, and he hurried to prepare the animal* symbolizes the union of goodness on the earthly plane with goodness on the rational plane; a *houseboy* is the earthly self. This can be seen from the meaning of a *houseboy* as one who serves and carries out orders. What he carries out or does is to *prepare* the young of the ox, which symbolizes earthly goodness, as shown.

To see better what the situation here is, you need to know that each person has an inner plane, an earthly plane, and a rational plane in between. These planes are different from each other. (For a discussion of them, see §§1889, 1940.) They need to harmonize closely enough to form a single whole, so rational-level goodness needs to harmonize with earthly-level goodness. Unless they harmonize and therefore unite, divine perception cannot exist. Since the subject here is the Lord's divine perception, on an inner level these images symbolize the harmony and union of the two.

2182   Genesis 18:8. *And [Abraham] took butter and milk and the young of an ox that he had prepared and placed it before them (and he was standing before them under the tree) and they ate.*

He took butter and milk and the young of an ox that he had prepared symbolizes all of them united in this way. *Butter* is the heavenly element of rationality; *milk* is the spiritual element that comes from it; and the *young of an ox* is something earthly that corresponds to these. *And placed it before them* means that this is how he readied himself to receive [the perception]. *And he was standing before them under the tree* symbolizes the perception that resulted; a *tree*, once more, is perception. *And they ate* symbolizes the communication that resulted.

2183   *He took butter and milk and the young of an ox that he had prepared* symbolizes all of them united in this way, as can be seen from the symbolism of *butter, milk,* and the *young of an ox,* discussed below.

The preceding verses spoke of the way the Lord's rational mind was equipped with heavenly qualities and with spiritual qualities growing out of them, symbolized by the flour-meal made into a cake (§§2176, 2177). They also spoke of heavenly qualities on the earthly plane, symbolized by the young of an ox (§2180). The same entities are now expressed with a different phrase—in terms of *butter* and *milk* and the *young of an ox,* which symbolize all of them united.

[2] It would be hard to describe them in a way most people could understand, though, because few realize that every person has an inner dimension, a rational dimension, and an earthly dimension. Few realize that these are very different from each other—so different, in fact, that they can disagree with one another. The rational dimension, which is called the rational self, can disagree with the physical or earthly dimension, which is the earthly self. The rational self can even see and perceive evil in the earthly self and (if it is truly rational) criticize it; see §1904.

Until the two come together, a person cannot be a whole person or enjoy peace and quiet, because each fights the other. The angels present with us govern our rational side, but the evil spirits present with us govern our earthly side, and this creates conflict. [3] If our *rational* side then wins, our earthly side is subdued, and as a result we receive the gift of conscience. If our *earthly* side wins, on the other hand, we become incapable of receiving conscience.

If our *rational* side wins, it is as if our earthly side then becomes rational too. If our *earthly* side wins, on the other hand, it is as if our rational side then becomes merely earthly.

Again, if our *rational* side wins, angels come closer to us and into us. They instill neighborly love into us, which is a heavenly quality that comes from the Lord by way of angels. Then evil spirits take themselves far away. However, if our *earthly* side wins, the angels move farther away. They shift more toward our deeper parts, but the evil spirits move closer to our rational mind and constantly attack it. They fill its lower reaches with hatred, vengefulness, deceit, and so on.

If our *rational* side wins, we gain peace and quiet, and heavenly peace in the next life. If our *earthly* side wins, though, things do seem quiet for as long as we live, but in the other life we enter into the unrest and agony of hell.

[4] This reveals what our situation is with regard to our rational side and our earthly side.

There is nothing, then, that can render us blessed and happy but an earthly side that matches or harmonizes with our rational side, and a union of the two. Only charity can unite them, and charity comes only from the Lord.

2184   *Butter* is the heavenly element of rationality; *milk* is the spiritual element that comes from it; and the *young of an ox* is something earthly that corresponds to these. This can be seen from the symbolism of *butter,* of *milk,* and of the *young of an ox.*

As for *butter,* in the Word it symbolizes something heavenly, because of its fat content. The first volume demonstrated that fat is a heavenly quality (§353) and that because oil is a fat it is heavenliness itself (§886). Butter is too, as Isaiah shows:

> Here, now, the virgin will deliver a child, and she will call his name Immanuel. He will eat *butter* and *honey,* in order to know to spurn what is evil and choose what is good. (Isaiah 7:14, 15)

This has to do with the Lord, who is Immanuel. Anyone can see that the butter does not mean butter, nor the honey, honey. Butter symbolizes his heavenly nature, while honey symbolizes what comes of that nature. [2] In the same author:

> And it will happen on account of the abundance of *milk*-making that he will eat *butter,* since *butter* and honey are what everyone who is left in the middle of the land will eat. (Isaiah 7:22)

This is about the Lord's kingdom and about people on earth who are in the Lord's kingdom. The milk stands for spiritual goodness; the butter, for heavenly goodness; and the honey, for the happiness they yield. [3] In Moses:

> Jehovah alone leads them, and there is no foreign god with them. He makes them ride on the heights of the earth and feeds them with the produce of the fields and makes them suck honey from rock, and oil from a flinty crag; the *butter of the herd* and the *milk of the flock,* together with the fat of lambs and of rams—the sons of Bashan—and of goats, together with the fat of the kidneys of wheat; and the blood of the grape you will drink as unmixed wine. (Deuteronomy 32:12, 13, 14)

No one can understand these images without knowing the inner meaning of each. The passage looks like a jumble of the kinds of phrases clever people use in their oratory. Each part, however, symbolizes a heavenly attribute, or something spiritual resulting from it, or the bliss and happiness these produce, one following the other in an elegant series. Butter of the herd is something heavenly on the earthly level as it exists in the rational mind; milk of the flock is something heavenly on the spiritual level as it exists there.

[4] As for *milk,* it symbolizes a spiritual attribute that comes of a heavenly one, or something heavenly on the spiritual level, as noted. For the definition of a heavenly-spiritual attribute, see §§1577, 1824, and quite a few other sections in volumes 1 and 2. The reason milk is a spiritual attribute that comes from a heavenly one is that water symbolizes what is spiritual (§§680, 739), but milk contains fat, so it symbolizes what is heavenly-spiritual. To say the same thing in other ways, it symbolizes truth that comes of goodness; faith that comes of love or charity; an intellectual grasp of the good things we will; a desire for truth that harbors a desire for good. To put it yet another way, it symbolizes a desire for knowledge on all levels springing from a feeling of charity for our neighbor. This is the type of desire we have when we love knowledge because we love our neighbor and use both religious knowledge and secular facts to strengthen ourselves in that love. Each of these is the same thing as a heavenly-spiritual attribute, and the subject at hand determines which one applies.

This symbolism of milk is also clear in the Word, [5] as in Isaiah:

> Everyone who is thirsty, come to the *water,* and whoever does not have silver, come, buy and eat! And come, without silver and without the price buy *wine and milk!* Why do you weigh out silver for what is not bread? (Isaiah 55:1, 2)

The wine stands for the spiritual side of faith; the milk, for the spiritual side of love. In Moses:

> He washed his garment in wine and his raiment in the blood of grapes. He had eyes redder than wine and *teeth whiter than milk.* (Genesis 49:11, 12)

This is the prophecy of Jacob (who by now was Israel) concerning Judah, and in it Judah depicts the Lord. "Teeth whiter than milk" symbolizes a heavenly-spiritual element in his earthly part. [6] In Joel:

> It will happen on that day that the mountains will shower down new wine, and the *hills will run with milk,* and all the brooks of Judah will run with *water.* (Joel 3:18)

This is about the Lord's kingdom, and the milk stands for what is heavenly-spiritual. The land of Canaan also represents and symbolizes the Lord's kingdom, and in the Word it is called a land flowing with milk and honey, as in Numbers 13:27; 14:8; Deuteronomy 26:9, 15; 27:3; Jeremiah 11:5; 32:22; Ezekiel 20:6, 15. The milk in these passages actually means heavenly-spiritual qualities in abundance, while the honey actually means the abundant happiness they yield. The land is the heavenly quality itself of that kingdom, which is the source of these blessings.

[7] As for the *young of an ox,* §2180 just above showed that it symbolizes something heavenly on the earthly plane, which is the same thing as earthly goodness, or goodness in our earthly part. Our earthly dimension, like our rational dimension, has its own goodness and its own truth (since the marriage of goodness and truth permeates everything, as noted above at §2173). The goodness that exists on the earthly plane is the satisfaction we take in charity, or in the friendship that characterizes charity. This satisfaction gives rise to a feeling of pleasure that, strictly speaking, belongs to the body. The truth that exists on the earthly plane is composed of facts that help us achieve that satisfaction. This shows what something heavenly on the earthly plane is.

2185   *And placed it before them* means that this is how he readied himself to receive [the perception]. This can be seen from the inner-level symbolism of *placing before them* in a passage speaking of the way the [Lord's] rational mind was being prepared to receive perception from his divine side. So it can be seen without further explanation.

2186   *And he was standing before them under the tree* symbolizes the perception that resulted. This follows from the symbolism of a *tree* as perception (discussed in §§103, 2163).

Above at verse 4, the three men who came to Abraham reclined under a tree, and it was said that this meant the Lord's divine side would move closer to his perceptive ability in the state he was then in [§2160]. Here, though, it says that Abraham stood under the tree, which means that the Lord moved closer to divine perception after he had prepared himself—a responding move of his own.

Anyone can see that the three men and Abraham would not both have been described as standing under the tree for no reason. They were described that way, then, for the sake of secrets lying hidden in the words.

2187   *And they ate* symbolizes the communication that resulted. This can be seen from the symbolism of *eating* as being communicated and also united—another symbolism evident in the Word.

The food consecrated by sacrifice that Aaron, his sons, the Levites, and the people ate in a holy place actually symbolized what is communicated to us, binds us together, and becomes our own. (This was said above at §2177 at the passage from Leviticus 6:16, 17.) Heavenly and spiritual nourishment was what the consecrated food they were eating symbolized, so [eating it symbolized] making it their own. The consecrated food came from the sacrifices that were not burned on the altar, and it was eaten either by the priests or by the people who had offered it. The many places that deal with sacrifices make this clear. Exodus 29:32, 33; Leviticus 6:16, 26; 7:6, 15, 16, 18; 8:31; 10:12, 13; and Numbers 18:9, 10, 11 say what the priests were to eat. Leviticus 19:5, 6; Deuteronomy 12:27; 27:7 and other passages tell what the people were to eat. Leviticus 7:19, 20, 21; and 22:4, 5, 6, 7 prohibited unclean people from eating it. The feasts were held in a holy place next to the altar, either at the doorway or in the courtyard of the tabernacle. Again, they simply symbolized heavenly kinds of good that are communicated to us, bind us together, and become our own, because they represented heavenly food. For a definition of heavenly food, see §§56, 57, 58, 680, 681, 1480, 1695. All of them were called *bread,* for the symbolism of which, see above at §2165. The fact that Aaron and his sons ate the loaves of showbread (or bread of presence) in a holy place (Leviticus 24:9) represented something similar.

[2] A law was laid down for Nazirites that they should not eat anything that came out of the wine-producing grape, from berries to skin, during the days of their Naziriteship (Numbers 6:4). The reason was that a Nazirite represented a heavenly person, and heavenly people by their very nature do not like even to mention spiritual things, as may be seen in §§202, 337, 880 (at the end), 1647 of the first two volumes. Wine and grapes and everything made from grapes symbolized something spiritual, so Nazirites were forbidden to eat any of it. In other words, they were forbidden to have any communication with it, unite with it, or make it their own. [3] Eating has a similar meaning in Isaiah:

> Everyone who is thirsty, come to the *water,* and whoever does not have silver, come, buy and eat! And come, without silver and without the price buy wine and milk! Why do you weigh out silver for what is not *bread* and labor for what does not *satisfy?* Listen closely to me and *eat what is good,* and your soul will revel in the fat. (Isaiah 55:1, 2)

So does the following instance in John:

Those who conquer I will grant to *eat from the tree of life* that is in the middle of God's paradise. (Revelation 2:7)

The tree of life is heavenliness itself and in the highest sense the Lord himself, since he is the source of everything heavenly, or in other words, of all love and charity. Eating from the tree of life, then, is the same as feeding on the Lord, and feeding on the Lord is receiving the gift of love and charity. So it is receiving the ingredients of heavenly life. As the Lord himself says in John:

"I am the *living bread* who came down from heaven; if any *eat of this bread,* they will live forever. Those who *feed on me,* they will live through me." (John 6:51, 57)

But they said, "This saying is hard." But Jesus said, "The words that I am speaking to you are spirit and are life." (John 6:60, 63)

This shows what eating means in the Holy Supper (Matthew 26:26, 27, 28; Mark 14:22, 23; Luke 22:19, 20); specifically, having communication, uniting, and taking things into oneself.

[4] These considerations also clarify what it means that the Lord said, "Many will come from east and west and *recline at [the table]* with Abraham, Isaac, and Jacob" (Matthew 8:11). The meaning is not that they will eat with them in God's kingdom but that they will enjoy the heavenly goodness symbolized by Abraham, Isaac, and Jacob. They will enjoy the deepest heavenly qualities of love (Abraham); lower ones, which are intermediate, like those of the rational mind (Isaac); and still lower ones, which are heavenly qualities of the earthly kind that exist in the first heaven (meant by Jacob). That is the inner sense of these words. The fact that Abraham, Isaac, and Jacob are these types of goodness may be seen in §1893 and everywhere else that they are discussed. It is all the same whether you speak of benefiting from that heavenly goodness or of benefiting from the Lord, whom the patriarchs represent; all heavenly goodness comes from the Lord, and the Lord is its all in all.

2188   Genesis 18:9. *And they said to him, "Where is Sarah, your wife?" and he said, "Look—she is in the tent."*

They said to him, "Where is Sarah, your wife?" means that rational-level truth was not visible at that point, because the Lord had achieved rational-level goodness. *And he said, "Look—she is in the tent,"* means that he was in a holy state.

They said to him, "Where is Sarah, your wife?" means that rational- **2189**
level truth was not visible at that point, because the Lord had achieved
rational-level goodness. This can be seen from the representation here of
Sarah as rational truth (discussed earlier at §2173).

What is the situation here and in what follows, where the state of the
Lord's rational mind (represented by Sarah) is the focus? This cannot be
explained intelligibly unless you know how things stand overall with the
state of the rational mind in regard to both goodness and truth. You also
need to know how things stood with the Lord's rational mind in regard to
both his divinity and the humanity then foremost in his consciousness.

[2] Rationality in a person begins with truth, as noted before, at §2072,
so it begins with a desire for truth. Truth comes first so that we can reform
and consequently regenerate. Religious and secular knowledge, which are
aspects of truth, are the means. They are constantly being grafted onto
goodness, that is, onto charity, so that we can receive a life of charity.
That is why the desire for truth predominates in our rational mind. The
fact of the matter is that in people who are reforming and regenerating, a
life of charity—heavenly life itself—is constantly being born and matur-
ing. It grows by means of truth, so the more truth we absorb, the more
fully we live a life of charity. *Charity in a human heart depends on the type
and amount of truth the person has.*

[3] These considerations to some extent show how the case stands
with human rationality.

Truth, however, does not contain life; goodness does. Truth merely
receives life, or in other words, receives goodness. Truth is like a covering or garment for goodness, so in the Word it is also called a covering or
clothing. When rationality actually consists of goodness, though, truth
disappears and seems to turn into goodness. Goodness then shines out
through truth. This is what happens with angels. When they appear in
clothes, radiance is what creates the illusion of a garment, as it also did
with the angels that the prophets saw.

[4] This, then, is what is meant by saying that rational-level truth
was not visible at that point, because the Lord had achieved rational-level
goodness—the symbolism of "They said to him, 'Where is Sarah, your
wife?'"

However, the Lord's rational-level goodness was then divine, which it
cannot be in any angel, so it can be described only by comparisons. It
needs to be illustrated by analogy with something similar but not identical.

2190   *He said, "Look—she is in the tent,"* means that he was in a holy state. This is established by the symbolism of a *tent* as holiness, which was dealt with in §§414, 1102, 1566, 2145. He is said to have been in a holy state because he was in a state of goodness. Anything good is described as holy because it partakes of love and charity, which come from the Lord alone.

The nature of the holiness, though, depends on the nature of the goodness. Goodness is formed, or in other words, born and raised, through religious truth, so its character is determined by the type and amount of religious truth grafted onto charity, as noted directly above at §2189. From this it can be seen that goodness, or holiness, differs from individual to individual. Although it looks similar on the outside, it is dissimilar on the inside, both with those outside the church and with those inside.

The good that comes of charity in us has more inside it than we could ever believe. Every aspect of our faith is contained in it, so every aspect of our faith is contained in the holy feelings we have during worship. The nature of our reverence in worship appears clear as day to the angels, even though all we are aware of is that we feel something vaguely holy. Millions of thoughts we have about religious goodness and truth and millions of feelings that result from the thoughts are present in our reverence.

More will be said elsewhere [§5459], however, about the general nature of reverence in worship, the Lord in his divine mercy willing.

2191   Genesis 18:10. *And [the man] said, "I will definitely return to you about this time of life. And look: a son for Sarah your wife!" And Sarah was listening at the door of the tent, and it was behind him.*

And he said symbolizes a perception. *I will definitely return to you about this time of life* symbolizes the union of divinity with the Lord's humanity. *And look: a son for Sarah your wife* symbolizes the divine rationality yet to come. *And Sarah was listening at the door of the tent* symbolizes rational truth that then stood near holiness. *And it was behind him* means near the goodness then occupying his rational mind and therefore separated from that goodness so far as it had something human in it.

2192   The symbolism of *and he said* as a perception can be seen from the symbolism of *saying* on the narrative level as perceiving, a symbolism discussed previously at §§1898, 1919, 2080.

2193   *I will definitely return to you about this time of life* symbolizes the union of divinity with humanity. This can be seen from the fact that Jehovah's coming to Abraham represented divine perception, which the Lord prepared himself to receive. So it represented union, as shown above

[§§2181–2183]. The fact that Jehovah would *definitely return to him,* then, has the same symbolism: union of divinity with humanity.

At this time of life means at the same time next year.

Look: a son for Sarah your wife symbolizes the divine rationality yet to come, as can be seen from the symbolism of a *son,* of *Sarah,* and of *Isaac,* who was to be born to her. Both a son and Sarah, and Isaac as well, symbolize some aspect of the Lord's rationality. A *son* symbolizes truth (see §§489, 491, 533, 1147); *Sarah* symbolizes rational truth (§2173); and *Isaac* symbolizes divine rationality (§§1893, 2066, 2083).

2194

The humanity in each of us germinates in the deepest part of our rational mind, as mentioned at §2106. The Lord's humanity did too. Everything above that level was Jehovah himself, unlike the higher levels in any other person.

Since humanity begins in the deepest part of the rational mind, and since the Lord made all the humanity in him divine, he started at the deepest point of his true rationality in transforming it. Isaac, as noted, represents and symbolizes his rationality once it had become divine.

And Sarah was listening at the door of the tent symbolizes rational truth that then stood near holiness, as can be seen from the following: *Sarah* represents rational truth, as treated of at §§2173, 2194. A *tent* symbolizes holiness, as treated of at §§414, 1102, 1566, 2145. So the *door of a tent* symbolizes entry to holiness, and therefore nearness to what is holy, as mentioned above at §2145. An explanation of these things now follows.

2195

And it was behind him means near the goodness then occupying his rational mind but separated from that goodness so far as something human remained in it. This can be seen from the fact that the door Sarah was standing in was said to be behind the man. *It was behind him* means that it was not united to him but lay at his back. What is separated from a person is represented by something more or less discarded behind the person's back. This can be seen from representations in the other world, described from experience in §§1393, 1875. The same idea is now expressed by the fact that the door where Sarah stood was behind the man.

2196

[2] The merely human rational truth then present in the Lord was separated from him when he united with his divinity, and this is why: Human rational truth does not grasp divine concepts, because they lie above the reach of its intellect. This kind of truth maintains ties with the facts our earthly self possesses. So far as it scrutinizes concepts that lie beyond it from the viewpoint of facts, it refuses to acknowledge those

concepts. Human rational truth, you see, becomes tangled up in appearances, unable to rid itself of them, and appearances are the product of sense impressions. The senses persuade us to believe that divine truth itself is exactly the same as appearances, when in reality it is free of all appearances. When divine concepts are put into words, this rational truth simply cannot believe them, because it does not comprehend them. Here are examples:

[3] Humans have no life except what the Lord gives them. On the basis of appearances, the rational mind thinks this means we cannot have any life that seems to be our own. The reality is that we truly come to life for the first time when we perceive that life comes from the Lord.

[4] On the basis of appearances, the rational mind thinks the good we do originates in us. The reality is that nothing good comes from us but from the Lord.

[5] On the basis of appearances, the rational mind thinks we earn salvation by doing good. The reality is that we cannot earn anything on our own; all the credit is the Lord's.

[6] On the basis of appearances, when the Lord withholds us from an evil path and keeps us on a good one, we think everything in us is good, just, and even holy. The reality is that everything in us is bad, unjust, and profane.

[7] On the basis of appearances, when charity inspires us to do good, we think we are acting from the willpower in us. The reality is that we are acting not from our willpower but from our intellect, which has charity planted in it.

[8] On the basis of appearances, we think there is no glory without worldly glory. The reality is that heaven's glory contains none of the world's glory.

[9] On the basis of appearances, we think none of us can love our neighbor more than ourselves, that all love begins with ourselves. The reality is that heavenly love has no self-love in it.

[10] On the basis of appearances, we think no light can exist that does not stem from the light of this world. The reality is that not a gleam of the world's light exists in the heavens, and yet the light there is so great that it surpasses the noonday light here by a thousand times.

[11] On the basis of appearances, we think the Lord cannot shine like the sun on all of heaven. The reality is that all of heaven's light comes from him.

[12] On the basis of appearances, we cannot imagine that people move around in the other world. The reality is that they seem to themselves to

move around in their dwellings, courtyards, and luxuriant gardens exactly the way we do on earth. Still less can we understand it if we hear that what looks like physical movement is really change in a person's state.

[13] On the basis of appearances, we also cannot fathom how spirits and angels invisible to the eye could appear or speak to anyone. The reality is that the inner eye—the eye of the spirit—sees them more clearly than we see each other on earth. The same with the audibility of their speech, not to mention thousands upon thousands of other realities that our rational mind can never see by its own meager light, which flows from the evidence of the senses and is therefore clouded.

In fact, our rational ability is blind even to earthly realities. It cannot comprehend, for instance, how inhabitants directly on the opposite side of the earth can stay on their feet and walk around, not to mention many other paradoxes. What then of spiritual and heavenly mysteries that lie far beyond the physical world?

[14] This being the nature of human rationality, it is here said to have been removed when the Lord was at one with his divinity at a time of divine perception. Such is the symbolism of the statement that Sarah (who is human rational truth here) stood at the door of the tent, which was behind the man.

Genesis 18:11. *And Abraham and Sarah were old, advancing in days; the way it is with women had ceased to be with Sarah.*

2197

Abraham and Sarah were old means that the humanity in the Lord would be stripped away. *Advancing in days* means that the time was at hand. *The way it is with women had ceased to be with Sarah* means a state of true rationality—the fact that it could no longer remain the same.

Abraham and Sarah were old means that the humanity in the Lord would be stripped away, as can be seen from the representation of *Abraham* and *Sarah* and the symbolism of *old people* or old age. *Abraham* here represents goodness on the Lord's rational plane, while *Sarah* represents truth on the Lord's rational plane, as noted several times before in the current chapter [§§2172–2173, 2189, 2194, 2195, 2196]. So they both represent the humanity in the Lord here, for the reason given above [§2172]: Jehovah was now present and talking to Abraham. Jehovah was the divinity itself in the Lord, which was not separate from him, even though it is being presented as separate in this representative story. It cannot be represented any other way in a story.

2198

[2] The statement that Abraham and Sarah were *old*, though, means that this humanity would be stripped away. Old age actually means a final stage. The Word frequently speaks of old age and also of peoples'

death, but the kind of old age and death that the body goes through is never perceived on an inner level. Something else that becomes evident from the sequence of ideas is perceived instead, because in the other life they do not know what old age or death is. The meaning perceived here can be seen from the sequence, as noted: the Lord would rid himself of his human side.

2199   *Advancing in days* means that the time was at hand, as follows from the above. A *day* in the Word symbolizes a state or condition, as does a year and even time in general. This was shown in §§23, 487, 488, 493, 893. On an inner level, then, *advancing in days* here means advancing to a state in which he would lay aside his humanity, so it means the time was at hand.

2200   *The way it is with women had ceased to be with Sarah* means that it could no longer remain the same. This can be seen from the remarks just made and so needs no explanation.

2201   Genesis 18:12. *And Sarah laughed within herself, saying, "After I have aged, will there be pleasure for me? And my lord is old."*
     Sarah laughed within herself symbolizes the emotional response that type of rational truth had to this event. *Saying, "After I have aged, will there be pleasure for me?"* means that type of truth did not like conditions to change. *"And my lord is old"* means the desire for truth was amazed at the way rational-level goodness (with truth attached to it) would shed its human side.

2202   *Sarah laughed within herself* symbolizes the emotional response that type of rational truth had to this event. This can be seen from the symbolism of *laughing* or laughter as the emotional response of truth, which was discussed above at §2072. An explanation of the ideas involved in these words now follows.

2203   *Saying, "After I have aged, will there be pleasure for me?"* means that type of truth did not like conditions to change, as can be seen from the following: *Aging* symbolizes laying aside the human part and therefore experiencing a change in condition, as discussed above at §2198. *Will there be pleasure for me?* means not wanting it. In other words, this was not its desire.
     What the case is here can be seen from the remarks above at §2196 about Sarah's standing at the tent door, which was behind the man. In other words, the truth present in human rationality is by its very nature incapable of understanding what a divine thought is, because it focuses on appearances. What it cannot understand it also fails to believe, and what it fails to believe does not touch it emotionally. The appearances in which our rational mind immerses itself are such that they do touch

it, because there is pleasure in the appearances themselves. If the rational mind were deprived of appearances, then, it would think that all pleasure was at an end. In reality, however, heavenly emotions are present not in appearances but in genuine goodness and truth. Because this is the nature of rational truth, it is excused for the shortcoming and allowed to remain under the sway of appearances, taking pleasure in them.

At a point when the Lord had bonded with his divinity, this kind of truth, which was immersed in appearances, was represented by Sarah. So the text says that she stood at the door and that she laughed and said, "After I have aged, will there be pleasure for me?" meaning that rational truth did not like conditions to change.

My lord is old means the desire for truth was amazed at the way rational-level goodness (with truth attached to it) would shed its human side, as the following establishes: Abraham, who is *my lord* here, represents goodness on the rational level at this point. Sarah represents truth on the rational level, as I said above at §2198 and elsewhere. And *aging* means shedding the human side, as I also said at §2198.

2204

Human goodness on the rational plane is such that it contains much worldly pleasure, because it is formed not only out of truth but also out of sensory pleasures and many other kinds of pleasure the world provides. When we are reforming and being reborn, the Lord weaves spiritual goodness into these pleasures, which then modifies the worldly element. Afterward we find our happiness in it.

The Lord, on the other hand, expelled absolutely everything of the world from his rational mind and in this way made it divine. That is what rational truth (meant by Sarah) was amazed at.

Genesis 18:13. *And Jehovah said to Abraham, "Why did Sarah laugh at this, saying, 'Will I really, truly give birth, when I have aged?'"*

2205

Jehovah said to Abraham symbolizes a perception the Lord had from his divine part. *Why did Sarah laugh at this?* symbolizes the way rational truth was thinking as a result of its emotions. *Will I really, truly give birth?* means this truth was amazed that the rational dimension would become divine. *When I have aged* means after it ceased to be what it had been.

Jehovah said to Abraham symbolizes a perception the Lord had from his divine part, as the following shows: *Saying* symbolizes perceiving, as discussed before in §§1898, 1919, 2080. And *Jehovah said* means perceiving from divinity. As shown quite often already, the real inner core of the Lord was Jehovah.

2206

Why did Sarah laugh at this? symbolizes the way rational truth was thinking as a result of its emotions, as can be seen from the following: *Laughing*

2207

or laughter symbolizes the emotional response of truth, as discussed above at §2072. And *Sarah* represents rational truth, as mentioned several times before in the current chapter [§§2172–2173, 2189, 2194, 2195, 2196, 2204].

This question involves the Lord's perception that something human lingered in his rationality.

2208   *Will I really, truly give birth?* means this truth was amazed that the rational dimension would become divine, as the inner-level symbolism here of *giving birth* shows. The Lord's divine rationality is represented by Isaac, as has been noted before and will become clear below [§§1893, 2066, 2083, 2194, 2632, 2658], so giving birth here symbolizes Isaac, or in other words, the fact that the Lord's rational dimension would become divine. The rational truth represented by Sarah could not comprehend this.

2209   *When I have aged* means after it ceased to be what it had been—human rather than divine. This symbolism and the fact that the human part would be stripped away can be seen from the symbolism of *aging* as discarding the human part, a symbolism mentioned above at §§2198, 2203.

To speak of rationality in general: When it delves into divine subjects, particularly on the basis of the truth it possesses, it cannot believe at all that matters really stand the way they do. For one thing it does not understand divine things. For another, appearances arising from the illusions of the senses cling tight, and the rational mind thinks in terms of those illusions and on the basis of them. This fact can be seen from the examples produced above at §2196. For the sake of illustration, let me add the following too.

[2] If the rational mind is consulted, can it believe that the Word has an inner meaning? One as remote from the literal meaning as I have shown? That the Word is therefore what unites heaven with earth, or in other words, what unites the Lord's kingdom in the heavens with his kingdom on earth?

Souls after death talk to each other clearly and distinctly and yet without using words. Even without words their speech is so comprehensive that they can say more in a minute than we can in an hour of our own speech. This is true of angels too, although their speech is even more complete, and is imperceptible to spirits. All souls come into the other life already knowing how to talk this way, though never taught the method. Is the rational mind capable of believing any of this?

Nor can it believe that angels perceive more in a single human emotion and in fact a single human sigh than can ever be expressed; that each of our emotions and in fact each of our individual thoughts holds an image of us within it; that this image miraculously holds every moment of our life within it; not to mention thousands upon thousands of other considerations like these.

[3] The rational mind gains its wisdom from sensory information and is steeped in the illusions produced by sense impressions. When it thinks about ideas like the ones above, it cannot believe they are so. That is because it is completely unable to form thoughts for itself unless it bases them on the kinds of information it perceives by some outward or inward sensation. Imagine, then, what happens when it considers divinely heavenlike or divinely spiritual notions, which are still higher! Our thought processes will always need at least some sense-based appearances to lean on. When those appearances are taken away, thought dies. Newly arrived spirits have made this clear to me, with their intense pleasure in the appearances they have brought with them from the world. They say that if these appearances were taken from them, they do not know whether they would be capable of thought.

Such is the rational mind viewed in itself.

Genesis 18:14. *"Will anything be [too] amazing for Jehovah? At the set time I will come back to you, about this time of life; and to Sarah, a son."*

Will anything be [too] amazing for Jehovah? means that anything is possible for Jehovah. *At the set time I will come back to you* symbolizes a future condition. *About this time of life; and to Sarah, a son* means that the Lord would then lay aside human rationality and put on divine rationality.

Will anything be [too] amazing for Jehovah? means that anything is possible for Jehovah, as is clear without explanation.

At the set time I will come back to you symbolizes a future condition. This can be seen from the symbolism of *time* as a condition or state, as noted above in §2199.

Here it says that Jehovah would come back *at the set time* and afterward that he would come *at this time of life,* or in other words, at the same time next year. Each involves something special. "The set time" means the overall nature of the condition symbolized by "this time of life." The overall nature of it is that it has yet to come, but how it will come is symbolized by "this time of life."

It is common for the Word—especially the Prophets—to describe states by the use of two terms that appear similar, when in reality one involves a general idea, while the other involves a narrowing down of the general idea.

2210

2211

2212

2213 *About this time of life; and to Sarah, a son* means that the Lord would then lay aside human rationality and put on divine rationality, as can be seen from the following: Returning *at this time of life,* or at the same time next year, symbolizes the union of the Lord's divinity with his humanity, as mentioned above in §2193. A *son to Sarah* symbolizes the divine rationality yet to come, which is also dealt with above, in §2194.

"This time of life," or the same time the following year, points to a time when Abraham would enter his hundredth year. The hundredth year symbolizes the union of the Lord's humanity with his divinity and of his divinity with his humanity, as shown above at §1988. A year now came in between, because in the Word a year means not a year but an entire period and so a whole span of time, whether it is a thousand years, or a hundred, or ten, or just a few hours. This was also demonstrated earlier, at §§482, 487, 488, 493, 893. The same is true of a week, as discussed at §2044.

2214 Genesis 18:15. *And Sarah denied it, saying, "I did not laugh," because she was afraid. And he said, "No, because you did laugh."*

And Sarah denied it, saying, "I did not laugh," because she was afraid means that human rational truth wanted to justify itself, because it sensed that it was not what it ought to be. *And he said, "No, because you did laugh,"* means it really was not quite right.

2215 *Sarah denied it, saying, "I did not laugh," because she was afraid* means that human rational truth wanted to justify itself, because it sensed that it was not what it ought to be. This is evident without explanation.

2216 *He said, "No, because you did laugh,"* means it really was not quite right, as is also evident without explanation.

The discussion above at §2072 about the symbolism of *laughing* or laughter can show how matters stand here. Laughter symbolizes an emotional response on the part of the rational mind, more specifically the rational mind's response to truth or falsity, which is the source of all amusement. As long as the emotion expressing itself in laughter stays on the rational level, it remains a bodily or worldly response and therefore a merely human one. Heavenly goodness and spiritual goodness do not laugh but have other ways of publishing their delight and good humor in look, word, and act. Laughter, after all, is complex. Usually it contains an element of contempt that may not show but still underlies the laughter. This mirth distinguishes itself clearly from high spirits, which also produce something like a laugh.

The state of the Lord's human rationality is depicted in Sarah's laughter, which symbolized the emotion with which the truth in his rational mind (separated at that point from goodness) regarded what was being said. What was being said was that human rationality would be taken off and divine rationality put on. Not that the truth in his rational mind laughed, but that his divine side gave it the perception to see what it was still like and how much of what was human remained, needing to be expelled. That is what Sarah's laughter symbolizes on an inner level.

Genesis 18:16. *And the men rose up from there and looked out toward the face of Sodom. And Abraham was going with them, to send them off.*   **2217**

The men rose up from there means that this perception came to an end. *And looked out toward the face of Sodom* symbolizes the condition of the human race; *Sodom* is every evil that comes of self-love. *And Abraham was going with them* means that the Lord, still present with the three, continued to have perceptions too, but the focus shifted to the human race. *To send them off* means that he wanted to get away from these perceptions.

The men rose up means that this perception came to an end. This can   **2218** be seen from the symbolism of *rising up* as leaving, and from that of the *men* as discussed above.

The coming of the three men (Jehovah) to Abraham represented the Lord's divine perception, as shown above. The perception the Lord received from his divine side at that time focused first on the divine Trinity, which is divinity itself, divine humanity, and their influence. Next the focus turned to the humanity in him, which was to put on divinity. Now there follows a perception from his divine part concerning the nature of the human race.

These three subjects are the topics of discussion in the current chapter, and they follow in sequence. That is to say, divinity took on a human side and made it divine in order to save the human race.

The Lord's perception concerning the first two subjects is what is being said to have ended, and this is what the rising of the men means in an inner sense. Their looking out toward the face of Sodom as Abraham went with them symbolizes, on an inner level, his perception concerning the nature of the human race. His going with them to send them off symbolizes his reluctance to remain in that perception. How all of this stands is clearer to see in the summary at the beginning of this chapter [§2140] and in the explanation of what follows.

They looked out toward the face of Sodom symbolizes the condition of   **2219** the human race, as can be seen from the symbolism of *looking out toward the face,* and here, *toward the face of Sodom.*

A *face* symbolizes everything inside us, both bad and good, because those things shine out from our face, as shown in §358 of the first volume. Here, since it is *the face of Sodom,* it symbolizes the inner evil that comes of self-love. This is the evil meant generally by Sodom, as the next section will make clear.

The worst evils of all trace their origin to self-love, because self-love is what destroys human society (as shown above at §2045) and heavenly society (§2057). Since the corruption of the human race is recognized by its self-serving evil, the face of Sodom here symbolizes the state of the human race.

[2] In addition, various sections in the first two volumes demonstrated what self-love is like: directly opposed to the divine pattern in which we were created [§§301, 987]. We have been given more rationality than animals so that we can wish each other well and do each other good, individually as well as collectively. This is the pattern we were created in. Love for God and for our neighbor constitute that pattern, then, and [if we lived by it] they would be our life, distinguishing us from brute animals. Love is also the pattern of heaven, which we would inhabit while living in the world. Inhabiting heaven means inhabiting the Lord's kingdom— the same kingdom we would pass into upon shedding the body that had served us on earth. There we would rise into an ever more perfect heavenly state.

[3] Self-love is the chief agent, in fact the only agent, that destroys these goals. Materialism is not as much to blame. It is true that materialism is directly opposed to the spiritual qualities of faith, but self-love is directly opposed to the heavenly qualities of love. Those of us who love ourselves do not love anyone else but work to destroy everyone who fails to worship us. We wish well and do well to no one but a subordinate, or someone who can be enticed into subordination, like some twig grafted onto our appetites and delusions. These considerations make it clear that love for ourselves is the wellspring of all kinds of hatred, vengefulness, and cruelty, and all kinds of horrendous deceit and fraud. So it is the wellspring of every unspeakable assault on the proper order of human society and the proper order of heavenly society.

[4] In fact, self-love is so degenerate that when the restraints on it are let loose—when given the opportunity to expand (especially in the worst type of people)—it runs so wild that it makes us want to control not only our neighbors and fellow citizens but the universe and even the supreme Deity himself. We do not know about this tendency, it is true, because we are bound by restraints we are mostly unaware of, but so far as the chains are undone, as noted, we go berserk. A great deal of experience [of people] in the other world has taught me this.

Because these traits lie hidden in self-love, people who love themselves and lack the bonds of conscience also hate the Lord more than anyone else does. They hate all religious truth too, since religious truths are the actual laws of order in the Lord's kingdom. Such people spurn them to the point of loathing them, which also makes itself obvious in the other life. What is more, self-love is the snake's head that the woman's seed (the Lord) tramples; for more on the subject, see §257 of the first volume.

[5] Self-love, however, is not always a love that looks outwardly like pride and arrogance, because sometimes people who seem proud and arrogant can actually feel charity for their neighbor. Some are born with that outward attitude, and some acquire it during their youth but later bring it under control, although it remains. The people who have real self-love are those who hold others in contempt and consider them worthless by comparison with themselves. They have no concern at all for the common good unless it benefits themselves, or unless they themselves *are* the common good, so to speak. Above all, they hate any who will not coddle and serve them; they persecute such people and, so far as they can, rob them of their belongings, position, reputation, and even life. If you plot things like this in your heart, be aware that you have more self-love than most.

The fact that *Sodom* is every evil that comes of self-love can be seen from the symbolism of Sodom in the Word. In the next chapter it seems as if Sodom symbolizes the evil of a vile form of adultery, yet in an inner sense it actually means the evil that comes of self-love. In the Word, abominations that well up out of self-love are represented by different kinds of adultery.

2220

In the second volume, §§1212, 1663, 1682, 1689 showed that Sodom symbolizes every evil in general that comes of self-love, while Gomorrah symbolizes every accompanying falsity, and the following passages in Scripture add evidence. In Jeremiah:

> "A sword upon the Chaldeans and on the inhabitants of Babylon, as in God's overthrowing *Sodom* and *Gomorrah* and its neighbors," says Jehovah. "Not a man will live there, and not a child of humankind will stay in it." (Jeremiah 50:35, 40)

This is about the people symbolized by the Chaldeans, who are those whose worship harbors profane falsity, as shown before in §1368. It is also about the people symbolized by Babylon, who are those whose worship harbors profane evil (§§1182, 1326). Their damnation is portrayed by the overthrow of Sodom (evil in general) and by the overthrow of Gomorrah (falsity in general), because their worship too contains the evil and falsity that rise out of self-love. [2] In Amos:

> I have overturned you as in God's overthrowing *Sodom* and *Gomorrah,* and you have become like a firebrand snatched from the blaze. (Amos 4:11)

This is about Samaria, which symbolizes the spiritual church corrupted. It is called Sodom in respect to the general evil in it that opposes charitable goodness. It is called Gomorrah in respect to the general falsity in it that opposes religious truth. It is called God's overthrowing, here as above, in respect to both. In Zephaniah:

> Moab will be like *Sodom,* and the children of Ammon like *Gomorrah:* a place abandoned to nettle, and a salt pit, and a ruin forever. This is theirs on account of their *pride,* because they taunted and spread out over the people of Jehovah Sabaoth. (Zephaniah 2:9, 10)

Sodom here stands for the evil that comes of self-love and Gomorrah for its accompanying falsity. Like "overthrow" above, the ruin here refers to both. The pride is self-love. Taunting the people of Jehovah Sabaoth is introducing evil into truth, while spreading out over them is introducing falsity into it. [3] In Ezekiel:

> Your big sister is Samaria, she and her daughters, living on your left. And the sister littler than you, living on your right, is *Sodom* and her daughters. Your sister *Sodom,* she and her daughters, have not done as you have done, you and your daughters. *Here, now, this was the wickedness of Sodom your sister: pride, a surfeit of bread, and the assurance of idleness was hers and her daughters'; and the hand of the wretched and poor she did not strengthen. And they became haughty and did an abomination before you.* (Ezekiel 16:46, 48, 49, 50)

The subject here is the abominations of Jerusalem, Jerusalem being depicted as Samaria and Sodom—as Samaria (rather than Gomorrah) in respect to falsity, and as Sodom in respect to evil. It specifies what *Sodom* symbolizes, since it says *this was Sodom's wickedness:* the self-love symbolized there by *pride.* The *surfeit of bread* symbolizes their distaste for doing anything to benefit their neighbor. The *assurance of idleness* means that they stopped trying. The fact that they did not *strengthen the hand of the wretched and poor* portrays their lack of mercy. And the fact that her *daughters became haughty* means that all greed is therefore saturated with self-love, the *daughters* being greedy impulses. [4] This indicates clearly what Sodom is, and consequently that its symbolism does not follow the sense of the story in the next chapter. Rather, on an inner level there it symbolizes the kinds of attributes described here in the prophet, specifically aspects of self-love. Sodom is described in comparatively mild terms here, since the passage is saying that Jerusalem's abominations were more serious than Sodom's. The Lord's words in Matthew make the same thing clear:

> Truly, I say to you: it will be more bearable for the land of *Sodom* and *Gomorrah* on judgment day than for that city. (Matthew 10:15; Mark 6:11; Luke 10:12)

In John:

> Their bodies will be on the street of the great city that is *spiritually* called *Sodom* and *Egypt*. (Revelation 11:8)

Obviously Sodom does not mean Sodom here, nor Egypt, Egypt, since it says the city is *spiritually* called Sodom and Egypt. Sodom stands for every evil, while Egypt (rather than Gomorrah) stands for every falsity, that develops out of self-love.

Abraham was going with them means that the Lord, still present with the three, continued to have perceptions, but the focus shifted to the human race. This can be seen from the logical progression of the inner meaning, because going with the three men—in other words, with Jehovah—means still having the perception. **2221**

To send them off means that he wanted to get away from these perceptions, as can be seen without explanation. The reason too is clear: his perception (received from his divine side) and so his thought that the human race was like this struck him with horror. The Lord's love for the whole human race was so immense that he wanted to save everyone forever, by uniting his human nature with his divine and his divine nature with his human. So when he perceived the character of the human race, he wanted to get away from the perception and the resulting thoughts. That is what his desire to *send them off* symbolizes. **2222**

Genesis 18:17. *And Jehovah said, "Shall I be hiding from Abraham what I am doing?"* **2223**

And Jehovah said symbolizes a perception. *Shall I be hiding from Abraham what I am doing?* means that nothing should be hidden from the Lord's eyes.

2224   *Jehovah said* symbolizes a perception. This is established by the symbolism of *saying* as perceiving, which was discussed before at §§1898, 1919, 2080. Since *Jehovah* spoke here, it means that the Lord received a perception from his divine part.

2225   *Shall I be hiding from Abraham what I am doing?* means that nothing should be hidden from the Lord's eyes. This can be seen from the representation of *Abraham* as the Lord at that stage, as discussed several times before in this chapter [§§2172, 2186]. It is easy to see that the rest of the verse symbolizes the inappropriateness of hiding anything. The literal meaning here is similar to the inner meaning, as it is in many other places, especially where the text deals with essential beliefs. Because these are necessary for salvation, the statement of them in the letter is the same as the reality in the inner meaning. An example in Moses:

> Jehovah our God is one Jehovah. And you shall love Jehovah your God with all your heart and with all your soul and with all your powers. And these words shall be on your heart. (Deuteronomy 6:4, 5, 6)

There are more passages like this.

2226   Genesis 18:18. *"And Abraham will unquestionably become a large and numerous nation, and all the nations of the earth will be blessed in him."*

Abraham will unquestionably become a large and numerous nation means that all goodness and all the resulting truth will come from the Lord. *And all the nations of the earth will be blessed in him* means that he will save everyone who lives in charity.

2227   *Abraham will unquestionably become a large and numerous nation* means that all goodness and all the resulting truth will come from the Lord, as can be seen from the following: *Abraham* represents the Lord, as frequently mentioned above. And a *nation* symbolizes goodness, as discussed in §§1159, 1258, 1259, 1260, 1416, 1849. A nation *large and numerous* here symbolizes goodness and the resulting truth. Goodness is described as *large* and truth as *numerous,* as other verses in the Word illustrate, although I will not quote them here.

The resulting truth, or truth that results from goodness, in a real sense is spiritual good.

[2] There are two different kinds of good: heavenly and spiritual. Heavenly good is that of love for the Lord; spiritual good is that of love for our neighbor. The latter, or spiritual good, comes from the former, or heavenly good, because no one can love the Lord without also loving other people. Love for the Lord contains love for our neighbor, because love for

our neighbor comes from the Lord and therefore from Love itself for the entire human race. Dwelling in love for the Lord is the same as dwelling in the Lord, and people who dwell in the Lord cannot help dwelling in his love, which is a love for the human race and so for the person next door. Accordingly, that love is present in both kinds of good, heavenly and spiritual. The former is truly genuine goodness, but the latter is the truth of that goodness, or the truth that results from it. This truth is spiritual good, as noted. The former is what "large" symbolizes, but the latter is what "numerous" symbolizes.

All the nations of the earth will be blessed in him means that he will save everyone who lives in charity. This can be seen from the symbolism of being *blessed* as being given everything good that comes from a heavenly origin, as discussed in §§981, 1096, 1420, 1422.

People who are given blessings from a heavenly origin—heavenly good and spiritual good, discussed just above in §2227—are also given eternal salvation. In other words, they are saved.

In an inner sense, *all the nations of the earth* means people who devote themselves to a loving and charitable goodness. This is evident from the symbolism of a *nation* as goodness (§§1159, 1258, 1259, 1260, 1416, 1849).

"All the nations of the earth" does not mean everyone everywhere in the four corners of the earth, as anyone can see, since many, many people are among those who are not saved. The phrase refers only to those governed by charity—that is, those who have acquired a life of charity.

[2] To prevent ignorance of how people are saved after they pass on, a few words must be said. Many say that we are saved by faith or, as they phrase it, simply by believing, but most of them do not know what faith is. Some imagine that it is nothing but a way of thinking, others that it is the acknowledgment of some necessary tenet, others that the entire theology of the faith must be accepted, and others other things. So they err even just in recognizing faith. As a result, they are also mistaken about what it is that saves us.

It is not simply a way of thinking, or an acknowledgment of a tenet, or a comprehensive knowledge of the theology. No one can be saved by any of this, because it cannot take root in anything deeper than thought. Thought saves no one. It is the life we have acquired for ourselves in the world by means of religious knowledge that saves us. This life remains, but any thinking that does not harmonize with our life fades away until it disappears. In heaven people associate with each other on the basis of the way they have lived, never on the basis of thought disconnected from

2228

life. Thoughts that are not attached to our life are hypocritical and are categorically rejected.

[3] There are two kinds of life, in general; one is hell's and the other is heaven's. We acquire a hellish life from all those aims, thoughts, and deeds that emanate from self-love and so from hatred for others. We acquire heavenly life from all those aims, thoughts, and deeds that belong to neighborly love. This is the life that everything called faith looks toward, and such a life is acquired through everything that belongs to faith.

This evidence shows what faith is: it is charity. Everything called a doctrine of faith leads toward charity. Charity contains all those doctrines, and all of them are derived from charity.

When bodily life ends, our soul reflects our love.

2229   Genesis 18:19. *"For I know him, because he will command his sons and his household after him, and they will keep the way of Jehovah, to perform justice and judgment, in order for Jehovah to bring on Abraham that which he spoke concerning him."*

For I know him means that it is true. *Because he will command his sons and his household after him, and they will keep the way of Jehovah, to perform justice and judgment* means that the whole theology of charity and faith comes from the Lord. *Sons* are people dedicated to truth; a *household* is people dedicated to goodness; a *way* is theology; *justice* is what theology says about goodness; *judgment,* what it says about truth. *In order for Jehovah to bring on Abraham that which he spoke concerning him* means that on this account the Lord's human nature would have to be joined to his divine nature.

2230   *For I know him* means that it is true, as can be seen from the symbolism of *knowing.* Strictly speaking, knowing someone is realizing she or he is such and such. By the same token, when applied to an abstraction or some other thing, knowing is realizing that it is such and such. The implication of "knowing," then, depends on what it is that is said to be known. To say that the thing suggested by the story line is known means that it is so, or true.

2231   *Because he will command his sons and his household after him, and they will keep the way of Jehovah, to perform justice and judgment* means that the whole theology of charity and faith comes from the Lord. This can be seen from the symbolism of a *son,* a *household,* a *way, justice,* and *judgment.* Taken collectively, or reduced to a single meaning, they symbolize the whole theology of charity and faith. *Sons,* you see, symbolize all who are dedicated to truth; a *household,* all who are dedicated to goodness; and a *way*, the theology they learn. What this theology says about goodness is symbolized by *justice*, and what it says about truth, by *judgment*. Teachings about goodness are the doctrine of charity, and teachings about truth are the doctrine of faith.

[2] Speaking generally, there is only one doctrine, which is the doctrine of charity, because every element of faith looks toward charity, as noted at §2228. Charity does not differ from faith any more than wanting what is good differs from thinking what is good. Anyone who wishes well also thinks well. So the difference is also the same as that between will and intellect. Those who reflect on it realize that will and intellect are two very different things. Even the scholarly world knows it, and it is obvious in people who intend ill and yet are inspired by their thoughts to speak well. This should make it clear to everyone that will and intellect are two different things. So the human mind is divided into two parts that do not make a united whole. Yet the intent in our creation was that the two halves form a single mind. To speak metaphorically, there was to be no other distinction than that between fire and the light it sheds. Love for the Lord and charity for our neighbor was to be like the flame, and all perception and thought was to be like the light it sheds. Love and charity were to have been the all-in-all of perception and thought; they were to have permeated each and every facet of it. Perception or thoughts about the nature of love and charity are what are called faith.

[3] But the human race began to wish ill. People started to hate their neighbor and to inflict revenge and cruelty on others. In the end, the part of the mind called the will became wholly depraved. In consequence, people started to distinguish between charity and faith. They began to put all the teachings of their religion in the category of faith and to label them with the single word *faith*. Finally they progressed so far as to say that they could be saved by faith alone—by which they meant their doctrinal precepts—as long as they believed those precepts, no matter how they lived.

In this way charity departs from faith, and then metaphorically speaking it is nothing more than light without fire. This light resembles the kind of sunlight that comes with winter, so bitterly cold that the earth's vegetation languishes and dies. Faith that comes of charity, on the other hand, is like the light of spring and summer, which enables everything to sprout and flourish.

[4] The same lesson can be learned from the consideration that love and charity are heavenly fire, while faith is the spiritual light it gives. Love,

charity, and faith also present themselves this way to the inner and outer eye in the other life, because the Lord's heavenly nature reveals itself to angels there as a fiery radiance like that of the sun, while his spiritual nature reveals itself as the light cast by that radiance. These phenomena touch the inner depths of angels and spirits in a way that mirrors the life of love and charity they live. That is the source of the joy and happiness in the other world, in all its variations.

This evidence shows how it is with the claim that faith alone saves us.

2232   The fact that *sons* are people dedicated to truth is established by the symbolism of a *son* in the Word as truth (discussed in §§489, 491, 533, 1147). In an abstract sense sons symbolize truth; but as applied to humankind, they symbolize everyone devoted to truth.

2233   The fact that a *household* is people devoted to goodness is established by the symbolism of a *household* or house as goodness (discussed in §§710, 1708, 2048). In an abstract sense, again, a household (or "those born in the house") symbolizes goodness; but as it applies to humankind, it symbolizes everyone devoted to goodness.

2234   The fact that a *way* means theology is established by the symbolism of a *way*. The Word speaks of a way or path in connection with truth because truths lead toward goodness and come from it, as can be seen from the passages quoted in §627 of volume 1. Since it is used in connection with truth, a way or path is theology, for the reason that theology gathers into one embrace everything that leads to goodness, or in other words, to charity.

2235   The fact that *justice* is what theology says about goodness, and *judgment,* what it says about truth, can be seen from the symbolism of *justice* and that of *judgment.*

The Word very often mentions justice and judgment together, but what they mean in an inner sense has not yet been recognized. In the most direct sense, justice relates to what is fair and judgment to what is right. We achieve what is just when we judge something in terms of goodness or benefit, in accord with our conscience. We achieve what is right, however, when we judge it in terms of the law and so in terms of legal justice—again in accord with our conscience—because the law is our guide. In an inner sense, on the other hand, justice is whatever comes of goodness, while judgment is whatever comes of truth. Goodness is everything related to love and charity; truth is everything related to the faith that comes of love and charity. Truth takes its nature from goodness and is called truth on the basis of goodness, just as faith draws on love; and judgment draws on justice in the same way.

[2] This symbolism of justice and judgment is visible in the following scriptural passages. In Jeremiah:

> This is what Jehovah has said: "Perform *judgment* and *justice,* and snatch spoil from the hand of the oppressor. Doom to those who build their house on what is not *justice* and their upper rooms on what is not *judgment!* Didn't your father eat and drink and perform *judgment* and *justice?* After that it was well with him." (Jeremiah 22:3, 13, 15)

Judgment stands for acts of truth; justice, for acts of goodness. In Ezekiel:

> If the ungodly turn back from their sin and perform *judgment* and *justice,* none of their sins that they sinned will be remembered of them; *judgment* and *justice* they have performed; they shall surely live. In the turning back of the ungodly from their ungodliness, if they perform *judgment* and *justice*—because of these things they shall live. (Ezekiel 33:14, 16, 19)

Again judgment stands for truth, which composes faith, and justice stands for goodness, which composes charity. [3] In Amos:

> Let *judgment* flow like the waters and *justice* like a mighty river. (Amos 5:24)

The same is true here. In Isaiah:

> This is what Jehovah has said: "Observe *judgment* and perform *justice,* because my salvation is about to come, and *my justice,* to reveal itself." (Isaiah 56:1)

In the same author:

> To peace there will not be an end, on the throne of David and on his kingdom, to establish it and to sustain it in *judgment* and *justice,* from now on forever. (Isaiah 9:7)

This stands for devotion to religious truth and neighborly good. In the same author:

> Jehovah has been exalted, because he inhabits the heights; he has filled Zion with *judgment* and *justice.* (Isaiah 33:5)

Judgment stands for faith, justice for love, and Zion for the church. Judgment comes first because love comes by means of faith; but where justice comes first, it means that love produces faith, as in Hosea:

> I will betroth you to me forever, and I will betroth you to me in *justice* and *judgment,* and in mercy and in compassion. And I will betroth you to me in *faith,* and you will know Jehovah. (Hosea 2:19, 20)

Justice and mercy, which have to do with love, come first here, while judgment and compassion, which have to do with the faith that love produces, come second. Both are called faith, or faithfulness. [4] In David:

> Jehovah, your mercy reaches the heavens, and your truth, to the heights of the sky. Your *justice* is like the mountains of God; your *judgments* are a great abyss. (Psalms 36:5, 6)

Here too both mercy and justice relate to love, while truth and judgments relate to faith. In the same author:

> Let *truth* sprout from the earth and *justice* look out from heaven. Yes, Jehovah will give what is good, and our land will yield its produce. (Psalms 85:11, 12)

Truth, which composes faith, stands for judgment here, and justice stands for love, or mercy. In Zechariah:

> I will bring them, and they will live in the middle of Jerusalem, and they will become my people, and I will become their God in *truth* and in *justice.* (Zechariah 8:8)

This verse too makes it clear that judgment is truth, and justice is goodness, because truth takes the place of judgment here. Something similar happens in David:

> One who walks unblemished and does *justice* and speaks *truth* . . . (Psalms 15:2)

[5] Because faith comes of charity, or in other words, because truth comes of goodness, true ideas that result from good are often called the judgments of justice. In this case, judgments symbolize almost the same thing as commandments. In Isaiah, for instance:

> Let them seek me day by day, and let them desire a knowledge of my ways, as a nation that performs *justice* and does not abandon the *rightful*

judgment of its God. Let them ask me about the *judgments of justice;* let them desire God's drawing near. (Isaiah 58:2)

David shows that they are commandments:

Seven times in a day have I praised you over the *judgments* of your *justice;* all your *commandments* are *justice.* (Psalms 119:164, 172)

The Lord is especially said to perform judgment and justice when he creates us anew, as in Jeremiah:

Over this let boasters boast: that they understand and know me, that I am Jehovah, performing mercy, *judgment,* and *justice* in the earth, because in these things I take pleasure. (Jeremiah 9:24)

In this verse mercy (an aspect of love) is depicted as judgment and justice. In the same author:

I will raise up for David a just offshoot, and he will reign as monarch, and he will act with understanding and perform *judgment* and *justice* in the land. (Jeremiah 23:5; 33:15)

[6] In consequence John says:

If I leave, I will send the Paraclete to you, and when he comes he will denounce the world regarding sin, regarding *justice,* and regarding *judgment:* regarding sin, because they do not believe in me; regarding *justice,* because I am going to my Father and you will no longer see me; regarding *judgment,* because the ruler of this world has been judged. (John 16:7, 8, 9, 10, 11)

In this passage sin stands for all faithlessness. To denounce the world regarding justice is to denounce it for anything that opposes what is good, despite the fact that the Lord united his humanity with his divinity in order to save the world. That is what "I am going to my Father and you will see me no longer" means. To denounce the world regarding judgment is to denounce it for anything that opposes truth, despite the fact that evil has been thrown down into its own hell, where it can no longer do any harm. That is what "the ruler of the world has been judged" means.

To take it as a whole, making a denunciation regarding sin, justice, and judgment means denouncing every faithless assault on goodness and truth. So it means that charity and faith are completely lacking, because in ancient times justice and judgment meant all the Lord's mercy and favor, and all human charity and faith.

2236 *In order for Jehovah to bring on Abraham that which he spoke concerning him* means that on this account the Lord's human nature would have to be joined to his divine nature. This is not as clear from the meaning of the words as from the fact that everything said in the Word has to do with the Lord's Coming on earth to unite his human nature with his divine nature and by uniting them, to save the human race. That is what is meant in an inner sense by his bringing on Abraham that which he had spoken concerning him.

2237 Genesis 18:20. *And Jehovah said that the outcry of Sodom and Gomorrah had become great and that their sin had become very heavy.*

Jehovah said symbolizes a perception. *That the outcry of Sodom and Gomorrah had become great and that their sin had become very heavy* means that the falsity and evil inherent in self-love had grown to its culmination; an *outcry* is falsity, and *sin* is evil.

2238 *Jehovah said* symbolizes a perception. This is established by the symbolism of *saying* in the narrative sense as perceiving, as discussed several times earlier.

When "Jehovah said" occurs in the stories of the Word, it symbolizes a perception that is not entirely continuous with the previous one but supplementary or perhaps entirely new. See also §2061.

2239 *That the outcry of Sodom and Gomorrah had become great and that their sin had become very heavy* means that the falsity and evil inherent in self-love had grown to its culmination, as can be seen from the following: *Sodom* symbolizes the evil that comes of self-love, and *Gomorrah*, falsity from the same source, as shown above at §2220. An *outcry* symbolizes falsity, while *sin* symbolizes evil, as will be dealt with just below. Clearly, then, *it had become great* (the outcry) and *it had become heavy* (the sin) mean that falsity and evil had reached their peak, or their culmination. What follows shows this more plainly, where verse 32 says that the city would be spared if ten were found there, meaning if any traces—any amount of goodness or truth—still remained. When humankind no longer has anything good or true inside, it faces spiritual devastation and ruin and therefore a culmination or end, as mentioned in the next verse [§2243].

2240 The fact that an *outcry* is falsity and *sin* is evil may be seen from the symbolism in the Word of an *outcry*. Without knowing the inner meaning of Scripture no one can see that an outcry symbolizes falsity. The term recurs several times in the Prophets. When those passages speak of devastation and ruin, they describe people as wailing and crying out, meaning that goodness and truth have been wiped out. The word *voice* also appears in those places, where in an inner sense it depicts falsity. In Jeremiah, for example:

> The *voice* of the shepherds' *outcry,* and the *wailing* of the powerful among the flock! For Jehovah is *devastating* their pasture. (Jeremiah 25:36)

The shepherds' outcry is their surrender to falsity, which causes devastation. [2] In the same author:

> Look! Water climbing from the north; and it will become a flooding river, and will flood the earth and its abundance, the city and those living in it; and humankind will *cry out,* and every resident of the land will *wail,* over the day for *devastation* that is coming. (Jeremiah 47:2, 4)

The subject here is the ruination of faith, which is accomplished by falsity. The flooding river is falsity, as shown in the first volume, §§705, 790. [3] In Zephaniah:

> A *voice of outcry* from the Gate of Fish, and a *wailing* from the Second [District], and great wreckage from the hills; and their riches will become plunder, and their houses a *ruin.* (Zephaniah 1:10, 13)

Here too the outcry is used to describe devastating falsity. [4] In Isaiah:

> On the way to Horonaim they will raise a *cry* for the wreckage, because the waters of Nimrim will be *wastelands,* because the grain has dried out, the grass has come to an end, there is no vegetation. (Isaiah 15:5, 6; Jeremiah 48:3)

In these verses, the wasting or ruination of faith and the end or culmination is depicted as a cry. [5] In Jeremiah:

> Judah has mourned, and its gates have drooped, people have been draped in black down to the earth, and *Jerusalem's cry* has risen up. And their notables have sent their little ones to the water; they came to the pits; they did not find water; they returned with their vessels empty. (Jeremiah 14:2, 3)

Jerusalem's cry in this verse stands for falsity, since the failure to find water is a failure to find knowledge concerning truth. The symbolism of water as knowledge of truth was illustrated in §§28, 680, 739 of the first volume. [6] In Isaiah:

> I will rejoice in Jerusalem and be glad in my people, and no longer will be heard in it the voice of weeping or the *voice of outcry.* (Isaiah 65:19)

The voice of weeping that will not be heard is wickedness, and the voice of outcry that will not be heard is falsity. Most of these details, including the outcry, cannot be understood from the literal meaning but only from the inner meaning. [7] In the same author:

> Jehovah waited for judgment, but look: a rash! For justice, but look: an *outcry!* (Isaiah 5:7)

This too deals with the devastation of goodness and truth. Here there is a kind of switch, as in many other passages in the Prophets. The switch involves the replacement of truth with evil (a rash instead of judgment) and of goodness with falsity (an outcry instead of justice). Judgment is truth, and justice is goodness, as demonstrated in §2235 above. [8] A similar kind of switch occurs in Moses, where he speaks of Sodom and Gomorrah:

> From the grapevine of *Sodom* comes their grapevine, and from the fields of *Gomorrah* come their grapes. Grapes of gall, clusters of bitterness are theirs. (Deuteronomy 32:32)

The language is similar here, because a grapevine portrays truth or falsity, while fields and grapes portray good or evil. So Sodom's grapevine is the falsity that grows out of evil, while Gomorrah's fields and grapes are the evil that grows out of falsity. There are two kinds of falsity, as discussed in §1212 of the second volume, so there are also two kinds of evil. The current verse offers symbols for both kinds of falsity and evil, in the outcry of Sodom and Gomorrah, which had become great, and their sin, which had become very heavy. The outcry is mentioned first and the sin second, yet the name of Sodom (evil growing out of self-love) appears first and that of Gomorrah (falsity growing out of self-love) second.

2241   Genesis 18:21. *"Let me go down, please, and I will see whether they have made an end of it according to its outcry, which has come to me; and if not, I will know it."*

Let me go down, please, and I will see symbolizes a visitation. *Whether they have made an end of it according to its outcry, which has come to me; and if not, I will know it* means whether evil has reached its peak.

Let me go down, please, and I will see symbolizes a visitation. This **2242** can be seen from the symbolism of *going down to see* as a judgment (discussed in volume 2, §1311) and so as a visitation. The Word refers to the final days of the church in general and of each individual in particular as a visitation; and visitation comes before a judgment. So a visitation is nothing but an examination into character—the character of the religious culture in general and of the individual in particular. This examination is expressed in the literal sense by Jehovah's *coming down* and *seeing*.

[2] This verse illustrates the nature of the literal meaning. Jehovah does not come down, because the Lord cannot be said to come down, since he is always at the highest heights. Neither does Jehovah look to see whether a thing is so, because this is another thing the Lord cannot be said to do, since he knows absolutely everything from eternity. Still, the idea is phrased this way because it seems to us to happen so. We live on lowly planes, and when an event occurs on those planes, we do not think about or even know what is happening higher up or how it influences us. Our thinking does not advance beyond the obvious, so we cannot help perceiving such an event as something like the act of coming down and seeing. What makes this perception more inevitable is the fact that we think no one knows what is going through our mind. In addition, we are thoroughly convinced such events do come from on high and, if God causes them, from the very highest heights, when in reality they come not from on high but from deep within. [3] This evidence shows what the literal meaning is like: it accords with appearances. If it did not, no one would understand or acknowledge the Word, so no one would accept it. Angels, however, are not so preoccupied by appearances as we on earth are. Since the letter of the Word is designed for us, then, its inner meaning is intended for the angels. The inner meaning exists also for the sake of people who while living in the world receive from the Lord in his divine mercy the gift of resembling angels.

[4] The Word often mentions visitation, which means either devastation (for the church or for everyone in it) or deliverance. So it means an examination into character.

It stands for devastation in Isaiah:

What will you do on the day of *visitation,* [which] will come from far away? To whom will you flee for help, and where will you leave your glory? (Isaiah 10:3)

In the same author:

> The stars of the heavens and their constellations will not shed their light; the sun will be shadowed over in its emergence, and the moon will not radiate its light. And I will *visit* evil on the world and their wickedness on the ungodly. (Isaiah 13:10, 11)

The stars and constellations that will not shine and the sun that will go dark and the moon that will not radiate its light symbolize a lack of love and charity; see §2120. Since this is the same as devastation, it is a day of visitation. [5] In Jeremiah:

> They will fall down among those who fall, and at the time of their *visitation* they will stumble. (Jeremiah 8:12)

This stands for a time when they are devastated, or purged of charity and faith. In Ezekiel:

> The *city's visitations* have come near, and a man [has taken] his weapon of destruction in his hand. (Ezekiel 9:1)

This too speaks of devastation, which is why the man has a weapon of destruction. In Hosea:

> The *days of visitation* have come; the days of retribution have come. (Hosea 9:7)

Likewise. In Micah:

> The day of your sentries—your *visitation*—has come; now they will have confusion. (Micah 7:4)

Here too it stands for the devastation or purging of charity. In Moses:

> On the day of my *visiting* I will *visit* their sin on them. (Exodus 32:34)

This is about the people [of Israel] when they were in the wilderness, after they had made themselves a golden calf.

The meaning of visitation as deliverance is clear from the following passages: Exodus 3:16; 4:31; Jeremiah 27:22; 29:10; Luke 1:68, 78; 19:41, 42, [44].

2243   *Whether they have made an end of it according to its outcry, which has come to me; and if not, I will know it* means whether evil has reached its peak. This can be seen from the symbolism of an *outcry* as falsity, a symbolism discussed just above at §2240. There are two kinds of falsity, as noted

at the end of that section: falsity that comes from evil and falsity that produces evil. Falsity that comes from evil is every thought we think when we
are acting badly—thoughts that cater to wickedness. Take, for instance,
the thoughts we have about adultery when we are committing it: that it is
legitimate, proper, one of life's central pleasures, a good way of increasing
the population, and so on. All these thoughts are falsities that come of evil.

[2] Falsity *produces* evil, though, when we form a principle on the
basis of our religious persuasion and therefore believe that it is good or
holy when it really is inherently evil. For example, if our religious beliefs
convince us that another person can save us, and we therefore worship and
revere that person, we are doing wrong as a result of the fallacy. The same
with the consequences of any other religious conviction that is intrinsically false.

Since falsity comes from evil and falsity produces evil, the word *outcry*
is used here, where it acts as a catchall term for the meanings it covers—
namely, for evil. The fact that the verse says "whether *they* have made an
end according to *its* outcry, which has come to me"—"*they* have made
an end" in the plural and "*its* outcry" in the singular—provides evidence
that this is true.

[3] Section 1857 in the second volume showed what an end or com-
pletion is. The same thing can also be comprehended from the various
churches. The earliest church, called "the human," was the most heavenly
of all. Over time its good and loving impulses degenerated so far that in
the end nothing heavenly remained, and then it faced its end, which is
depicted in the state of its people before the Flood [Genesis 6:1–7].

[4] After the Flood came the ancient church, which was called Noah
and was less heavenly. Over time it too abandoned its good and charitable
practices so completely that no charity remained. The church turned in
part toward sorcery, in part toward idolatry, and in part toward a kind of
dogmatism isolated from charity. That is when its end came.

[5] Another church, called the Hebrew church, took its place. This
one was still less heavenly and spiritual, since it had a somewhat sacred
worship in its outward rituals. Over time the church became deformed in
various ways and its superficial style of worship turned idolatrous. That is
when its end came.

[6] The religion that was then restored among Jacob's descendants—
the fourth church—had nothing heavenly or spiritual about it but only a
role representing such qualities. This religion, then, was a church representing what was heavenly and spiritual, because the people in it had no

idea what their rituals represented and symbolized. The religion was established to provide some remaining link between humankind and heaven—the kind of link that exists between representations of goodness and truth on one hand and actual goodness and truth on the other. This religion eventually deviated so far into falsity and evil that all its ritual became idolatrous, and that is when it faced its end.

[7] After the churches waned like this, one after another, the connection between the human race and heaven finally broke off altogether in the last one. So complete was the rift that the human race would have perished, because there was no church, and the church provides the connection and link (see §§468, 637, 931, 2054). So at that point the Lord came into the world. By making the divine nature one with the human in himself, he united heaven with earth and at the same time started a new church called the Christian church. Originally this church was dedicated to the good actions urged by faith, and its people lived in charity with each other like sisters and brothers. As time passed, though, it strayed in various ways until today it has come to such a state that people do not even know that the foundation of faith is love for the Lord and charity for our neighbor. Although theology teaches them to say that the Lord is the savior of the human race, that they will rise again after death, and that heaven and hell exist, few of them believe it. Since this is what the church has become, its end is not far off.

[8] This shows what an end or consummation is: a time when evil reaches its peak.

The situation is the same on the particular level, or in other words, for each individual. What a consummation is like for the individual in particular will be told below, the Lord in his divine mercy willing.

The Word frequently speaks of the final end, portraying the period before it as a time of devastation and ruin, followed by a visitation.

2244   Genesis 18:22. *And the men looked out from there and went toward Sodom; and Abraham was still standing before Jehovah.*

The men looked out from there symbolizes thoughts inspired in the Lord by his divine side. *And went toward Sodom* symbolizes thoughts about the human race and the amount of evil it was prey to. *And Abraham was still standing before Jehovah* symbolizes thoughts inspired in the Lord by his human side, which was joined [to his divine side] in the way mentioned above [§§2188–2196].

2245   *The men looked out from there* symbolizes thoughts inspired in the Lord by his divine side, as can be seen from the following: *Looking out* means thinking, since in an inner sense seeing means understanding, just as it does in everyday speech. The intellect is our inner eye, so looking out is thinking, which is the sight of the inner self, or the intellect.

The *men* symbolize the divine being. The current chapter sometimes mentions the men and sometimes calls them Jehovah. When it speaks of the men, they symbolize the Trinity—divinity itself, divine humanity, and their influence. The thinking the Lord did from this divine side is symbolized by the fact that the men looked out from there.

The Lord's thinking rose out of the human side of him in its union with his divine side. This union is discussed at the beginning of the chapter. But the perception on which his thinking was based came from his divine side. That is why this same verse soon mentions Jehovah, saying, "[Abraham] was standing before Jehovah." And when his humanity was united with his divinity, the influence emanating from him was also present.

They went toward Sodom symbolizes the human race and the amount **2246** of evil it was prey to. This can be seen from the symbolism of *Sodom* as evil that comes of self-love (dealt with above at §2220) and that of looking out toward the face of Sodom as looking at the condition of the human race (§2219).

The reason Sodom symbolizes the condition of the human race— that it was prey to so much evil—is that Sodom does not mean Sodom but everyone everywhere in the world who is afflicted with self-love. The description of Sodom represents the condition of a person who has fallen prey to that evil, as subsequent sections will show.

Self-love is the source of all evil and is therefore evil itself, as earlier remarks and evidence concerning it in §§2045, 2057, 2219 show. That is why I say here that the human race was prey to so much evil.

Abraham was still standing before Jehovah symbolizes thoughts inspired **2247** in the Lord by his human side, which was joined [to his divine side] in the way mentioned. This can be seen from the representation of *Abraham* in the current chapter as the Lord's human side. It follows without explanation that his *standing before Jehovah* was a way of thinking inspired by the Lord's human side, which was joined [to his divine side] in the way mentioned at the beginning of the chapter and above in §2245.

Genesis 18:23. *And Abraham came near and said, "Will you also destroy* **2248** *the just with the ungodly?"*

Abraham came near and said symbolizes thoughts inspired in the Lord by his human side, which attached itself more closely to his divine side.

Will you also destroy the just with the ungodly? symbolizes grief in the Lord because of his love for the human race, and his intervening to plead that there still be a connection with goodness, even though evil was present.

2249   *Abraham came near and said* symbolizes thoughts inspired in the Lord by his human side, which attached itself more closely to his divine side. This follows from the discussion above on the Lord's thinking about the human race, so it needs no explanation.

In its inner sense, then, the current chapter has a great deal of description concerning the Lord's state of thought and perception, and in the early verses, concerning the state of the union between his humanity and divinity. In the eyes of a person on earth, to be sure, this may not seem very important; but it is extremely important nevertheless. [2] To the eyes of angels, whose Holy Word is the inner meaning, these subjects are vividly presented with exquisite beauty in representative scenes. So are countless other concepts that follow on the heels of these subjects and bear a resemblance to them—concepts involving the Lord's bond with heaven, and the way angels receive his divinity in their humanity. Angelic ideas are such that angels possess more wisdom on these topics than on any other and also find the greatest pleasure in them. Such ideas also enlighten and confirm them more and more as to the union of the Lord's human nature with his divine.

Angels were once people on earth, and since they were, they could not help having thoughts about the Lord as a person and about the Lord as God, and also about the divine Trinity. They could not help forming various notions on these subjects for themselves, even though they had no way of evaluating the notions at the time. [3] One thing about heaven's secrets is that they lie wholly beyond our grasp, yet we each form some picture of them for ourselves. Nothing can possibly be kept in our memory (still less even begin to enter our thinking) except by means of some mental image, no matter how it is formed. [Angels] have necessarily formed such images from objects in the world or their parallels, and illusions due to misunderstanding have wormed their way in during that process. In the other life these illusions drive a wedge between an angel's own thoughts (although they are then deeper) and what faith teaches to be true and good. [4] In order to dispel such errors, the inner meaning of the current chapter speaks extensively of the bond between the Lord's humanity and divinity and of his perceptions and thoughts. When the Word is read, these subjects are presented to the senses of the angels in such a way that their earlier ideas, formed out of alien notions and the objections that so easily result from them, dissolve one by one. New ideas compatible with the light of truth that the angels enjoy enter in.

This is more the case with spiritual angels than with heavenly ones, because the purer angels' notions are, the better they become at accepting heavenly thoughts. That heaven is not pure in the Lord's sight is known [Job 15:15], but it is also true that its inhabitants are constantly improving.

Will you also destroy the just with the ungodly? symbolizes grief in the Lord because of his love for the human race, and his intervening to plead that there still be a connection with goodness, even though evil was present. This can be seen from the love and zeal that beam from the text here, and even more clearly from verse 25 below, which says, "Far be it from you to do according to this thing—to put the just to death with the ungodly, and that it should be the same for the just as for the ungodly. Far be it from you! Won't the judge of the whole earth perform judgment?" It can also be seen from the symbolism of the *just* as that which is good (discussed in §§612, 2235) and from the symbolism of the *ungodly* as something opposed to justness, or to what is good, and therefore as evil.

The current words and the remainder of the chapter also make it clear that it is an intervention.

The Lord intervened for the human race when he was in the world, specifically when he was feeling humbled, because at those times he talked to Jehovah as a separate person, as noted before [§§1745, 1999, 2004, 2159]. In a state of glorification, however, since his human nature has united with his divine and has itself become Jehovah, he no longer intervenes but rather shows mercy. His divine side reaches out to help us and saves us. Mercy itself is what intervenes, because that is its essential nature.

Genesis 18:24. *"Perhaps there are fifty just people in the middle of the city. Will you still destroy it and not spare the place for the sake of the fifty just people who are in the middle of it?"*

Perhaps there are fifty just people in the middle of the city means that truth can be full of goodness. *Will you still destroy it and not spare the place for the sake of the fifty just people who are in the middle of it?* means intervening out of love, so that they would not then be destroyed.

Perhaps there are fifty just people in the middle of the city means that truth can be full of goodness, as can be seen from the following: *Fifty* means full. The *just* symbolize what is good, as mentioned at §§612, 2235. The *middle* symbolizes the deepest core (§1074). And the *city* symbolizes truth (§402). So in an inner sense, *fifty just people in the middle of the city* means that at its core truth can be full of goodness.

2250

2251

2252

From the literal text no one can see that the words contain this meaning, because the narrative that makes up the literal meaning leads the mind in a completely different direction, into a very different way of thinking. This *is* how the words are perceived by people immersed in the inner meaning, however, as I know for sure. Not even the numbers (fifty here, and forty-five, forty, thirty, twenty, and ten below) are taken as numbers by people focusing on the inner meaning. Instead they are taken as attributes or as states, a fact demonstrated in §§482, 487, 575, 647, 648, 755, 813, 1963, 1988, 2075.

[2] The ancients also marked the different phases of their church by numbers. Their method of calculating can be seen from the numerical symbolism given in the sections referred to just above. This symbolism they took from representations that exist in the world of spirits. Any object there that seems to be counted or measured stands not for something defined by numbers but for either a quality or a state. This can be seen from passages alluded to in §§2129 and 2130 and in §2089 dealing with the number twelve as symbolizing all aspects of faith. The same is true of the numbers that follow in the current passage. This reveals what the Word is like in its inner meaning.

[3] The reason *fifty* means *full* is that it is the number coming next after seven times seven, or forty-nine, and therefore completes or fills it. As a result, in the representative church, the feast of seven Sabbaths came on the fiftieth day and the jubilee in the fiftieth year. This is what Moses says about the feast of seven Sabbaths:

> You shall count for yourselves from the day after the Sabbath; from the day that you bring the sheaf of the waved offering, *seven* whole *Sabbaths* there shall be. To the day after the seventh Sabbath you shall count *fifty days,* and you shall offer a new offering to Jehovah. (Leviticus 23:15, 16)

The same author on the jubilee:

> You shall count for yourself seven Sabbaths of years, seven times seven years, and the days of the seven Sabbaths of years shall be *forty-nine years* for you and you shall consecrate the *fiftieth year* and proclaim freedom in the land to all its inhabitants. A jubilee it shall be to you. (Leviticus 25:8, 10)

This shows that the count of Sabbaths is full with the fiftieth.

[4] What is more, everywhere the Word mentions the number fifty, it means fullness. For instance, the Levites were registered from a son of

thirty years and up, all the way to a son of *fifty* years (Numbers 4:23, 35, 39, 43, 47; 8:25). This stands for a full or final period of carrying out their ministry at that time.

A man who had lain with a girl, an unmarried woman, was to give her father *fifty pieces* of silver, and she would become his wife, and he could not divorce her (Deuteronomy 22:29). This stands for a full monetary penalty and full restitution.

David gave Araunah *fifty* shekels of silver for the threshing floor where he built an altar to Jehovah (2 Samuel 24:24), which stands for the full price fully paid.

Absalom made himself a chariot and horses and had *fifty* men running in front of him (2 Samuel 15:1). Adonijah too had chariots and riders and *fifty* men running in front of him (1 Kings 1:5). This stands for full superiority and greatness.

Because of the ancients, you see, [the people of Israel] viewed certain numbers as representative and symbolic. They honored the numbers, which were also commanded in their rituals, but few of them knew what they meant.

[5] Since *fifty* means fullness, then, and also had been a representative number, as I said, it has the same meaning in one of the Lord's parables. This involves a steward who said to a debtor who owed for oil, "How much do you owe my master?" The other said, "A hundred baths of oil." And the steward told him, "Take your note and sitting down quickly write *fifty*" (Luke 16:[5,] 6). Fifty stands for a full resolution. Because it is a number, it does seem as though it could not mean anything but that number. Everywhere in the inner meaning, though, this number means something full.

In Haggai too, for example:

> One came to the winepress to draw *fifty* [measures] from the press; there were twenty. (Haggai 2:16)

In other words, instead of fullness, there was not much. The prophet would not have mentioned fifty there if it had not had this meaning.

Will you still destroy it and not spare the place for the sake of the fifty just people who are in the middle of it? means intervening out of love, so that they would not be destroyed. This can be seen from the symbolism of *fifty*, the *just*, and the *middle of it* (the city), as discussed just above in §2252. All these words involve intervention out of love and the idea that the people would not be destroyed. For more on intervention, see above at §2250. The fact that it springs from love is also obvious

2253

When the Lord was in the world, he had no other life than the life of love for the entire human race, which he felt a burning desire to save forever. That vital energy is the very truest heavenly life, and through it he united himself to his divinity and his divinity to himself. His central being, or Jehovah, is nothing but mercy, the product of love for the whole human race; and his life was one of pure love, which is utterly impossible for any human.

Anyone who does not know what life is, or that one's life reflects one's love, will not understand this.

Clearly, then, the more we love our neighbor, the more of the Lord's life we receive.

2254   Genesis 18:25. *"Far be it from you to do according to this thing—to put the just to death with the ungodly, and that it should be the same for the just as for the ungodly. Far be it from you; won't the judge of the whole earth perform judgment?"*

Far be it from you to do according to this thing symbolizes the Lord's horror. *To put the just to death with the ungodly, and that it should be the same for the just as for the ungodly* means that what is good cannot die, because evil can be detached from it. *Far be it from you* symbolizes a more intense degree of horror. *Won't the judge of the whole earth perform judgment?* means that divine goodness cannot do this under the guidance of truth separated from good.

2255   *Far be it from you to do according to this thing* symbolizes the Lord's horror, as is clear without explanation.

2256   *To put the just to death with the ungodly, and that it should be the same for the just as for the ungodly* means that what is good cannot die, because evil can be detached from it. This can be seen from the symbolism of the *just* as that which is good and the *ungodly* as that which is evil, a symbolism discussed above at §2250. *To put the just to death with the ungodly,* then, is to put goodness to death along with wickedness. Because these events should not happen, and because the very thought arouses horror, the inner meaning lays them aside and replaces them with the idea that what is good cannot die because evil can be detached from it.

[2] Few if any know how matters stand here. It needs to be realized that anything good we have thought about or done from the time we were babies right up to the last hour of our life stays with us. So does everything evil; in fact not even the smallest particle of it entirely disappears. All of it remains written in our book of life. In other words, it remains written on both kinds of memory and on our nature—that is, on our mental and

emotional character. This is the material from which we have formed a life and a soul (so to speak) for ourselves, and it remains the same after death. Our virtues never mingle with our faults (nor our faults with our virtues) in such a way that they cannot be untangled, however. If they did mingle in this way, we would be destroyed forever. The Lord provides against it. When we come into the next life, if we have lived a life of loving, charitable goodness, the Lord filters out the evil and uses the good in us to lift us up to heaven. If on the other hand we have lived a life of evil—a life opposed to love and charity—the Lord filters out what is good in us and our wickedness takes us to hell. Such is everyone's lot after death. What is filtered out is merely detached, though; it is never removed completely.

[3] In addition, one of the two components of human life—our ability to will—has been completely ruined, so the Lord separates this unsalvageable part from our other, intellectual part. In the intellect of people who are regenerating (people who have conscience), he implants the goodness that comes of neighborly love, and by this means he implants a new will. So the Lord also detaches evil from goodness in an overall way.

These are the secrets meant in an inner sense by the idea that what is good cannot die, because evil can be separated from it.

The reason *far be it from you* symbolizes a more intense degree of horror is that the phrase is repeated. This too needs no explanation.

2257

Won't the judge of the whole earth perform judgment? means that divine goodness cannot do this under the guidance of truth separated from good. This can be seen from the symbolism of the *judge of the whole earth* and that of *judgment*.

2258

On an inner level, the *judge of the whole earth* symbolizes goodness itself, which produces truth. The priests who were also judges in the representative church represented the same thing. As priests they represented divine goodness, and as judges, divine truth. The judge of the whole earth represented both simultaneously, because of the symbolism of the *earth,* explained many times in the previous volumes. Bringing in the representational practices of that church to prove it here, though, would take too long.

Judgment, on the other hand, symbolizes truth, as shown earlier, at §2235.

The symbolism of these things and also the train of thought in the inner meaning show that *Won't the judge of the whole earth perform judgment?* means that divine goodness cannot do this under the guidance of truth separated from good

[2] How to understand these ideas? It needs to be known that the pattern governing all of heaven and therefore the whole universe has two components: goodness and truth. Goodness is the essential component of the pattern, and every facet of goodness is a facet of mercy. Truth is the secondary component of the pattern, and every facet of it is a facet of reality. Divine goodness judges everyone as worthy of heaven; divine truth condemns everyone to hell. If the Lord's mercy—his goodness—were not eternal, then, absolutely everyone would be damned. That is what it means to say that divine goodness cannot act this way under the guidance of truth separated from good. (See other remarks on this subject in volume 2, §1728.)

[3] The reason the evil are condemned to hell despite this fact is not that divine goodness is removed from divine truth but that we isolate ourselves from divine goodness. The Lord never sends anyone to hell; we send ourselves, as noted several times before [§§1093, 1683, 1857, 1861, 2121, 2258].

Divine goodness also intersects with divine truth in this: If bad people were not isolated from good, the bad would hurt the good and would constantly be trying to demolish the ordained pattern. Preventing harm to the good is merciful.

The situation here resembles that in the nations of the earth; if evil deeds were not punished, they would contaminate the whole country and therefore destroy it. So it is more merciful of a monarch or judge to punish wickedness and banish evildoers from society than to show them inappropriate mildness.

2259   Genesis 18:26. *And Jehovah said, "If I find in Sodom fifty just people in the middle of the city, I will spare the whole place for their sake."*

Jehovah said symbolizes a perception. *If I find in Sodom fifty just people* here as before means if truth is full of goodness. *I will spare the whole place for their sake* means that they will be saved.

2260   *Jehovah said* symbolizes a perception. This can be seen from the symbolism of *Jehovah said* on the narrative level, where it represents a perception received by the Lord from his divine side, a subsequent thought, and a kind of answer. For more on *Jehovah said,* see the discussion above at §2238.

2261   *If I find in Sodom fifty just people in the middle of the city* means if truth is full of goodness. This can be seen from the symbolism of *fifty* as fullness and that of the *middle of the city* as what lies at the core of truth, or what truth contains. This symbolism was mentioned above at §2252, which you may want to look at, since the words are the same.

One might imagine that people are inevitably saved if the truth they know is full of goodness, but it is important to see that we know very little truth. What truth we do know is devoid of life if it holds no goodness. If it does have something good in it, we are saved, but only out of mercy. As noted, we know very little truth, and the goodness it contains takes its nature from that truth and from the kind of life we live.

[2] Regarded in itself, truth does not give life, but goodness does. Truth is merely a vessel for receiving life—that is, for receiving goodness. As a consequence, no one at all can claim to be saved by truth—or faith alone, as people generally call it—unless the truth that composes the person's faith contains goodness. The goodness it needs to hold is that of love for others. Real faith, then, in an inner sense, is simply neighborly love, as shown above at §2231. People say that an acknowledgment of truth is the faith that saves, but it needs to be realized that people who live lives opposed to charity cannot possibly acknowledge truth. Instead they form a kind of self-persuasion, to which a life of self-love or materialism is attached. Such an acknowledgment contains none of the living energy of faith, or in other words, of love for others. The worst people of all are capable of seizing on religious truth and confirming it by many arguments. This they do at the inspiration of self-love or materialism, or in an effort to outshine others in what passes for understanding and wisdom and so to gain rank, prestige, and wealth. Despite their ability, though, the truth they acquire is dead in them.

[3] The living energy of truth and so of faith comes from the Lord alone, who is life itself. His life consists of mercy, which arises out of love for the entire human race. Some claim to believe the tenets of faith but despise other people in comparison with themselves. Whenever anything infringes on their life of self-love and greed, they react with hatred for their neighbor and take pleasure in their neighbor's loss of resources, position, reputation, and life. People doing such things can never partake of the Lord's life.

All the same, the fact is that religious truth is the means by which we are reborn, because it is the most genuine vessel for receiving goodness. The more accurate the truth, then, and the purer the goodness it contains, and the more perfect their union and therefore their ability to develop in the other life, the more blessed and happy our condition after death.

I will spare the whole place for their sake means that they will be saved. This follows as a conclusion from the sequence and so needs no explanation.

2262

A *place* symbolizes a state or condition, as shown in §§1273, 1378, so the city is called a place here to signify the fact that people who are in that state will be saved.

2263   Genesis 18:27. *And Abraham answered and said, "Here, I beg you, I have undertaken to speak to my lord, and I am dust and ash."*

Abraham answered and said symbolizes thoughts inspired in the Lord by his human side. *Here, I beg you, I have undertaken to speak to my lord, and I am dust and ash* symbolizes the humility of the Lord's human side concerning its relative nature.

2264   *Abraham answered and said* symbolizes thoughts inspired in the Lord by his human side. This can be seen from the representation of *Abraham* in the current chapter as the Lord's human side, dealt with several times above [§§2112, 2172, 2198, 2247].

2265   *Here, I beg you, I have undertaken to speak to my lord, and I am dust and ash* symbolizes the humility of the Lord's human side concerning its relative nature.

Several discussions have already focused on the Lord's state when his humanity was at the fore, his humbled state; and on the Lord's state when his divinity was at the fore, his glorified state. It has been mentioned that in humbled states he talked to Jehovah as another person but that in glorified states he addressed himself (see §1999).

Abraham represents the Lord in his humanity here, as noted, so in that state his human side is said to be dust and ash by comparison with his divinity. As a result, the state is called a humbled one. Humility comes of recognizing oneself to be relative dust and ash.

The Lord's humanity here does not mean his divine humanity but the humanity he inherited from his mother. This humanity he rid himself of completely, replacing it with a divine humanity. The former—the humanity he inherited from his mother—is what is being described as dust and ash. See the remarks above at §2159.

2266   Genesis 18:28. *"Maybe the fifty just people will lack five; will you ruin the whole city over five?" And he said, "I will not ruin it if I find forty-five there."*

"Maybe the fifty just people will lack five" means if there was any less. *"Will you ruin the whole city over five?"* means, will humankind be destroyed for the little it lacks? *And he said, "I will not ruin it if I find forty-five there,"* means that it would not be destroyed if these could be united.

2267   *Maybe the fifty just people will lack five* means if there was any less. This can be seen from the symbolism of *five* as a little, or less. The first volume deals with this symbolism in §649. Section 2252 above showed what *fifty just people* symbolize.

Will you ruin the whole city over five? means, will humankind be destroyed for the little it lacks? This is established by the symbolism of *five* as a little (mentioned just above) and that of a *city* as truth (also dealt with above [§§2252, 2261]).

2268

The Word compares truth in the human mind to a *city* and also refers to it as such. It compares the goodness present in that truth to a city's residents and again refers to them as such. After all, the two resemble one another. If the truth that we store in the different levels of memory and that our mind employs in its thinking lacks goodness, it is like a city without inhabitants, vacant and empty.

The angels can even be said to reside in the truth we know, infusing it with positive emotions that come from the Lord, provided we live lives of love for the Lord and charity for our neighbor. That is where they enjoy settling; in other words, they like living among such people.

The case is different with people who have some truth but none of the good qualities that embody charity.

And he said, "I will not ruin it if I find forty-five there," means that it would not be destroyed if these could be united. This can be seen from the symbolism of the number *forty-five* as union. It has been shown before that numerical factors keep their symbolism even when they are multiplied, so that large numbers have the same meaning as smaller ones [§482]. The same is true of the number forty-five, which is the product of five times nine. As a product of five and nine, it symbolizes the same thing five and nine do. Five symbolizes a little, as shown in §649, and nine symbolizes a union, or something united, §2075. Here, then, it means if goodness and truth are united to some extent.

2269

In the Word, numbers symbolize attributes or states, as earlier remarks on the number fifty at §2252 indicate and as previous discussions of numbers at §§482, 487, 575, 647, 648, 755, 813, 1963, 1988 showed.

[2] The fact that five symbolizes a little and forty-five symbolizes union explains why these numbers appear where they do in the current verse. It says, "Maybe the fifty just people will lack five," meaning if there was any less. Then, "Will you ruin the whole city over five?" meaning, will they be destroyed for the little they lack? Since five symbolizes a little, the verse does not repeat it again but says, "I will not ruin it if I find forty-five there," meaning that they would not be destroyed if these things could be united. Another reason it uses the number forty-five here instead of

saying "if five out of fifty are lacking" is that five symbolizes not only a little (as shown in §649) but also lack of unity (as also shown in the second volume, §1686). In order to symbolize union rather than disconnection, then, it mentions the number forty-five, since forty-five is a certain amount of interconnection, as noted above. So the individual pieces of the story follow each other in a beautiful series in the inner meaning.

[3] As far as the union of goodness with truth goes, it is a mystery that cannot be described intelligibly to most people. To say just a few words about it, the purer and more genuine truth is, the more easily it can serve as a vessel into which goodness from the Lord can be introduced. The less pure and genuine truth is, the harder it is for goodness from the Lord to be introduced into it. Goodness and truth need to correspond to each other. The better they correspond, the more they unite. Goodness can never be introduced into falsity as its proper vessel, nor can evil be introduced into truth as its [vessel], because their character and nature are opposite. The one spurns the other as its enemy. In fact, if they tried to come together goodness would spit evil out as poisonous, and evil would spit goodness out as nauseating. The Lord provides for this kind of hostility to exist between evil and goodness, to prevent them from ever mingling. If they did, humankind would be destroyed.

For frauds and hypocrites, the risk that evil and goodness will join together in them is not a distant one, but the Lord still takes scrupulous care to prevent it. That is why frauds and hypocrites in the other world suffer worse horrors than anyone else.

2270   Genesis 18:29. *And [Abraham] went on to speak to him further and said, "Maybe forty will be found there." And he said, "For the sake of forty, I will not do it."*

He went on to speak to him further symbolizes a thought. *And said, "Maybe forty will be found there,"* symbolizes people who have undergone spiritual trial. *And he said, "For the sake of forty, I will not do it"* means that they will be saved.

2271   *He went on to speak to him further* symbolizes a thought, as can be seen from the inner-level symbolism of *speaking. Speaking,* or speech, is just a product of thought. Since what is on the outside symbolizes what is on the inside—seeing means understanding, the eye symbolizes the intellect, the ear symbolizes obedience, and so on—speaking symbolizes thinking.

2272   *And said, "Maybe forty will be found there,"* symbolizes people who have undergone spiritual trial. This is established by the symbolism of the number *forty* as times of trial (discussed in volume 1, §730).

The logical progression here can be seen from our spiritual trials. We go through times of trial not only in order to be strengthened in the truth but also so that truth can be joined more tightly to goodness in us. At the time, we are fighting for truth against falsity. Because times of trial are times of deep anguish and of torment, they put an end to all pleasure in a life of greed and its attendant gratifications. Then goodness flows into us from the Lord, and we now view evil as abhorrent. This stirs up new thoughts contrary to our previous ones. Later we can be converted to these new ideas and therefore diverted from evil toward goodness, and this goodness can unite with truth. Spiritual trials, then, form a bond between goodness and truth, and since the previous verse [§§2266–2269] said that people in whom goodness could bond with truth would be saved, the same conclusion follows here, with the added idea that inward trials enable it to happen. This is the train of thought that people who know the inner meaning follow.

He said, "For the sake of forty, I will not do it," means that they will be saved, as can be seen without explanation.

2273

The previous verse said of the people symbolized by the number forty-five there, "I *will not ruin it* if I find forty-five." This meant that they would not be destroyed if goodness could be united with truth. This next verse speaks of the forty and says, "For the sake of forty, I *will not do it.*" This does not mean that they will be saved *because of* their trials; some people who undergo trials fail in them, and goodness does not unite with truth in those people. We also are not saved because of our trials if we take any credit for them, since if we do, it is the result of conceit. We boast about it, consider ourselves more deserving of heaven than anyone else, and contemplate our superiority over others, despising them in comparison with ourselves. All these impulses are contrary to mutual love and so to the blessings of heaven.

[2] The struggles we do win bring with them the belief that everyone else is more deserving than we are and that we have more of hell than heaven about us. These are the realizations that come to us in our trials. If we come into thoughts contrary to them after our inward challenges, then, it is an indication that we have not conquered. The thoughts we had while being tested are those toward which our thinking can be bent after the trials end; and if our later thoughts cannot be bent in the direction of our former thoughts, either we failed the test or we face the same test again—sometimes a heavier one. The trials continue until we are finally reduced to the sanity of believing we deserve nothing.

This evidence shows that the number *forty* here symbolizes people in whom spiritual trials form a bond between goodness and truth.

2274   Genesis 18:30. *And he said, "Please let anger not blaze in my lord and let me speak; maybe thirty will be found there." And he said, "I will not do it if I find thirty there."*

And he said, *"Please let anger not blaze in my lord and let me speak,"* symbolizes distress about the human race. *"Maybe thirty will be found there"* symbolizes a certain amount of struggle. *And he said, "I will not do it if I find thirty there,"* means that they will be saved.

2275   *And he said, "Please let anger not blaze in my lord and let me speak,"* symbolizes distress about the condition of the human race. This symbolism can be seen not so much from the words as from the emotion behind them.

There are two dimensions to the inner meaning of the Word: the spiritual and the heavenly. The spiritual dimension is to decipher the inner message as drawn out of the literal meaning (which serves as a springboard for the message, just as objects of sight sometimes serve as springboards for loftier thoughts). The heavenly dimension is to sense only the emotion behind the message of the inner meaning. Spiritual angels focus on the former; heavenly angels, on the latter. When people on earth read the actual text, angels who focus on the latter dimension (the emotion) instantly sense from the feeling alone what the literal meaning involves. From it they form heavenly thoughts for themselves with unending variety, by an indescribable method based on the way the heavenly qualities of love in the emotion follow each other in harmonious order. This description shows what the Lord's Word holds in its inner recesses.

When people read the words *please let anger not blaze in my lord and let me speak,* then, heavenly angels immediately sense a kind of distress, and in fact a distress born of love for the human race. At the same time, countless inexpressible thoughts are instilled in them about the loving anguish the Lord felt when he considered the state of the human race.

2276   *Maybe thirty will be found* symbolizes a certain amount of struggle, as can be seen from the symbolism of the number *thirty.*

The reason thirty symbolizes a certain amount or small measure of struggle is that the number is produced by multiplying five (symbolizing a small amount) times six (symbolizing hard work, or struggle), as demonstrated in §§649, 720, 737, 900, 1709 of the first two volumes.

[2] As a result the number symbolizes something relatively small wherever it appears in the Word, as in Zechariah:

I said to them, "If it is good in your eyes, give me my pay, and if not, decline to." And they weighed out my pay: *thirty silver [coins]*. And Jehovah said to me, "Throw it to the potter, the grand price at which I was appraised by them." And I took the *thirty silver [coins]* and threw it into the house of Jehovah, to the potter. (Zechariah 11:12, 13)

Here it stands for the small value they placed on the Lord's worth and on the redemption and salvation he offered. The potter stands for reformation and rebirth. [3] As a result, this appears in Matthew concerning the same thirty silver coins:

They took the *thirty silver [coins]*—the price of the one appraised, whom they bought from the children of Israel—and gave it for the potter's field, as the Lord commanded me. (Matthew 27:9, 10)

These words make it very clear that in the current instance thirty stands for the meager price that was assessed. A slave, who was not considered worth much, was valued at thirty shekels, as indicated in Moses:

If an ox gores a male slave or a female slave, [its owner] shall give *thirty shekels of silver* to the master of the slave, and the ox shall be stoned. (Exodus 21:32)

Verses 20 and 21 of the same chapter show how worthless a slave was considered. In an inner sense a slave stands for hard work. [4] Levites were accepted into the performance of their ministry (depicted as "one coming to carry out military service and do work in the tent") from a son of *thirty years* to fifty (Numbers 4:3, 23, 30, 35, 39, 43). The reason was that the number thirty symbolized people who were to be initiated and so could not yet carry out much military service, as understood in a spiritual sense. [5] There are other scriptural passages too that mention the number thirty. For instance, they were to offer a minha of *three tenths* [of an ephah of flour] on the young of an ox (Numbers 15:9). This was because the sacrifice of an ox represented goodness of an earthly type, as shown above in §2180, and earthly goodness is meager compared to spiritual goodness, which was represented by the sacrifice of a ram. It is even more meager compared to heavenly goodness, which was represented by the sacrifice of a lamb. These sacrifices involved a different ratio of tenths [of an ephah of flour] for the minha, as revealed by verses 4, 5, 6 of the same chapter [Numbers 15] and Numbers 28:12, 13, 20, 21, 28, 29; 29:3, 4, 9, 10, 14, 15. The ratios or proportions of tenths [of an ephah of flour] would never

---

have been commanded had they not involved heavenly secrets. [6] The number thirty also stands for a small amount in Mark:

> The seed that fell onto good earth yielded fruit rising up and growing, and one bore *thirty,* and another *sixty,* and another *one hundred.* (Mark 4:8)

Thirty stands for producing little and putting out little effort. These numbers would not have been specified had they not symbolized what they do.

2277 *He said, "I will not do it if I find thirty there,"* means that they will be saved. This can be seen without explanation from the train of thought in the inner meaning.

2278 Genesis 18:31. *And he said, "Here, I beg you, I have undertaken to speak to my lord; perhaps twenty will be found there." And he said, "For the sake of twenty, I will not ruin it."*

He said, "Here, I beg you, I have undertaken to speak to my lord," here as before symbolizes the humility of the Lord's human side in the presence of his divinity. *"Perhaps twenty will be found there"* means if there is no struggle but there is still something good. *And he said, "For the sake of twenty, I will not ruin it,"* means that they will be saved.

2279 *He said, "Here, I beg you, I have undertaken to speak to my lord,"* symbolizes the humility of the Lord's human side in the presence of his divinity. This can be seen from remarks above at §2265, where the same words occur.

2280 *Perhaps twenty will be found there* means if there is no struggle but there is still something good, as can be seen from the symbolism of *twenty.*

Since all numbers mentioned in the Word symbolize qualities or states, as has been said and shown in many places above (see §2252), so does the number twenty. Its symbolism can be seen from its roots, in that it is two times ten.

In the Word, ten and tenths symbolize a remnant, which means everything good and true that the Lord instills into us from infancy up to the last moments of our life; the next verse treats of this remnant. Two times ten (twenty, that is) or two tenths symbolizes the same thing—goodness—but a higher level of it.

[2] A remnant symbolizes three kinds of goodness: childhood goodness, uninstructed goodness, and a knowing goodness. Childhood goodness is the goodness instilled in us from the moment we are born up till we are old enough to start being taught and begin to know things. Uninstructed goodness is the goodness we have *while* we are being taught and starting

to know things. A knowing goodness is the goodness we have when we are able to ponder what is good and what is true. Childhood goodness lasts from infancy up to our tenth year. Uninstructed goodness lasts from then up to our twentieth year. After that we start to become rational and to develop the ability to think deeply about goodness and truth and to acquire a knowing goodness for ourselves.

[3] Blind goodness is what the number twenty symbolizes, because people who have it do not undergo any spiritual struggle. We are never tested until we are capable of contemplating what is good and true and perceiving it in our own way. The last two verses talked about people like this, people who have acquired good qualities through times of trial. The current verse is talking about the former kind—people who are not facing inward struggles but still possess some goodness.

[4] Because the number twenty symbolizes people who have the kind of goodness described as blind, everyone who left Egypt—"everyone going out into the army," as it is put—from a *son of twenty years* and up was registered. These individuals stood for people whose goodness was no longer blind. They are spoken of in Numbers 1:20, 24, 26, 28, 30, 32, 34, 38, 40, 42, 45; 26:4. For the same reason, everyone who was *over twenty years* old died in the wilderness (Numbers 32:10, 11), because they could be held responsible for their evil. They represented people who fail in their trials. Again it was for the same reason that one assessment valued a male at *twenty shekels* from a son of five years to a *son of twenty years* (Leviticus 27:5). Another assessment valued a male at fifty shekels from a *son of twenty years* to one of sixty (Leviticus 27:3).

[5] This is how the three kinds of goodness stand: A knowing goodness is best, because it is wise. The goodness that comes before it, or uninstructed goodness, is admittedly good, but because it is not very discerning it cannot be called wise. In itself childhood goodness is also admittedly good, but it is less good than the other two, because it is as yet untouched by any knowing kind of truth. It has not become a wise goodness but is merely a base on which wise goodness can form. Knowledge of what is good and true allows a human to gain human wisdom.

The childlike state that symbolizes innocence does not really belong to childhood but to wisdom, as will be easier to see from the commentary on children in the other world at the end of the chapter [§§2289–2309].

[6] The number twenty in this verse symbolizes no other kind of goodness than blind goodness, as noted. It is not only people under twenty, as mentioned, who can be described as blindly good but *everyone* who

practices charity in ignorance of the truth. This includes people in the church who practice charity but do not know what is true from a religious point of view, for whatever reason. Many, many of those who think well of their neighbor and reverently of God fall into this category. It also includes all those outside the church—people called Gentiles—who likewise practice charity in their lives. Although both kinds lack religious truth, still, because they have some goodness, they are capable of embracing such truth in the other world as readily as children do. Their intellectual side has not yet been tainted with false assumptions, and their volitional side has not been much hardened by an evil life, because they are ignorant of falsity and evil. A charitable life carries with it the ability for blind falsity and evil to change easily into truth and goodness. The same is not true for people who have justified themselves in attacking what is true and lived their lives as an attack on what is good.

[7] In other places in the Word *two tenths* symbolizes goodness that is both heavenly and spiritual. The *two tenths* [of an ephah of flour] that went into the making of each loaf of the bread of presence arranged in rows (Leviticus 24:5) symbolizes heavenly goodness and the spiritual goodness that grows out of it. The *two tenths* [of an ephah of flour] in the minha laid on a sacrificial ram (Numbers 15:6; 28:12, 20, 28; 29:3, 9, 14) symbolizes spiritual goodness. I will have more to say on this elsewhere [§§7978, 10140], with the Lord's divine mercy.

2281   *He said, "For the sake of twenty, I will not ruin it,"* means that they will be saved, as can be seen from the train of thought in the inner meaning and so without explanation.

2282   Genesis 18:32. *And he said, "Please let anger not blaze in my lord and let me speak just this once; maybe ten will be found there." And he said, "For the sake of ten, I will not ruin it."*

He said, "Please let anger not blaze in my lord and let me speak just this once," symbolizes lingering distress over the state of the human race. *"Maybe ten will be found"* means if there were still a remnant. *And he said, "For the sake of ten, I will not ruin it,"* means that they will be saved.

2283   *He said, "Please let anger not blaze in my lord and let me speak just this once,"* symbolizes lingering distress over the state of the human race. This can be seen from the emotion in the words, as discussed above at §2275, where the same words occur.

2284   *Maybe ten will be found there* means if there were still a remnant. This is established by the symbolism of the number *ten* as a remnant, dealt with in §§576, 1738 of volumes 1 and 2.

Various earlier sections, such as §§468, 530, 560, 561, 660, 661, 1050, 1738, 1906, have stated and illustrated what a remnant is. It is everything good and everything true that lies stored away in our memory and in our life. [2] People recognize that there is nothing good or true that does not come from the Lord. They recognize that goodness and truth are constantly flowing into us from the Lord but that we receive them in different ways, depending on how entrenched we have become in an evil life and false principles. These are the things that snuff out or choke off or overturn the goodness and truth that are constantly flowing in from the Lord. To prevent good from mixing with evil and truth with falsity, then, the Lord separates them; otherwise we would be destroyed forever. The goodness and truth we accept he hides in our inner self and refuses to release as long as evil and falsity are active in us. He lets it out only when we are in a reverent mood or anxious or dangerously sick and so on. What the Lord has hidden up in us this way is what is called a remnant, and the Word mentions it very often, but no one has yet realized that this is what it symbolizes. [3] The type and amount of our remnant, or of goodness and truth in us, determines the blessings and happiness we enjoy in the other life, since as noted they lie hidden away in our inner self and come into view only when we have left bodily and worldly concerns behind.

The Lord alone knows the nature and size of our remnant. We cannot possibly know, because human nature these days is such that we can put on a show of goodness even when we have sheer evil inside. Then again we can look evil even when we are good inside. That is why no one is ever allowed to judge the quality of another's spiritual life. Again, only the Lord knows this. Everyone, though, is allowed to judge the quality of another's private and public life, since this is a matter of concern to human society.

[4] It is extremely common for us to form an opinion about some religious tenet and then judge that other people cannot be saved unless they believe what we do, even though the Lord forbade this (Matthew 7:1, 2). However, much experience has taught me that people of every religious persuasion are saved as long as they have acquired a remnant of goodness and seeming truth through a life of love for others. That is the message of the words "If ten are found, for the sake of ten they will not be destroyed," meaning if there was a remnant they would be saved.

[5] A life of neighborly love involves thinking well of people, wanting what is good for them, and feeling personal joy in the notion that others too are saved. If we wish to see no one saved but those who believe as we

do, and particularly if we resent any other arrangement, our life is not one of neighborly love.

The truth of this can be seen simply from the fact that more non-Christians than Christians are saved. In the other life, non-Christians who have thought well of others and wished well to them accept the tenets of the faith better than those called Christian, and acknowledge the Lord more readily. (Nothing gives the angels more pleasure and happiness than teaching people who come into the other world from earth.)

2285 *For the sake of ten, I will not ruin it* means that they will be saved, as can be seen from the train of thought in the inner meaning and so without explanation.

2286 Genesis 18:33. *And Jehovah went, when he had finished speaking to Abraham. And Abraham returned to his place.*

Jehovah went, when he had finished speaking to Abraham means that the kind of perceptive state the Lord had been in now came to an end. *And Abraham returned to his place* means that the Lord went back to the state he had been in before he perceived these things.

2287 *Jehovah went, when he had finished speaking to Abraham* means that the kind of perceptive state the Lord had been in now came to an end, as can be seen from the symbolism of *speaking* and the representation of *Abraham*. In an inner sense, *speaking* symbolizes thinking, as shown above in §2271. Here, though, it means perceiving, since it is Jehovah who is said to have finished speaking to Abraham. To repeat, the Lord's thinking was a product of his perception, and his perception came from his inner core, which was Jehovah.

In the current chapter, though, *Abraham* represents the Lord in a human [rather than divine] state, as noted quite often already. This shows that *Jehovah went, when he had finished speaking to Abraham* in an inner sense means simply that the perceptive state the Lord had been in now came to an end.

See above at §2249 for the reason why this chapter in its inner meaning has so much to say about the Lord's perceptions and thoughts.

2288 *Abraham returned to his place* means that the Lord went back to the state he had been in before he perceived these things. This can be seen from the representation of *Abraham* in the current chapter as the Lord in a human [rather than divine] state, and from the symbolism of a *place* as a state, discussed in the second volume, §§1273, 1378. So in the inner meaning here, *returning to his place* means going back to the state he had been in earlier.

As has been said and shown before, the Lord had two phases when he lived in the world: a humbled one and a glorified one [§§1999, 2098, 2159, 2265]. His state was humble when the humanity he inherited from his mother was uppermost. It was glorified when the divinity he had from Jehovah his father was uppermost. The former condition—the human one inherited from his mother—he rid himself of completely. He took on a divine humanity when he passed out of the world, taking with him a human nature that had now become divine, and returned to the divine nature itself that was his from eternity (John 17:5). Both natures together are the source of the holiness that fills all of heaven. So the Lord rules the universe from his true divinity, by his divine humanity, through his holy influence.

The State of Children in the Other World

I have been allowed to learn for certain that all children who die, anywhere on the planet, are revived by the Lord and taken to heaven. **2289** There angels take care of them, raising and teaching them; and as they develop in understanding and wisdom, they grow up.

You can see, then, how vast the Lord's heaven is simply from the children there, since all of them are instructed in the truth that composes faith and the good actions that exhibit mutual love, and become angels.

People who know nothing about conditions in the life after death might **2290** imagine that the instant children enter the other world they gain angelic understanding and wisdom. Much experience has taught me, though, that the case is very different. Babies who pass away not long after birth have almost exactly the same kind of mind as babies on earth; their knowledge is no greater. All they have is an *ability* to learn, develop understanding, and become wise, in that order—which they do the more readily because they do not have a body but are spirits.

I have not only heard but seen that this is what they are like when they first reach heaven. Several times, by the Lord's divine mercy, groups of children were sent to me and I had the privilege of reading them the Lord's Prayer. At these times, I have been given the opportunity to perceive how the angels who accompanied them would introduce an idea of the prayer's message into the children's tender, rudimentary thoughts. The more the little ones' minds could take in, the fuller an idea the angels would give them. Afterward I saw how the children were given the ability to think similar sorts of thoughts seemingly on their own.

2291   While saying the Lord's Prayer I was also shown the undeveloped nature of their intellect, with which they were influencing the thoughts in my mind. Their intellectual power was so unformed that they knew hardly anything beyond the meaning of the words. Even so, their thinking in all its immaturity had a clear and open path all the way up to the Lord, or rather all the way down from the Lord. Particularly when acting on children's thoughts, the Lord works from the profoundest inner depths. Nothing has closed their minds yet, the way it has in adults. No false assumptions keep them from understanding truth. No life of evil keeps them from receiving goodness and consequently growing wise.

2292   This evidence shows that children do not come into an angelic state directly after death. No, they are gradually introduced into that state by learning about goodness and truth, and their progress follows the heavenly plan precisely. The smallest possible facets of their character are perceived with exquisite sensitivity there, and each and every stirring of their inclination is used to lead them to accept the truth that comes of goodness, and the goodness that grows out of truth. This process takes place under the Lord's unfailingly watchful eye.

2293   Above all, they are constantly being trained to see and then acknowledge the Lord as their only Father and to be aware that they receive life from him. The fact that they have life—truly human and angelic life—results from their intelligent understanding of truth and their wise embrace of goodness, and these come only from the Lord.

That is why children in heaven have no idea they were not born there.

2294   Very often organized groups of children who were still entirely child-like came to me. The sound they made was like a gentle chaos; they did not act as a single body yet, as they would later on after growing up. What surprised me was that the spirits present with me could not help trying to direct the children's thoughts and words. The desire to do so is innate in spirits, but I noticed that every time they tried, the youngsters would balk, not wanting to think or talk that way. Quite often I sensed this resistant, contrary reaction, combined with a kind of indignation, and when the children were given any chance to speak, all they said was,

"No!" I learned that this is how little children are tested in the other world. The goal is to introduce and accustom them not only to resisting falsity and evil but also to thinking, speaking, and acting for themselves. In this way they learn not to let anyone but the Lord lead them.

When children are not in that state but in a deeper, angelic environment, spirits cannot bother them in any way, even if the children are surrounded by the spirits.

2295

Sometimes the Lord sends children in the other life to children on earth, although earthly children are totally unaware of it. The other world's children take great pleasure in them.

Everything is instilled in children in the other world through joys and pleasures appropriate to their age, as was also shown to me. I had the opportunity to see them in beautiful clothes, wreathed about the chest and also round their tender arms with flower garlands radiant with the most charming, heavenly colors.

2296

Once I also had the privilege of seeing some children together with the young women who were their teachers. They were in a magnificent park made up not so much of trees as of a laurel-like plant with branches trained crosswise, forming arcades. The park was very elaborate, with pathways opening into the interior. The children themselves were dressed as before, and when they walked in, some flowers in a planter over the entrance shone out exuberantly. This gives some idea of the kinds of things that delight them. It also shows that pleasures and joys introduce them to the good impulses that innocence and love for others prompt—impulses that the Lord is constantly instilling in those joys and pleasures.

In addition, as the children develop, they are also surrounded with atmospheres that match their state of development. In the other world, atmospheres exist in countless varieties and inexpressible beauty, as experience has taught me; see volume 2, §1621. In particular youngsters see atmospheres composed of what seem to be children at play, at a size that is too small to see but that can be perceived, although only by the deepest power of thought. This gives them the heavenly idea that everything around them is alive and is part of the Lord's stream of life—a thought that gladdens them to the core.

2297

By a method of communication that is common in the next life, I was shown what goes through children's minds when they look at various objects. It was as if each and every one of the objects was alive, so that the individual concepts that went into their thinking had life.

2298

I perceived that children on earth have almost the same kind of notions when they are at play, because unlike adults they do not yet have the ability to ponder what an inanimate object is.

2299   The principal way of teaching children is through representative scenes suited to their frame of mind. No one could ever believe how beautiful and how full of inner wisdom these scenes are. Bit by bit they instill in the children an intelligence that takes its soul from goodness.

Let me report here just a single portrayal that I was permitted to see, from which the reader may draw conclusions about the others. [Teachers] represented how the Lord rose from the tomb and at the same time how he united his humanity with his divinity. The scene was performed with a wisdom surpassing all human wisdom and at the same time with child-like innocence. They also presented the image of a tomb. They did not present an image of the Lord along with it, except for one that was so abstract it could hardly be seen as the Lord except at a distance, so to speak. The reason was that the image of a tomb brings with it something having to do with death that they could push to the side in this way. [2] Later, very carefully, they allowed into the tomb a thin, vapory-looking atmosphere, by which they symbolized—again at a fitting distance—the spiritual life present in baptism.

Afterward I saw them represent the Lord going down to the prisoners and taking them up to heaven, a scene they produced with incomparable skill and reverence. When they represented the Lord among the prisoners in the underground realm, for the sake of the children they let down tiny, soft, very delicate little threads, almost invisible, with which they helped lift the Lord as he rose. All the time they felt a holy fear, not wanting any part of their portrayal to border on what was not spiritual and heavenly.

The children experience other types of representation too, which lead them into a knowledge of truth and a desire for goodness, just as child's play does when it is suited to their temperament.

2300   Furthermore, children have different bents of mind and different personalities, which they receive by inheritance from their parents and cumulatively from their grandparents and great-grandparents. Parents' actual deeds, entrenched by habit, become part of the parents' nature and are passed on to their children. Differences of inclination in the children are the result.

2301   To put it broadly, children have either a heavenly or a spiritual character. The heavenly ones are clearly distinguished from the spiritual ones. The former think, speak, and act very gently, so that hardly anything appears that is not an effect of their affectionate love for the Lord and for other children. The latter, on the other hand, do not proceed as gently. Instead, a quality reminiscent of beating wings reveals itself in all they do. Their character also manifests itself in an annoyance they display and in other signs as well. So every single child's personality differs from that of every other child, and the upbringing of each is adapted to that child's personality.

Taking care of children is the province of certain angelic communities (of which there are many) and particularly of women who had loved children with special tenderness during their bodily lives.   **2302**

When some children are more upright than the others, they offer them to the Lord, after a fashion.

Some angelic spirits who were above and in front of me talked to me in an angelic language that was not divided up into words. They said their state was of peace and quiet and that they had children with them too, whose company was a blessing to them. These spirits were likewise female.   **2303**

They continued by talking about children on earth, and what they said was this: Directly after birth, babies have angels from the heaven of innocence present with them. At the next stage they have angels from the heaven of peace and tranquillity, and later, angels from communities devoted to neighborly love. Then new angels come as the children get older and their innocence and love for others decrease. Eventually, when they grow up and enter on a life alien to charity, they still have angels with them, but at a distance. The distance depends on the goals the grown children have in life, which angels take particular charge of, always instilling good aims and turning aside evil ones. If the angels can, they influence them directly; if they cannot, they exert a more remote influence.

Many people may believe that children stay children in the other world and resemble baby angels. Because they are ignorant about angels, they can confirm this opinion from images found here and there in churches and elsewhere depicting angels as little children. The actuality is completely different. Understanding and wisdom make an angel, and as long as children lack these qualities, they are not angels, even though they live among angels. Not until they become understanding and wise do they become angels. In fact, surprising to say, that is the point at which they look like adults rather than children. By then their frame of mind is no longer that of a child but of a more mature angel. Understanding and   **2304** wisdom carry this consequence with them, since as anyone can see, intellect, good judgment, and a life based on them are the signs to ourselves and others that we are an adult.

I not only learned this from the mouths of angels but also talked once to a man who had died as a little child and now looked like a full adult. He talked to his brother, who had died as an adult, and the former's words held such a deep sense of mutual brotherly love that the latter absolutely could not keep from crying, saying it seemed exactly as if love itself were speaking. Not to mention other examples as well.

2305   There are some who identify innocence with childhood because the Lord said of children that they are the kind who make up heaven [Matthew 19:14; Mark 10:14; Luke 18:16] and that people who do not become like children cannot enter the kingdom of the heavens [Matthew 18:3; Mark 10:15; Luke 18:17]. But people who think this way do not know the Word's inner sense, so they do not know what is meant by the state of a child. It means the innocence that comes of understanding and wisdom. It involves the acknowledgment that we receive life from the Lord alone and that the Lord is our only Father. After all, if we are human, it is because we understand truth intelligently and embrace goodness wisely, and the capacity to do so comes only from the Lord. Innocence itself, which the Word is referring to when it mentions children, cannot possibly exist or dwell anywhere but in wisdom. In fact, the wiser we are, the more innocent we are. So the Lord, being wisdom itself, is innocence itself.

2306   Since children's innocence still lacks understanding and wisdom, it is only a kind of groundwork for real innocence, of which they receive more and more as they grow wise.

The nature of a child's innocence was represented to me by something wooden and almost completely inanimate that comes alive as the child becomes more well rounded through a knowledge of what is true and a desire for what is good.

Next the nature of real innocence was represented by a beautiful child, naked and full of life. The innocent in the deepest heaven, closest to the Lord, themselves look exactly like children to the eyes of other angels. In fact, they look like naked children, because unashamed nudity (like that of the first human and his wife in paradise, as we read [in Genesis 2:25]) represents innocence.

In a word, the wiser angels are, the more innocent they are, and the more innocent they are, the more they look to themselves like children. That is why childhood symbolizes innocence in the Word.

I will have more to say about the state of innocence later, though, with the Lord's divine mercy.

I spoke with some angels about children, asking whether they were **2307** not free of evil, since they have not actually committed any, as adults have. On the contrary I was told that they are immersed in evil just as much as adults and in fact that they too are nothing but evil. It is only that the Lord withholds them from evil and keeps them on a good path, as he does with all angels (so that it looks to them as though they keep themselves on that path). Once children in heaven grow up, then, sometimes they have to be prevented from forming a false impression of themselves, from thinking that the goodness in them comes from themselves rather than from the Lord. What happens is that they are let back into the evil urges they inherited and are left in them until they see, acknowledge, and believe that this is so.

One individual, who had died young but had grown to adulthood in heaven, once had just such an inflated opinion of himself, so he was let back into the evil life he had been born with. From the aura around him I was then able to tell that he had an instinct for tyranny and thought nothing of sexual misbehavior. These were the evils he had inherited from his parents. After he had acknowledged this nature in himself, though, the angels he had formerly lived among welcomed him back.

No one in the other world ever pays a penalty for inherited evil. It is **2308** not ours, so we are not responsible for having it. What we pay for is the evil we have actually committed, which *is* ours. As a result, the penalty depends on the extent to which we have made inherited evil our own by doing it in our lives, as noted before in §966.

When children who have grown up are returned to the condition created by their inherited evil, the point is not to penalize them for it but to show them that in themselves they are nothing but evil. They need to see that it is the Lord's mercy that removes them from the hell within and takes them to heaven, that they are in heaven not because they deserve it but because of the Lord. They need to avoid bragging to others about what is good in themselves, because to do so violates the goodness that characterizes mutual love, just as it violates the truth taught by faith.

From the details reported here the reader can see how children are **2309** raised in heaven: an understanding of truth along with wisdom about what is good introduces them to angelic life. Angelic life is love for the Lord and mutual love, both containing innocence.

Many children on earth, though, receive quite an opposite kind of upbringing, as I was able to see from just this one example: I was on the street of a large city when I saw some youngsters brawling. A crowd gathered excitedly to watch, and I learned that parents goad their own little children to fight like this. Some good spirits and angels were observing the scene through my eyes, and it repelled them so intensely that I could feel their horror. What appalled them the most was the idea that parents could egg their children on to this kind of activity. To do so, they said, is to extinguish all mutual love on the very threshold of life. It is to snuff out all the innocence children receive from the Lord and initiate them into hatred and revenge. By their own efforts the parents are banishing their children from heaven, where mutual love is everything.

Parents who wish their children well, then, had better steer clear of such behavior.

At the end of the preceding chapter, Genesis 17, there was a discussion of the Last Judgment [§§2117–2134]. Here at the end of this chapter, Genesis 18, is one on the state of children in the other world. Both are based on personal experience of events seen and heard in the world of spirits and in the heaven of angels.

A Disclosure of

SECRETS OF HEAVEN

Contained in

SACRED SCRIPTURE

or

THE WORD OF THE LORD

Those in

Genesis

Chapter 19

Together with Amazing Things Seen and Heard
in the World of Spirits & in the Heaven of Angels

At the End of the Current Chapter, Those Having to Do with
The Power of Recall That We Keep after Death
and Memories of What We Did during Bodily Life

Genesis 19

I have discussed the inner meaning of the Word a number of times already, but I know that few can accept the presence of such a meaning in every word of Scripture, not only in the prophetic but also in the narrative parts.

2310

Prophetic: It is easier to believe that this kind of meaning exists in the prophetic books, because they do not have the same kind of continuity, and they do contain strange language. This allows anyone to infer that they contain something hidden.

Narrative: It is not as easy, though, to see that the same is true of the narrative books. For one thing, the idea has never occurred to anyone before. For another, stories by their very nature seize our attention, distracting us from the thought that any deeper dimension lies hidden in them. For yet another, the narratives report events as they actually happened.

[2] Still, if you consider the following, you cannot help concluding that even the narratives contain a veiled message that is heavenly and divine:

First: The Word comes from the Lord and was sent down to us through heaven, so its original form is different. Many passages below will show what its origin is like and how different and distant it is from the literal meaning. In fact, its original form is so different that we cannot even see it, and as a result people who are merely worldly do not acknowledge it.

Second: Since the Word is divine, it was written not only for people on earth but also for the angels present with us. It exists to serve not only the human race but heaven as well. Accordingly, it is the means for uniting heaven and earth. The church is what unites the two, and specifically the Word in the church, which is why the Word has the nature it does and why it is unlike any other piece of literature.

[3] To address the narrative books in particular: If they too did not contain divine and heavenly themes separate from the literal meaning, no one who delves below the surface would ever be able to acknowledge them as part of a Word inspired down to every single jot. Would anyone expect God's Word to mention the revolting affair of Lot's daughters described at the end of the current chapter [Genesis 19:30–38]? How about the story in which Jacob peeled some rods, laying them bare down to the white and placing them in the water troughs to make the flock bear mottled, speckled, and spotted lambs [Genesis 30:37–39]? Not to mention many other accounts in the rest of Moses' books and in Joshua, Judges, Samuel, and Kings. They would lack any importance; it would be all the same whether we knew them or not, if they did not enfold a divine secret deep inside them. Otherwise they would not differ in any way from other histories, whose manner of expression sometimes seems more moving.

[4] The scholars of the world have no clue that divine and heavenly matters lie hidden in the narrative portions of the Word as well. If it were not for the holy veneration of the books of Scripture impressed on them since childhood, they would find it easy to tell themselves that the Word has no other holiness. Yet it is not this veneration that gives it holiness but rather the presence of an inner meaning. The inner meaning that sanctifies the Word is heavenly and divine, and it unites heaven with earth; in other words, it unites angelic minds with human ones and in the process unites human minds with the Lord.

2311   Another piece of evidence that the Word is like this and is therefore different from every other piece of literature has to do with symbolism. Not only do the names have symbolic meaning, as shown above (§§1224, 1264, 1876, 1888), but every word also has a spiritual sense, so that it means something else in heaven than on earth. This symbolism is utterly consistent in both the prophetic and the narrative parts. When these names and words are explained in their heavenly sense, according to their unchanging symbolism throughout the Word, what results is the inner meaning, or the Word as it exists among the angels.

This twofold meaning of the Word resembles a body and soul. The literal meaning is like a body, while the inner meaning is like a soul. Just as the body is kept alive by the soul, the literal meaning is kept alive by the inner meaning. The Lord's life flows into the literal meaning through the inner meaning in accord with the feelings of the person who is reading it.

These considerations make it clear how holy the Word is, even though it does not seem so to worldly minds.

Genesis 19

1. And the two angels came to Sodom in the evening, and Lot was sitting in the gate of Sodom. And Lot saw and got up to meet them and bowed down, face to the earth.

2. And he said, "Here, I beg you, my lords; please turn aside to the house of your servant and spend the night and wash your feet. And in the morning you may get up and go on your way." And they said, "No, because we will spend the night in the street."

3. And he pressed them very hard, and they turned aside to him and came to his house. And he made them a banquet and cooked unleavened loaves, and they ate.

4. Hardly had they lain down when the men of the city—the men of Sodom—circled the house, from youth to old man, all the people from the furthest limits.

5. And they shouted to Lot and said to him, "Where are the men who came to you at night? Bring them out to us and let us know them."

6. And Lot went out to them at the door, and the entrance he closed behind him.

7. And he said, "Please, my brothers, don't do wrong.

8. Look, please: I have two daughters who have not known any man. Please let me bring them out to you, and you may do with them as is good in your eyes. Only don't do anything to these men, because, you see, they have come into the shade of my roof beam."

9. And they said, "Get away!" And they said, "Didn't this one come to stay as an immigrant? And will he really judge us? Now we will do worse to you than to them!" And they put pressure on the man, on Lot, very hard, and they came up to break the entrance.

10. And the [angel] men put out their hand and brought Lot in to them, into the house, and closed the entrance.

11. And the men who were at the door of the house they struck with blindness, from small to large; and they had trouble finding the door.

12. And the men said to Lot, "Do you still have anyone here? [Your] son-in-law and your sons and your daughters and everyone you have in the city—take them away from the place.

13. Because we are destroying this place, because their outcry has grown loud before Jehovah, and Jehovah has sent us to destroy it."

14. And Lot went out and talked to his sons-in-law, the ones taking his daughters, and said, "Get up! Leave this place, because Jehovah is destroying the city." And it was as if he were fooling, in the eyes of his sons-in-law.

15. As dawn rose, the angels hurried Lot along, saying, "Get up! Take your wife and your two reclaimed daughters, to keep from being consumed in the wickedness of the city."

16. And he delayed, and the men took his hand and his wife's hand and the hand of his two daughters, in Jehovah's compassion on him, and brought him out and stood him outside the city.

17. And it happened when they brought them outdoors that [the angel] said, "Escape, on your soul! Don't look back behind you, and don't stop anywhere on the plain! Escape to the mountain to keep from being consumed."

18. And Lot said to them, "Please, no, my lords!

19. Look, please; your servant has found favor in your eyes, and you have enlarged the mercy that you have shown me, to keep my soul alive. But I cannot escape to the mountain or evil might cling to me and I might die.

20. Look, please: this city is nearby to flee to, and it is small. Let me escape there, please (isn't it small?), and let my soul live!"

21. And [the angel] said to him, "Here, now, I have also accepted your face in regard to this word, that I will not overthrow the city that you spoke of.

22. Hurry! Escape there, because I cannot do anything until you come there." Therefore they called the name of the city Zoar.

23. The sun came up over the earth, and Lot came to Zoar.

24. And Jehovah rained sulfur and fire from Jehovah out of the sky onto Sodom and onto Gomorrah.

25. And he overthrew those cities and all the plain and all the residents of the cities and what sprouted in the field.

26. And [Lot's] wife looked back behind him and turned into a pillar of salt.

27. And Abraham got up in the morning, at the place where he stood, there before Jehovah.

28. And he looked out opposite the face of Sodom and Gomorrah and opposite the whole face of the land of the plain, and he saw, and here, now, the smoke of the land rose like the smoke of a furnace.

29. And it happened, in God's destroying the cities of the plain, that God remembered Abraham and sent Lot out from the middle of the overthrow, in overthrowing the cities in which Lot had lived.

30. And Lot went up from Zoar and lived on the mountain, and his two daughters with him, because he was afraid to live in Zoar. And he was living in a cave, he and his two daughters.

31. And the firstborn said to the younger, "Our father is old, and there is no man in the land to come in to us according to the way of the whole earth.

32. Come, let's give our father wine to drink and lie with him and keep seed from our father alive."

33. And they gave their father wine to drink that night, and the firstborn came and lay with her father, and he was unaware in her lying down and in her getting up.

34. And it happened on the next day that the firstborn said to the younger, "Here, now, I lay yesterday with my father. Let's give him wine to drink tonight too, and come, lie with him and we will keep seed from our father alive."

35. And they gave their father wine to drink that night too, and the younger got up and lay with him, and he was unaware in her lying down and in her getting up.

36. And Lot's two daughters conceived by their father.

37. And the firstborn delivered a child, and she called his name Moab; he is the father of Moab right to this day.

38. And the younger, she also delivered a child, and she called his name Ben-ammi. He is the father of the children of Ammon right to this day.

Summary

I N the inner meaning of this chapter, Lot depicts conditions in a spiritual religion whose deeds are loving but whose worship is shallow, and the way such a church degenerates over time.   **2312**

Phase one: The people involved in this religion do loving deeds and acknowledge the Lord; he strengthens them in goodness (verses 1, 2, 3).   **2313**
They are saved (verse 12). *Phase two:* Evil starts to undermine goodness in them, but the Lord firmly withdraws them from evil and maintains them in what is good (verses 14, 15, 16). Their feebleness is portrayed (verse 18).

They are saved (verse 20). *Phase three:* No longer do they think and act from a desire for goodness but from a desire for truth (verses 18, 19, 20). They are saved (verse 23). *Phase four:* The desire for truth dies out (Lot's wife as a pillar of salt; verse 26). *Phase five:* An impure kind of goodness—goodness tainted with falsity—takes its place (Lot in the mountain cave; verse 30). *Phase six:* They adulterate and falsify this kind of goodness still more (verses 31, 32, 33). They do the same to truth (verses 34, 35). This results in the conception and birth of something that resembles a religion, whose so-called goodness is Moab and whose so-called truth is the son of Ammon (verses 36, 37, 38).

2314   Furthermore, the residents of Sodom in an inner sense depict conditions among people in that same religion who refuse to act in a loving way. It tells how wickedness and falsity build up in them as time passes, until in the end there is nothing in them that is not evil and false.

2315   *Phase one:* They oppose neighborly kindness and the Lord (verses 4, 5). *Phase two:* They are taught about doing good for others out of love and about the pleasurable feelings that come with it and that will be theirs. Even so, they dig in their heels and reject what is good (verses 6, 7, 8). They even try to demolish neighborly kindness itself, but the Lord protects it (verses 9, 10). *Phase three:* Eventually they become the type of people who cannot even see truth or goodness, let alone grasp the fact that truth leads to good (verse 11). So evil and falsity possess them, with the inevitable consequence that they are destroyed (verse 13). *Phase four:* Their annihilation (verse 24). Everything good and true is removed from them (verse 25).

2316   Good and evil people are separated—and the good are saved—by means of the Lord's humanity, which is now divine (verses 27, 28, 29).

Inner Meaning

2317   GENESIS 19:1. *And the two angels came to Sodom in the evening, and Lot was sitting in the gate of Sodom. And Lot saw and got up to meet them and bowed down, face to the earth.*

The two angels came to Sodom in the evening symbolizes a visitation that comes before a judgment. The *two angels* symbolize the Lord's divine humanity and holy influence, which is what passes judgment; *Sodom* symbolizes evil people, especially ones who are religious; and *evening* is a time of visitation. *And Lot was sitting in the gate of Sodom* symbolizes people whose deeds are loving but whose worship is shallow. They are *Lot* here; and they live among the evil, though isolated from them, which is to *sit in the gate of Sodom. And Lot saw* symbolizes their conscience. *And got up to meet them* symbolizes acknowledgment, and the effect that love for others has. *And bowed down, face to the earth* symbolizes humility.

The *two angels came to Sodom at evening* symbolizes a visitation that comes before a judgment. This can be seen from the words of the three men (that is, of Jehovah) in the previous chapter [§2242]; from the rest of the current chapter; and from the symbolism of *evening*. **2318**

In the previous chapter, Jehovah said, "Let me go down, and I will see whether the residents of Sodom and Gomorrah have made an end of it according to the outcry that has come to me. And if not, I will know it" (Genesis 18:20, 21). The explanation of these words [§2242] showed that they symbolize a visitation that comes before a judgment.

The current chapter depicts the actual visitation and then the judgment, as will be evident below.

Evening symbolizes a time of visitation, as will be evident below [§2323].

For a definition of visitation and the fact that it comes before judgment, see §2242.

The previous chapter focused on the corrupt condition of the human race, the Lord's grief for people who do evil but still retain some goodness and truth, and his intervention on their behalf. Accordingly, the text now turns to the salvation of those who do still have some goodness and truth—the people Lot represents in this chapter. At the same time it deals with the destruction of those completely under the sway of evil and falsity, who are symbolized by Sodom and Gomorrah here.

The *two angels* symbolize the Lord's divine humanity and holy influence, which is what passes judgment. This can be seen from two things: what *angels* symbolize in the Word, and the fact that there are said to be *two* of them here. **2319**

In the Word, *angels* symbolize some divine characteristic in the Lord, but the context reveals what specific characteristic it is, as shown before, in §1925. Here they symbolize the Lord's divine humanity and his holy influence, and the evidence is as follows: The three men who were with Abraham meant the Lord's true divinity, his divine humanity, and his holy influence (§§2149, 2156, 2288). Verse 24 calls them Jehovah. These considerations, and the symbolism of angels (§1925), make it quite clear that the two angels here mean the Lord's divine humanity and holy influence.

2320   Why were there only two angels here, when there were three with Abraham? This is a secret that cannot be explained briefly but can be seen to some extent from the following: The current chapter discusses judgment, or in other words, the salvation of the faithful and damnation of the faithless. The Word indicates that judgment is the province of the Lord's divine humanity and his holy influence. John shows that judgment belongs to his divine humanity: "The Father does not judge anyone but has given all judgment to the Son" (John 5:22). The Son means the Lord's divine humanity (see §2159). John also shows that judgment belongs to the holy influence emanating from the Lord's divine humanity: "If I leave, I will send the Paraclete to you, and when he comes he will denounce the world regarding sin, and regarding justice, and regarding judgment" (John 16:[7,] 8). The same author shows that this holy influence comes from the Lord: "He will not speak on his own authority but will take of what is mine and proclaim it" (John 16:13, 15). The same author again shows that this would happen when the Lord's humanity had become divine, that is, when the Lord had been glorified: "There was not the Holy Spirit yet because Jesus was not yet glorified" (John 7:39).

2321   The reason judgment is assigned to the Lord's divine humanity and holy influence is that the human race could no longer have been saved had the Lord not come into the world and united his divine with his human nature. If his humanity had not become divine, his salvation could never have come within our grasp again (§§1990, 2016, 2033, 2034).

The holy influence itself emanating from the Lord's divine humanity is what divides the evil from the good. Evil beings dread and fear the Lord's holiness so much that they cannot go near it. Instead they run far away from it, heading for their hells, each according to his or her own form of profaneness.

2322   *Sodom* symbolizes evil people, especially those who are religious. This is established by the symbolism of Sodom as the evil of self-love (discussed in §§2220, 2246) and therefore as people who fall prey to that evil.

People who take the Word at face value might imagine that Sodom means a foulness against the natural order of things. On an inner level, however, it symbolizes the evil of self-love. From this evil wells up all evil of every kind, and in the Word what wells up out of it is called and is depicted by adultery. The scriptural passages to be quoted at the end of the chapter [§2466] will bear witness to this fact.

Evening is a time of visitation, as can be seen from its symbolism. **2323**
The Word compares conditions in a religious culture both to seasons of the year and to times of day—the yearly seasons of summer, fall, winter, and spring, and the daily periods of midday, evening, night, and morning. Religious conditions resemble these times and seasons.

The condition of religion that is referred to as *evening* occurs when neighborly love dies out and so when faith starts to disappear. In other words, it occurs when religion comes to an end. This evening is the kind followed by night (see §22). Evening is also a time when neighborly love shines and faith accordingly does too. So it is a time when a new religion dawns. This kind of evening is the half-light that anticipates morning (see §883). Evening symbolizes both.

When one religion ends the Lord provides for a new one to rise, and to rise at the same time the other disappears. If the church did not exist somewhere in the world, the human race could not survive, because its connection with heaven would break, as shown in §§468, 637, 931, 2054.

[2] The current chapter deals with both states of religion: the dawn of a new one (represented by Lot) and the death of the old (symbolized by Sodom and Gomorrah). This can be seen from the summary [§§2312–2316]. That is why the text here says that two angels came to Sodom in the evening. That is also why it mentions what happened in the evening (verses 1–3), in the night (verses 4–14), in the morning as dawn rose (verses 15–22), and after the sun came up (verses 23–26).

[3] Since evening symbolizes those conditions in the religious culture, it also symbolizes a visitation that comes before a judgment. When judgment looms—the salvation of the faithful and the damnation of the faithless—first comes a visitation, or an examination into the character of the people to see whether any neighborly love or faith remains. This visitation occurs in the evening, so the visitation itself is also called evening time, as in Zephaniah:

> Doom to the inhabitants in the region of the sea, to the nation of the Cherethites! Jehovah's word is against you, Canaan, land of the Philistines, and I will destroy you, until there is no inhabitant. The survivors of the house of Judah will graze in the houses of Ashkelon. In the *evening* they will lie down, because Jehovah their God will *visit* them and bring them back from captivity. (Zephaniah 2:5, 7)

And Lot was sitting in the gate of Sodom symbolizes people whose deeds **2324** are loving but whose worship is shallow. They are *Lot* here; and they live among the evil, though isolated from them, which is to *sit in the gate of*

Sodom. This can be seen from the representation of *Lot* and from the symbolism of a *gate* and of *Sodom.*

The representation of *Lot:* When Lot was with Abraham, he represented the Lord's sensory level and so his outer level, as shown in §§1428, 1434, 1547 of the second volume. Now, when he has separated from Abraham, he no longer keeps his role as one who represents the Lord but instead represents people present with the Lord. To be specific, he represents the superficial individual in the church—that is, people whose deeds are loving but whose worship is shallow. [2] In fact, in this chapter Lot does not only represent a superficially religious person, or, what is the same, a superficial religion, such as it is at its beginning. No, he also represents that religion such as it is over time, and at its end too. The end of that religion is what Moab and the son of Ammon symbolize, as will be visible from the series of ideas in what follows [§§2465, 2466, 2468], the Lord in his divine mercy willing. In the Word, it is common for a single person to represent many consecutive stages, depicted in the consecutive deeds of the person's life.

[3] The symbolism of a *gate:* A gate is the place of entry to or exit from a city. In the current verse, then, sitting in the gate symbolizes living among the evil, to be sure, yet remaining separate from them. This is what religious people who practice the good of neighborly love often do. Although they live with evil people they are isolated from them—not so far as polite society goes but in their spiritual life.

Sodom symbolizes evil in general, or (interchangeably) evil people, especially religious ones, as noted above at §2322.

2325   *And Lot saw* symbolizes conscience—specifically, conscience in people who practice the good of neighborly love but whose worship is superficial— as can be seen from the symbolism of *seeing.* In the Word, *seeing* means understanding (see §§897, 1584, 1806, 1807, 2150). In an inner sense, though, it means believing (a symbolism to be discussed at Genesis 29:32, with the Lord's divine mercy).

The reason it symbolizes conscience here is that people who possess faith also have a conscience. The former is inseparable from the latter. They are so inseparable that it is all the same whether you say faith or conscience.

By faith I mean the faith that leads to neighborly love and the faith that comes of neighborly love. So I mean such love itself, because faith without love for others is no faith. Since faith cannot exist without love, neither can conscience.

And got up to meet them symbolizes acknowledgment, and also the **2326** effect that love for others has. This can be seen from the consideration that when the angels arrived, Lot immediately acknowledged them as angels. The men of Sodom did not. "They shouted to Lot," verse 5 says of them, "and said, 'Where are the men who came to you at night? Bring them to us so that we can know them.'" In an inner sense these words mean that people in the church who act out of love for others acknowledge the Lord's divine humanity and holy influence (meant by the two angels), but people who fail to act out of love do not.

The fact that the same words also involve the effect charity has is self-evident. It can also be seen from the fact that Lot invited the angels into his house, and Lot represents people who act out of love for others. In fact, he even symbolizes the good deeds that result from that love.

He bowed down, face to the earth symbolizes humility, as is evident **2327** without explanation.

In time past, especially in representative religions, people bowed so far down that they put their faces on the ground. The reason was that the face symbolized a person's inner depths (§§358, 1999). The reason they bent to the ground was that the dust of the earth symbolized whatever was profane and damned (§278), so in this way they represented a realization that of themselves they were profane and damned. That is why they prostrated themselves, lowering their faces to the earth, even rolling in dust and ash and throwing it on their heads. Lamentations 2:10, Ezekiel 27:30, Micah 1:10, Joshua 7:6, Revelation 18:19, and other passages demonstrate their use of these practices.

[2] By these practices they represented a state of true humility, and such a state is not possible in the least except for those who acknowledge that on their own they are profane and damned. It is not possible, then, except for those who acknowledge that by themselves they cannot turn to the Lord, where they will find only what is divine and holy. So the more clearly we recognize ourselves for what we are, the more true humility we can have, and the more reverence we will feel when worshiping. Humility has to be present in all worship. If humility is removed from it, there is no reverence, and consequently there is no worship.

[3] The reason a humble frame of mind is essential to genuine worship is that the more the heart humbles itself, the more self-love dies down, along with all the evil it spawns. The more they die down, the more goodness and truth, or charity and faith, flow into it from the Lord. The main obstacle to receiving goodness and truth is self-love, since this

love harbors contempt for others, hatred and vengeance toward people who fail to cultivate us, and ruthlessness and cruelty. That is to say, it harbors the very worst types of evil, in which goodness and truth can have no place, because they oppose one another.

2328   Genesis 19:2. *And he said, "Here, I beg you, my lords; please turn aside to the house of your servant and spend the night and wash your feet. And in the morning you may get up and go on your way." And they said, "No, because we will spend the night in the street."*

And he said, "Here, I beg you, my lords," symbolizes an inward acknowledgment and affirmation of the Lord's divine humanity and holy influence. *"Please turn aside to the house of your servant and spend the night"* means our inviting him to make his home in us; *to the house of your servant* means in our loving deeds. *"And wash your feet"* means his adapting to our earthly level. *"And in the morning you may get up and go on your way"* means being strengthened in goodness and truth in the process. *And they said, "No,"* symbolizes doubt, a common symptom of spiritual crisis. *"Because we will spend the night in the street"* means that [the Lord] seems to want to judge us on the basis of truth.

2329   *He said, "Here, I beg you, my lords,"* symbolizes an inward acknowledgment and affirmation of the Lord's divine humanity and holy influence. This can be seen from the acknowledgment and humility described just above. Here, affirmation follows directly on its heels, because Lot's words "Here, I beg you, my lords" are an affirmation.

Inward affirmation is affirmation of the heart; it occurs when we feel humble and want what is good. Outward affirmation, though, is affirmation of the lips; it can occur when we pretend to be humble and to want what is good. To pretend either of these is to do neither. Take people who profess a belief in the Lord for the sake of their own prestige (or rather their own adulation) and their own gain, for instance; what they affirm with their lips they deny at heart.

[2] It says "my lords" in the plural for the same reason the previous chapter mentions three men. Just as the three there symbolize the Lord's divinity itself, divine humanity, and their holy influence, the two here symbolize his divine humanity and holy influence, as noted above [§2319]. Everyone in the church knows that the two qualities are one, and since they are one, they are also referred to in the singular below. In verse 17, for example: "It happened when they brought them out that *he said*, 'Escape, on your soul!'" Verse 19: "'Look, please; *your* servant has found favor in *your* eyes, and *you have enlarged your* mercy that *you have shown* me.'"

Verse 21: "And *he said* to him, 'Here, now, *I have* also *accepted* your face in regard to this word, that *I will* not *overthrow* the city.'" Verse 22: "'Because *I cannot* do anything until you come there.'"

[3] Divinity itself, the divine humanity, and the holy influence are Jehovah, as can be seen throughout the previous chapter, where it refers to the three men as Jehovah. Specifically, in verse 13 there: "*Jehovah* said to Abraham." Verse 14: "Will anything be [too] amazing for *Jehovah?*" Verse 22: "Abraham was still standing before *Jehovah.*" Verse 33: "*Jehovah* went, when he had finished speaking to Abraham."

The divine humanity and holy influence are Jehovah too, then, and they are also referred to that way in the current chapter, in verse 24: "And *Jehovah* rained sulfur and fire from *Jehovah* out of the sky onto Sodom and Gomorrah." (For the inner meaning of these words, see below [§§2443–2447].) The Lord is Jehovah himself and is called this many times in the narrative and prophetic parts of the Old Testament (see §1736).

[4] True members of the church—people who love the Lord and treat their neighbor with charity—recognize and acknowledge that there is a Trinity, but they still humble themselves before the Lord and worship only him. This is because they know that no one can approach divinity itself (called the Father) except through the Son. They also know it is from the Son that any holy effect of the Holy Spirit emanates. When this is the picture that people have in mind, they worship none other than the one through whom and from whom everything comes. So they worship a single being [5] and do not spread their thoughts out over three, as many others in the church do.

This effect can be witnessed in many people in the other world, especially in scholars who imagined they had possessed more of the secret knowledge of faith than others during bodily life. In the other life their picture of the one God was examined to see whether they were thinking of three uncreated beings, three infinite beings, three eternal beings, three omnipotent beings, and three Lords. It could be seen clearly that they were indeed picturing three (since a person's thoughts are communicated to everyone there). And yet the [Athanasian] Creed says explicitly that there are not three uncreated beings, not three infinite beings, not three eternal beings, not three omnipotent beings, not three Lords, but one, as is the truth. So the scholars admitted that, yes, they had spoken of one God with their lips but had thought of three, and some had even believed in three. They said they could not unite the three in their minds but had to divide them. [6] The reason they could not is that absolutely all mysteries, even the very deepest ones, carry with them a mental image. Without an image we could not think or even remember a thing.

As a consequence, what kind of thought and therefore what kind of belief we have each formed for ourselves concerning the one God lies open as plain as day in the other world.

In fact, when Jews in the next life hear that the Lord is Jehovah and that there is only one God, they have nothing to say. When they see Christians split their image into three, though, they reply that *they* worship one God, but Christians, three. The claim is particularly justified when you consider that no one can unite the three beings separated in thought except one whose faith comes of love for others. With people like this, the Lord adapts their minds to his nature.

2330 *Please turn aside to the house of your servant and spend the night* means our inviting him to make his home in us, as can be seen without explanation.

2331 *To the house of your servant* means in our loving deeds. This is established by the symbolism of a *house* as heavenly goodness, which has everything to do with love and charity, as discussed in §§2048, 2231.

2332 *Wash your feet* means his adapting to our earthly level, as can be seen from the remarks at §2162 of the previous chapter, where the same words occur.

It used to be that when people saw the angel of Jehovah they thought they were about to die (Exodus 19:12, 21, 24; 20:19; Judges 6:22, 23; 13:22, 23), the reason being that when divine holiness touches the profaneness we have in us, its effect is like that of a consuming, devouring fire. When the Lord presents himself to people's sight, then, or even to angels' sight, he modifies and tempers the holiness emanating from him in a miraculous way so that they can endure it. To put the same thing another way, he adapts to their earthliness.

This, then, is the inner-level symbolism of Lot's words to the angels, "Wash your feet."

This interpretation reveals the nature of the inner sense, since the meaning given is not visible in the literal story.

2333 *"And in the morning you may get up and go on your way"* means being strengthened in goodness and truth in the process, as can be seen from the symbolism of *getting up in the morning* and of *going on one's way*. In the Word, *morning* symbolizes the Lord's kingdom and everything in it.

So the main thing it symbolizes is the good we do out of love and charity. (This will be corroborated from the Word at verse 15 [§2405].) A *way*, though, symbolizes truth (see §627). From this it follows that after they had entered his house and spent the night there (meaning that they had made their home in his loving deeds), they would get up in the morning and go on their way (meaning to be strengthened in goodness and truth in the process).

[2] From these remarks, as from all the others, it is clear how distant the inner meaning is from the literal and therefore how hard it is to see, especially in the narrative parts of Scripture. Clearly the inner meaning cannot reveal itself unless the individual words are explained according to their consistent symbolism in Scripture. When the literal meaning monopolizes our thinking, the inner meaning appears to be nothing more than a vague and shadowy something. On the other hand when the inner meaning monopolizes our thinking, the *literal* meaning looks vague. In fact, angels see it as a nonentity, because they no longer engage in worldly and body-centered thinking, as we on earth do, but in spiritual and heavenly thinking. When we read the Word, and it rises up from us to the dimension where angels are—to heaven—the literal words change into thoughts of just this kind in the most amazing way. The change is determined by a correspondence between spiritual subjects and worldly ones, and between heavenly subjects and bodily ones. The correspondence is absolutely constant, but its nature has never been revealed before, except in the current explanation of the inner meaning of the words, names, and numbers of Scripture.

[3] You may want to know what this correspondence is like, or in other words, how worldly and bodily thoughts convert into the corresponding spiritual and heavenly thoughts when they rise into heaven. Take *morning* and a *way* as examples. When we read the word "morning," as in the phrase *get up in the morning*, angels do not form an idea of any early part of the day but of morning time in a spiritual sense. So they treat it as it is treated in Samuel:

The rock of Israel—he is like the *morning* light when the sun rises, like a *morning* when there are no clouds. (2 Samuel 23:[3,] 4)

Also as in Daniel:

The Holy One said to me, "Up till the [day's second] evening, when it becomes *morning*, two thousand three hundred times." (Daniel 8:14, 26)

So they take the morning to be the Lord, or his kingdom, or the heavenly qualities of love and charity, which they perceive with great variety, depending on the story line of the Word in the part being read.

[4] Likewise, when we read the word "way," as in the phrase *go on your way*, they cannot form any picture of a physical path but of another kind of path that is spiritual or heavenly. In other words, they treat it as it is treated in John, when the Lord said:

> I am the *way* and the *truth*. (John 14:6)

And these words in David:

> Make *your ways* known to me, Jehovah; guide my *way* in the truth. (Psalms 25:4, 5)

And in Isaiah:

> He made the *way of understanding* known to him. (Isaiah 40:14)

So in both the narrative and the prophetic parts of the Word they take a way to be truth. Angels no longer care about the narrative details, since such details are completely incompatible with their thoughts. In place of them they perceive the kinds of things that have to do with the Lord and his kingdom, which follow one after another in a beautiful pattern and elegant sequence in the inner meaning. In order that angels too can benefit from the Word, then, all the historical events in it represent such subjects, and the individual words symbolize them. This characteristic is unique to the Word, as compared with any other type of writing.

2334   *And they said, "No,"* symbolizes doubt, a common symptom of spiritual crisis. This can be seen from their denial and from the fact that they still entered Lot's house. All inward trial contains doubt over the Lord's presence and mercy, over salvation, and so on. People undergoing such trials feel deep distress, even to the point of despair. They are usually kept in this despair in order to convince them eventually that they owe everything to the Lord's mercy, that he alone saves them, and that in themselves there is nothing but evil. If they win their battles, such beliefs grow stronger.

When their crisis passes, it leaves behind many impressions of truth and goodness. Afterward the Lord can bend their thoughts in the direction of these impressions whenever their thinking would otherwise plunge into insanity and turn their minds against anything true or good.

As noted [§2324], the text here uses the image of Lot to depict the first phase of a religious culture that acts out of love for others but lacks depth in its worship. Before people enter this phase, they have to reform, and this reformation is actually accomplished through a certain kind of crisis. If their worship is shallow, however, they undergo only mild challenges. That is the reason for the current passage, which describes only a measure of struggle. In other words, that is the reason that the angels first said they would spend the night in the street, that Lot pressed them, and that they therefore turned aside to him and came into his house.

"Because we will spend the night in the street" means that [the Lord] **2335** seems to want to judge us on the basis of truth, as can be seen from the symbolism of a *street* and of *spending the night.*

The Word mentions a *street* quite often, and on an inner level it symbolizes the same thing as a *way*—in other words, truth. A street, after all, is a way through a city. The next section will demonstrate this symbolism.

The fact that in this verse *spending the night* means passing judgment can be seen from the symbolism of *night.* Above in §2323, I showed that evening symbolizes the next-to-last phase of a religious culture, when faith starts to die, and also a visitation that comes before judgment. From this it is evident that the ensuing night is the final phase, when faith is gone, and also the judgment itself. Clearly, then, spending the night in the street, in an inner sense, is judging on the basis of truth.

[2] As far as judgment goes, there are two kinds: judgment from the standpoint of goodness and judgment from the standpoint of truth. Believers are judged from the standpoint of goodness, unbelievers from that of truth. It is obvious from Matthew 25:34–40 that believers are judged from goodness, and from verses 41–46 of the same chapter that unbelievers are judged from truth. People who are judged from goodness are saved, because they have welcomed goodness. People who are judged from truth, on the other hand, are damned, because they have rejected goodness. Goodness is the Lord's, and people who acknowledge this by the way they live and believe are the Lord's, so they are saved. People who do not acknowledge it by the way they live and who therefore fail to believe it cannot belong to the Lord, so they cannot be saved. As a result, they are judged by the deeds they have done and by their thoughts and goals. When they are judged by these, they are inevitably condemned, because the truth is that on our own we cannot do, think, or intend anything but evil. On our own we dash impetuously into hell, so far as the Lord does not hold us back.

[3] However, the fact of the matter concerning judgment based on truth is this: The Lord never judges anyone from anything but goodness. He wants to raise everyone into heaven, without exception. In fact, if he could he would lift us all right up to his own level. The Lord, you see, is mercy itself and goodness itself. Mercy itself and goodness itself could never condemn anyone. It is we who condemn ourselves, because we reject his goodness. Just as we had fled from goodness during bodily life, we flee from it in the other life, and consequently we flee from heaven and the Lord as well. The Lord, after all, can dwell only in goodness. He dwells in truth, too, but not in truth that is detached from goodness. He himself tells us in John that he does not damn anyone, or in other words, judge anyone to hell:

> God did *not* send his Son into the world so that he could *judge* the world but so that the world could be saved by him. This is the *judgment:* that the light came into the world but people loved the dark more than the light, since their deeds were evil. (John 3:17, 19)

And in the same author:

> If anyone listens to my words, yet does not believe them, *I do not judge* that person; because I did not come to *judge* the world but to save the world. (John 12:47)

In addition, see earlier discussions of this subject at §§223, 245, 592, 696, 1093, 1683, 1874, 2258.

[4] Where judgment was discussed above at §§2320, 2321, it was shown that all judgment belongs to the Lord's divine humanity and holy influence, in keeping with his words in John:

> "The Father does not *judge* anyone but has given all *judgment* to the Son." (John 5:22)

Yet it was just shown that the Lord does not judge anyone to damnation. This consideration indicates what the Word is like in the letter; if it were not taken in another, deeper sense, it could not be grasped. Only the inner meaning reveals how judgment actually works.

2336   The symbolism of a *street* as truth can be seen from many passages in the Word, like this one in which John describes the New Jerusalem:

> The twelve gates were twelve pearls; each gate was a single pearl; and the *city street* was pure gold, like transparent glass. (Revelation 21:21)

[2] The New Jerusalem is the Lord's kingdom. Because the goodness and truth of that kingdom are being portrayed, it is depicted in terms of walls, gates, and streets. The last—the streets—mean every facet of truth that leads to goodness, or in other words, every facet of faith that leads to love and charity. When truth leads to goodness, it *becomes* goodness and therefore turns transparent with goodness, so the street is said to be a mass of gold resembling transparent glass. In the same author:

> *From the middle of* its *street* and of the river, here and there, grew the tree of life, making twelve fruits. (Revelation 22:2)

This too depicts the New Jerusalem, or the Lord's kingdom. The middle of the street is religious truth that produces goodness and afterward becomes a product of goodness. The twelve fruits are what are called the fruit of faith, because twelve symbolizes every aspect of faith, as shown in §§577, 2089, 2129, 2130. [3] In Daniel:

> Know and perceive that from the issuing of the Word to restore and rebuild Jerusalem up to the time of Messiah the ruler, there will be seven weeks; and in sixty-two weeks *street* and moat will be restored and rebuilt. (Daniel 9:25)

This is about the Lord's Coming. The restoration of street and moat is the restoration of truth and goodness at that time. We know that Jerusalem itself was not restored or rebuilt at that point. Furthermore, anyone who focuses on the heavenly kingdom meant in an inner sense by Jerusalem, rather than on a worldly kingdom, can see that it was not about to be restored or built anew. [4] In Luke:

> The householder said to his slave, "Go quickly into the *streets* and *alleys* of the city and bring in there the poor, the maimed, the lame, and the blind." (Luke 14:21)

People who restrict themselves to the literal meaning glean nothing more from this than a command for the slave to go everywhere (which is what they take the streets and alleys to mean) and round up everyone (which is what they take the poor, maimed, lame, and blind to mean). Every single word, though, harbors secrets, because each word is the Lord's. Going into the streets and alleys means seeking everywhere for something genuinely true—for truth transparently radiant with goodness. Bringing in the poor, maimed, lame, and blind means bringing in the people who were described this way in the ancient church. Such people were poor, maimed, lame, and blind in their faith but still lived a good life and consequently needed to be taught about the Lord's kingdom; in other words, they were non-Christians who had not yet been instructed.

[5] Since streets symbolized truth, Jews had the representative practice of teaching in them, as is clear from Matthew 6:2, 5 and from Luke 13:26, 27.

In the Prophets, streets in an inner sense mean either truth or its opposite, wherever they are mentioned. In Isaiah, for instance:

> Judgment has been driven back, and justice has stood far off, since *truthfulness* stumbled in the *street*, and *uprightness* cannot approach. (Isaiah 59:14)

In the same author:

> Your children fainted and lay at the head of *all the streets*. (Isaiah 51:20)

In Jeremiah:

> Death climbed through the windows, it came into our palaces, to cut off the little ones in the *street*, the youths in the *avenues*. (Jeremiah 9:21)

[6] In Ezekiel:

> With the hooves of his horses Nebuchadnezzar will trample all your *streets*. (Ezekiel 26:11)

This is about Tyre, which symbolizes a knowledge of truth (§1201). Horses' hooves are facts that twist the truth. In Nahum:

> In the *streets*, the chariots run mad; they dash about in the avenues. (Nahum 2:4)

A chariot stands for the teaching of truth. It is said to run mad in the streets when falsity replaces truth. In Zechariah:

> Old men and old women will still live on the *streets* of Jerusalem, and the *city's streets* will be filled with boys and girls playing in the *streets*. (Zechariah 8:4, 5)

This is about people's emotional response to truth and about the joy and happiness that grow out of it. There are other passages as well, such as Isaiah 24:11; Jeremiah 5:1; 7:34; 49:26; Lamentations 2:11, 19; 4:8, 14; Zephaniah 3:6.

Genesis 19:3. *And he pressed them very hard, and they turned aside to him and came to his house. And he made them a banquet and cooked unleavened loaves, and they ate.* **2337**

He pressed them very hard symbolizes our mood when we win the struggle. *And they turned aside to him* symbolizes his making a home in us. *And came to his house* means our being strengthened in goodness. *And he made them a banquet* means living together. *And cooked unleavened loaves* means being purified. *And they ate* means making it our own.

The symbolism of *he pressed them very hard* as our mood when we win the struggle can be seen only by people who have suffered times of trial. **2338**

As I said [§2334], trial brings with it doubt concerning the Lord's presence and mercy and concerning salvation. The evil spirits then present with us, who bring on the crisis, inspire strong negativity. Good spirits and angels, however, on behalf of the Lord, use every method they can to do away with this doubt, keep hope always alive in us, and eventually reinforce a positive outlook. As a consequence, we hover between denial and affirmation during our inward struggles. When we fail, we continue to doubt, and sink into pessimism. When we win, on the other hand, we do still have doubts, but those of us who allow hope to set us on our feet remain optimistic.

During the battle, we seem to press the Lord (particularly in our prayers) to be with us, have mercy on us, help us, and free us from damnation. Here, then, where the focus is on the trials of people who are becoming part of the church, the idea is depicted by the fact that the angels first said no, they would spend the night in the street, but Lot pressed them very hard, so they turned aside to him and came into his house.

And they turned aside to him symbolizes his making a home in us. This can be seen from the symbolism of the same words above at §2330 and needs no further explanation. **2339**

And came to his house means our being strengthened in goodness. This can be seen from the symbolism of a *house* as heavenly goodness, discussed above at §§2233, 2331. From this symbolism and the train of thought in the inner meaning comes the fact that it means our being strengthened in goodness. **2340**

The fact that *and he made them a banquet* means living together can be seen from the symbolism of a *banquet.* **2341**

The Word often mentions *banquets,* and where it does, on an inner level they symbolize the act of living together, as in Jeremiah:

The word of Jehovah came to him: "A *banquet house* you shall not enter,
to sit with them, to eat and to drink." (Jeremiah 16:[1,] 8)

In this passage the prophet is given many messages representing a ban on
contact between good and evil, between truth and falsity. Among other
things, he was not to enter a banquet hall—meaning that goodness and
truth were not to reside in the same place as evil and falsity. [2] In Isaiah:

Jehovah Sabaoth will make for all peoples on this mountain a *banquet*
of rich foods, a *banquet* of mellow wines, of rich foods full of marrow,
of wines free of dregs. (Isaiah 25:6)

The mountain stands for love for the Lord (§§795, 1430). People who love
him live with him in goodness and truth, which is what the banquet
symbolizes. Rich foods and marrow are goodness (§353); mellow, purified
wines are the truth that grows out of goodness (§1071).

[3] The feasts of consecrated foods held in connection with sacrifices
in the Jewish religion actually represented the fact that the Lord lives with
us in the holy qualities of love symbolized by the sacrifices (§2187). The
same thing was later true of the Holy Supper, which was called a feast in
the early [Christian] church.

[4] Genesis 21:8 below mentions that Abraham held a grand banquet
on the day Isaac was weaned. This represented and therefore symbolized
the dwelling together of the Lord's divinity with his human rationality, and
the early bonding of the two.

Banquets symbolize the same thing on an inner level in other passages as well, as anyone can conclude from this: Banquets are held among
large groups of people who have love and charity for each other, become
attached to each other at heart, and share with each other the happiness
that love and charity foster in them.

2342   *And cooked unleavened loaves* means being purified, as can be seen
from the symbolism of *unleavened* or flat bread.

In the Word, bread symbolizes all heavenly and spiritual food in general, so it symbolizes absolutely everything heavenly or spiritual in general
(see §§276, 680, 1798, 2165, 2177). The aim that it be free of impurities
was represented by *unleavened* bread, because yeast symbolizes evil and
falsity that renders heavenly and spiritual qualities impure and profane.
This representation was the reason for requiring the people of the representative church not to offer any other bread (minha) in their sacrifices
than flat or unleavened bread. The prohibition appears in Moses:

No *minha* that you bring to Jehovah shall be made *with yeast.* (Leviticus 2:11)

In the same author:

You shall not offer the blood of my sacrifice on *yeast bread.* (Exodus 23:18; 34:25)

[2] For the same reason the people were also ordered not to eat any other bread on the seven days of Passover than flat or unleavened bread. The prohibition is expressed this way in Moses:

Seven days *you shall eat unleavened loaves;* yes, on the first day you shall make *yeast* cease from your houses, because everyone *eating yeast bread,* that soul shall be cut off from Israel. [This shall last] from the first day up to the seventh. In the first [month], on the fourteenth day of the month in the evening, *you shall eat unleavened loaves,* up to the twenty-first day of the month in the evening. For seven days, *yeast* shall not be found in your houses, because everyone *eating yeast bread,* that soul shall be cut off from the congregation of Israel, among the immigrant and the native of the land. (Exodus 12:15, 18, 19, 20)

It appears in other passages as well, such as Exodus 13:6, 7; 23:15; 34:18; Deuteronomy 16:3, 4. That is why Passover is called the Feast of Unleavened Bread in Leviticus 23:6; Numbers 28:16, 17; Matthew 26:17; Luke 22:1, 7.

[3] Passover represented the Lord's glorification and therefore the union of divinity with the human race, as will be shown elsewhere [§§3994, 7823, 9965, 10655], with the Lord's divine mercy. Since it is love and charity—and the faith that comes of them—that unite the Lord with the human race, the unleavened bread they were to eat during Passover represented these properties of heaven and of the spirit. The desire to keep these properties free from all taint of profanation was the reason yeast bread was so strictly forbidden that whoever ate any would be cut off. People who profane heavenly and spiritual things necessarily perish.

Anyone can see that if not for this hidden fact this ceremonial law would never have been laid down with such a severe penalty attached to it.

[4] All the requirements of that religion represented something secret, even the *cooking* itself. Take, for example, each of the actions the children of Israel took when they left Egypt. Specifically (Exodus 12:8, 9, 10), they were to eat that night the meat roasted with fire, and *unleavened loaves*

on bitter herbs. They were not to eat it raw, *nor cooked in water.* The head was to be atop the legs. They were not to leave any of it till morning; the remainder they were to burn with fire. The details here—eating at night, the meat roasted with fire, the unleavened loaves on the bitter herbs, the head atop the legs, not raw, not cooked in water, not leaving it till morning, and burning the remainder with fire—each represented something. The secret representation cannot possibly appear, though, unless revealed by the inner meaning. The only thing that *can* appear is that the whole is divine.

[5] The same is true of the ritual for a Nazirite in Numbers 6:19. The priest was to take the *cooked* flank of a ram and one *unleavened cake* from a basket and one *unleavened wafer* and put it onto the palms of the Nazirite, after he had cut the hair of his Naziriteship. If you do not know that a Nazirite represented a genuinely heavenly person, you also do not know that each and every aspect of the ritual involves a secret, heavenly meaning that is not visible in the letter. That includes the cooked flank of the ram, the unleavened cake, the unleavened wafer, and the cutting of the hair. From this it can be seen what kind of opinion people can form of the Word when they do not believe in an inner meaning; without inner content, the individual details have no importance. Take away the ceremony or the merely ritual aspect, however, and everything there becomes divine and holy. The same is true with every other aspect, and therefore with the unleavened bread, which is the holy quality of love, or something most holy, as it is even called in Moses:

> The remaining *unleavened loaves* shall be eaten by Aaron and his sons in a holy place, because *these are most holy.* (Leviticus 6:16, 17)

Unleavened bread, then, is pure love, and cooking unleavened bread is being purified.

2343   *And they ate* means making it our own. This can be seen from the symbolism of *eating* as sharing and bonding and so as making something our own, as discussed earlier, at §2187.

What the contents of this verse and the last are in the inner meaning and how they come together can be seen from the remarks and explanations just above: the angels symbolize the Lord's divine humanity and holy influence; turning aside to Lot means making a home in us; coming to his house means being strengthened in goodness; making a banquet means living together; cooking unleavened bread means being purified; and eating means making it our own. This clarifies the train of thought in the inner meaning, even though none of it appears anywhere on the narrative level.

[2] All parts of the Word contain an orderly sequence of thoughts like this one, but the actual sequence cannot disclose its true nature when each word is explained by itself. Such an explanation makes the words seem disconnected and breaks up the continuity of meaning. The sequence becomes clear only when we embrace all the words in a single view or perceive them all in a single glance of the mind, as people do who focus on the inner meaning and view everything by the Lord's heavenly light.

For such people, these words present before their eyes the whole process of reformation and rebirth for individuals who become part of the church—individuals represented here by Lot. To be specific, they first sense a measure of struggle, but when they persist and overcome, the Lord makes a home with them and strengthens them in goodness. He gathers them to himself, bringing them into his kingdom, and lives with them. There he purifies and perfects them, giving them goodness and happiness as their own. This he does through his divine humanity and holy influence.

[3] People in the church do know that all rebirth or new life and consequently all salvation come from the Lord alone; but few of them believe it. The reason they do not is that they do not act out of love for others. For people who do not do act out of love for others, it is as impossible to believe this as it is for a camel to go through the eye of a needle, because the good we do out of love for others is the very soil in which the seeds of faith are planted. Truth and goodness harmonize, but truth and evil have nothing in common whatever. They are of two opposing natures, and each loathes the other. So the more we dedicate ourselves to goodness, the more we can see the truth; in other words, the more charity we have, the more faith we have—especially in the primary religious principle that all salvation comes from the Lord.

[4] Many passages in the Word show that this is the chief principle of religion. In John, for instance:

> So much did God love the world that he gave it *his only Son,* so that anyone who *believes in him* may not be destroyed but have eternal life. (John 3:16)

In the same author:

> Those who *believe in the Son* have eternal life, but those who do not believe in the Son will not see life; instead, God's anger rests on them. (John 3:36)

In the same author:

> This is the work of God: that you *believe in him* whom the Father sent. (John 6:29)

In the same author:

> This is the will of him who sent me, that all who *see the Son* and *believe in him* should have eternal life, and that I should revive them on the last day. (John 6:40)

In the same author:

> Unless you *believe that I am,* you will die in your sins. (John 8:24)

In the same author:

> I am the resurrection and life; *those who believe in me,* even if they die, will live. But no one who lives and *believes in me* will ever die. (John 11:25, 26)

[5] It can also be seen in John that no one can believe in the Lord without doing good; that is, no one can have faith without having love for others:

> As many as did accept him, to them he gave the power to be God's children, to those *believing in his name,* who had their birth not from blood or from the will of the flesh or from a man's will, but from God. (John 1:12, 13)

And in the same author:

> I am the grapevine; you are the branches. Those who remain in me and in whom I remain bear much fruit; because without me you cannot do anything. If anyone does not remain in me, that person has been thrown out the door like a branch and has withered. Just as the Father has *loved* me, so I myself have *loved you;* remain in *my love.* This is my commandment: that *you love each other* as *I have loved you.* (John 15:5, 6, 9, 12)

[6] These passages show that love for the Lord and kindness toward our neighbor is the life of faith.

On the other hand, people who do bad things or live an evil life cannot possibly believe that the Lord is the source of all salvation. This was made clear to me by some who had come into the other life from the Christian world. They were among those who during bodily life had claimed to believe and even taught that without the Lord there is no salvation (just as the faith teaches) and yet had lived an evil life. These people, at the bare mention of the Lord, immediately filled the air with slander after slander. In the next world, what they are merely *thinking* is perceived by others, and these thoughts give off an aura that reveals what kind of faith they have (see §1394).

[7] In the same people I sensed something like clouds of dust at the bare mention of love or charity. These dust clouds were generated by an unclean type of love that by its very nature wanted to snuff out, choke off, and overturn any ability I had to perceive love for the Lord or charity for my neighbor. That is the nature of today's faith, which they claim will save us without any need for loving deeds.

[8] These same people were also asked what kind of faith they did have, if they did not have the faith they had avowed in physical life. They answered (none of us can hide what we are thinking in the other life) that they believed in God the creator of the universe. I prodded, though, to see whether this was true, and found that they did not believe in any God but ascribed everything to nature and dismissed anything they heard about eternal life. Anyone in the church who does not believe in the Lord but claims to believe in God the creator of the universe has this kind of faith. Truth cannot come from anywhere except the Lord, and the only soil in which the seed of truth can be planted is that of goodness received from him.

[9] The words spoken at the Holy Supper—"This is my body; this is my blood" [Matthew 26:26, 28; Mark 14:22, 24; Luke 22:19]—teach openly that the Lord's divine humanity and holy influence is the means and source of life and salvation. The body and blood are the Lord's divine humanity, which is plainly the source of all that is holy.

It is all the same whether you speak of the Lord's divine humanity, or of his body, or of his flesh, or of the bread, or of divine love. The Lord's divine humanity is pure love, and holiness has everything to do with love; any holiness faith has comes from love.

Genesis 19:4. *Hardly had they lain down when the men of the city—the men of Sodom—circled the house, from youth to old man, all the people from the furthest limits.*   **2344**

Hardly had they lain down means early in the visitation. *The men of the city* symbolize people under the sway of falsity. *The men of Sodom* symbolize people under the sway of evil. *They circled the house* means that they opposed any good done out of love for others. *From youth to old man* symbolizes falsity and evil both new and entrenched. *All the people from the furthest limits* means absolutely all of it.

2345 *Hardly had they lain down* means early in the visitation. This can be seen from the discussion of evening and night above at §§2323, 2335, showing that in the Word they symbolize visitation and judgment. It is true that neither evening nor night is mentioned in the current verse, but it does say, "when they had hardly lain down," and this means the time when evening turns to night, or night begins. So it means early in the time when the evil were being visited, as later verses also make clear. The inquiry into evil within the church—the evil meant by Sodom—starts here.

2346 *The men of the city* symbolizes people under the sway of falsity, and *the men of Sodom,* people under the sway of evil, as established by the symbolism of a *city* and *Sodom.* It was shown above in §402 that a *city* symbolizes truth, or else falsity (the opposite of truth), and in §§2220, 2246 that *Sodom* symbolizes evil of every kind.

Since the people were being explored (visited) for both falsity and evil, it says, "the men of the city, the men of Sodom." If both had not been meant, it would have said only "the men of Sodom."

2347 *They circled the house* means that they opposed any good done out of love for others, as can be seen from the following: A *house* symbolizes heavenly goodness, which is simply good done out of love and charity, as discussed at §§2048, 2231. And *circling* something means opposing it, or falling on and attacking it with hostile intent.

2348 *From youth to old man* symbolizes falsity and evil both new and entrenched, as can be seen from the symbolism of a *youth* and an *old man,* when these refer to falsity and evil. *Youths* symbolize falsity and evil that have not matured and therefore are new. *Old people* symbolize falsity and evil that have reached an advanced age and therefore have become entrenched. Young and old people are mentioned in a similar sense elsewhere in the Word too, as in Zechariah:

> *Old men* and *old women* will still live on the streets of Jerusalem, and the city's streets will be filled with *boys and girls* playing in the streets. (Zechariah 8:4, 5)

In this passage, Jerusalem stands for the Lord's kingdom and the church (§§402, 2117); the streets, for the truth that exists there (§2336). So the old men stand for truth confirmed; the old women, for goodness strengthened. The boys playing in the streets stand for fresh truth; the girls, for fresh goodness, along with the affections and happiness it inspires. This shows how heavenly and spiritual entities turn into narrative detail when they descend into worldly elements in the literal story. In the text, it is hard to see anything else as being meant than old men, boys, [old] women, and girls. [2] In Jeremiah:

> Pour it out on the *little one* in the street of Jerusalem and on the band of young adults, too; because even a man with his woman will be seized, the *elder* together with one *full of days*. (Jeremiah 6:11)

The street of Jerusalem stands for falsity that prevails in the church (§2336). In its newer and more mature forms it is called a "little one" and "young adults"; once aged and entrenched it is called an "elder" and a person "full of days." In the same author:

> In you I will scatter the horse and its rider, and in you I will scatter the chariot and its rider, and in you I will scatter man and woman, and in you I will scatter *elder* and *youth*. (Jeremiah 51:21, 22)

Here again the elder and the youth stand for confirmed truth and new truth. [3] In the same author:

> Death climbed into the windows, it came into our palaces, to cut off the *little ones* in the street, the *youths* in the avenues. (Jeremiah 9:21)

The little ones stand for truth that is cut off as soon as it is born, when death comes into the windows and the palaces, that is, into matters of intellect and matters of will. Windows are intellectual matters (see §§655, 658), and palaces or houses are matters of will (§710).

All the people from the furthest limits means absolutely all of it, as can be seen from the above. Youths and the old symbolize falsity and evil, both new and entrenched, so now the *people from the furthest limits* symbolize the entirety of it. In general, too, *people* symbolize falsity (see §§1259, 1260).

2349

[2] This now depicts the first phase of people in the church who oppose neighborly kindness and therefore oppose the Lord. The one necessitates the other, since no one can be united to the Lord except through love and charity. Love is spiritual union itself, as the very nature of love shows. And anyone who cannot unite with the Lord also cannot acknowledge him.

It can be seen in John that people who fail to do good are also unable to acknowledge the Lord, or in other words, to believe in him:

> The light came into the world, but people loved the dark more than the light, since *their deeds were evil*. Those who *do evil* hate the light, and they do not come to the light, for fear that their deeds will be exposed.

Those who act on the truth, however, come to the light to allow *their deeds* to be revealed, because they were done in God. (John 3:19, 20, 21)

This shows that anyone opposed to doing good out of love for others opposes the Lord. To put the same thing another way, anyone immersed in evil hates the light and does not come to the light. "The light" is faith in the Lord and is actually the Lord himself, as is clear in John 1:9, 10; 12:35, 36, 46. [3] Likewise in another place in the same author:

The world cannot hate you, but it does hate me, because I testify of it that *its deeds* are *evil.* (John 7:7)

It is stated even more openly in Matthew:

He will say to those who are on his left, "Go away from me, you cursed ones; because I was hungry and you did not give me anything to eat. I was thirsty and you did not give me a drink. I was a foreigner and you did not gather me in. Naked, and you did not put a robe around me. Sick and in prison, and you did not visit me. Truly, I say to you: so far as you did not do it for one of these least consequential ones, you also did not do it for me." (Matthew 25:41, 42, 43, 45)

[4] This shows how people who are against doing good out of love for others are against the Lord. It also shows that we are each judged according to the good we have done from love and not according to the truth we have believed in, if the truth is detached from any goodness. This too appears in Matthew, in another passage:

The Son of Humankind will come in the glory of his Father, with his angels, and then he will repay every person *according to that person's deeds.* (Matthew 16:27)

The deeds stand for good that is done out of neighborly love. Anything connected with love for others is also called the fruit of faith.

2350   Genesis 19:5. *And they shouted to Lot and said to him, "Where are the men who came to you at night? Bring them out to us and let us know them."*

They shouted to Lot and said to him symbolizes falsity growing out of evil, which rages at goodness. *Where are the men who came to you?* symbolizes denial of the Lord's divine humanity and holy influence. *At night* symbolizes the last days, when no one acknowledges them any longer. *Bring them out to us and let us know them* means that these people wanted to prove that it would be wrong to acknowledge their existence.

They shouted to Lot and said to him symbolizes falsity growing out of **2351**
evil, which rages at goodness, as can be seen from the symbolism of *shout-*
ing and *Lot,* and so from the emotion. The word *shout* is used of falsity
(as shown in §2240). *Lot* represents religious people who do good, so he
represents the good itself that they do (§2324). This, and the angry emotion of the words, shows that it symbolizes falsity growing out of evil,
which rages at goodness.

There are many kinds of falsity but two general categories: falsity produced by evil and falsity that produces evil (see §§1188, 1212, 1295, 1679,
2243).

[2] Within the church, the chief falsity to develop out of evil is falsity that promotes a wicked life. An example is the notion that it is not
goodness (that is, love for others) but truth (that is, faith) that makes
a person religious. This point of view says that it does not matter how
wickedly we live throughout the course of our life; we are saved as long
as we express some kind of belief—with apparent feeling—when bodily
concerns fade the way they do just before death. This type of falsity is
the main one to lash out at goodness, and it is symbolized by the people's
shouting to Lot.

Anything that tries to destroy the pleasure we receive from something
we love sparks anger. When evil attacks goodness, *anger* is the right word,
but when goodness rebukes evil, it is called *zeal.*

Where are the men who came to you? symbolizes denial of the Lord's **2352**
divine humanity and holy influence. This can be seen from the symbolism of the two *men* as discussed above at §2320; also from the emotion in
these angry words; and from what follows directly, where it says, "Bring
them out to us and let us know them." Clearly this involves denial.

To see that people who oppose doing good out of neighborly love also
oppose the Lord and deny him at heart, even though they claim to believe
in him because they love personal power and gain, see §§2343, 2349.

At night symbolizes the last days, when no one acknowledges [the **2353**
Lord's divine humanity and holy influence] any longer. This can be seen
from the symbolism of *night* as a dark time when matters of light are no
longer visible.

The angels did *not* come at night but in the evening; but since it
is the men of Sodom that spoke and shouted—in other words, people
immersed in falsity and evil—it does not say in the evening but at night.
In the Word, *night* symbolizes a time and condition when the light of
truth no longer exists, only falsity and evil. So it symbolizes a final period,

when there is a judgment. [2] The term appears in this sense in many places, as in Micah:

> Against the prophets who lead the people astray: You have *night* instead of visions, and *darkness grows out* of divination for you, and the *sun sets* on the prophets, and over them the day *blackens*. (Micah 3:5, 6)

The prophets stand for people who teach falsity. The night, darkness, sunset, and blackening of the day stand for falsity and evil. [3] In John:

> If any walk in the day, they do not stumble, but if any walk in the *night*, they do stumble, because there is no light in them. (John 11:9, 10)

The night stands for falsity that arises out of evil; the light, for truth that arises out of goodness. Just as truth's light comes entirely from goodness, falsity's nighttime comes entirely from evil. [4] In the same author:

> I have to do the work of him who sent me while it is still day. The *night*, in which no one can work, is coming. (John 9:4)

The day stands for a time and condition in which goodness and truth exist, but night stands for a time and condition in which evil and falsity exist. [5] In Luke:

> I say to you, *that night* there will be two on one bed; one will be accepted, the other abandoned. (Luke 17:34)

The night stands for the last days, when there is no longer any religious truth.

[6] Egypt, at the time the children of Israel left it, represented the ruination of goodness and truth in the church and the fact that nothing but falsity and evil was in control any longer. That is why they were commanded to leave *in the middle of the night* (Exodus 11:4) and why all the firstborn of Egypt were killed *in the middle of the night* (Exodus 12:12, 29, 30). The children of Israel, who represented people with goodness and truth, were guarded from the falsity and evil that surrounded them, as Lot was in Sodom. For this reason the night—from their point of view— is called a *night of watch-keeping for Jehovah* (Exodus 12:42).

2354   *Bring them out to us and let us know them* means that these people wanted to prove that it would be wrong to acknowledge the existence of them—of the Lord's divine humanity and holy influence. This can be seen from the symbolism of the two angels, as discussed above at §2320, and from the anger with which the words were said, since anything said in anger is negative.

[2] These words depict the first phase of a spiritually devastated religion—that is, one in which faith starts to disappear because charity does. In that phase, as noted, people oppose doing good out of neighborly love and so have no faith. In particular they refuse to acknowledge the Lord's divine humanity and holy influence. These are denied at heart by all who live a life of evil—who despise others in comparison with themselves, hate anyone that does not bow down to them, avenge themselves on such people, even enjoy cruelty, and consider adultery inconsequential. The Pharisees, who denied the Lord's divinity openly, nonetheless acted better in their day than their modern counterparts. Today's Pharisees worship the Lord with superficial devotion, for the sake of their own adulation and vile gain, while inwardly concealing this profane state of mind. The character they gradually adopt is depicted below by the men of Sodom and by the eventual overthrow of the city (verses 24, 25).

[3] The situation we find ourselves in, as noted several times before, is that we have both evil spirits and angels present with us. Through the evil spirits we communicate with hell, and through the angels, with heaven (§§687, 697). The more our life borders on evil, then, the more hell influences us. The closer our life approaches to being good, though, the more heaven and the Lord influence us. It stands to reason from this that people who live evil lives cannot acknowledge the Lord. Instead they privately invent countless charges against him, because delusions from hell pour into them and are accepted by them. People who live good lives acknowledge the Lord, because heaven flows into them, and in heaven, love and charity are the main focus. Heaven is the Lord's, and everything having to do with love and charity comes from him (see §§537, 540, 547, 548, 551, 553, 685, 2130).

Genesis 19:6, 7. And Lot went out to them at the door, and the entrance he closed behind him. And he said, "Please, my brothers, don't do wrong."

2355

Lot went out to them at the door symbolizes approaching cautiously. *And the entrance he closed behind him* means in order to prevent them from hurting the goodness born of neighborly love and denying the Lord's divine humanity and holy influence. *And he said* symbolizes a plea. *Please, my brothers, don't do wrong* means [a plea] that they not hurt those things; he says *brothers* because of the goodness motivating his pleas.

Lot went out to them at the door symbolizes approaching cautiously, as can be seen from the inner meaning of a *door* and *going out to a door*. In the Word, a *door* symbolizes something that leads (gives entrance) to truth or to goodness or to the Lord. For this reason, a door also symbolizes truth itself, goodness itself, and the Lord himself, because truth leads

2356

to goodness, and goodness leads to the Lord. That is what the door and veil to the tabernacle and the Temple represented (see §§2145, 2152, 2576). [2] This symbolism of a door is evident from the Lord's words in John:

> Whoever is not entering through the *door* into the sheepfold but climbs in from another place, that person is a thief and robber. But whoever is entering through the *door* is the shepherd of the sheep. For this person, the *doorkeeper* opens up. I am the *door of the sheep;* if any come in through me, they will be saved. (John 10:1, 2, 3, 7, 9)

The door stands for truth and goodness and so for the Lord, who is truth and goodness itself.

This explains the symbolism of being let into heaven through a door and consequently of the keys that open the door.

[3] In the current verse, however, the door symbolizes a type of goodness adapted to the psyche of the people besieging the house. The text distinguishes the door from the entrance here, the door being out in front of the house, as is clear from the fact that Lot went out and closed the *entrance* behind him. This particular type of goodness was something that would bless their lives (as will become clear in the discussion just below [§2363]), which he used in trying to persuade people engrossed in falsity and evil. People like this do not allow themselves to be persuaded by really genuine goodness, because they reject it. Clearly, then, going out to the door here means that he approached cautiously.

2357   *And the entrance he closed behind him* means in order to prevent them from hurting the goodness born of neighborly love and denying the Lord's divine humanity and holy influence, as established by the remarks just above. *Closing the entrance* is preventing people from entering—here, entering into the goodness symbolized by the house, and so coming into the presence of the Lord's divinity and holiness.

[2] Deeper secrets are also contained in these words, and when we read them, the meaning and the ideas lying on that deeper level come into angels' minds. The secret contained here is that people who live evil lives are not allowed to progress any further than simply knowing about goodness and about the Lord; they are not permitted to go so far as real acknowledgment and faith. This is forbidden because goodness lies beyond their reach as long as they are under the sway of evil, since no one can serve two masters at once. If we return to a life of evil after acknowledging and believing in [the Lord and his goodness], we profane everything good and holy, but if we do not acknowledge or believe in them, we also cannot

profane them. So the Lord in his providence takes care not to let us enter any further into true, heartfelt acknowledgment and belief than he can afterward maintain in us. He does this because of the penalty for profanation in hell, which is extremely heavy. [3] That is why so few today receive the grace to believe at heart that good done out of love and charity makes heaven in us and that the Lord possesses all divinity: people are leading evil lives.

This now is the deeper significance of Lot's closing the entrance behind him. The entrance was an inner door that led into the house proper, where the angels were; that is, it led to goodness that contains the Lord within it.

And he said symbolizes a plea. This can be seen from what follows directly and so needs no further explanation.

2358

Please, my brothers, don't do wrong means [a plea] that they not hurt those things—goodness born of neighborly love, and the Lord's divine humanity and holy influence. This can be seen from the symbolism of *wrongdoing* as hurting something.

2359

This makes it clear that the focus here is on people in the church, and that they are the ones meant by the men of Sodom. No one can inflict damage on those things but people who have the Word.

The extreme holiness of those things can be seen from this: No one can be let into the Lord's kingdom—heaven—without devotion to good done out of love and charity; and no one can be devoted to good done out of love and charity without acknowledging the Lord's divinity and holiness. What is divine and holy flows into us from the Lord alone, and in fact it flows into the goodness itself that comes from him. Divinity can act only on something divine, and it can be communicated to us only through the Lord's divine humanity and its holy influence. These considerations show what it means to say that the Lord is the all-in-all of his kingdom, and that nothing good in us is ours but is rather the Lord's.

He says *brothers* because of the goodness motivating his pleas, as can be seen from the symbolism of a *brother*. In the Word, a sibling symbolizes the same thing as a neighbor, because we each ought to love our neighbor as ourselves. The men here, then, are called brothers from love or (what is the same) from goodness. The reason for labeling or addressing a neighbor as a sister or brother is that the Lord in heaven is everyone's Father and loves us all as his children, and love therefore ties us together spiritually. As a result, heaven in its entirety resembles a single generation because of the love and charity there (§§685, 917).

2360

[2] So because all the children of Israel represented the Lord's heavenly kingdom, or in other words, a kingdom of love and charity, they called each other "brother." They also called each other "companion," although this label came from the presence of religious truth rather than a loving goodness. In Isaiah, for example:

> A man helps *his companion* and says to *his brother,* "Strengthen yourself." (Isaiah 41:6)

In Jeremiah:

> This is what you shall say, a man to *his companion* and a man to *his brother:* "What has Jehovah answered, and what has Jehovah spoken?" (Jeremiah 23:35)

In David:

> For the sake of *my brothers* and *my companions* I will speak: "Come, now; peace be in you!" (Psalms 122:8)

In Moses:

> They shall not press *their companion* or *their brother,* because an amnesty has been proclaimed to Jehovah. (Deuteronomy 15:2, 3)

In Isaiah:

> I will mix Egypt up with Egypt, and they will fight, a man against *his brother* and a man against *his companion.* (Isaiah 19:2)

In Jeremiah:

> Be careful, a man of *his companion,* and on no *brother* are you to put your trust; for every *brother* will ruthlessly supplant [his brother], and every *companion* will speak slander. (Jeremiah 9:4)

[3] It can be seen in Isaiah that all the people of that religion were called by the single term *brothers:*

> They will bring all *your brothers* out of all the nations, a gift to Jehovah, on horses, and in a chariot, and in coaches, and on mules, and on dromedaries, to my holy mountain, to Jerusalem. (Isaiah 66:20)

People such as Jews who know only the literal meaning believe that this is talking about no others than Jacob's descendants. Such people believe that those descendants will be brought back to Jerusalem on horses, and in a chariot, and in coaches, and on mules from the nations they call gentile. In reality, though, brothers mean everyone with goodness; the horses, chariots, and coaches mean different facets of truth and goodness; and Jerusalem means the Lord's kingdom. [4] In Moses:

> When there is among you a needy person, one of *your brothers,* in one of your gates, you shall not harden your heart, and you shall not shut your hand off from *your* needy *brother.* (Deuteronomy 15:7, 11)

In the same author:

> You shall put over you a monarch from the midst of *your brothers;* you cannot set over you a foreign man who is not your *brother.* And his heart shall not vaunt itself over *his brothers.* (Deuteronomy 17:15, 20)

In the same author:

> Jehovah your God will raise up for you a prophet from your midst, from among *your brothers,* resembling me; him you shall obey. (Deuteronomy 18:15, 18)

[5] These quotations show that Jews and Israelites all called each other brothers but called their allies companions. Wise only in the narrative and worldly aspects of the Word, they believed they had called each other brothers because they were all offspring of one father, Abraham. That was not why they were called brothers in the Word, though; it was because of the goodness they represented. In an inner sense, moreover, Abraham simply means love itself, that is, the Lord (§§1893, 1965, 1989, [2010,] 2011), and those of us with goodness are his children and are therefore siblings. In fact, this is true of everyone called a neighbor, as the Lord teaches in Matthew:

> One person is your teacher: Christ; all of you *are siblings.* (Matthew 23:8)

[6] In the same author:

> Any who are angry at *their brother* without cause will be subject to judgment. Any who say to *their brother,* "Raca!" will be subject to the Sanhedrin. If you offer your gift on the altar and with this remember that *your brother* has something against you, leave the gift there before the altar and first go reconcile with that *brother.* (Matthew 5:22, 23, 24)

In the same author:

> Why do you spy out the piece of straw that is in the eyes of *your brother?*
> How will you say to *your brother,* "Let me take the straw out of your
> eye"? (Matthew 7:2, 3, 4)

In the same author:

> If *your brother* sins against you, go and denounce him between you and
> him alone. If he hears you, you have gained *your brother.* (Matthew 18:15)

In the same author:

> Peter, approaching him, said, "Lord, how often will *my brother* sin against
> me and I have to forgive him?" (Matthew 18:21)

In the same author:

> So also will my heavenly Father do to you if you don't each forgive your
> *brothers* their offenses from your hearts. (Matthew 18:35)

[7] This makes it clear that all people everywhere who are our neighbor
are called brothers, and they are called this because we each ought to love
our neighbor as ourselves. So they are called this from love, or goodness.

Since the Lord is goodness itself, and looks on all of us with goodness, and is himself our neighbor in the highest sense, he also calls us his
brothers, as in John:

> Jesus said to Mary, "Go to *my brothers.*" (John 20:17)

And in Matthew:

> Answering, the king will say to them, "Truly, I say to you: so far as you
> did it for one of these least consequential *brothers of mine,* you did it for
> me." (Matthew 25:40)

From this it can now be seen that *brother* is a word of love.

2361 Genesis 19:8. *"Look, please: I have two daughters who have not known
any man. Please let me bring them out to you, and you may do with them as
is good in your eyes. Only don't do anything to these men, because, you see,
they have come into the shade of my roof beam."*

Look, please: I have two daughters who have not known any man symbolizes desires for goodness and truth. *Please let me bring them out to you*
symbolizes blessings that come from these desires. *And you may do with
them as is good in your eyes* means enjoying them, so far as they are perceived to come of goodness. *Only don't do anything to these men* means

that people should not hurt the Lord's divine humanity and holy influence. *Because, you see, they have come into the shade of my roof beam* means that they are to be found within the good done out of love for others; the *shade of a roof beam* means within a vague and general form of it.

Look: I have two daughters who have not known any man symbolizes **2362** desires for goodness and truth. This can be seen from the symbolism of *daughters* as feelings (discussed in §§489, 490, 491, [568]). The fact that they *had not known any man* means that falsity had not tainted them. A *man* symbolizes truth in the rational mind, and falsity too, in an opposite sense (§§265, 749, 1007).

There are two basic categories of desire: the desire for what is good and the desire for what is true (see §1997). The former—the desire for goodness—constitutes a heavenly religion, and the Word calls it both the daughter of Zion and the virgin daughter of Zion. The latter, though— the desire for truth—constitutes a spiritual religion, and the Word calls it the daughter of Jerusalem. [2] In Isaiah, for instance:

> The *virgin daughter of Zion* has spurned you, mocked you. Behind you the *daughter of Jerusalem* shakes her head. (Isaiah 37:22; 2 Kings 19:21)

In Jeremiah:

> What shall I compare to you, *daughter of Jerusalem?* What shall I equate with you, and [how] shall I comfort you, *virgin daughter of Zion?* (Lamentations 2:13)

In Micah:

> You tower of the flock, you slope of *Zion's daughter:* right to you it will come, and the former ruling power will come, the reign of *Jerusalem's daughter.* (Micah 4:8)

In Zephaniah:

> Shout for joy, *daughter of Zion!* Cheer aloud, Israel! Be glad and rejoice with your whole heart, *daughter of Jerusalem!* (Zephaniah 3:14)

In Zechariah:

> Rejoice immensely, *daughter of Zion;* cheer aloud, *daughter of Jerusalem!* See: your king will come to you! (Zechariah 9:9; Matthew 21:5; John 12:15)

[3] For further evidence that a heavenly religion (or the Lord's heavenly kingdom) is called the daughter of Zion because of a desire for goodness, or in other words, love for the Lord himself, see Isaiah 10:32; 16:1;

52:2; 62:11; Jeremiah 4:31; 6:2, 23; Lamentations 1:6; 2:1, 4, 8, 10; Micah 4:10, 13; Zechariah 2:10; Psalms 9:14. For further evidence that a spiritual religion (or the Lord's spiritual kingdom) is called the daughter of Jerusalem because of a desire for truth and so because of charity for others, see Lamentations 2:15.

The previous volumes dealt many times with these two types of religion, describing the nature of both.

[4] Because a heavenly religion is marked by love for the Lord, it is also marked by neighborly love, and for this reason it is compared in a particular way to an unmarried daughter, or in other words, a virgin. In fact, it is even called a virgin, as in John:

> They are the ones who have not been defiled with women, since they are *virgins*. They are the ones who follow the Lamb where he goes. For they are spotless before God's throne. (Revelation 14:4, 5)

In order for this to be represented in the Jewish religion as well, priests were directed not to take widows but virgins as wives (Leviticus 21:13, 14, 15; Ezekiel 44:22).

[5] The contents of this verse show how pure the Word is in its inner meaning, even if it looks quite different in the letter. Nothing but impure thoughts enter the mind—especially the minds of people who live an evil life—when they read these words: "Look, please: I have two daughters who have not known any man. Please let me bring them out to you, and you may do with them as is good in your eyes. Only don't do anything to these men." The explanation, however, reveals how chaste the words nonetheless are in their inner meaning, symbolizing as they do desires for goodness and truth and the blessings these desires yield in people who refuse to harm the Lord's divinity and holiness.

2363   *Please let me bring them out to you* symbolizes blessings that come from these desires—that is, from the desire for goodness and for truth. This can be seen from the meaning of the words when they apply to the desires meant by the daughters here.

Anyone who succumbs to evil and enjoys it is profoundly ignorant of the notion that blessing and happiness can be found only in the desire for goodness and truth. To such a person, the blessings that come of a liking for goodness and truth appear to be either nonexistent or dry. To some they seem depressing or even deadly. The demons and spirits of hell are like this. They imagine that if they were to be robbed of the pleasure they take in self-love and materialism and in the evil these desires lead to, no life could remain to them. If you show them that real life with all its blessings and happiness begins at that point, they sense a deep sadness in the loss of their pleasure. If you take them into the company of people who live such a life, pain and torment overwhelm them. In addition, they then start to feel a corpselike sensation in themselves, and something dreadfully hellish. As a result they refer to heaven (where blessings and happiness of this kind exist) as their hell. So far as they can escape and hide from the Lord's face, they do.

[2] Still, every bliss and happiness consists in a passion for the goodness that love and charity inspire and for the truth that leads to faith (so far as it leads to goodness). This is evident from the fact that heaven—angelic life—consists in the same passion, and that it touches angels from deep within, since it flows in from the Lord through their deepest inner reaches (see §§540, 541, 545). When it does, wisdom and understanding also enter and fill the inmost sanctuaries of the mind itself. They kindle the goodness there with heavenly fire and the truth there with heavenly light. With them they bring a sense of blessing and good fortune that can only be described as ineffable. People enjoying this state perceive how hollow, how grim, and how deplorable life is for those immersed in the evil of self-love and materialism.

[3] There is a way to see what this kind of life—a life devoted to love for ourselves and the material world—is like by comparison. In other words, there is a way to see what a life of arrogance, greed, envy, hatred, revenge, ruthlessness, and adultery is like: With any kind of mental gift, you can imagine to yourself the character of a person living this kind of life. If you are able, you can even paint your own mental portrait, drawing on images supplied by experience, knowledge, and reason. Keep working at the picture or sketch and you will see how ghastly those things are, that they are the Devil in form and contain nothing human. Anyone who finds life's highest pleasure in them turns into something diabolical after death as well, and the greater the pleasure, the more terrifying the form.

[4] On the other hand, if you picture to yourself the character of love and charity, or try to translate it into a physical shape in your mind, and if you work faithfully at the image or drawing, you will see that the form is an angel's. It will be rich with blessings and beauty, with something heavenly and divine. Does anyone believe that these two forms can coexist? Or that we can strip off the figure of the Devil and exchange it for the figure of neighborly love, simply through faith? A faith that we violate by the way we live? After all, our life awaits each of us after death. To put it

another way, what we love awaits us after death, since it then determines everything we think and therefore everything we believe. In this way our faith reveals itself, showing what it was like at heart.

2364 *And you may do with them as is good in your eyes* means enjoying [these desires], so far as they come of goodness. This too can be seen from the meaning of the words, when they apply to the desires symbolized by the daughters, and from the chain of ideas.

Lot's going out to them at the door meant that he approached cautiously (§2356), and the prudence he displayed in doing so is evident in these words and in the rest of the verse. In other words, they were to enjoy the blessings of a desire for goodness and truth so far as these came of goodness, which is what *doing with them as was good in their eyes* meant. Enjoying them so far as they come of goodness here is enjoying them so far as we can see that they are good. No one is asked to do more. The Lord bends all our lives in a good direction by means of what is good in our faith. So he leads non-Christians one way and Christians another, the untaught one way and the well-educated another, children one way and adults another. If we have filled our lives with evil, we bend in a good direction by refraining from evil and trying to do good, according to our conception of it. When we do so, it is our intent or aim that counts. Even if our actions are not inherently good, the purpose still lends them a measure of goodness and so of life, which creates the blessing in them.

2365 *Only don't do anything to these men* means that people should not hurt the Lord's divine humanity and holy influence, as the symbolism of the *men,* or angels, discussed above [§§2318–2319, 2352], establishes.

2366 *Because, you see, they have come into the shade of my roof beam* means that they are to be found within the good done out of love for others. This is established by the symbolism of a house as something good (§§710, 2233). Here it is called the *shade of a roof beam,* for reasons given below.

2367 The *shade of a roof beam* means within a vague and general form of that goodness, because when we perceive goodness or truth, we always do so vaguely. Even those of us that have been reborn perceive it only dimly, especially the people represented by Lot here—people whose worship is shallow. When we are caught up in bodily concerns (or in other words, while we are living in the body), our emotions, like our perceptions, are extremely general and consequently extremely vague, whether we believe it or not. There are millions of elements in every slightest one of our urges, and also in every thought that goes to make up our perception, but each urge and thought looks like a single whole to us. (By the Lord's divine mercy, this will come to be explained where feelings and thoughts are discussed [§§3078, 3189, 4005].) Sometimes we are able to examine and describe a few of the elements by reflecting on them, but a vast and even endless number of others remain hidden. These do not and cannot ever make their way into our conscious thought as long as we are living in our bodies, but they do reveal themselves after everything bodily and worldly has been snuffed out.

[2] The truth of this is clear enough from the consideration that when people who have acted out of love and charity pass into the other world, they move from a dim life to a brighter one. It is as if they are moving from night into day. The farther they come into the Lord's heaven, the farther they come into clarity. Eventually they come all the way into the light in which the angels live, who enjoy such radiant understanding and wisdom that it is beyond the power of words to describe. The very glimmer we live in is a dark shadow by comparison.

The text, then, says, "They have come into the shade of my roof beam," meaning that they are in a vague and general form. That is, the person knows little about the Lord's divinity and holiness but still acknowledges and believes that they exist. The person also believes that they are to be found within good done out of neighborly love, or in other words, with people who do that kind of good.

Genesis 19:9. And they said, "Get away!" And they said, "Didn't this one come to stay as an immigrant? And will he really judge us? Now we will do worse to you than to them!" And they put pressure on the man, on Lot, very hard, and they came up to break the entrance.   **2368**

And they said means an angry answer. *"Get away!"* means their angry threats. *And they said, "Didn't this one come to stay as an immigrant?"* symbolizes people whose theology was different and who lived differently. *"And will he really judge us?"* means, are they to teach us? *"Now we will do worse to you than to them!"* means that they rejected neighborly kindness even more than they rejected the Lord's divine humanity and holy influence. *And they put pressure on the man* means that they wanted to browbeat truth. *On Lot, very hard* means that they wanted to browbeat neighborly kindness as much as possible. *And they came up to break the entrance* means that they went so far as to try demolishing both.

And they said means an angry answer, as can be seen without explanation from the context above and below.   **2369**

"Get away!" means angry threats, specifically against neighborly goodness. This can be seen from the symbolism of Lot—the target and subject   **2370**

of the words—as good done out of neighborly love. The words themselves make it obvious that this is an angry threat. They also contain the idea that these people would completely reject such goodness if he said any more about it or tried to persuade them again, as the words that follow show. That is what "Get away!" means.

2371   *And they said, "Didn't this one come to stay as an immigrant?"* symbolizes people whose theology was different and who lived differently. This is established by the symbolism of *staying as an immigrant* as learning and living, and so as religious teachings and life (discussed in §§1463, 2025).

These words portray the condition of the church as it exists around the time of its end, when there is no faith because there is no charity. That is, because acts of neighborly love have disappeared entirely from its life, the church also banishes them from its theology.

[2] This passage is not talking about people who distort the truth about active charity, interpreting it to their own advantage, in order both to acquire supreme power and to obtain all worldly blessings. It is not talking about people who claim the right to hand out heavenly rewards and who in this way pollute charitable kindness with various tricks and stratagems.

It is referring instead to people who want to hear only about faith detached from acts of charity or good deeds, not about the deeds themselves. They rationalize their view by saying that we have nothing but evil inside us; that even the good we do is actually bad and therefore offers no salvation; that none of us can earn heaven or therefore be saved by any good that we do but only by a faith that acknowledges the Lord's merit. This is the theology that flourishes in the final days, when religion starts to breathe its last, and it is passionately taught and eagerly seized on. [3] However, to draw the conclusion that we can have virtuous faith along with an evil life is wrong. It is also wrong to think that because we have nothing but evil inside us we cannot receive goodness from the Lord—goodness that has heaven in it because it has the Lord in it, and that has bliss and happiness in it because it has heaven in it.

Finally, it is wrong to believe that since we cannot earn heaven through any good we do, we do not receive heavenly goodness from the Lord. This kind of goodness—in which personal credit is seen as something heinous—surrounds every angel, every regenerate person, and any who find pleasure and even bliss in goodness itself, or in the effect goodness has on them. This is what the Lord says in Matthew about such goodness, or such charity:

You've heard that it was said, "You shall love your neighbor and hate your enemy." I tell you, do good to those who hate you, and pray for those who wound and persecute you, so that you may be the children of your Father who is in the heavens. For if you love those who love you, what reward do you have? And if you greet your brothers and sisters only, what are you doing extra? Don't even the tax collectors do the same? (Matthew 5:43, 44, 45, 46, 47, 48)

Similar words appear in Luke, with this addition:

Do good and lend, not hoping for anything out of it; then your reward will be ample, and you will be children of the Highest One. (Luke 6:27–36)

[4] These passages describe the goodness we receive from the Lord and show that it is free of any desire to be repaid. That is why people who obey this impulse are called children of their Father who is in the heavens and children of the Highest One. Because the impulse holds the Lord within it, it is also a reward. In Luke:

When you make a luncheon or dinner, don't call your friends or your brothers and sisters or your relatives or your rich neighbors, or they might call you in return and it would become repayment to you. But when you make a banquet, call the poor, the maimed, the blind. Then you will be fortunate, because they have nothing to repay with; it will be repaid to you in the resurrection of the dead. (Luke 14:12, 13, 14)

Luncheon, dinner, and a banquet mean charitable goodness, in which the Lord lives together with us (§2341). So these words depict and explicitly reveal the fact that the reward is in the goodness itself, because the Lord is in it. After all, it says that repayment would come in the resurrection of the dead.

[5] People who make an effort to do good on their own, because the Lord has commanded it, are the ones who eventually welcome this kind of goodness. Once they have learned that all good comes from the Lord (§§1712, 1937, 1947), they acknowledge and believe it. They then reject any sense of credit for themselves so firmly that when they merely consider the possibility, it depresses them, and they sense their blessings and happiness accordingly shrinking with the thought.

[6] It is different with people who do not act this way but live an evil life, teaching and preaching that salvation consists in a detached faith. They

do not even know this kind of goodness is possible. Amazing to say—and I have had the opportunity to learn this from much experience—the same people in the other world feel that they deserve to go to heaven because of their good deeds! Such good deeds, that is, as they can remember. That is because they then realize for the first time that faith isolated from love for others offers no salvation. At that point, though, they are the people the Lord spoke of in Matthew:

> They will say to me on that day, "Lord! Lord! Haven't we prophesied in your name and cast out demons in your name and exercised many powers in your name?" But then I'll proclaim to them, "I do not know you. Leave me, you evildoers!" (Matthew 7:22, 23)

Clearly these people paid no attention whatsoever to all the Lord himself so often taught about doing good out of love and charity. These teachings were like clouds that flit away, or like visions in the night to them. They include the following: Matthew 3:8, 9; 5:7–48; 6:1–20; 7:16–20, 24–27; 9:13; 12:33; 13:8, 23; 18:21, 22, 23–end; 19:19; 22:35–40; 24:12, 13; 25:34–end; Mark 4:18, 19, 20; 11:13, 14, 20; 12:28–34; Luke 3:8, 9; 6:27–39, 43–end; 7:47; 8:8, 14, 15; 10:25–28; 12:58, 59; 13:6–10; John 3:19, 21; 5:42; 13:34, 35; 14:14, 15, 20, 21, 23; 15:1–8, 9–19; 21:15, 16, 17.

These ideas, then, and others like them are what was meant when the men of Sodom—that is, people immersed in evil (§§2220, 2246, 2322)—said to Lot, "Didn't this one come to stay as an immigrant? And will he really judge us?" In other words, "These people whose theology is different and who live differently—are they to teach us?"

2372   *"And will he really judge us?"* means, are they to teach us? This can be seen from the symbolism of *judging* as teaching. Section 2235 showed that justice is mentioned in connection with the exercise of goodness, but judgment with instruction in truth. That is why judging, in an inner sense, is instructing, or teaching.

Teaching truth is the same as teaching what is good, because all truth looks to goodness.

2373   *"Now we will do worse to you than to them!"* means that they rejected neighborly kindness even more than they rejected the Lord's divine humanity and holy influence, as can be seen from the following: Lot symbolizes kindness done out of neighborly love, because he represents people who do such kindness (§§2324, 2351, 2371). And the men (the angels), as mentioned above [§§2318–2319, 2352], symbolize the Lord, so far as his divine humanity and holy influence are concerned. From this it is clear that *doing worse to you than to them* has this meaning.

Why do people in the church who are under the sway of evil reject love for others more than they deny the Lord? Because this way they can use the pretense of religious principle to justify doing what they want to do while engaging in worship that is shallow and devoid of inner content. In other words, their worship springs from the lips rather than the heart. The more divine and sacred they make this worship out to be, the higher they rise in rank and the more they profit. There are many other reasons, too, which lie hidden and yet open.

Nevertheless, the fact of the matter is that people who reject the one (in their theology and their lives) also reject the other. If they do not dare to do it with their lips, they still do it in their hearts. This too is expressed in the literal story, by their coming up to break the entrance, meaning that they went so far as to try demolishing both. What stops their effort from bursting into action, though, is also no secret.

They put pressure on the man means that they wanted to browbeat **2374** truth. This can be seen from the symbolism of a *man* as our intellectual, rational side and therefore as truth, as discussed at §§158, 1007.

Browbeating truth is perverting tenets of faith. We pervert them when we separate them from charity and protest that they do not point toward living a good life.

On Lot, very hard means that they wanted to browbeat neighborly **2375** kindness as much as possible. This can be seen from the symbolism of *Lot* as neighborly kindness, discussed above at §§2324, 2351, 2371, 2373.

The words themselves here—*they put pressure on the man, on Lot, very hard*—show that a man symbolizes one thing and *Lot, very hard,* another. If not, one expression would have been enough.

They came up to break the entrance means that they went so far as to try **2376** demolishing both, as can be seen from the following: *Coming up* means trying. And an *entrance* symbolizes something that leads to goodness and the Lord, so it also symbolizes goodness itself, and the Lord himself, as discussed at §§2356, 2357. For more on the situation here, see above at §2373.

Genesis 19:10. *And the men put out their hand and brought Lot in to* **2377** *them, into the house, and closed the entrance.*

The men put out their hand symbolizes the Lord's powerful help. *And brought Lot in to them, into the house* means that the Lord guards people who act out of neighborly love. *And closed the entrance* means that he also blocks every opening leading to them.

2378   *The men put out a hand* symbolizes the Lord's powerful help, as is established by the following: The *men* symbolize the Lord, as mentioned above [§§2318–2319, 2352, 2373], and a *hand* symbolizes power, as discussed in §878.

2379   *They brought Lot in to them, into the house* means that the Lord guards people who act out of neighborly love, as can be seen from the following: *Lot* represents people who do good out of neighborly love, as mentioned above [§2375]. And *bringing him in to them, into the house* means guarding them. Being brought into the house is being brought into doing good; people who are brought into doing good are brought into heaven; and people who are brought into heaven are brought to the Lord. So they are safe from any assault on their souls.

In their souls, people devoted to goodness associate with angels. As a result, while they are still alive in their bodies they are also in heaven, even though they do not realize it at the time and cannot feel angelic joy. After all, they are taken up with bodily concerns and are being prepared. See §1277.

2380   *They closed the entrance* means that the Lord also blocks every opening leading to them. This can be seen from the symbolism of an *entrance* as something that leads in (§§2356, 2357, 2376) and so as an opening. That is why closing the entrance means blocking the opening.

In the next life, the opening is blocked by isolating the good from the evil. The point is to keep any atmosphere of persuasive lies and evil cravings from plaguing the good, since no wind blowing from hell can invade heaven. In bodily life, the opening is blocked by the fact that false assumptions and delusions have no effect on people governed by goodness, because of the angels present with them. As soon as they are subjected to any falsity that comes of evil, or any evil that comes of falsity, whether in an evil person's words or in thoughts suggested by an evil spirit or demon, these angels immediately deflect it. They bend it in the direction of some true idea or good impulse that the person has a firm hold on. It does not matter to such people if the infestation targets their body, because they consider their body insignificant compared to their soul.

[2] As long as bodily concerns continue to hold our attention, our thoughts and perceptions are so general and vague (§2367) that we hardly know whether we have charitable goodness or not. This is also because we do not know what charity is, or who our neighbor is. But we ought to know who does have that kind of goodness. Anyone who has a conscience

has charitable goodness—that is, anyone who refuses to deviate one bit from what is just and fair, good and true, and does so for the sake of justice and fairness itself, of goodness and truth itself. To refuse on these grounds is to refuse from conscience. People with charitable goodness, therefore, also think well of and wish well to their neighbor, even if that individual is their enemy; and they do so without any thought of being repaid. These are the people who do good out of love for others, whether they are outside the church or in. Those inside the church revere the Lord and willingly hear and do what he taught.

[3] On the other hand, people who are involved in evil have no conscience. They do not care what is just and fair, except so far as they can win a reputation for appearing to be just and fair. They do not know what is good or true or that it affects their spiritual life, which they reject as nonexistent. In addition, they think ill of and wish ill to their neighbor. If others do not fawn over them, they also treat them badly—even if these others are their allies—and take pleasure in doing so. If they do any good, it is to get something in return. People like this in the church deny the Lord secretly; or if they can do so without endangering their position, level of affluence, reputation, or life, they deny him openly.

[4] Still, it needs to be realized that some people believe they are *not* focused on goodness when they are, while others believe they *are* focused on goodness when they are not. The reason some people believe they are not focused on goodness when they are is that when they privately consider the possibility, immediately the angels they associate with inject the idea that they are not. The goal is to prevent them from attributing goodness to themselves and wandering off into self-righteousness and so into setting themselves above others. Otherwise they would fall into spiritual trial.

[5] The reason some believe they are focused on goodness when they are not is that when they consider the possibility, immediately the evil demons and spirits they consort with insist that they are. The evil, after all, equate goodness with pleasure. In fact, they hint that whatever good these people have done to others for the purpose of gaining personal power or material advantages is a kindness that ought to be repaid, in the other life as well [as this]. So they believe they deserve better than others, whom they despise and even consider worthless in comparison with themselves. Strange to say, if they thought otherwise, they would fall into spiritual trials in which they would fail.

Genesis 19:11. *And the men who were at the door of the house they struck* **2381** *with blindness, from small to large; and they had trouble finding the door.*

The men who were at the door of the house symbolize rational ideas, and doctrines growing out of them, which are used to browbeat neighborly kindness. *They struck with blindness* means that [the people being symbolized] were filled with falsity. *From small to large* means in particular and in general. *And they had trouble finding the door* means that they still could not see that truth of any kind would lead to goodness.

2382   *And the men who were at the door of the house* symbolize rational ideas, and doctrines growing out of them, which are used to browbeat neighborly kindness, as can be seen from the following: *Men* symbolize rational ideas, as discussed in §§158, 1007. A *door* symbolizes something that leads or opens into either truth or goodness, as discussed above at §2356, so it symbolizes a doctrine. And a *house* symbolizes neighborly kindness, as discussed many times above.

This phrase is talking about people who had come up to break the entrance, or in other words, who were trying to demolish both kindness done from love and the Lord's divinity and holiness (§2376). The men, then, mean evil in the rational mind and the false doctrines growing out of it, which are used to browbeat neighborly kindness.

2383   *They struck with blindness* means that [the people being symbolized] were filled with falsity, as can be seen from the symbolism of *blindness*.

In the Word, *blindness* is mentioned in connection with people who subscribe to falsity and also in connection with people who do not know truth; both are called blind. Which of the two is meant, though, can be seen from the context, especially that of the inner meaning.

The following passages show that people in the grip of falsity are called blind. In Isaiah:

> *His sentries are blind;* none of them know; they are all mute dogs; they cannot bark. (Isaiah 56:10)

Blind sentries stand for people whose rationalizations lead them into falsity. In the same author:

> We wait for light, and look: shadows; for brilliant days, [but] we walk in darkness. Like the *blind* we touch the wall. (Isaiah 59:9, 10)

In Jeremiah:

> They have wandered *blind* in the streets, they have defiled themselves with blood. Things that they themselves cannot touch they touch with their clothes. (Lamentations 4:14)

This is saying that all truth has been defiled. The street stands for the truth, in which they wandered or erred (§2336). [2] In Zechariah:

> On that day I will strike every horse with bewilderment and its rider with madness; every horse of the peoples I will strike with *blindness*. (Zechariah 12:4)

A horse here and elsewhere in the Word stands for the intellect. That is why it says a horse would be struck with bewilderment and a horse of the peoples would be struck with blindness—meaning that it would be filled with falsity. [3] In John:

> "For judgment I came into the world, in order that those who *do not see* may see but those who see become *blind*." Some of the Pharisees heard these things; they said, "Are we also *blind?*" Jesus said to them, "If you were *blind* you would have no sin. But now you say 'We see!' So your sin remains." (John 9:39, 40, 41)

This passage speaks of the blind in both senses: people given over to falsity and people ignorant of truth. In people who are part of the church and know what is true, blindness is falsity. In people who do not know what is true, including people outside the church, blindness is ignorance of truth, and they are blameless. [4] In the same author:

> *He has blinded their eyes* and closed off their heart to *prevent them from seeing with their eyes* and understanding at heart and being healed by me. (John 12:40; Isaiah 6:9, 10, 11)

This stands for the fact that since their lives are evil, it would be better for them to think false thoughts than true ones; if they learned truth, they would not only falsify it further but also pollute it with evil. The reason it would be better is the same as the reason that the men of Sodom were struck with blindness, or in other words, that their doctrines were filled with falsity. The reason was explained at §§301, 302, 303, 593, 1008, 1010, 1059, 1327, 1328, 2426.

[5] Since blindness symbolized falsity, the representative Jewish religion had a prohibition against sacrificing any blind animal (Leviticus 22:22; Deuteronomy 15:21; Malachi 1:8). It was also forbidden that any blind man among the priests approach to make an offering on the altar (Leviticus 21:18, 21).

[6] It is clear in Isaiah that blindness is mentioned in connection with ignorance of truth—the type of ignorance non-Christians have:

> On that day the deaf will hear the words of the Book, and out of the darkness and out of the shadows *the eyes of the blind will see.* (Isaiah 29:18)

The blind stand for people who do not know truth, especially people outside the church. In the same author:

> Lead forth a *blind people* (and they will have eyes) and the deaf (and they will have ears)! (Isaiah 43:8)

This is about a church among non-Jews. In the same author:

> I will lead the *blind* on a way they have not known; I will turn the darkness before them into light. (Isaiah 42:16)

[7] And in the same author:

> I will give you as a light for the people, to open *blind eyes,* to lead the prisoner out from jail, those sitting in darkness out of the prison house. (Isaiah 42:6, 7)

This is about the Lord's Coming and says that people who lacked a knowledge of truth would be taught then. People who commit themselves to falsity do not allow themselves to be taught in this way, because they know the truth and have hardened their minds against it. They have turned light into a darkness that is not dispelled. In Luke:

> The householder said to his slave, "Go quickly into the streets and alleys of the city and bring in here the poor and the maimed and the lame and the *blind."* (Luke 14:21)

This is about the Lord's kingdom. Obviously it is talking not about the poor, maimed, lame, and blind but about people who are like this spiritually. [8] In the same author:

> Jesus told them to report back to John that "the *blind* see, the *lame* walk, the *leprous* are cleansed, the *deaf* hear, the *dead* rise again, the *poor* have the gospel preached to them." (Luke 7:22)

In a literal sense the blind, lame, leprous, deaf, dead, and poor mean exactly that, because what he said was also happening: the blind were receiving sight; the deaf, their hearing; the leprous, a healing; and the dead, life. Nonetheless, in a deeper sense they mean the same people mentioned [9] in Isaiah:

Then the *eyes of the blind* will be opened, and the ears of the *deaf* will be opened, and the *lame* will spring up like a deer, and the *mute* will sing with their tongue. (Isaiah 35:5, 6)

This speaks of the Lord's Coming and a new religion at that time, called a church of Gentiles. The passage portrays them as the blind, deaf, lame, and mute—so called in relation to their theology and their lives. It needs to be realized that the miracles the Lord performed always involved and therefore symbolized the kinds of things meant in an inner sense by the blind, lame, leprous, deaf, dead, and poor. That is why his miracles were divine, as were those performed in Egypt, those performed in the wilderness, and any others mentioned in the Word. This is a secret.

From small to large means in particular and in general. This can be **2384** seen from the symbolism of these sizes on an inner level when they refer to rational ideas and the doctrines growing out of them, symbolized by the men who were at the door of the house. What is particular and what is general resemble size: particulars are small, so to speak, and general collections of particulars are large. For more about what is particular and what is general and the way they interrelate, see §§920, 1040, 1316.

And they had trouble finding the door means that they still could not **2385** see that truth of any kind would lead to goodness. This is established by the symbolism of a *door* as an entryway and opening and as truth itself, since this leads into goodness, as discussed above at §2356. Here, though, the door symbolizes knowledge that leads to truth, because the door was out in front of the house, [while the entrance was right on the house,] as noted above at §2356. After all, it says that Lot went out to the door and closed the entrance behind him (verse 6), so *having trouble finding the door* is not seeing that truth of any kind would lead to goodness.

[2] This is what happens to people who concoct doctrinal theories out of their rationalizations (especially in the final days) and who believe nothing unless they can first grasp it. Under those circumstances, the evil in their lives is constantly affecting their ability to reason. Like people who see apparitions by the glimmer of the moon, they see falsity as truth in the deceptive glow shed by their fiery passion for evil. That same falsity they then confirm in a multitude of ways, transforming it into doctrine. An example is the doctrine of those who say that the way we live (which is a matter of feeling) does not count but only what we believe (which is a matter of thought).

[3] Anyone can recognize that once we have adopted a principle we are capable of marshaling an unlimited wealth of arguments to prove it, no matter what its nature is—even if it is the height of falsity. Superficially, we can make it look as though it were the epitome of truth. That is how heresy arises, and from heresy we never back away, once we have confirmed it. However, everything that comes from a false principle is false thinking. Even if truth is injected, it still becomes falsified when used in support of the false principle, having been polluted with the quality of that principle.

[4] The situation is completely different if we adopt and confirm real truth as a principle. Take this proposition, for instance: Love for the Lord and charity for our neighbor underpin all the Law and form the subject that all the Prophets address. So love and charity are the essential ingredients of all theology and worship. If we took this as a premise, our minds would then be enlightened by vast numbers of passages in the Word that otherwise lie hidden in the murk of false assumptions. In fact, heresy would then vanish. All the churches would join into one, no matter how great the differences in doctrinal teachings derived from this premise or pointing to it, and no matter how great the differences in ritual.

[5] That is what the ancient church was like. It stretched through many countries: Assyria, Mesopotamia, Syria, Ethiopia, Arabia, Libya, Egypt, and Philistia all the way to Tyre and Sidon by way of Canaan on both the near and far sides of the Jordan. These peoples had different doctrines and different rituals but were still a single church, because charity was the vital element to them. In those days, the Lord's kingdom was "on earth as it is in the heavens," because that is what heaven is like (see §§684, 690). If this were how matters now stood, we would all be ruled as one person by the Lord. We would be like members and organs of a single body that, although they differ in form and function, are still connected to a single heart, on which they all depend, each in its own form, each different from the next. Then, no matter what our theology or what our outward form of worship, we would each say, "You are my kin; I see that you worship the Lord and that you are a good person."

2386   Genesis 19:12. *And the men said to Lot, "Do you still have anyone here? [Your] son-in-law, your sons, and your daughters, and everyone you have in the city—take them away from the place."*

The men said to Lot means that the Lord alerts people who act out of neighborly love. *Do you still have anyone here? [Your] son-in-law and your sons and your daughters and everyone you have in the city—take them away from the place* means that everyone and everything involved in neighborly kindness would be saved, as would those who concentrate on religious truth, if they pulled back from evil. *Sons-in-law* are truths attached to a desire for goodness (here, truths about to be attached to it). *Sons* are truths. *Daughters* are the desire for goodness and truth. *Everyone in the city* is whatever partakes at all of truth. A *place* is an evil state.

The men said to Lot means that the Lord alerts people who act out of neighborly love, as can be seen from the following: The *men* symbolize the Lord, as mentioned in §2378. *Saying* means alerting. And *Lot* represents people who act out of neighborly love, as discussed in §§2324, 2351, 2371. That is why *the men said to Lot* means that the Lord alerts people who act out of neighborly love.

Do you still have anyone here? [Your] son-in-law and your sons and your daughters and everyone you have in the city—take them away from the place means that everyone and everything involved in neighborly kindness would be saved, as would those who concentrate on religious truth, if they pulled back from evil. This can be seen from the symbolism of *sons-in-law, sons, daughters,* a *city,* and a *place,* dealt with below.

[2] The reason people who focus on religious truth are saved if they pull back from evil is this: True religious concepts are the actual vessels that receive goodness (§§1900, 2063, 2261, 2269), and they receive goodness so far as we move away from evil. What is good is always streaming into us from the Lord, but what is evil in our lives keeps it from being received in the truth we memorize or know. So the more we back away from evil, the more goodness enters into us and adapts to the truth we have. Then religious truth becomes religious goodness in us.

We might know truth; we might claim to believe it, spurred on by some worldly goal or other; we might even convince ourselves that it is true. Still, this truth does not come alive as long as we live an evil life. People who act this way are like a tree that has leaves but no fruit. Truth of this type resembles light without any warmth, like the light that shines in winter, when nothing grows. When it does contain warmth, however, it turns into the kind of light that shines in spring, when everything grows. The Word equates truth with light and even calls it light, but it equates warmth with love, which is also called spiritual warmth. In the next life truth also reveals itself as light, while goodness reveals itself as warmth. Truth without goodness reveals itself as a cold light, but with goodness it reveals itself as a springtime light. This indicates what religious truth devoid of neighborly kindness is. That is why Lot's sons-in-law and sons (symbolizing this kind of truth) were not saved, only Lot and his daughters.

[3] Since I say here that people who concentrate on religious truth are also saved, if they withdraw from evil, you need to know just who they are. They are champions of faith who do not think about charity at all, because that is how they have been taught. They do not know what charity is, since they imagine that it is only giving others what we have and having pity on everyone. They also do not know which neighbor they should show charity to, since they imagine that it is everyone in general, almost without distinction. Yet these people live lives of charity for their neighbor because they live a good life. It does them no harm to profess the same faith as everyone else, because within their faith lies charity. *Charity* means everything good we do in our lives, in general and particular. What charity is, then, and what the neighbor is, will be told later, by the Lord's divine mercy.

2389   *Sons-in-law* are truths attached to a desire for goodness and truth (here, truths about to be attached to that desire), as indicated by the symbolism of *sons-in-law*. In the Word, a man or husband symbolizes truth, and a wife, goodness (§§265, 749, 915, 1007), because truth and goodness have a kind of marriage (§§1432, 1904, 2173). That is why sons-in-law symbolize a knowledge of truth, to which the desire for goodness (the daughters) is attached. Here, though, it is about to be attached, because verse 14 below says that Lot went out and talked to the sons-in-law who were taking (that is, about to take) his daughters.

2390   *Sons* are truth or, to put it another way, people who focus on truth. This is established by the symbolism of *sons* as truth, as discussed in §§489, 491, 533, 1147.

2391   *Daughters* are the desire for goodness and truth or, to put it another way, people who desire goodness and truth. This is established by the symbolism of *daughters* as that desire, a symbolism discussed at §2362.

2392   *Everyone in the city* is whatever partakes at all of truth. This is established by the symbolism of a *city* as doctrine and so as truth, with all that it embraces, as discussed at §§402, 2268.

2393   A *place* is an evil state. This is established by the symbolism of a *place* as a state or condition, as treated of in §§1273, 1274, 1275, 1377. Here it symbolizes an evil state because it was Sodom, which symbolizes evil in general (§§2220, 2246, 2322).

2394   Genesis 19:13. *"Because we are destroying this place, because their outcry has grown loud before Jehovah, and Jehovah has sent us to destroy it."*

Because we are destroying this place means that the evil state the people were in would damn them. *Because their outcry has grown loud before Jehovah* means because of the amount of falsity inspired by evil in them. *And Jehovah has sent us to destroy it* means they will inevitably be destroyed.

Because we are destroying this place means that the evil state the people were in would damn them, as can be seen from the following: When the Lord is said to *destroy,* the sense of the inner meaning is that evil destroys, or damns. And a *place* symbolizes an evil state (§2393).

2395

Often the Word says that Jehovah destroys, but in an inner sense it means that we destroy ourselves. Jehovah—the Lord—does not destroy anyone, but it looks as though he does, because he sees absolutely everything and controls absolutely everything. So the Word speaks in these terms in many places, in order to maintain in us the general impression that everything comes under his gaze and under his supervision. Once we are caught and held by this notion, we can easily learn more. Explanations of the Word's inner meaning, you see, are nothing other than particulars that shed light on the general idea.

[2] Another objective is for people who lack love to be gripped by fear and therefore hold the Lord in awe, fleeing to him for deliverance.

This shows that it does no harm to take the Word literally (even if the inner meaning teaches differently) as long as we do so in simplicity of heart. This will be dealt with more fully below, however, at verse 24, §2447, where it says that Jehovah rained sulfur and fire onto Sodom and Gomorrah.

Because angels are caught up in the inner meaning, it is foreign to them to think that Jehovah (the Lord) destroys anyone—so foreign that they cannot stand even to imagine the possibility. So when we read these things and others like them in the Word, they toss the literal meaning over their shoulder, so to speak. Eventually it transforms into the idea that evil itself is what destroys us, that the Lord destroys no one. The example described in §1875 illustrates the point.

Because their outcry has grown loud before Jehovah means because of the amount of falsity inspired by evil in them, as can be seen from the symbolism of an *outcry.* The discussion in §2240 points out that the word is used in connection with falsity—here, falsity inspired by evil (§2351).

2396

Jehovah has sent us to destroy it means they will inevitably be destroyed. The case resembles that discussed above in §2395.

2397

We—the men or angels—are the Lord's divine humanity and holy influence, as shown above [§§2318–2319]. His divinity and holiness is what saved good people and destroyed the wicked—though the fate of the latter was determined by the law that wickedness itself is what destroys them. Because they were destroyed by this, and because the Lord's coming into the world is what triggered it, the text speaks in accord with the appearance: that the angels were sent to destroy them.

[2] More than once the Word says that the Lord was sent by the Father, just as it says here, "Jehovah has *sent* us." In every instance, however, *being sent* means *coming from,* on an inner level. In John, for instance:

They accepted and recognized truly that *I came from you,* and they believed that *you sent me.* (John 17:8)

The same thing is meant in other passages, as in the same author:

God did not *send his Son* into the world so that he could judge the world but so that the world could be saved by him. (John 3:17)

In the same author:

One who does not honor the Son does not honor the Father *who sent him.* (John 5:23)

There are many other places in addition, such as Matthew 10:40; 15:24; John 3:34; 4:34; 5:30, 36, 37, 38; 6:29, 39, 40, 44, 57; 7:16, 18, 28, 29; 8:16, 18, 29, 42; 9:4; 10:36; 11:41, 42; 12:44, 45, 49; 13:20; 14:24; 17:18; 20:21; Luke 4:43; 9:48; 10:16; Mark 9:37; Isaiah 61:1.

[3] Likewise it says that the holy operation of the Spirit would be sent—that is, come—from the Lord's divinity, as in John:

Jesus said, "When the Paraclete comes, whom *I am about to send* to you from the Father—the Spirit of Truth that *comes from* the Father—he will testify of me." (John 15:26)

In the same author:

If I leave, *I will send* the Paraclete to you. (John 16:5, 7)

For this reason the prophets were also said to have been sent, because the words they spoke came from the holy operation of the Lord's spirit.

Since all divine truth comes from divine goodness, the word *sent* in its proper sense applies to divine truth.

What *coming from* involves, though, is clear; someone or something that comes from another belongs to that other from whom it comes.

2398   Genesis 19:14. *And Lot went out and talked to his sons-in-law, the ones taking his daughters, and said, "Get up! Leave this place, because Jehovah is* *destroying the city." And it was as if he were fooling, in the eyes of his sons-in-law.*

Lot went out symbolizes people who act out of love for others, and such activity itself, too. *He talked to his sons-in-law, the ones taking his daughters,* means that he spoke with people who had the kind of truth to which a desire for goodness could be attached. *And said, "Get up! Leave this place,"* means that they should not stay in an evil state. *"Because Jehovah is destroying the city"* means that they would inevitably be destroyed. *And it was as if he were fooling, in the eyes of his sons-in-law* symbolizes ridicule.

Lot went out symbolizes people who act out of love for others, and such activity itself, too, as shown several times before [§§2318, 2324, 2334, 2371, 2373].

2399

One who represents people with some kind of goodness also symbolizes the goodness itself that they possess.

He talked to his sons-in-law, the ones taking his daughters, means that he spoke with people who had the kind of truth with which a desire for goodness could unite, as can be seen from the following: *Sons-in-law* symbolize a knowledge of truth and consequently truth itself, as mentioned above at §2389. *Daughters* symbolize the desire for goodness, also mentioned above, at §2362. And since it says that he talked to his sons-in-law, the ones taking his daughters, the meaning is that he spoke with people who had the kind of truth with which a desire for goodness could unite. Because they were capable of uniting, it says *sons-in-law;* but because they had not yet united, it says *the ones taking his daughters.*

2400

[2] The subject here is a third kind of religious people: ones who know truth but still live in evil. There are three types of religious people. The first is those who live lives of neighborly kindness, and they are represented by Lot. The second is those who give themselves over entirely to falsity and evil—who vigorously reject both truth and goodness—and they are the people represented by the men of Sodom. The third is those who do know truth but are involved in evil anyway; they are symbolized here by the sons-in-law. The foremost members of this class are people who teach, but the truth they teach does not root itself any deeper in them than is usual with rote memory. They learn truth (and flaunt their knowledge) purely for the sake of acquiring high rank and wealth. So since the soil that holds the seed of truth in them is made up of love for themselves and for material things, they have no belief in the truth, except for a certain dogmatic conviction arising out of that love. (The nature of this conviction will be described elsewhere, with the Lord's divine mercy [§§2682, 2689, 3895].) Such people are depicted here by the sons-in-law,

their flat refusal to believe Sodom would be overthrown, and their ridicule. The faith they hold in their hearts is as evil as they are.

2401   *He said, "Get up! Leave this place,"* means that they should not stay in an evil state, as can be seen from the symbolism of *getting up, leaving,* and a *place.*

Getting up or rising comes up frequently in the Word, but readers do not spend much time wondering what deeper meaning it may have, since it is one of the more common terms. In an inner sense, though, it involves an elevation—here, for instance, an elevation from evil to goodness, since our minds rise when we back away from evil (§2388). *Leaving* is going away, or not staying. A *place* is an evil state (§2393). This makes it clear that the verse has the meaning given.

[2] The nature of people who know truth but still live evil lives has been described several times already [§§2357, 2383, 2400]: As long as their lives are evil they have no faith, because it is simply impossible to intend and therefore do something evil on one hand and at the same time acknowledge and believe the truth on the other. Obviously, then, we cannot be saved by thinking and saying true things or even good things if all we want and willingly do is evil. Our will itself is what survives death, not so much our thinking (except so far as it flows from our will).

[3] Since we are what we will, you can see what opinion people might have of the religious truth they absorb and even teach, since it would damn them to hell. They are so far from basing their thoughts on that truth that they actually spurn it. In fact, so far as they are allowed to they blaspheme it, as the Devil's horde does.

People who have not been taught about life after death might imagine that these people will find it easy to develop faith then, when they see that the Lord governs all of heaven and hear that heaven consists of love for the Lord and for our neighbor. The evil, however, are as far from being able to develop faith—that is, from being able to will and consequently believe these things—as hell is from heaven. They are firmly mired in evil and so in falsity. You can recognize and sense from their approach or presence alone that they oppose the Lord and their neighbor. So they oppose goodness and therefore truth. They have a vile aura, given off by the vital force of their will and so of their thought (§§1048, 1053, 1316, 1504).

[4] If it were possible for people to believe and to transform their lives simply by receiving instruction when they reach the other world, not one person would be in hell. The Lord wants to lift absolutely everyone up to himself, into heaven. His mercy is infinite because it is divine and reaches out to the whole human race, to both the evil and the good.

Because Jehovah is destroying the city means that they would inevitably be destroyed, as is established by the explanation of almost the same words in §§2395, 2397.   **2402**

And it was as if he were fooling, in the eyes of his sons-in-law symbolizes ridicule. This can be seen from the meaning of *fooling* as being a kind of joke or piece of fiction or nonsense—something that would invite their ridicule. *In their eyes* means as presented to their rational mind, as can be seen from the symbolism of the *eyes* (§212).   **2403**

This makes it clear what people who know religious truth but do not live good lives are like.

Genesis 19:15. *And as dawn rose, the angels hurried Lot along, saying, "Get up! Take your wife and your two reclaimed daughters, to keep from being consumed in the wickedness of the city."*   **2404**

As dawn rose means when the Lord's kingdom comes near. *The angels hurried Lot along* means that the Lord would withhold people from evil and maintain them in goodness. *Saying, "Get up! Take your wife and your two reclaimed daughters,"* symbolizes religious truth and the desire for truth and goodness; *reclaimed* means detached from evil. *"To keep from being consumed in the wickedness of the city"* means to avoid being destroyed by the evil that comes of falsity.

As dawn rose means when the Lord's kingdom comes near, as can be seen from the symbolism of *dawn* or morning in the Word.   **2405**

Because this chapter focuses on different phases of the church in order, it started with what happened in the evening and then in the night. Now it follows with what happened in the half-light, and soon it will say what happened after the sun came up. The half-light is expressed here in the words *as dawn rose.* It is a time when the upright are separated from the evil, which is the subject from here to verse 22, embodied in the image of Lot's being brought out and saved, together with his wife and daughters.

The Lord's words in Matthew show that separation comes before judgment:

All nations will assemble before him, and he will *separate* them from each other, as a shepherd *separates* the sheep from the goats. (Matthew 25:32)

[2] The Word calls this period or phase dawn because it is when the Lord comes or, to put it another way, when his kingdom approaches. The same thing happens with good people, because at that time a kind of morning twilight or dawn shines in them. For this reason the Word compares the Lord's Coming to the morning and actually calls it morning. The comparison is made in Hosea:

Jehovah will bring us to life after two days; on the third day he will raise us up, and we will live before him, and we will know and press on toward knowing Jehovah. *His emergence is like the dawn.* (Hosea 6:2, 3)

The two-day period stands for the time and phase that comes first. The third day stands for the Lord's judgment, or his Coming, and so for the approach of his kingdom (§§720, 901), and the Coming or approach is compared to dawn. [3] In Samuel:

The God of Israel is like the *morning light:* The sun rises, a *morning* when there are no clouds. Because of the brightness, because of the rain, the shoot springs from the earth. (2 Samuel 23:[3,] 4)

The God of Israel stands for the Lord. The people of that religion meant nothing else by the God of Israel, since everything in the religion represented him. In Joel:

The day of Jehovah has come, because it is near: a day of shadow and darkness, a day of cloud and haze, like *dawn* spread over the mountains. (Joel 2:1, 2)

This too is about the Lord's Coming and his kingdom. It is a day of shadow and darkness because that is when the good are separated from the evil, as Lot here is being separated from the men of Sodom. After the good have been separated, the evil die.

[4] In Daniel the Lord's Coming or the approach of his kingdom is actually called rather than merely compared to morning:

A holy one said, "How long will the vision, the perpetual offering, and the devastating transgression continue?" He said to me, "Up till evening [and] *morning,* two thousand three hundred times; and the Holy One will become righteousness. The vision of evening and *morning* that has been told is truth." (Daniel 8:13, 14, 26)

Obviously the morning stands for the Lord's Coming. In David:

Yours is a willing people, on the day of your might, among sacred honors. From the womb out of the *dawn* you receive the dew of your birth. (Psalms 110:3)

The whole psalm is about the Lord and his victories in times of trial, which are his day of might and sacred honors. He himself—and therefore the divine love that moved him to fight—comes from the womb out of the dawn. [5] In Zephaniah:

> Jehovah the just is in the middle of it; he will not do wrong. *Morning* by *morning* he will offer his judgment as a light. (Zephaniah 3:5)

The morning stands for a period or phase in which there is a judgment, which is the same as the Lord's Coming, which is the same as the approach of his kingdom.

[6] This is the symbolism of morning, so for the sake of its representation as well, Aaron and his sons were commanded to make [the fire of] the lamp go up and to arrange it before Jehovah from *evening* till *morning* (Exodus 27:21). The evening here is the half-light that precedes morning (§2323). Likewise, the fire on the altar was to be kindled *every dawn* (Leviticus 6:12). None of the Passover lamb or of the food consecrated by sacrifice was to be left till *morning,* either (Exodus 12:10; 23:18; 34:25; Leviticus 22:29, 30; Numbers 9:12). This meant that when the Lord came, sacrifice would come to an end.

[7] In a broad sense "morning" applies to the time both when dawn glimmers and when the sun rises, and that being so, it is used for judgment on both the good and the evil, as in the current chapter:

> The sun came up over the earth, and Lot came to Zoar. And Jehovah rained sulfur and fire onto Sodom and Gomorrah. (Genesis 19:23, 24)

Again in David it stands for judgment on the evil:

> In the *mornings* I will destroy all the ungodly of the land, to cut off from the city of Jehovah all those doing wickedness. (Psalms 101:8)

And in Jeremiah:

> That man is like the cities that Jehovah overthrows and has no regrets over; and let him hear the outcry in the *morning!* (Jeremiah 20:16)

[8] Since in its proper sense morning symbolizes the Lord, his Coming, and so the arrival of his kingdom, it also symbolizes the dawn of a new religion (the church being the Lord's kingdom on earth). This dawn occurs both in general and in particular, and even in specific detail: in *general* when some church is being revived on earth; in *particular* when an individual is reborn and becomes a new person; in such people the Lord's kingdom then dawns, and each of them becomes a church; in

specific detail whenever love and faith have a good effect on this individual, because that is what the Lord's Coming consists in.

As a result, the Lord's resurrection on the *third* day in the *morning* (Mark 16:2, 9; Luke 24:1; John 20:1) involves all these meanings. It even involves the particular and specific ones, since he rises again in the minds of regenerate people daily and in fact from moment to moment.

2406 *The angels hurried Lot along* means that the Lord would withhold people from evil and maintain them in goodness. This can be seen from the symbolism of *hurrying someone along* as pressing that person urgently. The fact that it means being withheld from evil can be seen both from the inner meaning of these words and from those of the next verse.

The inner meaning is that when the church starts to fall away from neighborly kindness, the Lord withholds the people in it more firmly from evil than when it is maintaining its commitment to such kindness.

The next verse makes the same thing clear, since Lot still delayed, despite the pressure the angels put on him to leave the city, and since they took his hand and his wife's and his daughters' and brought them out and stood them outside the city. This symbolizes and depicts what we are like at that stage.

The current verse, you see, deals with the second stage of this church. Verses 1, 2, 3 of this chapter portrayed the first, in which people do loving deeds, they acknowledge the Lord, and he strengthens their goodness. The current passage depicts the second stage, in which evil starts to work against goodness in truly religious people. At that point the Lord withholds them firmly from evil and maintains them in goodness. The current and following verses (15, 16, 17) deal with this stage.

[2] As for the idea itself, few if any know that the Lord holds everybody back from evil, without exception, and with greater force than anyone could ever believe. All of us are constantly trying to do evil, both because of the heredity we were born with and as a result of the evil we have acquired for ourselves by acting on it. Our inclination is so strong that if the Lord did not hold us back, we would rush headlong for the lowest hell at every moment. The Lord's mercy is so immense, though, that at every moment, no matter how small, he lifts us up and keeps us from plunging into hell. Even with good people he does this, although there are differences, depending on the life of charity and faith they are living.

In this way the Lord constantly fights by our side and fights hell on our behalf, even though we do not see it.

The truth of this has been granted me to see from much experience, which will be discussed elsewhere [§§4564, 8206], the Lord in his divine mercy willing; see also §§929, 1581.

Saying, "Get up! Take your wife and your two reclaimed daughters," symbolizes religious truth and the desire for truth and goodness; *reclaimed* means detached from evil. This can be seen from the following: *Getting up* symbolizes being lifted up out of evil (§2401). A *wife* symbolizes religious truth here, as discussed at verse 26, which tells how Lot's wife changed into a pillar of salt [§2454]. And the *two daughters* symbolize the desire for truth and goodness, as discussed in §2362.

2407

The fact that *reclaimed* means detached from evil can also be seen, since it means being rescued.

These brief words portray this second phase of the church, in which people do not allow themselves to be led by goodness into truth, as before, but by truth into goodness. Even so, they have a vague desire for goodness. The more they follow the lead of truth, the dimmer goodness grows. The more they follow the lead of goodness, the more openly truth shines in its own light.

To keep from being consumed in the wickedness of the city means to avoid being destroyed by the evil that comes of falsity. This can be seen from the symbolism of *wickedness* as evil, and from that of a *city* as a doctrinal viewpoint, even a false one, as discussed in §402.

2408

What the evil that results from falsity is may be seen from remarks in §§1212, 1679 of the second volume.

Genesis 19:16. *And he delayed, and the men took his hand and his wife's hand and the hand of his two daughters, in Jehovah's compassion on him, and brought him out and stood him outside the city.*

2409

And he delayed symbolizes the resistance that evil naturally puts up. *And the men took his hand and his wife's hand and the hand of his two daughters* means that the Lord firmly withdrew them from evil and in the process strengthened the goodness and truth symbolized by Lot and his wife and daughters. *In Jehovah's compassion on him* means out of favor and mercy. *They brought him out and stood him outside the city* symbolizes his state at that time.

And he delayed symbolizes the resistance that evil naturally puts up, as can be seen from remarks above at §2406. The evil we have in us is constantly rebelling against the goodness sent by the Lord.

2410

The evil we inherit and commit clings to each of our thoughts and even to the very smallest elements in our thinking. It drags us downward, while the Lord, working through the goodness he instills into us, holds us back and lifts us up. As a result, we hang suspended between evil and good. If the Lord did not withhold us from evil every single second, we would spontaneously plunge downward. The religious people Lot now represents are in even greater danger under their current circumstances than they were before, in that they are beginning to think and act not so much from goodness as from truth. So in their thoughts and deeds they are beginning to stand somewhat removed from what is good.

2411   *The men took his hand and his wife's hand and the hand of his two daughters* means that the Lord firmly withdrew them from evil and in the process strengthened the goodness and truth symbolized by Lot, his wife, and his daughters. This can be seen from the following: The *men* symbolize the Lord, as mentioned above. A *hand* symbolizes power, as discussed at §878. *Lot* symbolizes doing good out of charity, as discussed at §§2324, 2351, 2371, 2399. A *wife* symbolizes religious truth, as mentioned below at verse 26 [§2454]. And *daughters* symbolize the desire for truth and goodness, as discussed at §§489, 490, 491, 2362. Finally, it can be seen from the discussion at §2388 showing that the more we are withheld from evil, the more we are influenced by goodness and truth from the Lord. Consequently, the goodness and truth symbolized by Lot, his wife, and his two daughters grow all the stronger.

[2] If you think about it, you can see the same thing from your own experience. The more we detach from a bodily and worldly focus, the more we come into a spiritual way of thinking—that is, the more we rise up toward heaven. This happens whenever we are worshiping devoutly, undergoing inward trials, or suffering misfortune or fatal illness. At those times, as people know, bodily and worldly advantages fade into the background. That is, a *love* of such advantages does. The reason, again, is that heavenly and spiritual influences from the Lord are always acting on us. What keeps us from accepting them is evil (and the falsity it spawns) and falsity (and the evil it produces), which our bodily and worldly interests inflict on us.

2412   *In Jehovah's compassion on him* means out of favor and mercy. This can be seen from the symbolism of *Jehovah's compassion* as favor and mercy; it cannot have any other meaning. To see that the Lord holds us back from evil and keeps us on a good path out of pure mercy, see §1049.

The reason for describing it as both favor and mercy is discussed in §§598, 981: People devoted to truth and therefore to goodness beg only for the Lord's favor; but people devoted to goodness and therefore to truth beg for his mercy. This comes from differences between the two groups in their attitude of humility and therefore of reverence.

And brought him out and stood him outside the city symbolizes his state at that time. This can be seen from the symbolism of *bringing him out* as holding him back, and from the symbolism of *standing him outside the city* as placing him away from falsity. His state at that time, then, was one in which the Lord strengthened what was good and true in him by holding him back from evil.

2413

Genesis 19:17. *And it happened when they brought them outdoors that [the angel] said, "Escape, on your soul! Don't look back behind you, and don't stop anywhere on the plain! Escape to the mountain to keep from being consumed."*

2414

And it happened when they brought them outdoors symbolizes a state in which they were being withheld from falsity and evil. *That he said, "Escape, on your soul!"* means that he was to take thought for his eternal welfare. *"Don't look back behind you"* means that he was not to look to doctrine. *"And don't stop anywhere on the plain"* means that he was not to spend time on any of the teachings. *"Escape to the mountain"* means resorting to a kind and loving goodness. *"To keep from being consumed"* means that otherwise he would perish.

And it happened when they brought them outdoors symbolizes a state in which they were being withheld from falsity and evil, as can be seen from remarks just above at §2413 and at §§2388, 2411.

2415

That he said, "Escape, on your soul!" means that he was to take thought for his eternal welfare, as stands to reason without explanation.

2416

Just how he was to see to his eternal welfare now follows.

Don't look back behind you means that he was not to look to doctrine, as can be seen from the symbolism of *looking back behind him* when the city was behind him and the mountain in front. A *city* symbolizes doctrine (§§402, 2268, 2449), but a *mountain* symbolizes love and charity (§§795, 1430). The explanation at verse 26 [§2454], which says that Lot's wife looked back behind him and turned into a pillar of salt, will make it clear that this is the symbolism.

2417

Anyone can see that these words, *looking back behind oneself*, contain some divine secret, one that lies too deeply hidden to detect. Looking behind us, after all, does not appear to be any sort of crime, but it is so weighty that the text says he would escape on his soul (see to his eternal welfare) by not looking back behind him. A discussion of what it is to look to doctrine will appear below [§2454].

[2] Here it is necessary only to say what doctrine is. There are two kinds of doctrine. One teaches about love and charity; the other, about faith. No church of the Lord's, in its beginning, when it still plays the role of a young, unmarried woman, possesses or loves any doctrine but one that teaches love for others, because this has to do with the way we live. The church gradually turns aside from this doctrine, though, until it starts to despise and finally reject it. After that it acknowledges no other doctrine than what is called the doctrine of faith. When it separates faith from neighborly love, doctrine enters into conspiracy with an evil way of life.

[3] This is what happened in the early [Christian] church (the church among non-Jews) after the Lord's Coming. At its start it had no other doctrine than one of love and charity, because the Lord himself taught the same thing (see §2371 at the end). After his time, though, the doctrine of faith gradually took hold as love and charity began to grow cold. With it came strife and heresy, which multiplied as people's fervor for that doctrine increased.

[4] It was similar in the ancient church, which followed the Flood and spread through so many kingdoms (§2385). In its beginning it too knew no other doctrine than the doctrine of charity, because this doctrine focused on life. It permeated people's lives, and by means of it they looked out for their eternal interests. Nevertheless, after a time some of them started to cultivate the doctrine of faith, which they eventually separated from charity. These people were called Ham, however, because they lived a life of evil (see §§1062, 1063, 1076).

[5] The people of the earliest church, which came before the Flood and more than any others was called "the human," lived in a genuine perception of love for the Lord and charity for their neighbor. As a result they had the doctrine of love and charity inscribed on them. Yet even then there were some who promoted faith, which they eventually separated from charity. They were then called Cain, because Cain symbolizes this kind of faith, while Abel, whom he killed, symbolizes charity (see the explanation at Genesis 4 [§§324–329, 338–369]).

[6] This shows that there are two kinds of doctrine, one having to do with charity and the other with faith. In reality, the two are basically one, since the doctrine of charity includes everything that belongs to faith. When doctrine is created solely out of teachings about faith, though, it is described as twofold, because faith is then detached from love for others.

The two are separate in modern times, as can be seen from the fact that no one has any idea what charity is or what a person's neighbor is. People who accept only the doctrine of faith do not realize that charity for their neighbor is anything more than giving what they have to others and taking pity on everyone (since they call everyone their neighbor, without regard for differences). The truth is that charity is absolutely everything good in us—everything good that touches our heart, everything good that we feel zeal for, and everything good that we do in life. Our neighbor is everything good in other people that touches our heart. Consequently people who display goodness are our neighbor, with all kinds of distinctions.

[7] People have charity and mercy, for example, when they exercise justice and judgment, punishing the evil and rewarding the good. Charity is present in the punishment they inflict, because zeal moves them to reform the wrongdoer and to protect others from the harm such a person might do. In the process they are looking out for the best interests of the wrongdoer, their enemy, and are wishing that person well. At the same time they are looking out for and wishing well to others, and to their country itself. All of this results from the charity they have for their neighbor.

The situation is the same with all other kinds of goodness in life. We cannot live a life of any good unless charity for our neighbor is what motivates us. Charity is what goodness looks to, and charity is what goodness requires.

[8] As I said, people have a very dim idea of what charity is and what a person's neighbor is, so now that the doctrine of faith has taken the leading role, clearly the doctrine of charity is a piece of lost wisdom. Despite this fact, it was the only doctrine the people of the ancient church pursued. In fact, they divided all the types of goodness belonging to charity for their neighbor, or in other words, all the people who did such good, into classes. They made many distinctions, which they also labeled, calling them the poor, wretched, oppressed, sick, naked, hungry, thirsty, prisoners in jail, immigrants, orphans, widows. There were also some that they called the lame, blind, deaf, mute, maimed, and many other things. The Lord spoke in accord with this doctrine in the Old Testament Word, which is why those terms come up so many times there. He also spoke in accord with it himself, as for instance in Matthew 25:35, 36, 38, 39, 40, 42, 43, 44, 45; Luke 14:13, 21; and many other places. That is why such terms have a different meaning on an inner level.

In order to restore the doctrine of charity, then, I will say below just who belongs to these categories and what charity and one's neighbor are generally and specifically, the Lord in his divine mercy willing.

2418   *Don't stop anywhere on the plain* means that he was not to spend time on any of the teachings. This can be seen from the symbolism of a *plain* as every aspect of a doctrine, to be discussed just below.

The reason he was not to spend time on any of the teachings will be discussed at verse 26, which speaks about the fact that Lot's wife looked back behind him [§2454].

The symbolism of a *plain* in the Word as every aspect of a doctrine can be seen in Jeremiah:

> A destroyer will come to every city, and no city will escape, and the valley will perish and the *plain* be destroyed. (Jeremiah 48:8)

The city stands for a false doctrine; the plain, for every element of that doctrine. In John:

> When the thousand years have ended, Satan will be released from his prison and go out to mislead the nations, Gog and Magog, in order to gather them for battle, their number being like the sand of the sea. So they went up over *all the plain of the earth* and surrounded the camp of the godly, but fire came down from God out of the sky and consumed them. (Revelation 20:7, 8, 9)

Gog and Magog stand for people whose worship is outward, not inward, and has therefore turned idolatrous (§1151). The plain of the earth stands for the church's doctrines, which they ravage. The camp of the godly stands for good done out of love and charity. The people consumed by fire from God out of the sky can be described in the same terms as the men of Sodom and Gomorrah in verse 24. In addition, doctrines teaching about charity are called cities of the mountain, while those teaching about faith are called cities of the plain in Jeremiah 33:13.

2419   *Escape to the mountain* means resorting to a kind and loving goodness. This can be seen from the symbolism of a *mountain* as love and kindness, or charity (discussed in §§795, 1430).

2420   *To keep from being consumed* means that otherwise he would perish, as can be seen without explanation.

2421   Genesis 19:18, 19. *And Lot said to them, "Please, no, my lords! Look, please; your servant has found favor in your eyes, and you have enlarged the mercy that you have shown me, to keep my soul alive. But I cannot escape to the mountain or evil might cling to me and I might die."*

Lot said to them, "Please, no, my lords!" symbolizes a weakness that prevented him. "*Look, please; your servant has found favor in your eyes*" symbolizes humility in response to truth. "*You have enlarged the mercy*" symbolizes a semblance of the humility that comes in response to goodness. *"That you have shown me, to keep my soul alive"* means because [the Lord] wished to save him. *"But I cannot escape to the mountain"* symbolizes doubt that he could exhibit neighborly kindness. *"Or evil might cling to me and I might die"* means that he would inevitably be inspired by evil at the same time, which would damn him.

Lot said to them, "Please, no, my lords!" symbolizes a weakness that prevented him, as can be seen from the emotion in the actual words and from what follows. **2422**

This passage is now speaking of the third phase of the religion that *Lot* represents in the current chapter. In this phase, people no longer think and act from a desire for goodness but from a desire for truth. When the desire for goodness starts to fade and more or less withdraw, this state comes next. Goodness is still present, but it has shrunk back more and more toward our inner depths, where it lies in the dark. It does reveal itself as a kind of emotional response called the desire for truth, though. For a definition of the desire for goodness and the desire for truth, see §1997 and just below in §2425.

We humans do not see that these phases occur, still less what they are like, but angels see them in a clear light, because angels are present in all our positive emotions. Our states also reveal themselves to us when we enter the other world. These emotions and their quality determine how the good are divided up into communities there (§685).

"Look, please; your servant has found favor in your eyes" symbolizes humility in response to truth. *"And you have enlarged the mercy"* symbolizes a semblance of the humility that comes in response to goodness. This can be seen from earlier remarks concerning *favor* and *mercy* (§§598, 981). **2423**

People who desire truth cannot humble themselves enough to acknowledge in a heartfelt way that everything is a gift of mercy, so they speak instead of grace, [or favor]. The more meager their desire for truth, the less humility they feel when they mention grace. On the other hand, the stronger a person's response to goodness, the more humility that person feels in mentioning mercy.

From this it is evident how much the reverence and therefore the worship of a person who loves truth differs from that of a person who loves goodness. Worship cannot exist without reverence, which cannot exist without humility, and this is true in each and every facet of worship. Now it is clear why the verse mentions both favor and mercy.

"That you have shown me, to keep my soul alive" means because [the Lord] wished to save him, as can be seen without explanation. **2424**

2425   *"But I cannot escape to the mountain"* symbolizes doubt that he could exhibit neighborly kindness—that is, that he could think and act with neighborly kindness. This can be seen from the symbolism of a *mountain* as love and charity (discussed in §§795, 1430).

[2] In regard to doubt, the case is this: In people who love truth, a desire for goodness lies within their desire for truth but is so faint that they are unaware of it. They do not know what a desire for goodness is, or what real charity is. They *think* they know, but they know only from truth and so from learning about it, not from goodness itself. Still, they do the good that charity requires, so far as they see the truth of it—not to earn a reward but from obedience. They allow the Lord to lead them out of their darkness concerning what is good by means of such truth as appears to them to be true.

For instance, when people do not know what the neighbor is, they benefit everyone they consider to be a neighbor. They do good especially to the poor, since these, in their lack of worldly wealth, call themselves poor; to orphans and widows, since that is what they are called; to immigrants, since that is what they are; and so on with all other categories. This is how they act as long as they fail to realize what is meant by the poor, orphans, widows, immigrants, and so on. However, within their affection for apparent truth lurks a vague desire for goodness, as noted, by which the Lord leads them to act this way. As a result, they possess goodness in their inner depths. Angels are present with them in that goodness and take pleasure in the appearances of truth that so touch their hearts.

[3] On the other hand, people dedicated to charitable goodness and the desire for truth that comes from it do all these things in a discriminating way. They have light, because the light of truth originates nowhere but in goodness, since it is through goodness that the Lord flows in. These people benefit the poor, orphans, widows, and immigrants not just because that is what they are called. They know that good people, rich or poor, are their neighbor above all others. A good person does good to others, so the more they benefit good people, the more they benefit others through them. They also know how to distinguish different kinds of good actions and therefore different kinds of good people.

The common good itself they call their neighbor still more, since it looks to the good of even larger numbers. The Lord's kingdom on earth (the church) they acknowledge to be their neighbor—and the object of their charity—still more again; and the Lord's kingdom in the heavens itself, still more again. But people who set the Lord before all these others, worship him alone, and love him more than anything, trace the origins of the neighbor back to him, because in the highest sense, only the Lord is our neighbor. All goodness is our neighbor, then, so far as it comes from him.

[4] People who look in the opposite direction, though, trace the origins of the neighbor back to themselves. The only individual they acknowledge as their neighbor is one that shows them favoritism and serves them. No one else do they call family or friend, and even at that they make distinctions, depending on how closely the person unites with them.

These considerations show what our neighbor is, in that we are to treat each according to what she or he loves. They also show that people who love the Lord and have charity for their neighbor are truly our neighbors, with all kinds of distinctions. So it is the goodness itself in each of them that makes the difference.

"*Or evil might cling to me and I might die*" means that he would inevitably be immersed in evil at the same time, which would damn him, as can be seen without explanation. **2426**

What is involved here can be seen from earlier explanations and demonstrations at §§301, 302, 303, 571, 582, 1001, 1327, 1328. These sections showed that the Lord constantly works to prevent evil from mingling with goodness. The more we turn to evil, the further we turn from goodness. It is better to be wholly wrapped up in evil than to come under the sway of both evil and goodness. If evil controls us, and goodness does too, we cannot help being damned forever.

Religious people who are deceivers and hypocrites are in more danger of this than others.

This then is the inner meaning of the words *evil might cling to me and I might die.*

Genesis 19:20. "*Look, please: this city is nearby to flee to, and it is small. Let me escape there, please (isn't it small?), and let my soul live!*" **2427**

Look, please: this city is nearby to flee to means that it would be acceptable to be motivated by religious truth. *And it is small* means to be motivated by the small amount he would have. *Let me escape there, please* means that it would be acceptable to look from truth to goodness. *Isn't it small?* means, wouldn't he have some small amount? *And let my soul live* means that in this way he just might be saved.

Look, please: this city is nearby to flee to means that it would be acceptable to be motivated by religious truth. This can be seen from the symbolism of a *city* as doctrine and so as religious truth, a symbolism discussed at §§402, 2268. It is described as *nearby* because truth is related to goodness. **2428**

Fleeing to it, then, means that being motivated by truth would be acceptable, since he could not be motivated by goodness (§2422).

2429   *It is small* means to be motivated by the small amount he would have. This can be seen from the symbolism of a city as truth (mentioned just above). The fact that the city was *small* means that he had little truth. Here it means that he would be motivated by the small amount he had, as appears from the words before and after it.

[2] Let me turn now to the matter at hand itself: that people with a passion for truth have relatively little truth, compared to people with a passion for goodness. The validity of this claim can be seen from the fact that they regard truth from the dim and scanty goodness they have. The truth we have relates directly to the goodness we have. Where there is little goodness there is little truth. The amount and the quality are the same. The two go hand in hand, as they say. This may seem puzzling, but it is still the case. Goodness is the real essence of truth, and truth without its essence is not true, even if it appears to be so. It is merely hollow noise and an empty vessel.

[3] If we want to possess truth, it is not enough that we learn it; we also have to acknowledge and believe it. When we do, we then possess it for the first time, because it then touches us and stays with us. When we merely learn the truth and do not acknowledge or believe in it, the situation is different; then we do not have the truth in us. That is what happens with very many people involved in evil. They are capable of learning truth—sometimes of learning it better than others—and yet they still do not possess it. In fact, all the less do they possess it because they deny it in their hearts.

[4] The Lord makes sure we go no further in receiving truth, that is, in acknowledging and believing it, than we do in adopting goodness.

That is why it says here about the city (symbolizing truth) that it was small, and later in the same verse, "Isn't it small?" In addition, verse 22 says that they called the name of the city Zoar, which means "small" in the original language. Smallness comes up repeatedly because this passage is focusing on people affected by truth and not so much by goodness.

2430   *Let me escape there, please* means that it is acceptable to look from truth to goodness, as can be seen from the words that come before and after. He had been told to escape to the mountain, which symbolizes a kind and loving goodness (§2419), but he answered that he could not do this but had to escape to the city, which symbolizes religious truth (§2428). So he was saying that he could look from truth to goodness or, what is the same, from faith to charity. What is more, the city was located at the bottom of the mountain, and later he went up from the city to live on the mountain, though in a cave there (verse 30).

Isn't it small? means, wouldn't he have some small amount? This can be seen from the remarks above at §2429 and so needs no further explanation.

2431

The reason for the question is that the Lord alone knows how much good there is in a true idea, and therefore how much truth there is in us.

Let my soul live means that in this way he just might be saved. This too can be seen without explanation. He *was* saved, too, because there was goodness in the truth he knew, as the following verses show. The answer he received in verse 21 is one example: "Here, now, I have also accepted your face in regard to this word, that I will not overthrow the city that you spoke of." The other is verse 23: "The sun came up over the earth, and Lot came to Zoar." The meaning here is that people are saved if they love truth, or in other words, if they believe, as long as it is goodness that they believe in.

2432

Genesis 19:21. And [the angel] said to him, "Here, now, I have also accepted your face in regard to this word, that I will not overthrow the city that you spoke of."

2433

He said to him, "Here, now, I have also accepted your face in regard to this word," symbolizes acquiescence, if the inner dimensions of truth partake at all of goodness. *"That I will not overthrow the city that you spoke of"* means in that case he would not be destroyed.

He said to him, "Here, now, I have also accepted your face in regard to this word," symbolizes acquiescence, if the inner dimensions of truth partake at all of goodness, as can be seen from the symbolism of the *face*. The Word mentions faces quite often, and when it does, they symbolize what lies inside, as shown in §§358, 1999. When Jehovah (the Lord) is spoken of as having a face, it also symbolizes mercy, peace, and goodness (§§222, 223). Here, then, it symbolizes the goodness that lies at the heart of truth. So *to accept someone's face* is to acquiesce, provided the inner dimensions of truth partake at all of goodness.

2434

In regard to this word means in this matter.

Truth is not true unless there is something good inside it; see §§1496, 1832, 1900, 1904, 1928, 2063, 2173, 2269, 2429. What blesses us and makes us happy after death is not truth but the goodness present in truth, §2261, so the more goodness there is in the truth we know, the more blessings and happiness we have.

Even the kind of goodness and truth to be found in worldly matters can demonstrate that goodness lies at the heart of truth and makes it true. In this arena, whenever we take up some value as a good thing, and acknowledge its goodness, we call whatever promotes it, true; but anything that does not promote it we reject and label false. (We are also capable of describing an idea that does not support it as true, but in this case we are presenting one thing and thinking another.) It is the same in spiritual matters.

2435

"I will not overthrow the city that you spoke of" means in that case he (anyone who possesses truth with something good inside it) would not be destroyed. This is established by the symbolism of a *city* as truth (dealt with in §§402, 2268, 2428).

Since earliest times people have debated whether charity or faith is the church's firstborn. We need the true ideas of faith in order to regenerate and become an individual church, but people who give priority to faith and make it the firstborn have always fallen into heresy and distortion. In the end, they completely annihilate charity, just as we read of Cain (who symbolizes this kind of faith) that he eventually killed his brother Abel (who symbolizes charity). The case was similar afterward with Reuben, Jacob's oldest child (also symbolizing faith), but what he did was to defile his father's bed (Genesis 35:22; 49:4). As a result he became unworthy, and the rights of the firstborn were handed to Joseph (Genesis 48:5; 1 Chronicles 5:1). That is why the Word contains so many disputes and laws relating to birthrights.

[2] People debated the subject because they did not know (any more than people do today) that the amount of charity we have determines how much faith we have. When we are being reborn, charity runs to meet faith or, to put the same thing another way, goodness runs to meet truth; it introduces itself into all aspects of faith, molds itself to fit, and causes faith to *be* faith. So charity is the church's true firstborn, even if it seems otherwise to us. None of this has been known. (See also §§352, 367.)

Since this subject comes up again and again later on, though, more will be said there, by the Lord's divine mercy.

2436

Genesis 19:22. *"Hurry! Escape there, because I cannot do anything until you come there." Therefore they called the name of the city Zoar.*

Hurry! Escape there means that he should stay there, seeing that he can go no farther. *Because I cannot do anything until you come there* means that before the evil are judged, people who love truth are to be saved. *Therefore they called the name of the city Zoar* means the desire for truth.

Hurry! Escape there means that he should stay there, seeing that he can go no farther. In other words, he should stay with religious truth and the desire for it, seeing that he could not handle charitable goodness itself and the desire for it. This can be seen from earlier sections [§§2421–2426].

2437

Because I cannot do anything until you come there means that before the evil are judged, people who love truth are to be saved, as can be seen from the following: *I cannot do anything* symbolizes a judgment on the evil, depicted soon afterward in the overthrow of Sodom and Gomorrah. *Until you come there* means that people who love truth (represented by Lot here) are to be saved first. The same thing is meant by *Lot came to Zoar* in verse 23.

2438

[2] Other passages in the Word also make it clear that good, upright people are saved before evil, unjust ones meet their end. One is the part of Matthew that talks about the Last Judgment, saying that the sheep were separated from the goats. The sheep were told they would enter the Lord's kingdom before the goats were told they would go away into eternal fire (Matthew 25:32, 34, 41).

When the children of Israel left Egypt, the same thing was represented by the fact that they were rescued before the Egyptians were drowned in the Suph Sea [Exodus 14:19–30].

[3] The same thing again is meant by events frequently mentioned in the Prophets—that after the faithful were brought back from captivity, their enemies would pay the penalty and die.

The same thing is also happening constantly in the other world: first the faithful are saved and then the faithless are punished. To put it another way, the Lord raises the former into heaven and the latter then plunge into hell.

The reason the two processes do not occur at the same time is that unless good people were snatched away from evil people, the evil cravings and persuasive lies constantly being spewed around like poison by the latter could easily destroy the former. Usually, though, before it comes to this, the good shed what is evil and the evil shed what is good so that the Lord can lift the former to heaven by means of their goodness and the latter can hurl themselves into hell by means of their evil. More will be said on this subject below at §§2449, 2451, by the Lord's divine mercy.

Therefore they called the name of the city Zoar means the desire for truth. This can be seen from the symbolism of the place as a desire for something good—namely, a desire for learning, or in other words, for truth, as discussed in §1589. It can also be seen from the symbolism of *culling*

2439

something's name as recognizing its character (discussed in §§144, 145, 1754, 2009). What is recognized here is that little truth is present, since in the original language *Zoar* means little or small. People who love truth have little of it, because they have little goodness compared to people who love what is good; see above at §2429.

[2] Furthermore, truth that is true in itself is more true in one person, less true in another, and completely untrue—false, in fact—in some people. Almost any inherent truth can serve to illustrate this fact, because true ideas change with the attitude of the person who holds them. Take the idea of doing good deeds, or acting on neighborly kindness, for example. It is true in itself that we ought to do this. In one person, the goodness is charitable because it springs from love for others. In another it is an act of duty because it springs from obedience. In some it is self-righteous because they want to earn salvation by doing it. In others, though, it is hypocritical, with a view to appearances. And so forth. The case is the same with any other concept that can be called religious truth.

This helps show that truth is abundantly present in people who love what is good and less present in those who love what is true. The latter view goodness as fairly remote from them, while the former view it as present in themselves.

2440   Genesis 19:23. *The sun came up over the earth, and Lot came to Zoar.*

The sun came up over the earth symbolizes the last days, which are called the Last Judgment. *And Lot came to Zoar* means that people with a desire for truth are saved.

2441   *The sun came up over the earth* symbolizes the last days, which are called the Last Judgment, as can be seen from the symbolism of *sunrise* in passages dealing with the periods and phases of a church. In an inner sense, times of day and seasons symbolize different stages of the church in order, as demonstrated before in §2323. Dawn, or the morning, symbolizes the Lord's Coming, or the approach of his kingdom (§2405). So now the sunrise, or the sun's *coming up over the earth,* symbolizes his actual presence. The reason for the meaning is that both the sun and the east symbolize the Lord. (For the fact that the sun has this meaning, see §§31, 32, 1053, 1521, 1529, 1530, 1531, 2120. For the fact that the east has this meaning, see §101.)

[2] The reason the Lord's presence is the same as the final days, which are called a judgment, is that his presence divides the good from the evil and causes the good to be taken up into heaven, and the evil to throw themselves into hell. The way things stand in the other world is that the

Lord is the sun throughout heaven (see §§1053, 1521, 1529, 1530, 1531). It is the heavenly divinity of his love that actually shines as the sun before angels' eyes and gives off the light itself of heaven. The more heavenly love people have, then, the more they rise up into that heavenly light that is beaming from the Lord. The farther they drift from heavenly love, the more they plunge away from that light into the shadows of hell.

[3] This is why a sunrise, symbolizing the Lord's presence, involves both the salvation of the good and the damnation of the evil. It is also why the text now says first that Lot came to Zoar (that is, the people Lot represents are saved) and then that Jehovah rained sulfur and fire onto Sodom and Gomorrah (that is, the evil are damned).

[4] Some people are wrapped up in the evils of self-love and materialism; they hate any hint of love for the Lord or charity for one's neighbor. To them the light of heaven looks for all the world like darkness. That is why the Word says that the sun turned black for them, meaning that they rejected any love or charity and welcomed anything opposed to it. In Ezekiel, for instance:

> When I blot you out I will *cover the heavens* and *blacken* their *stars; the sun* I will *cover* with a cloud, and the *moon* will not make its light shine. All the *lamps of light* in the heavens I will *blacken* above you, and I will bring darkness over your land. (Ezekiel 32:7, 8)

Anyone can see that covering over the heavens, blackening the stars, covering over the sun, and blackening the lamps of light mean something else. [5] Likewise in Isaiah:

> *The sun will be shadowed over in its emergence,* and the *moon* will not radiate its light. (Isaiah 13:9, 10)

And in Joel:

> The *sun* and *moon turn black,* and the *stars* hold back their rays. (Joel 2:2, 10)

It is possible to see, then, what these words of the Lord's in Matthew symbolize, when he is speaking of the church's final days, which are called a judgment:

> Immediately after the affliction of those days, the *sun* will *go dark,* and the *moon* will not shed its light, and *the stars* will fall down from the sky. (Matthew 24:29)

In other words, the sun does not mean the sun, the moon does not mean the moon, and the stars do not mean the stars. Instead, the sun symbolizes love and charity, the moon symbolizes faith reflected from them, and the stars symbolize a knowledge of what is good and true. They are said to go dark, lose their light, and fall down from the sky when there is no longer any acknowledgment of the Lord, no love for him, and no charity for others. When these have disappeared, self-love and the lies it spawns take up residence in us. The one is a consequence of the other.

[6] That is also the reason for the following in John:

> The fourth angel poured out his bowl *onto the sun,* and it was granted to him to scorch humanity with fire. Therefore humans burned with great heat and blasphemed the name of God. (Revelation 16:8, 9)

This too is speaking of the church's last days, when all love and charity are extinguished or, to put it in more familiar terms, when faith dies. The snuffing out of love and charity are meant by the pouring out of the bowl onto the sun. The resulting self-love and self-centered obsessions are meant by the scorching of humanity with fire and their burning with great heat. Blasphemy of God's name is the consequence.

[7] The people of the ancient church took the sun to mean nothing other than the Lord and the heavenly divinity of his love, which is why they had the ritual of facing the rising sun when they prayed, without even thinking about the sun itself. Later, though, their descendants lost all knowledge of the representation and symbolism in their ritual, including this, and they then started to worship the sun and moon in their own right. This worship spread to many other nations, to the point where they dedicated temples and erected pillars to these objects. The sun and moon then took on an opposite meaning, so they symbolize self-love and materialism, which are diametrically opposed to heavenly and spiritual love. As a result, the worship of sun and moon in the Word mean the worship of ourselves and the material world, [8] as in Moses:

> . . . to keep from lifting your eyes to the sky and seeing the *sun* and the *moon* and the *stars,* all the army of the heavens, and being driven to bow down to them and serve them. (Deuteronomy 4:19)

And in the same author:

> If they have gone and served other gods and the *sun* or the *moon* or the whole army of the heavens, as I did not command, then you shall stone them with stones and they shall die. (Deuteronomy 17:3, 5)

This is the kind of idolatry the worship of the ancients turned into when they no longer believed the rituals of the church had any inner meaning, only a superficial one. [9] Likewise in Jeremiah:

> At that time they will spread out the bones of Judah's monarchs, chieftains, priests, prophets, and residents of Jerusalem before the *sun* and the *moon* and the whole army of the heavens, [bones] that they loved and that they served. (Jeremiah 8:1, 2)

The sun stands for self-love and self-centered obsessions. Spreading out the bones means spreading out the hellish qualities that self-centered people possess. In the same author:

> He will smash the *pillars of the house of the sun* that is in the land of Egypt; and the houses of Egypt's gods he will burn with fire. (Jeremiah 43:13)

The pillars of the house stand for self-adoration.

And Lot came to Zoar means that people with a desire for truth are saved. This can be seen from the symbolism of *Zoar* as a desire for truth (discussed in §2439). This too shows that people who focus on faith are also saved, as long as goodness is present in their faith, or in other words, as long as they love religious truth for the sake of goodness, that is, at the call of goodness. The life within faith comes from no other source. **2442**

For the idea that charity is the essential ingredient of faith—actually *is* faith, in fact, since it is the core of faith—see §§379, 389, 654, 724, 809, 916, 1162, 1176, 1798, 1799, 1834, 1844, 2049, 2116, 2189, 2190, 2228, 2261, 2343, 2349, 2417.

Genesis 19:24. *And Jehovah rained sulfur and fire from Jehovah out of the sky onto Sodom and onto Gomorrah.* **2443**

Jehovah rained sulfur and fire onto Sodom and onto Gomorrah symbolizes the hell of people caught up in the evils of self-love and in the falsities produced by that evil. To *rain* is to be damned; *sulfur* is the hell where self-love rules; and *fire* is the hell where its resulting falsities rule. *From Jehovah out of the sky* means as a result of the laws of the ordained plan as they relate to truth, since these people cut themselves off from goodness.

Jehovah rained sulfur and fire onto Sodom and onto Gomorrah symbolizes the hell of people caught up in the evils of self-love and in the falsities produced by that evil. This can be seen from the symbolism of *raining* as being damned, of *sulfur* as the hell where the evils of self-love rule, and of *fire* as the hell where the falsities resulting from that evil rule, as discussed **2444** just below. It can also be seen from the symbolism of *Sodom* as the evil of self-love and the symbolism of *Gomorrah* as the resulting falsity—symbolism discussed at §§2220, 2246, 2322.

[2] This verse, unlike earlier verses in the chapter, also mentions Gomorrah, because Gomorrah symbolizes falsity rising out of the evil of self-love. In the church (whose last days, or judgment, are the focus here) this evil stands as the chief opponent of goodness, while the falsity it produces stands as the chief opponent of truth. The two are so tightly bound together that anyone who succumbs to the one also succumbs to the other, to an equal extent and an equal degree. It is true that this is not how things appear, but if they do not reveal themselves this way in the world, they certainly do in the next life.

Concerning the nature of self-love, the amount of evil it produces, and the fact that the hells are a product of it, see §§693, 694, 760, 1307, 1308, 1321, 1594, 1691, 2041, 2045, 2051, 2057, 2219.

2445　　　The fact that *raining* means being damned can be seen from the symbolism of *rain*. In the Word, rain symbolizes a blessing (and therefore salvation) when it has a positive meaning but a curse (and therefore damnation) when it has a negative meaning. Its symbolism as a blessing and consequent salvation can be seen from many passages, but its negative symbolism as a curse and consequent damnation is clear from the following. In Isaiah:

> A pavilion will serve as shade from the heat by day, and as a refuge, and as a hiding place from the *deluge* and from the *rain*. (Isaiah 4:6)

In Ezekiel:

> Say to the people applying foolish plaster that it will fall. There will be a *flooding rain* in which you, hailstones, will fall. In my anger there will be a *flooding rain,* and stones of hail in my wrath, until their final end." (Ezekiel 13:11, 13)

In David:

> He has sent them hail for their *rains, flaming fire* on their land, and has struck their grapevine and their fig tree. (Psalms 105:32, 33)

The above refers to Egypt, about which Moses says:

> Jehovah sent thunder and hail, and *fire* flashed over the land, and Jehovah *rained* hail on the land of Egypt. (Exodus 9:23, 24)

Sulfur is the hell where the evils of self-love rule, and *fire* is the hell **2446**
where its resulting falsities rule, as can be seen from the symbolism of
sulfur and its *fire* in the Word. Sulfur and fire symbolize self-love, the
passions that go with it, and the distortions that result, so they symbolize
hell, since that is what hell consists of. This symbolism of sulfur and fire
can be seen in David:

> On the ungodly *Jehovah will rain* snares, *fire,* and *sulfur.* (Psalms 11:6)

Clearly the fire and sulfur do not mean literal fire and sulfur but something else. One indication is the fact that it says Jehovah will rain snares.
In Ezekiel:

> I will argue my case with him by contagion and by blood; and a *flooding
> rain* and hailstones, *fire and sulfur I will rain down* on him and on his
> wings and on many peoples who are with him. (Ezekiel 38:22)

This refers to Gog, who devastates the land of Israel—that is, the church.
For what Gog means, see §1151. The fire stands for falsity. The sulfur
stands for the resulting evil, and also for the hells containing people who
sow this kind of destruction. In John:

> Those who worshiped the beast were thrown into a *lake burning with
> sulfur.* (Revelation 19:20)

The sulfur stands for hell. In the same author:

> The Devil was thrown into the *lake of fire and sulfur,* where the beast
> and the false prophet were, and they will be tortured days and nights
> forever and ever. (Revelation 20:10)

Obviously this stands for hell. In the same author:

> The despicable and murderers and adulterers and sorcerers and idola-
> ters and all liars have their share in the *lake burning with fire and sulfur.*
> (Revelation 21:8)

Again fire and sulfur plainly stand for hell.

[2] In Isaiah they stand for the evils of self-love and the falsities that
result, which give rise to hell:

> A day of vengeance for Jehovah, a year of redresses for Zion's dispute!
> And its rivers will turn into pitch, and its dirt into *sulfur,* and its land
> will become *burning pitch.* (Isaiah 34:8, 9)

Burning pitch here (in place of fire) stands for thick and dreadful falsity. The sulfur stands for the evil that comes of self-love. In the same author:

> Its pyre is *fire* and much wood; Jehovah's breath is like a *river of burning sulfur* in it. (Isaiah 30:33)

This is about Topheth. The river of burning sulfur stands for falsities rising out of the evils of self-love. In Luke:

> On the day Lot went out from Sodom, fire and sulfur rained from the sky and destroyed everyone. This is how it will happen on the day the Son of Humankind is revealed. (Luke 17:29, 30)

Anyone can see that fire and sulfur will not rain down at that time. Instead, the falsities and cravings of self-love, which are symbolized by fire and sulfur and constitute hell, will take control.

[3] In the Word, fire symbolizes our cravings and also the hells. The smoke from a fire symbolizes the false thinking our cravings produce, which permeates those hells; see §1861. And in John:

> I saw horses in the vision and people sitting on them, having breast-pieces of *fire* and *sulfur*. And the horses' heads were like lions' heads, and from their mouth went out *fire, smoke,* and *sulfur*. By these three a third of all human beings were killed—by the *fire* and by the *smoke* and by the *sulfur*. (Revelation 9:17, 18)

Fire, smoke, and sulfur stand for evil and falsity of every kind, which is where hell comes from, as noted.

2447   *From Jehovah out of the sky* means as a result of the laws of the ordained plan as they relate to truth, since these people cut themselves off from goodness. This can be seen only from the inner meaning, which reveals how matters stand in regard to punishment and damnation. Punishment and damnation never come from Jehovah, or the Lord, but from the person, evil spirit, or devil herself or himself. This results from the laws of the ordained plan as they relate to truth, because the people in question cut themselves off from goodness.

[2] The whole of the ordained plan comes from Jehovah, that is, the Lord. He governs absolutely everything according to that plan, but with many differences. Events can result because he *wills* them, *takes pleasure* in them, *accepts* them, or *tolerates* them. Whatever he wills or takes pleasure in results from the ordained laws as they relate to goodness. So do many of the things he accepts and even some of the ones he tolerates. When we

disconnect from what is good, though, we throw ourselves on the ordained laws that belong to truth isolated from goodness. By their very nature these laws are damning, because all truth condemns us and sends us to hell. From goodness, however—which is mercy—the Lord saves us and lifts us into heaven. This shows that we are the ones who damn ourselves.

[3] Most events the Lord tolerates belong in this category, as for instance when one devil punishes or torments another, not to mention countless other examples. These things result from the ordained laws that have to do with truth isolated from goodness. Without them, devils could never be held in check or stopped from assaulting all the good, honest people they can find and destroying them forever. Prevention of this possibility is a good outcome that the Lord looks to.

The case is the same as that of a kind and gentle monarch in the earthly world who intends and does only the best. He needs to allow his laws to punish evildoers and criminals, even though he himself punishes no one but rather grieves to know of people whose very character requires them to be punished by their own wickedness. If this monarch did not allow his laws to operate, he would leave his whole kingdom prey to such people, which would be the height of unkindness and the height of mercilessness.

[4] Clearly, then, Jehovah never rained down sulfur or fire. That is to say, he never condemned anyone to hell. It was the people themselves who did this—the ones involved in evil and therefore in falsity—because they had cut themselves off from what was good. In the process they had subjected themselves to the laws of the grand plan that stem from truth alone.

It now follows that this is the inner meaning of the current words.

[5] The Word attributes evil, punishment, curses, damnation, and more to Jehovah (the Lord), just as it says here that he rained down sulfur and fire. In Ezekiel:

> I will argue my case with him by contagion and by blood; *fire* and *sulfur* *I will rain down* on him. (Ezekiel 38:22)

In Isaiah:

> Jehovah's breath is like a *river of burning sulfur.* (Isaiah 30:33)

In David:

> On the ungodly Jehovah will rain snares, *fire,* and *sulfur.* (Psalms 11:6)

In the same author:

> *Smoke* went up *from his nose,* and *fire from* his *mouth. Embers sent flames* from him. (Psalms 18:8, 9)

In Jeremiah:

> May *my fury* not go forth like *fire* and *burn,* with no one to quench it. (Jeremiah 21:12)

In Moses:

> *A fire has kindled in my anger,* and it will *burn all the way to the lowest hell.* (Deuteronomy 32:22)

Similar statements appear in many other places besides. As I was saying, the Word attributes such things to Jehovah (the Lord), and the reason was explained in the first two volumes, §§223, 245, 589, 592, 696, 735, 1093, 1683, 1874. The possibility that they could come from the Lord is as remote as good is from evil, as heaven is from hell, or as divinity is from devilishness. Evil, hell, and the Devil commit these actions, never the Lord, who is mercy and goodness itself. Since it looks as though he does, however, they are attributed to him for the reasons given in the sections cited.

[6] The current verse says, "Jehovah rained (them) down from Jehovah out of the sky," so in the text it looks as though there were two Jehovahs— one on earth and one in the sky. The inner meaning teaches how even this is to be understood. The first mention of Jehovah refers to the Lord's divine humanity and holy influence (meant by the two men in this chapter). The second instance refers to divinity itself, which is called the Father (spoken of in the previous chapter [§§2149, 2218]). It is also saying that this Trinity exists in the Lord, as he himself says in John:

> Whoever has seen me has seen the Father. Believe me, that I am in the Father and the Father is in me. (John 14:9, 10, 11)

The same author on the Lord's holy influence:

> The Paraclete will not speak from himself; he will take from what is mine and proclaim it to you. (John 16:13, 14, 15)

So there is one Jehovah, even though two are mentioned here. The reason two are mentioned is that all the laws of his plan emanate from the Lord's fundamental divinity, divine humanity, and holy influence.

Genesis 19:25. *And he overthrew those cities and all the plain and all the residents of the cities and what sprouted from the ground.*

He overthrew those cities means that they were detached from any truth they knew, which left them with nothing but falsity. *And all the plain* symbolizes everything connected with truth. *And all the residents of the cities* means that they were detached from any goodness they had, which left them with nothing but evil. *And what sprouted from the ground* symbolizes every aspect of the church.

He overthrew those cities means that they were detached from any truth they knew, which left them with nothing but falsity. This can be seen from the symbolism of *cities* as doctrines and so as truth (discussed at §§402, 2268, 2428), since doctrines are made up of truth. They are said to be overthrown when falsity replaces truth. Here they are said to be overthrown when people are detached from any truth they know and from any goodness they have, which the current verse also speaks of. After all, it is talking about the final stage for those people in the church who immerse themselves in falsity and evil. And this is just what that stage is like.

[2] To show what that stage is like, a few words must be said. People who enter the other world all return to the kind of life they lived in their bodies. When they do, the ones who are good disengage from evil and falsity so that the Lord can raise them into heaven by means of their goodness and truth. The ones who are evil, however, disengage from goodness and truth so that their evil and falsity can carry them into hell; see §2119. This agrees perfectly with the Lord's words in Matthew:

> Those who have something will have it more abundantly; but from those who don't have anything, even what they have will be taken. (Matthew 13:12)

Elsewhere in the same author:

> All who have something will be granted to overflow with it; but from those who don't have anything, it will be taken from them. (Matthew 25:29; Luke 8:18; 19:24, 25, 26; Mark 4:24, 25)

The same thing is also meant by these words in Matthew:

> Let both grow together until the harvest, and it will happen in the time of the harvest that I will say to the harvesters, "First collect the tares and bind them into bundles to burn them. But gather the wheat into my barn." The harvest is the close of the age; just as the tares are collected

and burned with fire, so it will be at the close of the age. (Matthew
13:30, 39, 40)

This is also meant by the story of the dragnet cast into the sea that drew
in various kinds of fish. It says that the good kinds were then collected
into containers and the bad kinds thrown out, and that so it would be at
the close of the age (Matthew 13:47, 48, 49, 50). To see what the close of
the age is and that it involves a similar process in regard to religion, see
§§1857, 2243.

[3] The purpose of detaching good people from evil and falsity is to
prevent them from hanging indecisively between evil and goodness, so
that they can instead be lifted into heaven through what is good. The purpose of detaching evil people from goodness and truth is to prevent them
from using any remaining goodness in themselves to lead the upright
astray. It also allows them to be drawn away by their vices to join their evil
comrades in hell. In the other world all thoughts and feelings are shared
in such a way that the positive ones are communicated to good people
there and the negative ones are communicated to evil people (§§1388,
1389, 1390). So if the two were not separated, immense damage would
result, not to mention the fact that no connections would exist. In reality, though, everything is connected to everything else in a most exquisite
way. In the heavens, the ties that form reflect all the different ways angels
love the Lord and share that love with each other and therefore all their
different beliefs (§§685, 1394). In the hells, the ties reflect all the differences in spirits' obsessions and therefore in their delusions (§§695, 1322).

It needs to be known that having something detached is not having
it removed completely. No trait that we have possessed is ever taken completely away from us.

2450   *And all the plain* symbolizes everything connected with truth. This can
be seen from the symbolism of a *plain* as every aspect of doctrine and consequently as everything connected with truth, as discussed in §2418.

2451   *All the residents of the cities* means that they were detached from any
goodness they had, which left them with nothing but evil. This can be
seen from the symbolism of *residents* (when they are said to reside in a
city) as good qualities, a symbolism that many passages in the Word can
confirm. This also shows that since a city symbolizes truth (as shown), a
resident means something good, because truth is what goodness resides
in. Truth devoid of goodness is like an empty city, barren of inhabitants.

To see that the evil are detached from everything good in them, so
that they have nothing left but evil, see above at §2449.

What sprouted from the ground symbolizes every aspect of the church, **2452**
as can be seen from the symbolism of *what sprouts. Sprouts* mean crops and
also vegetation of every kind, and these symbolize goodness and truth, as
is evident throughout the Word.

It can also be seen from the symbolism of the *ground* as the church, a
symbolism discussed at §§566, 1068.

Goodness and truth constitute every aspect of religion, as people know.

Genesis 19:26. *And [Lot's] wife looked back behind him and turned into* **2453**
a pillar of salt.

His wife looked back behind him means truth turned its back on goodness to gaze in the direction of doctrine. *And turned into a pillar of salt*
means truth was purged of everything good about it.

His wife looked back behind him means truth turned its back on good- **2454**
ness to gaze in the direction of doctrine, as can be seen from the symbolism of *looking back behind him* and of a *wife.*

Looking back behind him means looking back toward doctrine (a matter of truth) and not toward a life in accord with doctrine (a matter of
goodness), as noted above at §2417. What is less important is said to be
behind him, and what is more important is described as being in front of
him. The fact that truth comes second, and goodness, first, has been shown
many times. After all, truth has everything to do with goodness, since good
is the essence and life of truth. Looking back behind him, then, is looking toward truth, which relates to doctrine, rather than toward goodness,
which relates to a life in accord with doctrine.

[2] This symbolism is quite plain from the Lord's words in Luke where
he speaks (as he does here) about the last days of the church, or the close
of the age:

> On that day, people who are on top of their house and whose belong-
> ings are in the house are not to go down to take those things. And
> people who are in the field likewise *should not turn back to behind them.*
> *Remember Lot's wife.* (Luke 17:31, 32)

These words of the Lord are not the least bit intelligible without the inner
sense—that is, unless we know what is meant by being on top of the
house, by the belongings in the house, by going down to take them, by the
field, and lastly by turning back to behind them. According to the inner
meaning, being on top of the house is having goodness, a house being
goodness (see §§710, 2233). The belongings or vessels in the house are
true ideas that contain something good, truth being a vessel for goodness

(see §§1496, 1832, 1900, 2063, 2269). Going down to take them, clearly, is turning away from goodness toward truth, since goodness is higher because it is more important, and truth is lower because it is less important. The field is the church (which is called a field because of the seed sown in it), and people who do the good deeds that doctrine teaches are therefore fields themselves, which can be seen from many passages in the Word. The symbolism of turning back to behind them is evident from these things, then; it symbolizes turning our back on goodness to gaze in the direction of doctrine. Accordingly, since doctrine is symbolized by Lot's wife, the passage adds the words "Remember Lot's wife."

It says she looked not "behind her" but "behind him," because Lot symbolizes goodness (see §§2324, 2351, 2371, 2399). That is why when Lot was addressed in verse 17 he was told, "Don't look back behind you." [3] The reason it says in Luke, "They should not turn back *to behind them,*" rather than "to what is behind them," is that those who are heavenly do not like even to mention anything that relates to doctrine (see §§202, 337). That is why the passage does not mention it but says *to behind them.*

The same situation is described this way in Matthew:

> When you see the ruinous abomination predicted by Daniel the prophet, then those who are in Judea should flee into the mountains. Those who are on top of the house should not go down to take anything from their house. And those in the field *should not turn back behind* to take their clothes. (Matthew 24:15, 16, 17, [18])

[4] The ruinous abomination is the condition the church is in when it has no love or charity. When love and charity have been ruined, abominations take over. Judea is the church—a heavenly church, in fact—as the Old Testament Word makes plain throughout both its narrative and its prophetic books. The mountains they were to flee into are love for the Lord and consequently charity for our neighbor (see §§795, 1430, 1691). The people who are on top of the house mean a loving goodness, as noted just above. Going down to take something from their house is turning away from goodness toward truth, as also noted above. People in the field are people in a spiritual religion, as is evident from the symbolism of a field in the Word [§§368, 3310]. "They should not turn back behind to take their clothes" means that they should not turn away from goodness toward truth in the form of doctrine. Clothes symbolize truth, because

truth acts as a garment for goodness (see §1073). Anyone can see that everything the Lord said about the end of the age in this passage means something very different and involves mysteries. This includes the fact that people in Judea were to flee into the mountains, that people on top of the house were not to go down to take anything from the house, and that people in the field were not to turn back behind to take their clothes. The same is true of the fact that Lot was not to look back behind him (verse 17) and that his wife did look back behind him (the current verse).

The same thing can again be seen from the symbolism of a *wife* as truth (discussed in §§915, 1468) and from that of Lot as goodness (discussed in §§2324, 2351, 2371, 2399), which is why it says "behind him."

[5] Truth is said to turn its back on goodness and gaze in the direction of doctrine when no one any longer takes to heart what kind of life a person in the church lives but only what kind of doctrine the person holds. Yet a life according to doctrine is what makes a person religious, not doctrine separated from life. When we disconnect doctrine from life, we destroy goodness, which is part and parcel of life, and as a result we also destroy truth, which is part and parcel of doctrine. That is, we turn it into a pillar of salt. Anyone can see that this is so. When people look only to doctrine, not to life, do they really—despite the teachings of doctrine—believe in resurrection, heaven, hell, the Lord himself, or any other doctrinal tenet?

She turned into a pillar of salt means truth was purged of everything good about it, as can be seen from the symbolism of a *pillar* and of *salt*. **2455**

The original language uses the same word for the pillar here as it uses for a garrison, not the word it uses for a pillar raised for worship or as a sign or as a witness. So the *pillar of salt* symbolizes the fact that the truth meant by Lot's wife (§2454) stood devastated. Truth is said to be devastated, [or purged,] when there is no longer any goodness in it. The actual process of devastation is symbolized by *salt*.

[2] Many words in Scripture have two meanings, positive and negative, and this is true also of salt. In a positive sense it means a desire for truth; in a negative sense it means stripping away a desire for truth. That is, it means stripping truth of anything good in it. For its symbolism as a desire for truth, see Exodus 30:35; Leviticus 2:13; Matthew 5:13; Mark 9:49, 50; Luke 14:34, 35. Its symbolism as the purging of a desire for truth, or the stripping of goodness from truth, may be seen in the following passages. In Moses:

Sulfur there will be, and *salt;* the whole land will be a conflagration. It will not be sown, it will not sprout, and no grass will come up in it, as in the overthrow of Sodom and Gomorrah, Admah and Zeboiim. (Deuteronomy 29:23)

The sulfur is the purging of goodness, while the salt is the purging of truth. Everything about the passage shows that it is talking about devastation. [3] In Zephaniah:

Moab will be like Sodom, and the children of Ammon like Gomorrah: a place abandoned to nettle, and a *salt pit,* and a ruin forever. (Zephaniah 2:9)

The place abandoned to nettle stands for goodness that has been devastated, and the salt pit, for devastated truth. The place of nettle, you see, refers to Sodom, which symbolizes evil (devastated goodness), while the salt pit refers to Gomorrah, which symbolizes falsity (devastated truth)—as has been demonstrated. The fact that it is talking about devastation is obvious, since it speaks of "a ruin forever." In Jeremiah:

Those who use flesh as their arm will be like a naked shrub in the desert and will not see when something good comes. And they will settle in the parched places in the wilderness—a *salt-filled land,* and one that is not inhabited. (Jeremiah 17:[5,] 6)

The parched places stand for devastated goodness; the salt-filled land, for devastated truth. [4] In David:

Jehovah makes rivers into a desert, and outlets of water into a dry gulch, a land of fruit *into a salty land,* because of the wickedness of those living in it. (Psalms 107:33, 34)

Turning a land of fruit into a salty land stands for purging or devastating truth of the goodness that is in it. In Ezekiel:

It has its marshes and its swamps, and they are not being cured; *they will be given over to salt.* (Ezekiel 47:11)

Being given over to salt stands for the total devastation of truth.

Since salt symbolized devastation and cities symbolized true doctrine, as shown in §§402, 2268, 2428, 2449, people used to sow with salt the cities they had destroyed, to keep them from being rebuilt (Judges 9:45).

This now is the fourth phase of the religion Lot represents—a phase in which all truth is purged of what is good about it.

Genesis 19:27, 28, 29. *And Abraham got up in the morning, at the place where he stood, there before Jehovah. And he looked out opposite the face of Sodom and Gomorrah and opposite the whole face of the land of the plain, and he saw, and here, now, the smoke of the land rose like the smoke of a furnace. And it happened, in God's destroying the cities of the plain, that God remembered Abraham and sent Lot out from the middle of the overthrow, in overthrowing the cities in which Lot had lived.*

2456

Abraham got up in the morning symbolizes the Lord's thoughts about the final days; here as before, *Abraham* is the Lord in that phase. *At the place where he stood, there before Jehovah* symbolizes the state of perception and thought he had been in earlier; a *place* is a state. *And he looked out opposite the face of Sodom and Gomorrah* symbolizes his thinking about their inner state as far as evil and falsity went. *And opposite the whole face of the land of the plain* symbolizes all the inner states resulting from that state. *And he saw, and here, now, the smoke of the land was like the smoke of a furnace* symbolizes the state of the falsity (the *smoke*) that developed from the state of their evil (the *furnace*) in the church (the *land*). *And it happened, in God's destroying the cities of the plain* means when they were destroyed by the falsities that grew out of their evil (the *cities of the plain*). *That God remembered Abraham* symbolizes salvation through the uniting of the Lord's divine nature with his human nature. *And sent Lot out from the middle of the overthrow* symbolizes the salvation of people focused on goodness and of people focused on truth that has goodness within it—all of whom are *Lot*. *In overthrowing the cities* means when people immersed in the falsities produced by evil were destroyed. *In which Lot had lived* means although even then some of the people immersed in them were saved.

There is no need to explain in detail, since most of this was explained in the previous chapter and in earlier places.

2457

These additional words were inserted in order to show that the good were separated from the evil and that the good were saved, but the evil, damned. It was only the uniting of the Lord's divine nature with his human nature that accomplished this. Otherwise, everyone represented here by Lot would also have been destroyed. That is what these words mean: "And it happened, in God's destroying the cities of the plain, that God remembered Abraham and sent Lot out from the middle of the overthrow, in overthrowing the cities in which Lot had lived." The inner meaning of this verse is that the uniting of the Lord's divine and human natures saved everyone who was focused on goodness, and also everyone who was focused on truth that had goodness within it (represented here by Lot). These were saved, while those caught up in the falsities produced by evil were destroyed, even though the ones who were saved had also fallen prey to falsity and evil.

So the contents of the current chapter are now connected with those of the previous chapter, which said that Abraham (the Lord in that phase) intervened on behalf of the people in Sodom and Gomorrah symbolized by the fifty, forty-five, forty, thirty, twenty, and ten. These people include everyone with goodness and everyone with truth that has some measure of goodness in it (as explained there), listed in order.

2458   Genesis 19:30. *And Lot went up from Zoar and lived on the mountain, and his two daughters with him, because he was afraid to live in Zoar. And he was living in a cave, he and his two daughters.*

Lot went up from Zoar means when these people no longer had a desire for truth. *And lived on the mountain* means they then resorted to a kind of goodness. *And his two daughters with him* means that the desires resulting from [the good represented by Lot] did the same. *Because he was afraid to live in Zoar* means because they were no longer able to look toward goodness from a desire for truth. *And he was living in a cave, he,* symbolizes goodness tainted with falsity. *And his two daughters* symbolize the feelings that develop out of [the tainted goodness represented by Lot]: a desire for this [tainted] goodness and a desire for this falsity.

2459   *Lot went up from Zoar* means when they no longer had a desire for truth. This can be seen from the symbolism of *Zoar* as a desire for truth (discussed at §2439). The verse says next that he lived on the mountain because he was afraid to live in Zoar, so the meaning is when they no longer had a desire for truth. The reason they no longer wanted truth was that truth had been stripped of everything good, as can be seen from verse 26 [§2455].

This now depicts the fifth phase of the church Lot represents, in which an impure kind of goodness—goodness tainted with falsity—pours in when there is no longer a desire for truth.

2460   *He lived on the mountain* means they then resorted to a kind of goodness. This can be seen from the symbolism of a *mountain* as love in all its forms: heavenly love and spiritual (§§795, 1430), and also self-love and love of worldly advantages (§1691). It has all these meanings because most words in Scripture also have a negative meaning. Since all goodness is connected with some variety of love, the mountain here symbolizes goodness, but the type of goodness it symbolizes is portrayed below [§2463]. To be specific, it was a dark type of goodness and became impure, since the text soon says that he lived in a cave and later that obscene things happened there [Genesis 19:30–35].

His two daughters with him means that the desires associated with [the good represented by Lot] did the same. This can be seen from the symbolism of *daughters* as desires (discussed in §§489, 490, 491, [568, 2362]). The nature of the desires, though, reflects that of the underlying goodness. Even false, impure goodness has its feelings, since we all find our hearts touched by the things we imagine to be good—no matter what their true character is—because we love them. **2461**

Because he was afraid to live in Zoar means because he was no longer able to look toward goodness from a desire for truth. This can be seen from the symbolism of *Zoar* as a desire for truth (§2439). When our desire for truth has been destroyed, we can no longer look toward goodness. We then fear all truth as well, because truth opposes anything that an impure love considers good. **2462**

And he was living in a cave, he, symbolizes goodness tainted with falsity, as can be seen from the symbolism of a *cave.* A cave is a type of mountain dwelling, but a dark one. Any kind of living space symbolizes goodness, as a house does (§2233), but it symbolizes a kind of goodness that resembles the type of dwelling. So in the current instance, since a cave is a dark place to live, it symbolizes a dark type of goodness. **2463**

Mountain caves are also mentioned many places in the Word, and in those passages they symbolize the same kind of thing on an inner level, as in Isaiah 2:19; 32:14. They also have the same meaning in the narrative books, such as when Elijah fled Israel and came to the *cave* on Mount Horeb, where he spent the night. There the word of Jehovah came to him telling him to go out and stand *on the mountain* before Jehovah. He then wrapped his face in his cloak and went out and stood at the *doorway of the cave* (1 Kings 19:9, 13). The cave here on an inner level symbolizes goodness that is dark and dim—the kind we experience in times of trial. Because it would not be capable of enduring the divine presence, Elijah wrapped his face in his cloak.

It is similar elsewhere in the narrative books. The children of Israel made themselves caves in the mountains because of Midian (Judges 6:2) and because of the Philistines (1 Samuel 13:6). The case with the historical details there is the same as here in Moses: they mean something else in an inner sense.

And his two daughters symbolize the feelings that develop out of [the tainted goodness represented by Lot]: a desire for this [tainted] goodness **2464** and a desire for this falsity. This can be seen from the symbolism of *daughters* as desires (§2461).

The type of goodness from which the feelings develop—the father from which the daughters had been born—is Lot. The truth from which they developed, though—the mother—was Lot's wife. When she has become a pillar of salt—when truth is stripped of its goodness—the kind of goodness symbolized by Lot lives in a cave, along with the kinds of feelings symbolized by his daughters, which develop out of it.

2465   Genesis 19:31, 32, 33, 34, 35, 36. *And the firstborn said to the younger, "Our father is old, and there is no man in the land to come in to us according to the way of the whole earth. Come, let's give our father wine to drink and lie with him and keep seed from our father alive." And they gave their father wine to drink that night, and the firstborn came and lay with her father, and he was unaware in her lying down and in her getting up. And it happened on the next day that the firstborn said to the younger, "Here, now, I lay yesterday with my father. Let's give him wine to drink tonight too, and come, lie with him and we will keep seed from our father alive." And they gave their father wine to drink that night too, and the younger got up and lay with him, and he was unaware in her lying down and in her getting up. And Lot's two daughters conceived by their father.*

[2] *The firstborn said to the younger* symbolizes desires, here as before [§2461]; the *firstborn* symbolizes a desire for this [tainted] goodness, and the *younger,* for this falsity. *Our father is old, and there is no man in the land* means no one any longer knows what goodness is or what truth is. *To come in to us* means with which they could unite. *According to the way of the whole earth* means according to doctrine; the *earth* is religion. *Come, let's give our father wine to drink* means that they were going to steep this kind of goodness in falsity (the *wine*). *And lie with him* means that this would unite them. *And keep seed from our father alive* means that this would be the start of a new religion. [3] *And they gave their father wine to drink* means they steeped this kind of goodness in falsity. *That night* means when everything was so dark. *And the firstborn came* symbolizes the desire for this type of good. *And lay with her father* means they consequently adapted. *And he was unaware in her lying down and her getting up* means that this general type of goodness suspected nothing. *And it happened on the next day* means later on. *That the firstborn said to the younger* means that the desire for this type of goodness made falsity convincing. *Here, now, I lay yesterday with my father* means that this would

unite them. *Let's give him wine to drink tonight too* here as before means that they would steep this kind of goodness in falsity when it was all so dark. [4] *And come, lie with him* means these too would unite. *And we will keep seed from our father alive* here again means that this would be the start of a new religion. *And they gave their father wine to drink that night too* means that in that dim state they steeped this kind of goodness in falsity. *And the younger got up and lay with him* means the desire for falsity did the same, so that falsity would look like truth, and they consequently united. *And he was unaware in her lying down and in her getting up* means that this general kind of goodness suspected nothing. *And Lot's two daughters conceived by their father* means that this gave rise to the kind of religiosity that Moab and Son-of-Ammon symbolize.

The fact that the symbolism on an inner level is as explained can be proved for every single word; but in the first place, most of it has already been confirmed. In the second, these words are the kind that wound the mind and injure chaste ears. The summary of the meaning is enough to show that the passage depicts the origin of the kind of religious culture that Moab and Son-of-Ammon symbolize in the Word. What that culture is like will be told below in the discussion of Moab and Son-of-Ammon [§2468]. Clearly it involves goodness that has been adulterated and truth that has been falsified.

2466

Adulteration of goodness and falsification of truth is usually depicted as adultery and whoredom in the Word and is also called by those names. The reason they are equated is that goodness and truth form a marriage with one another (§§1904, 2173). In fact—and hardly anyone will believe this—from that marriage as its true prototype comes the holiness of earthly marriage, and also the marriage laws laid down in the Word.

[2] The case is that when heavenly and spiritual qualities come down from heaven into a lower realm, they turn into a perfect image of marriage there. This results from the correspondence that exists between spiritual things and earthly ones. (There will be more on this correspondence elsewhere, the Lord in his divine mercy willing.) When spiritual things come down to a lower realm where evil demons and evil spirits live, however, they are perverted, and then they turn into the kinds of things that adultery and whoredom involve. That is why the contamination of goodness and corruption of truth is portrayed in the Word as adultery and whoredom and is also called by those names. This appears plainly in the following passages. In Ezekiel:

You *whored* because of your name, and you poured out your *whore-doms* on everyone passing by. You took some of your clothes and made yourself colorful high places and *whored* on them. You took the articles of your finery—made of my gold and of my silver, which I had given to you—and made yourself images of a male and *whored with them.* You took your sons and your daughters whom you bore to me and sacrificed them to those [images]. Was there too little of your *whoring?* You *whored* with the sons of Egypt, your neighbors, who were great in flesh, and multiplied your *whoredom* to provoke me. You whored with the sons of Assyria, and you *whored* with them and were not satisfied. And you multiplied your *whoredom* all the way to the land of trade, Chaldea, and even in this you were not satisfied. (Ezekiel 16:15, 16, 17, 20, 26, 28, 29, and following verses)

This is about Jerusalem, which here symbolizes a religion whose truth has been perverted. [3] Anyone can see that everything in the description means something very different. Plainly, corruption in the church is being called whoredom. The clothes there are perverted truth; the resulting falsities they worship are the colorful high places on which they whored. (For the symbolism of clothes as truth, see §1073, and for that of high places as worship, §796.) The articles of finery made of "gold and silver that I had given" are bits of knowledge concerning goodness and truth taken from the Word and used to prove false ideas. When false ideas look true, they are called images of a male, with which the people of Jerusalem whored. (The symbolism of gold as goodness, 113, 1551, 1552, and of silver as truth, 1551, 2048, makes it clear that articles of finery made of gold and silver are the knowledge of goodness and truth. Images of the male are the fact that they look true, 2046.) The sons and daughters they bore and sacrificed to the images are true ideas and good impulses that they per-verted, as is clear from the symbolism of sons and daughters (489, 490, 491, 533, 2362). Whoring with the sons of Egypt is perverting truth and goodness by means of secular knowledge, which is clear from the symbol-ism of Egypt as secular facts (1164, 1165, 1186, 1462). Whoring with the sons of Assyria is perverting them through sophistic reasoning, which is evident from the symbolism of Assyria as sophistry (119, 1186). Multiply-ing their whoredom all the way to the land of Chaldea is going so far as to profane truth, which is Chaldea (1368). This makes it transparently clear what the inner meaning of the Word is like within the literal meaning itself. [4] There is a similar passage elsewhere in the same prophet:

Two women, the daughters of one mother, *whored* in Egypt. In their youth they *whored*. Oholah is Samaria; Oholibah, Jerusalem. Oholah *whored* against me and *doted on her lovers,* the neighboring Assyrians. She bestowed her *whorings* on them, the choice part of all the sons of Assyria. Her *whorings* from [her time in] Egypt she did not abandon, because they had *lain* with her in her youth. Oholibah corrupted her love more than [Oholah], and her *whoredoms* above her sister's *whoredoms;* she lusted after the sons of Assyria. She added to her *whorings* and looked at images of *Chaldeans*. She *lusted after* them at one glance of her eyes. To her came the sons of Babylon, to her *love bed*. (Ezekiel 23:2, 3, 4, 5, 7, 8, 11, 12, 14, 16, [17,] and following verses)

Samaria is a religion that loves truth; Jerusalem, a religion that loves goodness. Their whoredoms with the Egyptians and the sons of Assyria are perversions of goodness and truth by means of secular facts and rationalizations, which they use in support of falsity. This is evident from the symbolism of Egypt (§§1164, 1165, 1186, 1462) and Assyria (119, 1186). They continue until they have profaned worship, which when profaned in regard to truth is Chaldea (1368) and when profaned in regard to goodness is the sons of Babylon (1182, 1326). [5] In Isaiah:

And it will happen at the end of seventy years that Jehovah will visit Tyre, and it will go back to its *wages as a harlot* and will *whore* with all the monarchies of the earth. (Isaiah 23:17)

Boasting about one's distorted thinking is what Tyre's wages as a harlot and its whoredom symbolize. (For Tyre's symbolism as knowledge of truth, see §1201, and for the symbolism of monarchies as truth, with which Tyre whored, §1672.) [6] In Jeremiah:

You *whored* with many companions, and you are coming back to me. Raise your eyes to the hills and look for a place where you have not been *debauched*. Beside the paths you have sat for them, like an Arab in the wilderness, and you have profaned the land with your *whorings* and your wickedness. (Jeremiah 3:1, 2)

Whoring, and profaning the land with whorings, is perverting and falsifying the church's truth (the land being the church; see §§662, 1066, 1068). [7] In the same author:

With the sound of her *whoredom* she profaned the land; she *committed adultery* with stone and wood. (Jeremiah 3:9)

To commit adultery with stone and wood is to pervert what is true and good in outward worship. (For the symbolism of stone as truth treated this way, see §§643, 1298; for that of wood as something good treated this way, §643.) [8] In the same author:

> Because of this they did folly in Israel and *committed adultery* with their friends' wives and spoke a word in my name, a false one that I did not command. (Jeremiah 29:23)

Committing adultery with friends' wives is teaching something wrong, supposedly on others' behalf. [9] In the same author:

> In Jerusalem's prophets I have seen a depravity, as they *commit adultery* and walk in falsity. (Jeremiah 23:14)

Committing adultery has to do with goodness that is being contaminated; walking in falsity, with truth that is being perverted. In the same author:

> Your *adulteries* and your whinnyings, the filth of your *whoredom* on the hills, in the field—I have seen your abominations. Doom to you, Jerusalem! You are not clean after this, for how much longer? (Jeremiah 13:27)

[10] In Hosea:

> *Whoredom* and *wine* and new wine have taken control of the heart. My people ask questions of wood, and their wand will point out [the answer], because a *spirit of whoredom* has led them astray. And they have *whored* against their god. On the mountain peaks they sacrifice, and on the hills they burn incense, under oak, poplar, and terebinth. Therefore your daughters are *whoring,* and your daughters-in-law are *committing adultery.* Won't I bring punishment on your daughters because they are *whoring,* and on your daughters-in-law because they are *committing adultery?* For [the men] divide with *whores* and sacrifice with *harlots.* (Hosea 4:11, 12, 13, 14)

What the individual items here mean in an inner sense can be seen from the following symbolism: Wine is falsity; new wine is the evil it produces. The wood that the people consult is whatever some pleasure urges on us as being good. The wand that will point out the answer is the imagined power of our own intellect. The mountains and hills are love for ourselves and love for worldly advantages. Oak, poplar, and terebinth are so many dull, coarse perceptions rising out of those loves—perceptions that we believe in. Daughters and daughters-in-law are emotions of the same character. From this it is clear what whoredom, adultery, and harlots symbolize here. [11] In the same author:

> Israel, you *whored* on your god; you delighted in the *wages you earned as a harlot* on all the grain-threshing floors. (Hosea 9:1)

The harlot's wages stand for boasting about one's false thinking. In Moses:

> Otherwise you might strike a pact with the inhabitants of the land, and [the people] might *whore after* their *gods* and sacrifice to their gods, and [the inhabitants] might call you, and you might eat of their sacrifices and take some of their daughters for your sons, and their daughters might *whore after* their *gods* and *make* your sons *whore after* their *gods.* (Exodus 34:15, 16)

In the same author:

> I will cut off all who *whore after him, whoring after* Molech, from the midst of their people. And the soul that looks to mediums and to soothsayers, to *whore after them*—I will set my face against those souls and cut them off from the midst of their people. (Leviticus 20:5, 6)

In the same author:

> Your children will be grazing in the wilderness forty years and will carry your *whoredoms,* until your bodies have been consumed in the wilderness. (Numbers 14:33)

In the same author:

> You are to remember all Jehovah's commandments and do them and not go seeking after your heart and after your eyes, which you *whore after.* (Numbers 15:39)

[12] The meaning is still more obvious in John:

> One angel said, "Come, I will show you the judgment on the *great whore* sitting on many waters, with whom the monarchs of the earth have *whored;* and those inhabiting the land have become drunk on the *wine of her whoredom.*" (Revelation 17:1, 2)

The great whore stands for people whose worship is profane. The many waters on which she sits are pools of knowledge (§§28, 739). The monarchs of the earth who whored with her are the true ideas of the church

(§§1672, 2015, 2069). The wine they became drunk on is falsity (§§1071, 1072). Since this is the symbolism of wine and drunkenness, verses 32, 33, 35 say that Lot's daughters gave their father wine to drink. [13] In the same author:

> Babylon has given some of the *wine* of her *whoredom's fury* to all the nations to drink, and the monarchs of the earth have *whored* with her. (Revelation 18:3)

Babylon (or Babel) stands for worship that looks devout on the outside but is profane on the inside (§§1182, 1295, 1326). The nations to which she gives drink are the good things that are profaned (§§1259, 1260, 1416, 1849). The monarchs that whored with her are true ideas (§§1672, 2015, 2069). In the same author:

> True and fair-minded are the judgments of the Lord God, because he has judged the *great whore* that polluted the earth with *her whoredom.* (Revelation 19:2)

The earth stands for the church (§§566, 662, 1066, 1068, 2117, 2118).

[14] It was because of this symbolism of whoredom, and the symbolism of daughters as feelings, that the daughter of a priest was so severely forbidden to prostitute herself, as stated this way in Moses:

> The daughter of a man who is a priest, if she has undertaken to engage in whoredom, is profaning her father; she shall be burned with fire. (Leviticus 21:9)

That was also why people were not to bring a harlot's wages into the house of Jehovah, because it was an abomination (Deuteronomy 23:18). And it was why there was such an elaborate procedure for investigating a wife whose husband had come to suspect her of adultery (Numbers 5:12–31); each and every part of the ritual relates to the adulteration of goodness.

[15] There are very many categories of adultery and sexual immorality, and even more particular types, and the Word speaks of them. This general kind, which is depicted by the lying down of Lot's daughters with their father, is what is called Moab and Son-of-Ammon, as spoken of next.

2467   Genesis 19:37, 38. *And the firstborn delivered a child, and she called his name Moab; he is the father of Moab right to this day. And the younger, she also delivered a child, and she called his name Ben-ammi. He is the father of the children of Ammon right to this day.*

The firstborn delivered a child symbolizes the culture of that religion in regard to what is good. *And she called his name Moab* symbolizes its nature. *He is the father of Moab right to this day* means it produced people of that nature. *And the younger, she also delivered a child* symbolizes the falsified truth of the same religion. *And she called his name Ben-ammi* symbolizes its nature. *He is the father of the children of Ammon right to this day* means it produced people of that nature.

Again there is no need to prove that this is the symbolism, since it is evident from the explanation itself and from the context above and below. What the religious culture symbolized by Moab and the children of Ammon is, though, and what its quality is, can be seen from their origin, as depicted. It can also be seen from very many passages in both the narrative and prophetic parts of the Word that mention them. In general, Moab and the children of Ammon are people who engage in outward worship that seems somewhat devout but not in inward worship. They take the shallower elements of worship to be good and true, but deeper elements they reject and sneer at.

[2] This kind of worship and this kind of religiosity settle on people who have a worldly goodness but despise others in comparison with themselves.

They are not too different from fruit that has no outward flaws but is moldy or rotten inside; from vessels made of marble whose contents are unclean or perhaps downright disgusting; from women whose face, body, and manner are pleasing enough but who deep inside are deathly ill and teeming with infection. There is a general kind of goodness in them, which looks at least somewhat attractive, but the particular qualities that go to make it up are quite unsavory. Such people are not like this at first, admittedly, but they do gradually become so, because they readily allow themselves to adopt any value that others call good. As a consequence they also soak up any kind of falsity, which they consider true because it supports their point of view. This is because they feel contempt for the deeper aspects of worship, which in turn results from the fact that they love themselves.

This type of character stems and develops from the type whose worship is strictly shallow (represented in the current chapter by Lot), and only when they have abandoned goodness based on truth.

These people are depicted in the Word, not only as they are in the beginning, when their goodness has not yet been polluted much, and as they are later, when it *has* been polluted. They are also depicted as they

2468

eventually become, when their goodness has been thoroughly polluted and they reject the deeper dimensions of worship and theology.

[3] *Their character in the beginning, when their goodness has not yet been polluted much.* In Daniel:

> At the time of the end, the king of the south will clash with [the king of the north]. Therefore the king of the north will storm onto him with chariot and riders and many ships and will come into various lands and flood them and pass through and come into the beautiful land, and many [lands] will cave in. These will be snatched from his hand: Edom and *Moab* and the *first fruits of the children of Ammon.* (Daniel 11:40, 41)

The king of the south stands for people devoted to goodness and truth; the king of the north, for those devoted to evil and falsity. The coming of the king of the north into various lands with chariot, riders, and ships, his flooding them, and his passing through stand for the eventual predominance of the evils and falsities symbolized by the chariots, riders, and ships. The places to be snatched from his hand—Edom, Moab, and the first fruits of the children of Ammon—stand for people whose goodness has not yet been polluted much, which is why they are called the first fruits of the children of Ammon. [4] In Moses:

> We crossed over by way of the wilderness, and Jehovah said to [me], Moses, "*You are not to assail Moab* or mix yourself with them in battle, because I will not give you any of his land as an inheritance, because to the *children of Lot* I have given Ar as an inheritance." (Deuteronomy 2:8, 9)

And concerning the children of Ammon:

> Jehovah spoke to Moses: "Today you are crossing *Moab's border,* Ar, and you shall approach from opposite the *children of Ammon.* And do not assail them, and you are not to mix yourself with them [in battle], because I will not give any of the *land of Ammon's children* to you as an inheritance, because to the *children of Lot* I have given it as an inheritance." (Deuteronomy 2:17, 18, 19)

Ar stands for this kind of goodness. Moab and the children of Ammon stand for people with this kind of goodness, but an early stage of it, which is why Moses is ordered not to assail them.

[5] This is the reason Moab drove out the Emim and Rephaim, who were like the Anakim. It is also the reason the children of Ammon drove

out the Rephaim, whom they called Zamzummim (Deuteronomy 2:9, 10, 11, 18, 19, 20, 21). The Emim, Rephaim, Anakim, and Zamzummim symbolize people steeped in delusions concerning evil and falsity (see §§581, 1673). Moab and the children of Ammon here symbolize people who have not yet been steeped in these delusions. When they too had absorbed them, though—when their goodness had also been polluted with falsity—they were banished as well (Numbers 21:21–31; Ezekiel 25:8, 9, 10, 11).

[6] *Depictions of their character when their goodness actually has been polluted.* In Jeremiah:

> *To Moab:* This is what Jehovah has said: "Doom upon Nebo, because it has been devastated; Kiriathaim has been shamed, seized; Misgab has been shamed and unnerved; the *praise of Moab* is no more. Give wing to *Moab,* because he will fly away, away, and his cities will become a ruin, no one living in them. Leave the cities and live in the rock, you *residents of Moab,* and be like a dove; it builds its nest across the mouth of the pit. I know his anger," says Jehovah, "and he is not dependable. [I know] his lies; they have not done what is right. Therefore over *Moab* I will wail and to all *Moab* I will cry. With the weeping of Jazer I will weep for you, grapevine of Sibmah. Your offshoots have crossed the sea; all the way to Jazer's sea they have reached. On your summer fruits and on your vintage a destroyer has fallen. Therefore over *Moab* my heart will throb like flutes. Doom to you, *Moab!* The people of Chemosh have perished, because your sons have been taken into captivity and your daughters into captivity. And I will bring *Moab* back from captivity in the end of days." (Jeremiah 48:1, 2, 9, 28, 30, 31, 32, 36, 46, 47)

[7] This whole chapter has to do with Moab; or rather under his image it has to do with people who have this kind of goodness and with the way they allow themselves to soak up falsity. That is why it says to give wing to Moab so he can fly away, and that his cities will become a ruin. However, they were to leave the cities, live in the rock, build nests like a dove across the mouth of the pit, and so on, all of which persuades them to keep their general kinds of goodness and truth. If they should then be enticed away from the kind of falsity that results from a lack of knowledge, in the end of days they would be brought back from captivity. Concerning those who do not do so, though, it says, "Over Moab I will wail and to all Moab I will cry, and over Moab my heart will throb." The falsity they absorb is symbolized by Nebo, Kiriathaim, Misgab, Sibmah, Jazer, Chemosh, and many other names in the same chapter. [8] In Isaiah:

A castoff nest the *daughters of Moab* will be. Offer counsel; exercise judgment. Lend all your shade in the middle of midday. Hide outcasts; do not expose a runaway. Let my outcasts stay in you, *Moab;* be a hiding place for them in the face of the destroyer. We have heard of *Moab's* pride; he is very proud. There is his haughtiness and his pride and his anger; his lies are not so. Therefore *Moab* will howl for Moab; it will all howl. Therefore my bowels will throb like a harp because of *Moab,* and my inside because of the city Heres. It will happen, when *Moab* has been seen to be exhausted on the high place, that he will come to his sanctuary to pray and will not be able to. In three years (like a hired servant's years) the praise of *Moab* will grow worthless in all his vast multitude, and the remainder will be a tiny pittance, not strong. (Isaiah 15:1, 2; 16:2, 3, 4, 5, 6, 7, 11, 12, 14)

This whole chapter too is about Moab and (under his image) about people with this kind of goodness. It depicts them throughout in terms similar to those of Jeremiah 48. Here too they are persuaded that they will keep their general kinds of goodness and truth and not allow themselves to soak up falsity. Their general kinds of goodness and truth are symbolized by their offering counsel, exercising judgment, hiding outcasts, not exposing a runaway, and being a hiding place from the destroyer for outcasts. All these acts symbolize the external motions of worship. They do allow themselves to absorb falsity, though, so it says, "In three years (like a hired servant's years) the praise of Moab will grow worthless in all his vast multitude, and the remainder will be a tiny pittance, not strong."

[9] Because they are easily led astray, Moab is called the stretching out of the Philistines' hand, and the children of Ammon are called their subservience, in Isaiah:

Jesse's root is what is standing as a banner of the *peoples,* it is what the nations will seek; and his resting place will be glorious. Ephraim's envy will withdraw, and Judah's foes will be cut off; Ephraim will not show envy toward Judah, and Judah will not assail Ephraim. And they will fly against the shoulder of the Philistines toward the sea; together they will plunder the children of the east: Edom, *Moab (the outstretching of their hand),* and the *children of Ammon (their subservience).* (Isaiah 11:10, 13, 14)

Jesse's root stands for the Lord. Judah stands for people with heavenly goodness; Ephraim, for people with spiritual truth. Philistines stand for people who know about truth but lack love for others; the children of the east stand for people who know about goodness but again lack love for others. Moab is said to be the outstretching of their hand, and the children of Ammon, their subservience, because they indoctrinate [the people represented by Moab and the children of Ammon] in falsity.

[10] *The eventual character of the people called Moab and the children of Ammon when their goodness has been thoroughly polluted by falsity.* This is depicted in David:

> God has spoken in his holiness: "I own Gilead, and I own Manasseh, and Ephraim is the strength of my head. Judah is my lawgiver. *Moab is my washbasin.*" (Psalms 60:6, 7, 8; 108:7, 8, 9)

A washbasin stands for goodness befouled with falsity. [11] In Jeremiah:

> The *praise of Moab* is no more. In Heshbon they thought up evil for him: "Go! Let's cut him off from nationhood." *Moab* had been placid from his youthful days and had been resting *on his dregs* and had not been emptied from vessel into vessel or gone into exile. Therefore *his flavor* stood firm in him, and *his aroma* did not change. On all the roofs of *Moab,* universal mourning, because I have broken *Moab* like a vessel in which there is no good pleasure. (Jeremiah 48:2, 11, 38)

The falsity that pollutes the goodness symbolized by Moab is being called dregs. Their flavor and aroma stand firm if goodness is not reformed—if it is not emptied from vessel into vessel, as this passage expresses it. The goodness itself is called a vessel in which there is no good pleasure, just as David speaks of a basin in which there is washing. In Isaiah:

> Jehovah's hand rests on this mountain, and *Moab* will be threshed under him, as *straw* is trampled *in the dung heap.* (Isaiah 25:10)

[12] *People with this kind of goodness care only about the shallower dimensions of worship and theology; the deeper dimensions they despise, reject, and even repudiate.*

As a result they have falsity in place of truth; in Ezekiel:

> Child of humankind, turn your face toward the *children of Ammon* and prophesy over them, and you are to say to the *children of Ammon,* "Listen to the word of the Lord Jehovih. This is what the Lord Jehovih has said: 'Since you say "Well done!" to my sanctuary because it has been profaned, and to the ground of Israel because it has been ruined,

and to the house of Judah because they have gone into captivity, I will make Rabbah the dwelling place of camels, and the *children of Ammon* the resting place of the flock.' The Lord Jehovih has said, 'Since you clapped your hand and stamped with your foot and rejoiced in all your contempt of soul at the ground of Israel, therefore watch: I myself will stretch my hand out over you and give you to the nations as prey and cut you off from the peoples and destroy you from the lands.'" (Ezekiel 25:2–11)

"'Well done!' to my sanctuary because it has been profaned, to the ground of Israel because it has been ruined, and to the house of Judah because they have gone into captivity," and "you clapped your hand, stamped with your foot, and rejoiced in all your contempt of soul at the ground of Israel" are words describing contempt, derision, and rejection for the deeper dimensions of worship and theology. Once these have been rejected, there is no health left in the superficial dimensions. They are given as prey to the nations (are beset by evil), cut off from the peoples (beset by falsity), and destroyed from the lands (lose all connection with the church). [13] In Zephaniah:

I have heard the *taunt of Moab* and the *blasphemies of Ammon's children,* who taunted my people, who spread out over their border. Therefore as I live, *Moab* will be like Sodom, and the *children of Ammon* like Gomorrah. A place abandoned to nettle, and a salt pit, and a ruin they will be forever. This is theirs on account of their pride, because they taunted and spread out over the people of Jehovah Sabaoth. (Zephaniah 2:8, 9, 10)

Taunting the people and spreading out over their border and over the people of Jehovah Sabaoth means demeaning and rejecting deep truth (this truth being the people of Jehovah Sabaoth). This turns goodness into the evil that comes of falsity (Sodom, a place abandoned to nettle) and truth into falsity (Gomorrah, a salt pit). It is the things on the inside that make the things on the outside good and true. [14] In David:

Your foes think up a secret, treacherous plan against your people; they consult over the ones you have hidden. "Go! Let's cut them off from nationhood, and let the name of Israel be mentioned no more." For they consult in their hearts together. The tents of Edom and the Ishmaelites, *Moab* and the Hagrites, Gebal and *Ammon* and Amalek, Philistia along with the residents of Tyre are cutting a pact against you. Assyria is also linked to them; they are an arm to the *children of Lot*. (Psalms 83:2–8)

Consulting over the hidden ones and cutting them off from nationhood so that the name of Israel is not mentioned anymore is repudiating deeper values entirely. The tents of Edom, the Ishmaelites, Moab, the Hagrites, Gebal, and Ammon are people who restrict themselves to the surfaces of worship and theology. Philistia along with Tyre is the fine words they speak about deeper qualities they do not bother to adopt. Assyria, the arm to Lot's descendants, is the rationalizations they use in fighting for superficiality and battling against anything deeper. [15] In Moses:

> A man shall not take his father's wife and shall not violate his father's wing; he shall not come severely crushed or bruised in the testicle into Jehovah's assembly. Neither a *Moabite* nor an *Ammonite* shall come into Jehovah's assembly; not even the tenth generation of them shall ever come into Jehovah's assembly. (Deuteronomy 22:30–23:7)

This shows clearly what Moab and Ammon are at the end of their days, or when they have become thoroughly steeped in falsity. Specifically, they are people in whom goodness has been adulterated and truth has been falsified by their contempt, their dismissal, and finally their utter repudiation of anything that has depth. That is why this passage mentions them after speaking about sordid types of adultery—taking the wife of one's father, and violating the "wing" of one's father. (These kinds of adultery are nearly the same as that ascribed to Lot's daughters, who gave birth to Moab and Ammon.) It also mentions them after speaking of men severely crushed or bruised in the testicle, who symbolize people that spurn any hint of love or charity. Jehovah's assembly is heaven, which they cannot enter because they have no remnant. It is only profound types of goodness and truth that produce a remnant, symbolized by the tenth generation (§§576, 1738, 2280).

[16] They were also among the nations that sacrificed their sons and daughters to Molech, which in an inner sense means that they wiped out truth and goodness. Moab's god was Chemosh, while the god of Ammon's descendants was Molech, or Milcom (1 Kings 11:7, 33; 2 Kings 23:13), to whom they sacrificed [their children] (2 Kings 3:27; on the point that sons and daughters symbolize truth and goodness, see §§489, 490, 491, 533, 1147).

[17] These things, then, are Moab and Ammon. The falsity they use in adulterating goodness and wiping out truth comes in many different kinds, which are listed in Jeremiah simply in the form of names, as follows:

> Judgment has come to the land of the plain—to *Holon* and to *Jahzah* and to *Mephaath,* and on *Dibon* and on *Nebo* and on *Beth-diblathaim,* and on *Kiriathaim* and on *Beth-gamul* and on *Beth-meon,* and on *Keri-oth* and on *Bozrah* and on all the cities of the *land of Moab* far and near. The horn of *Moab* has been cut off, and his arm has been broken. Get him *drunk,* because he made himself greater than Jehovah; and may *Moab* applaud in his own vomit. (Jeremiah 48:21–26)

These are the categories of falsity that come together in the people called Moab and Ammon. Exactly what their identity and character are, though, is visible from the symbolism of the individual names on an inner level. In the Word, names have a purely symbolic meaning, as shown many times.

The Power of Recall That We Keep after Death and Memories of What We Did during Bodily Life

2469   HARDLY anyone realizes yet that we each have two kinds of memory, one outer and one inner. Our outer memory belongs to our body, but our inner memory, to our spirit.

2470   While we are alive in our bodies, we can hardly even see that we have an inner memory, because during that time our inner power of recall acts almost in unison with our outer power. The individual thoughts that belong to our inner memory flow into the objects of our outer memory as containers designed for them. There the two kinds of memory unite.

The situation resembles the speech of angels and spirits with us. When they talk to us, the ideas they discuss among themselves flow into and unite with the words of our language. Their thoughts and our words combine so seamlessly that they themselves fully believe they are using our native tongue. In reality, though, the thoughts are theirs, while the words the thoughts flow into are ours.

I have talked with spirits about this phenomenon several times.

These two types of memory are completely different from one another. **2471**
Our outer memory is the one suited to us during our life in the world,
and it contains all vocabulary, impressions from the physical senses, and
worldly facts. Our inner memory contains the images that make up the
language of spirits (images seen by the inner eye) and all rational concepts
(whose ideas are the basis for thought itself).

Humankind does not realize that these two things are different from
one another, for two reasons. One is that we do not reflect on it. The other
is that bodily interests monopolize our attention, and as long as they do,
we have trouble drawing our minds up out of them.

That is why we can talk to each other only by using languages that are **2472**
broken up into distinct sounds (words) as long as we are living in our bodies. We cannot understand each other unless we know these languages,
because this kind of communication depends on the outer memory.

Spirits, on the other hand, talk to each other by means of a universal
language divided up into the ideas that compose thought itself. As a result
they can interact with any spirit, no matter what that spirit's language or
nationality had been in the world, because this kind of communication
depends on the inner memory.

We all take up this language directly after death, because we all become
aware of our inner memory, which (again) belongs to our spirit. See §§1637,
1639, 1757, 1876.

The inner memory is far superior to the outer memory. It compares **2473**
to the outer memory as a million compares to one, or as light compares to
darkness. Mental images by the tens of thousands from our inner memory enter into our outer memory as a single thought, where they present
one vague, general picture. The faculties that spirits have, then—both
their sensations and their thoughts and perceptions—are all fuller and
more perfect, and those of an angel are still more perfect.

Some examples can show how the inner memory is superior to the
outer. When you call to mind another person (friend or enemy) whose
character you know from years and years of personal dealings, what you
then think about that person presents itself as a single, vague picture. The
reason for the vagueness is that the thought rises from your outer memory. When you call that person to mind after you have become a spirit,
however, what you then think presents itself complete with all the impressions you have ever formed of her or him; and the reason for the richness
of thought is that it rises out of your inner memory.

The same is true in all other areas. Any subject you know about in depth presents itself to your outer memory as a single, dim whole but to your inner memory in all the detail you have ever acquired on it. What is more, it presents itself in the most amazing way.

2474   Whenever we hear, see, or feel touched by something, the picture we form of it and the goals we adopt concerning it are instilled in our inner memory without our awareness. There it stays, so that not a bit of it is lost, even if it is erased from our outer memory.

The inner memory, then, is such that everything—absolutely everything—we have ever thought, said, or done from early infancy to extreme old age is imprinted on it in the finest possible detail, even if it looks vague and shadowy to us.

When we go to the other world, we take the memory of all these things with us and are gradually led to recall each of them. This is our book of life, which is opened up in the other life and by which we are judged [Revelation 20:12–15]. People will have a hard time believing this, but it is absolutely true. All our purposes (which were unclear to us), all our thoughts, all our resulting words and deeds appear in that book, or in other words, in our inner memory, down to the smallest jot. Whenever the Lord allows it, they lie open clear as day for angels to view.

I have seen several demonstrations of this, and such a large number of my experiences bear it out that I have not a shred of doubt left.

2475   No one has yet recognized what the condition of a soul is after death in regard to its memory. Much experience over a long time (several years now) has taught me that after death we lose none of the information held in either kind of memory, outer or inner. Our retention is so full that nothing can be thought of, no matter how tiny or insignificant, that we do not take with us. When we die, then, we leave nothing behind at all but flesh and bones. These had no life of their own while we lived in the world but were animated by life from our spirit—our purer substance— which was merely linked with our physical parts.

2476   The case with our outer memory is that it contains everything about us in whole and in part; but after we die we are not allowed to use this memory, only our inner memory.

There are many reasons. The first, already given, is that in the next life our inner memory enables us to talk and interact with anyone anywhere. The second is that this memory belongs to our spirit and is suited to the state in which we then find ourselves, that of spirits. Things that are superficial—facts and worldly and bodily concerns—are suited to us here on earth and correspond to the state we experience when we are in the world and in our bodies. Deeper things—rational thoughts, spiritual concerns, and heavenly interests—are suited to spirits and correspond to them.

I once heard some spirits discussing the following idea among themselves: People can generate an endless supply of arguments in support of any premise they adopt, no matter what it is. Eventually, to those who have confirmed it for themselves, it can come to seem completely true, even if it is false. In fact, people are better at persuading themselves of falsity than of truth. To convince the spirits of this, I gave them a topic: I suggested they consider and discuss together whether it is helpful to spirits to use their outer memory. (Spirits are much better at discussing this kind of subject among themselves—each in accord with his or her own feelings—than we on earth could believe or even grasp.)

The spirits who were inclined toward bodily and worldly advantages argued copiously in favor of keeping the use of one's outer memory. These were their reasons: If they kept their outer memory, they would not be lacking anything they needed in order to be as human after death as before. They would also be able to come back into the world through that human side. Our outer memory supplies the highest joy in life. No other ability or gift provides us with understanding and wisdom. Not to mention many other points they piled up in support of their premise, until it seemed to them to be true.

[2] Others then thought and spoke for the opposite premise, knowing it was true because it agreed with the divine plan. This is what they said: If spirits were allowed to use their outer memory, they would suffer the same imperfections as before, when they were on earth. Under this system their ideas would be duller and dimmer than those of the inner memory. So they would not only grow more and more foolish, they would also sink lower instead of rising higher. Consequently they would not live forever, because to immerse themselves in worldly and bodily thinking would be to take on the condition of death. What is more, if spirits were allowed to use their outer memory, the human race would be destroyed. The Lord, you see, governs everyone on earth by means of spirits and angels. If spirits flowed into us from their outer memory, we would not be able to think from our own memory but only from theirs. So we would lose control of our own life and responsibility for ourselves and would be obsessed. This is exactly what obsession once was like. And so on with other arguments

2478 Two or three times, spirits were allowed to flow into me from their outer memory, in order for me to see what it would be like not to be able to think from one's own memory if they did. At those times I was fully convinced that what was not mine but the spirit's was really mine, and that what I had not thought before, I really had. I was not able to tell this was happening until they had left.

2479 One spirit, newly arrived, resented the fact that he could not remember much of what he had known during the life of his body. He was upset about the pleasures he had lost, which he had enjoyed tremendously. "You haven't lost a single, solitary thing," I told him. "You still have every bit of knowledge, but in the next life you don't have access to it. It's enough that you can now think and speak much better, much more perfectly. You will not be immersing your rational mind—as you did before—in the thick darkness of thinking based on matter and the body, which is useless in the realm you have now entered. You've left behind what belonged to the worldly realm and now possess everything you need for eternal life. This way and no other is the path to blessing and happiness.

"If you believe that all intelligent awareness dies in the other world when the use of your physical memory ends, you don't know anything. The reality is that the more we can draw our mind away from thoughts and urges rising out of our senses and body, the higher that awareness soars toward spiritual and heavenly ideas."

2480 It is because we have the use of our inner memory (which belongs to our rational mind) after death that people who in the world were more fluent than others in various languages cannot produce even a syllable of those languages. People with more book learning cannot produce a single fact, and are sometimes stupider than others.

Whatever we have absorbed by means of languages, however, and whatever we have absorbed through book learning has gone into the formation of our rational mind, so this we can put to use. The rationality we have gained from such sources is the basis of our thought and speech. If we have drunk falsity out of the cup of language and study, and have confirmed ourselves in it, falsity is the only basis for our logic. If we have drunk truth, though, we speak from truth. The desire is what gives it life. A desire for evil enlivens falsity, and a desire for goodness enlivens truth. Everyone thinks from desire; no one thinks without it.

2481 Much experience has taught me that people after death (spirits, in other words) have lost none of the contents of their outer or bodily memory.

Even though they are not allowed to dredge up the particulars of their life from it, they take with them their whole memory and everything in it, as the following account illustrates. Two men I had known during their physical lives met. They had been mutual enemies, and I heard one describing the other's personality to a crowd of bystanders and saying what his opinion of the man had been. He recited an entire letter the other had written to him, together with other details from his outer memory laid out in order. The other man acknowledged it all and remained silent.

Once I heard one man criticizing a second for having kept the first **2482** man's money and having refused to return it, describing the circumstances as recorded in his outer memory, to the second man's shame. I also heard the second man answer, going over the reasons he had done what he had. The whole conversation consisted of worldly particulars.

A certain woman was sent back into the state she had been in when **2483** she undertook to commit a crime in the world, and then everything she had thought and everything she had discussed with another woman came out clear as day.

One woman belonging to a company of sirens repeatedly denied that she had been the same kind of person during bodily life, and because of this she was taken back into the state of her physical memory. Her adulteries and offenses, which hardly anyone had been aware of during her life, were then laid open and listed in order, amounting to almost a hundred. The details of exactly where she was, whom she committed adultery with, and what she was trying to accomplish were all conveyed as vividly as if they lay open in broad daylight. In this way she was convicted.

Liabilities of this kind are brought out—with vivid realism, and with all the attendant circumstances—whenever we try to escape blame for what we have been.

Once a man I had not known in the life of his body was present with **2485** me. When I asked whether he knew where he came from, he said no. By means of my inner eyes, though, I led him through the cities where I was and finally through his home town. I took him through the streets and squares, all of which he recognized, and finally to the street where he had lived. If I had known how the houses were situated, I could even have known which was his.

Another piece of evidence for me that we take each and every bit of **2486** bodily memory with us has been an experience I very frequently had with people I knew during their bodily lives. When I would talk with them, they would recall everything they had done in my presence, everything they had said, and everything they had then thought.

These experiences and many others have taught me for certain that we carry all the contents of our outer or physical memory with us into the other world.

2487   I learned that the outer memory, regarded in itself, is just an organic phenomenon created by the objects of the senses (particularly sight and hearing) in the substances that are the origins of the nerve fibers. The impressions these objects make cause changes in form that can be reproduced. These forms vary and change as the state of a person's passions and persuasions changes.

The inner memory is also an organic phenomenon but a purer and more perfect one. It is formed from the objects of inner sight, arranged in certain patterns according to a design beyond our grasp.

2488   Like others, before personal experience taught me better, I supposed that no spirit could possibly see what was in my memory or in my thoughts. I imagined these things existed only inside me, well hidden. I can now attest, though, that the spirits present with us see and notice the very smallest elements of our memory and thoughts, and they do so much more clearly than we ourselves do. Angels even see our purposes. They observe how we swerve from good aims to bad ones, and from bad aims to good ones. They see far more of our intentions than we ourselves are aware of. They notice, for example, when we have immersed our intentions in the desire for pleasure and therefore in our own earthly character, so to speak. When we do this, we lose the ability to see what we are aiming at, because we can no longer raise our minds up above it to reflect on it.

Stop believing, then, that your thoughts are secret. Expect to be called to account for your thinking and also for your deeds, so far as they embody the nature of your thinking. (Our deeds derive their quality from our thoughts, and our thoughts, from our goals.)

2489   In the other world, the contents of the inner memory reveal themselves in a kind of aura that enables a spirit's character—a spirit's passions and persuasions—to be recognized at a distance. The aura arises out of the activity of the inner memory's contents. For more about these auras, see §§1048, 1053, 1316, 1504, and following sections.

2490   This is how it is with the inner memory: It holds not only everything we have ever seen or heard, everything we have thought, said or done from infancy on, but also the things we see and hear, and think, say, and do in the other life. There are differences in retention, however. People with distorted convictions and evil cravings soak up and retain whatever suits their convictions and cravings. They absorb it the way a sponge absorbs water. Other things do wash over them but so little is absorbed that the people hardly notice they exist. Individuals who believe what is true and love what is good, though, hold on to everything true and good and therefore are always being perfected. As a result they are capable of learning, and in the next life they do learn.

There are spirits who play the part of the inner memory. More will be said elsewhere about their place of origin, with the Lord's divine mercy. They wander about in crowds and have the most remarkable ways of drawing out other spirits' knowledge. Whatever they hear, they tell their friends.

2491

Sometimes the nature of the two kinds of memory is presented visually in the other world in forms that can be seen only there. (Many things are presented in visual images there that fall into mere thoughts with us.) The outer memory, then, presents itself to view in the form of a callus; the inner memory, in the form of a medullary substance like that of the human brain. These pictures also reveal what the two kinds of memory are like.

2492

With people who during physical life had put all their effort into memorization and so had failed to cultivate their rationality, the callus looks hard, and striated inside.

With people who had filled their memory with falsity, it seems to be covered with hair, because it contains a disorganized heap of ideas.

With people who had been prompted by conceit and greed to work at improving their memory, the callus looks as though it has been cemented together and hardened.

[2] With people who had wanted to pry into divine secrets by the use of factual knowledge (especially philosophy) and had refused to believe anything until persuaded by this knowledge, the callus looks very dark. The darkness is of a kind that absorbs rays of light and turns them into deep shadow.

With those who had been frauds and hypocrites, it looks as though it is made of bone and ebony that reflect rays of light.

With people who had devoted themselves to love with its goodness, on the other hand, and to faith with its truth, this kind of callus does not appear, because their inner memory sends rays of light into their outer memory. The light comes to rest in the objects of memory (or concepts) as its foundation, or its soil, and there it finds the most agreeable vessels to receive it. The outer memory is the last of a series, and when its contents are good and true, spiritual and heavenly influences gently come to rest in it and take up residence there.

2493   Talking with angels about the memory of the past and resulting worries about the future, I learned that the deeper and more perfect angels are, the less they care about the past or think about the future. That is why they are happy. From moment to moment, they said, the Lord shows them what to think and supplies them with blessings and happiness, so that they are free of worries and cares. This is what is meant in an inner sense by receiving manna from heaven *daily* [Exodus 16:4, 19–21], by the *daily* ration of bread mentioned in the Lord's Prayer [Matthew 6:11; Luke 11:3], and by being forbidden to worry about what we will eat or drink or how we will be clothed [Matthew 6:31].

Even though they do not care about the past or worry about the future, though, they still have a complete and perfect memory of the past and ability to see into the future, because for them the entire present moment holds both the past and the future. So they have a more perfect memory than could ever be imagined or expressed.

2494   While people who love the Lord and have charity for their neighbor are living in the world, they have angelic understanding and wisdom present inside, but it is hidden in the inmost depths of their inner memory. This understanding and wisdom remains completely invisible to them until they shed their bodies. Then the memory of particulars (described above [§§2481–2482]) goes to sleep, while they awaken into the use of their inner memory and eventually into the use of a truly angelic memory.

A Disclosure of

Secrets of Heaven

Contained in

Sacred Scripture

or

the Word of the Lord

Those in

Genesis
Chapter 20

Together with Amazing Things Seen and Heard
in the World of Spirits & in the Heaven of Angels

At the End of the Current Chapter, Those Having to Do with
The Lot and Condition in the Other World
of Nations and Peoples Born outside the Church

Genesis 20

IT has already been stated and demonstrated many times that the Word has an inner meaning that does not show in the literal meaning. The nature of the inner meaning becomes clear from the explanations given, starting with the first chapter of Genesis and continuing up to here.

Nonetheless, since not even the few today who believe in the Word realize that this kind of meaning exists, let me offer still more proof.

[2] The Lord describes the end of time (the last days of the church) in these terms:

> Immediately after the affliction of those days, the sun will go dark, and the moon will not shed its light, and the stars will fall down from the sky, and the powers of the heavens will be shaken. (Matthew 24:29; Mark 13:24, 25)

The sun here does not mean the sun, nor the moon, the moon, nor the stars, the stars. Instead, the sun symbolizes love for the Lord and charity toward our neighbor, the moon symbolizes the faith that comes of love and charity, and the stars symbolize knowledge of what is good and true. (This was demonstrated in §§31, 32, 1053, 1521, 1529, 1530, 1531, 2120, 2441.) So these words of the Lord's mean that at the end of time (in the last days), there will be no more love, no more charity, and therefore no more faith.

[3] Similar words of the Lord's in the Prophets show this to be the meaning, as in Isaiah:

Look—the day of Jehovah comes to make the earth a desert; and its
sinners he will destroy from it. For the *stars of the heavens* and their
constellations will not shed their light; *the sun will be shadowed over* in
its rising, and *the moon will not radiate light.* (Isaiah 13:9, 10)

This is also speaking of the church's last days, or the close of the age. In
Joel:

A day of shadow and darkness, a day of cloud and haze; before him the
earth shook. The heavens trembled, the *sun* and *moon* turned black,
and the *stars* gathered in their rays. (Joel 2:2, 10)

It is the same here. Elsewhere in the same author:

The *sun* will turn to darkness, and the *moon,* to blood, before the day of
Jehovah comes, great and fearsome. (Joel 2:31)

Again in the same author:

Near is the day of Jehovah; the *sun* and *moon* have gone black. And the
stars have withdrawn their rays. (Joel 3:14, 15)

In Ezekiel:

When I blot you out I will cover the heavens and blacken their *stars;*
the *sun* I will cover with a cloud, and the *moon will not make its glimmer shine.* All the *lamps of light* in the heavens I will blacken, and I will
bring darkness over your land. (Ezekiel 32:7, 8)

Likewise in John:

I looked as [the Lamb] opened the sixth seal, when suddenly a huge
earthquake occurred! And the sun turned black as sackcloth made of
hair, and the whole moon became like blood, and the stars fell onto the
earth. (Revelation 6:12, 13)

In the same author:

The fourth angel trumpeted, so that a third of the *sun* was struck and a
third of the *moon* and a third of the *stars,* and a third of them was shadowed over. (Revelation 8:12)

[4] These passages show that the Lord's words in the Gospels involve the
same thing as his words in the Prophets: that in the final days there will
be no charity or faith. From the same passages it can also be seen that this
is their inner meaning, as stands out still more clearly in Isaiah:

The *moon* will blush and the *sun* will feel shame because Jehovah Sabaoth will rule on Mount Zion and in Jerusalem. (Isaiah 24:23)

That is, faith (the moon) will blush and charity (the sun) will feel shame because that is what they are like. The moon and sun themselves cannot be said to blush or feel shame. And in Daniel:

The goat grew a horn toward the south and toward the sunrise, and it grew right to the *army of the heavens* and threw down to the ground some of the army and some of the *stars* and trampled them. (Daniel 8:9, 10)

Anyone can see that the army of the heavens here does not mean an army and that the stars do not mean stars.

Genesis 20

1. And Abraham traveled from there toward the land of the south and settled between Kadesh and Shur and stayed in Gerar.

2. And Abraham said [in regard] to Sarah his wife, "She is my sister"; and Abimelech, king of Gerar, sent and took Sarah.

3. And God came to Abimelech in a dream by night and said to him, "Look, you will die because of the woman that you took; and she is married to a husband."

4. And Abimelech had not gone near her, and he said, "Lord, will you kill even a righteous nation?

5. Didn't he say to me, 'She is my sister'? And she herself said, 'He is my brother.' In the integrity of my heart and in the blamelessness of my hands I did this."

6. And God said to him in a dream, "I do indeed know that you did this in the integrity of your heart, and indeed I kept you from sinning against me; therefore I did not give you [a chance] to touch her.

7. And now return the man's wife, because he is a prophet, and he will pray for you, and you will live. And if you do not return her, know that you will surely die, as will everyone who is yours."

8. And Abimelech got up early in the morning and called all his slaves and spoke all these words in their ears; and the men were extremely frightened.

9. And Abimelech called Abraham and said to him, "What have you done to us, and in what way have I sinned against you, that you have brought on me and on my kingdom an immense sin? Deeds that are not done you have done to me."

10. And Abimelech said to Abraham, "What have you seen, that you would do this thing?"

11. And Abraham said, "Because I said, 'Nevertheless there is no fear of God in this place, and they will kill me over the matter of my wife.'

12. And in addition she truly is my sister; she is my father's daughter—although not my mother's daughter—and she became my wife.

13. And it happened when God made me go from my father's house that I said to her, 'This is a kindness that you might do for me: every place that we come to, say [in relation] to me, "He is my brother."'"

14. And Abimelech took flock and herd, and male and female slaves, and gave them to Abraham, and restored to him Sarah his wife.

15. And Abimelech said, "Look: my land is before you; settle in the [part that is] good in your eyes."

16. And to Sarah he said, "Look, I have given a thousand pieces of silver to your brother; here now, for you it is a veil over the eyes of everyone who is with you, and of everyone [else], and you are vindicated."

17. And Abraham prayed to God, and God cured Abimelech and his wife and his female slaves, and they bore children,

18. because Jehovah had tightly closed every womb of Abimelech's house on that account, because of the matter of Sarah, wife of Abraham.

Summary

2496   CHAPTER 12 above [§§1401–1502] dealt with Abraham's stay in Egypt, which symbolized the secular knowledge the Lord acquired while he was still young.

The current chapter deals with Abraham's stay in Gerar, where Abimelech was. This period too symbolizes what the Lord learned, but what he learned about the doctrines concerning charity and faith.

In particular, the subject here is the *source* of the teachings about charity and faith. To be specific, those teachings are spiritual and come from a heavenly origin, not from logic.

2497   The text describes what the Lord's state was when he first started to inform himself about the doctrines concerning charity and faith. Kadesh and Shur symbolize the state itself; Abimelech, king of Gerar, symbolizes teachings on faith (verses 1, 2). At first the Lord considered inquiring of his rational mind (verse 2) but in the end did not (verses 3, 4, 8, 9). The reasons he thought this way (verses 5, 6, 10, 11, 12, 13). The doctrine concerning charity and faith is spiritual and comes from a heavenly origin (verse 7). That is what he was taught; and all logic and all factual knowledge then served him, the way a veil or garment would (verses 14, 15, 16). This completed and perfected his theology (verse 17). It would have gone differently if he had relied on logic (verse 18).

Inner Meaning

THE narrative details here, as everywhere else in the Word, hold divine secrets within them, as can be seen from the fact that Abraham called his wife his sister for a second time now. He did the same thing when he arrived in Egypt, since he then said to Sarah, "Please say you are my sister" (Genesis 12:13). Not only did Abraham do this but when Isaac arrived in Gerar he too said his wife Rebekah was his sister: "The men of the place asked about his wife, and he said, 'She's my sister'" (Genesis 26:6, 7). Many similar events recur in the same chapters, so that the same story is told three times, which never would have happened if the inner meaning had not provided a secret reason for it. **2498**

Genesis 20:1. *And Abraham traveled from there toward the land of the south and settled between Kadesh and Shur and stayed in Gerar.* **2499**

Abraham traveled from there toward the land of the south symbolizes the progress the Lord made in the good qualities and true ideas taught by faith; *Abraham* is the Lord at that stage. *And settled between Kadesh and Shur* is a specific symbol for the stage he had reached. *Kadesh* is a desire for the deeper truth that develops out of rational thinking; *Shur* is a desire for the more superficial truth that develops out of facts. *And stayed in Gerar* symbolizes what he learned about the spiritual aspects of faith.

Abraham traveled from there toward the land of the south symbolizes the progress the Lord made in the good qualities and true ideas taught by faith. This can be seen from the symbolism of *traveling* as making progress (mentioned at §1457), and from that of the *land of the south* **2500** as the goodness and truth of religion (mentioned at §1458). Chapter 12 above said that Abraham "traveled, going and traveling toward the south" when he went to Egypt (Genesis 12:9, 10). In an inner sense this meant that when the Lord was young he advanced into goodness and truth so far as his study of religious knowledge went (1456, 1459). The current verse says that Abraham traveled toward the land of the south, meaning further and deeper advancement, or in other words, progress in the goodness and truth taught by faith. That is why it says "the land of the south" here, because in its truest sense the land means the church, which is what doctrine exists for (566, 662, 1066, 2117, 2118).

[2] So far as the Lord's education in general goes, the nature it had shines out from the inner meaning of the current chapter. To be specific, he was taught through constant revelations and so through divine perceptions and thoughts originating in himself—in his divine side, that is. These thoughts and perceptions he introduced into his human understanding and wisdom until his human side achieved perfect oneness with his divine side. This path to wisdom is never open to any human being because what flowed into the Lord came from divinity itself (his inmost core), because it came from the Father, from whom he was conceived. So it came from divine love itself, which belonged to the Lord alone and was a desire to save the whole human race.

[3] Wisdom and understanding resides in love itself—a secret that hardly anyone knows yet—but its nature depends on the nature of the love. The reason wisdom and understanding resides in love is that anything that flows in flows into what we love or, to put it another way, what we see as good. So it flows into our very life. The wisdom and understanding of the angels, which is indescribable, comes from such inflow. So does that of people who love the Lord and show charity for their neighbor. Even if they cannot detect wisdom and understanding in themselves while they are living in their bodies, they come into the use of it after death, because it is present in love and charity itself. (See §2494.)

As for the Lord's love, it was infinitely far above the love that angels have, because it was divine love itself. Accordingly, it had the supreme distinction of containing within itself all wisdom and understanding. Still, since he was born human and was to develop like other humans, in accord with the divine plan, he led himself into the use of this gift gradually. In this way he was able to unite his humanity with his divinity and make it divine, and to do so under his own power.

2501   *Abraham* is the Lord at that stage. This is established by the representation of Abraham as the Lord—here, as the Lord at that stage, which is what he also represented earlier (§§1893, 1965, 1989, [2010,] 2011, 2172, 2198).

And settled between Kadesh and Shur is a specific symbol for the stage he had reached. This can be seen from the symbolism of *settling* or residing as living, a symbolism discussed in §1293. What comes before also points to this as the meaning. The text said, "Abraham traveled from there toward the land of the south," which symbolizes the progress the Lord made in the good qualities and true ideas taught by faith. Now it says that he settled between Kadesh and Shur, and it follows that this is in fact a specific symbol for the stage he had reached. That stage is depicted by Kadesh and Shur, to be discussed next. **2502**

Kadesh is a desire for the deeper truth that develops out of rational thinking, and *Shur* is a desire for the more superficial truth that develops out of facts, as can be seen from the symbolism of Kadesh and Shur. It has already been shown in §1678 that Kadesh symbolizes truth that is in dispute. So it symbolizes disputes over the origin of truth and whether it develops out of rational thinking, as becomes clear below. In the Lord, however, all truth came from a heavenly origin, so Kadesh symbolizes a *desire* for truth. **2503**

All religious people possess rational truth and factual truth. Rational truth is deeper; factual truth is shallower. The two differ in exactly the same way our two kinds of memory do, as described in §§2469–2473 and later sections. It follows, then, that there are also two kinds of desire for truth: a deeper desire, for rational truth, and a shallower desire, for factual truth. Kadesh here symbolizes a desire for the deeper truth that develops out of rational thinking, while Shur symbolizes a desire for the more superficial truth that develops out of facts. On the point that Shur symbolizes this kind of truth, see §1928.

It has been demonstrated already that names in the Word actually have a symbolic meaning (§§1224, 1264, 1876, 1888, and many times elsewhere).

And stayed in Gerar symbolizes what he learned about the spiritual aspects of faith. This can be seen from the following: *Staying* as an immigrant symbolizes being taught, as discussed in §§1463, 2025. And *Gerar* symbolizes the spiritual quality of faith. **2504**

Several passages in Genesis (10:19; 26:1, 6, 17, 20, 26) mention *Gerar,* and in them it symbolizes faith. Gerar was in Philistia, and Philistia symbolizes a knowledge of religious concepts (see §§1197, 1198). Gerar was also the place where the king of the Philistines himself lived, and that is why Gerar symbolizes faith itself (1209). The king of Gerar symbolizes the truth itself that is taught by faith, since in an inner sense a monarch is truth (1672, 2015, 2069). So Abimelech symbolizes the doctrine concerning faith, as dealt with below [2509–2510].

[2] Speaking generally, there are things we understand about religion through higher intuition, things we grasp rationally, and things we merely know about. This is the order the three come in, from inward to outward. The inmost aspect of faith is described as intuitional. What develops out of it is the rational aspect of faith, and what develops out of both of these again is the factual aspect of faith. These relate to each other as prior to posterior (to use the scholarly terms), or higher to lower, or inward to outward.

Admittedly, the aspect that seems to us to come first is factual knowledge about religion. A rational grasp seems to grow out of that knowledge, and intuitive understanding to develop last. The reason for this appearance is that these are the steps we take from youth onward. Even so, higher intuition is continually acting on the rational level, which is continually acting on the factual level, although we do not realize it. In our youth the influence of the higher levels is dim and vague; in our adulthood it is plainer; and finally, when we have been reborn, it is strikingly clear. Regenerate people can see that this is the arrangement, and in the other world they see it even better. (See §1495.)

All these factors are called spiritual aspects, which are divided (as explained) among the various levels and follow one another in order. The spiritual aspect of religion is composed exclusively of truth that stems from goodness or in other words, from a heavenly source. Anything that branches off from what is heavenly is a spiritual element of faith.

2505   Genesis 20:2. *And Abraham said [in regard] to Sarah his wife, "She is my sister"; and Abimelech, king of Gerar, sent and took Sarah.*

Abraham said symbolizes the Lord's thoughts. *[In regard] to Sarah his wife* symbolizes spiritual truth united to what is heavenly. *She is my sister* symbolizes rational truth. *And Abimelech, king of Gerar, sent* symbolizes teachings about faith; *Abimelech* is teachings that describe faith in rational terms. *And took Sarah* symbolizes a desire to consult logic.

2506   *Abraham said* symbolizes thoughts. This can be seen from the symbolism of *saying* in the narratives as perceiving and also thinking (discussed in §§1898, 1919, 2061, 2080, 2238, 2260, 2271, 2287).

2507   *[In regard] to Sarah his wife* symbolizes spiritual truth united to what is heavenly. This is established by the fact that *Sarah* as *wife* symbolizes intuitive truth united to divine goodness or, to put the same thing another way, spiritual truth united to what is heavenly. This is discussed at §§1468, 1901, 2063, 2065, 2172, 2173, 2198.

Spirituality and heavenliness have been defined quite often before; see §§1155, 1577, 1824, 2048, 2088. Whatever has to do with goodness, or in other words, with love for the Lord and charity for our neighbor, is called heavenly. Whatever has to do with truth, or in other words, with the faith that comes of love and charity, is called spiritual.

She is my sister symbolizes rational truth. This can be seen from the symbolism of a *sister* as intuitive rational truth, discussed at §1495.

2508

Only from the heavenly marriage can it be seen that rational truth is a sister. The attributes born from that marriage, you see, have closer or more distant ties to each other resembling those of blood relatives and other kin on earth, with unlimited variety. For more on this, see §§685, 917.

The real heavenly marriage forms only between divine goodness and divine truth. From that marriage, understanding and reason and knowledge are conceived in us. Unless these abilities are conceived from the heavenly marriage, we cannot possibly be endowed with them. As a result, we cannot possibly be human. So the more we draw on the heavenly marriage, the more human we are.

The heavenly marriage exists in the Lord himself, so that the Lord is that marriage itself, since he is both divine goodness and divine truth. Angels and people participate in the heavenly marriage to the extent that they dedicate themselves to love for the Lord, charity for their neighbor, and therefore faith. In other words, they participate in the heavenly marriage to the extent that they adopt the Lord's goodness and therefore his truth. When they do, they are called daughters and sons, and sisters and brothers to each other, although with differences.

The reason rational truth is called a sister is that it is conceived when divine goodness flows into a desire for rational truth. The goodness produced in the rational mind by this union is called a brother, and the truth produced there is called a sister. But this will be easier to see from Abraham's words in verse 12 of the current chapter: "And in addition she truly is my sister; she is my father's daughter—although not my mother's daughter—and she became my wife."

And Abimelech, king of Gerar, sent symbolizes teachings about faith, as established by statements above at §2504: Philistia symbolizes a knowledge of religious concepts (1197, 1198). *Gerar,* which was in Philistia, symbolizes faith (1209, 2504). A *king* symbolizes religious truth itself (1672, 2015, 2069). So *Abimelech* symbolizes teachings on faith, but teachings

2509

that describe faith in rational terms, as will become clear from the remarks just below.

2510   *Abimelech* is teachings that describe faith in rational terms. This can be seen from the fact that he viewed Sarah not as Abraham's wife but as Abraham's sister, and Sarah in her role as sister symbolizes rational truth (§2508). The same meaning is also evident from what follows [§§2516–2517, 2519], since it deals with the question of whether the doctrine of faith traces its origin to logic or to something heavenly. Abimelech, then, symbolizes teachings that view faith in logical terms.

Doctrine is said to turn toward logic when we acknowledge a teaching as true only if we can grasp it rationally, with the result that we examine all aspects of doctrine from the point of view of logic. However, the doctrine of faith does not develop out of logic but comes from a heavenly origin, as the inner meaning of the rest of the story will teach.

2511   *And took Sarah* symbolizes a desire to consult logic, as can be seen from the following: *Sarah* as a sister symbolizes rational truth, as discussed at §2508. And *taking* her indicates a desire for her and therefore, in an inner sense, a desire to consult logic.

The contents of the current verse involve the Lord's first thoughts about teachings on faith, whether it would be appropriate to consult his rational mind or not. The reason these were his first thoughts on the subject is that the Lord proceeded in entire accord with the divinely ordained plan. He had to strip himself of every merely human attribute he was born into and inherited from his mother, so that he could robe himself in divinity. Accordingly, he had to rid himself of this human question as well—whether to consult logic in regard to doctrinal teachings about faith.

2512   Genesis 20:3. *And God came to Abimelech in a dream by night and said to him, "Look, you will die because of the woman that you took; and she is married to a husband."*

God came to Abimelech symbolizes the Lord's perception concerning the doctrine of faith. *In a dream by night* symbolizes a dim one. *And said to him* symbolizes the resulting thought. *Look, you will die because of the woman* means that the doctrine of faith would cease to exist if he consulted logic in regard to its teachings. *And she is married to a husband* means that the true doctrine of faith is spiritual, and its teachings are wedded to something heavenly.

2513   *God came to Abimelech* symbolizes the Lord's perception concerning the doctrine of faith, as can be seen from the symbolism of *God's coming* and of *Abimelech.* Obviously *God's coming* symbolizes perceiving, because perception is simply God's arrival in or inflow into our intellect. *Abimelech* symbolizes the doctrine of faith, as shown above at §§2504, 2509, 2510.

In a dream by night symbolizes a dim perception, as can be seen from the symbolism of a *dream* and also of *night.* When the topic being discussed is perception, a *dream* (as compared to wakefulness) symbolizes something dim, especially when it is called a dream *by night.*   **2514**

The reason the Lord's first perception is being described as dim is that it came to his human side, and his human nature is what he had to rid himself of and clear away the shadows from. Although the Lord's perceptive ability came to him from his divine side, he received it in his human side, and human nature is such that it cannot receive true light in an instant but gradually, as the shadows in it are chased away. This vagueness in regard to teachings concerning faith did diminish, as symbolized in verse 6, which says that God returned to Abimelech in a dream but does not mention night. Eventually the Lord came into a clear perception, as symbolized by Abimelech's getting up early in the morning in verse 8.

And said to him symbolizes the resulting thought—that is, the thought produced by the perception. This can be seen from the symbolism of *saying* as perceiving and as thinking, a symbolism treated of above at §2506.   **2515**

Since I say here that the thought resulted from a perception, let me tell briefly how matters stand with thought.

Thoughts come from perception, from conscience, or from lack of conscience.

Thoughts produced by perception are possible only for those who are heavenly, or in other words, for those who love the Lord. It is the deepest kind of thinking to exist in humans and is present in heavenly angels in heaven. Perception from the Lord is the means and source of their thoughts. They cannot go against perception in their thinking.

Thoughts produced by conscience are not as lofty. They exist with those who are spiritual, or in other words, with those committed both in life and in belief to the doing of good out of charity and faith. Thought that goes against conscience is similarly impossible for them, because it goes against what the Lord tells them is good and true through their conscience.

[2] *Thoughts produced by lack of conscience,* however, exist in people who do not allow themselves to be ruled inwardly by goodness or truth but by evil and falsity. That is, they do not allow themselves to be ruled by the Lord but by themselves.

These last believe they think within themselves just as clearly as people who think from perception or conscience, because they do not know what conscience is, let alone perception. The difference, though, is as vast as that between hell and heaven. When people think thoughts devoid of conscience, they are inspired by all kinds of craving and delusion and so by hell. If they have any other inspiration, it is a desire to look good on the outside, for the sake of their reputation. When people think conscientious thoughts, on the other hand, they are inspired by a desire for goodness and truth and so by heaven.

The Lord's thoughts, however, transcended all human understanding, because they came directly from his divine nature.

2516   *Look, you will die because of the woman* means that the doctrine of faith would cease to exist if he consulted logic in regard to its teachings, as can be seen from the following: Abimelech *(you)* symbolizes the doctrine of faith. *Dying* means ceasing to exist. And a sister (called *the woman* here) symbolizes rationality, [or logic,] as discussed at §2508. Consequently, the idea that Abimelech would die because of the woman means that the doctrine of faith would cease to exist if logic were consulted.

[2] Logic does not yield teachings about faith because it focuses on what appears to be good and true, and these appearances are not actual truths, as shown before in §§2053, 2196, 2203, 2209. Besides, logic has an underpinning of illusions gathered from physical sensations confirmed by secular knowledge, which cast a shadow over those appearances. For the most part, logic is merely human, as even its birth shows. That is why no doctrine concerning faith can start with logic, much less be built on it. Instead, it must emanate from the divinity itself and divine humanity of the Lord. This is its source. In fact, the Lord *is* that doctrine itself, which is why the Word calls him the Word, the Truth, the Light, the Way, and the Door. It is a secret that every doctrinal teaching comes from divine goodness and divine truth and has the heavenly marriage inside it. If there is a doctrine that does not have the heavenly marriage inside it, it is not a genuine doctrine of faith. That is why the Word (the source of doctrine) contains an image of marriage at every point; see §§683, 793, 801.

[3] It is true that teachings about faith as they appear in the Word's literal or surface meaning seem to contain much of a rational nature, and even of an earthly nature. This, however, is because the Word is written for people on earth and is therefore adapted to them. In itself, the doctrine of faith is spiritual and comes from a heavenly origin. In other words, it comes from divine truth united to divine goodness.

What follows will provide examples to illustrate the idea that doctrine would cease to exist if logic were consulted in regard to its teachings.

She is married to a husband means that the true doctrine of faith is **2517** spiritual, and its teachings are wedded to something heavenly, as can be seen from the symbolism of being *married to a husband.* When a *husband* is mentioned by name in the Word, he symbolizes goodness and his wife symbolizes truth. Circumstances change when a husband is called a man, though. Then he symbolizes truth and his wife symbolizes goodness; see §915 and other sections. So in the current verse, Sarah's being married to a husband means that truth is united to goodness, and in such a way that that truth actually *is* goodness.

The same meaning can also be seen from the symbolism of Sarah as a wife, in that she is spiritual truth, and of Abraham, in that he is heavenly goodness, both of these being divine (discussed at §§2501, 2507). Since Sarah symbolizes divine, spiritual truth, as a wife she also means the true doctrine of faith itself, because doctrine is composed of truth.

Clearly, then, "she is married to a husband" means that the true doctrine of faith is spiritual, and its teachings are wedded to something heavenly.

Genesis 20:4. And Abimelech had not gone near her, and he said, "Lord, **2518** *will you kill even a righteous nation?"*

Abimelech had not gone near her means that in regard to the doctrine of faith [the Lord] had not consulted rational truth in any way. *And he said, "Lord, will you kill even a righteous nation?"* means, will everything good and true about this doctrine be wiped out?

Abimelech had not gone near her means that in regard to the doctrine **2519** of faith he had not consulted rational truth in any way, as established by the following: *Abimelech* symbolizes the doctrine of faith, as discussed at §§2504, 2509, 2510. And *going near her* (near Sarah as Abraham's sister, that is) means touching rational truth (Abraham's sister), or in other words, consulting it in any way (§§1495, 2508).

The reason he did not consult logic in any way was given before: teachings about faith all come from divinity, which is infinitely far above human logic. The rational mind receives its goodness and truth from divinity. Divinity can enter into logic but not the reverse. Likewise the soul can enter into the body and shape it, but the body cannot enter into the soul. Again, light can enter shadow and turn it different colors, but shadow cannot enter into light.

It does at first appear as though rationality ought to be involved, since that is what receives [doctrine]. As a result, the Lord's first thought here was to wonder whether it should in fact be consulted. He answered himself, however, by revealing that if it was, the doctrine would cease to exist. Accordingly, he did not consult it, which is meant here by "Abimelech had not gone near her."

2520   *And he said, "Lord, will you kill even a righteous nation?"* means, will everything good and true [about this doctrine] be wiped out? This can be seen from the symbolism of a *nation* as goodness (discussed in §§1259, 1260, 1416). Since the question is asked concerning the nation of Abimelech, who symbolizes the doctrine of faith, the *righteous nation* means truth as well as goodness, since doctrine teaches both.

[2] Obviously these words reflect a tender, loving zeal for the whole human race. The same love guided the Lord's thinking even when the human nature he had inherited from his mother came to the fore. Although he perceived from his divine side that the doctrines concerning faith come exclusively from a heavenly origin, he still wanted to look out for the human race. And we humans do not accept anything unless we can form some idea of it in our rational mind. That is why the text says, "Will you kill even a righteous nation?" meaning, will everything good and true taught by this doctrine be wiped out?

The thoughts we cherish concerning divine mysteries show that we do not accept anything unless we can form some idea of it in our rational mind. Some mental image of physical objects, or of things resembling physical objects, always clings to these thoughts. The image allows us to hold it in our memory and call it forth for consideration. Without some idea derived from physical objects, we cannot possibly think a single thought. As a consequence, if we were presented with the naked truth springing from a divine origin, we would never accept it. It would entirely exceed our grasp and therefore our belief—especially for those of us whose worship is superficial.

[3] Take the following examples by way of illustration:

Divinity itself can reside only in a divine being, so it can reside only in the Lord's divine humanity and through this with us. If we asked our rational mind, it would say that divinity itself can dwell in anyone's humanity.

Again, nothing holy exists except what comes from the Lord and so from a single, united Deity. If we used reasoning to examine this, we would say it could come from other sources.

[4] Again, we do not live on our own, do good on our own, or believe what is true on our own. We do not even think on our own. No, what is good and true comes from the Lord, while what is evil and false comes

from hell. Furthermore, not even hell thinks on its own, or rather not even the people in hell, but instead they likewise receive the Lord's goodness and truth. If we consulted logic, it would not comprehend the idea and so would reject it.

Once again, no one will be rewarded for doing what is good or teaching what is true. The outward act does not matter, only what is inside. What counts is how much of a passion for goodness is present in our doing of good, how much of a passion for the truth that comes from goodness is present in our teaching of truth, and how little of either is for our own sake. I could continue with a thousand other examples.

[5] Since this is what human rationality is like, the Word speaks in terms that we can understand and that suit our bent of mind. That is why the Word's inner meaning is different from its literal meaning. The Old Testament Word makes this fairly clear, since it speaks mostly in terms suited to the grasp and to the character of the people then living. This explains why it says so little—almost nothing—about life after death, eternal salvation, or the inner self. The people of Judah and Israel, with whom the church then existed, were such that if these subjects had been unveiled, they would not only have failed to understand them but would even have laughed at them. By the same token, if it had been disclosed to them that the Messiah, or Christ, was coming to save their souls forever, they would have rejected this too as inane. The same race as it exists today makes this clear. Even now, if you mention anything deep or spiritual to them, or tell them the Messiah will not be the supreme leader on earth, they sneer. [6] That is why the Lord's words so often resembled the prophets', and why even when they did not he spoke in parables, as he himself says in Matthew:

> Jesus said, "I speak to them in parables, because seeing, they do not see, and hearing, they do not hear or understand." (Matthew 13:13)

These people who see and hear are those in the church who, although they see and hear, still do not understand. And in John:

> He has blinded their eyes and closed off their heart to prevent them from seeing with their eyes and understanding at heart and turning and being healed by me. (John 12:40)

To say they would turn and be healed involves the idea that they would still reject his words in the end and profane them in the process, which carries eternal damnation with it. See §§301, 302, 303, 582, 1008, 1010,

1059, 1327, 1328, 2051, 2426. Still, the Lord revealed the inner depths of the Word in many places, but only for those wise enough to see.

2521   Genesis 20:5. *"Didn't he say to me, 'She is my sister'? And she herself said, 'He is my brother.' In the integrity of my heart and in the blamelessness of my hands I did this."*

Didn't he say to me? symbolizes his excuse for thinking this way. *"She is my sister"* means that logic was what he needed to consult. *And she herself said, "He is my brother,"* means that his rational mind itself told him so, saying that heavenly goodness would be attached to it. *In the integrity of my heart* means that he thought this way in innocence and simple goodness. *And in the blamelessness of my hands I did this* means in his desire for truth and therefore to the full extent of his ability.

2522   *Didn't he say to me?* symbolizes his excuse for thinking this way, as can be seen from everything the verse says and from the symbolism of *saying* as thinking, a symbolism mentioned in §2506.

2523   *She is my sister* means that logic was what he needed to consult—in other words, he had been thinking that logic was what he needed to consult. This can be seen from the symbolism of a *sister* in the current chapter as rational truth, a symbolism explained at §§1495, 2508.

The inner meaning of the Word tells what the Lord's whole future life in the world would be like, even down to his perceptions and thoughts. These were foreseen and provided for because they came from his divine side. The point in describing them was also to render them present at that time before the eyes of angels, who perceive the Word according to its inner meaning. The description would also present them with a picture of the Lord and the process by which he gradually laid aside his humanity and took on divinity. Unless these things had been kept before the eyes of angels by the Word and by all the rituals of the Jewish religion, the Lord would have had to come into the world immediately after the fall of the earliest church, called Humankind, or Adam. (A prophecy of the Lord's Coming did occur right then, as recorded in Genesis 3:15.) What is more, the human race as it then existed could not have been saved.

[2] As for the Lord's actual life, it consisted of the continual progress his human side made in approaching his divine side until they achieved absolute oneness, as noted many times before [§§1864, 2033]. It was from his human side that he had to fight and conquer the hells, because divinity never fights them. He chose, then, to clothe himself in a humanity like any other person's, to be a baby like any other, and to grow in secular and religious knowledge, as represented and symbolized by Abraham's stays in

Egypt (Genesis 12) and now Gerar. So like any other human he cultivated his rational mind, dispelling its clouds in the process and bringing it into the light; and all this he did under his own power.

You cannot doubt that the Lord advanced this way from humanity to divinity if you simply consider that he was a baby, learned to talk as a baby does, and so on. There *was* a difference, however: he had divinity itself inside him, since he was conceived by Jehovah.

She herself said, "He is my brother," means that his rational mind itself **2524** told him that heavenly goodness would be attached to it. This can be seen from the symbolism of a sister—*she herself*—as rationality (§§1495, 2508), and from that of a *brother* as the goodness that comes of truth (§§367, 2508).

Divine goodness and divine truth are united to one another in a kind of marriage. Their union gives rise to the heavenly marriage, and also to marital love even as it exists at the lower levels of creation. The goodness and truth of the rational mind, however, are bound to one another not in a kind of marriage but by the sort of blood tie that exists between brother and sister. The reason they are siblings is that rational truth is conceived when divine goodness acts on the desire for secular facts and religious knowledge (see §§1895, 1902, 1910), but good is conceived in the rational mind when divine goodness acts on that truth. Truth in the rational mind actually turns into the goodness that belongs to charity, and this goodness is the brother of faith or, to put it another way, of truth (§367).

[2] Rational goodness compares to rational truth in this way: rational goodness comes from divine goodness, but rational truth does not come from divine truth. We amass rational truth by means of facts and religious knowledge, which enter in through our senses, whether outer or inner, and so by an external route. As a result, many illusions acquired through our senses cling to rational truth and make it untrue. Still, when divine goodness acts on it and brings it to conception, it appears to be true and is acknowledged as true, even though it is only apparently true.

The shadows hovering in that truth then modify the goodness itself present there, and the nature of the goodness comes to resemble that of the truth. This is one secret that lies hidden in the verse—that the Lord's rational mind itself told him so, saying that heavenly goodness would be attached to it.

In the integrity of my heart means that he thought this way in inno- **2525** cence and simple goodness, as can be seen from the symbolism of *integrity* and of the *heart*

In the original language, *integrity* is expressed by a word that also means wholeness, perfection, and simplicity. The *heart* symbolizes love and charity, which relate to goodness, as everyone knows. That is why *in integrity of heart* means in innocence and simple goodness.

2526   *And in the blamelessness of my hands I did this* means in his desire for truth and therefore to the full extent of his ability, as can be seen from the symbolism of *blamelessness* and of *hands*. In the original language, blamelessness is expressed by a word that also means cleanliness and purity. *Hands* are mentioned in connection with truth and symbolize power, so they also symbolize ability (§878).

"In the integrity of my heart and blamelessness of my hands I did this," then, means that he thought this way in innocence and simple goodness, in his desire for truth, and therefore to the full extent of his ability. The reason it means this is that innocence renders goodness good, and goodness renders truth true, and when these are in order within us, we have a full range of ability. Clearly such ideas are involved in these words. After all, an upright, whole, or perfect heart, symbolizing goodness, is not possible unless innocence is present in the goodness, as noted, making it a simple goodness. Blameless, clean, or pure hands, mentioned in connection with truth, are not possible unless goodness is present in the truth, as also noted. This is to say that they are not possible unless a desire for truth is present. When we act with innocence and goodness and truth, we act to the full extent of our ability or power, which is also what hands symbolize (§878).

2527   Genesis 20:6. *And God said to him in a dream, "I do indeed know that you did this in the integrity of your heart, and indeed I kept you from sinning against me; therefore I did not give you [a chance] to touch her."*

God said to him in a dream symbolizes a perception that was less dim. *I do indeed know that you did this in the integrity of your heart* here as before means that he thought this way in innocence and in simple goodness, so that he was not to blame. *And indeed I kept you from sinning against me* means that no harm had been done. *Therefore I did not give you [a chance] to touch her* means that he had not consulted logic at all.

2528   *God said to him in a dream* symbolizes a perception that was less dim, as can be seen from the remarks and explanations above at §2514.

The reason this chapter speaks of God rather than Jehovah (except in the final verse) is that it is talking about something spiritual: doctrinal teachings about faith. Under these circumstances the name God is used, but when the subject is something heavenly—love and charity, in other words—the name Jehovah is used. See §§709, 732, 2001.

I do indeed know that you did this in the integrity of your heart means **2529** that he thought this way in innocence and in simple goodness, as established by the remarks above at §§2525, 2526, where the same words occur.

The text does not add "in the blamelessness of your hands" as above, for a secret reason: the desire for truth symbolized by the blamelessness of Abimelech's hands had a human element in it. Truth, you see, was instilled in the Lord partly through the human nature he received at birth, but his goodness came from divinity alone. This can be seen from the way goodness and truth emerged in his rational mind (§2524).

Indeed I kept you from sinning against me means that no harm had **2530** been done. That is, logic had not been consulted concerning the doctrine of faith, as the next clause also indicates. This can be seen without explanation.

Therefore I did not give you [a chance] to touch her means that he had **2531** not consulted logic at all, as can be seen from the following: *Giving [a chance] to touch* means consulting, as going near her also did, above at verse 4, §2519. And *Sarah as Abraham's sister—her*—symbolizes something rational, as discussed at §§1495, 2508.

[2] To see further how matters stand with teachings on faith—that they are spiritual and come from a heavenly origin—you need to know that they consist of divine truth derived from divine goodness. So they are divine through and through.

Anything divine lies beyond our grasp, because it surpasses all understanding, even the angels'. Still, this divine idea, which in itself is beyond our grasp, can enter our rational mind through the Lord's divine humanity. When it does, we receive it according to the truth we have in that part of our mind. So we receive it in various ways, one person differently than another. The more genuine the truth we possess, then, the more perfect our reception of the divine influence and the fuller our enlightenment.

[3] The Lord's Word contains real truth. Its literal meaning, though, contains truth adapted to the comprehension of people whose worship is shallow, while its inner meaning contains truth adapted for people with depth—people whose theology and life are both angelic. The rational minds of the latter consequently brim with so much light that it rivals the brilliance of the stars and sun (Daniel 12:3; Matthew 13:43). This shows how important it is for us to learn about and accept inner truth. Although

we can learn about such truth, we can never accept it unless we love or at least believe in the Lord. Just as he is divine goodness, he is also divine truth, and therefore he is the real doctrine. After all, everything the true doctrine of faith teaches looks to the Lord. It also looks to his kingdom, the church, and different features of his heavenly kingdom and the church; but all of these belong to him. They constitute intermediate goals, which look to the ultimate goal: the Lord.

[4] In John, the Lord himself teaches that he is the real doctrine, in respect to both its goodness and its truth, and doctrine therefore looks to him alone:

> Jesus said, "I am the way, the truth, and life." (John 14:6, 7)

The way is doctrine; the truth is everything doctrine teaches; life is everything good that gives life to truth. The Lord also teaches in John that love for him or at least faith in him is what accepts him:

> His own did not accept him. As many as did accept, though, to them he gave the power to be God's children, to those believing in his name, who had their birth not from blood or from the will of the flesh or from a man's will but from God. (John 1:11, 12, 13)

Those who have their birth from God are people who love and therefore believe.

2532   Genesis 20:7. *"And now return the man's wife, because he is a prophet, and he will pray for you, and you will live. And if you do not return her, know that you will surely die, as will everyone who is yours."*

Now return the man's wife means that he was to render the spiritual truth of doctrine safe from the harm of logic. *Because he is a prophet* means that then it would be taught. *And he will pray for you* means a revelation would result. *And you will live* means the doctrine would come alive as a result. *And if you do not return her,* here as before, means if he did not render the spiritual truth of doctrine safe from the harm of logic. *Know that you will surely die* means that any doctrine teaching truth or goodness would cease. *As will everyone who is yours* means together with everything it embraced.

2533   *Now return the man's wife* means that he was to render the spiritual truth of doctrine safe from the harm of logic, as can be seen from the following: A *wife* symbolizes spiritual truth, as discussed in §2507. And a *man* symbolizes doctrine itself. When Abraham, who represents the Lord at that stage, is called a man, he symbolizes heavenly truth, which is the same as doctrine from a heavenly origin. After all, in an inner sense a man means a property of the intellect; see §§158, 265, 749, 915, 1007, 2517. Clearly, then, returning the man's wife is rendering the spiritual truth of doctrine safe from harm. The reason it was to be rendered safe from the harm of logic is that it was Abimelech who was to return her, and he symbolizes teachings viewed in logical terms, or in other words, a logic-based approach to doctrine (§2510).

[2] As noted earlier [§2531], although the doctrine concerning faith is divine in itself and therefore exceeds all human and even angelic understanding, the Word was still delivered in a rational manner we could grasp. The situation is like that of parents teaching little boys and girls. When they teach, they explain everything in terms suited to the child's frame of mind, though they themselves think on a deeper or higher plane. Declining to adapt their lessons would be to teach what is not going to be learned, or to cast seed on stone.

The situation also resembles that of angels in the other world who teach the simple at heart. Although angels possess heavenly and spiritual wisdom, they do not go over the heads of the people they are teaching. They speak simply with them, gradually raising the level as their pupils learn more. If they spoke with angelic wisdom, their unsophisticated listeners would not understand a word and accordingly would not be led to the truth and goodness that make up faith. It would be the same if the Lord had not offered his scriptural lessons in a rational manner we could grasp. At the same time, the Word does rise to meet the understanding of angels in its inner meaning. Even so, at the highest height at which angels can see it, the Word they see is still infinitely far below the Divine. This clarifies what the Word is like in its origin and therefore in itself. Even though its text seems so trivial and unpolished, at every point it involves more than the whole of heaven is capable of grasping in the smallest way.

[3] The Lord is the Word because the Word is from him and he is in the Word, as can be seen in John:

> In the beginning there was the Word, and the Word was with God, and the Word was God. In him was life, and the life was the light of humankind. The Word became flesh and resided among us, and we saw his glory: glory like that of the Only-Born of the Father, who was full of grace and truth. (John 1:1, 4, 14)

See also Revelation 19:11, 13, 16. And since the Lord is the Word, he is also doctrine, because no other doctrine that is really divine is possible.

2534   *Because he is a prophet* means that then it would be taught, as can be seen from the symbolism of a *prophet.* The Word mentions prophets many times, and in a literal sense the term means people who receive a revelation and, in the abstract, revelation itself. In an inner sense, though, it means people who teach doctrine and, in the abstract, doctrine itself. Since the Lord is doctrine itself (as I said), or the Word that teaches us, he is being called a prophet, as he is in Moses:

> Jehovah your God will raise up for you a *prophet* from your midst, from your brothers, resembling me; him you shall obey. (Deuteronomy 18:15, 18)

The text says "resembling me" because Moses represented the Lord, as did Abraham, Isaac, Jacob, David, and others. Since people were waiting for him, it says in John:

> The people, seeing the sign that Jesus had performed, said, "Because this is truly the *Prophet* who was to come into the world." (John 6:14)

[2] The Lord is a prophet in the highest sense, and the testimony of Jesus is the spirit of *prophecy* (Revelation 19:10), which is why a prophet on an inner level of the Word means someone who teaches and, in the abstract, the doctrine taught. This can be seen plainly in the following passages. In Luke:

> You, child, will be called the *prophet of the Highest One.* (Luke 1:76)

This is what Zechariah said of his son, John the Baptist. John himself says that he was not the Prophet but one who was preparing the way by teaching and spreading the good news about the Lord's Coming:

> They asked him, "What are you? Are you Elijah?" But he said, "I am not." "Are you the *Prophet?*" He answered, "No." So they said to him, "Who are you?" He said, "I am the voice of one shouting in the wilderness, 'Straighten the Lord's path!'" (John 1:21, 22, 23)

[3] In Matthew:

> Many will say on that day, "Lord! Lord! Haven't we *prophesied* in your name?" (Matthew 7:22)

In this verse, obviously, prophesying is teaching. In John:

> It is necessary for you again to *prophesy* over many peoples and nations and tongues and monarchs. (Revelation 10:11)

Prophesying stands for teaching. It has already been said and shown in various places what peoples, nations, tongues, and monarchs are. In the same author:

> The nations will trample the holy city for forty-two months, but I will give my two witnesses [the task] to *prophesy* for a thousand two hundred sixty days dressed in sackcloth. (Revelation 11:2, 3)

Here too prophesying stands for teaching. In Moses:

> Jehovah said to Moses, "See, I have made you a god to Pharaoh, and Aaron your brother will be your *prophet*." (Exodus 7:1)

The prophet stands for a teacher, or a spokesperson for Moses. In Joel:

> I will pour out my spirit on all flesh, and your sons and your daughters will *prophesy.* (Joel 2:28)

The fact that they prophesy stands for the fact that they will teach. [4] In Isaiah:

> Jehovah has poured out a spirit of slumber on you and has closed your eyes. The *prophets* and your heads—*the seers*—he has put hoods over. And for you, everyone's vision has become like the words of a sealed book, which they give to one who knows his letters, saying, "Please read it," and that one will say, "I can't, because it has been sealed." (Isaiah 29:10, 11)

The prophets mean people who teach truth, while the seers mean people who see truth. They are said to be hooded when they do not know of or see any truth. In ancient times, people who taught were called prophets, so they were also called seers, because seeing meant understanding (§§2150, 2325). On their being called *seers,* see 1 Samuel 9:9; 2 Samuel 24:11. They were also called *men of God,* from the symbolism of a man (§§158, 265, 749, 915, 1007, 2517). On their being called men of God, see 2 Kings 1:9–16; 4:7, 9, 16, 21, 22, 25, 27, 40, 42; 5:8, 14, 20; 13:19; 23:16, 17.

[5] The whole of Jeremiah 23 and Ezekiel 13, which speak pointedly about prophets, and many passages elsewhere that mention them, make it clear that on an inner level prophets symbolize people who teach doctrine. As a consequence, false prophets symbolize people who teach falsities, as in Matthew:

> At the close of the age, many *false prophets* will arise and lead many astray. False Christs and *false prophets* will arise and do great signs and lead even the chosen, if possible, into error. (Matthew 24:[3,] 11, 24)

The false prophets mean no one else. The same is true of the *false prophet* in Revelation 16:13; 19:20; 20:10.

[6] The pictures we form of representative objects and practices in the Jewish religion cloud the Word's inner meaning. The degree to which they do so can be seen from the fact that whenever the Word mentions a prophet, we immediately picture the prophets that existed in Old Testament times. This image very effectively blocks us from seeing what they stand for. The wiser we are, however, the easier it is for us to put aside preconceptions formed from that kind of representative item. When the Temple is mentioned, for instance, people who think wisely do not picture the Temple at Jerusalem but the temple of the Lord. When Mount Zion is mentioned, or simply Zion, they do not picture the site of Jerusalem but the Lord's kingdom. When Jerusalem is mentioned, they do not picture the city that stood in the tribal territory of Benjamin and Judah but Jerusalem the Holy and Heavenly.

2535   *He will pray for you* means a revelation would result, as can be seen from the symbolism of *praying*.

Regarded in itself, praying is talking with God, while taking an inward view of the things we are praying about. In answer we receive a similar kind of inflow into the perceptions or thoughts of our mind, so that there is some opening of our inner depths to God. The experience varies, depending on our mood and the nature of the subject we are praying about. If we pray from love and faith and focus on or seek only what is heavenly and spiritual, something resembling a revelation emerges while we pray. It discloses itself in our emotions in the form of hope, comfort, or an inward stirring of joy. That is why praying, in an inner sense, means experiencing revelation—particularly here, because it is a prophet who is being said to pray and the prophet means the Lord. When the Lord prayed, he was simply talking inwardly to his divine aspect and experiencing a revelation. Luke makes it clear that revelation was involved:

> It happened, when Jesus was being baptized and *praying*, that heaven opened. (Luke 3:21)

In the same author:

> It happened, when Jesus (taking Peter, James, and John) went up into the mountain to *pray*; when he *prayed*, the appearance of his face became different and his garment became dazzling white. (Luke 9:28, 29)

In John, when he prayed, saying:

"Father, glorify your name." A voice then went out from heaven: "I both have glorified it and will glorify it again." (John 12:27, 28)

Clearly in the prayer of the Lord here he was talking with his divine aspect and there was then a revelation.

And you will live means the doctrine would come alive as a result, which stands to reason without explanation.　**2536**

And if you do not return her means if he did not render spiritual truth safe from the harm of logic, as shown by the remarks just above at §2533, where the same words occur.　**2537**

Know that you will surely die means that any doctrine teaching truth or goodness would cease, as again shown by remarks above, at §2516, where similar words also occur. Likewise, *everyone who is yours* means together with everything doctrine embraced. *Every one* means every thing in an inner sense because in the Word people have a symbolic meaning. So *everyone who was Abimelech's* symbolizes everything doctrine embraced.　**2538**

The discussion now indicates what the inner meaning of the words in this verse is: The Lord was to render the spiritual truth of doctrine safe from the harm of logic, and then it would be taught. He would experience a revelation, and the doctrine would come alive as a result. If he did not render spiritual truth safe from the harm of logic, however, any doctrine exhibiting truth or goodness would cease, down to every last one of its details.

[2] This is how theology works: The more the human element enters into it—that is, the more we rely on sensory, factual, and logical proof for our belief in it—the more it ceases to be theology. On the other hand, the further off to the side we move sensory, factual, and logical proof, or believe what theology teaches without that proof, the more theology comes alive, because divinity flows into it all the more. It is the distinctly human elements in us that keep divinity from flowing in, and keep us from welcoming it.

Still, to base our belief on logical thinking, factual knowledge, and sense impressions, and to consult these sources before we will believe, is very different from using them in support and confirmation of our belief. The nature of the difference will become clear in what follows, since the inner meaning of the current chapter deals with this question as well.

Genesis 20:8. *And Abimelech got up early in the morning and called all his slaves and spoke all these words in their ears; and the men were extremely frightened.*　**2539**

Abimelech got up early in the morning symbolizes clear perception and a confirmatory light shed by heavenly goodness. *And called all his slaves* means logic and facts. *And spoke all these words in their ears* means urging (these) to provide support, even to the point of submission. *And the men were extremely frightened* means even to the point of aversion.

2540   *Abimelech got up early in the morning* symbolizes clear perception and a confirmatory light shed by heavenly goodness, as can be seen from the symbolism of *getting up early,* of *Abimelech,* and of the *morning.* Sections 2333 and 2405 showed what the *early* part of the day symbolizes. Its meaning here as clear perception is plain from that demonstration. It is also plain from the series involved: at first the perception was dim (§§2513, 2514), but later it was less dim (§2528). *Abimelech* symbolizes doctrine that views faith in logical terms (see above at §§2509, 2510). The symbolism of *morning* is apparent from that of early day. Since the verse says, "He got up early in the morning," at this point it symbolizes not only clear perception but also a confirmatory light shed by heavenly goodness. Heavenly goodness, you see, is what radiates the corroborating light of truth. These remarks now show that the meaning of the clause is the one given.

[2] I have already explained one reason why the inner meaning has as much to do with the way the Lord perceived things in his human aspect as it does with his thinking about the role of logic in the doctrine of faith. Another is the angelic trait of thinking precisely distinguished thoughts about the Lord's life in the world and the way he rid himself of human logic and made his rationality divine, by his own power. At the same time they think about the nature of the doctrine of charity and faith when logic becomes mixed up with it. Not to mention many other subjects they consider that are central to religion and to humankind and that branch off from these. To us humans, who pour all our care and concern into worldly and bodily interests, these topics seem trivial and maybe even perfectly useless. To angels, though, who pour all their care and concern into heavenly and spiritual interests, they are valuable. Their thoughts and perceptions on these subjects are inexpressible.

This shows that angels have extremely high regard for many things that we see as trifling, because these things outstrip our capacity to understand them but enter into the light of angelic wisdom. Conversely, what we hold in highest regard because it is worldly and meets our comprehension is trifling to angels because it stands outside the light of their wisdom.

The same is more or less true of the Word's inner meaning in many places.

And called his slaves means logic and facts, as can be seen from the symbolism of *slaves* in the Word, to be discussed below at verse 14, §2567. **2541**

For a person in the Lord's kingdom, or in other words, a person who *is* a kingdom of the Lord, the heavenly, spiritual, rational, factual, and sensory dimensions are arranged in a hierarchy. The heavenly and spiritual dimensions come first and are the Lord's. The rational dimension comes under them and serves them. The factual dimension comes under the rational and serves it, and finally the sensory dimension comes under the factual and serves it. Anything that serves is a comparative slave, and that is what the Word calls it.

People who think only in terms of what their senses and the academic disciplines tell them do not realize that this kind of hierarchy exists. People who do know something about it still have only the vaguest idea, because they remain obsessed with bodily interests. Angels, though, have a perfectly distinct idea. Thousands and even millions of separate thoughts that angels think present only a single, vague idea to us. In regard to these words, for example—"Abimelech called his slaves and spoke all these words in their ears, and the men were extremely frightened"—angels discern secrets deeper than we could ever grasp or even believe. These secrets tell how the Lord reduced the rational and factual planes to submission, and in such a way that it was not logic and facts themselves that he subdued but the emotions rising up against heavenly and spiritual teachings. With these under control, logic and facts were reduced to submission, and also into order.

This is exceedingly common knowledge among angels but exceedingly obscure, perhaps, or even impossible to understand for people on earth.

And spoke all these words in their ears means urging (logic and facts) to provide support, even to the point of obedience, as established by the train of thought in the inner meaning and by the symbolism of *ears*. **2542**

The train of thought: There are many supporting arguments that lend themselves to any proposition the rational mind acknowledges. The rational mind will not acknowledge anything without proof. So when the rational dimension is forced into obedience, an appeal is made to the supporting arguments, since they are always standing ready, and spring forward, so to speak.

The symbolism of ears: In the Word's inner meaning, *ears* symbolize obedience. The reason for the symbolism is the correspondence that exists between hearing and obeying. The same correspondence exists in the actual word *hear*, and even more so in *heed*. The source of this correspondence is the other world, where people who obey and defer belong to the region of the ear. In fact, they correspond to the sense of hearing itself—a secret as yet unknown. These ideas will become clearer below, however, where correspondence will be treated of, by the Lord's divine mercy.

[2] Many passages in the Word show that this is the symbolism of ears. For the time being, let me offer just this verse from Isaiah:

> Make the heart of this people fat and make their *ears* heavy and smear over their eyes, to prevent them from seeing with their eyes and *hearing with their ears* and understanding in their heart. (Isaiah 6:10)

In this passage, seeing with the eyes is understanding, and hearing with the ears is perceiving affirmatively and therefore obeying. Nothing else is meant where the Lord says:

> Those who have an *ear to hear should listen.* (Matthew 11:15; 13:9, 43; Luke 8:8; 14:35)

2543   *The men were extremely frightened* means even to the point of aversion, as can be seen from the symbolism of *being frightened* here and of *men*.

Like any emotion, fear or *being frightened* has many aspects, even though it appears uncomplicated. On the worldly plane it includes fear of losing life, reputation, position, and wealth. On the heavenly plane it includes fear of losing what is good and true and therefore of the life that comes from them. Since it involves these things, it also involves aversion for whatever tries to destroy them. The more we love what is good and true, the more we loathe what tries to destroy them. The thing loathed is directly opposed to that love, so being frightened here means loathing. The extent of the Lord's aversion is evident from the zeal with which the words of the next verse were said. That zeal was for keeping doctrine from being tainted at all by logical thinking or bare fact.

Men symbolize logic and facts, or in other words, intellectual activity of various kinds, as shown in §§158, 265, 749, 915, 1007.

2544   Genesis 20:9. *And Abimelech called Abraham and said to him, "What have you done to us, and in what way have I sinned against you, that you have brought on me and on my kingdom an immense sin? Deeds that must not be done you have done to me."*

Abimelech called Abraham and said to him symbolizes what the doctrine concerning faith inspired the Lord to think. *What have you done to us, and in what way have I sinned against you?* symbolizes rebuking himself for thinking this way. *That you have brought on me and on my kingdom an immense sin* means that it put the doctrine of faith and all doctrines in danger. *Deeds that must not be done you have done to me* symbolizes horror.

Abimelech called Abraham and said to him symbolizes what the doctrine concerning faith inspired the Lord to think, as can be seen from the representation of *Abimelech* and *Abraham,* and from the symbolism of *saying,* all of which are dealt with several times earlier.

2545

What it is to think a thought inspired by the doctrine of faith cannot be explained intelligibly, because a perception of the matter falls only into angelic ideas. It is presented to angels' minds in such strong light, accompanied by heavenly pictures, that hardly any of it can be described. The difficulty will become evident if I say that the thought was inspired by intuitive truth, which lay above the Lord's rational mind, which relied on that truth for vision; while the perception from which the thought developed was inspired by divine truth.

What have you done to us, and in what way have I sinned against you? symbolizes rebuking himself for thinking this way. This can be seen from the emotion and zeal present in the words (as mentioned just above at §2543), because logic and facts wanted to rise up and intrude, and in this way establish a general presence in the doctrine of faith, which is divine.

2546

That you have brought on me and on my kingdom an immense sin means that it put the doctrine of faith and all doctrines in danger. This can be seen from the symbolism of Abimelech (to whom *me* refers) as the doctrine of faith, and from that of a *kingdom* as the truth present in doctrine, or doctrinal truth.

2547

It can be seen from the Word that on an inner level a kingdom symbolizes doctrinal truth and, in the opposite sense, doctrinal falsity, as in Jeremiah:

> He is the one who forms everything, and he is the scepter of his inheritance; Jehovah Sabaoth is his name. You are a hammer to me, the weapons of war, and in you I will scatter *nations* and in you destroy *kingdoms.* (Jeremiah 51:19, 20)

This is about the Lord. Clearly he is not about to scatter nations or destroy kingdoms but the things that nations and kingdoms symbolize: evil and falsity in doctrine. [2] In Ezekiel:

> See, now, I am about to take the children of Israel from among the nations where they have gone and gather them from round about and lead them into their own land. I will make them into one *nation* in the

land, on the mountains of Israel, and one monarch will serve them all as monarch. And they will no longer be as two *nations,* and they will no longer be split into two *kingdoms.* (Ezekiel 37:21, 22)

Israel stands for a spiritual religion. The nation stands for the good existing in that religion, or that theology. (For the fact that nations are goodness, see §§1259, 1260, 1416, 1849.) A kingdom stands for the truth existing there. Obviously the nations and kingdoms mentioned here mean something other than nations and kingdoms. After all it says of the children of Israel (or Israelites) that they were to be gathered and brought into the land, when in fact they had scattered among the nations and been absorbed into them. [3] In Isaiah:

I will mix Egypt up with Egypt, and they will fight, a man against his brother and a man against his companion, *city* against *city, kingdom* against *kingdom.* (Isaiah 19:2)

Egypt stands for sophistry about religious truth on the basis of mere facts (§§1164, 1165, 1186). A city stands for a doctrine, here a heretical one (§§402, 2268, 2449). A kingdom stands for falsity in doctrine. So city against city and kingdom against kingdom stand for heresies and falsities destined to fight each other. The meaning is similar to that of the words the Lord spoke concerning the close of the age, in Matthew:

Nation will be roused against *nation,* and *kingdom* against *kingdom.* (Matthew 24:7)

This stands for the fact that evil will be roused against evil, and falsity against falsity.

[4] Daniel's prophecies about the four kingdoms (Daniel 2:37–46; 7:17–end), about the kingdoms of Media and Persia (8:20–end), and about the kingdoms belonging to the monarchs of the south and north (chapter 11) mean nothing else. Neither do those of John in Revelation concerning various monarchs and kingdoms there. In all these cases, the kingdoms actually mean the condition of truth and falsity in the church. States of earthly monarchies and kingdoms as described in the Word's literal sense are states of the church and the Lord's kingdom in its inner sense, which contains only what is spiritual and heavenly. The Lord's Word, regarded in itself, is purely spiritual and heavenly, but to enable people in general to read and understand it, what has to do with heaven is conveyed by means of the things that exist on earth.

Deeds that must not be done you have done to me symbolizes horror. **2548**
This can be seen from the emotion in the words and from the train of
thought: the Lord felt aversion (§2543), rebuked himself with zeal (§2546),
and now was horrified.

Genesis 20:10, 11. *And Abimelech said to Abraham, "What have you* **2549**
seen, that you would do this thing?" And Abraham said, "Because I said,
'Nevertheless there is no fear of God in this place, and they will kill me over
the matter of my wife.'"

Abimelech said to Abraham symbolizes a further thought inspired by
teachings on faith. *"What have you seen, that you would do this thing?"*
symbolizes insight into the reason. *Abraham said* symbolizes a perception
received in answer. *Because I said, "Nevertheless there is no fear of God in*
this place," symbolizes the resulting thought that people would have no
esteem for spiritual truth in their present state. *"And they will kill me over*
the matter of my wife" means that the heavenly aspects of faith would be
destroyed too, then, if they thought only spiritual truth could be wedded
to heavenly goodness.

Abimelech said to Abraham symbolizes a further thought inspired by **2550**
teachings on faith, as can be seen from the remarks above at §2545, where
nearly the same words occur. Since this is the second time it has been
said, it means a further thought—specifically, a thought about the reason.

For what it is to think a thought inspired by the doctrine of faith, see
that same section [§2545].

What have you seen, that you would do this thing? symbolizes insight **2551**
into the reason. This is clear without explanation. It is also clear from the
discussion below, where the reason is given [§2553].

In this way, the inner meaning sets out in order what the Lord
perceived and thought about teachings on faith and about logic and
whether to consult it. The reason for setting it out this way is the tendency of angels to think about these subjects in this order. The Word's
inner meaning is designed especially for angels, so it is suited to their
perceptions and thoughts. They are in their element—and in fact in a
state of bliss and happiness—when they are thinking about the Lord,
his divinity and humanity, and the way his humanity was made divine.
They are surrounded by a heavenly and spiritual atmosphere that is full
of the Lord, so that they can be said to be in the Lord. Nothing, therefore, is more blissful or happier for them than to think thoughts that
fit with both the atmosphere they enjoy and the feelings arising from
that atmosphere. [2] At the same time they also receive instruction and

perfect their knowledge. The main thing they learn is how the Lord, as he grew, gradually and by his own power made the humanity into which he had been born divine. So they learn how he used the secular and religious knowledge he revealed to himself to develop his rational mind, chase away its shadows bit by bit, and bring it into divine light.

These and countless other concepts are presented to the view of angels in a heavenly and spiritual manner when the Word is being read, together with thousands upon thousands of representative pictures ablaze with a living light.

These ideas, which are so precious to the angels, seem trivial to us on earth, because they surpass our understanding and therefore lie in the shadows of our intellect. Conversely, the thoughts that we hold precious—those involving worldly concerns, for instance—are dismissible as far as angels are concerned, because they lie below the state of an angel's wisdom and therefore in its shadow. Strange to say, then, what departs into shadow for us and almost into our contempt passes over into light with the angels and into their affection. Much of the content of the Word's inner meaning is like this.

2552   *Abraham said* symbolizes a perception received in answer, as can be seen from the symbolism of *saying* in scriptural narrative, which has been discussed many times before, as in §§1791, 1815, 1819, 1822, 1898, 1919, 2061, 2080, 2238, 2260, 2271, 2287.

Abimelech said to Abraham symbolizes what the doctrine of faith inspired the Lord to think, while *Abraham said* symbolizes a perception he received in answer. This is how the matter stands: Perception is higher, and the Lord received it from divinity itself, but thought is lower, and the Lord received it from his intellect. Since his thoughts rose out of his perceptions, answering thoughts also rose out of perception. The phenomenon can be illustrated by something similar in humans. Heavenly people can think only from perception; spiritual people can think only from conscience (§2515). The perception of the former, like the conscience of the latter, comes from the Lord, but they do not see that. Their thoughts, on the other hand, come from their rational minds and seem to them to come from themselves. So when they think with their rational minds on any subject, the conclusion they reach, or the answer, also comes from either perception or conscience. The Lord, then, answers them in accord with the state of their life, with their passions, and with any doctrinal truth grafted or etched onto them in harmony with their state and passions.

2553   *Because I said, "Nevertheless there is no fear of God in this place,"* symbolizes the resulting thought that people would have no esteem for spiritual truth in their current state, as can be seen from the following: The *fear of God* symbolizes esteem for divine truth, or spiritual truth. And a *place* symbolizes a state or condition, as mentioned in §§1273, 1274, 1275, 1377.

To expand: We are not capable of grasping any doctrine that is purely spiritual and heavenly—divine, in other words—because such a doctrine infinitely exceeds our understanding and therefore our belief. All our thoughts are grounded in the earthly ideas provided by our senses. Anything we hear that does not grow out of these ideas or agree with them is something we do not comprehend. It dies, like a gaze cast out over the ocean or the universe with nothing to rest on. If doctrine were not explained to us in earthly terms, then, we absolutely would not accept it and so would have no esteem for it. The situation is fairly clear from particulars in the Word, where for the same reason things that are purely divine are expressed in earthly and even sensory terms. For example, it ascribes ears, eyes, a face, human emotions, anger, and so on to Jehovah.

[2] This applied even more at the time the Lord came into the world. People then did not even know what heavenly and spiritual qualities were or (still more surprising) what the inner realm was. What belonged to the earth and the world and so to the outer realm monopolized their attention. Take the apostles themselves. They imagined that the Lord's kingdom would resemble a worldly kingdom, so they asked to sit one on his right and the other on his left [Mark 10:37; Matthew 20:20–23]. For a long time they also thought they would sit on twelve thrones to judge the twelve tribes of Israel [Matthew 19:28; Luke 22:30], not yet realizing that in the other life they would not be able to pass even the most limited judgment on a single person (§2129 at the end).

The reason for this insight into the state of the human race was that the Lord, out of love, wondered at first whether he should consult logic in regard to teachings about faith. The love he had was a desire to seek the salvation of all and to keep the Word from being destroyed.

They will kill me over the matter of my wife means that the heavenly aspects of faith would be destroyed too, then, if they thought only spiritual truth could be wedded to heavenly goodness. This can be seen from the symbolism of *killing* as being destroyed, and from that of a *wife* as spiritual truth wedded to heavenly goodness (discussed in §2507).

This is a second reason why the Lord thought the way he did, and the explanation is that divine goodness (called heavenly goodness here) is united to divine truth (called spiritual truth here) in a kind of marriage (§2508). Although divine goodness is united only to divine truth

2554

in this way, it still flows into truth on lower levels and bonds with it. The bond is not like that of marriage, though. Divine goodness, you see, acts on and bonds with rational truth, which only seems to be true. In fact, it also acts on and bonds with secular truth and sensory truth, which are not much more than illusions. If it did not, none of us could ever have been saved (see the discussion of this in §§1831, 1832 of the second volume). This was also the reason the Lord came into the world: so that divine goodness could join with rational, secular, and sensory truth, enabling humankind to be saved. If the Lord's humanity had not become divine, no bond could possibly have been created, but through the Lord there *is* a bond.

[2] Still more secrets besides this one lie hidden in the words *they will kill me over the matter of my wife*, meaning that the heavenly aspects of faith would be destroyed, then, if they thought only spiritual truth could be wedded to heavenly goodness. Here is one such secret: Heavenly goodness would also be destroyed if people failed to esteem spiritual truth, because when the latter is rejected, the former is destroyed. Here is another: Unless people had been told to worship the Father, again the truth would not have been accepted, even though no one has access to him except through the Son [John 14:6], and whoever sees the Son sees the Father (John 14:8–12). Not to mention other secrets as well.

2555   Genesis 20:12, 13. *"And in addition she truly is my sister; she is my father's daughter—although not my mother's daughter—and she became my wife. And it happened when God made me go from my father's house that I said to her, 'This is a kindness that you might do for me: every place that we come to, say [in relation] to me, "He is my brother."'"*

And in addition she truly is my sister means that rational truth bore this kind of close relation. *She is my father's daughter but not my mother's daughter* means rationality was conceived by heavenly goodness as its father but not by spiritual truth as its mother. *And she became my wife* means that spiritual truth was united with what was heavenly by means of rationality. *And it happened when God made me go from my father's house* means when the Lord left behind secular facts and the appearances they generated, together with the pleasure he took in them, which is expressed as *his father's house*. *That I said to her* symbolizes the thought he then had. *This is a kindness that you might do for me* means that as a result he would then have this consolation. *Every place that we come to* symbolizes any conclusions he would later come to about rational truth. *Say [in relation] to me, "He is my brother,"* means it would be said that rational truth was attached to heavenly goodness.

In addition she truly is my sister means that rational truth bore this **2556** kind of close relation. This can be seen from the fact that Sarah in her role as *sister* represents rational truth, as discussed at §2508. It can also be seen from what follows directly after, which has to do with the birth of rationality and therefore with the way it was related.

In general it must be understood that in people who are truly rational, or in other words, regenerate, everything is related to everything else by a kind of blood tie or looser kinship. This includes everything involved in their feelings, their perceptions, and their thoughts, which are arranged in such a way that they interrelate the way the families of a single household do, each in its own, individual capacity. As a result the family ties that bind these feelings, perceptions, and thoughts determine how they reproduce—a characteristic traceable to heaven's influence, or rather to the Lord's influence by means of heaven. In a person who is truly rational (or regenerate), everything is arranged in the same pattern as heaven, and heaven's influence is what arranges it that way. From this we receive our ability to think, draw conclusions, make judgments, and reflect. These abilities are so amazing that they exceed all human knowledge and wisdom and immeasurably exceed any analysis the human mind has ever produced by means of them, despite its effort.

The reason no one has known any of this so far is that no one has believed that all our feelings, perceptions, and thoughts come to us from elsewhere. Evil ones come from hell and honorable ones come from heaven, so that they link with other feelings, perceptions, and thoughts outside us. This is not known or believed, even though our spirits are in fact joined to those of others outside us in such a way that if we were deprived of the connection we would not last a minute. We can see the truth of this from the fact that nothing disconnected exists anywhere, and that what *is* disconnected instantly perishes.

She is my father's daughter—although not my mother's daughter means **2557** rationality was conceived by heavenly goodness as its father but not by spiritual truth as its mother. This can be seen from the way the rational mind is conceived—by an inflow of divine, heavenly goodness into the desire for information, as described in §§1895, 1902, 1910.

There are two secrets here. One is that human rationality is conceived by divine, heavenly goodness, which serves as its father; otherwise no rationality comes into existence. The other is that rationality is not conceived by spiritual truth; spiritual truth does not serve as its mother.

The first secret—that human rationality is conceived by divine, heavenly goodness, which serves as its father, and that otherwise no rationality comes into existence—can be seen from previous discussions at §§1895, 1902, 1910. It can also be seen from considerations that anyone can recognize, upon reflection. [2] People know, after all, that we are not born with any knowledge or reason but only with the ability to gain both. By degrees we eventually absorb and learn everything, especially through the senses of hearing and sight, and as we absorb and learn, we become rational. Obviously this comes by a physical, or in other words, an external, route, since it comes by way of hearing and sight.

What people do not realize, however, because they do not reflect on it, is that something is always flowing into us from within—something that takes in what enters [from the outside] and absorbs it, and gives it a place in the overall pattern. This thing that acts on us, takes in what enters, and gives it a place, is divine, heavenly goodness, which comes from the Lord. This is the source of our life, of the overall pattern, and therefore of the "blood ties and kinships" among all our component parts, as noted. The evidence shows, then, that human rationality comes from divine, heavenly goodness, which serves as its father, according to the words of the current verse: "She is my father's daughter."

[3] The second secret—that rationality is not conceived by spiritual truth, that spiritual truth does not serve as its mother—can be seen from remarks at §1902. If spiritual truth acted on us from within the way goodness does, we would be born with full rationality and at the same time with full knowledge, so that we would not need to learn anything. By nature and heredity, though, we succumb to every kind of evil and so to every kind of falsity. As a result, if actual truth were also to flow in, we would adulterate and falsify it and be destroyed forever. So the Lord has provided that no truth come to us through our inward part, only through our outward part. This discussion demonstrates that human rationality does not arise from spiritual truth, and spiritual truth does not serve as its mother, in keeping with the current verse when it says, "although not my mother's daughter."

The Lord chose to form his rational mind by this same process, so that by his own power he could make the human elements in him divine, and so that he could graft and unite divine, spiritual truth to divine, heavenly goodness, and the reverse.

2558   *She became my wife* means that spiritual truth was united with what was heavenly by means of rationality. This can be seen from Sarah's representation as Abraham's *wife,* in that she is spiritual truth united to heavenly goodness, as mentioned in §2507, and from her representation as his sister, in that she is rational truth, as mentioned in §2508. So the fact that she became Abraham's wife after being his sister means that through rationality spiritual truth was united with what was heavenly. The remarks just above in §2557 show how the case stands with this.

It happened when God made me go from my father's house means when the Lord left behind secular facts and the appearances they generated, together with the pleasure he took in them, which is expressed as *his father's house*. This can be seen from the following: *Going from* symbolizes leaving behind. And a *house* symbolizes something good (§2233)—here, the good of the pleasure the Lord took in the appearances generated by secular facts and logic. Anything that gives pleasure seems good.

The reason the house of Abraham's father symbolizes pleasure in secular facts and logic and therefore in the appearances they generate is that they are ascribed to Abraham at the time that he left his father's house. At that point Abraham, along with his father's house, worshiped other gods (see §§1356, 1992). That is why the verb is plural in *God made me go*. It must be added that the original language also allows a rendering of *the gods made me stray,* but since Abraham represents the Lord, it must be expressed as *God made me go*.

The facts and therefore the rational ideas the Lord first acquired were human, tainted with his mother's heredity, and therefore not purely divine. That is why they are represented by Abraham's first stage. For how far representation goes, see §§665, 1097 at the end, 1361, 1992.

That I said to her symbolizes the thought he then had, which can be seen from the symbolism of *saying* as thinking, a symbolism discussed several times before.

This is a kindness that you must do for me means that as a result he would then have this consolation, as can be seen from what comes before and from what comes after and therefore without further explanation.

Every place that we come to symbolizes any conclusions he would later come to about rational truth. This can be seen from the symbolism of a *place* as a state (discussed in §§1273, 1274, 1275, 1377). The thing whose state is being spoken of here is the Lord's conclusion about rational truth—that rational truth would be described as being attached to heavenly goodness, as stated in the next section.

Say [in relation] to me, "He is my brother," means it would be said that rational truth was attached to heavenly goodness. This can be seen from the discussion above at §2524, where almost the same words appear.

§2559

§2560

§2561

§2562

§2563

2564   Genesis 20:14. *And Abimelech took flock and herd, and male and female slaves, and gave them to Abraham, and restored to him Sarah his wife.*

Abimelech symbolizes teachings concerning faith. *Took flock and herd* means that the teachings were enriched with goodness on the rational and on the earthly planes. *And male and female slaves* means also with truth on the rational and earthly planes and with the desire for this truth as well. *And gave them to Abraham* means that they were given to the Lord. *And restored to him Sarah his wife* means when divine spirituality had been joined with divine heavenliness.

2565   *Abimelech* symbolizes teachings concerning faith. This can be seen from the symbolism of *Abimelech* as the teachings on faith, a symbolism mentioned at §§2504, 2509, 2510.

2566   *Took flock and herd* means that the teachings were enriched with goodness on the rational and on the earthly planes, as can be seen from the symbolism of flock and herd. People in the church who are truly rational—people with depth—are called a *flock*. As a result, a flock also symbolizes genuine rational goodness, or inward goodness, in the abstract. For more on this symbolism of a flock, see §§343, 415, 1565. On the other hand, people in the church who are oriented toward the physical world—shallower people—are called a *herd*. So a herd also symbolizes genuine earthly goodness, or outward goodness, in the abstract. For more on this symbolism of a herd, see §2180. Animals have this kind of symbolism, as shown at §§45, 46, 142, 143, 246, 714, 715, 776, 1823, 2179.

Abimelech took and gave means that teachings on faith were enriched, because Abimelech symbolizes the doctrine of faith, as noted.

2567   *Male and female slaves* means also with truth on the rational and earthly planes and with the desire for this truth as well, as can be seen from the symbolism of *male and female slaves.* Slaves, or servants, are mentioned in many places in the Word, and on an inner level they symbolize qualities that are relatively lower and humbler, as rational and earthly things are in relation to spiritual and heavenly ones. Earthly truth means facts of every kind, because they belong to the earthly realm.

The fact that slaves symbolize these qualities in the Word is clear from the inner meaning of the words in passages where they come up. In Isaiah, for example:

> Jehovah will have mercy on Jacob and will yet choose Israel and will put them on their ground; and immigrants will cling to them and attach themselves to the house of Jacob, and the peoples will take them and

lead them to their place. And the house of Israel will inherit them upon the ground of Jehovah as *male* and *female slaves*. (Isaiah 14:1, 2)

[2] Jacob here stands for the outward church, Israel for the church within, immigrants for people who are being taught about truth and goodness (§§1463, 2025). Male and female slaves stand for truth on the earthly and rational planes, together with a desire for it, which will be of service to the religion meant by Jacob and Israel. Plainly the passage is not talking about Jacob and Israel, or Jews and Israelites, because having scattered among the surrounding nations they had become part of those nations. Jews still cherish this goal and expect it to come true in a literal sense: that immigrants will cling to them and the peoples will lead them and serve them as male and female slaves. In reality, though, where the prophetic parts of the Word mention Jews and Israelites, it has nothing in the least to do with them. They could see this clearly, too, by considering that in various passages Israel received as many promises as Judah that it would be brought back. [3] In the same author:

Look: Jehovah is emptying the earth and draining it, and he will deform its face and scatter its residents. And it will be for the priest as for the people, and for the master as for the *male slave,* and for the mistress as for the *female slave.* (Isaiah 24:1, 2)

The earth here stands for the church (§§662, 1066, 1068, 1850). The church is emptied and drained, its face is deformed, and its residents scatter, when there is no longer any inward truth and goodness (the people and priest) or outward truth and goodness (the male and female slaves). This happens when outward concerns overpower inward ones. [4] In the same author:

From Jacob I will produce seed, and from Judah, the heir to my mountains; and the ones I have chosen will own it, and my *servants* will live there. (Isaiah 65:9)

Jacob stands for the outer church; Judah, for the inner, heavenly church. The chosen ones stand for its goodness; servants, for its truth. [5] In Joel:

I will pour out my spirit on all flesh, and your sons and your daughters will prophesy. Also on *male slaves* and *female slaves* in those days I will pour out my spirit. (Joel 2:28, 29)

This passage is about the Lord's kingdom. Prophesying stands for teaching (§2534). Sons stand for truth itself (§§489, 491, 533, 1147); daughters, for goodness itself (§§489, 490, 491). Male and female slaves stand for lowlier kinds of truth and goodness, and Jehovah's spirit is said to be poured out on them when they provide support and confirmation. Here and elsewhere, it is not easy to see that slaves have these symbolic meanings, partly because of the general picture of slaves or servants, and partly because the literal meaning is more apparent. [6] In John:

> I saw an angel standing in the sun, who shouted in a loud voice, saying to the birds flying in midair, "May you eat the flesh of monarchs and the flesh of commanders, and the flesh of the mighty, and the flesh of horses and of the people sitting on them, and the flesh of all, free people and *slaves,* both small and great." (Revelation 19:17, 18)

Clearly it is not the flesh of monarchs, commanders, the mighty, horses, people sitting on them, free people, and slaves that they were to eat, but deeper and shallower religious truth, which had become [like] flesh to them.

[7] Male slaves symbolize truth—and female slaves, goodness—that serve spiritual and heavenly truth and goodness and are therefore slaves to it. Laws laid down for the representative religion concerning slaves make this quite clear. All those laws focus on conditions in the church and the Lord's kingdom in general and particular. They speak to the way lower kinds of truth and goodness (which are earthly and rational) have to serve spiritual and heavenly kinds and therefore divine kinds. For instance:

> A *male Hebrew slave* and a *female Hebrew slave* were to go free in the seventh year, and they were then to be given something from the flock, the threshing floor, and the winepress. (Exodus 21:2–6; Deuteronomy 15:12–15; Jeremiah 34:9, 14)

> A wife was to go free if she had entered slavery with [her husband], but if the master had given the slave's wife to the slave, the wife and her children were to be the master's. (Exodus 21:3, 4)

> Impoverished fellow Israelites who had been bought were not to serve as slaves but as hired servants or tenants, and were to leave at the jubilee, together with their children. (Leviticus 25:39–43)

> If fellow Israelites were bought by a resident foreigner, they could be redeemed and leave their slavery in the year of jubilee. (Leviticus 25:47 and following verses)

From the nations all around, male and female slaves could be bought, and also from the offspring of resident foreigners. They were to be the owner's permanent possession, and the owner could exercise complete control over them but not over the offspring of Israel. (Leviticus 25:44, 45, 46)

If a male slave did not want to leave his slavery, an awl was to be put through his ear at a doorway, and he was to be a permanent slave; the same with a female slave. (Exodus 21:6; Deuteronomy 15:16, 17)

If a master struck his male or female slave with a staff, so that the slave died, the slave was to be avenged; but if the slave survived a day or more, the master was to go free, because the slave was the master's silver. (Exodus 21:20, 21)

If a master struck the eye or tooth of a slave, the slave was to go free. (Exodus 21:26, 27)

If an ox gored a male or female slave, so that the slave died, the owner was to pay thirty shekels to the slave's master and the ox was to be stoned. (Exodus 21:32)

Slaves that had escaped from their master were not to be imprisoned but to live where they pleased and not be afflicted. (Deuteronomy 23:15, 16)

A slave bought with silver and circumcised was to eat the Passover. (Exodus 12:44)

Anyone's daughter who had been bought was not to leave her slavery as male slaves did. If she was bad, the master was not to sell her to a foreigner. If she was promised in marriage to his son, she was to be treated as a daughter. If the son took another woman, he was not to restrict her board, clothing, or marital rights. If he did not provide these things, she was to leave her slavery without charge. (Exodus 21:7–11)

[8] All these laws trace their origin to the laws of truth and goodness in heaven and refer to them in an inner sense, but partly by correspondence, partly by representation, and partly by symbolism. After representative and symbolic objects and practices—the very shallowest and lowliest aspects of worship—were eliminated from religion, the need for such laws also came to an end. If they were to be explained, then, in terms of the laws governing the divine plan for truth and goodness, and in terms of

their representation and symbolism, it would be clear what male and female slaves mean. Male slaves actually symbolize truth on the rational and factual planes—a lowly kind of truth that therefore ought to serve spiritual truth. Female slaves actually symbolize the goodness that goes with that truth, which is somewhat lowly as well and therefore ought to serve. This goodness serves in a different way, though, so the laws laid down for female slaves differ from those laid down for males. Regarded in itself, truth is more of a slave than is the goodness associated with it.

[9] The *royal prerogative* in Samuel also symbolizes nothing else on an inner level than the prerogative of truth—and also that of falsity, when it starts to overpower truth and goodness. This can be seen from an explanation of the words describing that prerogative:

> This will be the *right of the monarchs* who will reign over you: Your sons they will take and appoint them to themselves for their chariots and for their riders, and your sons will run before their chariots. Your daughters they will take as perfumers and as cooks and as bakers. Your *male slaves* and your *female slaves* and your best youths and your donkeys they will take and put to their own work. Your flock they will take a tenth of. In the end *you will become slaves.* And you will cry out on that day because of your monarch, whom you chose for yourselves, and Jehovah will not answer you on that day. (1 Samuel 8:11, 13, 16, 17, 18)

[10] Monarchs symbolize truth (see §§1672, 2015, 2069), so in a negative sense they symbolize what is not true—that is, falsity. The sons that they would appoint to themselves for their chariots and riders symbolize doctrinal truths that have to serve false premises (the chariots and riders). The daughters that they would take as perfumers, cooks, and bakers symbolize the teaching of what is good, which they will use to make the truth palatable and self-serving. The male slaves and female slaves, youths and donkeys that they would use to do their work symbolize the logic and secular facts they will use in confirmation. The flock of which they would take a tenth symbolizes the remnant of goodness that they will damage. The conversion of the people into slaves means that the monarchs will not allow the heavenly and spiritual elements of the Word and theology to dominate; instead, they will make those elements serve to confirm their false premises and justify their wicked appetites. There is no argument they cannot incorporate into their false theories as confirmation, through misapplication, deliberate misinterpretation, perversion,

and rejection of anything unsupportive. That is why the passage goes on to say, "If you cry out on that day because of your monarch, whom you chose for yourselves, Jehovah will not answer you on that day."

Earlier in this chapter it was said that doctrine would cease to exist if logic were consulted (§§2516, 2538) and that logic was not consulted (§§2519, 2531). Here, however, it is said that the doctrine of faith was enriched with goodness and truth on both the rational and earthly planes. At first glance, this seems to be inconsistent and self-contradictory, but it is not.

2568

[2] How it was with the Lord has been said, but how it is with us needs saying. In humans, it is one thing to look at teachings on faith from the viewpoint of logic, and something completely different to look at logic from the viewpoint of teachings on faith. To look at teachings on faith from the viewpoint of logic is to refuse to believe in the Word or the doctrine that comes from it until reason convinces us of its truth. To look at logic from the viewpoint of teachings on faith, on the other hand, is to believe in the Word first, or in the doctrine that comes from it, and then use reason to confirm what it says. The first way is backward and keeps us from believing anything, but the second way is the right way and increases our belief. The first is "You will die because of the woman," meaning that the doctrine of faith would cease if logic were consulted (§§2516, 2538). The second is "Abimelech gave flock and herd, and male and female slaves," meaning that teachings about faith were enriched with goodness and truth on the rational and earthly planes.

[3] The inner meaning of the Word has much to say about this, particularly where it speaks of Assyria and Egypt. When we look at the doctrine of faith from the viewpoint of logic—when we refuse to believe it until logic persuades us of its truth—not only does it die but we also deny everything it teaches. When we look at logic from the viewpoint of teachings about faith, though—when we believe the Word and then use logic to confirm it—doctrine lives, and we affirm everything it teaches.

[4] There are two principles, then. One leads to complete folly and insanity; the other, to all understanding and wisdom. The first is to deny everything. It is to say in our hearts, "I cannot believe these things until I am convinced of them by what I can understand or sense." This is the principle that leads to complete folly and insanity, and it should be called the negative principle. The other is to affirm the teachings of doctrine that come from the Word, or to think and believe inside oneself that they

are true because the Lord has said so. This is the principle that leads to all understanding and wisdom, and it should be called the affirmative principle.

[5] When people base their thinking on the negative principle, then the more they consult logic, and the more they consult secular facts, and the more they consult philosophy, the more they plunge and hurl themselves into darkness. In the end they deny everything. One reason is that no one can grasp what is above on the basis of what is below. In other words, no one can grasp spiritual or heavenly concepts from logic, secular facts, and philosophy—let alone divine concepts, because they transcend all understanding. Another is that the negative principle then wraps everything in doubt. Conversely, when people base their thinking on the affirmative principle, they are free to use any kind of logic, any kind of fact, and even any kind of philosophy they possibly can to support their position. All of these serve as confirmation for them and give them a fuller idea of the subject.

[6] In addition, there are people who doubt and then deny, and there are people who doubt but then affirm. People who doubt and then deny are those who lean toward living an evil life. When this life sweeps them away, then the more they think on such subjects, the more negative they become. People who doubt but then affirm, though, are those who lean toward living a good life. When they allow the Lord to bend them toward this kind of life, then the more they think about such subjects, the more affirmative they become.

Since this subject comes up again in the verses that follow, let me illustrate it more fully there, with the Lord's divine mercy; see §2588.

2569 *He gave them to Abraham* means that these things were given to the Lord. This can be seen from the representation of *Abraham* as the Lord— a representation discussed many times before.

And restored to him Sarah his wife means when divine spirituality had been joined with divine heavenliness. This can be seen from the symbolism of *Sarah* in her role as *wife,* in that she is spiritual truth attached to heavenly goodness, as mentioned in §2507.

The inner meaning of the words in this verse is clear from the discussion: When the human part had united with the divine part and the divine part with the human in the Lord, he possessed all knowledge. He possessed the knowledge not only of the divinely heavenly plane and the divinely spiritual plane but also that of planes below the heavenly and spiritual ones, or in other words, knowledge of the rational and earthly planes. Divinity itself, like a sun that radiates all the light there is, causes everything to be seen as immediately present.

Genesis 20:15. *And Abimelech said, "Look: my land is before you; settle in the [part that is] good in your eyes."*   **2570**

Abimelech said, "Look: my land is before you," symbolizes the Lord's perception of the theology of love and charity. *"Settle in the [part that is] good in your eyes"* means that he was present wherever there was anything good.

Abimelech said, "Look: my land is before you," symbolizes the Lord's perception of the theology of love and charity. This can be seen from the   **2571**
symbolism of *saying* as thinking (mentioned in §2506) and from that of the *land* here as the theology of love and charity. On an inner level, *land* symbolizes many different things (620, 636, 1066), but the context shows what its symbolism is. It symbolizes the outer self of a religious person, when heaven symbolizes the inner self (82, 913, 1411, 1733). It also symbolizes the area where the church is (662, 1066). It symbolizes the church itself, and more comprehensively the Lord's kingdom in the heavens and on earth, because that is what the land of Canaan, or the Holy Land, represented (1437, 1585, 1607). It is what the new heaven and the new earth represent as well (1733, 1850, 2117, 2118). Since the land represents a religious person, the church, and the Lord's kingdom, it also symbolizes their essence, which is love for the Lord and charity for one's neighbor, because love and charity are what they depend on (537, 540, 547, 553, 2130). So it symbolizes the theology of love and charity, which is what faith teaches and which is Abimelech's land here. Abimelech as king symbolizes the doctrine of faith, as shown, but his land—the place he came from and lived in—symbolizes the doctrine of love and charity, which is what faith comes from and dwells in.

[2] Up to this point, the Lord's thoughts had been about the doctrine of faith, but now they focused on the doctrine of love and charity. The reason is this: The Lord joined his humanity to his divinity through truth (which has to do with faith), even if he did so also through the divine goodness (which has to do with love) within that truth, according to plan. We too follow this plan when we become spiritual and heavenly, although we do not become divine beings with intrinsic life, as the Lord did. However, truth became wedded to goodness, and goodness to truth, in a divine marriage within the Lord, which is what Abimelech's restoration to Abraham of Sarah his wife symbolizes (§2569). Then the Lord's thoughts focused on the doctrine of love and charity. This too was according to plan, because when we become spiritual and heavenly, we no longer think in terms of

what is true but in terms of what is good. Still, we do not base our thinking on divine goodness united with divine truth, as the Lord did.

That is why the theology of love and charity is mentioned for the first time now, even though regarded in itself the doctrine of faith is identical with it, and the Lord's perceptions and thoughts on any aspect of faith always came from divine love.

So it is that the doctrine of love and charity is the divine doctrine itself. This was the teaching that the people of the earliest church cultivated, and since it was united with the doctrine of faith, they rejected anyone who split the two apart; see §2417.

2572   *Settle in the [part that is] good in your eyes* means that he was present wherever there was anything good. The most immediate meaning is that he was present in the goodness taught by doctrine. This can be seen from the symbolism of *eyes* as that which we understand, which relates to doctrine, and from that of *settling* as living a life (§1293). Here, settling means being, because it has to do with the Lord.

Being present wherever there is anything good means having complete awareness of everything divine, heavenly, spiritual, rational, and earthly, as a result of divine love, since divine love contains all knowledge of all these things (§2500).

[2] In addition, doctrine has a component of goodness and a component of truth. The goodness taught by doctrine is love and charity; the truth it teaches is faith. People who have the goodness taught by doctrine—love and charity—also have the truth, or faith.

It is one thing, however, to display goodness, or love and charity, and another to display a goodness based on theology. Children who have love for their parents and charity for other children exhibit goodness, but not as a result of doctrine. Consequently they are not awake to doctrinal truth, or in other words, faith. The people who display a goodness based on doctrine are people who have been reborn by means of the truth that composes faith. The more goodness they have, the more truth they have; in other words, the more love and charity they have, the more faith they have, and therefore the more wisdom and understanding they have.

[3] Because angels love the Lord and share in that love with others, they also possess all truth. As a result they possess all wisdom and understanding, covering not only heavenly and spiritual subjects but also rational and earthly ones. Love puts angels at the actual origins or source of these things; that is, it makes angels aware of purposes and causes. Love does this, because the Lord does it. To see a thing in terms of its origins,

or in terms of its purposes and causes, is to look from heaven at everything below, even on earth. Doing this is like standing on a tall mountain, and in a watchtower on the mountain. There you can look around at objects that are many miles below. Meanwhile, the people down below can hardly see many *feet* away, especially if they are in a valley or forest.

It is the same with people who have a goodness because of what they have been taught, compared to those who have a truth they have been taught detached from anything good. Although the latter imagine they can see much farther than the former, they cannot see anything good. They also cannot see anything true, except on the surface, in the most trivial way possible, and even at that it is tainted with falsity.

[4] Nonetheless, angels' wisdom and understanding is limited. In relation to the Lord's divine wisdom and understanding, it is so very limited as to amount to hardly anything. As evidence, take the fact that no ratio exists between the infinite and the finite (although the Divine in his absolute power does communicate with us). Take also the fact that the Lord is goodness itself and love itself. So he is the true essence of the goodness and love that exists with angels, which means that he is the true essence of their wisdom and understanding.

From this too it is clear that the Lord is present wherever there is anything good in heaven and on earth. Anyone who supposes that the Lord is present in truth detached from anything good, is seriously mistaken. The Lord is present only in what is good and consequently in what is true; that is, he is present only in love and charity and consequently in faith.

Genesis 20:16. *And to Sarah he said, "Look, I have given a thousand pieces of silver to your brother; here now, for you it is a veil over the eyes of everyone who is with you, and of everyone [else], and you are vindicated."*   **2573**

And to Sarah he said symbolizes a perception from spiritual truth. *Look, I have given a thousand pieces of silver to your brother* symbolizes a wealth of rational truth attached to heavenly goodness. *Here now, for you it is a veil over the eyes of everyone who is with you* means that rational truth resembles a veil or garment for spiritual truth. *And of everyone [else]* means so does the kind of truth that develops out of it. *And you are vindicated* means that there is consequently no blame or harm.

And to Sarah he said symbolizes a perception from spiritual truth, as can be seen from the following: As a wife *Sarah* represents divine, spiritual truth, as noted at §2507. As a sister she represents rational truth, as discussed in §2508. And *saying* symbolizes perceiving, as mentioned in   **2574**

§2506. This speech is addressed to Sarah both as Abraham's wife and as his sister. It is addressed to her as his wife because she had been restored to him (§2569). It is addressed to her as his sister because Abimelech says, "I have given a thousand pieces of silver to *your brother.*" What was said by Abimelech was perceived by Sarah in that state, so saying something to Sarah means perceiving from spiritual truth.

[2] Obviously these words involve secrets too deep to unfold intelligibly. If I were to explain them only in part it would be necessary first to explain many other things that people so far do not know: what spiritual truth is; what perception from spiritual truth is; that only the Lord perceived anything from spiritual truth; that just as the Lord grafted rational truth onto rational goodness, so he grafted spiritual truth onto heavenly goodness; that in this way he was continually grafting his humanity onto his divinity; and that at every point, then, there was a marriage of his humanity with his divinity, and of his divinity with his humanity. All this and more has to come first before the contents of the current verse can be explained in a comprehensible way.

Such matters are suited especially well to the minds of angels, who have the intelligence to understand them, since the Word's inner meaning exists for them. They see these things portrayed in a heavenly manner. Through the portrayals, and through the contents of the current chapter, they learn how the Lord gradually cast off the humanity he inherited from his mother until at last he was no longer her son. (He did not even acknowledge her as his mother, which is clear from Matthew 12:46, 47, 48, 49, [50]; Mark 3:31, 32, 33, 34, 35; Luke 8:20, 21; John 2:4.) By the same means the angels learn how he made his humanity divine, through his own power, until he was as one with the Father, as he teaches in John 14:6, 8, 9, 10, 11, and elsewhere. [3] All these ideas the Lord presents to the angels in full light through thousands upon thousands of images and pictures, each of them indescribable. These images are designed for the angels' way of thinking, as I said, and they enjoy the blessings of intelligence and the joy of wisdom while looking at them. What is more, when they were people on earth, they had formed the idea that the Lord's humanity resembled that of any other person. So since they are now angels, such misconceptions are dispersed by the Word's inner meaning, enabling them to coexist with heavenly angels in the other world (since thoughts inspired by good emotions bring people together there). In the process, they are perfected.

These considerations show how highly angels value the contents of the Word's inner meaning, even though such contents may appear insubstantial to a person on earth, whose thoughts on the subject are so vague as to be practically nonexistent.

Look, I have given a thousand pieces of silver to your brother symbolizes **2575** an infinite wealth of rational truth attached to goodness, as can be seen from the following: A *thousand* symbolizes a large amount or uncountable number—here, an infinite amount, or an infinite wealth, since it is ascribed to the Lord. This symbolism is discussed below. *Silver* symbolizes rational truth, as dealt with in §§1551, 2048. And a *brother* symbolizes heavenly goodness connected with rational truth, as a brother is connected with his sister (§§2524, 2557). Clearly, then, "I have given a thousand pieces of silver to your brother" symbolizes an infinite wealth of rational truth attached to goodness. The reason the wealth was given to goodness (the brother) rather than to truth is that truth comes from goodness, not the reverse.

For a description of that infinite wealth, see §2572.

[2] The following passages make it plain that in the Word a *thousand* symbolizes a large amount or uncountable number and, when ascribed to the Lord, an infinite amount. In Moses:

> I am Jehovah your God, God the Zealous, bringing the consequences of the parents' wickedness on their children, on the third ones and on the fourth ones, on those who hate me; and showing mercy to *thousands* who love me and keep my commandments. (Exodus 20:5, 6; 34:7; Deuteronomy 5:9, 10)

And in Jeremiah:

> Jehovah is showing mercy toward *thousands* and repaying the parents' wickedness onto the lap of their children after them. (Jeremiah 32:18)

The thousands do not mean any exact number but an infinite amount, because the Lord's mercy, being divine, is unlimited. In David:

> God's chariots: two *myriads, thousands doubled,* the Lord among them, Sinai in holiness. (Psalms 68:17)

The myriads and thousands stand for uncountable numbers. [3] In the same author:

> At your side will fall a *thousand,* and a *myriad* on your right; it will not come near you. (Psalms 91:7)

Here too a thousand and a myriad stand for uncountable numbers. Since it is about the Lord, who is meant by David in the Psalms, the thousand and the myriad stand for everyone hostile to him. In the same author:

> Our storehouses are full, supplying us from meal to meal; our flocks are giving birth to a *thousand*, and *ten thousand* in our streets. (Psalms 144:13)

Again in this verse the thousand and ten thousand (or myriad) stand for uncountable numbers. In the same author:

> A *thousand* years in your eyes are like yesterday when it has passed. (Psalms 90:4)

A thousand years stand for timelessness and consequently for eternity, which is infinite time. In Isaiah:

> *One thousand* will flee at the reproach of one; at the reproach of five you will flee, until you remain as a standing pole at the head of the mountain. (Isaiah 30:17)

One thousand, or a force a thousand strong, stands for a large, undefined number. Five stands for a few (§649). In Moses:

> May Jehovah the God of your ancestors add to you a *thousand times* [as much] as you are, and bless you. (Deuteronomy 1:11)

In this verse a thousand times stands for countless times, as it does in everyday speech, where we also use "a thousand" to mean many, as when we speak of saying something a thousand times or doing something a thousand ways. Likewise in Joshua:

> One man from among you will chase a *thousand*, because Jehovah your God is fighting for you. (Joshua 23:10)

[4] Because a thousand is a specific number in mathematics, it seems to mean a thousand in prophetic passages, especially where it is being woven into a story. In reality, though, it means a large or uncountable number, without any specific quantity. By its very nature, narrative detail focuses the mind on the most direct meaning of a word—on the word's own proper meaning—just as it focuses the mind on the names it mentions. Yet the numbers in the Word have symbolic meaning just as much as names do. This can be seen from previous demonstrations regarding numbers, §§482, 487, 575, 647, 648, 755, 813, 1963, 1988, 2075, 2252. That

is why some people also think that the thousand years referred to in Revelation 20:1, 2, 3, 4, 5, 6, 7 means a thousand years, or a thousand periods of time—because, as noted, the prophecies are set out as stories there. Still, the thousand years there just means a large, unlimited number, and in other places it can also mean infinite time, or eternity.

Here now, for you it is a veil over the eyes of everyone who is with you means that rational truth resembles a veil or garment for spiritual truth, as can be seen from the following: The symbolism of a *veil* is dealt with just below. The *eyes* symbolize the contents of the intellect, as is plain from very many passages in the Word. And seeing symbolizes understanding (§§2150, 2325).

Anyone can tell that the individual parts of this verse hold secrets that can be unfolded only from some kind of inner meaning. For instance, it says Abimelech gave a thousand pieces of silver, and that he gave it not to Sarah's husband but to her brother. He describes this as a veil over the eyes both of herself and of everyone who was with her, and in fact of everyone else too. And he says that this would vindicate her. Many guesses could be made from the literal words about the story's meaning, but none of them would contain anything spiritual, let alone divine; and the Word is divine.

[2] Here is why rational truth is like a veil or garment for spiritual truth: Whatever is deepest inside us belongs to our soul. What is on the surface belongs to our body. The things that are deepest inside are good urges and true thoughts, and our soul takes its life from them; otherwise the soul would not be a soul. Things on the surface take their life from the soul. They resemble a body or, to put the same thing another way, a veil or garment.

This is easiest to see from sights that appear in the other world, as, for instance, from angels. When they are presented to view, their inner depths shine out from their face. Their more external traits are represented both in their body and in their dress, so much so that everyone there can tell another's character simply from her or his clothing. The clothes are made of real substance, so they consist of an essence as it exists in a form.

The same is true of angels who appeared to people and whose faces and clothes are described in the Word. Take, for instance, those seen in the Lord's tomb (Matthew 28:3; Mark 16:5), the twenty-four elders around the throne (Revelation 4:4, 5), and others. Moreover, it is true not only of angels but also of everything else mentioned in the Word, even if it is inanimate; its outer part is a veil or garment. Take the ark of the covenant and the tent that surrounded it. The ark, which was at the center, represented the Lord himself, because it held the testimony, while the tent, which was outside it, represented the Lord's kingdom. Its hangings, or its veils and coverings, together and individually, represented the outward manifestations of heavenly and spiritual qualities in that kingdom, specifically in the three heavens. This can be deduced from the fact that the plan for all of it was shown to Moses on Mount Sinai (Exodus 25:9; 26:30). That is what gave the place its holiness, not the gold, silver, and carvings in it.

[3] Since the subject here is rational truth in its role as a veil or garment for spiritual truth, and Moses describes the hangings or coverings for the tent, including the veils over the entrance, let me explain the specific symbolism of those veils by way of illustration. (The symbolism of the overall coverings will be told elsewhere, with the Lord's divine mercy.)

There were three veils there. The first divided the Holy Place from the Holiest Place. The second is called the curtain for the door of the tent. The third is called the curtain for the gate of the courtyard. [4] This is what Moses says about the first, the true veil hiding the ark:

> You shall make a *veil* of blue-violet and red-violet and double-dyed scarlet and interwoven byssus, a work well designed; you shall make it with [images of] the guardian beings. And you shall place it on four pillars of sheetim overlaid with gold, whose hooks shall be of gold, on four bases of silver. And you shall place the *veil* under the clasps. And you shall bring in there, within the *veil,* the ark of the testimony; and the veil shall distinguish for you between the Holy Place and the Holiest Place. (Exodus 26:31, 32, 33, 34; 36:35, 36)

This veil represented the first and deepest face of rational goodness and truth—rational goodness and truth as *angels of the third heaven* see it. The blue-violet, red-violet, double-dyed scarlet, and interwoven byssus give a picture of it. The red in those materials represented the good effects of love; the white represented the truth that emerges from love. The gold and silver in the overlay on the pillars and in the hooks and bases represented the same thing. For the fact that colors represent something, see §§1042, 1043, 1053, 1624. For the fact that gold is the good that comes of love, see §§113, 1551, 1552. For the fact that silver is truth, see §§1551, 2048.

[5] From this you can see what the rending of the veil in the Temple symbolizes (Matthew 27:51; Mark 15:38; Luke 23:45). It means that the

Lord entered into true divinity after banishing all illusions. He also gave us access to divinity itself by making his humanity divine.

[6] This is what Moses says about the second veil, or the curtain for the door of the tent:

> You shall make a *curtain* for the doorway of the tent out of blue-violet and red-violet and double-dyed scarlet and interwoven byssus, the work of an embroiderer. And you shall make for the *curtain* five pillars of sheetim, and you shall overlay them with gold; their hooks shall be of gold; and you shall cast for them five bases of bronze. (Exodus 26:36, 37; 36:37, 38)

This curtain represented the way goodness and truth appears on a plane that is lower or shallower than the first—the plane of an intermediate kind of rationality. This is what *angels of the second heaven* are devoted to. It is depicted in almost the same terms, but with the difference that for this curtain there were five pillars and five bases. Five symbolizes a relatively small amount, because this appearance of goodness and truth is not as consistent or consequently as heavenly as that in the deepest or third heaven. For the symbolism of five as a little, see §§649, 1686. Since this face of goodness and truth looks toward earthly values, they were commanded to cast the bases of bronze, because bronze represented and symbolized an earthly kind of goodness (§§425, 1551).

[7] This is what Moses says about the third veil, or the curtain for the gate of the courtyard:

> For the gate of the courtyard a *curtain,* twenty cubits, of blue-violet and red-violet and double-dyed scarlet and interwoven byssus, the work of an embroiderer. The pillars [for the hangings], four; their bases, four; all the pillars of the courtyard all around strapped with silver, their hooks of silver but their bases of bronze. (Exodus 27:16, 17; 38:18, 19)

This curtain represented the way goodness and truth appears on a plane that is still lower or shallower—the plane of the lowliest kind of rationality. This is what *angels of the first heaven* are devoted to. Because it corresponds to the appearances on deeper planes, it is depicted in similar terms but with a difference: The pillars were not overlaid with gold but banded with silver, and the hooks were made of silver, symbolizing rational truth that traces its origin directly to facts. In addition, the bases were of bronze, symbolizing earthly goodness.

You can see from this that every feature of the tent without exception represented the heavenly and spiritual qualities of the Lord's kingdom. In other words, it was all designed to model the heavenly and spiritual qualities of the three heavens. You can also see that the hangings or coverings symbolized those aspects that surround the central core, or stand outside it, like a body or garment.

[8] Coverings, wraps, and garments or clothes symbolize truth that is relatively lowly, as many passages in the Word show. In Ezekiel, for example:

> Fine linen with embroidery from Egypt was *what you spread out;* blue-violet and red-violet fabric from the islands of Elishah was your *covering.* (Ezekiel 27:7)

This is about Tyre, which symbolizes a relatively deep knowledge of what is heavenly and spiritual and therefore people who have that knowledge (§1201). Embroidery from Egypt stands for secular facts. (For the symbolism of Egypt as secular facts, see §§1164, 1165, 1186, 1462.) Blue-violet and red-violet fabric from the islands of Elishah, serving as a covering, stand for ritual that corresponds to inward worship (§1156). [9] In the same author:

> All the chieftains of the sea will come down from upon their thrones and take off *their robes,* and *their embroidered clothes* they will shed. They will be dressed in terror. They will sit on the land. (Ezekiel 26:16)

This too is about Tyre. The robes and embroidered clothes stand for religious knowledge based on secular facts, and therefore for a lower kind of truth. [10] In the same author:

> I *clothed* you with embroidery and gave you shoes of badger and *swathed* you in fine linen and *covered* you in silk and decked you in finery and put bracelets on your hands and a necklace on your throat. You took some of your *clothes* and made yourself colorful high places and whored on them. You took *embroidered clothes* and covered [the images]. (Ezekiel 16:10, 11, 16, 18)

This is about Jerusalem, which symbolizes a spiritual religion. It is portrayed as it was in ancient times and also as it later became, after it had been corrupted. Its lowlier spiritual attributes and doctrines are the clothes made of embroidery, fine linen, and silk. [11] In Isaiah:

The Lord Jehovah Sabaoth is taking away out of Jerusalem and of Judah the whole staff of bread and the staff of water. Then a man will grab his brother of his parents' house: "You have a *garment!* You will be chieftain to us." He will take up [his answer] on that day, saying, "I will not be a binder [of wounds], and in my house there is no bread and no *clothing.* You are not to make me chief of the people." The Lord will cause a rash on the crown of the head of Zion's daughters. And on that day the Lord will take away the finery of the foot jewels and of the reticules and of the moon ornaments and of the pendants and of the chains and of the bangles; and the headdresses and the anklets and the sashes and the soul-houses and the earrings; the rings and the nose ornaments, the *ceremonial clothing* and the *robes* and the *mantles* and the needle cases, the mirrors and the muslins and the turbans and the wraps. (Isaiah 3:1, 6, 7, 17–24)

Jerusalem stands for a spiritual religion, and Judah, for a heavenly one. The staff of bread and the staff of water that will be taken away stand for goodness and truth. The garment belonging to the chieftain stands for truth taught by doctrine. The various kinds of clothing and other finery listed as belonging to Zion's daughters are all the categories and types of goodness and truth that would be stripped from them. If each of the items mentioned did not symbolize some particular aspect of religion, it would not be part of Scripture, every word of which holds something divine. They are ascribed to Zion's daughters, who symbolize attributes of religion, as may be seen in §2362. [12] In the same author:

Wake up! Wake up! Put on your strength, Zion! Put on *your finest clothes,* Jerusalem, you holy city, because the uncircumcised and unclean will not come into you any longer. (Isaiah 52:1, 2)

Zion stands for a heavenly religion; Jerusalem, for a spiritual one. The fine clothes stand for the holy qualities of faith. In the same author:

Their webs are not for *clothing,* and they are not *dressed* in their works; their works are works of wickedness. (Isaiah 59:6)

The webs stand for ideas that people pretend are true, which are not "for clothing"; clothing stands for the more superficial truth present in doctrine and worship. That is why it says they are not dressed in their works. [13] In the same author:

I will rejoice greatly in Jehovah; my soul will exult in my God, because he will dress me in *clothes of salvation;* with a *robe of righteousness* has he covered me. (Isaiah 61:10)

Clothes of salvation stand for religious truth. A robe of righteousness stands for neighborly goodness. In John:

You have a few names also in Sardis that have not defiled their *clothes* and will walk with me in white because they are worthy. Those who conquer will be dressed in *white clothes.* (Revelation 3:4, 5)

In the same author:

Fortunate are those who are watchful and keep their *clothes,* to avoid walking naked. (Revelation 16:15)

In the same author:

On the thrones I saw twenty-four elders sitting, dressed in *white clothes.* (Revelation 4:4, 5)

The clothes are obviously not clothes; they are spiritual qualities that have to do with truth. [14] The same applies to the Lord's words concerning the close of the age: that people should not turn back behind to take their *clothes* (Matthew 24:18; Mark 13:16). For the fact that the clothes in this verse are truth, see §2454. The same also applies to the Lord's remarks about the person who failed to dress in *wedding clothes* (Matthew 22:11, 12) and to his words about John:

What did you go out to see? A person dressed in *glistening clothes?* People who wear glistening clothes are in the houses of monarchs. (Matthew 11:8; Luke 7:25)

This stands for people who involve themselves in the inward depths of doctrine and worship rather than the outward show, which is why it adds:

What did you go out to see? A prophet? I tell you, even more than a prophet. (Matthew 11:9)

The prophet stands for the outward aspects of doctrine and worship.

[15] Since clothes symbolized truth of every sort, the children of Israel were given several commands regarding clothing. When they left Egypt, they were to borrow gold and silver and *clothes* and put these on their children (Exodus 3:22; 12:35, 36). They were not to wear *clothes of multiple*

types, that is, of mixed fibers (Leviticus 19:19; Deuteronomy 22:11). And they were to make themselves tassels on the *edges of their clothes,* put a blue-violet thread there, and remember and do the commandments when they saw it (Numbers 15:38, 39, 40).

[16] In time past they also tore their *clothes,* as is clear from Joshua 7:6; Judges 11:35; 1 Samuel 4:12; 2 Samuel 1:2, 11, 12; 3:31; 13:30, 31; 15:32; 1 Kings 21:27; 2 Kings 5:7, 8; 6:30; 22:11, 14, 19; Isaiah 36:22; 37:1. This symbolized a wound to the person's zeal for doctrine and for the truth. It also symbolized a humble awareness that what elegant clothes symbolize was lacking.

[17] The prophecy of Jacob (who by then was Israel) also makes it clear that coverings, wraps, and garments or clothes have this symbolism:

> He will tie his young animal to the grapevine and his jenny's foal to the choice vine. He will wash his *clothing* in wine, and his *garment* in the blood of grapes. (Genesis 49:11)

Without the help of the inner meaning, no one can see what is meant by these things—the grapevine, the choice vine, the young animal, the jenny's foal, the wine, the blood of grapes, the clothing, and the garment. Clearly it concerns the Lord, who is called Shiloh here. The subject of the prophecy is Judah, who represents the Lord's heavenly divinity. The clothing that he would wash in wine and the garment that he would wash in the blood of grapes symbolize the Lord's rational and earthly dimensions, which he would make divine. [18] Likewise in Isaiah:

> Who is this coming from Edom, stained in his *clothes,* from Bozrah, this one who is honorable in *his apparel,* marching in the abundance of his strength? Why is your *garment* red, and why is your *clothing* like that of one treading in the winepress? "And the winepress I have trodden, I alone, and from among the peoples there was not anyone with me. My victory over them was spattered on *my clothes,* and all my *garb* I defiled." (Isaiah 63:1, 2, 3)

Here too the garments and clothing stand for the Lord's humanity, which he made divine by his own power, through inward struggles and victories. That is why it says, "The winepress I have trodden, I alone, and from among the peoples there was not anyone with me." The fact that Isaac smelled the *smell of Esau's clothes* and so gave a blessing (Genesis 27:27) involves much the same meaning.

[19] The actual holiness of the Lord's divine humanity was also a garment, one that appeared like light and was dazzling white when he was transfigured. This is what Matthew says about it:

> When Jesus was transfigured, his face shone like the sun; his *clothes* became like the light. (Matthew 17:2)

In Luke:

> When Jesus prayed, the appearance of his face became different; his *garment, dazzling white.* (Luke 9:29)

And in Mark:

> When Jesus was transfigured, *his garments* became *radiant,* very white, like snow, such as a fuller on earth could not whiten them. (Mark 9:3)

The garments of holiness that Aaron wore when he entered inside the veil, which were linen, represented something similar (Leviticus 16:2, 4). Likewise the garments of holiness that were for glory and adornment, and the clothes of ministry, described in Exodus 28:2–end; 39:1–end. Every feature of those garments, without exception, represented something.

2577   *And of everyone [else]* means so does the kind of truth that develops out of it—specifically, facts and the evidence of the senses. This can be seen from the discussion above and from the progression of the story itself. After all, this is directly preceded by the words "Here now, for you it is a veil over the eyes of *everyone* who is with you," meaning rational truth, which resembles a veil for spiritual truth. Now it says *of everyone* again, which therefore symbolizes truth on a still lower plane, or the kind that develops out of rational truth. This kind is simply what people call truth in the form of facts and sense impressions. Both develop out of rational truth, as can be seen from the direction in which inflow moves. Deeper attributes flow into shallower ones or, to put it another way, higher attributes flow into lower ones, but not the reverse. It is true that the appearance is quite different; it looks as though sensory evidence and facts make us rational, but this is an illusion. Goodness from the Lord is always flowing in through our rational capacity and entering our consciousness; this good is constantly adopting facts as its own. The more of them it can adopt and organize properly, the more rational we become.

The case is the same as that with the goodness and truth that are said to belong to faith. Goodness from the Lord flows into truth and adopts it as its own. The more truth it can adopt, the more spiritual we become. This is so despite the appearance that the truth people describe as being part of faith flows in and makes us spiritual.

This appearance is also the reason people revere religious truth so much today and do not stop to think about neighborly kindness.

You are vindicated means that there is consequently no blame or harm, as can be seen from the whole previous discussion, which this clause sums up. **2578**

Genesis 20:17. *And Abraham prayed to God, and God cured Abimelech and his wife and his female slaves, and they bore children.* **2579**

Abraham prayed to God symbolizes a revelation. *And God cured Abimelech* symbolizes theology that is sound in regard to goodness. *And his wife* means in regard to truth. *And his female slaves* means in regard to desires for the teachings. *And they bore children* symbolizes fertility.

Abraham prayed to God symbolizes a revelation. This can be seen from the symbolism of *praying,* when the Lord is the one said to be doing it, as experiencing a revelation (discussed at §2535) and from the representation of *Abraham* as the Lord (mentioned many times). **2580**

In the literal story there are two people—one who prayed, and another to whom he prayed—since it says that Abraham prayed to God. In an inner sense, though, there are not two but one. The revelation came from God, or in other words, Jehovah within the Lord, since the Lord was conceived by Jehovah. To the extent that his humanity came from his mother, though, he was a separate person.

How matters stand here can only barely descend into thoughts we are capable of comprehending. It does descend into angelic thoughts, which present themselves in heaven's light, but not very easily into human thoughts, which do not perceive anything unless they are illuminated by rays of worldly light. Still less does it reveal itself to people for whom every ray of heavenly light is too dark to see.

And God cured Abimelech symbolizes theology that is sound in regard to goodness. This can be seen from the meaning of *curing* something as making it sound and from the representation of *Abimelech* as teachings that describe faith in rational terms (§2510). Clearly it means in regard to goodness, because Abimelech's wife is also said to have been cured, symbolizing theology that is sound in regard to truth. When the Word calls a husband a husband, and also when it mentions him by name, he symbolizes goodness and his wife symbolizes truth. When it calls a husband a man, though, he symbolizes truth and his wife symbolizes goodness. This was discussed in §§915, 1468, 2517 as well. **2581**

2582   *And his wife* means in regard to truth. This can be seen from the symbolism of a *wife* as truth, a symbolism mentioned directly above in §2581.

2583   *And his female slaves* means in regard to desires for the teachings. This can be seen from the symbolism of *female slaves* as desires for rational ideas and facts, as discussed in §§1895, 2567. Here they symbolize a desire for the teachings, because they are spoken of in connection with the teachings of faith, since they belonged to Abimelech, who symbolizes teachings about faith (§§2509, 2510). All nuances depend on the topic being discussed.

2584   *And they bore children* symbolizes fertility, as indicated by the symbolism of *giving birth* and being born. The Word's inner meaning contains nothing but the spiritual and heavenly attributes symbolized. So nothing else is meant in a spiritual sense when the Word mentions conception or conceiving, delivery or delivering, birth or being born, generation or generating. Nothing else is meant when the Word mentions people who reproduce (such as a father and mother) and the ones who are produced (such as sons and daughters). After all, in itself the Word is spiritual and heavenly. So too here with the bearing of children, which symbolizes fertility in regard to the teachings of theology.

[2] The following passages show that when the Word mentions the bearing of children, it means no other kind of giving birth. In Samuel:

> People filled with bread have been hired out, and the starving have taken a break from work, to the point that the *infertile woman has delivered seven, the one with many children* has collapsed. Jehovah kills and give life; he sends people down into hell, and he brings them up. (1 Samuel 2:5, 6)

In Jeremiah:

> *She* droops *who gives birth to seven;* she breathes out her soul. Her sun sets while it is still day. (Jeremiah 15:9)

In Isaiah:

> "Sing, *infertile woman!* (She has not *given birth.*) Break into song and shout for joy (she has not *gone into labor*), because the children of the desolate one are more numerous than the children of the married one," Jehovah has said. (Isaiah 54:1)

In David:

> Jehovah's voice *sends* the does *into labor* and strips the forests bare. And in his Temple, everyone who is his says, "Glory!" (Psalms 29:9)

In Isaiah:

> Blush, Sidon, because the sea, the stronghold of the sea spoke, saying, "I was not *in labor*, did not *give birth*, and did not bring up young men or raise young women." As when Egypt receives the news, they will *go into labor* over the news from Tyre. (Isaiah 23:4, 5)

In the same author:

> "Before she *goes into labor* she *gives birth*, and before pain came on her *she delivered a male*. Who has heard a thing like this? Who has seen things like those? Does the earth *labor* for one day and I *cause* it *to give birth?*" says Jehovah. "Am I, the *bringer of birth*, going to close up [the womb]?" says your God. (Isaiah 66:7, 8, 9)

In Jeremiah:

> Ask, please, and see if a *male is giving birth*. Why have I seen every man, his hands on his groin like those of a *woman giving birth?* (Jeremiah 30:6)

In Ezekiel:

> I will put fire in Egypt, and Sin will *be in strong labor*, and let No exist. (Ezekiel 30:16)

In Hosea:

> Ephraim—like a bird will their glory fly away, abandoning *birth* and the *womb* and *conception*. (Hosea 9:11)

In the same author:

> The pains of a *woman in labor* have come on Ephraim. He is an unwise child, because at the time when children *break open the womb*, he will not present himself. (Hosea 13:13)

In John:

> . . . a woman enveloped with the sun, and the moon under her feet, and on her head a crown of twelve stars. *Being pregnant*, she shouted out *laboring* and wracked with pain to *give birth*. The dragon stood before the woman who *was about to deliver* so that when she *had delivered* her child it could devour [the child]. So she *delivered* a male child, who was to shepherd all the nations with an iron rod. But the boy was snatched away to God and his throne. (Revelation 12:1, 2, 4, 5)

[3] Anyone can see from all these passages that no other kinds of conception and birth are meant than religious ones. The same can be seen from the words here concerning Abimelech: "God cured Abimelech, his wife, and his female slaves, and they *bore children,*" and "Jehovah had *tightly closed every womb* of Abimelech's house, because of the matter of Sarah, wife of Abraham." The explanation of these verses shows what they symbolize on an inner level: the status of teachings on faith when we regard them from the viewpoint of divine truth, and their status when we regard them from the viewpoint of logic. When we regard them from the viewpoint of divine truth—that is, from the Word—everything confirms them, whether it is a matter of reason or of secular fact. The situation changes when we regard teachings on faith from the perspective of human truth, or in other words, from reason and fact. Under those circumstances, nothing good or true is conceived. To examine a subject from the Word is to examine it with the Lord's help, but to do so from logic and secular fact is to do so on our own. To use the Lord's help is to be intelligent and wise in every way; to rely on our own devices is to be insane and stupid in every way.

2585   Genesis 20:18. *Because Jehovah had tightly closed every womb of Abimelech's house on that account, because of the matter of Sarah, wife of Abraham.*

Because Jehovah had tightly closed every womb of Abimelech's house on that account symbolizes doctrinal sterility. *Because of the matter of Sarah* means as a result of logic, if it had become involved. *Wife of Abraham* means in order to let spiritual truth unite with heavenly goodness.

2586   *Because Jehovah had tightly closed every womb of Abimelech's house on that account* symbolizes sterility—specifically, doctrinal sterility. This can be seen from the symbolism of *tightly closing the womb* as preventing conception itself, and from that of *Abimelech's house* as the goodness taught by faith. Clearly, then, sterility is symbolized.

Previously this chapter spoke of God, but now for the first time it refers to Jehovah, because God is mentioned when the focus is on truth, while Jehovah is mentioned when the focus is on goodness. Doctrine is always conceived by goodness as its father but is born of truth as its mother, a point made several times before. Since the current verse is talking about conception, and conception comes from goodness, it speaks of Jehovah. Since the text above talks about giving birth, though, and truth is what gives birth, it speaks of God. As the preceding verse says: "*God* cured Abimelech, his wife, and his female slaves, and they *bore children.*"

[2] Other passages in the Word dealing with conception are similar, as in Isaiah:

> *Jehovah* called me from the *womb. Jehovah,* who formed me from the *womb,* has said, . . . Then I will be precious to *Jehovah.* And my *God* will be my strength. (Isaiah 49:1, 5)

Strength is used to describe truth, which is why that clause mentions God. In the same author:

> This is what *Jehovah* has said, your maker and the one who formed you from the *womb.* (Isaiah 44:2, 24; and elsewhere)

That is why the current verse also speaks of *Abimelech's house,* symbolizing the goodness taught by faith. For the symbolism of a *house* as goodness, see §§2048, 2233. And for the symbolism of *Abimelech* as the doctrine of faith, see §§2509, 2510.

Obviously a divine secret lies within the fact that they bore children and that the wombs of Abimelech's house had been closed up because of Sarah. This secret is revealed only through the inner meaning.

2587 *Because of the matter of Sarah* means as a result of logic, if this had joined itself to it. This is established by the representation of *Sarah* in her role as a sister, in that she is logical truth, as discussed in §2508. The *matter* of Sarah means every event that had taken place—her being called Abraham's sister and Abimelech's taking her but not going near her.

The next section will say what else these words mean.

2588 *Wife of Abraham* means to let spiritual truth unite with heavenly goodness, as established by the following: Sarah as wife represents spiritual truth wedded to heavenly goodness, as noted in §§1468, 1901, 2063, 2065, 2172, 2173, 2198, 2507. And Abraham represents heavenly goodness wedded to spiritual truth, as noted at §§[2010,] 2011, 2172, 2198, 2501. It is all the same whether you say spiritual truth and heavenly goodness, or the Lord, because the Lord is truth itself and goodness itself. He is also the marriage itself of truth with goodness and of goodness with truth.

It is true that the explanation shows how the case stands in all this, but since it is among the harder topics to understand at the present day, let me shed as much light as possible on it.

The theme here is the doctrine of faith, which the Lord thought about in his youth. He asked himself whether it was allowable to delve into it by means of logic and in this way form thoughts about it for himself. It was because of his loving concern for the welfare of the human race that he considered this possibility, humankind being such that we refuse to believe what we cannot grasp rationally. Nevertheless, he perceived from his divinity that he should not do so, and as a result he revealed the doctrine to himself from his divine side. As a further result, he also revealed everything in the universe that is subordinate to that doctrine—namely, everything in the realms of logic and earthly learning.

[2] Section 2568 above explained what our situation is in regard to religious doctrines—that our thoughts on it spring from one of two principles, the negative or the affirmative. People who believe nothing unless convinced by reason and secular facts or even by the evidence of their senses base their thinking on the negative principle. People who believe a thing to be true because the Lord has said it in the Word—people who trust the Lord, in other words—base their thinking on the affirmative principle.

People whose attitude is negative toward the idea that everything in the Word is true say in their hearts, "When reason and fact persuade me, then I am willing to believe." Their plight is that they never come to believe, not even if the evidence itself of their physical senses—sight, hearing, and touch—convinces them. They are always coming up with new opposing arguments, until in the end they completely snuff out any spark of faith. At the same time they blot out the light of reason, turning it into darkness by falsifying it.

On the other hand, people whose attitude is affirmative believe a thing to be true because the Lord has said it. Their situation is one in which logic, fact, and even the evidence of the senses are always confirming their belief and lending light and strength to their ideas. It is only by means of reason and fact that we receive light; everyone relies on these. In the latter people, then, theology "surely lives," and they are said to *be cured* and *bear children.* In the former people theology "surely dies," and it is said of them that their *womb is tightly closed.*

This shows what it is to enter into religious doctrine by way of logic and what it is to enter into logic from religious doctrine. Now some examples to illustrate.

[3] The Word teaches that the first and foremost tenet of doctrine is love for the Lord and charity for our neighbor. If we regard this idea affirmatively, we can enter into any logical or factual analysis we want—even into analysis based on our senses—each of us according to our talents, knowledge, and experience. In fact, the more we enter into these kinds of

analysis, the more we strengthen ourselves in the idea, because the whole of creation is full of proof.

If we deny this first and foremost doctrinal premise, however, and demand at the outset to be convinced of its truth by fact and logic, we deny it at heart. Consequently we never do allow ourselves to be persuaded; instead we stand firm for some other principle we believe to be essential. Eventually, in shoring up our own premise, we blind ourselves so badly that we cannot even see what love for the Lord or love for our neighbor is. Because we harden ourselves in our opposition, in the end we also convince ourselves that no other pleasurable type of love can exist than love for ourselves and for the material world. In fact, we even embrace this hellish love in place of heavenly love in our lives, if not in our theology.

With people who are neither negative nor affirmative, though, but are hesitating before they deny or affirm, matters stand as described above at §2568. The people who lean toward living an evil life fall into denial, while the people who lean toward living a good life move toward affirmation.

[4] To take another example, one of the primary teachings of faith is that everything good is from the Lord and everything evil from humankind, or from ourselves. People who affirm that this is true can prove it to themselves by many rational arguments and facts, such as these: Nothing good can possibly enter us unless it comes from goodness itself, that is, from the source of what is good, and so from the Lord; goodness cannot take its start anywhere else. For affirmative people, everything they see in themselves, in others, in the larger community, and even in the whole of creation that is really good illustrates the truth of this proposition. For negative people, on the other hand, everything they ever think confirms them in the opposite opinion—so much so that eventually they cannot tell what is good. They wrangle with each other over the question of the highest good, profoundly unaware that heavenly and spiritual goodness from the Lord is what gives life to any lower kind of good and makes pleasure genuinely pleasurable. Some of them even believe that nothing good can come from anywhere if it does not come from themselves.

[5] Take as yet another example the idea that people who love the Lord and show charity for their neighbor can accept theological truth and have faith in the Word, but those who live a life of love for themselves and for worldly gain cannot. To put the same thing another way, people devoted to what is good can believe, but those devoted to evil cannot. Anyone who looks affirmatively on this proposition is capable of supporting it with countless arguments drawn from logic and fact. Logic

says that truth and goodness agree with one another but truth and evil do not. Just as all falsity dwells in evil, it also proceeds from evil. If certain evil people do possess truth, it rests on their lips, not in their hearts. Fact has much evidence to offer that truth shuns what is evil and evil spurns what is true.

People who view the proposition negatively, though, justify themselves with the consideration that any of us, no matter what we are like—even if we live a life of unceasing hatred, joy in vengeance, and deceit—can believe just as easily as others. They cling to this line of thinking until they finally rid theology of anything having to do with living a good life. Once they rid doctrine of goodness, they no longer believe anything.

[6] To shed still more light on the situation, take the example of people who affirm that the Word was written to have an inner meaning that is not visible in the letter. Again they are able to reinforce themselves at many points by the use of such logic as this: The Word provides humankind with a link to heaven. A correspondence exists between earthly phenomena and spiritual, though the correspondence is not visible. The thoughts of our inner mind are very different from the matter-based thinking we express in words. While we are living in the world we can also live in heaven because of the Word, which exists for both realms, since we have been born for both kinds of life. A kind of divine light flows into some people's perceptions and feelings when they are reading the Word. It is necessary for some document to exist that has come down from heaven, and such a document cannot be the same in its origin as it is in its literal text. It cannot be holy except as the result of a certain inner holiness. Affirmative people can also find support in facts such as these: In times past people made frequent use of representation, and the writings of the ancient church display this quality. As a result, the writings of many other nations were similar. Consequently this manner of writing was revered as holy among the churches and was admired for its learnedness in nations outside the church. One could also mention the books of many other authors.

People whose attitude is negative, however, do not believe any of this, even if they do not actually deny it. They persuade themselves that the Word is just as it appears to be in its literal text (which appears to be worldly) although it is still spiritual. Where its spirituality lies they do not care. Still, they do want it to be spiritual, for many reasons, and are able to prove in a multitude of ways that it is.

[7] To present the subject even to the grasp of the less educated, let me use an example from science as well. Sight belongs not to the eye but

to the spirit, which sees the objects of the world through the eye as an organ in its body. People who approach this idea affirmatively have many arguments with which to confirm it. For instance, the speech that we hear routes itself to a kind of inner eye and turns into something visual, which would not be possible if we did not have inner sight. Any thoughts we think also appear to our inner eye, more clearly in some of us and more dimly in others. Our imagination has a similar way of presenting itself in visual images. What is more, if the spirit inside the body did not see what the organic eye takes in, the spirit would not be able to see anything at all in the other life; yet in reality the spirit must necessarily be destined to see astounding sights beyond number that are invisible to the physical eye. In addition, people who are affirmative can reflect on dreams, especially those of the prophets, who also saw many, many things without using their eyes. Finally, if they are trained in philosophy, they can confirm the idea by this, that what is exterior cannot enter into what is interior, just as a compound cannot enter into its elements. By the same token, physical things cannot enter into spiritual things, only the reverse. Not to mention many other considerations. In the end, the affirmative person becomes convinced that vision is a function of the spirit and not of the eye except under the power of the spirit.

People whose attitude is negative, however, describe all these operations either as physical ones or as flights of fancy. If you tell them that the spirit enjoys much fuller powers of vision than people do in their bodies, they sneer and reject it as nonsense. They believe that once deprived of physical sight they will live in the dark, when to the absolute contrary they will then live in light.

[8] These examples show what it is to examine logic and fact from the viewpoint of truth, and what it is to examine truth from the viewpoint of fact and logic. To do the former is to follow the ordained plan; to do the latter is to violate it. When we follow the ordained plan, we gain light, but when we violate it, we are blinded. The importance of knowing truth and believing it, then, is crystal clear, since truth enlightens us and falsity blinds us. Truth opens up to the rational mind a field that is immeasurable and almost unbounded. Falsity by comparison opens hardly any field at all, even if the appearance is otherwise. That is why angels' wisdom is so vast—because they possess truth. Truth, after all, is the light itself of heaven.

[9] In times past, people who blinded themselves by refusing to believe anything they could not grasp with their senses—so much so that they finally believed in nothing—were called snakes in the tree of knowledge.

They spent a great deal of time creating logical constructs on the basis of sense impressions and the illusions these lead to (which humans find it easy to comprehend and accept), and they led many other people astray; see §§195, 196.

In the next life it is easy to tell them apart from other spirits because they argue over the truth of every tenet of faith. You can show them in thousands upon thousands of ways that a thing is true and they still raise doubts and objections to every single proof. This they would continue to do even if the debate went on forever. As a consequence they are so blind that they lack common sense enough to recognize goodness and truth. Yet they each imagine that they have more wisdom than anyone else in the universe, locating wisdom in their ability to break open any divine conundrum and reason their way to a conclusion on it from some starting point in what is physical. Many individuals admired as wise on earth have more of this character than others. The more ingenuity and book learning people have while maintaining a skeptical attitude, the more they outdo others in insanity. On the other hand, the more ingenuity and book learning they have while maintaining an affirmative attitude, the more wisdom they are capable of acquiring.

By no means are we forbidden to cultivate our rational mind by becoming educated; what we *are* forbidden to do is to make ourselves impervious to the religious truth in the Word.

[10] The inner meaning of the Word has much to say on this subject, especially where the prophetic parts speak of Assyria and Egypt. Assyria symbolizes sophistic reasoning (§§119, 1186), and Egypt symbolizes scholarly learning (§§1164, 1165, 1186, 1462).

Some people try to use fact and logic to investigate religious teachings and divine mysteries and are therefore insane. They are described this way in Isaiah:

I will mix *Egypt* up with *Egypt,* and they will fight, a man against his brother and a man against his companion, city against city, and kingdom against kingdom. And the spirit of *Egypt* will fail in its midst, and its counsel I will swallow up. The water will disappear from the sea, and the river will drain away and dry up. And the streams will recede; the rivers of *Egypt* will shrink and drain away. Reed and rush will wilt. Any seed of the stream will dry up. Jehovah has mixed up in its midst a spirit of perversities and made *Egypt* go astray in all its work, like the straying of drunkards in their own vomit. (Isaiah 19:2, 3, 5, 6, 7, 14)

In the same author:

> Doom to my defiant children, who leave to go down into *Egypt* (but have not asked of my mouth), to strengthen themselves with *Pharaoh's* strength, and to trust in *Egypt's* shadow. And for you *Pharaoh's* strength will turn to shame, and trust in *Egypt's* shadow to disgrace. (Isaiah 30:1, 2, 3)

In the same author:

> Doom to those going down into *Egypt* for help! And on horses they rely, and they trust in chariots (that they are numerous), but they do not look to the Holy One of Israel, and Jehovah they do not seek. And Jehovah will stretch out his hand; the helper will stumble and the one helped will fall, and they are all consumed together. And *Assyria* will fall by a sword that is not a man's, and a sword that is not a human's will devour him. (Isaiah 31:1, 3, 8)

In Jeremiah:

> Two evils my people have done: they have deserted me—the spring of living water—to carve out cisterns for themselves, broken cisterns that do not hold water. Isn't Israel a bondman? If he is a home-born [slave], why has he become plunder? Aren't you doing this to yourself, when you desert Jehovah your God at the time when he is leading you in the way? And now why should you go to *Egypt* to drink the waters of the Sihor, or why should you go to *Assyria* to drink the waters of the river? You [current] generation, see the Word of Jehovah! Have I been Israel's wilderness? A land of darkness? Why have my people said, "We will be in charge; we will not come to you anymore"? Why do you go so energetically to change your way? By *Egypt* as well you will be shamed, just as you were shamed by *Assyria*. (Jeremiah 2:13, 14, 17, 18, 31, 36)

In the same author:

> Listen to the word of Jehovah, remnant of Judah! This is what Jehovah Sabaoth God of Israel has said: "If you resolutely set your face to come into *Egypt*, and you come to stay there, then it will happen that the sword that you are fearing will seize you there in the land of *Egypt*, and the famine that you are dreading will cling to you there in *Egypt*, so that you die there. And it will happen that all the men who set their faces to come into *Egypt* to stay there will die by sword, famine, and contagion,

and they will not have a survivor or an escapee from the evil that I am bringing on you." (Jeremiah 42:15, 16, 17, and following verses)

In Ezekiel:

"And let all the inhabitants of *Egypt* recognize that I am Jehovah. Because these have been a staff of reed to the house of Israel, when you seize it in your palm, you will be shattered to pieces and split every shoulder of theirs, and when they lean on you, you will be broken and bring every haunch of theirs to a standstill." Therefore this is what the Lord Jehovih has said: "Watch: I am bringing a sword on you and will cut human and animal off from you, and the land of *Egypt* will become a ruin and wasteland—and they will know that I am Jehovah—because [Pharaoh] has said, 'The river is mine, and I myself have made it.'" (Ezekiel 29:6, 7, 8, 9, and following verses)

In Hosea:

Ephraim was like a stupid pigeon; on *Egypt* they called; to *Assyria* they went. When they go, I will spread my net out over them. Doom to them, because they wandered away from me! (Hosea 7:11, 12, 13)

In the same author:

Ephraim is grazing on a breeze and pursuing an east wind. Every day he multiplies lies and devastation; and with *Assyria* they strike a pact, and oil is carried off into *Egypt.* (Hosea 12:1)

In the same author:

Israel whored against her god; you delighted in the wage you earned on all the grain-threshing floors. Ephraim will return to *Egypt,* and in *Assyria* they will eat what is unclean. For look! They have left on account of the ruination. *Egypt* will gather them; Moph will bury them. What is desirable of their silver the thorn will possess; the thistle will be in their tents. Ephraim has been struck; their root has dried up; they will not make fruit. Even when they give birth, I will kill the desired things of their belly; my God will reject them because they did not hear him, and they will be wanderers among the nations. (Hosea 9:1, 3, 6, 16, 17)

In Isaiah:

Doom to *Assyria,* the rod of my anger! And he is the staff of my outrage in their hand. He thinks what is not right, and his heart contemplates what is not right, because it is in his heart to destroy, and to cut off not a few nations, since he says, "Aren't my chieftains all monarchs?" I will exact punishment on the fruit of the pride of heart of *Assyria's* king because he has said, "In the strength of my hand have I done this, and in my wisdom, because I have understanding; and I will move the borders of the peoples, and their treasuries I will rob, and as a mighty man I will cast down the inhabitants." Therefore the Lord of lords Sabaoth will send gauntness among his fat ones; and in place of his glory, a burning like the burning of fire will burn. (Isaiah 10:5, 7, 8, 12, 13, 16)

[11] In all these passages, Assyria symbolizes sophistic reasoning, as shown. Egypt and Pharaoh symbolize scholarly learning. Ephraim symbolizes the functions of the intellect, and here and in many other places he depicts the quality of human rationality in people who reason about religious truth from a negative standpoint.

A similar meaning was involved when the Rabshakeh was sent by the king of *Assyria* to speak against Jerusalem and King Hezekiah. The angel of Jehovah in the camp of *Assyria's* king then struck one hundred eighty-five thousand, as related in Isaiah 36, 37, which symbolizes the way people slaughter their rational powers when they argue against divine realities, even if it looks to the people themselves as though they are then being wise.

[12] In many places this kind of reasoning is also called whoredom with the sons of Egypt and with the sons of Assyria, as in Ezekiel:

You *whored with the sons of Egypt*, your neighbors, who were great in flesh, and multiplied your *whoredom*, and you *whored with the sons of Assyria*, without being satisfied. (Ezekiel 16:26, 28; 23:3, 5–21; see §2466)

[13] *But some people investigate logic and fact from the viewpoint of religious teachings and are therefore wise.* They are described in Isaiah:

On that day there will be an altar to Jehovah in the middle of the land of *Egypt*, and a pillar to Jehovah along its border, and it will serve as a sign and as a witness to Jehovah Sabaoth in the land of *Egypt*. For they will cry out to Jehovah because of their oppressors, and he will send them a deliverer and chieftain, who will rescue them. And Jehovah will become known to *Egypt*, and the *Egyptians* will recognize Jehovah on that day. And they will offer sacrifice and minha and swear an oath to Jehovah and fulfill it. (Isaiah 19:18–21)

In the same author:

On that day there will be a path from *Egypt* to *Assyria*, and *Assyria* will come into *Egypt*, and the *Egyptians* will serve *Assyria*. On that day Israel will be a third to *Egypt* and *Assyria,* a blessing in the middle of the earth, whom Jehovah Sabaoth will bless, saying, "A blessing on my people *Egypt* and on the work of my hands, *Assyria,* and on my inheritance, Israel!" (Isaiah 19:23, 24, 25)

This is about a spiritual religion. Its spiritual part is Israel, its rational part is Assyria, and its factual knowledge is Egypt, and these three constitute its intellectual possessions. The three come in this order, which is why it says, "On that day Israel will be a third to Egypt and Assyria," and "A blessing on my people Egypt, on the work of my hands, Assyria, and on my inheritance, Israel." [14] In the same author:

It will happen on that day that a large horn will be blown, and people perishing in the land of *Assyria* and outcasts in the land of *Egypt* will come and bow down to Jehovah on the holy mountain, in Jerusalem. (Isaiah 27:13)

In the same author:

This is what Jehovah has said: "The labor of *Egypt,* and the wares of Cush and of Seba's inhabitants—tall men—will pass over to you and will belong to you. They will walk after you, and to you they will bow down. To you they will pray: 'Only among you does God exist, and there is no other god besides.'" (Isaiah 45:14)

Cush and Seba's inhabitants are religious knowledge (§§117, 1171). In Zechariah:

Egypt will go up to Jerusalem to worship the King, Jehovah Sabaoth. (Zechariah 14:17, 18)

In Micah:

I am looking to Jehovah; I await the God of my salvation; my God will hear me. The day for building your bulwarks is this day, and they will come all the way to you from there, from *Assyria,* and [to] the cities of *Egypt,* and from there, from *Egypt,* all the way to the river. (Micah 7:7, 11, 12)

[15] In Ezekiel:

This is what the Lord Jehovih has said: "At the end of forty years, I will gather *Egypt* from the peoples where they have been scattered, and I will bring *Egypt* back from captivity." (Ezekiel 29:13, 14)

In the same author:

> Here, *Assyria* was a cedar in Lebanon, beautiful in its branch, and [forming] a shady forest, and lofty in its height; and its branch was surrounded by thickets. The water made it grow; with its rivers [the depth] was meandering around the place of its planting and sent out its channels of water to all the trees of the field. Therefore its height became higher than all the trees of the field, and its branches multiplied, and its branches grew long because of the many waters. In its branches every bird of the heavens nested, and under its branches every wild animal of the field gave birth, and in its shade all the great nations lived. And beautiful it became in its size, in the length of its branches, because its root was [going out] to many waters. The cedars did not hide it in the garden of God. The firs were not equal to its branches; no tree in God's garden was equal to it in its beauty. Beautiful I made it in the profusion of its branches, and all the trees of Eden in God's garden strove to match it. (Ezekiel 31:3–9)

These verses depict the earliest church (a heavenly church), the nature of its rationality, and so its wisdom and understanding. That church viewed lower things from the standpoint of divine things, so it viewed truth and therefore anything subordinate to truth from the standpoint of goodness itself. Assyria, the cedar, is rationality. The thickets surrounding its branch are facts. The rivers and water are spiritual kinds of goodness, which is where its root lay. The height and length of its branches is the extent of its reach. God's garden is a spiritual religion. The trees of Eden are perceptions.

This passage and the previous ones show what the rational and factual dimensions in a human being are like when they are subordinate to divine truth and serve to confirm it.

[16] The command to the children of Israel to borrow articles of gold and articles of silver and clothes from the *Egyptians* (Exodus 3:22; 11:2; 12:35, 36) represented and symbolized the fact that logic and facts serve as means to wisdom for people whose attitude is affirmative. So does the repeated statement in the Word that they would come into possession of the goods, houses, vineyards, olive groves, and so on of the surrounding nations. Likewise the claim that the actual gold and silver taken from those nations would become holy, as in Isaiah:

> Jehovah will visit Tyre, and it will go back to its wage as a harlot and will whore with all the monarchies of the earth on the face of the ground

And its merchandise and its harlot's wage will become *holy to Jehovah;* they will not be hidden away and will not be hoarded; because the people living in view of Jehovah will have its merchandise for eating till they are full and for an ancient covering. (Isaiah 23:17, 18)

Tyre's merchandise stands for religious knowledge (§1201), which serves as a harlot's wage for people whose attitude is negative but as a holy blessing for people whose attitude is affirmative.

Something similar is also meant by the Lord's words:

Make yourselves friends by unjust mammon, so that when you pass away, they will take you into the eternal dwelling places. If you do not become faithful in [using] unjust mammon, who will entrust the true [mammon] to you? (Luke 16:9, 11)

The Lot and Condition in the Other World of Nations and Peoples Born outside the Church

2589 THE general opinion is that people born outside the church—who are called pagans and Gentiles—cannot be saved because they do not have the Word and therefore know nothing about the Lord, without whom there is no salvation.

Yet this one train of thought can show that they too are saved: The Lord's mercy is universal; that is, it reaches out to every individual. People outside the church are born human, just like people in the church. Those in the church are fewer, and those outside the church are not to blame for not knowing the Lord.

By the Lord's divine mercy, their lot and condition in the other world has been shown to me.

2590 Many times I have been taught that non-Christians who have lived an ethical life, obeyed the laws, lived lives of mutual charity, and acquired some form of conscience in accordance with their religious tradition are welcomed in the other life. There, angels teach them about the values and beliefs of the faith with tender care. As pupils they are modest, perceptive, and wise, and quickly learn and accept what they are taught. They have adopted no premises that contradict the true tenets of the faith and need dispelling; much less have they created obstacles to belief in the Lord, as many Christians who lived evil lives have. What is more, they do not hate others, avenge any wrongs they do, or concoct plots and deceptions against them. In fact, they wish well to Christians, and yet Christians despise them in return and do their worst to hurt them, although the Lord delivers them from the Christians' ruthless ways and protects them.

[2] To compare Christians and non-Christians in the other world: Christians who have acknowledged religious truth and lived a good life are accepted more readily than non-Christians—but there are not many of them. On the other hand, non-Christians who have lived lives of obedience and mutual charity are accepted more readily than Christians who have not lived as good a life.

In his mercy the Lord accepts and saves anyone anywhere on the globe who has lived a good life, because goodness itself is what accepts truth. A good life is the actual soil in which seed, or truth, is planted. An evil life rejects the seed. With people who succumb to evil, you can teach them a thousand different ways—in fact they can become the best-educated people there are—yet religious truth still reaches no further than their memory. It does not penetrate to the feelings they have in their heart. As a result, the truth they have memorized dissolves in the other world and disappears.

As is true of Christians, though, there are non-Christians who are wise **2591** and non-Christians whose minds are untrained. I was given the opportunity to talk to both kinds, sometimes for several hours or even days, in order to learn what they were like. Hardly any wise non-Christians are found today, but there were very many of them in ancient times. They were especially numerous in the ancient church, whose wisdom spread to many nations. I was allowed to converse with some of these as friend to friend in order to find out what they were like. The superiority of their wisdom over modern wisdom can be seen from the reports that follow.

Once I had with me a spirit who had been among the wise of his day **2592** and who is therefore well known in the scholarly world. With him I discussed various subjects, and since I knew that he had been wise, I talked with him about wisdom, discernment, the ordained plan, the Word, and finally the Lord.

About wisdom, he said that no other wisdom is possible than the wisdom that comes of life. Wisdom cannot be attributed to anything but how we live.

About discernment, he said that it comes of wisdom.

About the ordained plan, he said that it comes from the supreme God, and that to live in harmony with that plan is to be wise and discerning.

[2] As far as the Word goes, when I read something from the prophetic parts out loud to him, it gave him intense pleasure, particularly because the individual names and words symbolized something deeper. He was astounded to hear that study of this symbolism does not interest modern scholars. I could tell clearly that the inner reaches of his thoughts—his mind—were open, while the minds of some Christians standing nearby were closed. The Christians were filled with envy of him, and with disbelief that the Word could have a symbolic meaning. In fact, when I read further from the Word, he said he could not stay there, because he felt that it was too holy for him to endure, so deeply did it affect him. In contrast, the Christians kept saying in an audible voice that they *could* stay there. This was because their inner depths were closed off and nothing holy touched their hearts.

[3] Finally I talked to him about the Lord—how he was born human but was conceived by God, how he shed his humanity and robed himself in divinity, and that he is the one who governs the universe. To this the man answered that he knew quite a bit about the Lord and sensed in his own way that it could not have happened any other way, if the human race was to be saved. All the while, some wicked Christians were reciting a long and varied list of reasons not to believe, but their words did not bother him. "I'm not surprised," he said to them, "because while you were living in your bodies, the ideas you absorbed on this subject were inappropriate. Until you shake off those ideas, you won't be able to take in others that support the truth, any more than people who don't know the truth can."

This man had been a non-Christian.

2593 I was also given the opportunity to talk with other people who had lived in ancient times and had been among the wiser of their day. They first appeared far out in front of me, and from there they could tell what I was thinking deep inside; so they were able to detect many things, and to see them in full. From a single image in my mind they could make out a whole train of thought, which they were able to enrich with delightful wisdom and charming representative scenes. This told me that they were some of the wiser people, and I learned they were from among the ancients. So they came closer, and when I then read out loud to them from the Word, they were extremely thrilled. Their actual pleasure and delight I was able to sense, and what inspired it most strongly was the fact that absolutely everything they were hearing from the Word represented and symbolized heavenly and spiritual qualities. They said that in their day, when they lived in the world, this was the way they thought, spoke, and wrote, and that this was what they studied in order to gain wisdom.

In regard to non-Christians on earth today, they are not as wise but for the most part are simple-hearted. Even so, the ones who have lived lives of mutual charity receive wisdom in the next life. Let me give the following account of them.

2594

I once was listening to the sound of a choral circle, but one that was more sluggish than such circles usually are. Their sound instantly revealed to me that they came from non-Christian nations. Angels told me they were non-Christians who had been revived from death just three or four days earlier. I listened to the circle, or chorus, for a number of hours and could tell even in the short amount of time I was listening that they were improving more and more. When I expressed my surprise, I was told that these people can be taught to form choruses and so to work in unison with each other in the space of a single night, while most Christians can hardly manage it in the space of thirty years.

2595

Choral circles consist of many people speaking in unison, all as one and each one as the whole. More will be said elsewhere about them, the Lord in his divine mercy willing.

Another chorus stood at a distance from me one morning, and from its emblems I was able to tell that its members were Chinese. They presented images of something like a woolly goat, a flat millet loaf, an ebony spoon, and the vision of a floating city.

2596

They wanted to come closer, and when they had approached they said that they wished to be alone with me in order to reveal their thoughts. "But you're not alone," I told them. "There are others, who are upset to hear you tried to get me to yourselves, even though you're guests here." Sensing the resentment of the others, they fell to considering whether they had sinned against their neighbor and tried to usurp what belonged to others. (In the next world, all our thoughts are shared with everyone.) I was able to perceive their agitation. It resulted from the admission that they may have hurt these people, from shame over it, and from other admirable emotions, all of which revealed that they possessed charity.

Soon afterward I talked with them, and eventually we spoke of the Lord. When I called him Christ, I sensed a resistance in them, but the reason then came out. They had developed this reaction in the world from seeing that Christians behaved more badly than they and lacked charity. When I called him simply the Lord, though, they were deeply moved.

Angels then taught them that Christian teachings more than any other teachings in the entire world call for love and charity, but that there are few who live according to them.

2597   There are non-Christians who learned from their own interactions and the reports of others when they lived in the world that Christians live terrible lives—lives of adultery, hatred and feuding, drunkenness, and so on. The non-Christians were horrified by this behavior because it went against their laws, their standards of conduct, and their religious tradition. In the next life, such non-Christians are more reluctant than others to accept the truth of the faith. Angels inform them, though, that Christian doctrine and faith itself teach just the opposite, and that Christians live less in harmony with their teachings than non-Christians do with theirs. When they grasp this, they accept the truth of the faith and revere the Lord, although this takes some time.

2598   Once I read Judges 17 and 18, concerning Micah and the idol, teraphim, and Levite stolen from him by the descendants of Dan. At that time a non-Christian spirit who had worshiped an idol during his bodily life was present, and he listened closely. When he heard what happened to Micah and how much Micah grieved for his idol that the Danites had stolen, he too was touched and overcome with grief, so much so that he hardly knew what to think for all his heartfelt sorrow. I sensed his grief and also the innocence of all his emotions.

Some Christian spirits were present as well, and they noticed and were amazed that this idol worshiper could be moved by such a strong feeling of innocent compassion.

Later, some good spirits talked to him, saying that it was wrong to worship idols. "As a human being," they said, "you're capable of understanding this. You ought to set aside carved images when you think about God the creator and ruler of all heaven and all earth. That God is the Lord."

While they were saying this, I was able to perceive the feelings that lay inside his worship (which were communicated to me), and they were much more reverent than they are in Christians. This made it clear that non-Christians go to heaven more easily than modern Christians whose hearts are not touched, which is what the Lord said in Luke 13:29, 30. In the state he was experiencing, this man was able to absorb everything the faith teaches and to accept it with deep affection. He possessed the compassion that is born of love, and within his ignorance lay innocence. When these are present in us, we accept everything faith teaches without hesitation and with joy.

Afterward he was taken up among the angels.

There was also another non-Christian who had lived a life of neighborly kindness, and he heard some Christian spirits arguing about creeds. (Spirits debate things in much more detail and with much greater subtlety than people on earth, especially when they are debating what is good and true, since goodness and truth belong to the other world.) Listening to them, he was surprised to hear them dispute this way. He did not want to listen, he said, because they were arguing from illusion. "If I am good," he taught them, "goodness itself shows me what is true, and whatever I do not know, I can learn." **2599**

For the most part, honest non-Christians in the other world are taught according to the stage of life they are in and according to their religious persuasions, as far as they can be. So there are different methods of teaching them. Let me describe just three here. **2600**

A state of calm resembling sleep is imposed on some of them, and in it they seem to themselves to be building miniature cities and hiding something secret —something they do not want anyone to hurt—in the middle of them. These cities they give as gifts to others, begging them not to damage the secret treasure in the center. In the process, innocence is instilled in them, as is love for others, along with the thought that the secret has to do with the Lord. They are kept in this state for fairly long, and it is a state of ignorance within which lies innocence. **2601**

Young children guard them, to keep anyone from hurting them.

I spoke with them and was much affected by the feeling of innocence and neighborly love in them. Their anxiety over finding a way to hide their secret, and their reverent fear that it might be violated, also touched me.

There is one nation (in southeast Asia, I am told) that has a religious tradition of worshiping the Greatest God with a ritual in which, during their devotions, they first glorify themselves and then directly afterward grovel like worms. It is also a traditional idea of theirs that this Greatest God sits above the universe (which they believe revolves) looking down to see what they are doing. **2602**

Because these had been their traditions, they return to them in the other world. I talked with them while they were creating images of this kind for themselves.

Most of them are modest, obedient, and simple-hearted.

Angels gradually free them from their fantasy through lessons that harmonize with their religious beliefs. They teach that the Greatest God is the Lord; that what they can pride themselves on is their ability to worship him; that they nonetheless do resemble worms; and that the Lord does see absolutely everything from on high.

So their tradition provides a suitable means for leading them into a knowledge of goodness and truth.

2603 Some non-Christians from areas where the people are black bring with them from life in the world a willingness to be treated harshly. They believe a person can come into heaven only through punishment and hardship. Afterward they expect to have happier times, which they describe as paradise.

Because they acquire this idea from their religious tradition and take it with them, they actually are treated harshly at first in the other life by certain people whom they call devils. Later they enter the marvelous gardens described in §1622. However, angels teach them that the Lord has turned their punishments and afflictions to good, as he does for people undergoing inward trials. "The gardens are not heaven," they explain. "They are your own longings for heavenly and spiritual qualities. You've been on the path of truth, so to speak, though you were walking in the shadow of ignorance."

These non-Christians talked with me for a long time. While they were actively being afflicted, they spoke with a kind of click, so they sounded different from others. When it was all over, though, and they had been taken up into the gardens, they no longer spoke that way but almost as the angels do.

Their tradition also gives them a desire for something deeper, they believe. They said that while they are being treated harshly they are black but that afterward they shed their blackness and take on a brightness. Although their bodies are black, they know, their souls shine brightly.

2604 When non-Christians who have worshiped a god in the form of an image, statue, or carving of some kind go to the other world, they are often introduced to people who stand in for their gods, or idols—the point being for them to discard their fantasies—and then after several days with them, they are taken away.

Sometimes those who have worshiped other people are also introduced to them, or to others who double for them. This happens with many Jews, who are introduced to Abraham, Jacob, Moses, and David.

When they perceive that these people are just as human as anyone else, though, and that they have no help to offer, they become embarrassed and move on to the place allotted to them according to the way they have lived.

The best-loved of the non-Christians in the next life are Africans, because they accept heavenly goodness and truth more easily than anyone else. They particularly want to be described as obedient, but they do not want to be called believers. They say that Christians can be referred to that way, since they possess the teachings of the faith, but not they themselves unless they accept the same teachings or, as they put it, *can* accept them.

I once talked with some people who had been part of the ancient **2605** church, who had known at the time that the Lord was going to come, and who had been imbued with religious goodness but had defected and become idolaters. They were out in front toward the left, in a shadowy spot, where their circumstances were wretched. Their speech had a reedy, droning quality and was almost devoid of rational thought. They said they had been there for many centuries and were sometimes freed to do ignominious work as a service to other people.

These people inspired me to think about the large number of Christians who are idolaters not on the outside but on the inside, who at heart deny the Lord and therefore the truth of the faith—and about the kind of lot that awaits them in the other world.

A Disclosure of

SECRETS OF HEAVEN

Contained in

SACRED SCRIPTURE

or

THE WORD OF THE LORD

Those in

Genesis

Chapter 21

Together with Amazing Things Seen and Heard
in the World of Spirits & in the Heaven of Angels

At the End of the Current Chapter, Concerning
The Way Marriage Is Viewed in Heaven
and the Way Adultery Is Viewed

Genesis 21

A N earlier name for the Old Testament Word was "the Law and the Prophets" [Matthew 22:40]. "The law" meant all the narrative books: the five books of Moses, and Joshua, Judges, Samuel, and Kings. "The Prophets" meant all the prophetic books—Isaiah, Jeremiah, Ezekiel, Daniel, Hosea, Joel, Amos, Obadiah, Jonah, Micah, Nahum, Habakkuk, Zephaniah, Haggai, Zechariah, Malachi—and the Psalms of David. **2606**

The narrative parts of the Word are also *called* Moses, so the text often refers to "Moses and the Prophets" instead of "the Law and the Prophets"; and the prophetic books are called Elijah (see the preface to Genesis 18).

In regard to the narratives, their contents are all historically true, except for those of the early chapters in Genesis, where the narrative is made up, as discussed in the second volume. **2607**

Although the narrative details are historically true, they still have an inner meaning. Like the prophetic parts, the narrative in its inner meaning speaks exclusively of the Lord. It does also deal with heaven, the church, and different aspects of both, but all these are the Lord's, so through them the account focuses on the Lord and consequently is part of the Word. All the historical events in it represent something, and each of the words in which the story is couched is symbolic. The explanations to this point involving Abraham show that the events represent something. Those to come involving Isaac, Jacob and his twelve sons, Egypt, the people's journey through the wilderness, their entry into Canaan, and all the rest will show the same thing, the Lord in his divine mercy willing.

[2] The fact that each of the words in the story has a symbolism is also plain from evidence offered above. One example is the fact that the names have symbolic meaning: Egypt symbolizes secular knowledge; Assyria, rationality; Ephraim, the intellect; Tyre, religious knowledge; Zion, a heavenly religion; Jerusalem, a spiritual religion; and so on with all the other names. So do the words. A king, for instance, symbolizes truth; a priest, goodness; and the rest all have their inner significance, too—a kingdom, city, house, nation, people, garden, vineyard, or olive grove; gold, silver, bronze, and iron; birds, animals, bread, wine, oil, morning, day, and light. The symbolism is consistent throughout both the narrative and the prophetic books, even though they were written by different authors at different periods. It would never have been so consistent had the Word not come down from heaven.

From this it can be seen that the Word has an inner meaning. The same thing can also be seen from the consideration that God's Word could not possibly be about mere humans like Abraham, Isaac, Jacob, their descendants (the worst of the nations), their kings, wives, sons, daughters, and harlots, their marauding, and so forth. In and of themselves, these things do not deserve even to be mentioned in the Word, unless they represent and symbolize the kinds of things that exist in the Lord's kingdom. That makes them worthy of the Word.

2608   Much of what is found in the Prophets is similar, such as the passages quoted in §1888 and this one in Isaiah:

> Moab will howl; all Moab will howl because of the foundations of Kirhareseth. You mourn, nonetheless, you who are worn down, because the fields of Heshbon have failed, the grapevine of Sibmah. The lords of the nations crush the branches; all the way to Jazer they reached; they wander in the wilderness; its offshoots have been pulled off. They crossed the sea; therefore I will weep for the grapevine of Sibmah with the weeping of Jazer. I will water you with my teardrop, Heshbon and Elealeh, because on the vintage and on your harvest the hedad has fallen. (Isaiah 16:7, 8, 9)

And in Jeremiah:

> A voice of outcry in Horonaim; devastation and a great crushing! Moab has been shattered. Its young ones have made their outcry heard, because on the ascent to Luhith, with weeping their weeping ascends, because in the descent to Horonaim, its foes have heard the outcry of their

shattering. Judgment has come to the land of the plain—to Holon and to Jahzah and to Mephaath and on Dibon and on Nebo and on Beth-diblathaim and on Kiriathaim and on Beth-gamul and on Beth-meon and on Kerioth and on Bozrah. (Jeremiah 48:3, 4, 5, 21, 22, 23, 24)

This is what the Word's prophetic parts are like in many places. If they did not have an inner meaning, they would be pointless. In reality, though, because the Word is divine, it has to hold within it the laws of the heavenly kingdom we are going to enter.

Commandments regulating life, however, serve a person's actual life, so they are useful in both the literal and deeper senses. These include everything in the Ten Commandments, and much of the Law and the Prophets. The contents of the literal meaning were for the people and populations of that time, who could not understand anything deeper. The contents of the inner meaning were for the angels, who have no interest in what lies on the surface.

2609

If the Ten Commandments did not also contain inner depths, they would never have been issued on Mount Sinai in such a miraculous way. After all, the rules they lay down—to honor one's parents, not to steal, not to kill, not to commit adultery, not to envy what belongs to another—are rules that non-Jews also acknowledge and have codified in their laws. The children of Israel, as human beings, should have known them anyway, without so grand an announcement. As noted, though, they were useful to people's lives on both levels, and they served as outward forms produced by inward laws (which correspond to one another), and that is why they came down from heaven to Mount Sinai in the miraculous way they did. Their inner meaning was spoken and heard in heaven, while their outer form was spoken and heard on earth.

[2] Take, for example, the rule that when people honored their parents their days would be lengthened on the land. Angels in heaven perceived that the parents meant the Lord. They perceived the land to be his kingdom, which people who worship him with love and faithfulness would possess forever as his children and heirs. People on earth, however, took parents to mean parents, the land to mean the land of Canaan, and the lengthening of days to be years of life.

Angels in heaven perceived the ban on theft to be a ban on taking anything away from the Lord or claiming any righteousness or merit as their own. People on earth, though, took it as a ban on theft. Clearly both senses of the commandments are valid.

Again, angels in heaven perceived the ban on murder to be a ban on hating anyone or choking off anything good or true in a person, but people on earth took it as a ban on killing their friends.

The same holds true for the other commandments.

Genesis 21

1. And Jehovah visited Sarah as he had said. And Jehovah did to Sarah as he had spoken.

2. And Sarah conceived and bore to Abraham a son for his old age, at the set time, as God had spoken with him.

3. And Abraham called the name of his son born to him—whom Sarah had borne to him—Isaac.

4. And Abraham circumcised Isaac his son, a son of eight days, as God had commanded him.

5. And Abraham was a son of a hundred years when Isaac his son was born to him.

6. And Sarah said, "God has made laughter for me; everyone who hears will laugh for me."

7. And she said, "Who would have said, 'For Abraham, Sarah will nurse sons'? For I have delivered a son for his old age."

8. And the child grew and was weaned, and Abraham made a grand banquet on the day when Isaac was weaned.

9. And Sarah saw the son of Hagar the Egyptian—whom she had borne to Abraham—mocking.

10. And she said to Abraham, "Throw out this slave and her son, because a slave's son must not be heir along with my son, with Isaac."

11. And the matter was very evil in Abraham's eyes on account of his son.

12. And God said to Abraham, "Don't let it be evil in your eyes because of your son and because of your slave. Everything that Sarah says to you, listen to her voice, because in Isaac your seed will be called yours."

*   *   *   *

13. "And also the slave's son I will make into a nation, since he is your seed."

14. And Abraham got up early in the morning and took bread and a flask of water and gave it to Hagar (he put it on her shoulder) and [gave her] the boy and sent her away. And she went and wandered in the wilderness of Beer-sheba.

15. And the water from the flask was used up, and she thrust the boy under one of the shrubs.

16. And she went and sat by herself opposite, distancing herself about a bowshot, because she said, "Don't let me see the death of the boy!" And she sat opposite and raised her voice and wept.

17. And God heard the voice of the boy, and God's angel cried out to Hagar from heaven and said to her, "What's the matter, Hagar? Don't be afraid, because God has heard the voice of the boy in the place where he is.

18. Get up; pick up the boy and strengthen the hold of your hand on him, because I will make him into a great nation."

19. And God opened her eyes, and she saw a well of water and went and filled the flask of water and gave the boy a drink.

20. And God was with the boy, and he grew and resided in the wilderness and was an archer.

21. And he resided in the wilderness of Paran, and his mother took for him a wife from the land of Egypt.

✳ ✳ ✳ ✳

22. And it happened at that time that Abimelech (and Phicol, the chief of his army) said to Abraham, saying, "God be with you in all that you are doing.

23. And now swear to me here by God, if you are lying to me or my son or my grandson, . . . ! As I have done kindness to you, so you are to do to me and to the land in which you are staying."

24. And Abraham said, "I will swear."

25. And Abraham denounced Abimelech on account of a well of water that Abimelech's slaves had seized.

26. And Abimelech said, "I do not know who has done this thing, and you did not point it out to me, either, and I did not hear, either, until today."

27. And Abraham took flock and herd and gave them to Abimelech, and they both struck a pact.

28. And Abraham set seven ewe lambs of the flock off by themselves.

29. And Abimelech said to Abraham, "What are these seven lambs here that you set by themselves?"

30. And he said, "Because you must take seven lambs from my hand; therefore let it serve as a witness for me that I dug this well."

31. Therefore he called the place Beer-sheba, because there they both swore.

32. And they struck a pact in Beer-sheba. And Abimelech (and Phicol, the chief of his army) rose, and they returned to the land of the Philistines.

33. And he planted a grove in Beer-sheba and called there on the name of the God of Eternity.

34. And Abraham stayed in the land of the Philistines for many days.

Summary

2610 THE first topic here in the inner meaning is the Lord's divine rationality, represented by Isaac (verses 1, 2, 3, 4, 5, 6, 7, 8).

2611 The next is his merely human rationality, which was then removed and which is the son of Hagar the Egyptian (verses 9, 10, 11, 12).

2612 After it has been removed, he—Hagar's son—along with his mother represents a spiritual religion, whose state is discussed next (verses 13, 14, 15, 16, 17, 18, 19, 20, 21).

2613 Verses 22 to the end have to do with human reasoning superimposed on teachings about faith, which in themselves are divine.

2614 The teachings that have human logic superimposed on them are Beer-sheba (verses 14, 31, 33).

❁❁❁❁❁❁❁❁❁❁❁❁❁❁❁❁❁❁❁❁❁❁❁❁❁❁

Inner Meaning

2615 GENESIS 21:1. *And Jehovah visited Sarah as he had said. And Jehovah did to Sarah as he had spoken.*

Jehovah visited Sarah symbolizes the presence of heavenly divinity within his spiritual divinity. *As he had said* means as he had perceived. *And Jehovah did to Sarah* symbolizes a state of union. *As he had spoken* means as he had thought.

2616 *Jehovah visited Sarah* symbolizes the presence of heavenly divinity within his spiritual divinity, as can be seen from the following: *Jehovah* symbolizes heavenly divinity—divine goodness, that is, or in other words, Being itself, which is composed of love and mercy and is therefore goodness itself. *Visiting* means being present. And *Sarah* symbolizes divine spirituality—divine truth, that is—as discussed in §§1468, 1901, 2063, 2065, 2507.

As he had said means as he had perceived. This can be seen from the symbolism of *saying* in scriptural narrative as *perceiving* (discussed at §§2238, 2260, 2552). **2617**

And Jehovah did to Sarah symbolizes the state of union of the Lord's spiritual divinity within his heavenly divinity. This can be seen from the symbolism of *doing*, when used of the Lord's divinity, as every result and consequently as a state; and from the symbolism of *Jehovah* and *Sarah*, given just above at §2616. **2618**

About the state of union of the Lord's spiritual divinity within his heavenly divinity: This union is the marriage itself of goodness and truth, from which comes the heavenly marriage, which is the Lord's kingdom in the heavens and on earth. That is why the Lord's kingdom is so often called a marriage or compared to a marriage in the Word. The reason, which is a mystery, is that the marriage of divine goodness and truth—and of divine truth and goodness—in the Lord is the source of all married love. Through this it is the source of all heavenly and spiritual love.

None of the other secrets hidden in these words—"Jehovah visited Sarah as he had said, and Jehovah did to Sarah as he had spoken"—can be verbalized, because they are inexpressible. After all, they embrace the state itself of the union between the Lord's divinity and humanity. The Lord uses different kinds of heavenly light to present this union to angels in a visible way, and he illustrates it with indescribable representations. He cannot present it to people on earth in this way, though, because it would require the use of objects visible by worldly light, and to such objects it is inaccessible. In fact, to describe it in worldly terms would only make it more obscure.

As he had spoken means as he had thought. This is established by the symbolism of *speaking* as thinking—a symbolism discussed in §§2271, 2287. The perception symbolized by "Jehovah had said" came from the Lord's heavenly divinity. The thought symbolized by "Jehovah had spoken," though, came by way of his spiritual divinity from his heavenly divinity. That is why the literal sense of the words contains the near repetition "as he had said" and "as he had spoken." **2619**

The light the world offers, however, does not enable even the most brilliant people to grasp what it is to perceive from heavenly divinity and what it is to think from heavenly divinity by means of spiritual divinity. How well anyone can grasp the rest in all its infinity, then, is evident. (Thought stems from perception; see §§1919, 2515.)

In humans, goodness is the source of perception, while truth is the means of thought. Goodness is a matter of love and of the emotions that go to make up love, so perception rises out of these. Truth, though, is a matter of faith, so faith is a matter of thought. The former is symbolized in scriptural narrative by *saying,* but the latter by *speaking.* On the other hand, when the word *say* is used by itself, it can symbolize either perceiving or thinking, because it involves both.

2620   Genesis 21:2. *And Sarah conceived and bore to Abraham a son for his old age, at the set time, as God had spoken with him.*

She conceived and bore means that it existed and emerged. *Sarah [conceived and bore] to Abraham* means from the uniting of the Lord's spiritual divinity with his heavenly divinity. *A son* symbolizes divine rationality. *For his old age* means when the moment was ripe for him to shed his humanity. *At the set time* means when his rationality had developed the ability to receive [divinity]. *As God had spoken with him* means as [the Lord] wished.

2621   *She conceived and bore* means that it existed and emerged. Specifically (as mentioned below), divine rationality existed and emerged from the uniting of the Lord's spiritual divinity with his heavenly divinity. This can be seen from the symbolism of *conceiving* and *bearing.*

On the Word's inner level, only spiritual and heavenly conception and delivery are meant (see §2584). Here, though, divine conception and delivery are meant, because the subject is the Lord's rational mind after it had become divine. Existence and emergence apply mainly to the Lord, because he alone exists and emerges.

Further in respect to existence and emergence, it seems as if the two were almost the same, but they are not. Everyone and everything has its existence from being conceived, but its emergence from being born. So just as conception comes before birth, existence comes before emergence.

[2] Our soul is our actual being, while our ability to sense things, or our body, is what manifests us, because the soul manifests itself in the body.

Heavenly and spiritual love is the core being of a person who is regenerating, while rationality and sensation permeated with that love is what enables the same person to emerge into presence. The situation is the same with absolutely everything in the universe; nothing is at all possible that does not have its conception, allowing it to *exist,* and its birth, allowing it to *emerge.*

Another consideration can shed light on the same thing, but only scholars will appreciate it: Every result has its means, and every means has its goal. The goal is what exists within the means, and the means are the way the goal emerges. Likewise the means are what exist within the result, but the result is the way the means emerge.

Sarah [conceived and bore] to Abraham means from the uniting of the **2622** Lord's spiritual divinity with his heavenly divinity, as can be seen from the following: *Sarah* represents spiritual divinity, or divine truth, as dealt with in §§1468, 1901, 2063, 2065, 2172, 2173, 2198, 2507. And *Abraham* represents heavenly divinity, or divine goodness, as dealt with in §§1989, [2010,] 2011, 2172, 2198, 2501.

On the union of his spiritual divinity with his heavenly divinity, see the remarks above at §2618.

A son symbolizes divine rationality, as the symbolism of a *son* shows: **2623** in the Word's inner meaning, a son symbolizes truth (§§489, 491, 533). Since truth is the main component of the rational mind (§§2072, 2189), a son also symbolizes rationality. Here it symbolizes divine rationality, whose primary component is goodness. Goodness is also what Isaac—the son mentioned here—represents, as will be discussed below [§2658].

For his old age means when the moment was ripe for him to shed his **2624** humanity. This can be seen from the symbolism of *old age* as the stage at which he would shed his humanity and put on divinity (discussed at §2198). Abraham was then an old man of a hundred years, and a hundred symbolizes a condition of full oneness, as the explanation at verse 5 will show [§2636].

At the set time means when his rationality had developed the ability to **2625** receive [divinity], as can be seen from the symbolism of a *time*.

Two things seem indispensable to us while we are living in the world, because they are hallmarks of our nature: space and time. To live in space and time, then, is to live in the world—the physical world. Both disappear in the other life. In the world of spirits they still seem to exist, because spirits recently released from their bodies bring with them a mental image of earthly phenomena, but eventually they realize that no space or time exists there. Instead they have states. States in the next life correspond to space and time in the physical world. A state of being corresponds to space, and a state of becoming, to time. For more on space and location, see §§1274, 1379, 1380, 1382.

[2] While living in the world of nature, then, how well can we comprehend what we hear about the next life and other secrets of faith? It should be plain to everyone that we will not be willing to believe such concepts until we use what we know about this world, and even what we learn through our senses, to grasp them. We cannot help thinking

that if we discarded the idea of space and time (and especially if we discarded space and time itself), we would completely disappear. We presume nothing would be left for us to feel or think with aside from a vague, incomprehensible something-or-other. The truth, though, is exactly the opposite. Angelic life, which is the wisest and happiest of all, is free of space and time.

[3] That is why various ages in the Word do not symbolize ages, on an inner level, but conditions. So old age in the current verse does not mean old age. The numbers do not mean numbers, either, but certain particular conditions. A hundred years is an example, as discussed below [§§2635–2636].

This now shows that a *set time* symbolizes a condition in which the Lord's rationality had developed the ability to receive.

[4] We can now turn to the subject at hand, which is this: Divine rationality existed and emerged from the union of the Lord's spiritual divinity with his heavenly divinity when the moment was ripe for him to shed his humanity and when his rationality had developed the ability to receive [divinity]. Such is the inner-level symbolism of the words *Sarah conceived and bore to Abraham a son for his old age, at the set time.* In this regard, it needs to be known that humanity begins in the deepest reaches of the rational mind (see §§2106, 2194). It also needs to be known that the Lord gradually advanced to the point where his human nature became one with his divine nature, and his divine nature one with his human (1864, 2033, 2523). This he did under his own power (1921, 2025, 2026, 2083) through constant inward struggles and victories (1690, 1737, 1813) and constant revelations from his divine side (1616, 2500). Finally he rid himself completely of the humanity he had received from his mother (1414, 1444, 2574). In this way he made the rational part of his humanity divine, as the contents of the current verse describe.

This shows how to understand the explanation, "when the moment was ripe for him to shed his humanity and when his rationality had developed the ability to receive [divinity]."

[5] Some idea of this process can be formed from the experiences of people who are being reborn. The Lord implants the heavenly qualities of love and the spiritual qualities of faith in them not all at once but gradually. When these qualities turn our rational mind into something that is open to receiving them, we are first reborn—largely through inner struggles in which we win. When this happens, the moment is ripe for us to shed our old self and put on a new one. For more on a person's rebirth, see §§677, 679, 711, 848, 986, 1555, 2475.

As God had spoken with him means as [the Lord] wished. This can be **2626** seen from the symbolism of *speaking* as thinking (discussed in §§2271, 2287, 2619). The reason it means wishing here is that God is the one being said to have spoken; for God, to think is to will.

Genesis 21:3. *And Abraham called the name of his son born to him—* **2627** *whom Sarah had borne to him—Isaac.*

Abraham called the name of his son born to him means that its nature was divine. *Whom Sarah had borne to him* means existing and emerging from spiritual divinity united with heavenly divinity. *Isaac* symbolizes divine rationality.

Abraham called the name of his son born to him means that its nature **2628** was divine, as can be seen from the following: *Abraham* represents the Lord's heavenly divinity, or his divine goodness, as mentioned many times before. *Calling* [or giving] *a name* symbolizes identifying the character, as discussed at §§144, 145, 1754, 1896, 2009. A *son* symbolizes the rational mind, as mentioned in §2623. And *born to him* means emerging from divinity. This shows that "Abraham called the name of his son born to him" means that its nature was divine.

To people who focus on the inner meaning these few words reveal three secrets. (1) The Lord's divine humanity emerged from divinity itself, as dealt with further in the current verse. (2) The Lord's divine humanity was not only conceived but also born from Jehovah. As a result, the Lord in his divine humanity is called the Son of God and the Only-Born (John 1:14, 18, 49; 3:16, 18, 35, 36; 5:19–27; 6:69; 9:35; 10:36; 11:27; 14:13, 14; 17:1; 20:31; likewise in the rest of the Gospels). (3) The Lord's divine humanity is Jehovah's name; in other words, the Lord's divine humanity is his nature. See John 12:28.

Whom Sarah had borne to him means existing and emerging from spir- **2629** itual divinity united with heavenly divinity, as can be seen from the following: *Bearing* symbolizes emerging, a symbolism dealt with in §2621. Birth presupposes conception, and birth (or emergence) comes from spiritual divinity, while conception (or existence) comes from heavenly divinity. At this point, the two had become one, so bearing here symbolizes both existence and emergence. And *Sarah* represents spiritual divinity united with heavenly divinity; see §§1468, 1901, 2063, 2065, 2172, 2173, 2198, 2507.

These secrets are too deep to explain or even to illustrate by means of worldly analogies. They are for the minds of angels, to whom they are presented visually in heaven's light in indescribable ways.

Isaac symbolizes divine rationality, as established by previous remarks **2630** concerning Abraham, Isaac, and Jacob in §§1893, 2066, 2083: Abraham represents the Lord's highest level of divinity; Isaac represents his divine rationality; and Jacob represents his earthly divinity. This will also become clear below where Isaac is discussed [§§2637, 2643, 2648–2649, 2658].

2631   Genesis 21:4. *And Abraham circumcised Isaac his son, a son of eight days, as God had commanded him.*

Abraham circumcised Isaac his son symbolizes purification of his own rational mind. *A son of eight days* symbolizes a beginning and continuation. *As God had commanded* means in accord with the divinely ordained plan.

2632   *Abraham circumcised Isaac his son* symbolizes purification of his own rational mind. This can be seen from the symbolism of being *circumcised* as being purified (discussed in §2039) and from the representation of *Isaac* as divine rationality (mentioned in §2630).

[2] The Lord's earliest rationality came into being the same way it does with others: through secular and religious knowledge. This was mentioned earlier [§§1893, 2078], in a discussion of Ishmael, who represents that rational ability. Because it came into being through secular and religious knowledge and therefore (as it does with others) by an external route—the route of the senses—much of what the Lord possessed had necessarily come from the world. That is where the rational mind acquires its notions. This was all the more true because he had received a heredity from his mother. Those worldly notions (and this heredity) were what the Lord gradually shed from his rational mind, which he continued to do until he had developed the ability to receive divinity (2624, 2625). At this point the Lord's divine rationality, represented by Isaac, was born (2630). It came into being not through an external route (the route of the senses), as his earlier rational ability had, but by way of an inner route, from divinity itself (2628, 2629). Because this did not happen all at once but over time (1690, 2033), it was purified, and purified constantly, which is what is meant by the statement that Abraham circumcised his son, a son of eight days.

John too indicates that the Lord gradually made his rational mind divine and continually purified it:

> Jesus said, "Father, glorify your name." So a voice went out from heaven: "I both have glorified it and will glorify it again." (John 12:28)

Glorifying something is making it divine; see §§1603, 1999.

[3] In the ancient church, circumcision actually represented and symbolized a person's purification from self-love and materialism—again, a gradual and constant purification. See §§2039, 2046 at the end, 2049, 2056. We become particularly pure when we are born anew, or regenerated. At

that point, the Lord's influence reaches us by an inner way—through goodness in our conscience—and gradually and constantly detaches the evil that clings to us by heredity and by actual deed.

A son of eight days symbolizes a beginning and continuation. This can **2633** be seen from the symbolism of the eighth day, the day of circumcision, as every new beginning and so as a continuation, which was treated of at §2044.

As God had commanded means in accord with the divinely ordained **2634** plan, as can be seen from the symbolism of *God's commanding,* or the commandments. God's commandments, or the things he has commanded, are all the laws of his divinely ordained plan, in whole and in part. In fact, the divine plan is equivalent to God's perpetual command. Living according to God's commandments and within God's commandments, then, is living according to the divine plan and within the divine plan. This is why "God had commanded" means in accord with the divine plan.

It was in accord with the divine plan that every male be circumcised on the eighth day after his birth. It was not that circumcision accomplished anything, or that the circumcised rather than the uncircumcised would enter God's kingdom. Instead, the point was that this ritual in a representative religion corresponded to purification of the heart. (This correspondence will be discussed elsewhere, with the Lord's divine mercy [§§2799, 4462, 7044–7045].)

It is in accord with the divine plan that the heart—our inner depths— be gradually and constantly purified of evil in the form of cravings, and of falsity in the form of resulting delusions. Commandments about purification of the heart are all without exception part of the divine plan. To the extent that we live within these commandments, then, we live within God's plan. And to the extent that we live within God's plan, the Lord rearranges everything inside us—both the thoughts of our reasoning and the facts we know—in accord with the pattern he creates in the heavens. As a result we become heaven on a small scale, corresponding to heaven on the largest scale.

Genesis 21:5. *And Abraham was a son of a hundred years when Isaac his* **2635** *son was born to him.*

Abraham was a son of a hundred years symbolizes a state of full union. *When Isaac his son was born to him* means when the Lord's rational mind became divine.

Abraham was a son of a hundred years symbolizes a state of full union, **2636** as can be seen from the following: A *hundred* symbolizes completeness, as the remarks just below will show. And *years* symbolize a state, as discussed in §§482, 487, 488, 493, 893—here, a state of union.

It is not easy to describe intelligibly the state in which the Lord's divinity is fully united to his humanity—or, what is the same, to his rationality, since humanity begins in the deepest part of the rational mind (§§2106, 2194). Still, it can be illustrated by the state that is described as complete when a person is reforming and regenerating.

[2] People know that we cannot be reborn before we are grown up, because that is when we first gain the use of reason and judgment and so are capable of receiving goodness and truth from the Lord. Before we reach that stage, the Lord prepares us by instilling in us the kinds of things that can serve as soil for the seeds of truth and goodness. They include many states of innocence and love for others, a knowledge of what is good and true, and thoughts that grow out of both. This goes on for many years before we are reborn. When we have been permeated with them and are therefore ready, our state is described as complete, because our inner depths are then prepared to receive. In humankind, all the gifts the Lord gives before regeneration and as the means *for* regeneration are called a remnant. In the Word, a remnant is symbolized by the number ten (§§576, 1738, 2284), and also by a hundred, when conditions are ripe for regeneration (§1988).

[3] This explanation can illustrate what it means to speak of a state in which humanity was fully united to divinity in the Lord. It means the point at which he had acquired enough divinity within his humanity— that is, within his rational mind—that he could make divinity itself one with the divinity acquired in his rational mind. This he did under his own power, through the battles and victories of his inward trials and through the powers of divine wisdom and understanding.

It was for the sake of representing this state that Isaac was not born to Abraham until Abraham had reached a hundred years of age, despite the many years he spent in Canaan.

These are the secrets contained in this number: Abraham's one hundred years.

[4] Other scriptural passages can also show that a hundred symbolizes completeness, as in Isaiah:

> No longer will there be a days-old baby or an old person from there who does not *fulfill* his or her days, because a youth will die *at the age of a hundred years,* and a sinner will be cursed *at the age of a hundred years.* (Isaiah 65:20)

Clearly a hundred stands for completeness here, since it says, "No longer will there be a days-old baby or an old person who does not fulfill his or her days," and mentions a youth and a sinner of a hundred years—that is, at a time when their state is complete. [5] In Matthew:

> Everyone who leaves behind houses or brothers or sisters or father or mother or wife or children or fields for my name will receive *a hundredfold* and will inherit *eternal life*. (Matthew 19:29; Mark 10:29, 30)

The hundredfold stands for completeness, or for good measure pressed down, shaken, and overflowing (Luke 6:38). [6] In Luke:

> Some seed fell on good earth, and it bore fruit sprouting *a hundredfold*. (Luke 8:8; Matthew 13:8, 23; Mark 4:20)

Here too a hundred stands for completeness. The number would not have been mentioned had it not symbolized this. Likewise in the place where the Lord speaks metaphorically about some debtors of which one owed a *hundred* baths of oil, and another, a *hundred* kors of wheat (Luke 16:5, 6, 7). Likewise again in other places where the number is mentioned. The meaning resembles that of a thousand, for a discussion of which, see §2575.

When Isaac his son was born to him means when the Lord's rational mind became divine. This can be seen from the symbolism of *being born* as emerging into reality (discussed at §§2584, 2621, 2629) and from the representation of *Isaac* as divine rationality (mentioned in §2630). This rationality is said to have been born *to Abraham* when it became divine, as also above in verse 3: "Abraham called the name of his son *born to him*." See §2628.

2637

Genesis 21:6, 7. *And Sarah said, "God has made laughter for me; everyone who hears will laugh for me." And she said, "Who would have said, 'For Abraham, Sarah will nurse sons'? For I have delivered a son for his old age."*

2638

Sarah said symbolizes a perception from spiritual divinity. *God has made laughter for me* symbolizes a desire for heavenly truth. *Everyone who hears will laugh for me* means that everything involved in that desire will have an effect. *And she said* means a thought. *Who would have said, "For Abraham, Sarah will nurse sons"?* means that by his own strength the Lord implanted his humanity in his divinity. *For I have delivered a son for his old age* means that this happened when the days were completed.

Sarah said symbolizes a perception from spiritual divinity. This can be seen from the symbolism of *saying* as perceiving (mentioned frequently)

2639

and from the representation of *Sarah* as spiritual divinity, or divine truth (mentioned at §2622).

2640   *God has made laughter for me* symbolizes a desire for heavenly truth. This can be seen from the symbolism of *laughter* as a desire for truth (discussed in §§2072, 2216) and from that of *God's making* as its heavenly source.

2641   *Everyone who hears will laugh for me* means that everything involved in that desire will have an effect, as can be seen from the symbolism of *hearing* and *laughing*. In the Word, *hearing* relates to the whole concept of desire, but *laughing* relates to the whole concept of thought. Many passages in the Word demonstrate this, as do correspondences; see §2542. Because the current context concerns the desire for heavenly truth, it says *everyone hearing,* which symbolizes everything involved in the desire.

For the idea that *laughing* means being affected by truth, or having a desire for it, see §§2072, 2216, 2640.

2642   *And she said* means a thought. This is established by the symbolism of *saying* as perceiving and also as thinking, a symbolism mentioned quite often; see the end of §2619.

2643   *Who would have said, "For Abraham, Sarah will nurse sons"?* means that by his own strength the Lord implanted his humanity in his divinity, as can be seen from the representation of *Abraham* and *Sarah* and from the symbolism of *nursing* and *sons. Abraham* represents divine goodness, and *Sarah,* divine truth, as shown. Milk is something spiritual that comes from a heavenly source, or in other words, truth that comes of goodness (see §2184), so *nursing* is implanting it. *Sons* are truth, and here they are truth in the rational mind, as can be seen from the symbolism of sons, §§489, 490, 491, 533.

The reason these words in an inner sense mean that the Lord implanted his humanity in his divinity by his own strength is that divine truth is the same as divine humanity. When it is said to nurse sons for Abraham, the meaning is that he implanted his humanity in his divinity; and because it is his humanity [that is said to nurse sons], it means he did it by his own power.

It is hard to explain these words to the intellect more clearly. If the explanation were drawn out further, the meaning would grow still dimmer. The subject is divine, after all, and it can be presented to angels only through heavenly and spiritual images. If it were presented to people in some lofty style, it would sink down into the kind of ideas that people have—ideas connected with matter and with the physical body.

[2] In addition, it is important to know that the nature of the Lord's divine rationality when it was first born is described in these words: "*God has made laughter for me; everyone who hears will laugh for me.*" *And she said, "Who would have said, 'For Abraham, Sarah will nurse sons'?"* It was an ancient custom when a baby was born to give the child a name symbolizing conditions and then to mention what those conditions were as well. Examples occur when Cain was born to Eve and Adam (Genesis 4:1); when Seth was born to them (Genesis 4:25); when Noah was born to Lamech (Genesis 5:29); when Esau and Jacob were born to Isaac (Genesis 25:25, 26); when Jacob's twelve sons were born to him (Genesis 29:32, 33, 34, 35; 30:6, 8, 11, 13, 18, 20, 24; 35:18); when Perez and Zerah were born to Tamar (Genesis 38:29, 30); when Manasseh and Ephraim were born to Joseph (Genesis 41:51, 52); and when Gershom and Eliezer were born to Moses (Exodus 2:22; 18:4). The description attached to each name as it is given embraces that individual's representation and inner-level symbolism. So too here with that of Isaac. The representation and symbolism involved is somewhat visible from the general explanation, but secrets still deeper remain hidden within. They remain hidden because they are divine and therefore cannot be expressed in any term or turn of speech.

For I have delivered a son for his old age means that this happened when the days were completed. This can be seen from the explanation of almost the same words in verse 2, which were discussed in §§2621, 2622, 2623, 2624.　**2644**

Genesis 21:8. *And the child grew and was weaned, and Abraham made a grand banquet on the day when Isaac was weaned.*　**2645**

The child grew symbolizes further development of the Lord's rational mind. *And was weaned* symbolizes the removal of merely human rationality. *Abraham made a grand banquet* symbolizes living together and becoming one. *On the day when Isaac was weaned* symbolizes the state of removal.

The child grew symbolizes further development of the Lord's rational mind. This can be seen from the symbolism of *growing* as developing and from that of a *child* or son as the Lord's divine rationality (mentioned in §2623).　**2646**

And was weaned symbolizes the removal of merely human rationality. This can be seen from the symbolism of *being weaned* as being removed, as babies are from their mother's breasts.　**2647**

The chapter goes further in depicting the way the rationality that was purely human was removed, representing it by Hagar's son in his banishment from the household.

2648   *Abraham made a grand banquet* symbolizes living together and becoming one. This can be seen from the symbolism of a *banquet* as living together (discussed in §2341). Here it also means becoming one, because it has to do with the Lord, whose humanity united with his divinity, as did his divinity with his humanity. Since this is the union being discussed, the text speaks of a *grand* banquet.

2649   *On the day when Isaac was weaned* symbolizes the state of removal. This is established by the symbolism of a *day* as a state (discussed in §§23, 487, 488, 493, 893) and from that of *being weaned* as being removed (dealt with in §2647).

The theme so far, from the first verse of the chapter, has been the uniting of the Lord's divine nature with his human nature, dealt with in this order: The presence of his divinity within his humanity, for the sake of their union (verse 1). The presence of his humanity within his divinity, and therefore a reciprocal union (as discussed in §2004; verse 2). That union made his humanity divine (verse 3). It occurred gradually and constantly while the Lord was alive in the world (verse 4). It started when his rationality had reached a stage where it could receive [divinity] (verse 5). What the state of oneness was like, depicted; together with divine secrets (verses 6, 7). The sequel from here deals with the removal of the humanity he received from his mother and continues all the way to verse 12. In the current verse, the removal is symbolized by the weaning of Isaac. Below [§§2657–2658], it is represented by Hagar's son in his banishment from the household.

The union of the Lord's divinity with his humanity (and of his humanity with his divinity) is the actual marriage of goodness and truth. So it is the heavenly marriage, which is the same as the Lord's kingdom. That is why the text mentions the grand banquet Abraham made when Isaac was weaned, symbolizing the beginning of the marriage, or of the union. If the banquet (and the weaning too) had not symbolized something hidden, it would never would have been mentioned.

[2] What follows now has to do with the removal of the human nature the Lord had at first, from his mother, and with its eventual and complete eradication. It needs to be known, then, that the Lord worked gradually and constantly—right to the end of his life, when he became divine—to remove from himself what was merely human and rid himself of it. What was merely human was what he inherited from his mother, and this he stripped away until at last he was no longer her child but God's, both in his conception and in his birth. Consequently he was one with the Father, and therefore was Jehovah himself.

The Lord's words in John make it very clear that he removed everything human he had received from his mother and rid himself of it, so that he was no longer her son:

When the wine ran out, Jesus' mother said to him, "They don't have wine." Jesus says to her, "*What do we have to do with one another, woman?*" (John 2:3, 4)

In Matthew:

A man said, "Look—your mother and your siblings are standing outside asking to talk to you." But Jesus answering said to the one who had said it, "*Who is my mother,* and who are my siblings?" And stretching out his hand over his disciples he said, "*Look: my mother* and my siblings. For whoever does the will of my Father, who is in the heavens, is my brother and sister and *mother.*" (Matthew 12:47, 48, 49, 50; Mark 3:32, 33, 34, 35; Luke 8:20, 21)

In Luke:

Raising her voice from among the people a woman said to him, "Blessed is the belly that delivered you and the breasts that you sucked!" but Jesus said, "Blessed are those who hear God's word and keep it!" (Luke 11:27, 28)

[3] Whereas the woman is talking about his mother, here, the Lord is talking about the people in the previous quotation: "Anyone who does the will of my Father is my brother, sister, and mother." They are the same as the latter—the blessed ones who hear God's word and keep it. In John:

Jesus, seeing his mother and the disciple whom he cherished standing by, he said to his mother, "*Woman,* look: your son!" Then he said to the disciple, "*Look: your mother!*" So from that very hour the disciple took her to live with him. (John 19:26, 27)

These words demonstrate that the Lord spoke in the same terms she was thinking in as she looked at him on the cross, but he calls her not "mother" but "woman." They also demonstrate that he transferred the name "mother" to the people that the disciple symbolizes, which is why he said to that disciple, "Look: your mother!" The Lord's own words in Matthew make the same thing even more obvious:

Jesus questioned the Pharisees, saying, "How does it seem to you concerning the Christ? Whose child is he?" They say to him, "David's."

He says to them, "How, then, can David in the spirit call him Lord? Saying, 'The Lord said to my Lord: "Sit on my right till I make your enemies your footstool."' *If David, then, calls him Lord, how is he his child?"* And no one could answer him a word. (Matthew 22:41–end; Mark 12:35, 36, 37; Luke 20:42, 43, 44)

So he was no longer David's descendant in regard to his flesh.

[4] To understand any more about the removal and eradication of the humanity the Lord had from his mother is not possible for people whose image of the Lord's humanity is purely physical. It is not possible for people who view his humanity the same way they view anyone else's. Such ideas create obstacles for them. They do not realize that our life determines who we are; that from conception the Lord had the divine essence—Jehovah—at the core of his life; and that the same living essence became manifest in his humanity when the two became one.

2650   Genesis 21:9. *And Sarah saw the son of Hagar the Egyptian—whom she had borne to Abraham—mocking.*

Sarah saw symbolizes the Lord's insight from his spiritual divinity. *The son of Hagar the Egyptian* means into his merely human rationality; *Hagar the Egyptian* is a desire for knowledge, which as mother gives birth to that kind of rationality. *Whom she had borne to Abraham* means that it emerged from heavenly divinity, which served as its father. *Mocking* means that it did not harmonize with or promote divine rationality.

2651   *And Sarah saw* symbolizes the Lord's insight from his spiritual divinity, as is established by the following: *Seeing* symbolizes understanding (discussed at §§897, 2150, 2325), which is the same as the sight of the mind's eye. And *Sarah* represents spiritual divinity, or divine truth, as discussed in §2622. *Sarah saw* means that spiritual divinity had an insight, which is the same as saying that the Lord had an insight from his spiritual divinity.

2652   *The son of Hagar the Egyptian* means into his merely human rationality; *Hagar the Egyptian* is a desire for knowledge, which as mother gives birth to that kind of rationality. This can be seen from the symbolism of the *son*, Ishmael, as the Lord's early form of rationality, which was discussed where Hagar and Ishmael were treated of in Genesis 16 [§§1893, 1895–1896, 1920]. It can also be seen from the representation of Ishmael and that of his mother, *Hagar the Egyptian,* which is also discussed there.

On the point that this first or purely human rationality in the Lord was conceived by heavenly divinity (which served as its father) and was born from a desire for knowledge (which served as its mother), see §§1895, 1896, 1902, 1910.

Whom she had borne to Abraham means that it emerged from heavenly divinity, which served as its father. This can be seen from the symbolism of *giving birth* as emerging (discussed at §§2621, 2629) and from the representation of *Abraham* as the Lord's heavenly divinity (discussed at §§1989, [2010,] 2011, 2172, 2198, 2501). **2653**

On the point that this rationality emerged from the Lord's heavenly divinity, which served as its father, see §§1895, 1896, 1902, 1910.

Mocking means that it did not harmonize with or promote divine rationality. This can be seen from the symbolism of *mockery*, which results from an emotion that opposes whatever does not harmonize with or promote it. **2654**

The previous verse said that the child grew and was weaned and that Abraham made a grand banquet when Isaac was weaned. This meant that when the Lord's rationality became divine, his first rationality was removed.

So the focus now turns immediately to the son of Hagar the Egyptian, by whom is meant that first rationality, as the explanation concerning Ishmael and Hagar in Genesis 16 showed. This also makes it clear that the contents of the inner meaning follow each other in an unbroken series.

[2] The Lord's first rationality was born as it is in any other person: out of secular learning and religious knowledge. As a consequence, it inevitably fell prey to seeming truth, which is not true in itself, as the points brought out in §§1911, 1936, 2196, 2203, 2209, 2516 show. Since this initial rationality focused on seeming truth, that truth could not harmonize with it or promote truth that is free of appearances, as divine truth is. For one thing, such rationality is unable to grasp that kind of truth; for another, that kind of truth is hostile to it. But let some examples shed light on the situation.

[3] Human rationality is rationality born from worldly experiences taken in through the senses, and later from something analogous to worldly experiences taken in through learning and knowledge. This kind of rationality virtually laughs, or mocks, if you say it does not live on its own but only *seems* to live on its own. It ridicules the idea that the less we believe we live on our own, the more alive we are—that is, the more wisdom and understanding and the more bliss and happiness we have in our lives. It jeers at the claim that angels live this way, especially the heavenly ones, who are the deepest, or closest to the Lord, because those angels know that none live on their own but Jehovah, or in other words, the Lord.

[4] The same kind of rationality would also sneer if you told it that it possesses nothing of its own, that possession is an illusion or appearance. It would scoff even louder if you said that the more it accepts the illusion that it possesses something of its own, the less it really does, and the reverse. Likewise if you said that anything we think or do on our own is evil, even if it seems good, and that we do not begin to be wise until we believe and sense that everything evil comes from hell, while everything good comes from the Lord. All angels believe this and even perceive it. Paradoxically, they have a fuller sense of self than anyone, but they know and perceive that this selfhood comes from the Lord, even though it seems exactly as though it is their own.

[5] Again, this rationality would make fun of it if you said that the greatest in heaven are the ones who are least; that the wisest are those who least believe and perceive themselves to be wise; that the happiest are those who most want others to be happy and least care whether they themselves are; that heaven is wanting to be at the bottom, while hell is wanting to be at the top; and that heaven's glory therefore contains absolutely nothing that the world's glory contains.

[6] This rationality would also deride you if you said that there is no space or time in the other world but only states that yield the appearance of space and time. It would do the same if you said that life becomes more and more heavenly the further we move from anything related to space and time and the closer we move toward that which constitutes eternity. Eternity contains not the least trace of the idea of time, nor any trace of anything analogous to time.

Likewise on countless other points.

[7] The Lord saw that his merely human rationality held these kinds of attitude and that it would therefore mock anything divine. In fact, he saw this from his spiritual divinity, which is symbolized by Sarah's seeing the son of Hagar the Egyptian (§§2651, 2652).

From within, we can have insight into those aspects of ourselves that lie below, as people endowed with perception (and even those with conscience) know from experience. They are clear-sighted enough to denounce their own thoughts. So people who have been reborn are able to see what the rationality they had before rebirth is like. In us, this perception comes from the Lord, but the Lord's perception of it came from himself.

2655   Genesis 21:10. *And she said to Abraham, "Throw out this slave and her son, because this slave's son must not be heir along with my son, with Isaac."*

She said to Abraham symbolizes a perception received from his divine side. *Throw out this slave and her son* means that the thinking of his merely human rationality would be expelled. *Because this slave's son must not be heir along with my son, with Isaac* means that neither the truth nor the goodness in his merely human rationality could share in the living energy of his divine rationality.

She said to Abraham symbolizes a perception received from his divine side. This can be seen from the symbolism of *saying* in scriptural narrative as perceiving (dealt with many times before) and from the representation of *Abraham* as heavenly divinity, or divine goodness (mentioned in §2622).

2656

Throw out this slave and her son means that the thinking of his merely human rationality would be expelled, as can be seen from the following: *Throwing out* means expelling. A female *slave* symbolizes a desire for logic and facts and therefore for something good in them, as discussed in §2567. And a *son* symbolizes truth in that kind of rationality; see §§264, 489, 533, 1147. The goodness and truth associated with this first or merely human rationality, though, only appear to be good and true. That is why "Throw out this slave and her son" means that the thinking of his merely human rationality would be expelled.

2657

In many earlier places I have stated and shown that the Lord's first rationality was expelled when his divine rationality took over. Since the current passage deals with it specifically, though, a few more words of explanation are needed.

[2] Everyone who is being reborn has two kinds of rationality: one before rebirth and the other after.

Our first rationality, before rebirth, we acquire from sensory experience, reflection on the issues of public and private life, secular studies, reasoning sparked and facilitated by our secular studies, and the spiritual knowledge we gain from religious doctrine—that is, from the Word. At the time, none of this reaches much higher than the images present in our bodily memory, which are quite closely tied to the material world, relatively speaking. So whatever thoughts we then think, they stem from these kinds of origins; or if we also want to see with our inner eye, the eye of true understanding, we present ourselves with comparisons based on simile or analogy. That is what our first rationality—the rationality we have before regeneration—is like.

[3] After regeneration, our rational mind is formed by the Lord through the desire for spiritual goodness and truth. The Lord has a miraculous way of grafting this desire onto the truth present in our first rationality. In this way, he takes anything present there that is harmonious and supportive and brings it to life. The rest is removed as useless. This process continues

until spiritual goodness and truth are finally gathered into bundles, so to speak. Anything incompatible, anything that cannot be brought to life, is more and more shoved off to the side as spiritual goodness and truth grow and our desire for them becomes increasingly alive. This shows what our second rationality is like.

[4] The way it works can be illustrated by comparison with fruit on a tree. In the beginning, our first rationality resembles immature fruit, which gradually ripens, until it finally develops seeds inside itself. When it reaches the stage where it starts to separate from the tree, its state is complete, as described above in §2636.

Our second rationality, though, which the Lord gives us as a gift when we have been reborn, resembles the same fruit in good soil, where the flesh surrounding the seed rots. The seed sends forth roots from inside itself, and above ground a sprout, which grows into a new tree. The new tree gradually develops until at last it produces new fruit, then gardens and whole parks, all in keeping with the urge for goodness and truth that it receives. See Matthew 13:31, 32; John 12:24.

[5] Since examples are more convincing, take as an example the sense of autonomy we have before rebirth and the sense of autonomy we have afterward. Our first rationality (which we acquire by the means outlined above) gives us to believe that we think what is true and do what is good on our own, under our own power. This first rationality cannot see it any other way, even if you teach it that all the good impulses of love and all the true ideas of faith come from the Lord.

When as adults we have been reborn, however, our second rationality (which the Lord gives us) allows us to begin thinking that goodness and truth do not come from us or our own ability but from the Lord, although it still seems to us as though we do good and think truth on our own (see §§1937, 1947). The stronger this idea grows in us, the more we are brought into true light concerning the subject. In the end we believe that everything good and true comes from the Lord. Then the sense of self present in our first rationality is removed bit by bit and we receive the gift of a heavenly selfhood from the Lord. This selfhood becomes that of our new rationality.

[6] Take another example: In the beginning, our first rationality recognizes no other kind of love than love for ourselves and for the material world. Despite hearing that heavenly love is completely different, we do not grasp it. Whatever good we do after that, the only pleasure we find in it is that we think we have earned another person's gratitude, or that people view us as Christian, or that we are securing the joy of eternal

life by our deeds. Our second rationality, on the other hand, which we receive from the Lord through regeneration, starts to sense some pleasure in goodness itself and truth itself. We feel this pleasure not on any account of our own but on account of what is good and true. When this delight takes hold of us, we reject any credit for it, to the point where we spurn such an idea as an outrage. This pleasure keeps growing and growing in us and becomes bliss, and happiness in the other life, and our very heaven.

From this it can now be seen what the case is with the two kinds of rationality in a person who is being reborn.

[7] It is important to know, however, that even when we are being reborn, absolutely everything belonging to our first rationality remains. It is only detached from our second rationality, which the Lord accomplishes by miraculous means.

The Lord did obliterate his first rationality, though, so that none of it remained. Nothing that is merely human can coexist with divinity. As a consequence, he was no longer Mary's child but Jehovah as to both his natures.

Because this slave's son must not be heir along with my son, with Isaac **2658** means that neither the truth nor the goodness in his merely human rationality could share in the living energy of his divine rationality, as can be seen from the following: *Being heir* means having someone else's vital energy, as discussed just below. A *slave's son* symbolizes a merely human rationality in respect to its truth and goodness, as mentioned at §2657. And *my son, Isaac* symbolizes both truth in the Lord's divine rationality ("my son") and goodness there ("Isaac"), as mentioned at §§2623, 2630. Isaac means goodness in the Lord's divine rationality because laughter, for which he was named, symbolizes a desire for truth, or something good that develops out of truth, as can be seen in verses 6 and 7, §§2640, 2641, 2643. This shows that "this slave's son must not be heir along with my son, with Isaac" means that neither the truth nor the goodness of a merely human rationality can share in the living energy of divine rationality.

[2] A single consideration shows that purely human rationality cannot share in that living energy: divinity is life itself and therefore possesses life in itself. Conversely, anything merely human is an organ designed to receive life and therefore possesses no life in itself. When the Lord's humanity became divine, it was no longer an instrument or container of life but was life itself, or the kind of life that belongs to Jehovah himself. He first received this capacity purely by conception from Jehovah, as his own words in John make plain:

Just as the Father *has life in himself,* so he has granted the Son *to have life in himself.* (John 5:26)

His divine humanity is what is being called the Son here (§§1729, 2159, 2628). In the same author:

In him was *life,* and the *life* was the light of humankind. (John 1:4)

In the same author:

Jesus said, "I am the way, the truth, and *life.*" (John 14:6)

In the same author:

Jesus said, "I am the resurrection and *life;* those who believe in me, even if they die, will *live.*" (John 11:25)

In the same author:

The bread of God is the one who comes down from heaven and gives *life* to the world. (John 6:33)

On the point that we humans, on the other hand, are not life but an instrument or container of life, see §2021 and many other places. This clarifies the fact that when the Lord became Jehovah even in respect to his human side, any part that was not intrinsically alive—any part that was merely human—was banished. That is what Sarah's refusal to let her slave's son be heir with her own son Isaac symbolizes.

[3] Where the text speaks of the Lord, *being an heir* in an inner sense is having the Father's life and therefore having life in himself. Where the text speaks of us, it means having the Lord's life, or in other words, receiving life from the Lord. Many passages in the Word reveal this fact. To have life in oneself is to have the very essence of life, or Jehovah, in oneself. Conversely, to have the Lord's life, or to receive life from the Lord, is to welcome the Lord with love and trust. Since people who accept the Lord with love and trust are in the Lord and are the Lord's, they are called his heirs and children.

[4] The Old Testament Word relates inheritance both to heavenly qualities, or goodness, and to spiritual qualities, or truth, but it uses different words for each. The former term can be translated as *possess as an inheritance,* and the latter as *inherit.* The former term in the original language directly implies possession, while the latter is merely derived from a word for possession. This is the relationship that heavenly and spiritual things (or goodness and truth) have to one another. In the current verse, where Isaac

represents divine rationality, or the Lord's divine humanity, the word used is the one that has to do with possession as an inheritance. The Lord's divine humanity is the only owner and heir, as he also teaches by parable (Matthew 21:33, 37, 38; Mark 12:7; Luke 20:14); and in many places he declares that everything that is the Father's is his.

[5] A passage in John shows that where the Word speaks about us, "possessing as an inheritance" and "inheriting" mean receiving life from the Lord and therefore receiving eternal life, or heaven (since only those who accept the Lord's life receive heaven):

> Those who conquer will *inherit* everything, and I will be their God, and they will be my children. (Revelation 21:7)

In Matthew:

> Everyone who leaves behind houses or brothers or sisters for my name will receive a hundredfold and will *inherit eternal life.* (Matthew 19:29; 25:34; Mark 10:17; Luke 18:18)

Heaven is called eternal life here, and elsewhere it is simply called life, as in Matthew 18:8, 9; 19:17; John 3:36; 5:24, 29. The reason they are equated is that the Lord is life itself, and anyone who receives life from him is in heaven. [6] In David:

> God will save Zion and rebuild the cities of Judah, and they will live there and *possess it as an inheritance,* and the seed of his slaves will *inherit* it, and those who love his name will live in it. (Psalms 69:35, 36)

In these verses, people with heavenly love are said to possess as an inheritance, while people with spiritual love are said to inherit. In Isaiah:

> The one who trusts in me will *inherit* the land and will *possess* my holy mountain *as an inheritance.* (Isaiah 57:13)

Likewise. [7] In Moses:

> I will bring you to the land over which I lifted my hand, to give it to Abraham, Isaac, and Jacob, and I will give it as an *inherited possession.* (Exodus 6:8)

In a literal sense these words mean that the land of Canaan would be given to them as an inherited possession, which did happen. In an inner sense they mean that heaven would be given to people who love and believe in the Lord. Just as Abraham, Isaac, and Jacob represent the Lord, they also symbolize love itself and faith itself, and therefore people who have love and faith, or who in other words are in the Lord. The same is true of Abraham, Isaac, and Jacob as mentioned in Matthew 8:11, with whom many would recline at a table in the kingdom of the heavens. No one in heaven knows anything at all of Abraham, Isaac, or Jacob. All they know is what the three represent and symbolize, just as they know what reclining at a table, or in other words, eating with them, means. All names in the Word have symbolic meaning (see §§1224, 1264, 1876, 1888). The land of Canaan is the heavenly Canaan, or heaven (§§1585, 1607, 1866). It is also called simply the land (§§1413, 1607, 1733, 2571), as it is in Matthew:

> Fortunate are the wretched, because they will *inherit the land*. (Matthew 5:5)

2659   Genesis 21:11. *And the matter was very evil in Abraham's eyes on account of his son.*

The matter was very evil in Abraham's eyes symbolizes the Lord's state when he first thought about removing that kind of rationality from himself. *On account of his son* means because he cherished it.

2660   *The matter was very evil in Abraham's eyes* symbolizes the Lord's state when he first thought about removing that kind of rationality from himself—specifically, a state of grief rising out of love, as is evident without explanation.

2661   *On account of his son* means because he cherished it (his first rationality). This can be seen from the symbolism of a *son* (the slave's) as the Lord's merely human rationality, or his first rationality, a symbolism mentioned before [§§1893, 2652–2653, 2657–2658].

It is true that the reason for Abraham's grief is not mentioned here, but what follows makes it plain. Clearly it grew out of love, because the text says "of his son," and that is whom verses 13 to 21 below focus on. Still, to see why sorrow is expressed here—why it says, "The matter was very evil in Abraham's eyes on account of his son"—let the brief treatment that follows serve to provide some light.

[2] The Lord came into the world not to save heavenly individuals but to save the spiritual. The earliest church, which was called "the human," was a heavenly one. If it had maintained its integrity, the Lord would have had no need to be born as a person. As soon as it started to fail, then, the Lord foresaw that heavenly religion would be utterly wiped off the earth. That is why a prediction was immediately made about the Lord's arrival in the world (Genesis 3:15). No heavenly religion remained after that church's era, only spiritual religion. The ancient church, which came after the Flood, was a spiritual religion, as mentioned quite often in the first volumes.

This church, or the people in it, could not have been saved had not the Lord come into the world. That is the meaning of the Lord's words in Matthew:

> The well do not need a doctor, only the ill. I did not come to call the righteous but sinners to repentance. (Matthew 9:12, 13)

Also of these words in John:

> And other sheep I have that are not from this fold. Those too I must bring, and they will hear my voice, and there will come to be one flock and one shepherd. (John 10:16)

It is also the meaning of the parable of the hundred sheep in Matthew 18:11, 12, 13.

[3] Now, since Isaac represents the Lord's divine rationality, he also symbolizes heavenly people, who are called the Lord's heirs. And as Ishmael represents the Lord's merely human rationality, he also symbolizes spiritual people, who are termed the Lord's children. (The remarks above in §2658 show the same thing.) It was from divine love, then, that his grief—or the words of the current verse—sprang. So do those that follow in verses 13 to 21, where Hagar's son and his mother represent spiritual religion and the theme is the state of that religion, or of the people in it (§2612).

These secrets cannot be spelled out further. It can only be said that when the Lord was in the world, all the states of religion were represented in him, as was the method by which he would save them. As a result, the same states of religion are symbolized by the same names.

Genesis 21:12. *And God said to Abraham, "Don't let it be evil in your eyes concerning your son and concerning your slave. Everything that Sarah says to you, listen to her voice, because in Isaac your seed will be called yours."* **2662**

God said to Abraham symbolizes a perception the Lord received from his divine side. *Don't let it be evil in your eyes concerning your son and concerning your slave* symbolizes a change of state regarding that rationality. *Everything that Sarah says to you, listen to her voice* means that he was to do what spiritual truth told him to. *Because in Isaac your seed will be called yours* means that the Lord's divine humanity is the source of all salvation for people with goodness.

God said to Abraham symbolizes a perception the Lord received from his divine side. This can be seen from the symbolism of *saying* in scriptural narrative as perceiving, a symbolism mentioned many times before. Because the perception came from his divine side, the wording is *God said to Abraham*. Both—God and Abraham—mean the Lord. The stories **2663** that compose the literal meaning split different ideas apart, but the inner meaning reunites them, as the following thoughts show: In the literal sense of this narrative, there are two parties conversing—God and Abraham. In an inner sense, though, there is one, and that one is the Lord in his divinity. From this it is also clear that when the letter speaks of three, they are one in the inner meaning. Father, Son, and Holy Spirit, for instance, are not three gods but one. Furthermore, the whole Trinity is full and complete in the Lord; the Father is in him, as he says [John 10:38; 14:10–11, 20], and the holy operation of the Spirit comes from him, as he also says.

2664   *Don't let it be evil in your eyes, concerning your son and concerning your slave* symbolizes a change of state regarding that rationality. The inner meaning most closely related to the words is that he was not to grieve over the removal of his merely human rationality. He did not grieve, either, because he perceived from his divine side that the removal was imperative, since otherwise the human race could not have been saved. This is the change of state symbolized.

2665   *Everything that Sarah says to you, listen to her voice* means that he was to do what spiritual truth told him to. This is established by the representation of *Sarah* as spiritual divinity, or divine truth (mentioned at §2622), and by the symbolism of *listening to someone's voice* as doing what the person says (discussed in §2542).

It is not easy to explain to the intellect how one does what spiritual truth says. It would be easier to explain it to perception, which people aware of the inner meaning have. If I were to explain it in the terms in which these people perceive it, hardly any others would accept it. What is more, the many secrets involved would first need to be revealed and in fact believed before the concept could be incorporated into a person's religious thinking. The general meaning can be explained to some slight extent by saying that the Lord in his human divinity would come to a decision and carry it out; so he would be acting under his own power. Divine truth was the means by which he united his humanity with his divinity, while divine goodness was the means by which he united his divinity with his humanity—the union being reciprocal (see §2004).

2666   *In Isaac your seed will be called yours* means that the Lord's divine humanity is the source of all salvation for people with goodness, as can be seen from the following: *Isaac* represents divine rationality, as noted before [§§1893, 2066, 2083, 2194, 2632, 2658], and therefore divine humanity, since humanity starts in the inmost depths of rationality (§2106). And *seed,* which is being connected with Isaac, symbolizes a heavenly rationality or, to put the same thing another way, people who are heavenly, as discussed in §§2085, 2661. So *your seed will be called yours* means that they will be heirs and therefore that they will find salvation. People who are spiritual are also seed, but they are the seed of a slave's son, as noted in the next verse: "And also the slave's son I will make into a nation, since he is your seed." They too will find salvation, then, if they have goodness, as the inner meaning of those words will show. The Lord teaches the same thing in many places, and explicitly in John:

> As many as did accept him, to them he gave the power to be God's children, to those *believing in his name,* who had their birth not from blood or from the will of the flesh or from a man's will but from God. (John 1:12, 13)

The first seven verses of the current chapter concentrated on the uniting of the Lord's humanity with his divinity and of his divinity with his humanity and on the fact that this union made his humanity divine. See the contents of the individual verses as listed in §2649.

2667

Next the chapter spoke of the Lord's merely human rationality. That rationality was removed (verse 8), because it did not harmonize with divine rationality (verse 9). Neither the truth nor the goodness in it was able to share in the living energy of his divine rationality (verse 10). At first its removal grieved the Lord (verse 11), but he received a perception from his divine side that the human race could not be saved in any other way (verse 12).

From here on the chapter deals with people in a spiritual religion, who are symbolized by Hagar's son after he was banished.

*　　*　　*　　*

Genesis 21:13. *"And also the slave's son I will make into a nation, since he is your seed."*

2668

Also the slave's son I will make into a nation symbolizes a spiritual religion that will accept the goodness that rises out of faith. *Since he is your seed* means that the Lord's divine humanity will bring *them* salvation too.

Also the slave's son I will make into a nation symbolizes a spiritual religion that will welcome the goodness that rises out of faith, as can be seen from the symbolism of a *slave's son* and a *nation.*

2669

When the *slave's son*—Ishmael—was in Abraham's household, or in other words, living with Abraham, he represented the Lord's first rationality, as shown in §§2652, 2653, 2657, 2658. Now, however, when that rationality had been removed, he took on another representation: that of a spiritual religion (2666). Something similar happened earlier with Lot. When he was with Abraham he represented the Lord's outer self (1428, 1429, 1434, 1547, 1597, 1598, 1698), but when he separated from Abraham, he represented a shallow religion and the many states of that religion (2324, 2371, 2399, 2422, 2459, and throughout Genesis 19).

A *nation* symbolizes goodness; see §§1159, 1258, 1259, 1260, 1416, 1849. Here it symbolizes the goodness that rises out of faith, because the term is being applied to a spiritual religion. The current words, then ("also the slave's son I will make into a nation"), symbolize a spiritual religion that will welcome the goodness that rises out of faith—in other words, neighborly love.

[2] The Lord's kingdom in the heavens and on earth is heavenly and spiritual, so the angels are divided into heavenly and spiritual angels; see §§202, 337. Heavenly angels see the Lord as the sun; spiritual angels, as the moon (1053, 1521, 1529, 1530, 1531). People too are divided into the heavenly and the spiritual. The people of the earliest church, which preceded the Flood, were heavenly, as discussed in §§607, 608, 784, 895, 920, 1114–1125. The people of the ancient church, which came after the Flood, were spiritual; see §§609, 640, 641, 765. For the difference between the two churches, see §§597, 607; for that between heavenliness and spirituality, 81, 1155, 1577, 1824, 2048, 2069, 2088, 2227, 2507.

[3] Heavenly individuals are those of whom the Lord said this:

> He calls his own sheep by name and leads them out, and when he has led his own sheep out, he goes before them, and the sheep follow him, because they know his voice. (John 10:3, 4)

Concerning spiritual individuals, on the other hand, he says this:

> And other sheep I have that are not from this fold; those too I must bring, and they will hear my voice, and there will come to be one flock and one shepherd. (John 10:16)

The goodness that rises out of love is what composes a heavenly religion, while the goodness that rises out of faith is what composes a spiritual one. The truth taught by faith does not constitute religion, but it does introduce us into it.

2670   *Since he is your seed* means that the Lord's divine humanity will bring *them* salvation too, as the remarks above at §2666 show.

On the point that *seed* is faith (but only the faith that comes of neighborly love), see §§255, 880, 1025, 1447, 1610, 1940.

From here in verse 13 to verse 21, the general topic is the Lord's spiritual kingdom; the specific topic is people who are becoming spiritual. It follows their progress from the first stage of reformation to the last. The condition they are in before reformation, when they wander confused among religious doctrines (verse 14). They are reduced to ignorance, lacking any awareness of truth (verse 15). This grieves them (verse 16). Then the Lord comforts and helps them (verse 17). He also enlightens them (verse 18). They learn from the Word (verse 19). Even so, their condition after reformation is relatively dim, compared to that of heavenly people (verse 20). Light from the Lord's divine humanity does shine, though, on the affection they feel for facts and for semblances of truth (verse 21).

2671

Genesis 21:14. And Abraham got up early in the morning and took bread and a flask of water and gave it to Hagar (he put it on her shoulder) and [gave her] the boy and sent her away. And she went and wandered in the wilderness of Beer-sheba.

2672

Abraham got up early in the morning symbolizes a clear perception the Lord received from his divine side. *And took bread and a flask of water* symbolizes what is good and true. *And gave it to Hagar* means implanting it in her life. *And put it on her shoulder* means as much as she could handle. *And the boy* symbolizes spiritual truth. *And sent her away* means that he left her sense of autonomy to her. *And she went and wandered in the wilderness of Beer-sheba* symbolizes a state of confused wandering among religious doctrines.

Abraham got up early in the morning symbolizes a clear perception the Lord received from his divine side. This can be seen from the symbolism of *morning* and *getting up early* as perceiving clearly (discussed in §2540, where the same words occur) and from the representation of *Abraham* as the Lord's divinity (mentioned many times before).

2673

The clear perception the Lord received from his divine side concerned conditions in his spiritual kingdom. It showed what the people in that kingdom (or in that religion) are like in the beginning, what they are like at later stages, and what they become in the end. The inner meaning of verses 13 to 21 in the current chapter delineates precisely and fully every state they experience.

And took bread and a flask of water symbolizes what is good and true. This can be seen from the symbolism of *bread* as what is heavenly, or

2674

good (discussed in §§276, 680, 2165), and from the symbolism of *water* as what is spiritual, or true (discussed in §§28, 680, 739).

The text speaks of a *flask* of water because the amount of truth we are given is very small to start with. Specifically, we are given as much as we can handle at that point, which is what putting it on her shoulder symbolizes (§2676).

This part of the story contains hidden mysteries, as anyone can see from Abraham's behavior here. Although he was rich in flock and herd and in gold and silver, he banished his slave, who had given him a son, and the boy Ishmael, whom he loved very much, giving them only some bread and some water in a flask. He could foresee that they would die when these were gone—and that is exactly what would have happened if an angel had not brought them help. Besides, these details of some bread and a water flask and of putting them on Hagar's shoulder are not important enough in themselves to mention. Still, it happened this way and was recounted because the details imply and symbolize the first stage people go through when they are becoming spiritual. They start with some goodness and some truth and are in fact given very little by way of provisions. Eventually their water runs out and they then receive help from the Lord.

2675   *And gave it to Hagar* means implanting it in her life. This can be seen from the symbolism of *Hagar* as the vital energy (or life) of the outer self (dealt with at §§1895, 1909). The vital energy of the outer self is a desire for knowledge, a desire that Hagar the Egyptian specifically symbolizes.

In people who are becoming spiritual, the Lord implants goodness and truth in their desire for knowledge. To be more specific, he implants it in their longing to see and learn what is good and true for the goal and purpose of becoming rational and also spiritual. A desire for facts is the mother that gives birth to the kind of rationality that has a spiritual core (§§1895, 1896, 1902, 1910). The Lord does exert the same kind of influence on everyone, admittedly, but the only people who accept it for that goal and purpose are the ones who can be reformed. The rest receive it with other aims, which are too many to count and which focus on themselves and the material world.

2676   *He put it on her shoulder* means as much as she could handle. This is established by the symbolism of a *shoulder* as all a person's might (treated of at §1085) and so as the most goodness and truth that a person can handle.

2677   *And the boy* symbolizes what is spiritual. This can be seen from the symbolism of the *boy* as that which is called spiritual. Ishmael, the slave's son, here represents people in a spiritual religion, and since at this point he represents them as they are in the beginning, he is called a boy.

He sent her away means that he left her sense of autonomy to her. **2678** This can be seen from the symbolism of being *sent away* when Abraham (who represents the Lord) is the one doing the sending, and from the first phase people go through when they are reforming and becoming spiritual. In this phase they imagine that they can do good and think truth on their own, autonomously. At that point they do not know otherwise at all. When you tell them that everything good and true comes from the Lord, they do not actually reject the idea, but they do not acknowledge it in their hearts. They do not sense and are unable to perceive inwardly that anything does flow into them from any source but themselves. Since all who are reforming first go through this phase, the Lord leaves them to their sense of independence but still leads them by means of it without their knowledge.

And she went and wandered in the wilderness of Beer-sheba symbolizes **2679** a state at that time of confused wandering among religious doctrines, as can be seen from the following: *Going and wandering in the wilderness* symbolizes a state of confused wandering. And *Beer-sheba* symbolizes theology, as discussed at the end of the current chapter [§2723] where it says that Abraham and Abimelech struck a pact in Beer-sheba (verse 32) and that Abraham planted a grove there (verse 33).

This verse depicts that the state of people just starting to reform is one that carries them wandering into various errors. The Lord puts it into their hearts to spend time thinking about eternal life and therefore about religious truth. However, since all the thoughts come out of their own selves, as I said, they cannot help wandering to and fro in their lives, just as they do in their theology. They take the truth to be whatever has been drilled into them from infancy, or whatever someone else has pressed on them, or whatever they themselves think up. In addition, various passions they are unaware of make off with them. They are like fruit as yet unripe, which cannot instantly develop shape, beauty, and flavor. They are like tender seedlings that cannot instantly sprout into bloom or produce grain.

What then enters our minds, though, even if it is mostly mistaken, is still capable of serving to promote growth. Afterward, when we reform, part of it is removed; part helps generate nourishment and sap for future life; part is capable of incorporating the goodness and truth the Lord later engrafts; and part serves as the ultimate receiving ground for spiritual attributes. So time and again these first, inaccurate notions function as a means of reforming—means that form an orderly, unbroken chain. The Lord, after all, foresees the smallest particulars of everything in regard to us and provides for our future condition to eternity. This he does with his eye on our welfare, as much as he possibly can, and as much as we allow him to lead us.

2680   Genesis 21:15. *And the water from the flask was used up, and she thrust the boy under one of the shrubs.*

The water from the flask was used up means the stripping away of truth. *And she thrust the boy under one of the shrubs* symbolizes despair because of an inability to perceive any truth or goodness.

2681   *The water from the flask was used up* means the stripping away of truth. This can be seen from the symbolism of being *used up* as being stripped away and from the symbolism of *water* as truth (discussed in §§28, 680, 739).

2682   *And she thrust the boy under one of the shrubs* symbolizes despair because of an inability to perceive any truth or goodness, as can be seen from the following: A *boy* symbolizes spiritual truth, as mentioned in §§2669, 2677. And a *shrub* or bush symbolizes perception, but so little perception as to be hardly any (which is why it says "under *one* of the shrubs"). It symbolizes the same thing as a tree but at a reduced level, and trees symbolize perceptions (see §§103, 2163). The meaning of the clause can also be seen from the emotion behind the action, which is one of despair. This shows that "she thrust the boy under one of the shrubs" symbolizes despair because of an inability to perceive anything true or good.

Job makes it clear that being cast under one of the shrubs is being stripped of what is true and good, to the point of despair:

> Alone in poverty and in hunger they are fleeing to drought, the spent night, *desolation,* and *devastation.* They are picking the mallow on the *shrub,* to live in the crevice of valleys, in openings in the dirt and rocks. *Among the shrubs they were moaning;* under the thistle they were banding together. (Job 30:3, 4, 6, 7)

This is about the stripping away or desolation of truth. It is being described in expressions familiar to the ancient church (since Job is a book of the ancient church), such as being alone in poverty and hunger; fleeing to drought, the spent night, desolation, and devastation; living in the crevices of valleys and of rocks, picking the mallow on the shrub, and moaning among the shrubs. The same is true in Isaiah:

They will all come and rest in the rivers of the *remote wilds,* in the crevices of rocks, and *in all the bushes,* and in all the channels. (Isaiah 7:19)

This too is about desolation, which is described by similar expressions— resting in the rivers of the remote wilds, in the crevices of rocks, and in bushes.

[2] The current verse has to do with the second stage of people who are reforming, a stage during which they are reduced to ignorance, so that they lack any awareness of truth, to the point where they despair.

The reason they are reduced to this level of ignorance is to snuff out the light of dogmatism. This light is such that it illuminates falsehood and truth equally. It uses truth to make us believe falsity, it uses falsity to make us believe truth, and it also leads us to feel smug. Another purpose is to teach us by actual experience that nothing good and nothing true comes from us or our own ability; it comes only from the Lord.

People who are reforming are reduced to such ignorance that they despair, and then they receive comfort and enlightenment, as the verses that follow show. After all, the light of truth from the Lord cannot flow into self-serving dogma because dogma by its very nature blots out that light. In the other world, dogmatism appears to resemble winter's light. As soon as heaven's light approaches, though, the wintry light turns into a darkness that contains ignorance of all truth.

This stage is called the stage in which truth is stripped away from people who are reforming. The Word's inner meaning actually has many things to say about it.

[3] Few can know much about that stage, however, because few today regenerate. To people who are not regenerating, it is all the same whether they do or do not know truth, and whether what they know is true or not, as long as they can pass *something* off as truth. In contrast, people who are regenerating spend a lot of time thinking about theology and life, because they spend a lot of time thinking about their eternal salvation. So if *their* supply of truth runs out, they grieve to the core, because truth is dear to their minds and hearts.

The following line of reasoning shows what the state of each is like: While we are in our body, our spirit is alive in heaven and our body is alive in the world; we are born into both. What is more, we are created in such a way that we can actually be with angels as to our spirit at the same time that we are with other people by means of our body and everything that belongs to it. However, few believe they have a spirit that will live on after death, and as a result few are reborn. When people believe they have a spirit, the next life monopolizes their thoughts and feelings, and the material world is relatively unimportant. When people do not believe it, the material world monopolizes their thoughts and feelings, and the next life is relatively unimportant. The former are people who can be reborn; the latter are people who cannot.

2683   Genesis 21:16. *And she went and sat by herself opposite, distancing herself about a bowshot, because she said, "Don't let me see the death of the boy!" And she sat opposite and raised her voice and wept.*

She went and sat by herself opposite symbolizes a thoughtful mood. *Distancing herself about a bowshot* symbolizes the gap between this mood and true theology; a *bow* is true theology. *Because she said, "Don't let me see the death of the boy!"* symbolizes grief that [spiritual truth] would be destroyed this way. *And she sat opposite* symbolizes a thoughtful mood. *And raised her voice and wept* symbolizes a higher level of grief.

2684   *She went and sat by herself opposite* symbolizes a thoughtful mood. This can be seen from the symbolism of *going,* of *sitting by herself,* and of doing so *opposite,* in relation to what comes before and after in the text. *Going*—leaving the boy—means moving away from spiritual truth. The idea is expressed again more precisely when it says that she distanced herself about a bowshot. *Sitting by herself* symbolizes a solitary mood like the thoughts we experience in grief and despair. *Opposite* means so that she could look and not look. (Looking is thinking; see §2245.) The idea is expressed again more precisely when it says that she said, "Don't let me see the death of the boy!" and sat opposite. These words, then, involve the thoughtful mood of people who have been stripped of truth and who consequently despair.

2685   *Distancing herself about a bowshot* symbolizes the gap between this mood and true theology. This can be seen from the meaning of *distancing oneself* as being far away and from that of a *bow* as true theology, to be discussed just below. A *shot* means that it was as far away as it possibly could be, or as far an arrow could be shot from a bow.

The term *bowshot* is used here because a bow is mentioned in connection with spiritual people, and Ishmael was an archer. As verse 20 below says of him, "And he resided in the wilderness and was an archer."

2686   The fact that a *bow* is true theology can be seen from its symbolism. Wherever the Word describes or mentions wars, the only kind of wars it symbolizes on an inner level are spiritual ones (§1664). The ancient church also had some books titled *The Wars of Jehovah,* as you can see in

Moses (Numbers 21:14, 15, 16). Written in a prophetic mode, they had an inner meaning and focused on the struggles and trials of the Lord, of the church, and of the people in the church. This can be seen from the fact that Moses quoted from those books, and also from some other books of the same church called *The Books of the Prophetic Utterances*. These books are mentioned in Numbers 21:27, 28, 29, 30, which uses almost the same words as a passage in Jeremiah; compare Numbers 21:28 and Jeremiah 48:45. These facts lead to the conclusion that the ancient church had both narrative and prophetic writings that were divine and inspired. In an inner sense these writings dealt with the Lord and his kingdom, and they were his Word to those people, just as the narrative and prophetic books are to us, dealing as they do in a literal sense with Jews and Israelites but in an inner sense with the Lord and whatever is his.

[2] In the Word, as in the books of the ancient church, war symbolized spiritual war. Consequently, all weapons—sword, spear, shield, buckler, arrows, darts, and bow—symbolized particular tools of war understood in a spiritual sense. The specific symbolism of each weapon will be given elsewhere, by the Lord's divine mercy. Here that of a bow will be given. A bow symbolizes true theology, because of its arrows, which are the doctrines that form the instruments and tools of battle, especially in the hands of people who are spiritual. At one time such people were therefore called archers.

[3] The following passages show that a bow symbolizes true theology. In Isaiah:

> Jehovah's *arrows* are sharp, and *all* his *bows* are bent; the hooves of his horses are considered to be like rock, and his wheels, like windstorms. (Isaiah 5:28)

This has to do with theological truth. The arrows are spiritual truth; the bow is theology; the horses' hooves are earthly truth; the wheels are theology based on that truth. They are said to be Jehovah's because they symbolize these things, although they can be described as his only in a spiritual sense. Otherwise the words would be meaningless and inappropriate. In Jeremiah:

> The Lord *bent his bow* like an enemy. His right hand stood like a foe, and he killed everything that was desirable to the eye in the tent of Zion's daughter. He poured his anger out like fire. (Lamentations 2:4)

The bow stands for true theology, which seems inimical and foelike to people ruled by falsity. The Lord cannot be described as having any other kind of bow. In Habakkuk:

> Jehovah, you ride on your horses; your chariots are salvation. *Your bow* will be completely bared. (Habakkuk 3:8, 9)

Here too the bow is theology that is good and true. In Moses:

> They will vex him and *shoot arrows; the archers* will hate him. He will sit *in the firmness of his bow,* and his arms and hands will be strengthened by the hands of mighty Jacob, from whom comes the Shepherd, the Stone of Israel. (Genesis 49:23, 24)

This is about Joseph. The bow stands for theology that is good and true. [4] In John:

> I looked, when there! A white horse! And one sitting on it, *having a bow,* who was given a crown. (Revelation 6:2)

The white horse stands for wisdom. The one sitting on it stands for the Word, as it says explicitly in Revelation 19:13, where the white horse appears again. Since the one sitting on the horse is the Word, clearly the bow is true theology. In Isaiah:

> Who has stirred justice up from the east? Called that one to follow him? Yielded up the nations before him, and made him rule over monarchs? Made them like dust with his sword, like straw driven by *his bow?* (Isaiah 41:2)

This is speaking of the Lord. The sword stands for truth; the bow, for theology that comes from him. In the same author:

> I will put a mark on them and send some of them—escapees—to the nations Tarshish, Pul and Lud *(drawing the bow),* Tubal and Javan. (Isaiah 66:19)

Those drawing the bow stand for people teaching theology. For the symbolism of Tarshish, see §1156. For that of Lud, 1195, 1231. For that of Tubal, 1151. For that of Javan, 1152, 1153, 1155. [5] In Jeremiah:

> Because of the sound of a rider and of one *shooting a bow,* the whole city is fleeing. They have entered fogs, and onto crags they have climbed. The whole city has been deserted. (Jeremiah 4:29)

The rider stands for people who say what is true. The bow stands for true doctrine, which people given to falsity flee from, or are afraid of. In the same author:

> Draw up a battle line against Babylon all around. All you who *bend the bow*, *shoot* at [the city]; do not spare the *arrow*, because it has sinned against Jehovah. (Jeremiah 50:14, 29; 51:2, 3)

People shooting and bending the bow stand for people who speak and teach true theology. [6] In Zechariah:

> "I will cut the *chariot* off from Ephraim and the horse from Jerusalem," and the *war bow* will be cut off, and he will speak peace to the nations. (Zechariah 9:10)

Ephraim stands for the church's understanding of truth; the bow, for theology. In Samuel:

> David lamented a lament over Saul and over Jonathan his son and said, "to *teach the children of Judah the bow*." (2 Samuel 1:17, 18)

This is not about a bow but about religious doctrine. In Ezekiel:

> The Lord Jehovih has said, "This is the day of which I spoke, and the residents of Israel's cities will go out and kindle and burn weapons, and buckler and shield, *bow* and *arrows*, and handstaff and spear. And they will kindle them with fire for seven years." (Ezekiel 39:[8,] 9)

The weapons named here are all weapons of spiritual war. The bow with its arrows stands for theology and its truth.

In the other world, truth itself, separated from anything good, also looks like arrows, when it is presented visually.

[7] Just as a bow symbolizes true theology, in a negative sense it symbolizes false theology. (In many places it has been said and shown that the same object in the Word usually has two opposite meanings.) In Jeremiah, for example:

> Look: a people is coming from the north, and a large nation will be stirred up from the flanks of the land. *Bow* and spear they *grasp*. It is a cruel [nation], and they will not show mercy. Their voice will be boisterous like the sea; they will ride on horses. [Each] is equipped as a man for war against you, daughter of Zion. (Jeremiah 6:22, 23)

The bow stands for false theology. In the same author:

> Look: a people coming from the north, and a large nation; and many
> monarchs will be stirred up from the flanks of the land. *Bow* and spear
> they hold; they are cruel and will not show mercy. (Jeremiah 50:41, 42)

Likewise. In the same author:

> They bend their tongue; *their bow is a lie* and is not for *truth.* They are
> very strong in the land, because they have marched out from evil to
> evil; and they do not know me. (Jeremiah 9:2, 3)

[8] Obviously the bow is false theology, because it says that they bend their
tongue and that their bow is a lie and is not for truth. In the same author:

> Jehovah Sabaoth has said, "Here, now, I am *breaking the bow of Elam,*
> the beginning of its might." (Jeremiah 49:35)

In David:

> Go observe the works of Jehovah, who makes barrens on the earth,
> stopping wars all the way to the end of the earth. *The bow he breaks;* he
> chops off the spear; wagons he burns with fire. (Psalms 46:8, 9)

In the same author:

> God is known in Judah; in Israel his name is great, and his tabernacle
> will be in Salem, and his dwelling place, in Zion. There he *broke the bow's*
> *flaming arrows,* the shield, and the sword, and war. (Psalms 76:1, 2, 3)

In the same author:

> Look: the ungodly *bend the bow;* they ready *their arrows on the string,* to
> *shoot* in darkness those who are upright in heart. (Psalms 11:2)

The bow and arrows clearly stand for false doctrines.

2687 *Because she said, "Don't let me see the death of the boy!"* symbolizes grief
that [spiritual truth] would be destroyed this way. This can be seen from
the symbolism of *seeing death* as being destroyed, and from that of a *boy*
as spiritual truth (mentioned above [§2677]). This symbolism, and the
feeling of despair over the loss of truth, make it clear that deep grief is
what these words hold.

2688 *And she sat opposite* symbolizes a thoughtful mood, as shown by the
remarks above at §2684, where the same words occur.

The reason the verse repeats the clause is that the reflective mood
grows and intensifies until the grief reaches its peak, as the words "Don't

let me see the death of the boy!" just above and the words "She raised her voice and wept" below make plain.

And raised her voice and wept symbolizes a higher level of grief. This can be seen from the symbolism of *raising one's voice and weeping* as the peak of grief, because that is the time of crying out loud.

2689

The current verse depicts a condition in which truth is stripped from people who are becoming spiritual and distances itself from them. A brief explanation of the situation is necessary. People who cannot be reformed have no idea what it is to grieve over the loss of truth. They cannot imagine anyone feeling distress over such a thing. The only anguish they consider possible is that which results from being deprived of bodily and worldly advantages, such as health, position, prestige, wealth, and life.

People who *can* be reformed, on the other hand, see it very differently. The Lord maintains positive emotions and true thoughts in them, so when they are deprived of either, they start to feel distress.

[2] People know that distress and grief always result from losing what touches our hearts, or what we love. Those who are touched by or love only what belongs to the body and the world mourn when they are deprived of it, but those who are touched by and love what is spiritually good and true mourn when they are deprived of this. Everyone's life consists solely of affection, or love. From this you can see what conditions are like for people who are attached to or love what is good and true and are stripped of it: their grief is heavier because it is deeper. In their loss of goodness and truth they see the specter not of physical death (which would not bother them) but of eternal death. Their state is the one portrayed here.

[3] You might also want to know just who can and who cannot be held by the Lord in a desire for goodness and truth, and therefore who is and is not capable of being reformed and becoming spiritual, so a few words must again be said. In youth, when we are first being trained in goodness and truth, the Lord always preserves in us the positive attitude that what our parents and teachers tell us and teach us is true. In people who can become spiritual, secular and religious knowledge shores up this attitude, because any related information they gain adds to their positive attitude and reinforces it. They assimilate it more and more until they come to feel affection for it. These are the people who become spiritual (with a spirituality that matches the character of the truth they believe in) and who win in their inward struggles.

The case is very different with people who cannot become spiritual. Despite their positive attitude in youth, they develop doubts when they reach the next stage of life, breaking the positive hold that goodness and truth had on them. Once they reach full adulthood, they entertain negative thoughts, to the point of preferring falsity. If they underwent spiritual trial, they would fail completely. As a result, they are exempted from it.

[4] The real cause of the doubts and eventually of the negative thinking they develop originates entirely in a life of evil. People who live evil lives cannot possibly help having such an attitude. To repeat, everyone's life consists of affection, or love. The nature of our affection or love determines the nature of our thoughts. Evil desire never unites with true thinking. When they seem to unite (although they do not actually do so) the result is thoughts of truth devoid of any desire for truth. In people who try to unite the two, then, truth is not truth but only empty noise, words on their lips, far from their heart. Even the worst types can learn this kind of truth, and sometimes they learn it better than others.

Some people's dogmatic belief in truth appears so genuine that no one can tell otherwise; but if they do not live a good life, it is not genuine. The desire aroused by self-love or materialism is what creates this kind of conviction, which they also defend with all the energy of apparent zeal. They even condemn anyone who does not accept it or think the same way they do. Such truth resembles its source in the individual, however: the more forceful the believer's self-love or materialism, the more forceful the truth. Such truth is born alongside evil, admittedly, but it does not bond with evil, so it is obliterated in the other life.

Things are different with people who live a good life. Genuine truth finds its receiving ground, its heart, and its God-given life in them.

2690   Genesis 21:17. *And God heard the voice of the boy, and God's angel cried out to Hagar from heaven and said to her, "What's the matter, Hagar? Don't be afraid, because God has heard the voice of the boy in the place where he is."*

God heard the voice of the boy symbolizes help received then. *And God's angel cried out to Hagar from heaven* symbolizes comfort. *And said to her, "What's the matter, Hagar?"* symbolizes a perception about her state. *"Don't be afraid, because God has heard the voice of the boy in the place where he is"* symbolizes hope of receiving help.

2691   *God heard the voice of the boy* symbolizes help received then, as can be seen from the following: in a literal sense *God's hearing someone's voice* means in an inner sense bringing help. And a *boy* symbolizes spiritual truth, as mentioned before [§§2669, 2677]. Here it symbolizes the state of the Lord's spiritual side in respect to truth, for the following reason: It says

God heard the *voice of the boy;* just afterward in the same verse it says he heard the voice of the boy *in the place where he was,* or in other words, in the state he was in; and the preceding discussion showed that the Lord was in the deepest possible state of grief over his loss of truth.

The reason it says God heard the boy's voice rather than Hagar's is that the focus here is on conditions in spiritual people. The boy, Ishmael, represents people in a spiritual religion. His mother, Hagar, represents their desire to know truth, and it is this desire that grieves.

The desire for knowledge, as mother, is what gives birth to our rational mind (§§1895, 1896, 1902, 1910, 2094, 2524), but our spirituality is born from a desire to know any truth that theology and particularly the Word can teach us. Here, the boy is spirituality itself; Hagar is the desire to know truth.

And God's angel cried out to Hagar from heaven symbolizes comfort, as can be seen from the symbolism of *crying out from heaven,* of *God's angel,* and of *Hagar. Crying out from heaven* symbolizes an inflow. *God's angel* symbolizes the Lord (§§1925, 2319). And *Hagar* symbolizes a desire to know truth (§2691). When we are in deepest grief over the loss of something we desire, the Lord's inflow into our desire for truth comes in the form of comfort.

What flows into us from the Lord is said to be cried out from heaven, because it comes by way of heaven. There his influence is plain to see but in our perceptions or thoughts it is hard to see. It reveals itself only as a change in the state of our feelings, which is how it revealed itself here when Hagar felt comforted.

He said to her, "What's the matter, Hagar?" symbolizes a perception about her state. This can be seen from the symbolism of *saying* in the stories of the Word as perceiving (discussed earlier) and from that of *What's the matter, Hagar?* as the state she was in. Here it means that the Lord knew her state, even though he questioned her and said, "What's the matter, Hagar?" In a literal sense this is an inquiry by the Lord, but in an inner sense it is his infinite perception of everything. The Word often says that people are asked about their state, but that is because we cannot believe anyone knows what we are thinking, let alone how we are feeling. The goal is also for them to have the comfort of being able to bring what is on their mind out in the open—often a healing experience. See §§1701, 1931.

"Don't be afraid, because God has heard the voice of the boy in the place where he is" symbolizes hope of receiving help, as can be seen from the

2692

2693

2694

following: *Don't be afraid* means not despairing, because when fear is removed, hope takes its place. And *hearing the voice of the boy* symbolizes help, as noted above at §2691, where similar words occur.

The previous verses dealt with the stage at which people who are reforming and becoming spiritual are stripped or purged [of truth]. Now the focus is on that which is restored to them—here, comfort and hope of help.

[2] These days people do not realize that anyone who is reforming is reduced to ignorance or a stripping away of the truth, to the point of grief and despair. They do not realize that this is the point at which such a person first receives comfort and help from the Lord. The reason it is unknown is that few today are reforming. People who *are* capable of reforming go through this stage in the next life, if not in physical life. In the other world, the state is very familiar, and it is called devastation, or desolation, which is discussed to some extent in the second volume; see §1109 there. People undergoing this kind of devastation or purging are reduced even to the point of despair, and when they reach that stage, they then accept comfort and help from the Lord. Eventually they are taken from that state to heaven, where among the angels they essentially relearn what there is to know about religious goodness and truth.

The main purpose of this devastation and desolation is to shatter the veneer of self-serving dogmatism; see §2682. Another purpose is to make it possible for people to receive a perception of goodness and truth, which they cannot do until the self-serving dogmatism is softened up, so to speak. A state of distress and grief that intensifies to the point of despair accomplishes just that. We cannot tell precisely what is good, or even what is blissful or happy, without first going through a phase that is not good, blissful, or happy. From the experience we develop a field of sensitivity, and the worse the negative phase has been, the more sensitive we become. The perspectives we form through actual experience create the field of perception and determine how far it reaches. These, along with many others, are the reasons for devastation or desolation.

Let me offer some examples for illustration, though. [3] Take people who credit everything to their own prudence and little or nothing to divine providence. You can overwhelm them with thousands upon thousands of reasons for believing that divine providence is universal (but that it is universal because it attends to the most trivial details). You can prove decisively that not a hair of their head falls—that is, not the smallest thing can happen—that has not been foreseen and provided for. Even so, it does not change their state of thought concerning their own prudence, except for the brief moment in which they feel convinced by the arguments. In fact, if the same thing is proved to them by actual experience, they admit to it while they are observing or living through the experience but return to their former opinion a few moments later. Such tools of persuasion have some passing effect on their thinking but not on their feelings, and unless their emotional state is broken, the state of their thinking remains the same. It is our feelings that give our thoughts their credibility and vital energy.

However, when the recognition that they can do absolutely nothing on their own forces them into distress and grief to the point where they give up hope, their conviction is broken and their state changes. Then they can finally be persuaded to believe that they are incapable of anything on their own, and that all strength, prudence, understanding, and wisdom come from the Lord.

The case is the same with people who believe that faith originates in themselves or that goodness does.

[4] Take another example by way of illustration. Some people develop the conviction that once God has made them righteous they no longer have any evil inside themselves, that it has been totally wiped away and erased, and that they are therefore pure. You can try to enlighten them with thousands of arguments showing that nothing is wiped away or erased, but that the Lord withholds people from evil and keeps them on a good path if the character they have developed by living a virtuous life in the world allows it. You can go further and attempt to persuade them by the lessons of experience that on their own they are nothing but evil and in fact are filthy bundles of evil. Even so they continue to believe in their own opinion. When they are reduced to a state in which they see hell in themselves, though, and see it so vividly that they despair of ever being saved, that is when their conviction is first shattered. At the same time, their conceit, their contempt for others in comparison with themselves, and their arrogance in imagining that they alone are saved are broken. They can then be brought to acknowledge with genuine belief not only that everything good comes from the Lord but also that it is all a gift of his mercy. Lastly, they can adopt heartfelt humility before the Lord, which is not possible until they admit the truth about themselves.

These considerations now make it clear why people who are reforming or becoming spiritual are reduced to a condition in which they are devastated or purged, as dealt with in the verses above. The same considerations also make it clear that when they reach a point of despair in that state, they first receive comfort and help from the Lord.

2695 Genesis 21:18. *"Get up; pick up the boy and strengthen the hold of your hand on him, because I will make him into a great nation."*

Get up symbolizes raising one's mind. *Pick up the boy* symbolizes the spiritual plane in respect to truth. *And strengthen the hold of your hand on him* means being supported by it. *Because I will make him into a great nation* symbolizes a spiritual religion.

2696 *Get up* symbolizes raising one's mind, as can be seen from the symbolism of *getting up* in the Word. When it is mentioned, it involves some kind of elevation, as noted in §2401. Here it involves raising one's mind, because it involves enlightenment. In the next verse it involves learning truth.

2697 *Pick up the boy* symbolizes the spiritual plane in respect to truth. This can be seen from the symbolism of a *boy* as spirituality, particularly in regard to truth, as noted in §§2677, 2687.

People in a spiritual religion seem to be reborn through religious truth. They do not realize that they are reborn through the goodness that goes with truth, because this good is not visible. It reveals itself only in their desire for truth and afterward in a life lived according to the truth. No one can possibly be reborn through truth unless the truth carries goodness with it, because truth without goodness has no life. Truth detached from goodness, then, is not a means to new life, and new life is what we gain by rebirth.

2698 *And strengthen the hold of your hand on him* means being supported by it. This can be seen from the symbolism of being *strengthened* as being supported, and from that of a *hand* as power (discussed in §878), which is required for support. *On him* (the boy) means by it—by the spiritual plane in respect to truth.

People in deep grief and in despair over the loss of truth are lifted up and supported solely by truth, because it is truth they are grieving and despairing over.

When people desire goodness, the good in them yearns for goodness, as the hungry yearn for bread, but when they desire truth, the good in them yearns for truth as the thirsty yearn for water.

Without the inner meaning, no one will understand what "strengthen the hold of your hand on him" is here.

2699 *Because I will make him into a great nation* symbolizes a spiritual religion. This is established by the symbolism of a *great nation* as a spiritual religion that will welcome the goodness that rises out of faith, as discussed above in §2669. The text speaks of a great nation because the spiritual kingdom is the Lord's secondary kingdom, as also discussed in that section.

Just as Ishmael represents people in the spiritual church, he also represents that church itself, and the Lord's spiritual kingdom in the heavens as well. The image and likeness of the one is in the other.

The previous verse depicted the first stage people go through after they have been purged as a time of comfort and of hope that help will arrive. The second stage they go through after they have been purged is portrayed in the current verse as a time when they are enlightened and therefore restored.

[2] The world knows nothing about these stages, because few in modern times are reborn, as I said above [§§2682, 2694], so let me tell what their second stage is like in the other world, where its nature is very well known. After the ones there who had been devastated or purged have been comforted with the hope that they will receive help, the Lord takes them up into heaven. So he takes them from a condition of shadow, which is one of ignorance, into a condition of light, which is one of enlightenment and therefore renewal, and accordingly into a joy that touches their inmost depths. The light they come into is real and is a kind of light that illuminates not only their eyes but also their minds. The extent to which it restores them can be seen from the opposite state, from which they were freed. Some of them, whose minds had been childlike and whose faith had been simple, now appear to themselves to be wearing brilliant, white clothes. Some seem to be wearing crowns. Some travel around to different communities of angels and are welcomed lovingly everywhere as sisters and brothers; there, any kindness that can grace their new life is performed for them. Some are given the opportunity to see the vastness of heaven, or the Lord's kingdom, and to sense the bliss of the inhabitants. Not to mention countless other experiences that are indescribable.

This is what the first stage of enlightenment and therefore renewal is like for people who are coming out of desolation.

Genesis 21:19. *And God opened her eyes, and she saw a well of water and went and filled the flask of water and gave the boy a drink.*   **2700**

God opened her eyes symbolizes understanding. *And she saw a well of water* symbolizes the Lord's Word—a source of truth. *And filled the flask of water* symbolizes the truth that comes from it. *And gave the boy a drink* means learning about spiritual subjects.

God opened her eyes symbolizes understanding. This can be seen from   **2701** the symbolism of *opening,* of *God opened,* and of *eyes* as giving someone understanding. *Eyes* symbolize the intellect (see §212), just as sight and seeing do (§§2150, 2325).

God is said to open our eyes when he opens our inner sight, or our intellect. This he does by acting on our rational mind, or rather on the spiritual part of our rational mind. His influence comes by way of our soul, or in other words, by an inward way we are unaware of. It creates a state of enlightenment in us, in which the truth we hear or read is confirmed for us by a kind of perception deep in our intellect.

This phenomenon we believe to be located inside us and to be produced by our own intellectual ability, but we are as wrong as can be. It is a result of an inflow from the Lord through heaven into our obscurity, error, and trust in appearances. The goodness that flows into us turns our beliefs into something resembling truth. But only people who are spiritual are blessed with enlightenment in the spiritual aspects of faith; and that is what God's opening of Hagar's eyes symbolizes.

[2] The reason the eye symbolizes the intellect is that physical sight corresponds to the sight of the spirit, which is the intellect. Since they correspond, almost everywhere the eye is mentioned in the Word it symbolizes the intellect, even where people think otherwise. Take, for instance, the place in Matthew where the Lord says:

> The *lamp* of the body is the *eye;* if the *eye* is sound, the whole body is light. If the *eye* is bad, the whole body is dark. So if the light is darkness, how immense the darkness! (Matthew 6:22, 23; Luke 11:34)

The eye in this passage is the intellect, whose spiritual aspect is faith, as can also be seen from the explanation it contains ("So if the light is darkness, how immense the darkness!"). Likewise in the same author:

> If your right eye makes you stumble, dig it out and throw it from you. (Matthew 5:29; 18:9)

The left eye is the intellect, but the right eye is its desires. The need to dig out the right eye is the need to tame our desires if they make us stumble. [3] In the same author:

> Your *eyes* are *fortunate* because they *see,* and your ears because they hear. (Matthew 13:16)

And in Luke:

> Jesus said to his disciples, "Fortunate are the *eyes* that *see* what you see." (Luke 10:23)

The eyes that see symbolize understanding and faith. After all, seeing the Lord and his miracles and deeds did not make anyone fortunate; that effect is produced only by grasping them intellectually and believing them (which is seeing with one's eyes) and obeying them (which is hearing with one's ears). For the idea that to see with the eyes is to understand and also to believe, see §§897, 2325. The intellect, you see, is the spiritual form of sight, and faith is the spiritual form of the intellect. The sight of the eye comes from the world's light; the sight of the intellect comes from heaven's light as it shines on the things that the world's light illuminates; but the sight of faith comes from heaven's light. That is why we speak of seeing with the mind's eye and seeing with the eye of faith. On the point that hearing with the ear is obeying, see §2542.

[4] In Mark:

> Jesus [said] to his disciples: "Don't you know or *understand* yet? Do you still have your heart hardened? *Having eyes, don't you see,* and having ears, don't you hear?" (Mark 8:17, 18)

Clearly, having eyes and not seeing means not wanting to understand and not believing. In Luke:

> Jesus, speaking of the city: "If you knew what [leads] to peace for you! But it has been hidden from *your eyes*." (Luke 19:41, 42)

And in Mark:

> This was done by the Lord, and it is amazing in *our eyes*. (Mark 12:11)

From the meaning of eyes even as used in everyday conversation everyone knows that what is "hidden from the eyes" and "amazing in the eyes" in these verses is hidden from and amazing to the intellect.

And she saw a well of water symbolizes the Lord's Word—a source of truth, as can be seen from the following: A *well of water* and a spring symbolize the Word and also theology drawn from the Word. So they symbolize truth itself, too, as discussed just below. And *water* symbolizes truth.

Many passages show that a *well* with water in it and a spring symbolize the Lord's Word, theology drawn from the Word, and therefore truth itself. Because the current subject is spiritual religion, the text speaks of a well rather than a spring, as it also does later in the chapter: "Abraham denounced Abimelech on account of a *well* that Abimelech's slaves had seized" (verse 25). The same is true in Genesis 26:

2702

All the *wells* that the slaves of Isaac's father dug in the days of Abraham his father, the Philistines stopped up. And Isaac returned and dug the *wells of water* that they had dug in the days of Abraham his father and that the Philistines kept stopping up after Abraham's death. And Isaac's slaves dug in the valley and found there a *well of living water.* And they dug another *well,* and they feuded over it, too. And he moved on from there and dug another *well,* and they did not feud over it. And it happened on that day that Isaac's slaves came and told him the account of the *well* that they had dug and said to him, "We've found *water."* (Genesis 26:15, 18, 19, 20, 21, 22, 25, 32)

The wells actually mean teachings that they did and did not quarrel over. Otherwise the digging of the wells and the repeated strife over them would not have been significant enough to mention in the Word of God.

[2] A well likewise symbolizes the Word, or theology, concerning which Moses says:

They traveled to *Beer.* This is the *well* of which Jehovah said to Moses, "Gather the people and I will give them *water."* Then Israel sang this song: "Gush up, you *well!* Give answer from it! A *well* that the chieftains dug, the willing among the people excavated, in [the name of] the Lawgiver, with their staffs." (Numbers 21:16, 17, 18)

The fact that a well symbolized these things explains Israel's mystical song, which speaks of true theology, as all the particulars of the inner meaning show. It also explains the name Beer, the name Beer-sheba, and its inner-level symbolism as theology itself.

[3] A theology that contains no truth, however, is called a pit, or a dry well, as in Jeremiah:

Their notables have sent their little ones to the *water;* they came to the *pits;* they did not find *water;* they returned with their vessels empty. (Jeremiah 14:3)

The water stands for truth; the pits where they did not find water, for theology that contains no truth. In the same author:

Two evils my people have done: they have deserted me—the *vein of living water*—to carve out for themselves *pits, broken pits* that cannot hold water. (Jeremiah 2:13)

Here too pits stand for doctrines that are not true. The broken pits stand for doctrines that have been cobbled together.

[4] A spring symbolizes the Word, theology, and therefore truth. In Isaiah:

> The afflicted and needy are seeking *water,* and there is none. Their tongue has failed from thirst. I Jehovah will listen to them; the God of Israel will not desert them. I will open *rivers* on the slopes, and *springs* in the middle of valleys; I will make the desert into a *lake of water,* and dry land into *outlets of water.* (Isaiah 41:17, 18)

This passage is talking about deprivation of truth, which is symbolized by the fact that the afflicted and needy were seeking water and there was none, and by the fact that their tongue failed from thirst. Then (like the current verses concerning Hagar) it turns to the comfort, restoration, and instruction they receive after their deprivation. These things are symbolized by Jehovah's promise to open rivers on the slopes, set springs in the middle of valleys, and make the desert into a lake of water and dry land into outlets of water. All of these have to do with true theology and a desire for it. [5] In Moses:

> Israel has lived securely, alone, at *Jacob's spring,* in a land of grain and new wine; its skies also drizzle dew. (Deuteronomy 33:28)

Jacob's spring stands for the Word and true doctrine taken from it. Since Jacob's spring symbolized the Word and true doctrine from it, when the Lord came to Jacob's spring he spoke with a Samaritan woman and taught her the significance of a spring and water. This is what John says about it:

> Jesus came into a city of Samaria called Sychar. *Jacob's spring* was there. So Jesus, worn out with travel, therefore sat down at the *spring.* A woman from Samaria came to draw water, to whom Jesus says, "Give me something to drink." Jesus said, "If you knew God's gift, and who it is that says to you, 'Give me something to drink,' you would ask him to give you *living water.* Anyone who drinks this water will be thirsty again. But those who drink the *water* that I give them will never be thirsty to eternity; instead, the *water* that I give them will become a *spring of water* gushing up in them to provide eternal life." (John 4:5, 6, 7, 10, 13, 14)

Jacob's spring symbolized the Word, water symbolized truth, and Samaria symbolized spiritual religion, as these terms very frequently do in the Word. That is why the Lord talked with the woman from Samaria and taught her that true theology comes from him, and that when it comes from him or (to put the same thing another way) from his Word, it is a spring of water gushing up to provide life. He also taught her that truth itself is living water. [6] Likewise in the same author:

> Jesus said, "If any are thirsty, let them come to me and drink; any who believe in me, as the scripture says, from their belly will flow *rivers of living water.*" (John 7:37, 38)

And in the same author:

> The Lamb who is in the middle of the throne will pasture them and lead them to *lively springs of water,* and God will erase every tear from their eyes. (Revelation 7:17)

In the same author:

> To the thirsty I will give a drink from the *spring of the water of life* for free. (Revelation 21:6)

Rivers of living water and lively springs of water stand for truth from the Lord, or from his Word, since the Lord is the Word. A loving and charitable goodness, which comes from the Lord alone, is the life force of truth. People who love and desire truth are called thirsty; no one else can feel that thirst. [7] These truths are also called springs of salvation in Isaiah:

> You will draw *water* in happiness from *springs of salvation,* and you will say on that day, "Acclaim Jehovah; call on his name!" (Isaiah 12:3, 4)

It is also plain in Joel that a spring is the Word, or theology from it:

> It will happen on that day that the mountains will shower down new wine, and the hills will run with milk, and all the *brooks* of Judah will run with *water,* and a *spring* will issue from Jehovah's house and water the river of the sheetim. (Joel 3:18)

The water stands for truth; the spring from Jehovah's house, for the Lord's Word. [8] In Jeremiah:

> Watch: I am bringing them from the land of the north, and I will assemble them from the flanks of the land; among them are the blind and the lame. They will come with weeping, and I will bring them with prayers to *springs of water on the path of uprightness;* they will not stumble on it. (Jeremiah 31:8, 9)

Springs of water on the path of uprightness clearly stand for true doctrines. The land of the north stands for ignorance, or a complete loss of truth; weeping and prayers, for a time of grief and despair among the people involved. Being brought to springs of water means being restored and taught truth—just as in the current verse, which speaks of Hagar and her son. [9] Isaiah speaks of the same people this way:

> Wilderness and desert will rejoice in them, and the wasteland will exult and bloom like the rose; it will sprout luxuriantly, and also exult greatly with singing. The glory of Lebanon has been given to it, the honor of Carmel and Sharon; they will see the glory of Jehovah, the honor of our God. Make limp hands firm, and to sinking knees give strength. The eyes of the blind will be unclosed, and the ears of the deaf will open. In the *wilderness, water* will burst forth, and *rivers* in the wasteland, and dry land will turn into a *lake,* and the thirsty place into *wellsprings of water.* (Isaiah 35:1, 2, 3, 5, 6, 7)

The wilderness stands for loss of truth. The water, rivers, lake, and wellsprings of water stand for truth, which will refresh and gladden people who have been devastated, whose joy is portrayed at length in this passage. [10] In David:

> Jehovah sends *springs* forth in *valleys;* among the mountains they will run. They will supply drink to every wild animal of the fields; wild donkeys will break their thirst. He waters the mountains from his *chambers.* (Psalms 104:10, 11, 13)

Springs stand for truth; mountains, for love of goodness and truth; supplying drink, for teaching. Wild animals of the fields stand for people whose lives depend on all these things; see §§774, 841, 908. Wild donkeys stand for people who focus only on logic-based truth; see §§1949, 1950, 1951. [11] In Moses:

> The child of a fertile woman is Joseph, the child of a fertile woman beside the *spring.* (Genesis 49:22)

The spring stands for a theology that comes from the Lord. In the same author:

> Jehovah your God will bring you into a good land, a land of *rivers of water, springs, gulfs* issuing in the valley and on the mountain. (Deuteronomy 8:7)

The land stands for the Lord's kingdom and church (§§662, 1066, 1068, 1262, 1413, 2571), which is described as good because of its loving, charitable goodness. The rivers, water, springs, and gulfs stand for truth that develops out of that goodness. In the same author:

The land of Canaan—land of mountains and valleys—drinks up *water* at the *raining* of the sky. (Deuteronomy 11:11)

[12] Water is truth on the planes of the spirit, of reason, and of fact, as the following passages show. In Isaiah:

> Look: the Lord Jehovah Sabaoth is taking away from Jerusalem and from Judah the whole staff of bread and the whole staff of *water.* (Isaiah 3:1)

In the same author:

> Bring *water* to meet the thirsty; approach the wanderers with bread for them. (Isaiah 21:14)

In the same author:

> Fortunate are you who sow seed along *all the waters.* (Isaiah 32:20)

In the same author:

> Those who walk in justice and speak what is upright will live on the heights; they will be given their bread, their *dependable waters.* (Isaiah 33:15, 16)

In the same author:

> Then they will not grow thirsty; in the wilderness he will lead them; *water* from rock he will bring flowing out for them. And he splits rock, and *water* gushes out. (Isaiah 48:21; Exodus 17:1–8; Numbers 20:11, 13)

[13] In David:

> He splits rocks in the *wilderness* and gave the people *gulfs* (as it seemed) to drink much from; he brought *rivulets* out from rock and sent *water* down like a *river.* (Psalms 78:15, 16)

The rock stands for the Lord. The water, rivers, and gulfs coming from it stand for truth that comes from him. In the same author:

> Jehovah makes *rivers* into a *desert,* and *outlets of water* into a dry gulch. He makes the *desert* into a *lake of water,* and thirsty land into *outlets of water.* (Psalms 107:33, 35)

In the same author:

> Jehovah's voice is upon the *waters;* Jehovah is upon *many waters.* (Psalms 29:3)

In the same author:

> A *river*—its currents will gladden the city of God, the sanctuary of the dwelling places of the Highest One. (Psalms 46:4)

In the same author:

> By Jehovah's word were the heavens made; and by the spirit of his mouth, the whole army of them. He is gathering the *waters of the sea* like a heap; he is putting *abysses* in his treasuries. (Psalms 33:6, 7)

In the same author:

> You visit the earth and take great pleasure in it; you enrich it; *God's brook is full of water.* (Psalms 65:9)

In the same author:

> The *waters* saw you, God; the *waters* saw you; the *abysses* shook. The clouds *gushed out water.* On the *sea* is your route, and your path is on *many waters.* (Psalms 77:16, 17, 19)

Anyone can see that the waters here do not mean waters, that the abysses did not shake, and that Jehovah's route is not on the sea nor his path on the waters. Instead, the waters are spiritual ones—that is, spiritual qualities, which are forms of truth. Otherwise the text would be a heap of meaningless words. In Isaiah:

> Oh, everyone who is thirsty, come to the *water,* and whoever does not have silver, come, buy! (Isaiah 55:1)

In Zechariah:

> It will happen on that day that *living water* will go out from Jerusalem, half of it to the eastern sea and half of it to the western sea. (Zechariah 14:8)

[14] Moreover, where the Word describes the planting of a church (as either a future or a past event) and depicts the church as a paradisal park, a garden, a grove, or trees, it commonly speaks as well in terms of the water or rivers that water such a place. They symbolize spiritual, rational, and factual matters, which are forms of truth. One example is paradise (Genesis 2:8, 9), which is also described in terms of its rivers (Genesis 2:10–14). The rivers symbolize facets of wisdom and understanding; see §§107–121. It is the same in many other passages in the Word, such as this one in Moses:

They are planted as valleys are, as *gardens beside the river;* like sandalwoods has Jehovah planted them, like *cedars beside the water.* The *waters* will flow down from his buckets, and his seed will be on *many waters.* (Numbers 24:6, 7)

In Ezekiel:

[An eagle] took some of the seed of the land and put it in a field suitable for sowing; [the eagle] took it *beside many waters.* It sprouted and became a luxuriant *grapevine.* (Ezekiel 17:5, 6)

A grapevine and vineyard symbolize a spiritual church; see §1069. In the same author:

Your mother was like a *grapevine* that resembled you, *planted* next to the *water;* fruitful and full of branches she became because of the *many waters.* (Ezekiel 19:10)

In the same author:

Look—Assyria, [a cedar] in Lebanon: *The water made it grow;* the *abyss* made it tall; with *its rivers* [the abyss] was meandering all around its planting-place and *sent out its channels of water to all the trees of the field.* (Ezekiel 31:[3,] 4)

[15] In the same author:

Look: on the *bank of the river,* very *many trees* on this side and that! He said to me, "*This water* is going out to the eastern boundary, and it runs down onto the plain and goes toward the *sea,* having been sent down into the *sea,* and the *water* [of the sea] is cured. And it will come about that every living soul that creeps in any place where [the water] of the *two rivers* goes will survive. And the fish will be very numerous, because *this water* goes there and is cured, so that everything may live, wherever the *river* goes. It has its marshes and its swamps, and they are not being cured; they will be given over to salt." (Ezekiel 47:7, 8, 9, 11)

This is about the New Jerusalem, or the Lord's spiritual kingdom. Water going out to the eastern boundary symbolizes spiritual elements that grow out of heavenly ones, or truth from a heavenly origin—that is, faith that develops out of love and charity (§§101, 1250). Running down onto the plain means flowing down into doctrines present in the rational mind

(2418, 2450). Going toward the sea means approaching knowledge, the sea being a body of knowledge (28). The living soul that creeps symbolizes the pleasure these things give (746, 909, 994). Such pleasure survives on the water of the river, or in other words, on spiritual traits that come from a heavenly source. Numerous fish stand for a wealth of useful facts (40, 991). Marshes and swamps stand for those that are useless and impure; turning to salt stands for being purged (2455). In Jeremiah:

> Blessed is the man who trusts in Jehovah. He will be like a *tree planted by the water*, and by the *brook* he will send out his roots. (Jeremiah 17:7, 8)

In David:

> They will be like a *tree planted beside brooks of water* that will yield its fruit in its season. (Psalms 1:3)

In John:

> He showed me a *pure river of the water of life*, brilliant as crystal, going out from the throne of God and the Lamb; in the middle of its street and of the *river*, on this side and that, was the *tree of life*, making twelve fruits. (Revelation 22:1, 2)

[16] Now, since in the Word's inner meaning, water symbolizes truth, the priests and Levites of the Jewish religion were ordered to *wash with water* when they came up [to the altar] to minister. (This was for the sake of the representation in the eyes of the angels, who looked at ritual from a spiritual viewpoint.) They were to do so in the *washbowl* between the tabernacle and the altar, and later in the *bronze sea* and the other washbowls around the Temple, which stood in place of a spring. The custom of the *sin water* or purifying water that was to be spattered on the Levites was likewise established for the sake of the representation (Numbers 8:7). The same holds true for the *water for removing [sin]*, made from the ashes of a red cow (Numbers 19:2–19). Plunder from the Midianites was to be cleansed by *water* (Numbers 31:19–25). [17] The *water that came from the rock* (Exodus 17:1–8; Numbers 20:1–13) represented and symbolized an ample supply of spiritual elements—religious truth, in other words—from the Lord. The *bitter water* that was cured with wood (Exodus 15:22–25) represented and symbolized unpleasant truth rendered welcome and pleasing by goodness, or positive desires. Wood symbolizes something good in our desires, or our will; see §643.

This evidence now reveals what water means in the Word and so what it means in baptism, of which the Lord said this in John:

Unless people have been born of *water* and *spirit* they cannot enter God's kingdom. (John 3:5)

To be specific, water is the spiritual side of religion, while spirit is the heavenly side. So baptism is a symbol of being regenerated by the Lord through religious truth and goodness. Not that baptism regenerates us, but rather the kind of life baptism symbolizes—the life that Christians need to enter into, since they possess religious truth because they have the Word.

2703   *And filled the flask of water* symbolizes the truth that comes from it. This is established by the symbolism of *water* as truth (discussed directly above).

2704   *And gave the boy a drink* means learning about spiritual subjects. This can be seen from the symbolism of *giving a drink* as teaching someone what is true, and from that of a *boy* as the spiritual plane in respect to truth (discussed in §2697).

The stage dealt with in the current verse—a stage of instruction—is the third stage for people who are coming out of devastation or a time of purging. The previous verse, verse 18, depicts a stage of enlightenment, or heavenly light (see §2699), and when they enter that stage, they want to learn and know the truth. When that is what they want, they readily and almost spontaneously absorb true ideas. Those on earth learn them from the Lord's Word, or from doctrine. Those in heaven learn them from angels, to whom nothing gives more bliss or happiness than teaching their new sisters and brothers, and training them in the principles and values that form the ordained plan of heaven and therefore lead to the Lord.

2705   Genesis 21:20. *And God was with the boy, and he grew and resided in the wilderness; and he was an archer.*

God was with the boy symbolizes the Lord's presence among spiritual people. *And he grew* symbolizes increases. *And resided in the wilderness* symbolizes what is relatively dim. *And was an archer* symbolizes an adherent of a spiritual religion.

2706   *God was with the boy* symbolizes the Lord's presence among spiritual people, as can be seen from the symbolism of *God's being with someone* and a *boy.*

God's being with someone symbolizes the Lord's presence, as can be seen without explanation. The Lord truly is present with all of us (there is no other source of life) and regulates the very smallest things about us, even in the worst of us and in hell itself; but he does so in different ways, depending on how we receive his life. When we receive his life (the vital energy of love for goodness and truth) in a bad way, and twist it into a love for evil and falsity, the Lord is present and turns our aims to a good end, so far as possible. His presence with us in this case, though, is called absence; and the further our evil stands from goodness, and our falsity from truth, the greater the absence.

When we do receive the Lord's life (the vital energy of love for goodness and truth), however, it is called presence; and the more we receive, the greater the presence.

The situation can be compared to that with the sun, which is present by means of its warmth and light in the world's vegetation, again depending on how it is received.

A *boy* symbolizes the spiritual plane in respect to truth, as noted above [§§2697, 2704]. Here it symbolizes spiritual people, because it represents an individual in a spiritual religion, and spiritual religion itself. In a comprehensive sense it represents the Lord's whole spiritual kingdom. When I say that someone symbolizes something spiritual—as the boy here symbolizes the spiritual plane in respect to truth—that person necessarily symbolizes spiritual people as well, because a spiritual quality is not possible without an individual to possess it. The same is true with any other statement I have expressed abstractly.

And he grew symbolizes increases, as can be seen without explanation.　**2707**

And resided in the wilderness symbolizes what is relatively dim. This　**2708**
can be seen from the symbolism of *residing* as living (see §2451) and from that of the *wilderness* as something barely alive (discussed in §1927)— here, something dim, but only relatively so. "Relatively dim" refers to the condition of a spiritual religion compared to that of a heavenly religion, or the condition of spiritual people compared to that of heavenly people. Heavenly people are drawn to goodness; spiritual people, to truth. Heavenly people have perception, but spiritual people have the voice of conscience. Heavenly people see the Lord as the sun, but spiritual people, as the moon (§§1521, 1530, 1531, 2495). Just as the former receive light to see by from the Lord, they also receive light to perceive goodness and truth by, and this light resembles the sunlight of day. The latter receive a light from him that resembles moonlight at night, so things are relatively dim for them. The reason for the difference is that heavenly people dwell in love for the Lord and so in life itself from him, while spiritual people dwell in charity for their neighbor and in faith. They do dwell in the

Lord's life, then, but more dimly. That is why those who are heavenly never debate about religion or religious truth. Goodness gives them an intuition for truth, so they simply say "Yes." The spiritual, though, talk and argue about religious truth, because truth gives them a conscience for goodness. Another reason is that heavenly people have a loving goodness planted in the voluntary part of their mind, where a person's main life resides. Spiritual people have it planted in the intellectual part of their mind, where a person's secondary life resides. This explains why that loving goodness is relatively dim in spiritual people. (See §§81, 202, 337, 765, 784, 895, 1114–1125, 1155, 1577, 1824, 2048, 2088, 2227, 2454, 2507.) The relative dimness is called a wilderness here.

[2] In the Word, a *wilderness* means a place sparsely inhabited and little tamed, and also a place completely uninhabited and untamed; so it is used in two senses. When it means a place sparsely inhabited and little tamed—a place where there are a few dwellings and where there are sheepfolds, pastures, and water—it symbolizes things or people with relatively little life and light. This is what spiritual qualities or people are like in comparison with heavenly qualities or people. Where it means a place completely uninhabited and untamed, however—a place where there are no dwellings, sheepfolds, pastures, or water—it symbolizes people who have been stripped of goodness and purged of truth.

[3] The following passages show that a wilderness means a place of relatively little habitation or development, or in other words, where there are a few dwellings and where there are sheepfolds, pastures, and water. In Isaiah:

> Sing Jehovah a new song! His praise comes from the farthest part of the earth. Those that go down to the sea and the things that fill it, the islands and their inhabitants, will lift up the *wilderness* and *its cities*. Kedar will inhabit the courtyards. Those who live on the rock will sing; from the head of the mountains they will shout. (Isaiah 42:10, 11)

In Ezekiel:

> I will strike a pact of peace with them and bring an end on the earth to the evil wild animal, and they will *live* securely *in the wilderness* and sleep in forests, and I will make them—and the environs of my hill—a blessing. The tree of the field will yield its fruit, and the earth will yield its fruit. (Ezekiel 34:25, 26, 27)

This is about what is spiritual. In Hosea:

> I will lead her into the *wilderness* and speak to her heart and give her her vineyards from there. (Hosea 2:14, 15)

This passage deals with the stripping away of truth, followed by consolation. In David:

> The *sheepfolds of the wilderness* drip with rain, and the hills gird themselves with exultation. Meadows clothe the flock, and the valleys are covered with grain. (Psalms 65:12, 13)

[4] In Isaiah:

> I will make the *wilderness* into a lake of water, and thirsty land into outlets of water. I will set in the *wilderness* a cedar of sheetim, and a myrtle, and an oil tree. I will put in the *wilderness* a fir, so that they can see and know and store [in mind] and understand, all together, because the hand of Jehovah has done this, and the Holy One of Israel has created it. (Isaiah 41:18, 19, 20)

This is about the rebirth of people who do not know the truth, or in other words, of people outside the church. It is also about the enlightenment and instruction of people who are desolate; they are referred to as the wilderness. The cedar, myrtle, and oil tree stand for truth and goodness in the inner self; the fir, in the outer self. In David:

> Jehovah makes rivers into a *wilderness,* and outlets of water into a desert. He makes the *wilderness* into a lake of water, and thirsty land into outlets of water. (Psalms 107:33, 35)

Likewise. In Isaiah:

> *Wilderness* and desert will rejoice in them, and the wasteland will exult and bloom like the rose; it will sprout luxuriantly. Water has gushed in the *wilderness,* and rivers in the wasteland. (Isaiah 35:1, 2, 6)

In the same author:

> You will be like a watered garden and like an outlet of water, whose waters do not prove false, and they will rebuild from you the ancient *wildlands.* (Isaiah 58:11, 12)

In the same author:

> . . . until the spirit is poured out on us from on high; and the *wilderness* will become Carmel, and Carmel will be considered a forest. And in the *wilderness* integrity will reside, and virtue in Carmel. (Isaiah 32:15, 16)

These verses speak of spiritual religion, which is being called a relative wilderness, even though it is inhabited and developed. (After all, it says, "In the wilderness integrity will reside, and virtue in Carmel.")

The fact that a wilderness is a relatively dim state is plain from passages in which it is called a wilderness and also a forest. It is quite clear in Jeremiah:

> You [current] generation, see the Word of Jehovah! Have I been a *wilderness* to Israel? A *land of shadows?* (Jeremiah 2:31)

[5] It can also be seen from the Word that a wilderness means a place completely uninhabited and untamed, or in other words, where there are no dwellings, sheepfolds, pastures, or water. So it symbolizes people who have been stripped of goodness and purged of truth. Mention of this kind of wilderness comes up in two senses; it is used of people who eventually reform and also of people who cannot be reformed. In Jeremiah it is used of people who eventually reform (as it is used here of Hagar and her son):

> This is what Jehovah has said: "I remembered you, the mercy of your youthful days, when you walked after me in the *wilderness,* in a land unsown." (Jeremiah 2:2)

This is about Jerusalem, which in this case is the ancient church—a spiritual religion. In Moses:

> Jehovah's lot is his people; Jacob is the rope of his inheritance. [Jehovah] found them in a *wilderness land,* and in devastation, lamentation, wastelands; he enveloped them, enlightened them, guarded them as the pupil of his eye. (Deuteronomy 32:9, 10)

In David:

> They wandered in the *wilderness,* in a desert path; a habitable city they did not find. (Psalms 107:4)

This is about people who are being stripped of truth and are reforming. In Ezekiel:

> I will bring you to the *wilderness of peoples,* and I will subject you to judgment there, as I subjected your ancestors to judgment in the *wilderness of the land of Egypt.* (Ezekiel 20:35, 36)

This too is about the stripping and purging of people who are reforming.

[6] The travels and wanderings of the Israelite people in the wilderness in fact represented the devastation and purging of the faithful before their reformation, and therefore their times of trial (since undergoing spiritual trials means being devastated and purged). This too is visible from the following in Moses:

> Jehovah carried them in the *wilderness*, as a man carries his child, on the path, right to this place. (Deuteronomy 1:31)

And in another passage:

> Remember all the path by which Jehovah your God led you forty years now in the *wilderness* to afflict you, *to test you* and know what was in your heart, whether you would keep his commandments or not. He afflicted you, he made you hungry, he fed you manna—which you did not recognize and your ancestors did not recognize—so you would know that humankind does not live by bread alone; but by everything that issues from Jehovah's mouth does humankind live. (Deuteronomy 8:2, 3)

And again:

> Do not forget that Jehovah led you in a large and fearsome *wilderness*, where there was serpent, fire snake, and scorpion, a thirsty place, where there was no water, bringing water out of the flinty rock for you. He fed you manna in the *wilderness*—which your ancestors did not recognize—to afflict you, *test you*, and to do good in your final days. (Deuteronomy 8:15, 16)

The wilderness stands for being stripped and purged, as happens to a person in times of trial. The traveling and wandering of the people in the wilderness for forty years depicts every phase of the church when it engages in battle—how it fails on its own but wins when it relies on the Lord.

[7] In addition, the woman described by John as fleeing into the wilderness actually symbolizes the church's trials. John says this of her:

> The woman who had delivered the male child fled into the *wilderness*, where she has a place prepared by God. The woman was given two wings of a large eagle to fly into the *wilderness*, to her place. And the serpent hurled water like a river from its mouth after the woman to cause her to be swallowed up by the stream, but the earth helped the woman. For the earth opened its mouth and gulped down the river that the dragon had hurled out of its mouth. (Revelation 12:6, 14, 15, 16)

[8] Isaiah speaks this way about a wilderness in connection both with a religion and with people who have been entirely stripped of goodness and truth and cannot reform:

> I will make the rivers a *wilderness;* their fish will stink from lack of water and die of thirst; I will clothe the heavens in darkness. (Isaiah 50:2, 3)

In the same author:

> Your holy cities were a *wilderness;* a *wilderness* was Zion; Jerusalem was deserted. (Isaiah 64:10)

In Jeremiah:

> I looked, and here, Carmel was a *wilderness,* and all its cities had been destroyed before Jehovah. (Jeremiah 4:26)

In the same author:

> Many shepherds spoiled my vineyard, trampled my allotment, turned the allotment I desired into a *desolate wilderness.* They made it a desolation; it mourned over me, desolate; all the land is made desolate, because no one takes it to heart. Over all the slopes in the *wilderness* have come the destroyers. (Jeremiah 12:10, 11, 12)

In Joel:

> Fire devoured the *sheepfolds of the wilderness,* and flame kindled all the trees of the field; brooks of water dried up; *fire devoured the sheepfolds of the wilderness.* (Joel 1:19, 20)

In Isaiah:

> He made the world a *wilderness,* and its cities he destroyed. (Isaiah 14:17)

This is about Lucifer. In the same author:

> An oracle of the *wilderness beside the sea:* Like windstorms in the south, from the wilderness it comes, from a fearsome land. (Isaiah 21:1 and following verses)

The wilderness beside the sea stands for truth devastated by secular knowledge and logic based on it.

[9] The examples above reveal what the following words about John the Baptist mean:

The saying of Isaiah: the voice of one shouting in the *wilderness,* "Prepare the way for the Lord! Straighten his paths!" (Matthew 3:3; Mark 1:3; Luke 3:4; John 1:23; Isaiah 40:3)

What they mean is that the church was then completely devastated, so that there was no longer any goodness or truth. This becomes obvious when you consider that no one then knew that people had any inner dimension, or that the Word did either. So they did not know that the Messiah, or Christ, was coming to save them forever.

The same thing also shows what the following mean: John was in the *wildlands* up to the day of his presentation to Israel (Luke 1:80). He preached in the *wilderness of Judea* (Matthew 3:1 and following verses). And he baptized in the *wilderness* (Mark 1:4). In doing so, he too represented the condition of the church.

The symbolism of a wilderness also shows why the Lord so often withdrew into the *wilderness,* as in Matthew 4:1; 15:32–end; Mark 1:12, 13, 35–37, 45; 6:31–36; Luke 4:1; 5:16; 9:10 and following verses; John 11:54. The symbolism of a mountain shows why the Lord withdrew onto *mountains,* as in Matthew 14:23; 15:29, 30, 31; 17:1 and following verses; 28:16, 17; Mark 3:13, 14; 6:46; 9:2–9; Luke 6:12, 13; 9:28; John 6:15.

And was an archer symbolizes an adherent of a spiritual religion. This **2709** is established by the symbolism of an arrow as truth, and by that of a bow as theology (discussed above at §2686).

People in a spiritual religion were once called *archers* because they use truth to defend themselves and because they debate truth, unlike people in a heavenly religion, who are protected by goodness and do not debate truth; see §2708 above. The truth which people in a spiritual religion use for defense and which they debate springs from the theology they acknowledge.

[2] Further evidence in David shows that in times past a spiritual person was called an archer, theology was called a bow and a quiver, and theological truths (doctrines, in other words) were called arrows:

Ephraim's armed sons—*archers*—turned tail on the day of battle. (Psalms 78:9)

Ephraim stands for the intellectual side of religion. In Judges:

You who are riding on white jennies, sitting on middim, and walking on the way, meditate! With the voice of *archers* among those drawing

water, they will discuss Jehovah's virtues there, the virtues of his town in
Israel. (Judges 5:10, 11)

In Isaiah:

> Jehovah called me from the womb; from my mother's belly he men-
> tioned my name and made my mouth a sharp sword. In the shade of
> his hand he hid me and made me a *polished arrow.* In *his quiver* he con-
> cealed me and said to me, "You are my servant, Israel, because in you I
> will glory." (Isaiah 49:1, 2, 3)

Israel stands for a spiritual religion. [3] In David:

> As *arrows* in the hand of a mighty man, so are the children of one's
> youthful days. Fortunate are all who have filled *their quiver* with them.
> (Psalms 127:4, 5)

The quiver stands for theology that is good and true. In Habakkuk:

> The sun, the moon stood in their places; at the *light of your arrows* they
> will move on, at the radiance of your lightning spear. (Habakkuk 3:11)

At Elisha's command, Joash, king of Israel, used a *bow* to shoot an *arrow*
through a window, and Elisha said, "*The arrow of Jehovah's salvation! The
arrow of Jehovah's salvation* against Syria!" (2 Kings 13:16, 17, 18). This symbolizes secrets concerning a theology that is good and true.

[4] Just as most things in the Word also have a negative meaning, so
do arrows, a bow, and an archer. They symbolize false ideas, false theology, and people who adopt falsity. In Moses, for instance:

> The child of a fertile woman is Joseph, the child of a fertile woman
> beside her daughters' spring; she stepped over the wall, and the *archers*
> treated him with bitterness and *shot arrows* and hated him. (Genesis
> 49:22, 23)

In Jeremiah:

> They have *shot forth* their tongue; *their bow* is a lie and is not for truth.
> An *outstretched arrow* is their tongue; it speaks deceit. (Jeremiah 9:3, 8)

In David:

> They sharpened their tongue like a sword. They *bent their "arrow"*—a bit-
> ter word—to *shoot* the upright person in secret; they will *shoot* suddenly,

and will not fear the person. They will corroborate an evil matter to themselves; they will tell ensnaring tales in order to hide. (Psalms 64:3, 4, 5)

In the same author:

Look: the wicked *bend the bow;* they ready *their arrow* on the string, to *shoot* in deep darkness those who are upright in heart. (Psalms 11:2)

In the same author:

His truth is a shield and buckler; you will not be afraid of the horror at night, of the *arrow* [that] flies by day. (Psalms 91:4, 5)

This verse, then, depicts the condition of a spiritual religion as being dim in comparison with the condition of a heavenly religion, and as being embattled. People in a spiritual religion recognize truth only from theology, not from goodness itself, as people in a heavenly religion do. **2710**

Genesis 21:21. *And he resided in the wilderness of Paran, and his mother took for him a wife from the land of Egypt.* **2711**

He resided in the wilderness of Paran symbolizes the life of a spiritual person in regard to goodness. Here as before, the *wilderness* is relative dimness; *Paran* is enlightenment from the Lord's divine humanity. *And his mother took for him* symbolizes a desire for truth. *A wife from the land of Egypt* symbolizes a desire for knowledge among people in a spiritual religion.

He resided in the wilderness of Paran symbolizes the life of a spiritual person in regard to goodness. This can be seen from the symbolism of *residing,* a word used in connection with the good effects of truth, or spiritual goodness, which is to say the goodness of a spiritual person. His residing in the wilderness of Paran depicts the nature of that goodness, as discussed directly below. **2712**

Many passages in the Word show that residing is spoken of in connection with the good effect of truth, or a desire for truth. These passages are ones that mention cities—which symbolize truth—saying that they will lack residents, who symbolize what is good (§§2268, 2449, 2451). Truth is inhabited by goodness, and truth without goodness is like a city in which no one lives, as in Zephaniah:

I have devastated their streets, so that none is passing through; their *cities* have been deserted, *so that no one is living* there. (Zephaniah 3:6)

[2] In Jeremiah:

> Jehovah was bringing us through the wilderness; not a man passed through in [the land], and not a person *resided* there. They made the land a desert; its *cities* were burned, so that there was not a *resident.* (Jeremiah 2:6, 15)

In the same author:

> Every *city* has been abandoned, and nobody is *living* in them. (Jeremiah 4:29)

In the same author:

> In the deserted streets of Jerusalem there is no person and no *resident* and no animal. (Jeremiah 33:10)

The streets stand for truth (§2336). "No person" stands for an absence of heavenly goodness; "no resident," for an absence of spiritual goodness; "no animal," for an absence of earthly goodness. In the same author:

> Moab's *cities* will become deserted land, *none living in them.* (Jeremiah 48:9)

[3] Every clause in the Prophets contains a marriage of truth and goodness, so when a deserted city is mentioned, the text adds that there was not a resident in it, because a city symbolizes truth, and a resident, goodness. Otherwise, when a city has already been described as deserted, it would be superfluous to say that there was not a resident.

Likewise there are standard terms to symbolize facets of heavenly goodness, facets of spiritual goodness, and facets of truth, as in Isaiah:

> Your seed will *possess* the nations, and deserted cities they will *inhabit.* (Isaiah 54:3)

Possessing here has to do with heavenly goodness; inhabiting, [or residing,] with spiritual goodness. In the same author:

> The ones I have chosen will *possess* it, and my servants will *reside* there. (Isaiah 65:9)

Likewise. [4] In David:

> God will save Zion and *rebuild* the cities of Judah, and they will *live* there and *possess* it, and the seed of his servants will *inherit* it, and those who love his name will *live* in it. (Psalms 69:35, 36)

Living and at the same time possessing has to do with heavenly goodness; living by itself has to do with spiritual goodness. In Isaiah:

> He is saying to Jerusalem, "You will be *inhabited,*" and to the cities of Judah, "You will be *rebuilt.*" (Isaiah 44:26)

Inhabiting is connected here with the goodness of a spiritual religion, which is Jerusalem.

So consistently do the terms in the Word refer to their own forms of goodness and truth that simply being aware what a word like this refers to enables a person to tell what the general topic is.

The fact that a *wilderness* symbolizes relative dimness is apparent from the symbolism of a *wilderness* as something dim, when it is mentioned in connection with a spiritual person as compared to a heavenly one. This is discussed above at §2708.

2713

Paran here means enlightenment from the Lord's divine humanity, as can be seen from the symbolism of *Paran* as the Lord's divine humanity. This symbolism is clear from passages in the Word that mention it, as in the prophet Habakkuk:

2714

> Jehovah, I have heard of your fame; I have trembled, Jehovah, at your work. In the middle of the years, bring it to life; in the middle of the years, make it known; in your merciful zeal, remember. God will come out of *Teman,* and the Holy One from *Mount Paran;* selah. His majesty covered the heavens, and the earth is full of his praise. And there was radiance and light; he has horns coming from his hand, and in them is the hiding place of his strength. (Habakkuk 3:2, 3, 4)

Clearly this is about the Lord's Coming, which is symbolized by "bringing it to life in the middle of the years" and "making it known in the middle of the years." His divine humanity is portrayed by the promise that God would come out of Teman, and the Holy One, from Mount Paran; the text says "from Teman" in respect to heavenly love, and "from Mount Paran" in respect to spiritual love. The fact that the Lord's divine humanity would radiate enlightenment and power is symbolized by "there was radiance and light; he has horns coming from his hand." The radiance and light are enlightenment; the horns are power. [2] In Moses:

> Jehovah came from Sinai and dawned from *Seir* on them; he shone out from *Mount Paran* and came with the holy myriads. From his right hand came the fire of a law for them; yes, he loves the peoples. All his

holy ones were in your hand and came together at your foot, and he will take up some of your words. (Deuteronomy 33:2, 3)

This too is about the Lord, whose divine humanity is depicted in his rising out of Seir and shining out from Mount Paran. The text says "out of Seir" in respect to heavenly love, "from Mount Paran" in respect to spiritual love. Spiritual individuals are symbolized by the peoples he loves and by the ones joining together at [Israel's] foot. The foot symbolizes something lowlier in the Lord's kingdom, and therefore something dimmer. [3] In the same author:

> Chedorlaomer and the kings with him struck the Horites on their mountain *(Seir)*, all the way to *El-paran,* which is up in the wilderness. (Genesis 14:5, 6)

For the point that Mount Seir and El-paran symbolize the Lord's divine humanity, see §§1675, 1676. In the same author:

> It happened in the second year, in the second month, on the twentieth of the month, that the cloud rose up from upon the tabernacle of the testimony. And the children of Israel traveled on their travels from the wilderness of Sinai, and the cloud settled in the *wilderness of Paran.* (Numbers 10:11, 12)

[4] All the people's travels in the wilderness symbolize conditions in the church when it is embattled, and its inward struggles, in which its members fail but which the Lord wins for them. As a result, those travels symbolize the Lord's own struggles and victories. This will be demonstrated elsewhere, with the Lord's divine mercy. Since it was the Lord's human divinity that endured these trials, the wilderness of Paran here symbolizes his human divinity too. So do the following words in the same author:

> Afterward the people traveled from Hazeroth and camped in the *wilderness of Paran;* and Jehovah spoke to Moses, saying, "Send yourself some men and have them scout out the land of Canaan, which I am giving to the children of Israel." And Moses sent them out of the *wilderness of Paran* on Jehovah's command. And they came back both to Moses and to Aaron and to the whole assembly of the children of Israel, to the *wilderness of Paran* in Kadesh, and they brought word back to them and showed them the fruit of the land. (Numbers [12:16]; 13:1, 2, 3, 4, 26)

[5] Their traveling from the wilderness of Paran to scout out the land of Canaan means that these people—the children of Israel, or in other words, spiritual people—receive the Lord's heavenly kingdom (symbolized by Canaan) through the Lord's divine humanity. The fact that the Israelites then lost heart, however, symbolizes the frailty of such people. [The passage also involves the idea] that the Lord would therefore fulfill everything in the law, suffer times of trial, and overcome. In this way his divine humanity would bring salvation to people who possess a faith that develops out of love for others, and to people who face trials in which the Lord was victorious. For this reason, when the Lord was tested, it took place in the wilderness (Matthew 4:1; Mark 1:12, 13; Luke 4:1); see above at §2708.

There are two secrets here. One is that a spiritual person's goodness is relatively dim. The other is that the Lord's divine humanity sends light into this dimness.

2715

As for the first—that a spiritual person's goodness is relatively dim—this can be seen from the comparison of a spiritual person's condition with a heavenly person's, as presented above in §2708. The comparison of the two states makes it quite obvious. In heavenly people, goodness is planted in the voluntary part of their mind, which sheds light on the intellectual part. In spiritual people, on the other hand, the voluntary part is completely destroyed. In consequence, they receive nothing good from their voluntary side, and for this reason the Lord plants goodness in the intellectual side; see §§863, 875, 895, 927, 928, 1023, 1043, 1044, 2124, 2256. The voluntary part has the primary life in us; the intellectual part lives from it. The voluntary part in spiritual people is so badly damaged that it contains nothing but evil, and evil continually and constantly pours from it into their intellectual side, or their thinking. Clearly, then, the goodness there is relatively dim.

[2] That is why spiritual people do not love the Lord the way heavenly people do. So they do not feel the same humility, which is an essential ingredient in all worship and a conduit for goodness from the Lord. A proud heart can never receive goodness from him; only a humble one can.

The spiritual also do not love their neighbor the same way the heavenly do. Self-love and materialism are constantly streaming in from their voluntary side and obscuring the benefits of that love. Anyone who reflects on it can see this from the fact that when we help others, it is for the sake of a worldly goal. Although we do not acknowledge it openly, we are thinking about a reward, either from the people we help or from the Lord in the next life. Our goodness, then, is still defiled with the sense that we are owed something. Another piece of evidence is the fact that whenever we do good, if we have a chance to mention it and set ourselves up as better than others, we are at the peak of our happiness. The heavenly, though, love their neighbor more than themselves, never think about being repaid, and never consider themselves superior to others in any way.

[3] What is more, goodness is obscured in spiritual people by dogmatic convictions based on various principles rising (again) out of self-love and materialism. Concerning the nature of dogmatism, including dogmatic belief in truth, see §§2682, 2689 at the end. This too is a result of the evil flowing in from their voluntary side.

[4] Here is yet more evidence that the goodness in spiritual people is comparatively dim: They do not recognize truth from any kind of perception, as heavenly people do, but from their parents' and teachers' lessons and from the creed they were born into. To this mix they add something of themselves and their own cogitations, and then their sense impressions and power of logic usually hold sway over them. So do the illusions of the senses and seemingly logical notions. These things make it almost impossible for spiritual people to acknowledge the pure truth that heavenly people acknowledge. Nonetheless the Lord plants goodness in this "truth," although it is false truth, or a semblance of truth; but the goodness consequently fades, qualified as it is by the truth to which it is tied. The situation here resembles that of sunlight when it flows into objects; the nature of the objects receiving it makes the light look a certain color there. The color is beautiful if the form and the way it receives the light is attractive and harmonizes with the light. The color is ugly if the form and the way it receives the light is not attractive and therefore does not harmonize with the light. In the same way, genuine goodness is qualified by truth.

[5] From this it is also plain that spiritual people do not recognize evil. They believe hardly anything is bad unless it violates the Ten Commandments. The evils that show up in our feelings or thoughts—and there are countless types—are beyond their knowledge. They do not reflect on them or call them evil. They never regard any of the pleasures that greed and indulgence bring us as anything but good. The pleasures of self-love they actually pursue and approve of and justify, not realizing that these pleasures are what shape their spirit, that this is what they will become through and through in the other world.

[6] This in turn shows that spiritual people do not realize that goodness is the essential element of faith, even though the whole Word speaks of hardly anything but the good inspired by love for the Lord and by love for our neighbor. They do not even know what love and charity are in their essence. What they do know about faith—which they consider the essential thing—they argue over, debating whether it is true (unless they have had it confirmed for them by plentiful life experience). Heavenly people never debate this way, because they recognize and sense that truth is true. That is why the Lord said in Matthew 5:37, "Let your conversation be 'Yes, yes,' 'No, no.' Anything beyond these comes from evil." Heavenly people have the truth itself; spiritual people debate its validity. Since heavenly people have the truth itself, they can see unlimited ramifications of that truth, so in a manner of speaking, their light allows them to see the whole of heaven. Since spiritual people argue over the validity of truth, as long as they are doing so they cannot approach the outermost limit of heavenly people's light, let alone see anything by that light.

As for the second—that the Lord's divine humanity sends light into **2716** this dimness that exists in spiritual people—it is a secret that cannot be explained intelligibly. To do so would be to describe the inflow of the Divine. Only the following provides any idea of it: If Supreme Divinity itself were to exert an influence on the kind of goodness described above— polluted as this goodness is with so much evil and falsity—it could not be received. If some of it *were* received, that goodness (which is to say people with that kind of goodness) would suffer the tortures of hell and would therefore be destroyed. The Lord's divine humanity, on the other hand, *can* influence them and shed light on that kind of goodness, just as the sun shines on thick clouds, which take on the multicolored faces of dawn early in the morning. Still, the Lord cannot appear to them as sunlight but as moonlight.

This shows that the purpose of the Lord's coming into the world was to save the spiritual; see §2661.

And his mother took for him symbolizes a desire for truth. This can be **2717** seen from the symbolism of a *mother* as a religion (treated of in §289). Since a spiritual religion (which is what is being represented here) has a desire for truth, and this desire makes it a religion, the mother here symbolizes this desire.

A wife from the land of Egypt symbolizes a desire for knowledge among **2718** people in a spiritual religion. This is established by the symbolism of a *wife* as a desire, or some goodness (discussed in §§915, 2517), and by that of *Egypt* as secular knowledge (discussed in §§1164, 1165, 1186, 1462).

This verse depicts the kind of goodness that people in a spiritual religion have, or the essential nature of their life. It portrays the goodness in them as dim but also as having light shed on it by the Lord's divine humanity. From this light, a desire for truth emerges in their rational mind, and a desire for knowledge in their earthly mind.

The type of desire for goodness heavenly people have cannot be born in spiritual people. Instead, spiritual people have a desire for truth. Goodness is implanted in the intellectual part of their minds, where it is fairly dim, as shown in §2715. From this dim goodness, no other emotion can be produced or derived in their rational mind than a desire for truth, and through this, in their earthly mind, a desire for knowledge.

By "truth" no other kind of truth is meant than the kind a person believes to be true, even if it is not inherently so. By "knowledge" is meant not the arts and sciences known to scholars but any kind of knowledge from public life, doctrine, or the Word that a person can absorb from experience or through hearing about it. It is for these things that a person in a spiritual religion has a desire.

[2] To disclose what it is to have a desire for truth, and what it is to have a desire for goodness, a few words must be said. People who desire truth ponder, investigate, and discuss whether a thing is true and valid. When they are sure it is true and valid, they ponder, investigate, and discuss what it is. So they stop on the very threshold, unable to be admitted into wisdom until they have quelled all doubt within themselves. By contrast, people who desire goodness recognize and sense from the very goodness in them that a thing is true. So they stand not on the near side of the threshold but inside the hall, having been admitted into wisdom.

[3] Take, for example, the idea that *heavenliness consists in thinking and acting on a desire for goodness or on goodness itself.* People who are moved by truth debate whether this is true, whether it is possible, and what it is. As long as they are mulling doubts about it, they cannot be admitted [into wisdom]. People who are moved by goodness, though, do not debate or mull doubts but say, "Yes, it's true"; so they are admitted. People moved by goodness (the heavenly) start where people moved by truth (the spiritual) stop, so that what is the end for the latter is the beginning for the former. As a consequence, the heavenly receive the opportunity to see, know, and sense that there are countless ways to be moved by goodness—as many different ways as there are communities in heaven.

They also see that the Lord joins all these communities together into a heavenly form, so that essentially they constitute a single human being. At the same time it is possible for them to perceive and distinguish the general category and specific type of each individual emotion.

[4] Or take another example: *All pleasure, blessing, and happiness is purely a matter of love; but the type of love determines the type of pleasure, blessing, and happiness.* Spiritual people tie their minds in knots wondering whether this is true. Aren't there other sources of happiness, such as social life, conversation, reflection, and scholarship? Isn't pleasure to be found in possessions, high position, public esteem, and consequent glory? All the while these people fail to confirm in themselves the idea that these things are unimportant, that what matters is the feeling of love we invest in them and the quality of that feeling. Heavenly people, however, do not get bogged down in these preliminaries but say, "Yes, it's true." Accordingly, they concern themselves with purpose itself and usefulness. In other words, they concern themselves with the actual feelings produced by love, which cannot be counted, each of which contains ineffable thoughts that continue to vary in pleasure, blessing, and happiness forever.

[5] Again, take for example the idea that *we should love our neighbors for the good in them.* People who respond to truth ponder, investigate, and discuss whether this is true, or whether it is valid, what a neighbor is, and what goodness is. They never venture any further, so they shut the door to wisdom on themselves. People who respond to goodness, though, say, "Yes, it's true," so they do not shut the door on themselves but enter in. From goodness they see, know, and sense who is more their neighbor than another and how much more of a neighbor that person is. They also see that everyone is a neighbor to a different extent. So they have access to indescribable wisdom, compared to those who respond only to truth.

[6] For yet another example take the idea that *if we love our neighbors for the good in them, we love the Lord.* People who are moved by truth investigate the validity of this. You can tell them that if we love our neighbors for the good in them, we love what is good, and since everything good comes from the Lord and contains his presence, when we love what is good we also love him, because he is its source and substance. Once again they examine whether this is so, what goodness is, and whether the Lord is more present in goodness than in truth. As long as they are stuck on these questions, they cannot see wisdom even at a distance. People who are moved by goodness, though, recognize intuitively that it is so and immediately see laid before them the whole field of wisdom leading to the Lord.

[7] All of this indicates the source of the dimness that besets people who desire truth (spiritual people) compared to people who desire goodness (heavenly people).

Still, they can move from their darkness into the light as long as they are willing to look affirmatively on the idea that all goodness is a matter of love for the Lord and charity for one's neighbor; that love and charity are spiritual closeness, the source of all blessing and happiness; and consequently that heavenly life consists in the good inspired by love for the Lord, not in the truth taught by faith in isolation from goodness.

✳   ✳   ✳   ✳

2719   The current chapter dealt first with the way the Lord's rational mind became divine (this rationality being Isaac) and with the removal of his merely human rationality (this being the son of Hagar the Egyptian).

Next it spoke of the spiritual church (this kind of religion being Hagar and her boy), which was saved by the Lord's divine humanity.

Now it turns to teachings about faith that will be useful to this church. What it says is that human logic, based as it is on factual knowledge (this logic being Abimelech and Phicol), is superimposed on those teachings. The pact that Abraham struck with Abimelech and Phicol symbolizes the bond between these. Such logic consists of appearances that stem not from a divine but from a human origin. The reason they are superimposed is that a spiritual church would not understand and therefore would not accept theology without them. As shown in §2715, people in a spiritual religion live in relative dimness. Their theology, then, needs to be clothed in the kinds of appearances that conform to human thinking and emotion and do not clash so sharply that divine goodness cannot find a kind of home in them.

A subsequent chapter (26 [§§3356–3471]) again speaks of Abimelech and a pact he made (though with Isaac this time) and, on an inner level, of logic and factual knowledge added a second time to teachings on faith. Let me just summarize the contents of the inner meaning on this subject, therefore, since it will become clearer in the explanation of chapter 26.

2720   Genesis 21:22. *And it happened at that time that Abimelech (and Phicol, the chief of his army) said to Abraham, saying, "God be with you in all that you are doing."* 23. *"And now swear to me here by God, if you are lying to me or my son or my grandson, . . . ! As I have done kindness to you, so you are to do to me and to the land in which you are staying."* 24. *And Abraham said, "I* *will swear." 25. And Abraham denounced Abimelech on account of a well of water that Abimelech's slaves had seized. 26. And Abimelech said, "I do not know who has done this thing, and you did not point it out to me, either, and I did not hear, either, until today." 27. And Abraham took flock and herd and gave them to Abimelech, and they both struck a pact. 28. And Abraham set seven ewe lambs of the flock off by themselves. 29. And Abimelech said to Abraham, "What are these seven lambs here that you set by themselves?" 30. And he said, "Because you must take seven lambs from my hand; therefore let it serve as a witness for me that I dug this well." 31. Therefore he called the place Beer-sheba, because there they both swore. 32. And they struck a pact in Beer-sheba. And Abimelech (and Phicol, the chief of his army) rose. And they returned into the land of the Philistines.*

[2] *It happened at that time* symbolizes the Lord's state when his rational mind had become divine. *That Abimelech (and Phicol, the chief of his army) said to Abraham* symbolizes human logic (based as it is on factual knowledge) that was to be superimposed on teachings concerning faith (which in themselves are divine). *Saying, "God be with you in all that you are doing,"* means that these were divine in each and every particular.

[3] *"And now swear to me here by God"* symbolizes affirmation. *"If you are lying to me"* means free of doubt. *"Or my son or my grandson"* means concerning the tenets of faith. *"As I have done kindness to you"* symbolizes the rational ideas the Lord had already learned about. *"So you are to do to me and to the land in which you are staying"* symbolizes reciprocation.

[4] *And Abraham said, "I will swear,"* symbolizes total affirmation.
And Abraham denounced Abimelech symbolizes the Lord's indignation. *On account of a well of water that Abimelech's slaves had seized* symbolizes teachings about faith and the way factual knowledge was eager to attribute those teachings to itself.

[5] *And Abimelech said* symbolizes an answer. *"I do not know who has done this thing"* means that his rational mind stated otherwise. *"And you did not point it out to me, either"* means that it did not come from his divine side. *"And I did not hear, either, until today"* means that now it was being revealed for the first time.

[6] *And Abraham took flock and herd and gave them to Abimelech* symbolizes divine goodness grafted onto the theological reasoning symbolized by Abimelech. *And they both struck a pact* symbolizes the resulting bond between these.

And Abraham set seven ewe lambs of the flock off by themselves symbolizes holy innocence.

[7] *And Abimelech said to Abraham, "What are these seven lambs here that you set by themselves?"* means in order to learn and acknowledge.

And he said, "Because you must take seven lambs from my hand," means that his divine side was the source of holy innocence. *"Therefore let it serve as a witness for me"* symbolizes the certainty. *"That I dug this well"* means that the theology came from his divine side.

Therefore he called the place Beer-sheba symbolizes the state and nature of that theology. *Because there they both swore* means as a result of the bond between them.

[8] *And they struck a pact in Beer-sheba* means that human logic was superimposed on teachings concerning faith. *And Abimelech (and Phicol, the chief of his army) rose, and they returned to the land of the Philistines* means that human logic still had no part in the doctrine itself.

2721 Genesis 21:33. *And he planted a grove in Beer-sheba and called there on the name of the God of Eternity.*

He planted a grove in Beer-sheba means theology, along with the knowledge it imparts, and its character. *And called on the name of the God of Eternity* means the worship it inspired.

2722 *He planted a grove in Beer-sheba* means the theology that resulted, along with the knowledge it imparts, and its character, as can be seen from the symbolism of a *grove* and that of *Beer-sheba.*

In regard to *groves,* the sacred worship of the ancient church took place on mountains and in groves. It took place on mountains because they symbolized heavenly aspects of worship, and in groves because they symbolized its spiritual aspects. As long as that church—the ancient church—remained pure, its worship on mountains and in groves remained holy, because of the representation. Whatever was tall and lofty, as mountains and hills are, represented heavenly qualities, which have to do with love and charity. Whatever bore fruit and leaves, as gardens and groves do, represented spiritual attributes, which develop out of heavenly ones.

The people of that church started to turn their representative and symbolic objects into idols, however, which they did by venerating the outward shell devoid of any inward significance. When they did, their sacred worship became profane. For that reason they were forbidden to hold their worship on mountains and in groves.

[2] What Genesis 12 says about Abraham shows that the ancients held their sacred worship on mountains:

> He moved from there onto a *mountain* to the east of Bethel and spread his tent (Bethel being toward the sea and Ai toward the east) and *built*

an altar there. And he *called on* Jehovah's *name.* (Genesis 12:8; §§1449–1455)

The same thing can also be seen from the symbolism of a mountain as the heavenly quality of love (§§795, 796, 1430). The words of the current verse—"Abraham planted a *grove* in Beer-sheba and *called there on the name of the God of Eternity*"—show that the ancients held their sacred worship in groves too. The same thing can also be seen from the symbolism of a garden as intelligence (§§100, 108, 1588) and of trees as perceptions (§§103, 2163).

The following passages show that this kind of worship was forbidden. In Moses:

> You shall not plant yourself a *grove of every tree* beside the altar of Jehovah your God that you shall make for yourself. And you shall not set up for yourself a pillar, which Jehovah your God hates. (Deuteronomy 16:21, 22)

In the same author:

> The altars of the nations you shall destroy, their pillars you shall smash, and their *groves* you shall demolish. (Exodus 34:13)

> The *groves* they were also to burn with fire. (Deuteronomy 12:3)

[3] Jews and Israelites, who were introduced to the representative rituals of the ancient church, concentrated exclusively on superficial things. They were nothing but idolaters at heart, not knowing (and not wanting to know) what the inner dimension was, what life after death was, or that the Messiah's kingdom was a heavenly one. Consequently, whenever they found themselves free to, they conducted profane worship on mountains and hills, and in groves and forests. They also made themselves "high places" to replace the mountains and hills, and carved images of a grove to replace the groves, as many passages in the Word reveal. In Judges, for instance:

> The children of Israel served baals and *groves.* (Judges 3:7)

In Kings:

> Israel made *groves* to provoke Jehovah. (1 Kings 14:15)

And in another place:

> Judah built itself *high places* and pillars and *groves* on every *tall hill* and under every *leafy tree.* (1 Kings 14:23)

In another place:

> Israel built itself *high places* in all the cities and set up pillars and *groves* on every *tall hill* and under every *leafy tree*. (2 Kings 17:9, 10)

And in another place:

> Manasseh, king of Judah, raised altars to Baal and made a *grove*, as Ahab, king of Israel, had done, and he placed a *carved image of a grove* that he had made in God's House. (2 Kings 21:3, 7)

This makes it clear that they did in fact make themselves carved images of a grove. The same book informs us that these were destroyed by King Josiah:

> Josiah caused to be brought out of Jehovah's Temple all the vessels made for Baal and for the *grove*, for the sun and moon, and for the whole army of the heavens, and he burned them outside Jerusalem, and the houses that the women had woven there for the *grove*. He also cut down the *groves* that Solomon had made, and also the *grove* in Bethel that Jeroboam had made. (2 Kings 23:4, [5,] 6, 7, [13,] 14, 15)

In addition, King Hezekiah tore down the same kinds of objects, as that book also reports:

> Hezekiah, king of Judah, took away the *high places* and broke the pillars and cut down the *grove* and smashed the snake of bronze that Moses had made. (2 Kings 18:4)

[4] Plainly the bronze snake was sacred in Moses' day; but when people venerated the outward object, it became profane and was smashed to pieces for the same reason worship on mountains and in groves was forbidden.

These facts become still clearer in the Prophets. In Isaiah:

> You were growing hot for your gods under every *leafy tree*. You were slaughtering your offspring in rivers under rock bluffs. Even for the rivers you poured out your libation; you offered your gift on a *high mountain,* and in a *lofty* place you put your dwelling, and there you offered sacrifice. (Isaiah 57:5, 6, 7)

In the same author:

> On that day, humankind will regard its maker, and its eyes will look to the Holy One of Israel; and it will not regard the altars, the work of its

hands, and what its fingers have made it will not see, neither *groves* nor sun pillars. (Isaiah 17:7, 8)

In Micah:

> I will cut down your carved images and your pillars from your midst, and you will not bow down anymore to the work of your hands, and I will pluck your *groves* from your midst and destroy your cities. (Micah 5:13, 14)

In Ezekiel:

> . . . so that victims of stabbing lie amid their idols, around their altars, at every *high hill,* on all the *heads of the mountains,* and under every *leafy tree,* and under every tangled *oak,* [in] the place where they offered a restful smell to all their idols. (Ezekiel 6:13)

[5] This now shows where idolatrous worship took its start: with the worship of representative and symbolic objects. The earliest people, who lived before the Flood, saw something to represent and symbolize the Lord's kingdom absolutely everywhere. They saw it in mountains, in hills, in plains, and in valleys. They saw it in gardens, groves, and woods, in rivers and water, in fields and crops, in trees of every kind, in animals of every kind as well, and in heavenly bodies. They never fastened their eyes, though, let alone their minds, to these objects. For them, such items were a means of thinking about the heavenly and spiritual wonders of the Lord's kingdom. So much was this the case that nothing at all in the whole of creation failed to serve them as inspiration. It is also inherently true that each and every component of nature represents something, which in modern times is a mystery, believed by hardly anyone.

After the heavenly frame of mind that comes of love for the Lord died out, however, the condition of the human race changed, so that physical objects no longer inspired people to see the heavenly and spiritual qualities of the Lord's kingdom. [6] Still, the ancients (who lived after the Flood) realized from their traditions and from the collected sayings of certain mentors that these objects had symbolic meaning. Since they were symbolic, the ancients also considered them holy, and that is how the representative worship of the ancient church arose. The ancient church was a spiritual church, so it did not perceive what the symbolism was but only knew that the symbolism existed, because it lived in relative dimness (§2715). Even so, the people of that church did not worship what they saw on the outside. Rather, outward objects reminded them of inward qualities, so when they were immersing themselves in the representation and symbolism of these things, they were immersing themselves in holy worship. This they could do because they had spiritual love, or in other words, charity, which they considered the crucial element of worship. As a result, holiness from the Lord was able to flow into their worship.

Eventually, though, the condition of the human race changed so much and became so corrupt that it exempted itself from neighborly kindness. In consequence, people no longer believed in a heavenly kingdom or in life after death but decided that circumstances are the same for humans as for animals, except that we can think. (Modern people see it this way too.) When humanity reached this point, representative worship turned from being holy to being idolatrous, and people started to worship superficialities. So the worship of many non-Jews at that time, and also of Jews and Israelites, was not representative worship but worship of representative and symbolic items. In other words, it was worship of outward things devoid of inward meaning.

[7] As regards groves specifically, they symbolized different things to the ancients, depending on the type of tree they contained. Those with olive trees symbolized the heavenly elements of worship. Those with grape-vines symbolized the spiritual elements. Those with fig trees, cedars, firs, poplars, and oaks symbolized various heavenly and spiritual entities. The current verse simply mentions a grove, or stand of trees, which symbolizes logical reasoning superimposed on theology and on the knowledge it imparts. After all, trees in general symbolize perceptions (§§103, 2163), but when they are mentioned in connection with a spiritual religion, they symbolize knowledge, because people in a spiritual religion receive perceptions only through knowledge gained from religious teachings or the Word. This knowledge becomes part of their religion, so it becomes part of their conscience, which is where their perception comes from.

2723   As for *Beer-sheba,* it symbolizes theology in a certain state and with a certain character—divine, but with human logic imposed on or added to it. This can be seen from the series of topics dealt with from verse 22 up to this point (§§2613, 2614). It can also be seen from the meaning of the word itself in the original language as "the well of the oath" or "the well of seven." A well is teachings about faith (see §§2702, 2720). An oath is a bond (2720), as is the pact sealed by an oath (1996, 2003, 2021, 2037). And seven is holiness and therefore divinity (395, 433, 716, 881). All of this stands as evidence that the name symbolizes a theology that in itself is divine but has human logic, or human appearances, added to it. [2] Abraham's words make it plain that this is the source of the name Beer-sheba: "Abraham said, 'Because you must take *seven* lambs from my hand; therefore let it serve as a witness for me that I dug this *well.' Therefore he called the place Beer-sheba,* because there they both *swore.* And they struck a *pact* in *Beer-sheba"* (verses 30, 31, 32). Isaac's words in chapter 26 below imply the same thing:

> It happened on that day that Isaac's slaves came and told him the account of the *well* that they had dug, and they said to him, "We've found water," and he called it *Sheba* [oath or seven]. Therefore the name of the city is *Beer-sheba* up to this day. (Genesis 26:32, 33)

This passage too speaks of wells, strife over them with Abimelech, and a pact struck with him. Beer-sheba here symbolizes human reasoning again imposed on teachings about faith. Because it is the second time such logic was imposed, adapting the theology to human comprehension, it is called a city. A city means all doctrine collectively (see §§402, 2268, 2449, 2451).

Beer-sheba occurs with the same inner-level meaning in other places too: Genesis 22:19; 26:23; 28:10; 46:1, 5; Joshua 15:28; 19:1, 2; 1 Samuel 8:2; 1 Kings 19:3. It occurs in a negative sense as well, in Amos 5:5; 8:13, 14.

[3] How far the heavenly and spiritual attributes of theology extend is symbolized on an inner level in places where the extent of Canaan is described as being "from Dan all the way to Beer-sheba." After all, the land of Canaan symbolizes the Lord's kingdom, and the church, so it symbolizes the heavenly and spiritual attributes of theology. In Judges, for instance:

> All the children of Israel went out, and the assembly gathered as one man from *Dan all the way to Beer-sheba.* (Judges 20:1)

In Samuel:

> All Israel from *Dan all the way to Beer-sheba . . .* (1 Samuel 3:20)

In another place:

> . . . causing the kingship to pass from the house of Saul, and raising the throne of David over Israel and over Judah, *from Dan all the way to Beer-sheba.* (2 Samuel 3:10)

In another place:

> Hushai to Absalom: "Let all Israel be gathered *from Dan all the way to Beer-sheba.*" (2 Samuel 17:11)

In another place:

> David told Joab to traverse all the tribes of Israel *from Dan all the way to Beer-sheba.* (2 Samuel 24:2, 7)

In another place:

> There died of the people, *from Dan all the way to Beer-sheba,* seventy thousand men. (2 Samuel 24:15)

In Kings:

> Judah lived under its own grapevine and under its own fig tree, *from Dan all the way to Beer-sheba,* all the days of Solomon. (1 Kings 4:25)

2724   *And called there on the name of the God of Eternity* means the worship it inspired. This can be seen from the symbolism of *calling on God's name* as worship (discussed in §440).

The people of the ancient church did not take a name to mean a name but the whole quality; see §§144, 145, 340, 768, 1754, 1896, 2009. So they took *God's name* to stand collectively for every means of worshiping God and so for every expression of love and faith.

When inward worship died out, though, and only the shell remained, they started to view God's name as nothing more than a name, so much so that they worshiped the name itself, not caring what kind of love or faith inspired them. Accordingly, nations started to differentiate themselves by the names of their gods. Jews and Israelites considered themselves better than any others because they worshiped Jehovah. They made the mentioning and invoking of this name the most important part of worship, when in reality the worship of a name alone is no worship at all. Even the worst people are capable of worshiping this way, and in doing so they deepen their profanation.

[2] Since God's name symbolizes every aspect of worship—that is, every aspect of the love and faith with which we worship him—you can see what *may your name be held sacred* in the Lord's Prayer means (Matthew 6:9). You can also see what the Lord meant when he spoke the following words:

> You will be hated by everyone because of *my name.* (Matthew 10:22)

If two agree in *my name* on earth concerning any matter, whatever they seek will be done for them by my Father who is in the heavens. Where two or three are gathered in *my name,* there I am in their midst. (Matthew 18:19, 20)

Whoever leaves behind houses or brothers or sisters or father or mother or wife or children or fields for *my name* will receive a hundredfold and will inherit eternal life. (Matthew 19:29)

Hosanna to the Son of David! A blessing on the one who comes in the *Lord's name!* (Matthew 21:9)

Jesus said, "You will not see me from now on until you say, 'A blessing on the one coming in the *Lord's name!*'" (Matthew 23:39)

You will be hated by all the nations because of *my name.* In fact, many will then stumble and betray each other and hate each other, and all this because of *my name.* (Matthew 24:9, 10)

As many as did accept him, to them he gave the power to be God's children, to those believing in *his name.* (John 1:12)

Those who do not believe have already been judged, because they have not believed in the *name of God's only Son.* (John 3:17, 18)

Jesus said, "Whatever you ask in *my name,* that I will do." (John 14:14, 15; 15:16; 16:23, 24, 26, 27)

Jesus said, "I have revealed *your name* to the people." (John 17:6)

Holy Father, preserve in *your name* those whom you gave to me, so that they can be one, as we are. (John 17:11, 12)

I made *your name* known to them, and I will make it known, so that the love with which you loved me can exist in them, and I in them. (John 17:26)

. . . so that you can believe that Jesus is Christ, the Son of God, and so that as believers you can have life in *his name.* (John 20:31)

Not to mention many passages of the Old Testament in which the name of Jehovah or God means not a name but every impulse of love and faith that inspires worship.

[3] Concerning people who do worship the name alone, though, without love or faith, this appears in Matthew:

> Many will say to me on that day, "Lord! Lord! Haven't we prophesied in *your name* and cast out demons in *your name* and exercised many powers in *your name?*" But I'll proclaim to them, "I do not know you. Leave me, you evildoers!" (Matthew 7:22, 23)

When people in the church lost their depth and became shallow, as noted above, and started to equate worship simply with use of the name, they no longer acknowledged one God but many. You see, it was customary for the ancients to add something to Jehovah's name in order to call to mind some benefit or attribute of his, as in the current verse: "He called on the *name of the God of Eternity.*" In the next chapter:

> Abraham called the name of that place *Jehovah Jireh.* (Genesis 22:14)

—that is, "Jehovah will see."

> Moses was building an altar and called its name *Jehovah Nissi.* (Exodus 17:15)

—that is, "Jehovah my banner."

> Gideon was building an altar to Jehovah and called it *to Jehovah Shalom.* (Judges 6:24)

—that is, "Jehovah of peace." There are other passages too. That is how it came about that people who equated worship with use of the name alone acknowledged so many gods. It is also why people outside the church (especially in Greece and at Rome) acknowledged and worshiped so many gods, even though the ancient church, from which those epithets came, never worshiped more than one. The reason they revered this one God under so many names was that by a name they meant a quality.

2725   Genesis 21:34. *And Abraham stayed in the land of the Philistines for many days.*

Abraham stayed in the land of the Philistines for many days means that the Lord superimposed on teachings about faith much that he gleaned from a study of human knowledge.

2726   *Abraham stayed in the land of the Philistines for many days* means that the Lord superimposed on teachings about faith much that he gleaned from a study of human knowledge, as can be seen from the following: *Staying* as a foreigner means instructing, as discussed in §§1463, 2025. *Abraham* represents the Lord, as discussed in §§1965, 1989, [2010,] 2011, 2501. The *land of the Philistines,* or Philistia, symbolizes the study of religious knowledge, as discussed in §§1197, 1198. And *days* symbolize the state of affairs, as discussed in §§23, 487, 488, 493, 893. Here, since the theme is knowledge gleaned from facts and logic, and the text says "many days," it means a relatively large amount.

The focus of the text from verse 22 to this point has been human reasoning based on knowledge and superimposed on teachings about faith, as is clear from the explanation. Here we reach the end of that thread.

As regards the actual topic, in itself it is quite deep. For this reason, and because Genesis 26 below has much to say on the same subject, let me put off further explanation of it.

The Way Marriage Is Viewed in the Heavens and the Way Adultery Is Viewed

F EW today know what real marriage love is or where it comes from, because few experience it. Almost everyone believes that it is inborn and therefore results from a certain "natural instinct"—all the more so because the impulse comes out even in animals. In reality, though, the difference between marriage love in people and the mating urge in creatures is as great as the difference in condition between humans and brute animals. **2727**

Because (again) there are few today who know what real marriage love is, I will describe it from information disclosed to me. **2728**

Marriage love traces its origin to the marriage of divine goodness and truth and therefore to the Lord himself.

The fact that this is the source of marriage love is not apparent to the senses or the intellect but *can* be seen by considering how it flows in and what it corresponds to, not to mention what the Word says about it.

How it flows in: Goodness and truth united as one flow in [to heaven] from the Lord, as a result of which heaven is compared to marriage and is called a marriage. *What it corresponds to:* When goodness united to truth flows down from there into a lower realm, it presents itself as a uniting of minds. When it flows into a still lower realm, it presents itself as marriage.

So the union of minds that develops out of the union between goodness and truth provided by the Lord is marriage love itself.

2729 Evidence that this is the origin of real marriage love can also be seen in the fact that the only people who experience it are those who allow the Lord to endow them with the goodness that comes of truth and the truth that comes of goodness.

Another piece of evidence is the fact that real marriage love holds within it the bliss and happiness of heaven. Everyone who enjoys that love enters heaven, or in other words, the heavenly marriage.

Another piece of evidence is the fact that when angels discuss the bond between goodness and truth, a scene representing marriage presents itself to good spirits on a lower level. Among evil spirits, however, a scene representing adultery presents itself. That is why the union of goodness and truth is called a marriage in the Word, while adulteration of goodness and falsification of truth are called adultery and whoredom there. See §2466.

2730 More than any others on this planet, the people of the earliest church lived lives of genuine married love, because they were heavenly. They had truth as a result of having goodness; they interacted with angels in the Lord's kingdom; and they found heaven in that love.

Their descendants, however, among whom the church deteriorated, began to love their children rather than their spouses. The evil are capable of loving their children, but only the good can love their spouse.

2731 From these earliest people I heard that marriage love by its very nature wants to belong wholly to the other, and to do so mutually. When that love is mutual and reciprocal, the partners enjoy heavenly gladness. I also learned that the joining of minds by its very nature is mutual and reciprocal in absolutely every facet of life—that is, in every last bit of emotion and in every last bit of thought.

That, I was told, is why the Lord ordained that wives would embody the will's positive emotions, while husbands would embody the intellect's true ideas. From this would come marriage—marriage like that between will and intellect, and between all the capacities, in whole and in part, of a person who possesses the goodness that comes of truth and the truth that comes of goodness.

2732 I talked to angels about the nature of this mutual, reciprocal quality, and here is what they said: The image and likeness of one is in the mind of the other, so they live together not only in the superficial details of life but also in its inmost depths. The Lord's love and mercy can flow into this oneness with blessing and happiness.

Moreover, people who had this kind of married love during their bodily lives live and dwell together in heaven as angels, sometimes even with their offspring. Very few from the modern Christian world live this way, but everyone from the earliest church (which was heavenly) does, and many from the ancient church (which was spiritual) do.

On the other hand (they continued), people who have lived in marriages in which they were united not by married love but only by lust are separated in the other world, because nothing lewd is tolerated in heaven. People who disliked one another are separated by an even greater distance, and those who hated one another by a greater distance still. Usually they meet up as soon as both have reached the other world, but after they suffer difficulties, they split apart.

Once, some spirits attacked me with a unique skill that they had acquired by practice during bodily life. They acted on me in a rather gentle, pulsating way often used by honest spirits, but I could tell that their activity harbored tricks and ruses intended to captivate and deceive me.

2733

Eventually I spoke with one of these spirits. He told me that he had been an army general when he was alive in the world. Since I detected something lecherous in his thoughts, I talked to him about marriage. (We used the kind of language spirits use, in which representative pictures illustrating their thoughts appear, giving those ideas full and very rapid expression.)

[2] He said that in the life of the body he had not felt that adultery counted for anything. "Adultery is unutterably wicked," I was permitted to reply, "even though to adulterers it appears otherwise—and in fact seems perfectly legitimate—because of the pleasure they've felt in it, which persuades them.

"What's more, you could have seen this by considering that marriages are the breeding grounds for the human race and so for the heavenly kingdom. Marriage ought never to be violated, then, but held sacred.

"You could also have realized it because you ought to know, now that you're in the next world where you can perceive it, that marriage love comes down through heaven from the Lord. And it gives birth to mutual love, the foundation of heaven.

"Yet another indication should have been that as soon as adulterers draw near any community in heaven they become aware of their own stench and hurl themselves down from there toward hell.

"At the very least, you could have seen that violating marriage is against divine law, against civil law everywhere, and against the genuine light of reason, because it goes against proper order, both divine and human. Not to mention many other considerations."

[3] But he answered that he had known nothing of the kind during his bodily life and had never even given it any thought. He wanted to debate the validity of the idea, but I said, "Truth is not a topic for debate in the afterlife, because rationalizations tend to favor pleasure and therefore defend evil and falsity.

"First you ought to think about the things I said, because they're true. Or you ought to base your thinking on the principle—very familiar in the world—that we should not do to others what we don't want them to do to us. You once loved your wife, as everyone does when first married, and if anyone had seduced her as you seduced others, you would have been in a fury over it. Surely you yourself, speaking under the influence of that rage, would have reviled adultery as well. And since you're gifted, wouldn't you have come up with even more arguments against it than others would? Wouldn't you in fact have damned it to hell? So you could have judged yourself on your own experience."

2734 People whose marriages during bodily life were happy because they genuinely loved their spouse have happy marriages in the next world too. Their happiness carries over from one life into the next, where it becomes a oneness of minds, which holds heaven within it.

I have been told that even the most general types of heavenly and spiritual happiness rising from that of marriage are beyond number.

2735 Real marriage love is an image of heaven. When it is portrayed visually in the other life, it is represented by the most gorgeous things the eye could ever see or the mind could ever grasp. It is portrayed as a young woman of indescribable beauty enveloped in a bright white cloud—so lovely that she can be called the essence and form of beauty itself. I have been told that all beauty in the next world comes from marriage love. The emotions and thoughts associated with it are represented by diamond-bright atmospheres that seem to shimmer with rubies and garnets, bringing a pleasure that touches the inmost depths of the mind.

As soon as lust intrudes in any way, however, these sights vanish.

2736 I was taught that real marriage love is innocence itself, which dwells in wisdom. People who have lived lives marked by love for marriage are wiser than anyone else in heaven, yet when others look at them they resemble little children flourishing in the springtime of their life. Whatever happens to them at that stage gives them joy and happiness.

They live in the deepest heaven, which is called the heaven of innocence. Through this heaven the Lord flows into the love of marriage, and from this heaven angels are present with people on earth who live lives of married love. They are also present with children in the children's early years.

In people who live lives of married love, the inner reaches of the mind **2737** open all the way to the Lord by way of heaven, because that love flows in from the Lord through a person's inmost core. So they have the Lord's kingdom inside themselves, and as a result they truly love children, for the sake of the Lord's kingdom. For this reason, they are more receptive to heavenly kinds of love than anyone else. They also reciprocate love more than anyone else, because mutual love comes from marriage love as a brook flows from its source.

The kind of mutual love that exists in heaven differs from marriage **2738** love. Marriage love is the desire to be part of another person's life, as one with that person; mutual love is wishing better to others than to ourselves. The latter is the kind of love parents show toward their children. It is also the kind of love people show when they seek to do good, not for their own sakes but simply because it gives them joy. This angelic type of love stems from marriage love, and is born to it as a baby is born to its parents—which is also why parents have this love for their children. The Lord preserves it in parents even when they lack married love, in order to keep the human race from dying out.

From the marriage of goodness and truth in the heavens descend all **2739** the different kinds of love. These have the same relationship to each other that exists between the love of parents for their children, the love of siblings for each other, the love of more distant relatives for each other, and so on, in all their various degrees in order.

These varieties of love, which develop only out of goodness and truth, or in other words, out of love for and faith in the Lord, direct the formation of all the communities in heaven. The Lord binds these communities together in such a way that they resemble a single human being, and for that reason heaven is also called the universal human. The variations are beyond description, and all trace their origin and source to the union of goodness and truth from the Lord, this union being the heavenly marriage.

As a result, marriages on earth form the source of all blood relationships and other family ties. Different degrees of love should descend from each other in a similar way, but since marriage love does not currently exist, relationships and connections are documented on the basis of marriage, but do not reflect relationships between types of love.

In the earliest church, different kinds of love did descend from each other this way, so in the heavens, varieties of love dwell together divided into "nations," "clans," and "households," all of which acknowledge the Lord as their only parent.

2740   True married love is not possible except between two spouses—that is, except in a marriage of one husband and one wife—and never with more partners simultaneously. Married love is mutual and reciprocal. The life of one spouse resides in that of the other, and the reverse, so that they resemble one individual. This kind of oneness is possible between two people, not more. A plurality of spouses fragments the love.

With the people of the earliest church, who were heavenly and perceived what was good and true, as angels do, each man had only one wife. They said that they sensed heavenly pleasures and happiness with one wife, and that the mere mention of other partners made them shudder.

As noted [§§2728–2729, 2731], the marriage of one husband and one wife develops out of the marriage of goodness and truth, or the heavenly marriage, which is monogamous, as the Lord's words in Matthew make very clear:

> Jesus said, "Haven't you read that the one who made them from the beginning made them male and female? And said, 'Therefore shall a person leave father and mother and cling to his wife, and the two will become one flesh'? So they are no longer two but one flesh. What God has joined as a pair, then, a human is not to separate. Moses, because of the hardness of your heart, allowed you to put your wives away. From the beginning, though, it was not this way. Not everyone will grasp this word, only those to whom it has been given." (Matthew 19:3–12)

2741   Goodness and truth constantly flow into all of us from the Lord, and consequently real marriage love does too, but we receive it in different ways. The way we receive it determines who we are. With the lewd it turns into lechery, with adulterers it turns into adultery; heavenly gladness then turns into unclean pleasure, so heaven turns into hell. The situation resembles that of sunlight flowing into physical objects, which receive it according to their form. They turn it blue, red, yellow, green, or murky, and even black, depending on how they take it in.

2742   Some people experience a kind of substitute for married love, but it is not the real thing if they do not love what is good and true; it is a love that resembles married love but springs from the same causes as self-love and materialism. The goal of such people is to be waited on at home; to maintain stability; to live idly; to be taken care of in sickness and old age; or to ensure that their children, whom they love, are looked after. It is forced on some by fear of their spouse, fear for their reputation, or fear of evil consequences. With some, unclean lust is what creates the appearance. At first it mimics married love, because at that point the partners pretend to some degree of innocence. They play together like children and feel a joy that resembles a bit of heavenly joy. As time passes, though, they do not unite more deeply and closely, as spouses who love one another do, but drift apart.

Married love also differs in the partners themselves. It can be more or less present in one, diminished or absent in the other. Since it differs, it can be heaven for one and hell for the other. A person's desire for it and manner of receiving it determines which it is.

I saw a large dog resembling Cerberus and asked what it symbolized. I **2743** was told that this kind of dog symbolizes protection against passing back and forth between the heavenly pleasure in marriage love and a hellish pleasure in it. People who have true married love enjoy heavenly pleasure, while people who live a life of adultery enjoy a pleasure that is hellish, although it seems heavenly to them. The dog, then, represents a blocking of the passage between these two opposite types of pleasure.

I was shown how the pleasures found in marriage love advance toward **2744** heaven on one hand and toward hell on the other. As they rose into heaven they developed into ever more numerous blessings and joys, until they could no longer be counted or expressed. The deeper they went, the more countless and indescribable these pleasures became, until they turned into heavenly bliss and happiness itself as it exists in the deepest heaven—the heaven of innocence. Utter freedom was the means to this end, because all freedom comes of love, and the greatest freedom therefore comes of marriage love, which is heavenly love itself.

Next I was shown how the pleasures of marriage love move toward hell, edging away from heaven bit by bit (just as freely, or so it seems) until hardly anything human remains to them. The deadly and hellish pleasure in which they end, and which I saw, cannot be described.

A certain spirit then accompanying me, who also witnessed these changes, rushed forward toward some sirens (whose pleasures turn hellish in this way). The spirit was shouting that he would show the sirens what their pleasures were like, and at first he managed to hold on to his idea of pleasure. When he had gone a short distance forward, however, his thoughts moved toward hell, just as the pleasures had, until they finally came to the same kind of horrifying end.

Sirens are women who are convinced that whoredom and adultery are honorable. Other people admire them for being this way while living an elegant lifestyle. Most of the ones arriving in the next life come from the Christian world. For more about them, see §§831, 959, 1515, 1983, 2483.

2745 There are women who do not love their husbands but instead despise them and come to consider them utterly worthless. The character of these women was represented by a rooster, a wildcat, and a dark-colored tiger. I was told that such women start talking endlessly, then scold, and finally take on the nature of a tiger. Some countered that women like this do love their children, but I answered that the kind of love they have is not human. It flows just as easily into the hearts of evil people, and even affects certain animals strongly enough that they too love their offspring more than themselves. I added that these women have no marriage love.

2746 Once there was a spirit moderately high above my head whose bodily life had been a debauched one. What he enjoyed was variety, so he never loved any woman for long but spent his life in brothels. As a result he slept with numerous women and then cast each aside. This meant that he cheated a large number of them and consequently snuffed out any desire within himself for marriage or for having children. In other words, he developed an unnatural nature.

All of this came out in the open, and he was punished horribly, in plain view of some angels. Afterward he was thrown into hell.

For more on the hells of adulterers, see §§824–830 in the first volume.

2747 Because adultery is contrary to marriage love, adulterers cannot coexist with angels in heaven. Another reason they cannot is that they engage in pursuits opposed to goodness and truth and therefore do not participate in the heavenly marriage. Yet another is that their thoughts about marriage are all foul. When just the mention or idea of marriage comes up, instantly their minds turn to lust, obscenity, and unspeakable perversions. Again, when angels converse about anything good or true, adulterers think the opposite. After death we have the same kind of feelings and resulting thoughts that we had in the world.

Adulterers have the urge to destroy society. Many of them are cruel (§824). So at heart they attack kindness and mercy and laugh at other people's misery. They want to rob everyone, and so far as they dare, they actually do. They find satisfaction in tearing down friendships and building up enmity. They make an attempt at religion in claiming to acknowledge the creator of the universe, and providence too, but only a very general form of it. They also claim to believe that salvation comes of faith, denying that they can be any worse off than others. When their inward character is examined, however—which happens in the other life—they do not believe even in these things; not in the universe's creator but rather in nature, not in an overarching providence but rather in no providence at all. They do not give any thought to faith. All these things, because they constitute adultery, stand in total opposition to what is good and true. You can judge for yourself, then, how likely they are to go to heaven.

Once some spirits who had lived a life of adultery in the world came to talk with me. I sensed that they had not been in the other world long, because they did not know they were there. They thought they were still in the world, because the ability to reflect on where they were had been taken from them. I was allowed to tell them they were in the next life, but they soon forgot, asking where to find homes they could worm their way into.

"Don't you have any respect for spiritual values?" I asked. "Specifically for married love, which is alienated by these kinds of enticements? Seduction violates the heavenly order." They paid no attention, though, and did not even understand.

"Aren't you afraid of the law or of legal penalties?" I added; but they scoffed. When I suggested the possibility that they might receive a vicious beating by the household servants, though, they did admit to fear on this one point.

Afterward I was able to perceive their thoughts, because thoughts are shared with everyone in the other life. The adulterers' thoughts were so revolting and obscene that a good person could not help being horrified by them. Yet in the other world these thoughts are exposed publicly to spirits and angels in all their detail.

This too shows that people like them cannot live in heaven.

Through adultery, some people develop a distaste and revulsion for marriage. When any amount of pleasure, blessing, or happiness from heaven with its angels reaches them, it turns into something that offends and nauseates them. Then it becomes painful and finally starts to stink, to the point that they hurry away from it toward hell.

Angels have taught me that when people commit adultery on earth, heaven is immediately closed to them, and afterward they live with an eye toward worldly and bodily concerns alone. Then, even if they hear talk about different facets of love and faith, it does not penetrate to their inner levels. Anything they themselves say on the subject comes not from deep within them but only from their memory and their lips, at the urging of vanity or greed. Their inner depths are closed and cannot be opened, except through serious repentance.

2748

2749

2750

2751   Diagonally up in front of my left eye was a clump of people who in physical life had plotted secretly and with exceptional skill. They were adulterers and were still in the world of spirits, having arrived fairly recently. They were in the habit of sending certain members of the group out in different directions to scheme not only against married love but also against goodness and truth and especially against the Lord. The agents return to them and tell what they have heard, and in this way they consult together.

They also sent one of their number to me, thinking I was a spirit, since I spoke the spirits' language. When the messenger spoke, he babbled on, presenting various impediments to belief, especially to belief in the Lord. It was as if he was composed of nothing but barriers to faith.

"Stop talking that way," I answered. "I know what ball of dung you come from. As far as the Lord goes, I know without any doubt that he is one with the Father and that the whole of heaven is his. I know that he is the source of all innocence, peace, love, charity, and mercy, the source of all marriage love, and the source of everything good and true, all of which is divine. I know that Moses and the Prophets—that is, each and every word of Scripture in its inner meaning—has to do with him. I know that all the rituals of the Jewish church represented him. And now, since I am so sure of all this that there is no doubt in my mind, what more do you want?" At this he retreated in shame. The reason I said all I did was so that he would report it back to the adulterers that constituted the unholy clump that had sent him.

2752   More than others in the next life, those who are addicted to adultery want to take possession of us and so return through us into the world. The Lord keeps them in hell, though, to prevent them from joining the ranks of the spirits who keep us company. Most spirits like this come from the Christian world; few come from anywhere else.

2753   There are some in the world who are swept away by lust and seduce young women wherever they can find them—in convents, in the shelter of their families, still with their parents, or even living a married life. These men ingratiate themselves by various ruses and pretty words. By the time they reach the other world they are used to acting this way and have therefore taken it on as their character, so they retain the knack of using flattery and pretense to worm their way into various circles. Because their thoughts come out in the open, though, they are thrown out. As a result they travel from one community to another, but everywhere they go they encounter rejection and even retaliation for trying to steal the pleasures and blessings of others. Eventually no community will open its doors to them, and after they have been punished severely they form a connection with others like themselves in hell.

The most deceitful of them often appear high above my head even though their hell is far below my heel. They are modern antediluvians. They use innocence as a cover, and mercy, and various positive emotions accompanied by persuasive arguments. When they lived in the world they were flagrant adulterers. Any time they came across a beautiful woman, whether married or single, they walked in without a pang of conscience and used their wiles to manipulate her into sexual disgrace. They are undetectable and take pains not to be exposed, because they operate in secret. They are also cruel. They cared only about themselves, and even if the whole world had been destroyed for their sake, it would have meant nothing to them.

There is a large number of people like this today, and I have heard that they come from the Christian world.

Their hell is the grimmest of all.

Adulterers have many, many hells. The inhabitants love nothing more than filth and excrement; this is what they enjoy in that life. You can see the same thing in many people of the same sort during their physical life— people who find it delightful to both think and talk about vile things, although they abstain from acting on them, simply for propriety's sake.

The thrill of adultery turns into filth like this in the other world. The situation is comparable to the effect of the sun's warmth—even the pleasant warmth of spring—on excrement or a dead body.

There are also people who believed in wife sharing. In the other life they talk like good people, but they are wicked and deceitful. Their punishment is horrible. They are gathered into a bundle, so to speak, and something like a snake is represented as stretching out and tying them all into a tight little ball. Trussed this way, they are cast aside.

When I was being led through a series of residential areas, I came to one where my feet and groin started to grow warm. I was told that it was occupied by people who had indulged in sensual pleasure but had not extinguished the physical longing to bring forth children.

True marriage love is heaven, and this fact is represented in the kingdoms of nature. Nothing exists anywhere throughout creation that does not in some way represent the Lord's kingdom as a whole. The physical realm traces its entire origin to the spiritual kingdom. Whatever does not arise from something prior to itself is nothing. Nothing exists that is not linked to its cause and therefore to its purpose. Anything that lacks connection instantly collapses and disappears. This, then, is why the Lord's kingdom is portrayed in the kingdoms of nature.

The fact that marriage love is heaven can be seen in the metamorphosis of larvae into nymphs or chrysalises and then into flying creatures. When their wedding day arrives—that is, when they shed their earthly, wormlike form, sprout beautiful wings, and become capable of flight—they soar into the air, which is their heaven. There they frolic together, marry, lay eggs, and feed on the sap of flowers. They are then at their loveliest, too, because they have wings adorned with pretty flecks of gold, silver, and other colors.

That is the effect the urge to marry produces even in tiny, insignificant creatures like these.

2759   A kind of swell surged up from the underground realm on my right. I learned that it was composed of a large number of spirits from among the common people, uneducated but not immoral. They were peasants and other simple people. When I spoke with them, they said they knew the Lord and commended themselves to his name. Beyond this they knew little of faith or its mysteries. Later, there rose up another group that knew a little more. I sensed that their inner depths were capable of opening up. (This is something that can be perceived plainly in the other world.) They had a conscience, which was communicated to me so I would know, and I learned that they had led lives of simple love for their married partners. They themselves said they loved their spouses and shunned adultery. Clearly this was a matter of conscience for them, because they said, "We *have* to; anything else would go against our will."

In the other life, people like this receive instruction and learn to love goodness and believe truth more fully. In the end they are welcomed among the angels.

[Continued in Volume 4]

Biographical Note

EMANUEL SWEDENBORG (1688–1772) was born Emanuel Swedberg (or Svedberg) in Stockholm, Sweden, on January 29, 1688 (Julian calendar). He was the third of the nine children of Jesper Swedberg (1653–1735) and Sara Behm (1666–1696). At the age of eight he lost his mother. After the death of his only older brother ten days later, he became the oldest living son. In 1697 his father married Sara Bergia (1666–1720), who developed great affection for Emanuel and left him a significant inheritance. His father, a Lutheran clergyman, later became a celebrated and controversial bishop, whose diocese included the Swedish churches in Pennsylvania and in London, England.

After studying at the University of Uppsala (1699–1709), Emanuel journeyed to England, the Netherlands, France, and Germany (1710–1715) to study and work with leading scientists in western Europe. Upon his return he apprenticed as an engineer under the brilliant Swedish inventor Christopher Polhem (1661–1751). He gained favor with Sweden's King Charles XII (1682–1718), who gave him a salaried position as an overseer of Sweden's mining industry (1716–1747). Although Emanuel was engaged, he never married.

After the death of Charles XII, Emanuel was ennobled by Queen Ulrika Eleonora (1688–1741), and his last name was changed to Swedenborg (or Svedenborg). This change in status gave him a seat in the Swedish House of Nobles, where he remained an active participant in the Swedish government throughout his life.

A member of the Royal Swedish Academy of Sciences, he devoted himself to studies that culminated in a number of publications, most notably a comprehensive three-volume work on natural philosophy and metallurgy (1734) that brought him recognition across Europe as a scientist. After 1734 he redirected his research and publishing to a study of anatomy in search of the interface between the soul and body, making several significant discoveries in physiology.

From 1743 to 1745 he entered a transitional phase that resulted in a shift of his main focus from science to theology. Throughout the rest of his life he maintained that this shift was brought about by Jesus Christ, who appeared to him, called him to a new mission, and opened his perception to a permanent dual consciousness of this life and the life after death.

He devoted the last decades of his life to studying Scripture and publishing eighteen theological titles that draw on the Bible, reasoning, and his own spiritual experiences. These works present a Christian theology with unique perspectives on the nature of God, the spiritual world, the Bible, the human mind, and the path to salvation.

Swedenborg died in London on March 29, 1772 (Gregorian calendar), at the age of eighty-four.